THE ABC OF THE OPT

Israel's half-a-century long rule over the West Bank and Gaza Strip and some of its surrounding legal issues have been the subject of extensive academic literature. Yet, to date, there has been no comprehensive, theoretically-informed, and empirically-based academic study of the role of various legal mechanisms, norms, and concepts in shaping, legitimizing, and responding to the Israeli control regime. This book seeks to fill this gap, while shedding new light on the subject. Through the format of an A-Z legal lexicon, it critically reflects on, challenges, and redefines the language, knowledge, and practices surrounding the Israeli control regime. Taken together, the entries illuminate the relation between global and local forces – legal, political, and cultural – in Israel and Palestine. The study of the terms involved provides insights that are relevant to other situations elsewhere in the world, particularly with regard to belligerent occupation, the law's role in relation to state violence, and justice.

Orna Ben-Naftali holds the Emile Zola Chair for Human Rights in the Striks School of Law, Israel.

Michael Sfard is an Israeli human rights lawyer and the legal adviser to several Israeli human rights organizations and peace groups.

Hedi Viterbo is Lecturer in the School of Law at the University of Essex.

The ABC of the OPT

A LEGAL LEXICON OF THE ISRAELI CONTROL OVER THE OCCUPIED PALESTINIAN TERRITORY

ORNA BEN-NAFTALI

Haim Striks School of Law, The College of Management
Academic Studies, Israel

MICHAEL SFARD

Michael Sfard Law Office, Israel

HEDI VITERBO

University of Essex

CAMBRIDGE
UNIVERSITY PRESS

CAMBRIDGE
UNIVERSITY PRESS

University Printing House, Cambridge CB2 8BS, United Kingdom

One Liberty Plaza, 20th Floor, New York, NY 10006, USA

477 Williamstown Road, Port Melbourne, VIC 3207, Australia

314-321, 3rd Floor, Plot 3, Splendor Forum, Jasola District Centre, New Delhi - 110025, India

79 Anson Road, #06-04/06, Singapore 079906

Cambridge University Press is part of the University of Cambridge.

It furthers the University's mission by disseminating knowledge in the pursuit of education, learning and research at the highest international levels of excellence.

www.cambridge.org
Information on this title: www.cambridge.org/9781316609934
DOI: 10.1017/9781316661376

First published 2018
First paperback edition 2018

A catalogue record for this publication is available from the British Library

Library of Congress Cataloging in Publication data
NAMES: Ben Naftali, Orna, author. | Sfard, Michael, 1972– author. | Viterbo, Hedi.
TITLE: The ABC of the OPT : a legal lexicon of the Israeli control over the occupied Palestinian territory / Orna Ben-Naftali, Striks School of Law, Israel; Michael Sfard, Michael Sfard Law Office, Israel; Hedi Viterbo, University of Essex.
DESCRIPTION: Cambridge, United Kingdom ; New York, NY, USA : Cambridge University Press, 2018.
IDENTIFIERS: LCCN 2017050590 | ISBN 9781107156524 (hardback)
SUBJECTS: LCSH: Law – West Bank. | Law – Gaza Strip. | Military government – Israel. | Palestinian National Authority – Foreign relations – Israel. | Israel-Arab War, 1967 – Occupied territories. | Palestine – International status. | Palestinian Arabs – Legal status, laws, etc. – Israel. | BISAC: LAW / International.
CLASSIFICATION: LCC KMM506.3 .B46 2018 | DDC 349.5694/2–dc23
LC record available at https://lccn.loc.gov/2017050590

ISBN 978-1-107-15652-4 Hardback
ISBN 978-1-316-60993-4 Paperback

Contents

Acknowledgments		*page* vii
List of Abbreviations		viii
	Introduction	1
A	Assigned Residence	26
B	Border/Barrier	43
C	Combatants	60
D	Deportations	78
E	Export of Knowledge	95
F	Future-Oriented Measures	118
G	Geneva Law	141
H	House Demolitions	162
I	Investigations	182
J	Jewish Settlements	200
K	Kinship	218
L	Lawfare	243
M	Military Courts	264

N   Nomos   277

O   Outside/Inside   301

P   Proportionality   327

Q   Quality of Life   343

R   Regularization Law   362

S   Security Prisoners   383

T   Temporary/Indefinite   399

U   Usufruct   417

V   Violence   431

W   War Crimes   448

X   X Rays   475

Y   Youth   499

Z   Zone   516

Index   548

Acknowledgments

Orna Ben-Naftali is grateful for the superbly intelligent research assistance given to her by Rafi Reznik and for the generous hospitality and support offered to her by the faculty and researchers of the Law Department of the European University Institute, Florence; the Max Planck Institute for Comparative Public Law and International Law, Heidelberg; and the Haim Striks School of Law, Israel.

Michael Sfard would like to express his boundless gratitude to Orna Ben-Naftali, for her vision, her comments, her advice, and her friendship. He would also like thank Maya Johnston, who has translated parts his text from Hebrew.

Hedi Viterbo's contribution to this book was generously supported by a grant from the Leverhulme Trust.

The authors also wish to thank Avital Amrani for her dedicated format editing.

Abbreviations

ACHR	American Convention on Human Rights
ACRI	Association for Civil Rights in Israel
AP I	Protocol Additional to the Geneva Conventions of 12 August 1949, and relating to the Protection of Victims of International Armed Conflicts
AP II	Protocol Additional to the Geneva Conventions of 12 August 1949, and relating to the Protection of Victims of Non-International Armed Conflicts
CAT	UN Committee Against Torture
CCPR / ICCPR	International Covenant on Civil and Political Rights
CESCR	UN Committee on Economic, Social and Cultural Rights
CIHL	Customary International Humanitarian Law
CRC	Convention on the Rights of the Child
GC I	Geneva Convention (I) for the Amelioration of the Condition of the Wounded and Sick in Armed Forces in the Field
GC II	Geneva Convention (II) for the Amelioration of the Condition of the Wounded, Sick and Shipwrecked Members of Armed Forces at Sea
GC III	Geneva Convention (III) relative to the Treatment of Prisoners of War
CV IV	Geneva Convention (IV) relative to the Protection of Civilian Persons in the Time of War
Eur Ct HR / ECHR	European Court of Human Rights
GA	General Assembly of the UN
GSS	General Security Services of Israel

HCJ	Supreme Court of Israel sitting as the High Court of Justice
HRC / UNHRC	UN Human Rights Committee
ICC	International Criminal Court
ICCPR	International Convent on Civil and Political Rights
ICCSt	Statute of the International Criminal Court
ICESCR	International Covenant on Economic, Social and Cultural Rights
ICJ	International Court of Justice
ICL	International Criminal Law
ICRC	International Committee of the Red Cross
ICTY	International Criminal Tribunal for the former Yugoslavia
IDF	Israeli Defense Forces
IHL	International Humanitarian Law
IHRL	International Human Rights Law
ILAC	International Law of Armed Conflict
IPS	Israel Prison Service
Inter-Am Ct HR	Inter-American Court of Human Rights
LCR	Levy Committee Report
MAG	Military Advocate General of the IDF
MilA	Military Appeal
MilC	Military Case
NIAC	Non-International Armed Conflict
OECD	Organisation for Economic Co-operation and Development
OPT	Occupied Palestinian Territory
PA	Palestinian Authority
SC	Security Council of the UN
UDHR	Universal Declaration of Human Rights
UNESCO	UN Educational, Scientific and Cultural Organization
UNICEF	UN Children's Fund

Introduction

1 ISRAEL'S CONTROL OF THE PALESTINIAN TERRITORY AS A LEGAL LABORATORY

1.1 Subject Matters

Beginning on June 5 and ending six days later, the 1967 war was brief. During these few days, Israel gained control over the West Bank of the Jordan River, the Gaza Strip, the Sinai Peninsula, and the Golan Heights.[1] Within pre-1967 Israel, East Jerusalem (located in the West Bank) has been subsumed into pre-1967 Jerusalem. Jewish settlements began to be built in the OPT in 1967.[2] Half a century later, there are more than 586,000 Israelis living in the West Bank, including East Jerusalem.[3] Most Palestinians and Israelis know no other reality. Law has played a significant role in the making and maintaining of this reality. This role is the focus of *The ABC of the OPT*.

---

[1] In 1967, the West Bank, including East Jerusalem, was under Jordanian control; the Gaza Strip and the Sinai Peninsula were under Egyptian control; and the Golan Heights were under Syrian control. The Sinai Peninsula was returned to its Egyptian sovereign pursuant to a peace treaty signed in 1979 (Treaty of Peace Egypt-Israel, March 26, 1979, reprinted in (1979) 18 International Legal Materials 362). The Golan Heights were fully annexed, and their residents were given Israeli citizenship (Golan Heights Law, 1981). East Jerusalem was annexed as well, although its residents were only given residency status, rather than citizenship (Basic Law: Jerusalem, Capital of Israel). The rest of the West Bank, as well as the Gaza Strip, was occupied, and Jewish settlements were established there. In 2005 Israel effected its unilateral disengagement plan, whereby it withdrew its ground forces from the Gaza Strip, evacuated the settlements, and dismantled them.

[2] The first settlement was Kfar Etzion. The territory on which the settlement had been established was officially seized by the military commander for military purposes, following a governmental decision to resettle the Hebron area; see CivA (Jerusalem) 2581/00 *G.A.L Ltd v. State of Israel* (October 30, 2007) [Hebrew]. On the settlements, see entries J: Jewish Settlements and R: Regularization.

[3] See Central Intelligence Agency, The World Factbook – Middle East: The West Bank, https://www.cia.gov/library/publications/the-world-factbook/geos/we.html.

The acronym OPT – short for "the Occupied Palestinian Territory" – is widely used in reference to the West Bank and Gaza Strip under Israel's control. In Israeli Jewish discourse, in contrast, these territories have been designated as "administered" rather than "occupied," and the West Bank has been commonly referred to by the biblical names of "Judea and Samaria," claiming a historical link with the Jewish people. From the perspective of international law, however, this form of control has been framed as "belligerent occupation,"[4] and this normative framework is considered to still apply,[5] five decades later, to the West Bank, including East Jerusalem and possibly also to the Gaza Strip.[6]

At the same time, Israel's protracted and highly institutionalized rule over the Palestinian territories, coupled with the mass Jewish settlement project, the de facto incorporation of the West Bank (but not its Palestinian residents) into Israel, and the broader political and legal porosity of the borders between "Israel" and "Palestine,"[7] may well indicate that the Israeli control regime has far transgressed the normative bounds of occupation. Therefore, while the title of this book invokes the commonly used term "OPT," it avoids reducing Israel's rule over the West Bank and Gaza Strip to "occupation" by using the broader term "control" instead. This introduction, and the book in general, oscillates between the concepts "occupation," "control," and "rule," depending on the context under examination and the analytical approach.

Indeed, if viewed through the conceptual prism of "belligerent occupation," the Israeli control of the OPT is possibly the most legalized such regime in world history. This is mainly evidenced by four interrelated factors. The first is the extensive involvement of government lawyers in designing and carrying out Israel's rule over the West Bank and Gaza Strip, since its beginning.[8]

---

[4] On the normative framework governing the OPT see Section B.2.2 and entry G: Geneva Law.

[5] On the indeterminacy between occupation and non-occupation and between Occupied and Administered Territories, see entries G: Geneva Law and N: Nomos. See also A. Gross, *The Writing on the Wall: Rethinking the International Law of Occupation* (Cambridge: Cambridge University Press, 2017), pp. 38–51; G. H. Fox, *Humanitarian Occupation* (Cambridge: Cambridge University Press, 2008).

[6] On the debate over the status of the Gaza Strip since Israel dismantled the Jewish settlements in that territory and withdrew its ground forces, see entries Z: Zone (specifically Section Z.2.2.1) and X: X Rays (specifically Section X.2.6). The situation in Gaza is also the focus of entry Q: Quality of Life.

[7] On this porosity, see entry O: Outside/Inside.

[8] M. Shamgar, "Legal Concepts and Problems of the Israeli Military Government – The Initial Stage," in M. Shamgar (ed.), *Military Government in the Territories Administered by Israel 1967–1980 – The Legal Aspects* (Jerusalem: Sacher Institute, 1982), pp. 13, 24–25, 27, 50–51; I. Zertal and A. Eldar, *Lords of the Land*, V. Eden (trans.) (New York: Nation Books, 2007), pp. 341, 343–344, 361–371.

The second is the Israeli military legal system, which tries thousands of Palestinians each year, and which has produced thousands of enactments governing Palestinian lives.[9] A third factor is the unprecedented decision of the Israeli supreme court, operating in its capacity as a high court of justice (HCJ),[10] to open its gates to petitions emanating from the OPT,[11] and to determine such petitions in the light of international law[12] as well as Israeli law.[13] Lastly, the Israeli rule over the Palestinian territories is the longest – and, accordingly, the most entrenched and institutionalized – belligerent occupation in modern history. Taken together, these facts have generated a profusion of law and, concurrently, voluminous legal scholarship.[14]

[9] See entries M: Military Courts, S: Security Prisoners.

[10] Basic Law: The Judiciary, Article 15(c) provides that the supreme court of Israel may also sit as a high court of justice, and "when so sitting, it shall hear matters in which it deems it necessary to grant relief for the sake of justice and which are not within the jurisdiction of another court."

[11] This decision was first made in 1972. See HCJ 337/71 *The Christian Society for the Holy Places* v. *The Minister of Defence* (1972) 26(1) PD 574 [Hebrew; an English summary is available at (1972) 2 *Israel Yearbook of Human Rights* 354–357]. Note that the decision is unprecedented within the paradigm of belligerent occupations but not within the colonial paradigm. See S. Ben-Nathan, "The Supreme Court and the Territories: The Last Diamond in the King's Throne," in I. Menuchin (ed.), 50 *Concepts, Testimonies and Representations of Occupation* (Mevaseret Zion: November Books, 2017) [Hebrew].

[12] International humanitarian law (hereinafter: IHL) in general; the law of belligerent occupation in particular; and, to a lesser extent, international human rights law (hereinafter: IHRL). While Israel's official position has been that IHRL does not apply to the Palestinian territories, since 2002 the HCJ has occasionally applied it as a complementary source to IHL. See HCJ 7957/04 *Mara'abe* v. *The Prime Minister of Israel* (September 15, 2005) [Hebrew; English translation available at http://elyon1.court.gov.il/files_eng/04/570/079/a14/04079570.a14.pdf]. On the applicable law and its interpretation by the HCJ, see entry G: Geneva Law.

[13] Israeli administrative law and, to the extent Jewish settlers are involved, constitutional law. In HCJ 1661/05 *Gaza Coast Regional Council* v. *The Israeli Knesset* (2005) 59(2) PD 481, ¶¶ 78–80, the court decided that the Israeli Basic Laws (which comprise the nascent Constitution of Israel), including the Basic Law: Human Liberty and Dignity, apply *in personam* to Israelis in the occupied territories, leaving open the question of the application of these laws to the Palestinian residents of the same territories.

[14] A search in online data bases supports this assessment. E.g., the term "Israeli Occupation" currently generates some 19,000 results in the Google Scholar interdisciplinary database, http://scholar.google.co.il/scholar?hl=iw&q=%22israeli+occupation%22&btnG=, and more than 1,300 in the law journal database "HeinOnline," http://heinonline.org/HOL/LuceneSearch?spe cialcollection=&typea=text&termsa=%22israeli+occupation%22&operator=AND&typeb=title& termsb=&operatorb=AND&typec=creator&termsc=&operatorc=AND&typed= text&termsd=&operatord=AND&typee=text&termse=&operatore=AND&typef=text&terms f=&collection=journals&yearlo=&yearhi=&sortby=relevance&only_vol=&collection_true=&se archtype=field&submit=Search&sections=article&sections=comments&sections=notes&sectio ns=reviews&sections=legislation&sections=case&sections=decisions&sections=misc&section s=index&sections=editorial&sections=external&other_cols=yes.

Yet, it seems that more laws, arming to the teeth trailing troops of lawyers, legal advisors, judges, and scholars, have not operated to limit state violence. Instead, more often than not, law has enabled this violence, cloaking the use of force required to sustain the Israeli regime with a mantle of legitimacy.[15] Judicial review exercised by the HCJ, for example, has rejected the over-whelming majority of the petitions challenging the legality of various deci-sions and actions of the occupying power.[16] The very few (though highly publicized) rulings in favor of petitioners have had no significant long-run impact on Israel's conduct in the OPT, other than, in some cases, "legalizing" oppressive state practices or propelling Israel to pursue alternative legal justifications.[17] Scholarly work, in the main, has followed the footsteps of the judiciary and other state agents, engaging in an assessment of the legality of specific decisions and institutional practices rather than analyzing, in their light, the role of law in structuring and sustaining the regime. Such an analysis is at the heart of this study.

1.2 *The Aims of the Study*

This study is designed to accomplish several objectives. First, it sets out to offer a detailed account of the ways in which international and domestic law has been implicated in the multitude of measures taken by the Israeli authorities to establish and maintain their control over the OPT. The first

[15] See, e.g., Judge A. Kozinski: "In the end, we do not believe that more law makes for better law," in *Hart v. Massanari* 266 F 3d 1155, 1180 (9th Cir 2001). This notion can be traced to Cicero's dictum "The more law, the less justice" (Cicero, *De officiis* I (44 BC; Oxford: Oxford University Press, 1994), pp. 10, 33). On the unbridgeable gap between law and justice see Section 3.

[16] R. Shamir, "'Landmark Cases' and the Reproduction of Legitimacy: The Case of Israel's High Court of Justice" (1990) 24 *Law & Society Review* 781, 783, provides data on judgments rendered by the HCJ between the years 1967–1986, indicating that 99 percent of Palestinian petitions were rejected. Y. Dotan, "Judicial Rhetoric, Government Lawyers, and Human Rights The Case of the Israeli High Court of Justice during the Intifada" (1999) 33 *Law & Society Review* 319, 334, provides data according to which in the years 1986–1995, 98.5 percent of Palestinian petitions were wholly rejected, and some additional 3 percent were partly accepted. He further notes that during the first Oslo Accord negotiations (1991–1993), the Israeli military attorney general's office tended to treat Palestinians differently according to their factional affiliation: those affiliated with factions supporting the negotiations were treated relatively leniently, while those affiliated with factions actively trying to undermine the negotiations were handled as harshly as possible. Throughout the 1990s, the Israeli military continued arresting and prosecuting Palestinians for actions committed during the Intifada. L. Hajjar, *Courting Conflict: The Israeli Military Court System in the West Bank and Gaza* (London: UC Press, 2005), pp. 124–126. Our own data up to 2014 indicates that some 99 percent of Palestinian petitions were rejected.

[17] Shamir, "Landmark Cases," p. 797.

decades of the twenty-first century have witnessed a resurrection of the concept of "belligerent occupation," with the 2003 military occupation of Iraq by the US-led coalition forces, the Ugandan occupation of parts of the Congo, Ethiopia's 2006 occupation of parts of Somalia, Nicaragua's occupation of Isla Calero in 2010, and Russia's occupation of certain areas of Georgia in 2008 and Crimea in 2014. There have also been similar regimes, even if labeled with ostensibly less disturbing names, such as "transformative/humanitarian occupations" or "post-bellum regimes."[18] Against the backdrop of these developments, a careful scrutiny of the experiments carried out in Israel's legal laboratory may well generate lessons that are relevant to other situations, and indeed to the course of the development of international law itself.

Second, the study seeks to highlight the nexus between the normative legal text and the narrative context within which it is written and that endows it with meaning. While decisions on the legality of a specific measure affecting the occupied population often accept the normative relevance of international law, they are neither made *in abstracto* nor by abstracted decision-makers. The legal text is written in a national context by domestic decision-makers (judges, legal advisors, and legislators) and, in most cases, its argumentation is directed primarily at the national constituency.[19] The interaction between an international legal norm and a national narrative is among the key factors determining the *nomos* of the regime. Insofar as "[n]o set of legal institutions exists apart from the narratives that locate it and give it meaning,"[20] it is necessary to elucidate this nomos in order to understand the role international law has played in instituting and maintaining Israel's rule over the West Bank and Gaza Strip.[21]

---

[18] On the allegedly changing faces of foreign control/occupation reflected, inter alia, in their different names, see e.g., Gross, *The Writing on the Wall*, pp. 38–51; Fox, *Humanitarian Occupation*; S. Ratner, "Foreign Occupation and International Territorial Administration: The Challenges of Convergence" (2005) 16 *European Journal of International Law* 695; R. Wilde, *International Territorial Administration: How Trusteeship and the Civilizing Mission Never Went Away* (Oxford: Oxford University Press, 2008).

[19] As a general rule, judgments of the HCJ are written and published in Hebrew. Some landmark decisions – notably those that are based on a sophisticated application of international law coupled with an evocative narrative about the subjection of the executive to legal restraints even in the face of terrorism – are published in English as well as Hebrew. It is interesting to note that while Arabic, not English, is both an official language in Israel and the petitioners' language, the judgments are not translated into Arabic.

[20] R. M. Cover, "The Supreme Court 1982 term – Foreword: Nomos and Narrative" (1983) 97 *Harvard Law Review* 4.

[21] See entry N: Nomos.

Third, by analyzing specific cases, measures, institutions, and legal concepts, this study aims to provide insights into the immensely convoluted legal architecture of the Israeli control regime. The book thus offers not merely a comprehensive but also a detailed study of law's role in constructing and maintaining this regime, tracing the Ariadne's thread woven by legal *dentelièrs* into the fabric of the regime.

Finally, the study delves into the relationship between the rule, the norm, and the exception, as well as the ways in which this relationship informs and is affected by Israel's control of the West Bank and Gaza Strip. This issue, the relevance of which exceeds well beyond the Israel/Palestine context, is discussed in detail in Section 2. This jurisprudential discussion includes an exposé of the main methodologies used in the various entries comprising this volume to explore the law–rule–exception relationship. Section 3 focuses on the structure of this book and explains the methodological choice to opt for the format of a lexicon for the study of law's role in the making and shaping of Israel's rule over the Palestinian territories conquered in 1967.

2 THE LAW–RULE–EXCEPTION RELATIONSHIP

2.1 *General Overview*

The law–rule–exception triad has been at the core of a rich jurisprudential literature. Carl Schmitt conceptualized an exceptional situation as one that poses a threat to the existence or survival of the state. Legal norms cannot fully foresee every exceptional situation, nor can such situations, which are never self-evident, be simply grounded in fact. Therefore, according to Schmitt, in order to enable the state to overcome the exception, the sovereign must be entrusted with deciding on the existence of an exception, and, subsequently, with suspending the law previously in force.[22] Many have drawn on this formulation of the law–exception relationship (while rejecting Schmitt's authoritarian prescription), to examine various situations that either constitute, or are comparable to, a state of emergency.[23] This section touches upon central themes of the jurisprudential discourse on the exception, including reference to Walter Benjamin and Giorgio Agamben, whose highly influential

---

[22] C. Schmitt, *Political Theology: Four Chapters on the Concept of Sovereignty*, G. Schwab (trans.) (Chicago: University of Chicago Press, 1988).

[23] However, in Schmitt's own writing, the state of exception (*Ausnahmezeustand* in German) is not simply equivalent to a state of emergency. S. Weber, "Taking Exception to Decision: Walter Benjamin and Carl Schmitt" (1992) 22 *Diacritics* 5, 9.

writing on this topic both engages with, and substantially diverges from, Schmitt's thinking.[24]

In particular, this book sheds light on law's role in shaping or transforming distinctions between the rule and the exception in relation to the occupied territories, as well as on the architecture and effects of specific rules and exceptions deployed by the Israeli authorities. Two overarching lines of critique, via which the book's entries address these themes, will now be described.

The first, which enshrines concepts such as "the rule of law" and "legal normalcy," largely comports with a mode of thinking and operating that Patricia Ewick and Susan Silbey have labeled "before the law."[25] This approach generally tends to treat legal norms (here, especially international legal norms) as "distinctive, yet authoritative and predictable," as "a formally ordered, rational, and hierarchical system of known rules and procedures." In this critique, legality appears, more often than not, "as something relatively fixed," if not in practice then in principle. In so doing, and in investigating law's operation in light of the premises of the dominant international legal discourse, this critique tells international "law's story of its own awesome grandeur ... Objective rather than subjective," international legal norms are "defined by ... [their] impartiality."[26]

The second line of critique amalgamates two other modes of thinking and acting. The first, toward which this critique primarily leans, can be termed, following Ewick and Silbey, "critiquing against the law." It includes what they have described as "exploit[ing] the interstices of conventional social practices to forge moments of respite" – ideationally and concretely – "from the power of law. ... [P]art of the resistance inheres in ... passing the message that legality can be opposed, if just a little." The second mode, which on the basis of Ewick and Silbey's terminology can be called "critiquing with the law," involves "playing" law "as a game ... in which pre-existing rules can be deployed and new rules invented to serve the widest range of interests and values." The concern is less with protecting or respecting (international) "law's

---

[24] On the dialogue (actual and ideational) between Benjamin and Schmitt, see Weber, "Taking Exception to Decision." Agamben's writing refers to Schmitt and Benjamin extensively, as discussed, e.g., in D. McLoughlin, "The Fiction of Sovereignty and the Real State of Exception: Giorgio Agamben's Critique of Carl Schmitt" (2016) 12 *Law Culture and the Humanities* 509, http://journals.sagepub.com/doi/pdf/10.1177/1743872112469863.

[25] This use of this phrase clearly differs from its use in F. Kafka "Before the Law," in *Wedding Preparations in the Country and Other Stories*, W. Muir and E. Muir (trans.) (Longon: Penguin Books, 1978), p. 127.

[26] P. Ewick and S. S. Silbey, "The Social Construction of Legality," in *The Common Place of Law: Stories from Everyday Life* (Chicago: University of Chicago Press, 1998), p. 47.

power than ... [with] the power ... to successfully deploy and engage with the law."[27]

By juxtaposing and/or combining these critiques, this study aims to produce a multilayered analysis, richer than would have been possible through a single perspective.

2.2 *Critiquing Before the Law*

The normative point of departure for this line of critique is the foundational principle of the Westphalian international order: namely, a presumption of sovereign equality between states, each exercising effective control over its territory, and people.[28] Under current international law, while said sovereignty is still attached mostly to states, it is increasingly understood as vested in the people, giving expression to their right to self-determination.[29] The latter is conceived as the sine qua non for realizing freedom in its negative (freedom from coercion) and positive (freedom of choice) senses.[30] From this normative perspective, a situation of belligerent occupation is the exception that suspends the norm: it consists of a foreign military force exercising effective control over a territory, despite having no sovereign title over that territory and without the sovereign's volition.[31] In this manner, the link between sovereignty and effective control is severed and the normal order concerning

---

[27] *Ibid.*, pp. 48–49.   [28] Article 2(1) of the UN Charter.

[29] On the right to self-determination, see generally, e.g., A. Cassese, *Self Determination of Peoples: A Legal Reappraisal* (Cambridge: Cambridge University Press, 1995); S. Oeter, "Self Determination," in B. Simma et al. (eds.), *The Charter of the United Nations: A Commentary*, Volume 1, 3rd edn. (Oxford: Oxford University Press, 2012), p. 313. In the Palestinian context, see, e.g., M. Halberstam, "Nationalism and the Right to Self-Determination: The Arab-Israeli Conflict" (1993–1994) 26 *NYU Journal of International Law and Politics* 573; R. J. Tyner, "Wars of National Liberation in Africa and Palestine: Self-Determination for Peoples or for Territories" (1978–1979) 5 *Yale Studies in World Public Order* 234; J. Quigley, *The Statehood of Palestine: International Law in the Middle East Conflict* (Cambridge: Cambridge University Press, 2010).

[30] The exposé of the normative framework provided here reproduces, mutatis mutandis, pp. 543–546 of O. Ben-Naftali, "Belligerent Occupation: A Plea for the Establishment of an International Supervisory Mechanism," in A. Cassese (ed.), *Realizing Utopia: The Future of International Law* (Oxford: Oxford University Press, 2012). It is noteworthy that the common distinction between so-called "negative" and "positive" rights (or duties), invoked by the present line of critique, is highly problematic. For criticism see, e.g., H. Shue, *Basic Rights: Subsistence, Affluence, and US Foreign Policy* (Princeton: Princeton University Press, 1980); J. P. Sterba, "The Welfare Rights of Distant Peoples and Future Generations: Moral Side-Constraints on Social Policy" (1981) 7 *Social Theory and Practice* 99.

[31] E. Benvenisti, *The International Law of Occupation*, 2nd edn. (Princeton: Princeton University Press, 2004), p. 4.

the occupied territory is suspended.[32] Once the suspension of the norm loses its temporariness, the exception becomes normalized. The normalization of the exception severely affects the occupied population's fabric of life, the occupying power's legitimacy, and, indeed, the very notion of the rule of law.

As Giorgio Agamben has observed, the space where the temporary suspension of the rule is indistinguishable from the rule has generated the conditions of possibility for the concentration camp,[33] but is not limited to Nazi Lagers. It is paradigmatic of every situation where the political machinery of the modern nation state finds itself in a continuous crisis and decides to take it upon itself to defend the nation's biological life, collapsing human rights into citizens' rights,[34] subsuming humanity into citizenry and making the former the "exceptionless exception."[35] In such a situation, the enemy, stripped of human rights, is also stripped of her/his humanity. Having been excluded from the body politic, s/he has only her/his own body as a political tool and it is through this political body that s/he interacts with the body politic that has thus reified her/him.[36]

The reason for the indeterminacy of the state of exception – Agamben has argued, adapting Schmitt – is the absence of any necessary relation between the decision on the state of exception and its factual existence. This allows for an indefinite suspension of the norm, explains how the Nazis produced an

---

[32] This notion of suspension was already recognized in the first attempt to codify the law of belligerent occupation in the Brussels Declaration. See Final Protocol and Project of an International Declaration Concerning the Laws and Customs of War (Brussels, 27.8.1874) reprinted in D. Schindler and J. Toman (eds.), *The Laws of Armed Conflict. A Collection of Conventions, Resolutions and Other Documents* (The Hague: Brill, 1988), p. 25.

[33] G. Agamben, *Homo Sacer: Sovereign Power and Bare Life*, D. Heller-Roazen (trans.) (Stanford: Stanford University Press, 1988), pp. 166–168.

[34] *Ibid.*, pp. 126–131, 174–176. Agamben, noting the very ambiguity of the title *Declaration des droits de l'Homme et du Citoyen*, refers in this context to Arendt's discussion of the paradox wherein "The Conception of human rights, based upon the assumed existence of a human being as such, broke down at the very moment when those who professed to believe in it were for the first time confronted with people who had indeed lost all other qualities and specific relationships – except that they were still human." See H. Arendt, *The Origins of Totalitarianism* (San Diego: Harcourt Brace, 1973), p. 299. Thus, says Agamben, in the nation-state system, human rights that are considered inalienable have become meaningless once they cannot be attached to the citizens of a nation-state. The refugee, the person who was supposed to be the "human rights" person par excellence, has thus become the paradigm of "bare life."

[35] A term coined by Gross in his analysis of Schmitt's theory of the exception. See O. Gross, "Exception and Emergency Powers: The Normless and Exceptionless Exception: Carl Schmitt's Theory of Emergency Powers and the 'Norm-Exception' Dichotomy" (2000) 21 *Cardozo Law Review* 1825.

[36] Agamben, *Homo Sacer*, pp. 187–188.

ostensibly "normal" constitutional structure characterized by the legal indeterminacy of the emergency situation, and also explains why the sovereign
cannot distinguish between the norm and the exception, thus failing to meet
the task Schmitt's *Political Theology* assigned to it.[37] In Schmittian terms, the
result may be conceptualized as blurring the line between law and fact: the
law continues to operate despite its suspension but no longer signifies "the rule
of law": those subject to the state of exception are stripped of the legal rights
that would protect them, yet are still subject to law's violence: "insofar as law is
maintained as pure form in a state of virtual exception, it lets bare life ...
subsist before it."[38] The *Goldstone Report* captured this problem when noting,
in one of its concluding observations, that "a line has been crossed, what is
fallaciously considered acceptable 'wartime' behavior has become the
norm."[39]

International law has contributed significantly to the blurring of this line.
And so has Israel's use of this law over the years, with regard to a wide range of
measures designed to sustain, expand, and deepen Israeli control over the
OPT (while simultaneously perpetuating Israel's self-perception and external
image as a law-abiding "defensive democracy" fighting "with one hand tied
behind its back").[40] Against this backdrop, the central proposition this line of
critique advances is that once law becomes implicated in obfuscating the
rule–exception relationship, it becomes itself infected and its legitimacy is
jeopardized. This proposition rests on several observations this critique seeks
to substantiate. First, the application of law to individual cases would typically
resort to various sophisticated interpretative techniques and methodologies
designed to advance the occupying power's interests at the occupied people's
expense. More often than not the result would frustrate the original purpose of
the rule at hand and would operate as a legitimizing device, encouraging
a discourse of various specific violations of human rights carried out in the
name of security to be perceived as exceptional, thereby concealing the reality
wherein said violations have become the rule, not the exception. Second, such
application of the law would contribute to and facilitate the formation of an

[37]   G. Agamben, *State of Exception*, K. Attell (trans.) (Chicago: University of Chicago Press,
       2005), p. 58.
[38]   Agamben, *Homo Sacer*, p. 55 (and the discussion pp. 50–55).
[39]   UN Human Right Council, Report of the United Nations Fact-Finding Mission on the Gaza
       Conflict, "Human Rights in Palestine and other Arab Occupied Territories," September 25,
       2009, A/HRC/12/48, ¶ 1433.
[40]   This is a recurrent narrative in the judgments of the HCJ pertaining to the OPT. See, e.g.,
       HCJ 7015/02 *Ajuri* v. *IDF Commander in the West Bank* (2002) 56(6) PD 352 [Hebrew;
       English translation available at http://elyon1.court.gov.il/Files_ENG/02/150/070/A15/02070
       150.A15.pdf].

environment, indicative of a state policy of tolerance toward systemic violations of human rights and the institutionalization of a culture of impunity.[41] Third, over time, the resulting chain of specific anomalies would generate the perception among the occupied population that the justice system itself is an instrument not merely of power but of unpredictable violence, of arbitrariness, where the absence of law is carried out under the name of law. Constant exposure to law's violence would engender violence.[42]

International law seeks to regulate the interruption created by belligerent occupation. Such regulation signifies the need to distinguish both order from chaos and the rule from the exception. In distinguishing between order and chaos, its function is to govern the situation; to prevent anarchy by entrusting the occupying power with governing the occupied territory. In distinguishing between the rule and the exception, its function is to establish the conditions that would enable as swift as possible a return to the normal order of the international society.

This, according to the present line of critique, is the role of the law of belligerent occupation, a body of law that bears strong structural resemblance to the normative framework applicable to an emergency regime. This regime, the roots of which date back to the Roman-Commissarial model, rests on three precepts: exceptionality, limited scope of powers, and temporary duration.[43] The assumption on which this model is based is that a situation of emergency is exceptional, hence separated from the ordinary state of affairs. For this reason, its duration must be limited and it must not generate permanent effects. This is also the reason for regarding the norm as superior to the exception: the existing legal order defines the terms under which it is suspended, and the powers granted in such a situation are to be used for the purpose of an expeditious re-establishment of normalcy.[44] Indeed, as modern studies of emergency situations concerned with the derogation from human rights law thereby occasioned have concluded, "[a]bove and beyond the rules ... one principle, namely, the principle of provisional status, dominates all others. The right of derogation (of human rights) can be justified solely by the concern to return to normalcy."[45]

---

[41] See, e.g., entry W: War Crimes.   [42] See, e.g., entry V: Violence.

[43] See T. E. Mommsen, *The History of Rome* (New York: Meridian Books, 1958), pp. 325–326; For later references to this classical model, see, e.g., N. Machiavelli, *The Discourses*, L. J. Walker (trans.) (London: Penguin Books, 1970), pp. 194, 198; J. J. Rousseau, *The Social Contract and Discourse*, G. D. H. Cole (trans.) (London: Everyman, 1993), pp. 293–296.

[44] For the essential features of the traditional model of emergency powers, see Gross, "Exception and Emergency Powers," pp. 1836–1839.

[45] N. Questiaux, *Study of the Implications for Human Rights of Recent Development Concerning Situations Known as State of Siege or Emergency* (1982) UN ESCOR 35th

The basic tenets of the normative regime of occupation largely conform to this constitutional model, transporting it to the international arena: the normal order is based on the principle of sovereign equality between states that are, at least to some extent, presumed to be founded on the ideas of self-government and self-determination. The severance of the link between sovereignty and effective control, and life under foreign rule – both features of occupation – constitute an exceptional situation. The law of occupation recognizes it as an exception to be managed so as to ensure expeditious return to normalcy. This is why the occupant has only limited powers in terms of both scope and time, and is not permitted to act in a manner designed to generate permanent results.

As noted earlier, this mode of critique takes as its normative framework the law of belligerent occupation, consisting of the 1907 Hague Regulations Respecting the Laws and Customs of War on Land,[46] the Fourth Geneva Convention Relative to the Protection of Civilian Persons in Times of War,[47] and the Additional Protocol I of 1977.[48] Over the past decades it has been accepted that IHL provides the specific – though not exclusive – law governing occupation (*lex specialis*), and that it is complemented by IHRL.[49] Three basic tenets, extractable from this body of law, will now be articulated.[50]

Session, Agenda item 10, 69 UN Doc E/CN.4/Sub.2/1982/15, p. 20. Also see O. Gross and F. NíAoláin, "To Know Where We Are Going, We Need To Know Where We Are: Revisiting States of Emergency," in A. Hegarty and S. Leonard (eds.), *Human Rights: An Agenda for the 21st Century* (London: Cavendish Publishing, 1999), p. 79.

[46] The Hague Convention (IV) Respecting the Laws and Customs of War on Land and its annex: Regulations concerning the Laws and Customs of War on Land, The Hague, October 18, 1907, 205 CTS 277; 36 Stat 2277 [hereinafter: the Hague Regulations].

[47] Geneva Convention Relative to the Protection of Civilian Persons in the Time of War, Geneva, August 12, 1949, 75 UNTS 287 [hereinafter: *GC IV*].

[48] Protocol Additional to the Geneva Conventions of August 12, 1949, and relating to the Protection of Victims of International Armed Conflicts (Additional Protocol I), Geneva, June 8, 1977, 1125 UNTS 3 [hereinafter: *AP I*].

[49] See, e.g., Legality of the Threat or Use of Nuclear Weapons, Advisory Opinion, 1996 ICJ 226, ¶ 25; Consequences of the Construction of a Wall in the Occupied Palestinian Territory, Advisory Opinion, 2004 ICJ 136, ¶ 106; Armed Activities on the Territory of the Congo (*Democratic Republic of the Congo* v. *Uganda*), Judgment, 2005 ICJ 168, ¶¶ 216–217. See generally, O. Ben-Naftali (ed.), *International Human Rights and Humanitarian Law* (Oxford: Oxford University Press, 2011). For the position that the application of IHRL together with IHL may not necessarily achieve its purpose and may indeed harm more than ameliorate the human rights of "protected people," see A. Gross, *The Writing in the Wall*, pp. 338–396.

[50] For a comprehensive exposé of these basic tenets, see O. Ben-Naftali, A.M. Gross, and K. Michaeli, "Illegal Occupation: The Framing of the Occupied Palestinian Territory" (2005) 23 *Berkeley Journal of International Law* 551.

2.2.1 Occupation Neither Transfers Sovereignty Nor Confers Title

Effective control by foreign military forces suspends, but does not transfer sovereignty. The prohibition on annexing an occupied territory is the normative consequence of this principle.[51] Under current international law, and in view of the principle of self-determination, sovereignty remains vested in the occupied people. This principle is currently undisputed. Its development merits attention primarily because history – that is, change over time – is hardly ever a linear process of progression; regression to imperial domination remains an ever-present possibility. It is thus worthwhile to take account, albeit briefly, of this development.

The roots of the principle of the inalienability of sovereignty date back to the post-Napoleonic wars and the restoration of a European order, designed to protect the ruler's sovereignty from intervention by another state. Given that the political legitimacy of European rulers at the time was based on either dynastic monarchy or popular democracy, the principle was designed to accommodate both systems and minimize disruption by preventing one from overthrowing the other.[52] In the relationship between the European and the non-European world, conquest remained a legally valid way to acquire sovereignty until the twentieth century.[53] The international community's gradual renunciation of the use of force as an acceptable policy, coupled with decolonization processes and the ensuing right to self-determination, have internationalized this hitherto exclusively European order. Accordingly, the prohibition on annexation of territory, differentiating between occupation and sovereignty, coheres with the corpus of general international law core principles of sovereign equality, self-determination, and nonintervention.[54]

Given, however, that such principles have not been inscribed on a tabula rasa, it is little wonder that the very occurrence of an occupation echoes the sorry story of the "civilizing mission," and that "alien occupation" of whatever type has been grouped together with colonial domination, racist regimes,[55] and related practices of subjugation, domination, and

---

[51] S. P. Sharma, *Territorial Acquisition, Disputes and International Law* (Leiden: Kluwer Law International, 1997), p. 148.

[52] E. Benvenisti, "The Origins of the Concept of Belligerent Occupation" (2008) 26 *Law and History Review* 621. N. Bhuta, "The Antinomies of Transformative Occupation" (2005) 16 *European Journal of International Law* 721.

[53] S. Korman, *The Right of Conquest: The Acquisition of Territory by Force in International Law and Practice* (Oxford: Oxford University Press, 1996), p. 9.

[54] See Articles (2), 2(1), 2(4), 2(7) and 55 of the UN Charter.   [55] Article 4 of AP I.

exploitation.[56] This sensibility runs through the divide between sovereignty and foreign occupation, and implies that the very phenomenon of occupation is viewed with suspicion and is likely to generate resentment and resistance. This is a fortiori the case with prolonged occupations and with "transformative occupations" – that is, occupations that purport to replace the sociopolitical system of the occupied territory with a system akin to that of the occupying power. The association between such attempts and imperialism may well explain why the various international interventions of the 1990s shied away from either describing themselves as occupations or indeed from referring to the law of belligerent occupation. From this perspective, former president George W. Bush's admission that the American and British troops occupying Iraq were "welcomed, but it was not a peaceful welcome" should not have come as a surprise,[57] nor should the subsequent resurgence. Foreign occupation connotes subjugation, not liberation. Reflecting this understanding are the distinction between sovereignty and occupation (as discussed in Section 2.2.2) and the consequential limits placed on the occupant's governmental authority (as discussed in Section 2.2.3).

2.2.2 An Occupation Is a Form of Trust Precluding the Introduction of Major Systemic Change

The basic rule regulating the occupant's governmental authority is articulated in Article 43 of the Hague Regulation. Under this rule, the occupant is vested with the authority "to take all the measures in his power to restore, and ensure, as far as possible, public order and safety/civil life, while respecting, unless absolutely prevented, the laws in force in the country."[58] This rule, thus, imposes two categories of obligations on the occupant: (a) to protect the

---

[56] See Declaration on Principles of International Law Concerning Friendly Relations and Co-operation among States in Accordance with the Charter of the United Nations, UN General Assembly, October 24, 1970, A/RES/2625(XXV).

[57] In an interview with Brian Williams, *NBC News* (December 12, 2005), cited in A. Roberts, "Transformative Military Occupation: Applying the Laws of War and Human Rights" (2006) 100 *American Journal of International Law* 580, 616.

[58] The authoritative French version uses the phrase "l'ordre et la vie publics." The English translation reads: "public order and safety." Since the authoritative text of the Hague Regulations is in the French language, the English text has no legal standing. For the discussion of the difference between the French and the English versions of Article 43 of the Hague Regulations, see Y. Dinstein, "Legislation under Article 43 of the Hague Regulations: Belligerent Occupation and Peace-Building" *Harvard Program on Humanitarian Policy and Conflict Research, Occasional Paper No.1* (2004), pp. 2–4.

inhabitants' life, property, and livelihood; and (b) to respect the existing legal, economic, and sociopolitical institutions in the territory.

The first category reflects humanitarian concerns.[59] It has evolved over time to incorporate the concept of trusteeship, the beneficiaries of which are the inhabitants of the territory.[60] Admittedly, this is a sui generis form of trust insofar as it carries with it a potential conflict of interests between the occupant's security needs and the inhabitants' welfare. In the nineteenth century, this framework produced two primary rules: the occupant was mainly incumbent with the negative duty of refraining from infringing on the inhabitants' most basic rights, while the latter were incumbent with a duty of obedience to the occupant.[61] Over time, the scale began to tip to the inhabitants' side: the GC IV seems to reject the idea that the occupied population was under any obligation to obey the occupant.[62] In parallel, it has considerably expanded the protection due to the inhabitants, in respect of both negative and positive duties. This process has culminated in the coapplication of IHL and IHRL to occupied territories. Nevertheless, the GC IV explicitly subjects some of the guarantees afforded to the population to military necessity and conditions[63] and empowers the occupant to take various measures against "protected persons."[64] It is thus clear that situations where the occupation either is met with strong resistance in general (such as the occupation of Iraq), or produces such resistance (the occupation of the Palestinian Territory being the quintessential example), threaten the viability of this precarious balance.

The second category of obligations, which prohibits the occupant from instituting major changes in the occupied territory, has its origins in the above-discussed preservation of the sovereignty (inclusive of the domestic governmental system) of the ousted rulers in Europe. This limitation on the

---

[59] Originating in the principle of distinction between civilians and combatants, see Benvenisti, "Origins of the Concept of Belligerent Occupation," pp. 624–627.

[60] Construction of a Wall, ¶ 88; Separate Opinion of Judge Koroma, ¶ 2, explicitly stated that occupied territories "constitute ... a sacred trust, which must be administered as a whole in the interests both of the inhabitants and the legitimate sovereign or the duly constituted successor in title"; cf. Separate opinion of Judge Higgins, ¶ 2; Separate opinion of Judge Kooijmans, ¶ 33.

[61] R. R. Baxter, "The Duty of Obedience to the Belligerent Occupant" (1950) 27 *British Yearbook of International Law* 235.

[62] E.g., the terms "war rebellion" and "war treason" were not incorporated in the Convention. Furthermore, while providing the occupant with the right to take measures against "protected persons" who carry out acts detrimental to the occupant's security (GC IV, Articles 27, 64), it nevertheless preserves most of their rights under the Convention (*ibid.*, Articles 5, 68).

[63] E.g., *ibid.*, Articles 27, 49, 51, 53.

[64] Promulgating penal laws (*ibid.*, Article 64); assigning residence (*ibid.*, Article 78); and internment (*ibid.*, Article 42).

occupant's authority was incorporated and further detailed in the *GC IV*.[65] Currently known as the "conservation principle," it highlights the distinction between temporary occupation and sovereignty.[66] Given that the latter is attached to the occupied people, the principle protects local self-determination. In this context too, both transformative and prolonged occupations threaten the viability of this principle: the former because the objective of redesigning the existing system stands in direct conflict with its conservation;[67] the latter because maintaining the status quo may well become a mandate for stagnation and defy the obligation to promote the inhabitants' welfare.[68] This point invites a discussion of the third tenet of the law of belligerent occupation.

2.2.3 An Occupation is a Temporary Form of Control

The idea that an occupation is a temporary form of control that may not generate permanent results is undisputed. Indeed, it is implicit in both the principle that occupation does not confer title and in the conservation principle. The notion of limited duration further coheres with the exceptionality of the regime and highlights the need to resume, as quickly as possible, the normal international order of sovereign equality.

---

[65] *Ibid.*, Article 64.

[66] J. L. Cohen, "The Role of International Law in Post-Conflict Constitution-Making: Toward a Jus Post Bellum for 'Interim Occupations'" (2006–2007) 51 *New York Law School Law Review* 496, 498–499.

[67] Viewed from the perspective of the conservation principle, a "transformative occupation" mocks the law. When measured against the idea that an occupation is distinct from sovereignty and that, therefore, it is necessary to preserve the sovereign's decision-making capacity in matters pertaining to its sociopolitical and economic profile, that is, its right to self-determination, the very concept of "transformative occupation" is an oxymoron which challenges the basic assumptions of the law of belligerent occupation. See Bhuta, "Antinomies of Transformative Occupation"; N. Bhuta, "New Modes and Orders: The Difficulties of a Jus Post-Bellum of Constitutional Transformations" (2010) 60 *University of Toronto Law Journal* 799.

[68] Viewed from the perspective of human rights, however, "transformative occupations," designed to substitute a democratic for a despotic form of government, arguably create the conditions of possibility for self-determination. From this perspective, the argument has been made that a law that fails to advance this objective is anachronistic and should be updated. See, e.g., G. H. Fox, "The Occupation of Iraq" (2004–2005) 36 *Georgetown Journal of International Law* 195. A somewhat less radical variation of this view holds that resort to dynamic interpretations, which reads broadly the "unless absolutely prevented" proviso, allows for the reconciliation of transformative objectives with the conservation principle without a legislative reform. See, e.g., Roberts, "Transformative Military Occupation," pp. 620–622.

The greatest challenge to this principle comes not only from reality, but from law itself: the law of occupation, while providing for the provisional status of the occupation regime, does not set time limits on its duration. In this particular regard, the present critique departs from its overall location "before the law," as described in Section 2.2. This absence of time limits has been construed to mean that an occupation can continue indefinitely.[69] This construction obfuscates the crucial distinction between the "temporary" and the "indefinite": a temporary situation definitely has an end; an indefinite situation may or may not have an end. Indeed, if an occupation could continue indefinitely, the interests it is designed to protect would all become meaningless: (i) the inhabitants' interest in regaining control over their life and exercising their right to self-determination; (ii) the interest of the international system in resuming the normal order of sovereign equality between states; and (iii) the interest of the international rule of law in maintaining the distinction between the norm (the principle of sovereign equality) and the exception (occupation).[70]

2.3 *Critiquing Against/With the Law*

Another critical approach, interwoven throughout some of this book's entries, presents various challenges to dominant legal frameworks, while refraining (unlike the former approach) from committing itself to any totalizing normative agenda.[71] This critique differs from the former one in at least five respects. While these differences raise complex theoretical questions, a succinct overview suffices for the purpose of this introduction.

---

[69] Shamgar, "Legal Concepts and Problems of the Israeli Military Government," p. 43.

[70] GC IV, Article 6, is the only provision that tackles directly the issue of the duration of an occupation. It does so, alas, in an implausible manner, providing for the continued applicability of only some of the Convention's provisions. This may well be construed by occupying powers as limiting their obligations toward the inhabitants precisely in situations where greater protection is needed. Indeed, the text indicates the drafters' assumption that occupations would normally be of short duration. Once it became clear that this assumption was defied by reality and that it may generate counterproductive results, the provision was abrogated: AP I, Article 3(b), provides for the application of the law of belligerent occupation until the termination of the occupation. It does not, however, provide for time limits for its duration. See Construction of a Wall, Separate Opinion of Judge Elaraby, ¶ 3.1; Separate Opinion of Judge Koroma, ¶ 2. See entry T: Temporary/Indefinite.

[71] This position is also influenced by the post-structuralist skepticism toward totalizing grand-narratives. See, e.g., J.F. Lyotard, *The Postmodern Condition: A Report on Knowledge*, G. Bennington and B. Massumi (trans.) (Minneapolis: University of Minnesota Press, 1984). On post-structuralism generally see, e.g., I. Buchanan, A *Dictionary of Critical Theory* (Oxford: Oxford University Press, 2010), p. 381.

First, for the present line of critique, concepts such as "legal" and "norm" – and their counters, "illegal" and "exception" (or "fact") – are not self-evident givens from which conclusions can be deduced, but are complex, elusive, and contestable products of legal discourse and action.[72] Consequently, the rule–exception distinction is treated as an object of inquiry rather than as a point of departure. The task therefore becomes to carefully scrutinize the construction, deployment, and interplay of the (so-designated) "rule" and "exception," and the effects thereof.

Second, a conceptual distinction between "the exception" and "the rule" can be maintained while acknowledging, at the very least, that these terms are neither historically nor structurally antithetical. Historically, as Walter Benjamin famously observed, "the tradition of the oppressed teaches us that the state of emergency in which we live is not the exception but the rule."[73] Indeed, for at least a century now, the apparent exception has been anything but exceptional. Across the globe, emergency powers have drastically increased in scope, and the definition of "emergency" has been broadened far beyond military conflicts to justify routine governmental powers serving the interests of socioeconomic elites.[74] The fact that Israel has been in a declared state of exception since its establishment underscores the point.[75] Structurally, the state of exception is powerfully tied to the legal rule. For Carl Schmitt (and

[72]   On meaning as the product of use, see, e.g., J. L. Austin, *How to Do Things with Words*, 2nd edition (Cambridge, MA: Harvard University Press, 1975); J. Derrida, *Writing and Difference*, A. Bass (trans.) (Chicago: University of Chicago Press, 1980); L. Wittgenstein, *Philosophical Investigation*, P. M. S. Hacker and J. Schulte (eds.), G. E. M. Anscombe et al. (trans.) (4th edn., Hoboken: Wiley-Blackwell, 2009). On international law as a realm of practices and discourses producing distinctions between, for example, "compliance" with and "violation" of international law, or between "wartime" and "peacetime," see D. Kennedy, *Of War and Law* (Princeton: Princeton University Press, 2006). On law (generally) as revolving around the production of such distinctions, see N. Luhmann, "Operational Closure and Structural Coupling: The Differentiation of the Legal System" (1988) 15 *Journal of Law and Society* 153. Though a relevant source of reference in this regard, Luhman's writing has important limitations in other regards. For criticism see, e.g., M. Valverde, *Law's Dream of a Common Knowledge* (Princeton: Princeton University Press, 2003), pp. 6–7. On law as subject to an endless deference of meaning see J. Derrida, "Before the Law," in J. Derrida and D. Attridge (eds.), *Acts of Literature* (London: Routledge, 1991). See also text and note 91.

[73]   W. Benjamin, "Theses on the Philosophy of History," in H. Arendt (ed.), *Illuminations: Essays and Reflections*, H. Zohn (trans.) (Berlin: Schoken, 1969), p. 257.

[74]   See, e.g., M. Neocleus, "The Problem with Normality: Taking Exception to 'Permanent Exception'" (2006) 31 *Alternatives* 191.

[75]   See HCJ 3091/99 *The Association for Civil Rights in Israel v. The Knesset* (May 8, 2012) [Hebrew]. An international legal manifestation of this constant state of emergency, which will not be discussed in this book, is Israel's declaration to the UN upon ratifying the International Convent on Civil and Political Rights in 1991. The declaration states that Israel does not see itself bound to Article 9 of the Convent, which forbids arbitrary detention,

later, Giorgio Agamben), the state of exception retains a link to the suspended legal order by establishing the conditions for its reapplication after its suspension, thereby maintaining law's authority.[76] A critique "against/with the law," however, construes this link as even stronger, in two interrelated respects: first, far from being a lawless or extralegal space, the state of exception brims with law – with legal texts, procedures, mechanisms, and discourses;[77] second, to a large extent, many of the oppressive practices and policies associated with the (assumed) exception actually reproduce or originate from practices and policies in the supposedly normal legal order.[78]

A third difference is that the present critique, rather than regarding international law (and law generally) as its normative basis, treats it as inherently violent. Put explicitly, violence is viewed as integral to the so-called "normal" legal order, not as an aberration from this order.[79] It is in line with this violence, and also due to law's malleability to diverse (and often competing) interpretations, that law provides a framework not only for engaging with the limits of belligerent control, but also for continuing war and state violence by

in light of Article 4, which reads: "In time of public emergency ... the States Parties to the present Covenant may take measures derogating from their obligations," International Convent on Civil and Political Rights, opened for signature December 19, 1966, 999 UNTS 171 (entered into force March 23, 1976). For a discussion of this issue, see J. Quigley, "Israel's Forty-Five Year Emergency: Are There Time Limits to Derogations from Human Rights Obligations?" (1994) 15 *Michigan Journal of International Law* 491.

[76]   Schmitt, *Political Theology*, pp. 12–15; Agamben, *State of Exception*, p. 58. It is also a significant element of the inclusive exclusion characteristic of the Israeli occupation. See the aptly titled A. Ophir et al. (eds.), *The Power of Inclusive Exclusion: Anatomy of Israeli Rule in the Occupied Palestinian Territories* (New York: Zone Books, 2009).

[77]   See, e.g., P. Fitzpatrick and R. Joyce, "The Normality of the Exception in Democracy's Empire" (2007) 34 *Journal of Law and Society* 65; N. Hussain, "Beyond Norm and Exception: Guantánamo" (2007) 33 *Critical Inquiry* 734, 737–750; F. Johns, "Guantánamo Bay and the Annihilation of the Exception" (2005) 16 *European Journal of International Law* 613.

[78]   See entry O: Outside/Inside. For discussion beyond the Israeli–Palestinian context, see, e.g., J. Forman, Jr., "Exporting Harshness: How the War on Crime Helped Make the War on Terror Possible" (2009) 33 *NYU Review of Law and Social Change* 331; E. Hernández-López, "Guantánamo as Outside and Inside the US: Why is a Base a Legal Anomaly?" (2010) 18 *Journal of Gender, Social Policy and Law* 471; J. T. Parry, "Torture Nation, Torture Law" (2009) 97 *Georgetown Law Journal* 1001; W. R. Levi, "Interrogation's Law" (2009) 118 *Yale Law Journal* 1434; N. T. Saito, "Colonial Presumptions: The War on Terror and the Roots of American Exceptionalism" (2009) 1 *Georgetown Journal of Law and Modern Critical Race Perspectives* 67; A. Anghie, "The Evolution of International Law: Colonial and Postcolonial Realities" (2006) 27(5) *Third World Quarterly*, 739–753; C. Jochnick and R. Normand,"The Legitimation of Violence: A Critical History of the Laws of War" (1994) 35(1) *Harvard International Law Journal* 49–95.

[79]   See especially entries L: Lawfare and V: Violence.

other means. Indeed, states all too often rely on, and resort to, international law to shape and legitimize their violent actions.[80]

Fourth, in this account, the so-called "normal" political order is no less perilous than the "normal" legal order to which it is inextricably tied. Therefore, this critique does not share the previous critique's lament over the purported suspension of the international order by the prolonged belligerent occupation. Nor does it share the tendency of legalistic approaches to fetishize the principle of state sovereignty,[81] upon which the international order is based. In short, from this critical perspective, neither state-centrism nor a reversion to the dominant international order should be extolled as an ideal solution to the ills of belligerent control.

Lastly, just as legal and political norms are not necessarily praiseworthy, so the exception is not, by definition, deplorable. Moreover, in certain circumstances, the exception can open a space for justice. This insight follows Walter Benjamin's assertion that in normal situations, the state employs oppressive "law-preserving violence" to protect its monopoly on violence, whereas in the state of exception the bell tolls for the oppressed: "pure violence" erupts, destroying or suspending the law. An example of such "pure violence," Benjamin claimed, is the proletarian general strike, which – unlike the instrumental violence of partial and political general strikes – demands radical transformation of the state-enforced capitalist labor system.[82] Giorgio Agamben and Jacques Derrida have each developed this notion in different, but potentially related, directions. Agamben advocated a "real" state of exception, neither statal nor juridical, which would obliterate, or at least undermine, the normalized (and in this regard "fictitious") state of exception that has been imposed on humanity.[83] Derrida, in comparison, defined responsibility as, among other things, "the experience of absolute decisions made outside of . . . given norms, made therefore through the very ordeal of the undecidable."[84] "[F]or a decision to be just and responsible," maintained Derrida, "it must . . . conserve the law and also destroy it or suspend it enough

---

[80] See, e.g., Kennedy, *Of Law and War*; Jochnick and Normand, "The Legitimation of Violence."

[81] For criticism of this tendency, see K. McEvoy, "Beyond Legalism: Towards a Thicker Understanding of Transnational Justice" (2007) 34 *Journal of Law & Society* 411, 421–424.

[82] W. Benjamin, "Critique of Violence," in P. Demetz (ed.), *Reflections: Essays, Aphorisms and Autobiographical Writings* (Berlin: Schoken, 1986), pp. 277, 290–292, 300.

[83] Agamben, *Homo Sacer*; Agamben, *State of Exception*, p. 59. For discussion of this aspect of Agamben's writing see McLoughlin, "Fiction of Sovereignty."

[84] J. Derrida, *The Gift of Death*, D. Wills (trans.) (Chicago: University of Chicago Press, 1995), p. 5. For discussion of the US detention facility at Guantánamo Bay through the prism of Derrida's notion of responsibility, see Johns, "Guantánamo Bay," pp. 615, 633–634.

to have to reinvent it in each case … Each case is other, each decision is different and requires an absolutely unique interpretation, which no existing, coded rule can or ought to guarantee absolutely."[85]

This critical approach aims to pursue this perhaps-impossible yet imperative ideal of simultaneously conserving and destroying the law.

2.4 *Convergence and Divergence*

The question of how these two lines of critique relate to each other is open to interpretation. On the one hand, given the different angles from which they address the Israeli control regime, some may regard them as mutually exclusive, at least in some senses. On the other hand, in many respects, they can be viewed as potentially complementary, and in some cases seemingly contrasting views are merely differences of emphasis. This book leaves room for these different interpretations, with some entries endeavoring to tie these lines of critique together, whereas others lean exclusively toward one or the other. Whichever way one interprets the interrelation of these critiques, their important commonalities are undeniable, including the realization, discussed earlier, that Israel's rule over the West Bank and Gaza Strip, far from being a space of lawlessness, is in fact filled to the brim with legalism.

Neither of these lines of critique – it is important to stress – is simply "internal" or "external" to law, especially considering the porosity, elasticity, and contestability of law's (imagined) boundaries.[86] Instead, these critiques exemplify different types of "legal consciousness" – "before," "with," and "against" the law – as defined in Ewick and Silbey's insightful, if inevitably schematic, writing on the subject. Ewick and Silbey explain:

> Legality is not inserted into situations; rather, through repeated invocations of the law and legal concepts and terminology, as well as through imaginative and unusual associations between legality and other social structures, legality is constituted … We use the phrase "legal consciousness" to name participation in the process of constructing legality. … The production [of legality]

---

[85] J. Derrida, "Force of Law: The Mystical Foundations of Authority" (1990) 11 *Cardozo Law Review* 919, 961. For discussion see, e.g., P. Goodrich, "Postmodern Justice," in A. Sarat, M. Anderson, and C. O. Frank (eds.), *Law and the Humanities: An Introduction* (Cambridge: Cambridge University Press, 2009).

[86] See, e.g., P. Schlag, "The Dedifferentiation Problem" (2009) 42 *Continental Philosophy Review* 35. Characterizing law's boundaries as "imagined" does not diminish the "realness" of their consequences. For a similar claim in relation to the category "nationality" see B. Anderson, *Imagined Communities: Reflections on the Origin and Spread of Nationalism* (New York: Verso, 1983).

may include innovations as well as faithful replication. . . . Consciousness is
not merely a state of mind. Legal consciousness is produced and revealed in
what people *do* as well as what they *say*.[87]

Seeing law and legality as ever-changing products of discourse, imagination, and practice – a view long shared by prominent jurists[88] – also sheds light
on the nature of law in Israel's control of the West Bank and Gaza Strip.
In addition to Israel's formal legal institutions and texts, there are also, no less
importantly, Israeli soldiers on the ground. While not professionally lawyers,
they too engage in the sort of activity Ewick and Silbey would characterize as
"legal consciousness." Among other things, soldiers produce various, and at
time concurrent, narratives of legality and illegality in the OPT, narratives that
largely revolve around the question of the ability, or the authority, to locate
and identify the rule and the exception. Thus, in testimonies of Israeli ex-
soldiers, the OPT is sometimes described as a space of lawlessness, where
"there is no law, only Jewish interests." According to another narrative, the
OPT is in fact replete with law, but since soldiers "only follow orders" they are
somewhat distinguishable and remote from that law. In yet another narrative,
soldiers not only perform but actually embody the law, a dynamic that finds its
ultimate manifestation whenever a soldier asserts: "I am the law."[89]

Thus, Israel's control of the West Bank and Gaza Strip, on the one hand,
and this study, on the other hand, engage in and produce different legal
formations. To reflect the particular legal patchwork of the Israeli control
regime, this book is organized in the form of a legal lexicon, as explained in the
following section.

3 THE LEXICON FORMAT

The book is structured in a lexical format, comprising 26 alphabetically
ordered entries. Each entry, from A: Assigned Residence to Z: Zones, focuses
on a legal, administrative, and/or military term/concept that is central to the
modus operandi of Israel's rule over the West Bank and Gaza Strip. Each entry
begins descriptively, with a definition, description, or presentation of the legal
doctrine relative to the term/concept as a terminus a quo for the ensuing
discussion. The latter focuses on the actual use, or role, of the term/concept

---

[87] Ewick and Silbey, "Social Construction of Legality," pp. 43–46.
[88] See, e.g., Cover, "Nomos and Narrative"; R. M. Cover, "Violence and the Word" (1986) 95
      Yale Law Journal 1601.
[89] M. Zagor, "'I am the Law!' – Perspectives of Legality and Illegality in the Israeli Army" (2010)
      43 *Israel Law Review* 551. See entry W: War Crimes.

under examination, and on its impact on life under Israeli rule. This format thus encompasses both the traditional function of a lexicon, as an instrument for the organization of knowledge, and the function of reflecting on this knowledge in a critical manner that challenges and redefines it.

These analytical and deconstructive moves take place at both the level of each separate entry and also, through abundant cross-references, at the level of their interaction. Indeed, to a large degree, the meaning of each term or concept is to be found in its relation to the other terms and concepts discussed in this book. This conception of meaning as relational is inspired in part by Ludwig Wittgenstein's "family resemblance" theory, and in part by Derrida's writing on "différance." According to Wittgenstein, certain words acquire their meaning not by standing for certain objects, but by the relationship between their different uses.[90] Derrida's argument is more far reaching: that meaning always entails an endless movement/play of differences, in which words are defined by appealing to their (ever unstable) differences from other words that have been, or will be, used.[91]

A lexical format has been adopted in, and adapted to, a wide variety of genres, covering the whole gamut from autobiographies[92] to televised documentaries,[93] literary criticism,[94] journals of political philosophy,[95] and international human rights law,[96] to name a few. This format was also used in the 1980s, to provide information on facts, agencies, and institutions affecting life in the West Bank.[97]

---

[90] Wittgenstein, *Philosophical Investigation.*

[91] J. Derrida, "Différance," in *Margins of Philosophy*, A. Bass (trans.) (Chicago: University of Chicago Press, 1982); Derrida, *Writing and Difference.* Derrida was not the first to argue that terms acquire meaning through their relation to other terms, but one of the differences between him and, for example, structuralist linguist Ferdinand de Saussure, is his emphasis on the inherent instability of conceptual differences, distinctions, and oppositions. Cf F. de Saussure, *Course in General Linguistics*, W. Baskin (trans.) (New York: Philosophical Library, 1959).

[92] E.g., C. Milosz, *Milosz's ABC*, M. Levine (trans.) (New York: Farrar, Straus and Giroux, 2002).

[93] *L'Abécédaire de Gilles Deleuze, avec Claire Parnet* (1996) (A French documentary television program produced in 1988–1989, consisting of an eight hours series of interviews with Deleuze, organized from Animal to Zigzag).

[94] R. Barthes, *The Pleasure of the Text*, R. Miller (trans.) (New York: Hill & Wang, 1975) (literary criticism from "Affirmation" to "Voice").

[95] Mafte'akh – Lexical Review of Political Thought, http://mafteakh.tau.ac.il/en.

[96] S. Marks and A. Clapham, *International Human Rights Lexicon* (Oxford: Oxford University Press, 2005).

[97] M. Benvenisti et al., *The West Bank Handbook: A Political Lexicon* (Boulder: Westview Press, 1986).

The methodological choice to opt for the format of a lexicon for the study of law's role in the making and shaping of the Israeli control regime rests primarily on the centrality of language to law and, more specifically, on the performative nature of legal language.[98] Legal language does more than merely describe reality, and even more than enable or limit action: it creates reality, and shapes both experience and consciousness.[99] The alphabetical order that serves as the organizing principle of this book underscores both the centrality of language to law and the performativity of a (local) dialect of the (international) legal language, in two nuanced ways.

First, the Israeli control regime itself maintains an order that at times may seem arbitrary and at times carefully designed. To an extent, the lexicon reflects and responds to this highly complex order: its alphabetical structure is somewhat arbitrary, but the terms and concepts under examination have been carefully selected and interlinked. At the same time, as Michel Foucault has shown generally,[100] and as this book demonstrates in relation to the Israeli regime, an apparently arbitrary order, if closely inspected, can be highly valuable for revealing the dominant epistemic forces at play.

Second, the lexicon allows for attention to detail: its formality may be analogized to a fisherman's net, which yields definitive shapes from what

---

[98] Austin, *How to Do Things with Words*; J. R. Searle, *Speech Acts: An Essay in the Philosophy of Language* (Cambridge: Cambridge University Press, 1969); J. R. Searle, "A Taxonomy of Illocutionary Acts," in K. Günderson (ed.), *Language, Mind and Knowledge*, volume VII (Minneapolis: University of Minneapolis Press, 1975); P. F. Strawson, "Intention and Convention in Speech Acts" (1964) 73 *Philosophical Review* 439; K. Bach and M. Harnish, *Linguistic Communication and Speech Acts* (Cambridge, MA: MIT Press, 1979). The concept of performative speech has had an enormous impact on social theory; see, e.g., M. Foucault, *The Archaeology of Knowledge*, A. M. Sheridan Smith (trans.) (London: Routledge, 2002); J. Butler, *Excitable Speech: a Politics of the Performative* (London: Rutledge, 1997). International legal scholarship has also been thus influenced; see, e.g., W. G. Werner and J. H. de Wilde, "The Endurance of Sovereignty" (2001) 7 *European Journal of International Relations* 28.

[99] It is little wonder that such discursive practices characterize the world of law: performative speech acts are made, for the most part, by reference to a law or a convention (i.e., in conventionally designated circumstances), by authorized people exercising their authority in conformity with the relevant conventions. See K. Bach, "Speech Acts," in *Concise Routledge Encyclopaedia of Philosophy* (London: Routledge, 1999).

[100] M. Foucault, "Preface," in *The Order of Things: An Archaeology of the Human Sciences* (New York: Pantheon Books, 1970), p. xvi (using the example of the seemingly arbitrary, fantastic, and fictitious taxonomy of animals depicted by Jorge Luis Borges in his *The Analytical Language of John Wilkins* as a point of departure for discussing the epistemic structures of the human sciences). For a critique of the postmodern mistrust of structural classifications in reference to Foucault's example, see A. Peters and H. Schwenke, "Comparative Law Beyond Post-modernism'" (2000) 49 *International and Comparative Law Quarterly* 800, 825–826.

otherwise appears to be an infinite and indefinite river.[101] At the same time, the fish and other treasures caught in the net do come from the same river, opening the possibility to learn about the environment in which they were bred and cultivated. The lexicon format does just that: focusing on specific terms and concepts and pointing to their interconnectedness, it offers an opportunity to consider the nomos of the regime – that is, law's interrelation to the vocabularies that constitute and traverse it in the OPT.

---

[101] A metaphor used by Israeli novelist, Dan Tsalka, in the introduction to his alphabetically structured autobiography; see D. Tsalka, *Sefer Ha'Alef-Beit [Book of ABC]* (Tel Aviv: Hargol, 2003) [Hebrew].

A

Assigned Residence

Orna Ben-Naftali

A.1 INTRODUCTION: THE LEGAL PARAMETERS OF ASSIGNED RESIDENCE

A.1.1 *The Normative Framework of Assigned Residence*

Assigned residence is an uncanny legal idiom: the dissonance between the sterility of the term and its impact on the person whose residence is being assigned produces, literally, an *unheimlich* effect.[1] For that person it usually means that what used to be *home* has become forbidden territory; that s/he has been exiled from life as s/he has known it, by law but without trial.[2] The law does not conceive of this power to crumble the building blocks of a person's life and indeed, personhood,[3] as a punishment for past crimes executed pursuant to a judicial process, but as an administrative means of prevention.[4]

---

[1] S. Freud, *The Uncanny*, D. McLintock (trans.) (London: Penguin Classics, 2003). (In German, "das Heim" translates into a "home" in English.)

[2] Note that it can mean confinement to one's residence, but this is not how it has been used by Israel.

[3] Margaret Radin argues that "[t]he home is a moral nexus between liberty, privacy, and freedom of association . . . There is also the feeling that it would be an insult for the state to invade one's home because it is the scene of one's history and future, one's life and growth. In other words, one embodies or constitutes oneself there." M. J. Radin, "Property and Personhood" (1982) 34 *Stanford Law Review* 957, 991–992.

[4] On the nexus between a home and personhood and its normative ramifications in the Israeli context, see, e.g., M. Birnhack, "Just Property: Three Concepts of Property" (2005) 21 *Bar Ilan Law Studies* 439 [Hebrew]; A. Gross, "Property as a Constitutional Right and Basic Law: Human Dignity and Liberty" (1998) 21 *Tel-Aviv University Law Review* 405 [Hebrew]; See also Justice Edmond E. Levy's dissent in the Gaza Strip "disengagement" judgment, arguing that the legitimate expectation of the Jewish residents in the Gaza Strip to continue living there, and the nexus between their homes and their right to human dignity, are factors that can contribute to the illegitimacy of a political decision of national security: HCJ 1661/05 *Gaza Coast Regional Council v. The Israeli Knesset* (2005) 59(2) PD 481, 797. Sensitivity to the traumatic effect of being forced to leave one's home also characterized the narrative of the

The law is articulated in Article 78 of the Fourth Geneva Convention (GC IV).[5] This provision authorizes the occupying power to restrict the freedom of movement of a "protected person"[6] who has not violated the applicable penal code, for "imperative reasons of security." Such restriction may be effected by two administrative measures: (i) internment, or administrative detention, and (ii) assigning a place of residence. Both are exceptional measures of precaution, not punishment; both are subject to various procedural safeguards; and both demand individual, as distinct from collective, consideration, that is, that the measure be applied to a person against whom there is solid administrative evidence that otherwise s/he will present a real danger to the security of the territory.[7]

The level of control the occupying power has over an interned person is higher than that exercised over a person whose residence is assigned. From the perspective of freedom of movement, a perspective that falls short of capturing the full experience, the assignment of a place of residence is the

justices who comprised the majority: e.g., "the disengagement disconnects the evicted Israeli from his home, from his environment, from his synagogue and from the cemetery in which his dead relatives are buried. It hurts his personality" (¶ 82); "whether we agree with the evicted Israelis' way or oppose it, we understand their pain. Behind the law stands the person … We stressed the historical character of the disengagement. Its traumatic character should also be recognized" (¶ 482). On the meaning of home for Palestinians in the OPT, as a site of continuity, memory, solidarity and an empowering vision generally, and for women most particularly, see N. Shalhoub-Kevorkian, "When Laws are Tools of Oppression: Palestinian Women Counter Discourse against the Policy of House Demolition," in D. Barak-Erez, S. Yanisky-Ravid, Y. Bitton, and D. Pugach (eds.), *Studies in Law, Gender and Feminism* (Tel Aviv: Nevo, 2007), p. 463 [Hebrew]; N. Shalhoub-Kevorkian, "Hunted Homeplaces" in *Security Theology, Surveillance and the Politics of Fear* (Cambridge: Cambridge University Press, 2015), pp. 73–115. See entry H: House Demolitions.

5 Geneva Convention Relative to the Protection of Civilian Persons in the Time of War, Geneva, August 12, 1949, 75 UNTS 287 [hereinafter: GC IV], Article 78, provides: "If the Occupying Power considers it necessary, for imperative reasons of security, to take safety measures concerning protected persons, it may, at the most, subject them to assigned residence or to internment. Decisions regarding such assigned residence or internment shall be made according to a regular procedure to be prescribed by the Occupying Power in accordance with the provisions of the present Convention. This procedure shall include the right of appeal for the parties concerned. Appeals shall be decided with the least possible delay. In the event of the decision being upheld, it shall be subject to periodical review, if possible every six months, by a competent body set up by the said Power. Protected persons made subject to assigned residence and thus required to leave their homes shall enjoy the full benefit of Article 39 of the present Convention."

6 *Protected persons* are defined as "those who, at a given moment and in any manner whatsoever, find themselves, in case of a conflict or occupation, in the hands of a Party to the conflict or Occupying Power of which they are not nationals." *Ibid.*, Article 4.

7 J. S. Pictet (ed), *The Geneva Conventions of 12 August 1949, Commentary – IV Geneva Convention Relative to the Protection of Civilian Persons in Time of War* (Geneva: International Committee of the Red Cross, 1958), p. 367.

less restrictive measure. The occupying power is required to ensure the livelihood of the person whose residence is assigned, and that of his or her dependents.[8] The assigned residence must be within the confines of the occupied territory,[9] lest it amounts to impermissible deportation or forcible transfer.[10]

The legal validity of orders issued by the military commander of the "West Bank" (a.k.a. "Judea and Samaria"[11]), which assigned the residence of three protected persons from the West Bank to the Gaza Strip, was the subject matter of the *Ajuri* case.[12]

A.1.2 *The Context of the Judicial Text*

The Palestinian uprising known as the second Intifada broke out on September 29, 2000. Reflecting as it enhanced the disenchantment of both Israelis and Palestinians with the Oslo peace process, the renewed cycle of violence in 2002 led to the reoccupation of most of the West Bank area.[13] The decision to assign the residence of family members of Palestinians engaged actively in attacks against Israeli targets, including suicide bombings, from the West Bank to the Gaza Strip, was reached by the ministerial committee for

---

[8] *GC IV*, Article 39. [9] Pictet, *Geneva Conventions*, p. 368.

[10] *GC IV* Article 49 provides: "Individual or mass forcible transfers, as well as deportations of protected persons from occupied territory to the territory of the Occupying Power or to that of any other country, occupied or not, are prohibited, regardless of their motive"; Grave breaches are defined in Article 147 as "those involving any of the following acts, if committed against persons or property protected by the present Convention: . . . unlawful deportation or transfer or unlawful confinement of a protected person . . . not justified by military necessity and carried out unlawfully and wantonly"; Deportation or forcible transfer of population are also listed as crimes against humanity in the Rome Statute of the International Criminal Court (Rome, July 17, 1998, entered into force July 1, 2002), 2187 UNTS 90, Article 7 § 1(d), while unlawful deportation or transfer are war crimes, Article 8 § 2(a)(vii). See, e.g., *Prosecutor* v. *Krstić* (Trial Chamber Judgment), case no IT-98–33-T (August 2, 2001) §§ 521–522.

[11] Language is a powerful tool in the construction of consciousness. The area the international community refers to as the "West Bank" is referred to in Israel as "Judea and Samaria" to emphasize the historical justification of the claim to the land. See, J. Peteet, "Words as Interventions: Naming in the Palestine – Israel Conflict" (2003) 26 *Third World Quarterly* 153. For further discussion, see entry G: Geneva Law.

[12] HCJ 7015/02 *Ajuri* v. *Commander of the IDF in Judea and Samaria* (2002) 56(6) PD 352 [Hebrew; English translation available at http://elyon1.court.gov.il/Files_ENG/02/150/070/A15/02070150.A15.pdf].

[13] *Ibid.*, § 3. For a concise account, see O. Ben-Naftali and A. Gross, "The Second Intifada," in A. Dworkin, R. Gutman, and D. Rieff (eds.), *Crimes of War (0.2): What the Public Should Know* (New York: W. W. Norton & Company, 2007). Note that the IDF re-entered parts of the West Bank, but not of the Gaza Strip.

national security on July 31, 2002.[14] It was taken in view of doubts regarding the legality and effectiveness of other means designed to prevent and to deter the Palestinian uprising, primarily house demolition[15] and deportation.[16] The following day the military commanders of the West Bank and the Gaza Strip issued complementary orders, giving effect to this decision.[17] Pursuant to this general order, the military commander of the West Bank issued three specific orders requiring three residents of the West Bank – Amtassar Ajuri, Kipah Ajuri, and Aber Asida – to leave their respective homes and reside for two years in the Gaza Strip. The three residents appealed the orders before an appeals board set up by the military commander. The board rejected their appeal and they petitioned the High Court of Justice (HCJ).[18] The judgment is the focus of this entry.

From a normative perspective, this is the first judgment of the HCJ that was based solely on an analysis of the *GC IV*. Its conclusion was that the measure undertaken by the military commander qualifies as permissible assigned residence rather than impermissible deportation or forced transfer. The court framed its normative analysis within a contextual narrative that was later reiterated in numerous judgments. The proposition advanced in this entry is that the assigned residence of the petitioners was, in fact, prohibited deportation. In order to substantiate this proposition, Section A.2 describes the judgment in terms of the narrative, the normative discourse, and the application of the law to the facts.

---

[14] *Ajuri*, ¶ 4. Prior to this decision, the power to restrict movement was exercised only within the West Bank, but not between the West Bank and the Gaza Strip.

[15] GC IV Article 53 provides: "Any destruction by the Occupying Power of real or personal property belonging individually or collectively to private persons, or to the State, or to other public authorities, or to social or cooperative organizations, is prohibited, except where such destruction is rendered absolutely necessary by military operations." For a legal analysis of house demolitions, see D. Kretzmer, *The Occupation of Justice: The Supreme Court of Israel and the Occupied Territories* (Albany: SUNY Press, 2002), pp. 145–164. Note that since 2014, the IDF has resumed the policy of house demolitions. Petitions challenging the legality of said measure have been rejected by the HCJ; see HCJ 8091/14 *Center for the defense of the Individual v. The Minister of Defense* (December 31, 2014) [Hebrew]. The same legalization of house demolitions has continued in numerous decisions since. For a detailed discussion, see entry H: House Demolitions.

[16] GC IV Article 49. For a legal analysis of deportations, see entry D: Deportations.

[17] The background to the decision to issue orders assigning residence is discussed in E. Benvenisti, "Scrutiny: Ajuri et al. – Israel High Court of Justice, 3 September 2002" (2003) 9 *European Public Law* 481; R. Zigler, "Case Note: The 'Assigned Residence' Case" (2002) 36 *Israel Law Review* 179, 179–183; D. Barak-Erez, "The International Law of Human Rights and Constitutional Law: A Case Study of an Expanding Dialogue" (2004) 2 *International Journal of Constitutional Law* 611, 620.

[18] *Ajuri*, ¶ 7.

Section A.3 offers a critical analysis of the judgment, focusing on both the interpretative techniques the court used and on its application of the law to the facts, to posit that the measure amount to impermissible deportation. Section A.4 concludes by juxtaposing the judicial narrative with its normative analysis.

A.2 THE *AJURI* JUDGMENT

The central question before the court was whether the orders assigning the residence of the petitioners were a valid exercise of the authority of the military commander under Article 78 of the GC IV, or an invalid exercise which amounted to forcible transfer or deportation, a measure prohibited under Article 49 of the GC IV.[19] The court determined that the general order was valid under international law (and Israeli law), but in applying the law to the facts of the case, invalidated one of the three specific orders.[20]

A.2.1 *The Narrative Framework*

The unanimous judgment, written by then chief justice Barak presiding over a panel of nine judges,[21] is framed within a narrative. The latter has been reiterated in later judgments[22] and indeed reflects the *nomos* of HCJ.[23] It is thus worthwhile to cite it at some length.

---

[19]   *Ibid.*, ¶ 13. Note that in the past, the HCJ, making a distinction between mass and individual deportation, approved individual deportation orders from the West Bank to foreign countries. See HCJ 785/87 *Abed El-Apu v. Commander of the IDF in the West Bank* (1988) 42(2) PD 4 [Hebrew; English translation available at (1990) 29 ILM 139 or at http://elyon1.court.gov.il/files_eng/87/850/007/Z01/87007850.z01.pdf]. See entry D: Deportations.

[20]   Later judgments of the HCJ, referring to the *Ajuri* judgment, upheld such specific orders. See, e.g., HCJ 9552/03 *Abed v. Commander of the IDF in the West Bank* (December 31, 2003) [Hebrew]; HCJ 9586/03 *Salame v. Commander of the IDF in the West Bank* (2003) 58(2) PD 342 [Hebrew].

[21]   Decisions of the supreme court are usually made by a panel of three judges. The court may decide to constitute a panel comprising a larger uneven number of judges to determine matters that involve fundamental legal questions and constitutional issues of particular importance.

[22]   See, e.g., HCJ 769/02 *Public Committee Against Torture v. Government of Israel* (2006) 62(1) PD 507 [Hebrew; English translation available at http://elyon1.court.gov.il/Files_ENG/02/690/007/a34/02007690.a34.pdf]; HCJ 316/03 *Mohammad Bakri v. Films and Plays Censorship Board* (2003) 58(1) PD 249 [Hebrew].

[23]   See R. M. Cover, "The Supreme Court 1982 term – Foreword: Nomos and Narrative" (1983) 97 *Harvard Law Review* 4. Cover uses the term "nomos" to refer to a normative universe, comprising both rules and the narratives that give them meaning. See entry N: Nomos.

Its opening paragraphs read as follows:

Since the end of September 2000, fierce fighting has been taking place in Judaea, Samaria and the Gaza Strip ... Within this framework, approximately 14,000 attacks have been made against the life, person and property of innocent Israeli citizens and residents, the elderly, children, men and women. More than six hundred citizens and residents of the State of Israel have been killed. More than 4,500 have been wounded, some most seriously. The Palestinians have also experienced death and injury. Many of them have been killed and wounded since September 2000 ... Bereavement and pain overwhelm us. Israel's fight is complex.

The Palestinians use, *inter-alia*, guided human bombs. These suicide bombers reach every place where Israelis are to be found ... They sew destruction and spill blood ... Indeed, the forces fighting against Israel are terrorists; they are not members of a regular army; they do not wear uniforms; they hide among the civilian Palestinian population in the territories, including in holy sites; they are supported by part of the civilian population, and by their families and relatives. The State of Israel faces a new and difficult reality, as it fights for its security and the security of its citizens.

In its struggle against terrorism, Israel has undertaken – by virtue of its right of self-defence – special military operations ... The purpose of the operations was to destroy the Palestinian terrorism infrastructure and to prevent further terrorist attacks ...

The special military operations did not provide an adequate response to the immediate need to stop the grave terrorist acts ...[24]

The judgment ends with the following words:

the State of Israel is undergoing a difficult period. Terror is hurting its residents. Human life is trampled upon. Hundreds have been killed. Thousands have been injured. The Arab population in Judaea and Samaria and the Gaza Strip is also suffering unbearably. All of this is because of acts of murder, killing and destruction perpetrated by terrorists ... The State of Israel is a freedom-seeking democracy. It is a defensive democracy acting within the framework of its right to self-defence – a right recognized by the charter of the United Nations. The State seeks to act within the framework of the lawful possibilities available to it under the international law to which it is subject and in accordance with its internal law. As a result, not every effective measure is also a lawful measure. Indeed, the State of Israel is fighting a difficult war against terror. It is a war carried out within the law and with the tools that the law makes available. The well-known saying that "In battle laws are silent" ... does not reflect the law as it is, nor as it should be. Indeed, "even

---

[24] *Ajuri*, ¶¶ 1–4.

when the cannons speak, the military commander must uphold the law. The power of society to stand against its enemies is based on its recognition that it is fighting for values that deserve protection. The rule of law is one of these values" ... Indeed, the position of the State of Israel is a difficult one. Also our role as judges is not easy. We are doing all we can to balance properly between human rights and the security of the area. In this balance, human rights cannot receive complete protection, as if there were no terror, and State security cannot receive complete protection, as if there were no human rights. A delicate and sensitive balance is required. This is the price of democracy. It is expensive, but worthwhile. It strengthens the State. It provides a reason for its struggle.[25]

The judicial analysis of the legal validity of the contested orders assigning the residence of the three petitioners, unfolds within and coheres with this narrative framework. It is structured deductively along three phases: (i) the normative framework for the determination of the authority of the military commander to issue orders assigning residence; (ii) the analysis of the applicable law in order to determine the conditions for the exercise of said authority and its scope; and (iii) the application of the law to the specific facts relative to the petitioners. The court's line of reasoning is detailed in Sections A.2.2–A.2.4.

A.2.2 *The Normative Framework*

The applicable normative framework, says the court, is the laws of belligerent occupation, comprising the rules of the 1907 Hague Regulations and the GC IV. The former apply by virtue of their customary nature; the latter by virtue of the longstanding practice reflecting the decision of the government of Israel to act according to its humanitarian parts.[26] The authority of the military commander derives from these rules and they determine the extent of the permitted restriction on human rights as a result of a forcible assignment of residence.[27]

The issue before the court is governed entirely by Article 78 of the GC IV. This provision allows an occupying power, if it considers it necessary for

---

[25]   *Ibid.*, ¶ 41.
[26]   The court noted that the legal arguments supporting the Israeli position regarding the applicability of the GC IV "are not simple," but saw no need make a decision on the issue. The court further noted that alongside the international legal rules, "the fundamental Israeli of administrative law, such as the rules of natural justice, also apply. Indeed, every Israeli soldier carries in his pack both the rules of international law and the basic principles of Israeli administrative law," *ibid.* The thesis that the GC IV is inapplicable is presented and critically discussed in entry G: Geneva Law.
[27]   *Ibid.*, ¶ 16.

imperative security reasons, to take safety measures concerning protected persons. Such measures include, at most, assigned residence or internment and are subject to a certain procedure.[28] Article 78, says the court, constitutes *lex specialis*. As such, the measures indicated therein are permitted even if a general provision prohibits them. It follows that Article 49, which prohibits forcible transfer or deportation, is irrelevant to the case at hand. The order at issue was an order to assign residence, and Article 78 "provides a comprehensive and full arrangement," in this respect: it is "both a source for the protection of the right of a person whose residence is being assigned and also a source for the possibility of restricting this right."[29]

A.2.3 *Analysis of Article 78*

Having thus determined the normative framework, the court proceeded to analyze Article 78 in the light of two main arguments made by the petitioners. The first argument related to the area within which assigned residence may be permissible. The petitioners argued that the new place of residence should be within a single territory subject to belligerent occupation, and that since the Gaza Strip is situated outside that territory, the assignment of their residence from the West Bank to Gaza is impermissible under Article 78, and amounts to deportation prohibited under Article 49. The court, having accepted that that the area to which a protected person is assigned is indeed a parameter that distinguishes between Article 49 and Article 78, had to determine whether the West Bank and Gaza form one territory or two separate territories. It decided that the fact that the territories were conquered from different states (Jordan and Egypt, respectively) and are managed by two distinct military commanders does not suffice to conclude that they are separate territories: both areas form one territorial unit. This conclusion was based on two grounds: first, a teleological reading of Article 78 generates the conclusion that it restricts the validity of assigned residence to one territory, characterized by "societal, linguistic, cultural, social and political unity" so as to minimize the harm caused to the person whose residence is being assigned, and that the West Bank and Gaza are thus united under one belligerent occupant. Second, both Israel and the Palestinian Authority view the West Bank and the Gaza Strip as a single territorial unit, as is evidenced, inter alia,

---

[28]   *Ibid.*, ¶ 18. While the court says that it sees no need to determine the legality of orders of deportation and that this matter can be decided at a later date, the reference to the measures that the military commander is authorized "at most" to take seems to contain an implicit rejection of the permissibility of deportation of *protected persons*.

[29]   *Ibid.*, ¶17.

in clause 11 of the Israel-Palestinian Interim Agreement on the West Bank and the Gaza Strip.[30]

The second argument of the petitioners concerned the considerations governing the military commander's exercise of authority. The court accepted their position that the prevention of a danger from the person whose residence is being assigned, a danger that the assignment is to avert, is the essential and necessary condition for exercising this authority. This determination too was based on a teleological interpretation of the *GC IV* in general, and of Article 78 in particular. This interpretation emphasizes the particularly severe nature of this exceptional measure. It further determined that such an interpretation is in accordance with "our Jewish and democratic values."[31] The exceptionality of the measure further decrees that the authority is to be exercised only if there is convincing administrative evidence that if residence is not assigned, there is a reasonable possibility that the person will present a real danger to the security of the territory, and that the measure meets the standard of proportionality.[32] Nevertheless, the court proceeded to determine, once it is clear that the authority was exercised as a preventive measure to avoid danger from a specific person, the military commander is authorized to also take into account the consideration of deterring others. Such reading of the scope of the authority, said the court, is consistent with the *GC IV*, which regards assigned residence as a legitimate measure for the security of the territory, and is especially required by harsh ground realities – realities which call for a dynamic interpretation of the law.[33] It is to be noted that in its first concluding remark, the court repeated the need for a dynamic interpretation in the face of the new reality of "living bombs" Israel is facing, a reality "the drafters of article 78 never anticipated."[34]

A.2.4 *Applying the Law to the Facts*

Having thus analyzed the law, the court proceeded to determine whether the military commander has used his authority accordingly with respect to each of the petitioners. The orders assigning the residence of two of the three petitioners, were issued because they assisted the "terrorist Ahmed Ali Ajuri" to whom "much terrorist activity is attributed ... including sending suicide bombers with explosive belts."[35] Amtassar Ajuri, his sister, is an unmarried woman aged 34. The court was satisfied that she was aware of her brother's forbidden activities, knew that he was armed and had hidden an

---

[30] *Ibid.*, ¶¶ 20–22.   [31] *Ibid.*, ¶ 24.   [32] *Ibid.*, ¶ 25.   [33] *Ibid.*, ¶ 27.   [34] *Ibid.*, ¶ 40.
[35] *Ibid.*, ¶ 31.

assault rifle in the apartment, and assisted him by sewing explosive belts. Kipah Ajuri, his brother, is a 38-year-old married man and the father of three children. He too knew of his brother's activities and aided him by acting as a look-out and, on occasion, bringing food to his brother's group. In the case of both, the court found that the decision to assign their residence was a reasonable exercise of authority, as both pose a grave danger to the security of the area. The court found, however, that the activities of the third petitioner, Abed Asida, a 38-year-old married man and brother of the "terrorist" Nasser Asida, consisting of knowledge of his brother's activities, driving him and another person to a hospital after they were injured by an explosive, and occasionally lending his brother his car, fall short of the level of danger required for adopting the measure of assigned residence, and that therefore assigning residence in this case exceeds "the zone of reasonableness."[36]

A.3 CRITICAL ANALYSIS OF THE JUDGMENT

A.3.1 *A Dynamic and Teleological Interpretation*

The *Ajuri* case is noteworthy for being the first judgment that deals with a security issue to have been determined entirely on the basis of an in-depth analysis of IHL, and particularly on the basis of the *GC IV*. From this perspective, while the court still refrained from a clear determination regarding the applicability of the *GC IV* as a matter of a legal obligation, the decision appeared nevertheless to be a positive development insofar as the incorporation of international law into the Israeli legal discourse is concerned.[37] Appearances, however, are notoriously deceptive.[38] The assessment of the nature of this development depends on the objectives it is designed to achieve –that is, on whether its purpose is to ensure that the exercise of power is limited, rather than facilitated by law. The interpretative and narrative methodologies employed by the court in the *Ajuri* case shed a

---

[36] *Ibid.*, ¶¶ 31–39.
[37] It is instructive to note that this change was probably related to developments in international criminal law, and especially to the establishment of the International Criminal Court, the exercise of universal jurisdiction and an appreciation of the implication of the principle of complementarity. It is also quite probable that the implicit rejection of the legality of deportation of protected persons, noted in note 28, was equally thus motivated.
[38] In reference to the language used by Judge Krylov in his dissenting opinion in Conditions of Admission of a State to Membership in The United Nations, Advisory Opinion, 1948 ICJ 57, 107.

dim light on the purposes the resort to the *GC IV* was designed to, and did in fact, achieve.[39]

The court, as described above, employed a dynamic as well as a teleological method of interpretation of Article 78. The justification for a dynamic interpretation was articulated as follows: "we doubt whether the drafters of the provisions of article 78 ... anticipated protected persons who collaborated with terrorists and living bombs. This new reality requires a dynamic interpretation."[40] In reality, however, the drafters of the *GC IV* did anticipate that protected persons would participate in hostilities against an occupying power, and it is precisely because of this anticipation that the convention contains certain provisions, including Article 78, which authorize the occupant to take security measures against protected persons who perpetrate or otherwise assist in such hostilities.[41] It does not follow that a dynamic interpretation is unwarranted, but the dubious justification given for advancing it informs, and indeed provides, the Ariadne's thread for the understanding of the interpretive path paved by the HCJ.

There is little doubt that a dynamic interpretation designed to align normative provisions with the nature of present warfare is often necessary. This indeed was the methodology employed by the International Criminal

---

[39] The following analysis is based on the critical review of the judgment in O. Ben-Naftali and K. Micaheli, "The Call of Abraham – Between Deportation and Assigned Residence: A Critique of the Ajuri Case" (2004) 9 *Hamishpat* 107 [Hebrew].

[40] *Ajuri*, ¶ 40.

[41] GC IV Article 5 provides: "Where, in the territory of a Party to the conflict, the latter is satisfied that an individual protected person is definitely suspected of or engaged in activities hostile to the security of the State, such individual person shall not be entitled to claim such rights and privileges under the present Convention as would, if exercised in the favor of such individual person, be prejudicial to the security of such State. Where in occupied territory an individual protected person is detained as a spy or saboteur, or as a person under definite suspicion of activity hostile to the security of the Occupying Power, such person shall, in those cases where absolute military security so requires, be regarded as having forfeited rights of communication under the present Convention. In each case, such persons shall nevertheless be treated with humanity, and in case of trial, shall not be deprived of the rights of fair and regular trial prescribed by the present Convention. They shall also be granted the full rights and privileges of a protected person under the present Convention at the earliest date consistent with the security of the State or Occupying Power, as the case may be." Article 68 provides: "Protected persons who commit an offence which is solely intended to harm the Occupying Power, but which does not constitute an attempt on the life or limb of members of the occupying forces or administration, nor a grave collective danger, nor seriously damage the property of the occupying forces or administration or the installations used by them, shall be liable to internment or simple imprisonment, provided the duration of such internment or imprisonment is proportionate to the offence committed."

Tribunal for the former Yugoslavia (ICTY) in the *Tadić* case.[42] The ICTY resorted to a dynamic interpretation in order to broaden the protection afforded to the civilian population. The HCJ, by contrast, employed it in order to broaden the scope of the discretion of the occupying power at the expense of the protection offered to the occupied population,[43] while at the same time turning a blind eye to the main reality the drafters of the convention did not anticipate: a prolonged occupation, the end of which is indefinitely deferred, and the cause-and-effect relationship between this reality and Palestinian resistance. It is not inconceivable that had the drafters contemplated such a situation, they would have changed the balance of power between the occupant and the protected persons in favor of the latter insofar as the limitations the convention imposes on resisting an occupation are concerned.[44] The net result of the above is that the dynamic interpretation employed by the HCJ is incongruous with the teleological interpretation of the GC IV, the main purpose of which is to protect the civilian population, as is indeed otherwise acknowledged by the court.[45]

The teleological interpretation of Article 78 ostensibly employed by the court becomes all the more problematic when considered in the light of another ground reality – namely, the lesser control Israel exercised over the Gaza Strip, when compared to its control over the West Bank.[46] The court, as was discussed above, resorted to this interpretative method to conclude that Gaza and the West Bank are indeed one territory, stating that:

> [t]he purpose underlying the provisions of Article 78 ... and which restricts the validity of assigned residence to one territory, lies in the societal,

---

[42] The ICTY canceled, in effect, the condition stipulated in article 4 of the GC IV, according to which the nationality of the protected person should be different from the nationality of the occupying power, on the grounds that the drafters of the Convention did not anticipate the situation where ethnicity rather than nationality is the source of the conflict. See Tadić, Appeal Chamber Opinion and Judgment, ICTY-94-1-A (July 15, 1999) ¶ 168; Aleksovski, Appeal Chamber Judgment, IT-95-14/1-A (March 24, 2000) ¶¶ 151–152; Delalić, Mucić, Delić, Landźo, Appeal Chamber Judgment, IT-96-21-A (February 20, 2001) ¶¶ 82–84.

[43] By permitting the military commander to base its decision to assign residence on considerations of general deterrence in addition to the danger emanating from the individual whose residence is being assigned, see text between notes 32–33. Note that the expansion of Israel's legal and political discretion is characteristic of various control mechanisms it employs in the OPT and indeed enables such control. See, e.g., the entry M: Military Courts.

[44] Pictet, *Geneva Conventions*, pp. 35–36.   [45] *Ajuri*, ¶ 24.

[46] Ben-Naftali and Gross, "The Second Intifada." Note that some of the briefs submitted by the petitioners posited that since there were no Israeli forces in Gaza at the relevant time, it was not under Israeli effective control; that therefore the law of belligerent occupation did not apply to it at all; and that the military commander of the West Bank had as much authority to assign their residence to Gaza as it had to assign it to Birmingham, England. See Ajuri.

linguistic, cultural, social and political unity of the territory, out of a desire to restrict the harm caused by assigning residence to a foreign place.[47]

This conclusion is less clear-cut than it appears to be: a teleological interpretation of the *GC IV* is indeed driven by a wish to offer the occupied people as broad a protection as possible. Meeting this objective, however, calls for a strict rather than a wide interpretation of the scope of the territory, so as to minimize the harm to a protected person who is being removed from his home, family, social network, and work – that is, from his/her life. Between the Gaza Strip and the West Bank, there is no territorial continuity and they are, and were at the relevant time, separated by Israeli-controlled borders. While they are connected nationally and linguistically, their distinct history accounts for significant differences in social, cultural, economic, and political terms. It was thus not unreasonable to assume that the alienation the petitioners would have felt in Gaza would not have been that different from what they would have felt in an altogether foreign country. This line of reasoning becomes all the more poignant when considered in the light of two additional points: first, the petitioners themselves indicated that they would rather be detained than dispatched to Gaza.[48] The second point relates to the original purpose of assigned residence, a purpose the court was silent about: the clear rationale behind authorizing the assignment of residence of a protected person was to allow the occupying power to exercise greater and more effective control over that person's actions.[49] The assignment of the petitioners from the West Bank to Gaza, a territory over which Israel exercised far less effective control, seems to defy that purpose. Indeed, if the idea was to isolate the petitioners from being in contact with hostile factors, then greater support is lent to their position that Gaza is a separate territory and that therefore the measure amounts to deportation rather than to assignment of residence.

A.3.2 *Application to the Facts*

The above critique of the interpretive methodology of the judgment is strengthened when one takes a closer look at the application of the law to

---

[47]   *Ajuri*, ¶ 22 (emphasis added). Benvenisti, "Ajuri," pp. 485–487, notes, first, that it is effective control rather than the cultural determinants that are relevant from the perspective of the law of belligerent occupation, and that given the lack of effective control over Gaza, the assignment of residence to Gaza was impermissible; and, second, that the lack of effective control means that there would have been no possibility to offer the persons whose residence was assigned the protection and livelihood required under Article 78.

[48]   Application of the petitioners to the court in *Ajuri*, www.acri.org.il/he/?p=477.

[49]   Pictet, *Geneva Conventions*, p. 256.

the facts of the case as they relate to the sister and the brother of Ahmed Ali Ajuri. The commentary to Article 42[50] clarifies that in order for a protected person to be considered as presenting such a grave danger as to sanction assigned residence, "the State must have good reason to think that the person concerned, by his *activities, knowledge or qualifications*, represents a real threat to its present or future security."[51] It is clear from the judgment that the activities the siblings performed, and not any particular knowledge or qualifications, justified the security concern: indeed, the activities required neither special skills nor knowledge. It is equally clear that the tasks they had performed related directly to their essential role as the brother and the sister of Ahmed Ali. It does not, of course, follow that because he is their brother they are allowed to violate the law without consequences, but it does provide the proper context for their actions. It is against this context that the question regarding the security danger they pose, a danger justifying the assignment of their residence, should be evaluated. Ostensibly, the answer is apparent: it is reasonable to assume that if they assisted their brother in the past in a manner that endangered security, they are likely to continue to do so, unless otherwise prevented. Appearances, however, are indeed deceptive, and often attest to blind spots rather than to clear vision: the brother, Ahmed Ali, had been killed by the IDF on August 6, 2002 – that is, about a month before the judgment was rendered. This fact was known to, but ignored by, the court.[52] Given that assisting their brother was the reason for their predicament, his death renders the likelihood that they will pose a danger in the future improbable and the proportionality of assigning their residence quite excessive, strengthening the conclusion that rather than being subjected to a permissible assignment of residence, they were, in reality, subjected to deportation or forcible transfer.

A.4 CONCLUSION

The interplay of law and fiction is most apparent when legal texts narrate not merely the story but also the history of their subjects. Judicial decisions participate in the construction of the collective memory of the imagined

---

[50] *GC IV* Article 42 provides: "The internment or placing in assigned residence of protected persons may be ordered only if the security of the Detaining Power makes it absolutely necessary."

[51] Pictet, *Geneva Conventions*, p. 258 (emphasis added).

[52] Both the petition of Amtassar Ajuri and the Respondent's brief referred to this fact. The point was noted by Amnesty International; see Amnesty International, Forcible transfers of Palestinians to Gaza constitutes a War Crime (September 3, 2002), www.amnesty.org/en/documents/mde15/134/2002/en.

communities of which they are part. They frame past experiences in a manner designed to advance present and future public consciousness, a particular ideology. That construction benefits from the value of objectivity attached to law and courts, but it is not less, and is perhaps more fictional for that.[53] Judges, however, unlike historians and novelists, are empowered to determine the fate of both the participants in the judicial process and the law.

In the *Ajuri* case, the dynamic interpretation employed by the court, far from establishing a normative limit to the exercise of power by the occupant, has enabled it, supplying the Israeli narrative with a normative umbrella. This narrative indeed effects more than a "dynamic interpretation"; it controls the dynamics of the conflict and determines the legal outcome of the specific case. Thus, for instance, the narrative within which the court frames its judicial review, at both the beginning and the end of the judgment, posits that Israel is acting pursuant to its right to self-defense.[54] This indication is stated as a fact. It is, however, a normative proposition that is as debatable as it is irrelevant to the case at hand: it is debatable primarily because Israel is the belligerent occupant, exercising effective control over the OPT; it is irrelevant because the question of whether or not power is exercised in self-defense has little to do with the question of whether the power (the authority to order the assignment of residence) has been exercised according to the rules of IHL. The first question is a *jus ad bellum* issue; the second, a *jus in bello* issue.[55] The judicial reference to the right to self-defense, consciously blurring the boundaries between the two otherwise distinct legal arenas, indeed served no normative purpose in the judgment; its only implication was to advance a particular narrative: the Israeli narrative with which the court identifies and which it exports to the international community.

The repetitive reference in the judgment to the "terrorists" whom Israel is fighting equally serves no normative purpose and is designed to advance the Israeli narrative in the rhetorical battleground: as the court itself admits, IHL recognizes only two statuses: a combatant and a noncombatant (i.e., a

---

[53] See, e.g., A. Sarat and T. R. Kearns, "Writing History and Registering Memory in Legal Decisions and Legal Practices: An Introduction in History" in A. Sarat and T. R. Kearns (eds.), *Memory and the Law* (Ann Arbor: Michigan University Press, 2002), pp. 1–2; D. Barak-Erez, "And Thou Shalt Tell Thy Son: History and Memory in the Court" (2002) 26 *Tel Aviv University Law Review* 773 [Hebrew].

[54] *Ajuri*, ¶¶ 3, 41.

[55] For views that posit a different appreciation of the distinction between *jus ad bellum* and *jus in bello*, see, e.g., C. Stahn, "'Jus in bello, Jus ad bellum – Jus post Bellum'?: Rethinking the Conception of the Law of Armed Force" (2006) 17 *European Journal of International Law* 921; E. Benvenisti, "Rethinking the Divide Between Jus ad Bellum and Jus in Bello in Warfare against Non-State Actors" (2009) 34 *Yale Journal of International Law* 541.

civilian).[56] Both may perform illegal acts, and be engaged in terrorist activities, but it does not follow that there is either a third status, a terrorist, or that the "war on terror" is otherwise exempt from the normative constraints imposed by IHL. The court is well aware of that.[57]

The articulation of the dominant Israeli narrative finds further expression in the court's assignment of blame for the "harsh reality in which the State of Israel and the territory are situated": "All of this," says the court "is because of acts of murder, killing and destruction perpetrated by terrorists."[58] Further, "the forces fighting against Israel are terrorists; they are not members of a regular army."[59] This narrative thus not merely extracts the situation from its political context – the indefinite occupation, which is not even mentioned – but further engages in a reversal of the relationship between cause and effect: the Palestinians seem to be responsible for, rather than victims of, their lack of "regular army." The latter is the privilege of sovereign states; Israel is thus the victim, not the perpetrator, of the denial of Palestinian statehood. Competing narratives, ascribing the harsh reality to the continuation of the Israeli control over and expropriation of Palestinian land, exploitation of Palestinian resources and disregard for Palestinian life and dignity, are not hard to find.

In the court's narrative, however, Israel is not only a victim of its own privileged status and the power it exercises over the Palestinians, it is also "a freedom-seeking democracy. It is a defensive democracy."[60] One may wonder, however, if it is indeed the democracy which is defending itself, or rather the hegemonic Jewish ethnos, safeguarding exclusively the freedom of Jews, including their freedom to settle in the OPT at the expense of Palestinian individual and collective human rights, thus defending its ethnocratic and not its democratic regime.[61]

The problem does not emanate solely from the fact that judges in Jerusalem empathize with and advance the official Israeli narrative, but rather from the privileged position this narrative enjoys in relation to the law: the national

---

[56] See entry C: Combatants.
[57] *Ajuri,* ¶ 41: "not every effective measure is also a lawful measure." For a discussion of the status of combatants, and the affirmation by the HCJ that IHL recognizes only two categories – combatants and noncombatants – see entry C: Combatants.
[58] *Ibid.,* ¶ 41. [59] *Ibid.,* ¶ 3. [60] *Ibid.,* ¶ 41.
[61] See O. Yiftachel, *Ethnocracy Land and Identity Politics in Israel/Palestine* (Philadelphia: University of Pennsylvania Press, 2006); Y. Peled and D. Navot, "Ethnic Democracy Revisited: On the State of Democracy in the Jewish State" (2005) 20 *Israel Studies Forum* 3; S. Smooha, "The Regime of the State of Israel: Civil Democracy, Non-Democracy, or Ethnic Democracy?" (2000) 2 *Israeli Sociology* 565 [Hebrew]; A. Azoulay and A. Ophir, *The One-State Condition* (Stanford: Stanford University Press, 2013), p. 205.

narrative determines the court's "dynamic interpretation" of IHL, and the latter reflects the power relations of a legal order which includes "protected persons," primarily through their exclusion from its protection. The result in this particular case is that a specific order designed to punish and deter is read as a preventive security measure, and an impermissible order of deportation or forcible transfer is being legitimated as a permissible order to assign residence. The military commander can now lawfully drop the Ajuri siblings at the outskirts of the Gaza Strip, for theirs is a "bare life," suspended, as it were, between inside and outside, bereft of any legal protection.[62] The cumulative result of such a narrative, which has reached the status of a judicial mantra, is that the judiciary, more than effecting "checks and balances" vis-à-vis governmental policies in the OPT, has operated as the latter's executive agency.

---

[62] G. Agamben, *Homo Sacer: Sovereign Power and Bare Life*, D. Heller-Roazen (trans.) (Stanford: Stanford University Press, 1995), pp. 127–128.

B

Border/Barrier

Michael Sfard

B.1 INTRODUCTION: CAN A WALL HAVE ONLY ONE FACET?

A state needs a *border*. From the perspective of positive international law, borders are an existential issue for states. This is what the Montevideo Convention teaches us through its requirement that states have a defined territory as one of the conditions for being endowed with the international legal personality of statehood.[1] State borders must form a geometric shape – that is, they must delineate a territory within a geographic space. Thus, a borderline both defines a country and the area over which it has sovereignty, and, at the same time, affirms and respects the sovereignties that stretch out beyond its outer limits. Borders divide the entire world into "inside" and "outside."[2] The Inside is where a country may exercise the powers and liberties of "making or interpreting of Laws, the declaring of Wars, imposing of Taxes, levying or quartering of Soldiers, erecting new Fortifications ... or reinforcing the old Garisons."[3] And, in more modern terms: "the capacity to make authoritative decisions with regard to the people and resources within [its] territory."[4]

---

[1] Convention on the Rights and Duties of States, Montevideo, December 26, 1933, 165 LNTS 19 (hereinafter: Montevideo Convention).

[2] This division is, however, subjective. Given that the earth has a finite amount of space, the areas on either side of the border are surrounded by it, and anyone standing on either side could argue that they are the ones surrounded by the border, and therefore, "inside."

[3] Article LXV of the Treaty of Westphalia: Peace Treaty Between the Holy Roman Emperor and the King of France and Their Respective Allies, Munster, October 24, 1648, printed in: F. L. Israel (ed.), *Major Peace Treaties of Modern History 1648–1967* (New York: Chelsea House Publishers, 1967), vol. I, p. 27.

[4] International Commission on Intervention and State Sovereignty, *The Responsibility to Protect* (International Development Research Centre Publications, 2001), p. 12.

Outside, foreign sovereignties have equal rights and powers with respect to their own territory,[5] together with political independence that prohibits interference in their affairs.[6] Inside, the home of the *locals*, subjects of the sovereignty are entitled to status within it; outside, the home of the *foreigners* who will receive their status from the sovereignty that is in power on the other side of the border.[7] The border is theoretically one-dimensional – that is, it has only length, not width, which guarantees full planar coverage of sovereignty.[8] In practice, however, borders are often two-dimensional; their width creates a no man's land where there is either no sovereignty at all, or partial and limited multiple sovereignties, but no single full one. Either way, a border or a no man's land has two sides, with a single, distinct sovereignty on each. Borders prevent sovereignties from spilling over into one another, which is why they are a requirement for independent statehood.

A *barrier* is a physical divide installed in a geographic space, which prevents or impedes passage from one side to another. A barrier, like a border, has two sides, and it too splits the geographic space. When a barrier forms a geometric shape – that is, when one end of it, or of a chain of physical barriers, meets the other – that barrier, like a border, divides the world into *inside* and *outside*.

Roughly speaking, a border is a political-legal geographic divide and a barrier is a physical geographic divide.[9] Physical and legal divides sometimes overlap. For instance, the fence between my lawn and my neighbor's lawn is a physical divide preventing each of us from trespassing on the other's territory.

---

[5]   Article 4 of the Montevideo Convention; Article 2(1) of the Charter of the United Nations, United Nations, October 24, 1945, 1 UNTS XVI (hereinafter: UN Charter).

[6]   Article 8 of the Montevideo Convention; Article 2(7) of the UN Charter.

[7]   For a discussion of the liquidity of the inside/outside dichotomy, see entry O: Outside/Inside.

[8]   To be precise, the border, stretches to the airspace above land and to the depth underneath the surface, hence the border can be seen as two-dimensional and as creating a spatial rather than planar division. For the recognition of sovereignty over airspace, see Article 1 of the *Convention Relating to the Regulation of Aerial Navigation*, Paris, October 13, 1919, and Article 1 of the *Convention on International Civil Aviation [italics above also?]*, Chicago, December 7, 1944, both declaring "The High Contracting Parties recognise that every Power has complete and exclusive sovereignty over the air space above its territory." Sovereignty over the undersurface was partially recognized by the laws of sovereignty over natural resources: see GA Res 1803 (XVII), 15 / UN Doc A/5217 (December 14, 1962), "Permanent sovereignty over natural resources"; see also Article 1(2) common to the International Covenant on Economic, Social and Cultural Rights (ICESCR), General Assembly, December 16, 1966, 933 UNTS 3 and the International Covenant on Civil and Political Rights (ICCPR), General Assembly, December 19, 1966, 999 UNTS 17 – although sovereignty over natural resources is ascribed to *Peoples and Nations* (in the GA resolution, those terms and "State" are used interchangeably). However, the underlying assumption is that peoples and nations exercise their sovereignty over their wealth and natural resources through the polity of a state.

[9]   On the legal production of space, see entry Z: Zone, Section Z.1.

Property law, civil law, and even criminal law create a legal divide that occupies the same place as the physical fence between our homes.

Borders and barriers at times maintain a symbiotic and at others a dialectical relationship. Sometimes a physical barrier is installed on a borderline.[10] Sometimes a borderline is determined according to a natural barrier that is already there (a river or a mountain range).[11] Physical barriers are used to regulate border crossings, and even in an age of technology that allows the monitoring and control of movement through territories that are not separated by physical obstacles,[12] such obstacles remain popular. Mass migration of asylum seekers from conflict areas[13] and international terrorism, the major causes of public anxiety in the Western world of the first decades of the twenty-first century, have produced a public demand to tighten border controls. In many places – Israel, Hungary, France, and the United States, to name a few – politicians who have promised to fortify borders with concrete, barbed wire, and observation towers enjoy great popularity.[14]

---

[10]   The most obvious example of a physical barrier placed on a border line is the Berlin Wall, erected on the political line that separated West Berlin from East Berlin, between the German Democratic Republic (East Germany) and the Federal Republic of Germany (West Germany). The border between the two Germanies was a border between sovereignties, and since each of these sovereignties had the power to regulate entry and exit from its territory, the border was also a legal barrier. The wall itself was built more than 15 years after the border was created, and it was meant to bolster the legal barrier with a physical one. For a political-historical account of the events leading up to its construction, see D. Heller and D. Heller, *The Berlin Wall* (New York: Walker and Company, 1962). Another example is the Great Wall of China, built to set the boundary of the Chinese empire and foreigners incursions. "The wall is the sign of separation," wrote the American explorer William Edgar Geil, who is said to have traveled its entire length; see W.E. Geil, *The Great Wall of China* (New York: Sturgis & Wanton, 1909), p. 6.

[11]   Some examples of a natural barrier that created a political one are parts of the border between Canada and the USA, determined by the course of the Niagara River; the Rhine River that determined the border between Germany and France; the Dead Sea and Jordan River, which form the border between Jordan and Israel; and the Pyrenees, which created the political border between France and Spain.

[12]   See entry X: X Rays, Section X.2.5: "Surveillance Technologies 3.0: 'Smart' Techno-occupation."

[13]   Z. Bauman, *Strangers at our Door* (Malden: Polity, 2016).

[14]   The clearest and most recent example is Donald Trump's pledge to build a wall on the US–Mexican border to prevent immigrants from entering. See, for example: "Trump Says Would Raise Visa Fees to Pay for Mexican Border Wall," *Reuters* (August 16, 2015), www .reuters.com/article/us-usa-election-trump-immigration-idUSKCN0QL0NN20150816.
On the French so-called "great wall of Callais" meant to stop influx of illegal immigrants, see G. McAuley and M. Birnbaum, "France and Britain Just Beat Donald Trump to Building a Border Wall," *The Washington Post* (September 29, 2016), www.washingtonpost.com/world/europe/france-and-britain-just-beat-donald-trump-tobuilding-a-border-wall/2016/09/28/345e35 2a-8000-11e6-ad0e-ab0d12c779b1_story.html?utm_term=.c40775bf70cf. For the Hungarian

Given these definitions, borders and barriers are concepts that cover the same ground and signify a two-way spatial restriction on those located inside and outside: When one *walls out* others, one is simultaneously *walled in*. That is the *objective* trait of a physical barrier: it excludes on both of its sides. So does a border: bordering is simultaneously an act of defining the *interior* and the *exterior*, claiming sovereignty in the *interior* and acknowledging the *other's* sovereignty over the *exterior*, simultaneously including and excluding local status to residents of each side.

This entry concerns Israel's separation fence project.[15] The separation fence is made up of a physical barrier and a legal barrier. The barrier purportedly separates Palestinians from Israelis. In other words, it has a Palestinian side and an Israeli side. A very small portion of the route chosen for the fence overlaps with the Green Line, which is currently internationally recognized as the eastern limit of Israeli sovereignty.[16] The rest of it penetrates into the West Bank. Unlike the international community, Israel has never recognized the Green Line as an international border and maintains it has claims to the West Bank.

The proposition advanced in this entry is that Israel has enlisted the separation fence to serve its political territorial ambitions.[17] It has done so by creating a barrier whose sides are not merely geographic (east v. west) but also, and more so, national (Israeli v. Palestinian), and by making it a one-way barrier on the national plane. This one-way barrier functions like a one-way mirror. Both deflect (people or light) from only one side. In the case of the separation fence, it is the Palestinian side that gets deflected. For Palestinians, the fence is both a physical barrier and a borderline. For Israelis, the fence is neither. The fact that the barrier has only one side gives Israel an *inside*, without having to recognize that the area on the other side of the fence is an *outside*. While a border establishes distinct sovereignties on either side of it, this one-way fence with sovereignty only on one side creates *moving lines of sovereignty*. The border is a process, a verb rather than a noun.

border fence, see M. Birnbaum, "Refugees Race into Hungary as Border Fence Nears Completion," *The Washington Post* (September 25, 2016), www.washingtonpost.com/world/europe/refugees-race-into-hungary-as-border-fence-nears-completion/2015/08/25/91f6e9c8-4aac-11e5-9f53-d1e3ddfd0cda_story.html?tid=a_inl&utm_term=.fdc520aa73aa.

[15]   For a fuller account of the legal issues surrounding the separation fence, the entry should be read in conjunction with entries P: Proportionality and Z: Zone.

[16]   The Green Line was delineated as an armistice line in the armistice agreement signed in 1949 between Israel and Jordan: Jordanian-Israeli General Armistice Agreement, April 3, 1949, 1949 UN Doc S/1302/Rev.

[17]   This vision is discussed in entry N: Nomos.

This alteration to how a barrier/border functions is also what allows Israel to both deny the political meaning of the fence, brushing off the accusation that it is engaging in illegal annexation and to effectively impose its own sovereignty in the area that stretches all the way to the fence, without acknowledging a foreign sovereignty beyond it. In accepting the claim that the fence is not a political border, the High Court of Justice (HCJ) misapplied the rationale for the prohibition on the annexation of occupied territory.[18] The issue is not the finality of the border line created, but rather the power to make unilaterally long-term decisions regarding the area and its inhabitants.

To substantiate this proposition, Section B.2 of this entry describes the Israeli separation fence project, focusing on the special legal traits that make it a one-sided border/barrier. Section B.3 discusses and analyzes the HCJ jurisprudence in cases challenging the legality of the separation fence. Section B.4 concludes.

B.2. THE EASTWARD EXPANSION: THE SEPARATION FENCE PROJECT

B.2.1 *The Re-partitioning of Palestine – Eretz Israel*[19]

Israel's separation fence project placed a physical barrier in the heart of Mandatory Palestine–Eretz Israel, dividing the area between the Mediterranean and the Jordan River. The Partition Plan, adopted by the UN General Assembly on November 29th, 1947,[20] was also set to divide the same territory, but it was never implemented, as Arab countries did not accept it. Instead, Palestine–Eretz Israel was ultimately divided according to the outcome of the 1948 War, with the Green Line marking the armistice on the Israel–Jordan front. The Rhodes Agreements, which established the Green Line, explicitly state that it would have no political meaning and that it was "dictated exclusively by *military considerations.*"[21] The 1967 war reshuffled the cards of this territorial arrangement.

---

[18] The legality of the separation barrier has been subject to international and Israeli jurisprudence generating substantial scholarly writing. For a comprehensive critical review including references, see A. Gross, *The Writing on the Wall: Rethinking the International Law of Occupation* (Cambridge: Cambridge University Press 2017), pp. 265–337.

[19] For a more detailed description of the separation fence project and its background, see entry P: Proportionality, Section P.2.1: "Israel's Separation Fences and Walls Project."

[20] The Partition Plan, GA Res. 181 (II), UN Doc A/RES/181(II) (November 29, 1947).

[21] Article 2II of the Jordanian-Israeli General Armistice Agreement: "It is also recognized that no provision of this Agreement shall in any way prejudice the rights, claims and positions of either Party hereto in the ultimate peaceful settlement of the Palestine question, the provisions of this Agreement being dictated exclusively by military considerations."

When the West Bank was occupied by Israel in 1967, the territory between
the Mediterranean and the Jordan River returned once more to be under one
rule, although the regime was divided: a belligerent occupation in the West
Bank, and civil rule, with separation of powers and an elected legislature, in
Israel. In 2002, pursuant to a wave of suicide terror attacks on Israeli streets,
cafes, and buses undertaken in the context of the second Palestinian uprising
(Intifada) and to popular public demand to seal entry points from the West
Bank into Israel, the Israeli government decided to build a system of fences,
walls, patrol roads, and military posts, known collectively as "the separation
fence."[22] The route chosen for it was marginally congruent with the Green
Line (only about 15 percent[23]) and most of it ran within the West Bank,
creating what Israel calls "the seam zone" between the fence and the Green
Line. Although the plan originally included a vast seam zone (some 16 percent
of the territory of the West Bank) international pressure and HCJ judgments[24]
produced significant changes in the route of the fence, and today the seam
zone covers a little more than 8 percent of the West Bank. The entire route of
the fence spans 720 kilometers (more than twice the length of the Green Line,
which spans 320 km). At the time of this writing, some 500 km of the separation
fence have been completed.

B.2.2 *What Is Barred by the Barrier?*

The separation fence is a contiguous physical barrier, but it does have gates
and openings[25] that allow crossing to the other side. As stated, parts of the
separation fence do lie on the Green Line itself. In these sections, the fence

[22] The disagreements regarding the project were translated into wars of terminology: for the IDF
it is "the security barrier" or "security fence"; for those opposing it, it is known as the
"separation wall" and even "the Apartheid wall." Most Israelis refer to it as the "separation
fence."

[23] UN Office for the Coordination of Humanitarian Affairs, *Barrier Update* (July 2011), p. 3. www
.ochaopt.org/sites/default/files/ocha_opt_barrier_update_july_2011_english.pdf.

[24] The standard for routing the fence was set primarily in the *Beit Sourik* case, which merited
a rerouting of large segments of it: HCJ 2056/04 *Beit Sourik Village Council* v. *Government of
Israel* (June 30, 2004), p. 828, http://elyon1.court.gov.il/files_eng/04/560/020/A28/04020560.a28
.pdf (hereinafter: *Beit Sourik*).

[25] There are more than 70 gates along the route of the fence. The military refers to 6 of them as
"fabric of life" crossings. They are open between 12 to 24 hours a day. The remaining gates are
agricultural and seasonal. They open for several hours a day during several days of an
agricultural season. In addition to these, there are several gates for use by security forces
exclusively. See B'Tselem, *Arrested Development: The Long Term Impact of Israel's Separation
Barrier in the West Bank* (October 2012), p. 28, www.btselem.org/download/201210_arrested_
development_eng.pdf.

serves as the physical manifestation of the border. The restrictions on crossing it westward stem from a legal apparatus that prevents unmonitored entry into the state of Israel. The same holds true for all parts of the fence built on the Jerusalem municipal boundary. Israel has annexed East Jerusalem, and therefore, under domestic law, and despite the international community's lack of recognition for the annexation, Israeli law does apply in these areas. The Entry into Israel Law requires non-Israeli citizens to obtain a visa from the Ministry of Interior in order to enter the area bound by the Green Line and East Jerusalem.[26] For Palestinian residents of the OPT there is a special arrangement in place, whereby the military commander has the power to grant them entry and stay permits to enter Israel for work, medical treatments, or special humanitarian reasons.[27] Basic Law: Human Dignity and Liberty, which is considered the pillar of Israel's constitutional order, sets forth that: "Every Israeli citizen who is abroad is entitled to enter Israel."[28] Regarding exiting Israel, the law stipulates: "Every person is free to exit Israel." In plain English, the part of the separation fence that is built on the Green Line and around East Jerusalem forms a barrier to persons who are not Israeli citizens who wish to cross it westward. Israelis can cross it freely.

As noted, the parts of the separation fence that were built inside the West Bank created the seam zone. There is no barrier separating the seam zone from the area beyond the Green Line. The seam zone itself was declared a closed military zone that can be accessed only with a permit,[29] and a bureaucracy was put in place to handle applications for permits made by Palestinians. The permits are issued under four categories of interests the applicants may have in entering the seam zone: cultivating farmland, on condition that the applicant has proven proprietary ties to land in the seam zone; conducting business, provided that the applicant has a business or business contacts in the seam zone that require his/her physical presence; and humanitarian purposes such as attending a wedding or funeral or visiting a sick relative and the likes.[30] The fourth category is for residents of the seam zone, provided that they can prove they actually reside in it.[31]

---

[26] Article 1(a) of the Entry into Israel Law, 1952.

[27] Articles 3b–3c of the Citizenship and Entry into Israel Law (Temporary Order), 2003. This enactment is discussed in entry K: Kinship.

[28] Article 6(b) of the Basic Law: Human Dignity and Liberty.

[29] Order Regarding Defense Regulations (Judea and Samaria) (No. 378), 1970, Declaration Regarding Closure of Area No s/2/03 (Seam Area).

[30] Standing Orders for the Seam Zone, 2017 (Coordinator of Government Activities in the Territories, Civil Administration).

[31] On the seam zone and its attendant permit regime see entry Z: Zone, Section Z.2.2.4.

These are the rules for Palestinians. For Israelis, the restrictions on accessing and remaining in the seam zone are irrelevant. The proclamation of the
seam zone as a closed military zone stated when issued that it does not apply
to Israeli citizens and permanent residents.[32] It also exempted potential
citizens of Israel, under its Law of Return – that is, anyone of Jewish
descent,[33] thereby adopting the cornerstone of Israel's immigration policy.
A general permit signed the same day as the proclamation itself granted
anyone holding a valid Israeli visa (i.e., tourists) a permit to enter and remain
in the seam zone. The net result is that Palestinians are the only group of
people who need an individual permit to enter and remain in the seam
zone.[34]

Israelis and visa holding-tourists may cross the fence eastward, deeper into
the West Bank, by virtue of a general permit granting them entry into the West
Bank that has been in place since the occupation began.[35]

Thus, the separation fence is not a barrier to Israelis and tourists visiting
Israel. They can freely enter and leave the seam zone in any direction, while
Palestinians (including thousands who live in the seam zone[36]) must obtain
a permit from the military commander to enter the area and remain in it.
Palestinians wishing to cross the fence, whether into the seam zone or
beyond the Green Line, must prove they have a legitimate need. They
need a reason.

In summary, the separation fence – made up of fences and walls, augmented by the attending legal regime which determines who has a right to travel
through its openings – has created a barrier for Palestinians, and only for them.
They are thereby excluded both from entry into Israel and from free movement across their own land.

---

[32]   Article 4(a)(1) Declaration Regarding Closure of Area No s/2/03 (Seam Area) (see note 29)
      stipulates that the proclamation is not applicable to any "Israeli." "Israeli" is defined in
      Article 1.

[33]   *Ibid.*, Article 1, definition of "Israeli."

[34]   In May 2004, the Proclamation was amended: the exemption of Israelis was vacated, and
      a general permit was issued for them instead. That did not change the fact that only
      Palestinians need to apply for a permit while Israelis, Jews and tourists do not.

[35]   General Entry Permit (No. 5) (Israeli and Foreign Residents) (Judea and Samaria), 1970.
      It was preceded by an entry permit from 1967. Incidentally, the general permit grants entry
      only during the day, and a longer stay requires a permit. This provision has become a dead
      letter that is not followed. See response of the IDF Spokesperson's Office to a query from
      HaMoked: Center for the Defence of the Individual (October 25, 2010), www.hamoked.org.il
      /Document.aspx?dID=Documents1306 [Hebrew].

[36]   According to an OCHA estimate. Once the construction of the barrier is completed, about
      25,000 Palestinians will find themselves as residents of the seam zone: OCHA, Barrier
      Update, p. 3.

B.2.3 *To Be or not to Be a Border?*

The first government of Israel resolution approving the fence states:

> The fence ... is a security measure. The construction of the fence does not express a political or any other border.[37]

A Security Cabinet resolution approving a segment of the separation fence states:

> The barrier that shall be constructed per this resolution, like the other segments thereof in the "seam zone" is a security measure to prevent terrorist attacks and does not express a political or other border.[38]

These statements, and many similar ones,[39] echo the statement contained in the Rhodes Agreement that the Green Line is not a political border and that it was "dictated by military considerations." They also seem to conform to Israel's official stance that the future of the West Bank will be determined through negotiations.[40] Simultaneously, however, they are defied by material reality occasioned by Israel's actions on the ground in the seam zone.[41]

The seam zone, created by the route of the fence, was formed such that it keeps more than 70 settlements, and East Jerusalem,[42] on the so-called Israeli side of the fence. It is where 425,000 of the half a million Israeli settlers[43] in the West Bank live. The number of Palestinians who live in the seam zone is much smaller: about 11,000 in total,[44] though about 150 Palestinian villages

---

[37] Government Resolution No. 2077 (June 23, 2002).

[38] National Security Cabinet Resolution (September 9, 2003) regarding Phase 3 of the Barrier in the Jerusalem Envelope Area (excluding Maale Adumim).

[39] On October 20, 2003, then Prime Minister Ariel Sharon declared on the Knesset podium that "the separation fence is not a political border, it is tool to prevent terror attacks" (reported in Israeli news site Nana10: http://news.nana10.co.il/Article/?ArticleID=84463). The same position was conveyed to the American national security advisor, Condoleezza Rice, in June 2003. See "Rice: the US Views the Separation Barrier as an Israeli Attempt to set a Political Border," *Globes* (June 29, 2003), www.globes.co.il/news/article.aspx?did=701242.

[40] "[T]he West Bank is best regarded as territory over which there are competing claims which should be resolved in peace process negotiations," Israeli Settlements and International Law, Israeli ministry of foreign affairs website, www.mfa.gov.il/mfa/foreignpolicy/peace/guide/pages/israeli%20settlements%20and%20international%20law.aspx. For a thorough analysis of Israel's normative approach to the OPT, see entry N: Nomos.

[41] For a discussion of the gap between Israel's declared positions on the future of the OPT and its deeds, see entry R: Regularization.

[42] OCHA, Barrier Update, p. 4.

[43] Around 190,000 of the seam zone settlers reside in East Jerusalem. Figures are relevant to 2005 – "The Separation Barrier," *B'Tselem* (January 1, 2011), www.btselem.org/separation_barrier/map.

[44] Figures are relevant to 2013 – "The Separation Barrier," *B'Tselem* (January 1, 2011), www.btselem.org/separation_barrier/map.

have land in it.[45] The seam zone is also where Israel's larger industrial areas in the West Bank are located and it is connected to Israel's metropolitan areas by major roads.

The municipal jurisdiction of the settlements located in the seam zone cover it almost entirely, a fact that is extremely important given the law applicable in the settlements. Throughout the years, large parts of Israeli law were imported into the West Bank and applied to the jurisdictions of the settlements, turning them into enclaves of Israeli law in the OPT. In fact, this practice has been called "enclave law,"[46] and it is implemented through a technique called "pipelining": military orders which constitute primary legislation in the OTP cite laws enacted by the Israeli parliament, mostly administrative law, as applying in the jurisdictions of the Israeli local councils in the West Bank. This gives Israel's bureaucracy administrative powers in the settlements.[47] Pipelining Israeli laws is thus what gives the Israeli Ministry of Education the ability to apply statutory powers provided for in Israeli law to the school system in the settlements. It is what gives the bureaucracy of the Ministry of Health regulatory powers over medical facilities there, and so on.

Side by side with the "enclave law," extraterritorial legislation by the Knesset has applied parts of Israeli law to Israelis in the West Bank on a personal basis. An obvious example of this is Israeli criminal law, which has been applied on a personal basis to Israelis in the West Bank.[48] This personal application follows Israelis wherever they go in the West Bank, whether inside the seam zone or east of it.

Once the separation fence seals off a section of the seam zone and access to it becomes subject to the permit regime, Palestinians' presence there depends on their ability to withstand the bureaucratic via dolorosa of obtaining an entry permit. Israeli military authorities practice a policy of issuing agricultural

[45] OCHA, *The Humanitarian Impact of the Fence* (July 2013), www.ochaopt.org/documents/ocha_opt_barrier_factsheet_july_2013_english.pdf.

[46] "Enclave law" is a term coined by Prof. Amnon Rubinstein: see A. Rubinstein, "The Changing Status of the Territories – From Trust to Legal Hybrid" (1987) 11:439 *Iyunei Mishpat* 450 [Hebrew].

[47] Section 2 of the Order regarding Administration of Local Councils (Judea and Samaria) (No. 982), 1981, empowered the military commander to promulgate a bylaw for Israeli local councils in the OPT. Local Council by Law, 1981, promulgated pursuant to this section, has applied hundreds of Israeli laws to the territories of local councils.

[48] Defense (Emergency) Regulations (Judea and Samaria – Adjudication of Offenses and Legal Assistance), 1967. For more, see Association for Civil Rights in Israel, *One Rule, Two Legal Systems: Israel's Regime of Laws in the West Bank* (October 2014), www.acri.org.il/en/wp-content/uploads/2015/02/Two-Systems-of-Law-English-FINAL.pdf.

permits only for the harvests, making the permitted Palestinian presence in the seam zone extremely limited. In addition, the military denies permits to many Palestinians who do have one of the acknowledged legitimate reasons to cross into the seam zone and are theoretically eligible for them because of "security blocks." These are people denied entry by either the Israeli police or the General Security Service (GSS) into an area where many settlements are located and which provides unhindered access to areas beyond the Green Line. These objections usually rely on some sort of intelligence information alleged to be in the possession of the GSS but which remains undisclosed.[49]

Data collected by Israeli human rights organizations that have been monitoring the implementation of the permit regime ever since its inception show that both the number of seam-zone permits the civil administration issues to Palestinians and their duration plummeted over the years.[50] Research conducted by the UN revealed that the yield produced by Palestinian-owned olive trees west of the fence is 60 percent lower than that of trees to the east of it because farmers are unable to cultivate the groves freely and fully.[51]

The barrier's traits have turned the entire seam zone into an area that provides all the conditions for flourishing, thriving Israeli civilian life, while at the same time draining and gradually erasing Palestinian presence there. The same hand that unraveled the binds that tied the seam zone to the remainder of the West Bank, physically, economically, socially, and in terms of infrastructure, has been weaving new, increasingly strong bonds that tie it to Israel proper.

The separation fence Israel has declared "does not express a political or any other border" has brought dramatic changes to all aspects of life in the area it has sealed off to Palestinians. Demographically, normatively, economically, and in terms of infrastructure and commerce, the area became Israeli. At the same time, Israel's denial that the fence constitutes a border has allowed it to avoid recognizing that a *different* sovereignty lies to the east of it and has left Israeli claims to areas east of the fence intact. In practice, the fact that, in terms of the law, the fence is transparent to Israelis has also ensured that its construction would not undermine Israeli presence to the east of the fence. Indeed, Israelis are free to cross the fence eastward, ensconced in the bubble of Israeli law that has been applied to them on a personal basis and continue to

[49] On the bureaucracy of the permit regime and the role of the GSS in this context see entry Z: Zone Section Z.2.3.

[50] HaMoked: Center for the Defence of the Individual, *The Permit Regime: Human Rights Violations in West Bank Areas Known as the Seam Zone* (March 2013), pp. 15–19.

[51] OCHA, *The Monthly Humanitarian Monitor* (December 2011), p. 8.

enjoy Israeli administrative law, which is still applied in the jurisdiction of settlements that remained east of the fence.

B.3 DE FACTO WHAT? THE ANNEXATION ARGUMENT AND THE HCJ SEPARATION FENCE JURISPRUDENCE

B.3.1 *The Annexation Argument – It Walks like a Duck*

The situation in the seam zone, described above, has led two UN Special Rapporteurs to conclude that the fence and its attendant legal regime constitute the annexation of the seam zone into Israel. Prof. John Dugard, the UN Special Rapporteur on the OPT, wrote in September 2003:

> The word "annexation" is avoided as it is too accurate a description and too unconcerned about the need to obfuscate the truth in the interests of anti-terrorism measures. However, the fact must be faced that what we are presently witnessing in the West Bank is a visible and clear act of territorial annexation under the guise of security. There may have been no official act of annexation of the Palestinian territory in effect transferred to Israel by the construction of the Wall, but it is impossible to avoid the conclusion that we are here faced with annexation of Palestinian territory.[52]

The Special Rapporteur on the Right to Food, Jean Ziegler, has also addressed that year the construction of the separation fence as an act of de facto annexation:

> As the fence/wall does not follow the 1967 border between Israel and the OPT, but cuts through Palestinian lands in the West Bank, it effectively annexes Palestinian land.[53]

The ICJ, which addressed the issue when asked by the UN General Assembly to provide an advisory opinion on the ramification of the construction of the fence, voiced concern that the fence would create de facto annexation:

> The Court considers that the construction of the wall and its associated regime create a "fait accompli" on the ground that could well become

---

[52] Commission on Human Rights, The Situation of Human Rights in the Palestinian Territories Occupied by Israel since 1967: Report by the Special Rapporteur John Dugard, E/CN.4/2006/29 (January 17, 2006), p. 6.

[53] Commission on Human Rights, Addendum – Mission to the Occupied Palestinian Territories: Report by the Special Rapporteur Jean Ziegler, E/CN.4/2004/10/Add.2 (October 31, 2003), p. 16.

permanent, in which case, and notwithstanding the formal characterization of the wall by Israel, it would be tantamount to de facto annexation.[54]

The legal view that the fence is an act of annexation, despite Israel's official position that it is not a political border and the fact that it has not taken any official legal steps toward annexation, such as applying Israeli legislative powers directly to the seam zone, is predicated on a substantive analysis of the issue rather than on a formal one. Such analysis looks at the rationale underlying the absolute prohibition international law places on the annexation of occupied land and examines whether Israel's actions and the reality they produce violate the value protected by the prohibition.

The prohibition on annexation is a customary norm, reflecting the foundational principle of the legal regime of belligerent occupation that an occupation does not confer title and that an acquisition of territory by force amounts to prohibited conquest.[55] Currently, it reflects the principle of self-determination.[56] The prohibition on annexation of occupied territory was codified back in the 1930s, in the Montevideo Convention, where the state was the object of protection,[57] and again after WWII, in the GC IV, where civilians are the object of protection from annexation.[58] The prohibition can be violated and annexation effected even in the absence of an *official* change

---

[54] Consequences of the Construction of a Wall in the Occupied Palestinian Territory, Advisory Opinion, 2004 ICJ 136, ¶ 121.

[55] On this principle, see Introduction, Section 2.2.1.

[56] The principle of self-determination has a long history and was enshrined throughout the UN Charter: Articles 1(2) and 55 list promoting self-determination as the goal of the UN; Article 76(b) affirms that the objective of the trusteeship system is to promote the "progressive development" of the inhabitants of the trust territories toward "self-government or independence." See also: Common Article 1 of the Human Rights Covenants (ICCPR, ICESCR), Legal Consequences for States of the Continued Presence of South Africa in Namibia (South West Africa) notwithstanding Security Council Resolution 276 (1970), Advisory Opinion, 1971 ICJ 16, ¶ 52; Western Sahara, Advisory Opinion, 1975 ICJ 12, ¶¶ 54–59.

[57] Article 11 of the Montevideo Convention stipulates that "The contracting states definitely establish as the rule of their conduct the precise obligation not to recognize territorial acquisitions or special advantages which have been obtained by force whether this consists in the employment of arms, in threatening diplomatic representations, or in any other effective coercive measure."

[58] Article 47 of the Geneva Convention Relative to the Protection of Civilian Persons in the Time of War, Geneva, 12 August 1949, 75 UNTS 287 provides that "Protected persons . . . shall not be deprived, in any case or in any manner whatsoever, of the benefits of the present Convention by any change introduced, as the result of the occupation of a territory, into the institutions or government of the said territory, nor by any agreement concluded between the authorities of the occupied territories and the Occupying Power, nor by any annexation by the latter of the whole or part of the occupied territory."

to the borders of the annexing state that brings the annexed territory within its jurisdiction. Substantive annexation is the de facto application of sovereignty by the annexing state over the occupied territory in a manner that exceeds temporary administration and forfeits the trust function required in a regime of occupation.[59] Substantive annexation is the application of a policy that defies the principles of temporariness and conservation,[60] entrenches the occupier's long-term hold over the occupied territory, undercuts the occupied people's ability to exercise its right to self-determination, and pushes it farther out of reach.[61]

It is difficult to think of a clearer example of substantive, or de facto, annexation than the reality Israel has forced on the seam zone. As the UN Special Rapporteurs and the ICJ noted, this is a reality that creates a fait accompli whose impact is not temporary.[62] The principle of conservation is openly and profoundly breached. With the fence and the legal regime applied to it and to the seam zone, Israel has freed itself of the restrictions the laws of occupation place on the administration of occupied land, and, using security as an excuse, created de facto sovereignty. In parallel, it has been engaged in engineering the demographics, economy, and law of the seam zone with effects that will reverberate far into the future. To the extent that any human endeavor may be considered permanent, this annexation is. It translates the vision of "Greater Israel" into a political, material, and legal reality. The HCJ, as discussed in the following subsection, has been complicit in the transportation of the Israeli *nomos*, comprising law and the narratives which endow it with meaning, into the West Bank.[63]

B.3.2 *The HCJ Fence Jurisprudence – Form over Substance, Words over Deeds*

The de facto annexation argument was raised in the two main HCJ cases challenging the legality of constructing the separation fence inside the West

---

[59]   The foundational principles of the regime of occupation and their interrelations are discussed in the Introduction, Section II.B.

[60]   For more on the conservation principle, see Introduction and entry G: Geneva Law.

[61]   O. Ben-Naftali, A. Gross, and K. Michaeli, "Illegal Occupation: The Framing of the Occupied Palestinian Territory" (2005) 23(3) *Berkeley International Law Journal* 551 (hereinafter: Illegal Occupation).

[62]   Temporariness as a feature (and principle) of occupation is discussed in both the Introduction and in entry T: Temporary/Indefinite.

[63]   See R. M. Cover, "The Supreme Court 1982 term – Foreword: Nomos and Narrative" (1983) 97 *Harvard Law Review* 4. For a discussion of the concept and the different nomoi inhabited by Israel and by the international community, see entry N: Nomos.

Bank:[64] the Beit Sourik case[65] and the Alfei Menashe case.[66] Israel denied it vehemently. State counsel argued that the fence was built for security purposes only and that its route was dictated solely by the need to protect Israel and Israelis from Palestinian terrorists.

An affidavit signed by General Office Commander (GOC) of the Central Command Maj. Gen. Moshe Kaplinsky and submitted in the Beit Sourik case stated: "This is not a permanent fence, but a temporary one, built for security purposes."[67] Given that international law decrees that an occupation is temporary but fails to set precise time limits on its duration, that this lacuna has produced the Israeli thesis that equates the temporary with the indefinite;[68] and the past successes in convincing the HCJ that long-term projects were temporary,[69] it is little wonder that in this instance too, the principle of temporariness was used to deflect the de facto annexation argument.

And it worked. The court accepted the state's position lock, stock, and barrel. Relying on the text of the resolutions passed by the government and by the national security cabinet,[70] then chief justice Aharon Barak, who presided in both cases, ruled that the motivation for the construction of the fence was security,[71] that Israel's ultimate final borders did not factor into the determination of its route,[72] and that it was "inherently temporary."[73] When petitioners proved that the future expansion plans for settlements formed the basis for the route at various locations such as Bil'in,[74] 'Azzun,[75] and Aflei Menashe,[76] the justices took it as a regrettable aberration from the security basis for the project rather than as the exposure of its true political character. When Israel's then minister of justice said at a public event, sitting next to the

---

[64] Domestic and ICJ Litigation focused on the de facto annexation and proportionality arguments. A third possible argument that no physical barrier even on an international recognized border is legal, was not argued. For an analysis of the "left out argument," see Y. Blank, "Legalizing the Barrier: the Legality and Materiality of the Israel/Palestine Separation Barrier" (2010–2011) 46 *Texas International Law Journal* 309.

[65] *Beit Sourik*, p. 828.

[66] HCJ 7957/04 *Mara'abe v. Prime Minister of Israel* (2005) 60(2) IsrSC 477, http://elyon1.court .gov.il/files_eng/04/570/079/A14/04079570.a14.pdf (hereinafter: Alfei Menashe). The author of this entry served as the attorney for the petitioners.

[67] Affidavit signed on April 19, 2004, quoted in *Beit Sourik*, p. 830.

[68] See entry T: Temporary/Indefinite.   [69] See entry J: Jewish Settlements.

[70] For the resolutions, see notes 37–38.   [71] *Beit Sourik*, p. 830; Alfei Menashe, ¶ 98.

[72] *Beit Sourik*, p. 820; Alfei Menashe, ¶ 98.   [73] *Alfei Menashe*, ¶ 100.

[74] HCJ 8414/05 *Bil'in Village Council Chairman v. The Government of Israel* (2007) TakSC 2007(3) 3557.

[75] HCJ 2732/05 *Head of 'Azzun Village Council v. Government of Israel* (June 15, 2006). English translation available on the website of HaMoked: Center for the Defence of the Individual: www.hamoked.org/files/2015/6654_eng.pdf.

[76] Alfei Menashe, ¶ 113.

then deputy chief justice Mishael Cheshin, that in its rulings on the separation fence, the HCJ was "drawing the country's borders," Cheshin chastised her, saying: "That is not what you have contended in court."[77] Yet, even this statement did not steer the HCJ away from following Israel's official statements: the fence is merely a security barrier. It is not a border.

The HCJ preferred form over substance, text over context, purported intentions over expected outcomes. In the courtroom, it was official declarations – words – rather than deeds – ground realities – that dictated the judicial conclusion.

B.4 CONCLUSION: SOVEREIGNTY WITHOUT BORDERS

Israel erected a system of fences and walls that functions as a one-way barrier and restricts Palestinian movement only. As a border, it represents the line of de facto sovereignty Israel has managed to force on the seam zone, but not its final territorial claims on the eastern front. On one side of it, the regime "makes authoritative decisions with regard to the people and resources" without any real restrictions, while on the other side of it, sovereignty is in suspension. Israel's denial that the route of the fence expresses a political border must be understood in the context of the denial – in the Rhodes Agreements – that the Green Line is a political border. In both cases, the line is proclaimed not to be a border as a way of maintaining claims to sovereignty over areas to the east of it. In both cases, the creation of a legal status of a border, which Israel perceives more as preventing its expansion eastward than cementing its sovereignty west of it, is avoided by the assertion that the route was determined by security considerations and that it is temporary.

The HCJ analysis was based on embracing the virtual reality created by the state's declarations. In accepting Israel's official position that there was no annexation, it ignored the substantive questions that attribute decisive weight to the impact the construction of the fence has on the Palestinian right to self-determination. In axiomatically accepting the declaration that the fence is temporary, the justices absolved themselves of the need to face the magnitude of the long-term changes the fence would create in the area it seals off. Finally, the HCJ misinterpreted the undertone of the Israeli government's declaration that the route of the fence was not a border. The judgments issued by the HCJ consider this statement as deriving from the position that, pending any other

---

77 Y. Yoaz and The Associated Press, "Justice Minister: West Bank Fence Is Israel's Future Border," *Haaretz* (December 1, 2005), www.haaretz.com/news/justice-minister-west-bank-fence-is-israel-s-future-border-1.175645.

agreement, the Green Line is the border of sovereign Israel. Yet this assumption overlooked the fact that the fence is effectively a continuation of what is stated in the Rhodes Agreements – i.e., that the Green Line *is not a border* and, as a result, that the eastern limit of Israel's sovereignty is not defined either by the Green Line or by the fence.

The separation fence is a barrier/border mutation, wrought by the fact/norm, temporary/indefinite, annexation/nonannexation indeterminacies of the Israeli control over the Palestinian Territory.[78] With the legal regime it applied to the fence and the space between it and the Green Line, Israel managed to create a physical and legal line that preserves the empowering characteristics of a barrier and of a border, while casting away its limiting characteristics. This genetic mutation created a uni-national barrier which is also a one-sided border.

---

[78] Ben-Naftali, Gross and Michaeli, "Illegal Occupation," pp. 612–613.

C

Combatants

Orna Ben-Naftali

C.1 STATUS MATTERS

War engages risk. Armed fighters present a threat and a challenge to an adversary party that unarmed civilians do not. The idea that this difference matters had been floating around for some two centuries before it became positive law in the 1860s.[1] Thus, the 1863 Lieber Code states:[2]

> As civilization has advanced during the last centuries, so has likewise steadily advanced ... the distinction between the private individual belonging to a hostile country and the hostile country itself, with its men in arms. The principle has been more and more acknowledged that the unarmed citizen is to be spared in person, property, and honor as much as the exigencies of war will admit.

The principle of distinction, decreeing that the parties to the conflict must always distinguish between civilians and combatants and that attacks may only be directed against the latter,[3] became the cornerstone of IHL in the 1868 St. Petersburg Declaration, the preamble of which provided that "the only legitimate object which States should endeavour to accomplish during war is

---

[1] G. Best, "The Restraint of War in Historical and Philosophic Perspective," in A. J. M. Delissen and G. J. Tanja (eds.), *Humanitarian Law of Armed Conflict Challenges Ahead* (The Hague: Martinus Nijhoff, 1991), p. 17.

[2] Instructions for the Government of Armies of the United States in the Field (Prepared by Francis Lieber and promulgated as General Order No 100 by President Lincoln, 24.4.1863), reproduced in D. Schindler and J. Toman (eds.), *The Laws of Armed Conflict. A Collection of Conventions, Resolutions and Other Documents* (The Hague: Brill, 1988), p. 3, Article XXII.

[3] J.M. Henckaerts and L. Doswald-Beck (eds.), *Customary International Humanitarian Law, Volume 1: Rules* (reprinted with corrections; Cambridge: Cambridge University Press, 2009), p. 14.

to weaken the military forces of the enemy."[4] It is considered one of the "cardinal principles" of IHL and one of the "intransgressible principles of customary international law."[5] It also incorporates an image of a war between states' armies, thus excluding fighters who do not belong to such armies, either because there is no state or because it is the state which their fighting opposes.[6]

The principle dictates not merely the distinction between combatants and civilians, but also that each status confers different rights and obligations: combatants participate, and are entitled to participate, in the fighting. Ergo, they are a legitimate military target and, if captured, cannot be prosecuted and acquire prisoner-of-war status.[7] Civilians are not a legitimate military target because they do not participate in hostilities.[8] If they do, they lose the special protection to which they are entitled, and they may be prosecuted for their participation in hostilities. The question of identifying, who is entitled to which status, is thus of utmost importance.

For the purpose of the principle of distinction, customary international law currently defines combatants in both international and noninternational armed conflicts, as the organized armed forces – groups and units which are under a command responsible to a party to a conflict for the conduct of its

---

[4] Declaration of St. Petersburg Renouncing the Use, in Time of War, of Explosive Projectiles Under 400 Grammes Weight (St. Petersburg, 11.12.1868), reproduced in Schindler and Toman, *Laws of Armed Conflict*, p. 102. Note that both the Lieber Code and the First Geneva Convention of the Amelioration of the Condition of the wounded in the armies in the Field (Geneva, 22.8.1864), reproduced in Schindler and Toman, *Laws of Armed Conflict*, p. 280, attached neutrality to the sick and wounded, thus implicitly incorporating the principle of distinction.

[5] Legality of the Threat or Use of Nuclear Weapons, Advisory Opinion (diss. Op. Koroma), 1996 ICJ 226, p. 343.

[6] F. Mégret, "From 'Savages' to 'Unlawful Combatants': A Postcolonial Look at International Humanitarian Law's 'Other'," in A. Orford (ed.) *International Law and Its Others* (Cambridge: Cambridge University Press, 2006), p. 265.

[7] Geneva Convention (III) relative to the Treatment of Prisoners of War (Geneva, August 12, 1949), 75 UNTS 135 [hereinafter: GC III], Article 4A; Protocol Additional to the Geneva Conventions of 12 August 1949, and relating to the Protection of Victims of International Armed Conflicts (Additional Protocol I), (June 8, 1977), 1125 UNTS 3 [hereinafter: AP I], Article 44. This does not preclude the possibility of prosecuting them for acts which do not constitute legitimate fighting tactics, such as war crimes.

[8] Save the exceptional circumstances in which a civilian population rises spontaneously against an invader as a *levée en masse*. See The Hague Convention (IV) Respecting the Laws and Customs of War on Land and its annex: Regulations concerning the Laws and Customs of War on Land, The Hague, October 18, 1907, 205 CTS 277; 36 Stat 2277, Article 2; Geneva Convention (I) for the Amelioration of the Condition of the Wounded and Sick in Armed Forces in the Field (Geneva, August 12, 1949), 75 UNTS 31 [hereinafter: GC I], Article 13(6); Geneva Convention (II) for the Amelioration of the Condition of the Wounded, Sick and Shipwrecked Members of Armed Forces at Sea (Geneva, August 12, 1949), 75 UNTS 85 [hereinafter: GC II], Article 13(d); GC III Article 4A(b).

subordinates.[9] "Armed forces" includes not only regular armies but also militia, volunteer corps, and organized resistance movements, provided they meet certain conditions.[10] The two main treaties defining combatants for the purposes of international armed conflicts, the *GC III* and the *AP I*, differ on the scope and substance of these conditions. The difference attests to the controversy surrounding the designation of fighters who do not fit the traditional image of states' armies as combatants, each time IHL was renegotiated.[11]

The *GC III* enumerates four qualifying conditions for the status of combatants: (a) being commanded by a person responsible for his subordinates; (b) having a fixed distinctive sign recognizable at a distance; (c) carrying arms openly; and (d) conducting their operations in accordance with the laws and customs of war.[12] The postcolonial negotiations of the *AP I* generated a far less restrictive definition of combatants: First, it extended the scope of international armed conflicts to include national liberation movements that hitherto would have been classified as internal armed conflicts.[13] Second, it recognized that there are situations where, due to the nature of the hostilities, an armed combatant cannot distinguish himself, and provides that "he shall nevertheless retain his status as a combatant, provided that, in such situations, he carries his arms openly: (a) during each military engagement, and (b) during such time as he is visible to the adversary while he is engaged in a military deployment preceding the launching of an attack in which he is to participate."[14]

Israel is a party to the Geneva Conventions, but it is not a party to the *AP I* and is indeed a persistent objector to both the transformation of national liberation struggles into international armed conflicts and the consequential expansion of the combatants' category.[15] Its military and civil courts have

---

[9]   Henckaerts and Doswald-Beck, *Customary IHL*, p. 14. In Interational armed conflicts, this customary rule is codified in *AP I* Article 43(1).

[10] Henckaerts and Doswald-Beck, *Customary IHL*, p. 15. This rule is codified in *GC III* Article 4; *GC I* Article 13; and *GC II* Article 13.

[11] N. Berman, "Privileging Combat? Contemporary Conflict and the Legal Construction of War" (2004) 43 *Columbia Journal of Transnational Law* 1, 6.

[12] *GC III* Article 4.   [13]   *AP I* Article 1(4).

[14] *AP I* Article 44(3). See also Article 48, emphasizing the obligation not to harm noncombatants. Note that while the requirement to respect the laws of war has been lifted, the *AP I* nevertheless retained the requirement to have an internal disciplinary system. See Henckaerts and Doswald-Beck, *Customary IHL*, p. 16.

[15] See E. Gross, "Thwarting Terrorist Acts by Attacking the Perpetrators or their Commanders as an Act of Self-Defense: Human Rights Versus the State's Right to Protect its Citizens" (2001) 15 *Temple International and Comparative Law Journal* 195, 203–205; C. C. Burris, "Re-examining the Prisoner of War Status of PLO Fedayeen" (1997) 22 *North Carolina Journal of International Law and Commercial Regulation* 943, 975–976. On the debate over the

refused, from the very beginning of the occupation, to grant combatant status to Palestinian fighters. That refusal still holds, and neither the establishment of the Palestinian Authority (PA), nor the security coordination between Israel and the PA has changed it.[16]

Given the underlying rationale for differentiating combatants from civilians, it is clear that the status of combatants is inextricably linked to the status of civilians. Indeed, the definition of "civilians" is residual: civilians are noncombatants. This customary norm is codified in Article 50 of *AP I*.[17]

The normative consequence of enjoying civilian status is articulated in Article 51(2) of *AP I*, codifying the customary norm that "[t]he civilian population as such, as well as individual civilians, shall not be the object of attack. Acts or threats of violence, the primary purpose of which is to spread terror among the civilian population, are prohibited."[18] The International Criminal Tribunal for the former Yugoslavia (ICTY) held that to constitute a violation of distinction, the act must have been committed willfully, "intentionally in the knowledge ... that civilians or civilian property were being targeted."[19]

---

transformation of wars of national liberation into an international armed conflict, see the Official Records of the Diplomatic Conference on the Reaffirmation and Development of International Humanitarian Law Applicable in Armed Conflicts, Geneva, III, CDDH/III/209 (1974–1977). Note that the USA decided not to ratify *AP I* for similar reasons. See R. Reagen "Letter of Transmittal" (1987) 81 *American Journal of International Law* 910. The decision of the United States was made pursuant to an Israeli campaign. Justice Rubinstein of the Israeli supreme court proudly made that disclosure in CFH 5698/11 *State of Israel v. Dirani* (January 15, 2015) [Hebrew]: "I had at the time ... the privilege, as legal advisor to the Ministry of Foreign Affairs and as the Israeli Delegate to Washington DC, to contribute to persuading the US not to exceed these protocols."

[16] See, e.g., Israeli Military Court at Ramallah 4/69 *Military Prosecutor v. Kassem* [Hebrew]; CrimC 1158/02 *State of Isarel v. Barghouti* (May 20, 2004) [Hebrew].

[17] *AP I* Article 50(1) (Definition of Civilians and Civilian Population): "A civilian is any person who does not belong to one of the categories of persons referred to in Article 4 A(1), (2), (3) and (6) of the Third Convention and in Article 43 of this Protocol. In case of doubt whether a person is a civilian, that person shall be considered to be a civilian." Note that no reservation has been made to this provision. This customary norm is applicable in international armed conflicts. It also applies to noninternational armed conflicts, although practice is ambiguous as to whether members of armed opposition groups are considered members of armed forces or civilians, Henckaerts and Doswald-Beck, *Customary IHL*, p. 18.

[18] The ICRC notes that this provision "is one of the most important articles in the Protocol. It explicitly confirms the customary rule that innocent civilians must be kept outside hostilities as far as possible." See Y. Sandoz, C. Swinarski, and B. Zimmermann (eds.), *Commentary on the Additional Protocols* (The Hague: Martinus Nijhoff, 1987), p. 615.

[19] *Prosecutor v. Blaškić*, Trial Chamber Judgment, IT-95–14-T (March 3, 2000), ¶ 180. The term "willfully" incorporates recklessness, but excludes simple negligence. See *Prosecutor v. Galić*, Trial Chamber Judgment and Opinion, IT-98–29-T (December 5, 2003), ¶ 54.

The international laws of war recognize only two categories: combatants and civilians. Both may perform unlawful acts, but there is no status of either "unlawful combatant", "unlawful civilian" or "terrorist." At the same time, the rationale underlying the principle of distinction also decrees, that a civilian who poses a risk to the adversary by directly engaging in hostilities risks forfeiting the protection offered by the status s/he otherwise enjoys. In international armed conflicts, this customary norm is expressed in Article 51(3) of *AP I*: "Civilians shall enjoy the protection afforded by this Section, unless and for such time as they take a direct part in hostilities."[20]

Israel's "targeted killing policy" takes place in the shadow-land inhabited by people who do not occupy comfortably either of the two recognized categories. Its legality, revolving around the status of the targets, was the subject matter of the *Targeted Killings* judgment.[21] The judgment could have contributed to greater clarity regarding the principle of distinction. In effect, it obfuscated the nature of the conflict and generated further erosion of this principle. This erosion produces an inverse relation between law's inclusive reach and law's exclusive protection in a manner that further obfuscates the ostensible distinction between law and violence or between the rule of law and rule by law. It has also become the most (in)famous Israeli legal export. In order to substantiate this proposition, Section C.2 focuses on the context of the judgment. The judgment is detailed in Section C.3 and critiqued in Section C.4. Section C.5 concludes.

C.2 THE CONTEXT OF THE JUDICIAL TEXT

The "targeted killing policy" was developed as one of the means to quash the second Intifada which erupted in late September 2000.[22] On November 9, 2000, at around 11:00 a.m., Hussein 'Abayat, aged 37, drove his car along one of

---

[20]   *AP I* Article 13(3) reiterates the same norm with respect to noninternational armed conflicts.
[21]   HCJ 769/02 *Public Committee Against Torture v. Government of Israel* (2006) 62(1) PD 507 [Hebrew; English translation available at http://elyon1.court.gov.il/Files_ENG/02/690/007/a 34/02007690.a34.pdf] [hereinafter: Targeted Killings].
[22]   The second Intifada broke out as an immediate reaction to a visit, on September 28, 2000, to Temple Mount/Haram al-Sharif by the then-opposition leader, Ariel Sharon. The following day, in response to stones thrown at Jewish worshippers from the *al-Aqsa* Mosque in Jerusalem, Israeli security services entered the area around the Mosque and fired rubber-coated metal bullets and live ammunition at the crowd, killing five Palestinians and injuring about 200 more. Palestinian demonstrations throughout the territories and within Israel followed, and the vicious circle of vengeful violence known as the *al-Aqsa* or second Intifada began. For a brief summary of the deeper causes for the Intifada, see O. Ben-Baftali and A. Gross, "The Second Intifada" in A. Dworkin et al. (eds.), *Crimes of War* (o.2): *What the Public Should Know* (New York: W. W. Norton & Company, 2007).

the crowded streets of his village, Beit Sahur, in Area A in the West Bank;[23] an Israeli Defense Forces (IDF) helicopter circling above went into a dive and fired three missiles at him, killing him as well as two women, Rahmeh Shahin and 'Aziza Muhammad Danun, both in their fifties, who were standing outside a house awaiting a taxi. A few other people were injured.[24] These were the first victims of Israel's official, publicly stated policy of targeted killing. As of the date of the judgment and up until "Operation Protective Edge" (July 2014), 112 Palestinians had been killed as a result of this policy; 49 of them, including 17 children, were innocent bystanders.[25]

Israel is not the only state that pursues a policy of liquidating its opponents. At the time, however, it was the only state that confirmed publicly that such activity reflects a deliberate and long-term state policy. Indeed, shortly after the operation, the IDF Spokesman issued the following announcement:[26]

> During an IDF-initiated action in the area of the village of Beit-Sahur, missiles were launched by IDF helicopters at the vehicle of a senior *Fatah/Tanzim* activist. The pilot reported an accurate hit. The activist was killed, and his aide, who accompanied him, was wounded . . . The action this morning is a long-term activity undertaken by the Israeli Security Forces, targeted at the groups responsible for the escalation of violence.

In the second decade of the twenty-first century, "targeted killing" has become so prevalent and so global in scope[27] that it is hard to believe that this 2000 acknowledgment was unprecedented in comparison to the secrecy that

---

[23] Under the terms of the Interim Agreement on the West Bank and Gaza Strip, an incremental transfer of authority from Israel to the Palestinian Authority was delineated. See Israeli-Palestinian Interim Agreement on the West Bank and the Gaza Strip, September 28, 1995, Isr-PLO, 36 ILM 557. Under the terms of Oslo II, Area A was transferred to a full Palestinian civilian and military authority. On the zoning of the OPT, see entry Z: Zone.

[24] See Amnesty International, *Israel and the Occupied Territories: State Assassinations and other Unlawful Killings* (February 2001), p. 9, www.amnesty.org/download/Documents/128000/md e150052001en.pdf.

[25] Since 2000 and up until July 2014 ("Operation Protective Edge"), 459 Palestinians lost their life due to "targeted killings" operations in the Gaza Strip and the West Bank, 186 of whom were innocent bystanders. Since the judgment was rendered in December 2006, 112 people, 49 of whom were innocent bystanders, were killed in the Gaza Strip. See B'Tselem: www .btselem.org/statistics. According to files provided by former National Security Agency contractor Edward Snowden, Israeli armed drones have been launching attacks in the OPT since 2004, indicating the figures may be even higher. See C. Currier and H. Molte, "Spies in the Sky," *The Intercept* (January 29, 2016), https://theintercept.com/2016/01/28/isr aeli-drone-feeds-hacked-by-british-and-american-intelligence.

[26] Amnesty International, *State Assassinations*, pp. 9–10.

[27] Tellingly, the current discourse on targeted killings focuses on the means used to execute it, especially on drones and their ability to comply with IHL, and not on the lawfulness of the policy as such – that is, on the tactical as distinct from the strategic issues. See, e.g.,

hitherto surrounded such activities carried out by other governments.[28] Indeed, it stood in sharp contrast with Israel's own vehement refutation of allegations that it had been engaged in such operations in the not so distant past.[29]

Thus, by publicly admitting the policy of targeted state killings, Israel had set a precedent in terms of both the political discourse and the international legal discourse. In the context of the latter, this transparency was designed to posit that far from engaging in the illegal activity of extrajudicial executions, state assassinations or willful killings,[30] Israel is acting in a lawful manner under IHL.[31] This is the position challenged in the *Targeted Killings* appeal.

C.3 THE JUDGMENT

C.3.1 *The Key Issue*

The central question before the court was whether the Israeli policy "of preventive attacks that cause the death of terrorists ... who plan, dispatch, or

Directorate-General for External Policies of the European Union, Policy Department, Human Rights Implications of the Usage of Drones and Unmanned Robots in Warfare (May 2013) EXPO/B/DROI/2012/12; Human Rights Watch & The International Human Rights Clinic, Human Rights Program at Harvard Law School, Losing Humanity: The Case Against Killer Robots (November 2012); N. Melzer, *Targeted Killing in International Law* (Oxford: Oxford University Press, 2008); J. J. Paust, "Self-Defense Targeting of Non-State Actors and Permissibility of US Use of Drones in Pakistan" (2010) 19 *Journal of Transnational Law & Policy* 237; O. Ben-Naftali and Z. Triger, "The Human Conditioning: International Law and Science Fiction" (2013) *Law, Culture and the Humanities*, http://lch.sagepub.com/content/early/2013/09/06/1743872113499215.full.pdf.

[28]   See S. Krasmann, "Targeted Killing and Its Law: On a Mutually Constitutive Relationship" (2012) 25 *Leiden Journal of International Law* 665, 668–670.

[29]   See, e.g., "The IDF categorically rejects such accusations ... There has never been, nor will there ever be an IDF policy of intentional killing of wanted fugitives ... The sanctity of life is a basic IDF value – there has been no change in this principle nor will any in this matter ever be tolerated"; cited in N. Yashuvi, B'Tselem, Activity of the Undercover Units in the Occupied Territories (Position Paper, May 1992), www.btselem.org/publications/summaries/199205_undercover_units, p. 81.

[30]   The terms "extra-judicial / extra-legal killings" and "state-assassinations" are used by intergovernmental and nongovernmental human rights organizations; see, e.g., UNHRC Report of the Special Rapporteur on Extrajudicial, Summary or Arbitrary Executions, Philip Alston, Addendum: Study on Targeted Killings (May 28, 2010) UN Doc A/HCR/14/24/Add.6; Amnesty International, *State Assassinations*; Y. Stein, B'Tselem, Israel's Assassination Policy: Extra-Judicial Executions (Position Paper, January 2001).

[31]   For further discussion, see entry L: Lawfare. On the role of "Lawfare" in the context of "Targeted Killings," see L. Hajjar, "Lawfare and Armed Conflict: Comparing Israel and US Targeted Killing Policies and Challenges Against Them" (Research Report, Issam Fares Institute for Public Policy and International Affairs 2013), www.aub.edu.lb/ifi/international_affairs/Documents/20130129ifi_pc_IA_research_report_lawfare.pdf.

carry out terror attacks" in Israel and in the OPT against both civilians and soldiers, is lawful.[32] The response to this question rests primarily on the status of the targeted persons.

A previous attempt to subject the policy of targeted killings to judicial review failed when the court accepted the state's position that the matter is not justiciable.[33] This position was reversed in the instant case.[34] The court's unanimous conclusion reads:[35]

> The result of the examination is not that such strikes are always permissible or that they are always forbidden. The approach of customary international law applying to armed conflicts of an international nature is that civilians are protected from attacks by the army. However, that protection does not exist regarding those civilians "for such time as they take a direct part in hostilities" (§51(3) of *The First Protocol*). Harming such civilians, even if the result is death, is permitted, on the condition that there is no other means which harms them less, and on the condition that innocent civilians are not harmed. Harm to the latter must be proportional.[36]

C.3.2 *The Normative Framework*

The starting point of the judgment is that since September 2000, a continuous situation of armed conflict has existed between Israel and "various terrorist organizations."[37] In the court's view, this armed conflict is of an international character because it "crosses the borders of the state."[38] Therefore, the applicable normative framework is the international law of armed conflicts. This law is part of IHL and includes the laws of belligerent occupation.[39] Substantial parts of this law are customary and, as such, part of Israeli law.[40] IHL is the *lex specialis*, to be supplemented, in cases of lacuna, by human rights law.[41] Israeli law requires soldiers of the IDF to act pursuant to the laws of armed conflict.

---

[32] Targeted Killings, opening (unnumbered) paragraph. The judgment further refers to the fact that such attacks at times harm innocent civilians. For a broader critique of the so-called "preventive" practice, see the entry F: Future-Oriented Measures.

[33] HCJ 5872/01 *Barakeh* v. *Prime Minster* (2005) 56(3) PD 1 [Hebrew].

[34] The Israeli supreme court is not bound by the *stare decisis* principle; see Basic Law: Judicature, 38 LSI 101 (1984), Article 20(2).

[35] Targeted Killings, ¶ 60. The main judgment was written by president (emeritus) Barak. President Beinisch and vice president Rivlin concurred and appended individual opinions.

[36] Note that the HCJ categorical assertion "on the condition that civilians are not be harmed" is immediately compromised by the sentence which follows: "Harm to the latter must be proportional." On the HCJ construction of proportionality, see entry P: Proportionality.

[37] Targeted Killings, ¶ 16.   [38] *Ibid.*, ¶ 18.   [39] *Ibid.*, ¶ 20.

[40] *Ibid.*, ¶ 19. The applicable normative framework is detailed in entry G: Geneva Law.

[41] *Ibid.*, ¶¶ 18–21.

If they act contrary to these laws "they may be, *inter alia*, criminally liable for their actions."[42]

C.3.3 *The Principle of Distinction*

International humanitarian law, said the court, is based on a balance between human rights and military requirements, thus reflecting "the relativity of human rights and the limits of military needs."[43] The principle of distinction, differentiating between two categories of people, combatants, and civilians, is a central consideration in this balance: combatants are legitimate military targets; civilians are not.[44] IHL, at present, does not recognize a third category of "unlawful combatants."[45] The Palestinian militants fail to meet the qualifying conditions set in the Hague Regulations and in the Geneva Conventions for combatants. Consequently, they are civilians. They are not, however, entitled to the full protection granted to civilians who do not take a direct part in the hostilities.[46]

C.3.3.1 Interpreting Article 51(3) of AP I

According to the customary norm codified in Article 51(3) of *AP I*, civilians who take a "direct part in hostilities" do not lose their status as civilians. However, "for such time" as they take part in the hostilities they become legitimate objects of attack, without enjoying the rights of combatants.[47] The interpretation of this provision should be dynamic, adapting the rule to new realities.[48]

   Article 51(3) of *AP I* comprises three cumulative components: (i) *hostilities*; (ii) *direct part*; and (iii) *for such time*. The court interpreted *hostilities* as acts intended to cause damage to the army or to civilians. A civilian takes a direct part in hostilities when he engages in, or prepares himself for, such acts.[49] Noting the lack of an agreed-upon customary standard for (ii) and (iii), the

---

[42]   *Ibid.,* ¶ 19.   [43]   *Ibid.,* ¶ 22.
[44]   *Ibid.,* ¶¶ 23–26 discusses the definitions of each status and its respective scope of protection.
[45]   *Ibid.,* ¶ 28.   [46]   *Ibid.,* ¶ 26.
[47]   *Ibid.,* ¶ 30. Combatant status brings with it a host of privileges, which include, inter alia, rights to medical treatment and religious services, food, clothing, and adequate conditions of detention. See GC III Articles 21–22, 25, 26, 27, 33–37 respectively. Most importantly, combatant status entails the right to legal immunity from prosecution for the (legal) actions which the combatant has performed during the war, which otherwise would have been criminal offenses. This customary rule is universally accepted. See D. Jinks, "The Declining Significance of POW Status" (2004) 45 *Harvard International Law Journal* 367, 376, note 38.
[48]   Targeted Killings, ¶ 28.   [49]   *Ibid.,* ¶ 33.

court concluded that "there is no escaping going case by case, while narrowing the area of disagreement."[50] It thus offered guidelines and examples in respect of these two elements.

A civilian takes a "direct part" in hostilities when he is physically engaged in them and when he plans, decides on, and sends others to be thus engaged. At one end of the spectrum, a civilian bearing arms who is on his way to (or from) the place where he will use (or had used) them is clearly taking a direct part in hostilities. At the other end are cases of indirect support, including selling of supplies and financing hostile acts. In between are the hard cases, where the function the civilian performs determines the directness of the part he takes in the hostilities (e.g., collecting intelligence, servicing weapons, and functioning as a "human shield" are direct acts of participation).[51]

A similar methodology is followed in respect of the third element: "for such time." At one end of the spectrum is the civilian taking part in the hostilities once or sporadically, thereafter detaching himself from such activity. He is not to be attacked for his past participation. At the other end is the active member of a terrorist organization for whom a rest between hostilities is but "preparation for the next hostility."[52] He is a civilian who has lost his immunity. The wide spectrum in between is where the "gray" cases are. Each requires a case-by-case examination. The test involves four elements. First, targeting decisions must be grounded in well-based and thoroughly verified information regarding the identity and activities of the individual. Second, no attack is permitted if a less harmful means exists. This requirement, grounded in the principle of proportionality, reflects that "trial is preferable to use of force."[53] Its practicality is related to the status of the territories as occupied. Third, a retroactive independent examination must be undertaken regarding, inter alia, the precision of the identification of the target. In appropriate cases, compensation for harm to innocent civilians should be paid. Finally, every effort should be made to minimize harm to innocent civilians; any such collateral damage must be proportional.[54]

---

[50] *Ibid.*, ¶ 34 (regarding "direct") and ¶ 39 (regarding "for such time").   [51] *Ibid.*, ¶¶ 34–37.

[52] *Ibid.*, ¶ 39.

[53] *Ibid.*, ¶ 40. Note that classified documents leaked by Anat Kamm to HaAretz journalist Uri Blau disclose that the IDF defied the court's ruling with respect to Palestinians who were targeted despite the possibility of arresting them. See U. Blau, "IDF Ignoring High Court on West Bank Assassination," *Haaretz* (November 26, 2008), www.haaretz.com/print-edition/ne ws/idf-ignoring-high-court-on-west-bank-assassinations-1.258296. The allegation was later refuted by then attorney general Menachem Mazuz; see D. Izenberg, "Stamp of Approval from the Attorney-General," *The Jerusalem Post* (April 13, 2010), www.jpost.com/Israel/Stamp-of-approval-from-attorney-general.

[54] *Ibid.*, ¶¶ 38–40.

Proportionality, opined the court, is a general principle of customary international law. Its application in international armed conflicts requires a proper proportion between the military advantage of an attack and the damage caused to innocent civilians harmed by it.[55] Thus, shooting at "a terrorist sniper shooting at soldiers or civilians from his porch"[56] is proportionate, even if innocent civilians are harmed. An instance that fails the proportionality test is an aerial bombarding of a building where "scores of its residents and passersby are harmed."[57] In between fall the hard cases, necessitating a case-by-case determination.[58]

C.3.4 *Justiciability*

The court proceeded to reject the state's preliminary argument regarding nonjusticiability, on the following grounds: (a) cases involving impingement to human rights are justiciable; (b) the disputed issues are legal; (c) the disputed issues are examined by international tribunals; and (d) judicial review will intensify the objectivity of the ex post examination of the conduct of the army.[59] Focusing on the scope of judicial review of military decisions to engage in targeted killings, the court differentiated between questions regarding the applicable law, which fall within its expertise, and operational decisions, which fall within the professional expertise of the executive.[60]

In conclusion, the court situated the decision within the context of previous judgments where it had reviewed military measures, stating that

> Every struggle of the state – against terrorism or any other enemy – is conducted according to rules and law ... There are no "black holes" ... The state's struggle against terrorism is not conducted "outside" the law. It is conducted "inside" the law, with tools that the law places at the disposal of democratic states.[61]

---

[55] *Ibid.*, ¶¶ 41–45.   [56] *Ibid.*, ¶ 46.   [57] *Ibid.*
[58] For a discussion of "Proportionality," see entry P: Proportionality.
[59] Targeted Killings, ¶¶ 47–54. Note that justiciability is a preliminary matter: when a court determines justiciability, it normally does so before proceeding to the merits of a case, as the discussion may obviate the need to proceed. In the present case, however, the order is reversed: having analyzed the question on the merits, the judgment proceeds to discuss the issue of justiciability. On the significance of this reversal, see O. Ben-Naftali, "A Judgment in the Shadow of International Criminal Law: the Decision of the Israeli High Court of Justice on the Legality of Targeted Killings" (2007) 5 *Journal of International Criminal Justice* 322.
[60] Targeted Killings, ¶¶ 55–59.
[61] *Ibid.*, ¶ 61. The discussion of the legal limits imposed on a democracy extends to ¶ 62.

C.4 CRITICAL ANALYSIS OF THE JUDGMENT[62]

The *Targeted Killings* judgment is the first ever comprehensive judicial attempt to clarify the legal status of, and the rules applicable to, civilians taking direct part in hostilities, embodied in Article 51(3) of *AP I*.[63] Given the lack of consensus on the issue, and concern over the progressive erosion of traditional distinctions between civilians, combatants, terrorists, guerilla fighters, and civilian contractors, the judgment could have contributed to the progressive development of international law. This, alas, it failed to do. The controversy attached to both the process and the final product of the ICRC study of the concept of "Direct Participation in Hostilities" underscores the point.[64]

The crucial (though widely overlooked) difficulty with the *Targeted Killings* judgment is the court's jumbling of the two main instruments comprising the legal framework of the decision, that is, the Geneva Conventions and *AP I*.[65] This mishmash does not seem to reflect an innocent mistake. Indeed, it is easily traced to the outset of the decision, where the court refrains from clearly

---

[62] The analysis reproduces, mutatis mutandis, a case note; see O. Ben-Naftali and K. Michaeli, "The Public Committee against Torture in Israel v. Government of Israel" (2007) 101 *American Journal of International Law* 459.

[63] Even the ICTY has refrained from thoroughly addressing the phrase "taking direct part in hostilities." See Tadić, Trial Chamber Opinion and Judgment, ICTY-94-1-T (May 7, 1997), ¶ 16.

[64] The ICRC concluded in 2005 that "there is still no precise definition of the term "direct participation in hostilities""; see Henckaerts and Doswald-Beck, *Customary IHL*, pp. 23–24. Attempting to clarify the matter, the ICRC conducted, in cooperation with the TMC Asser Institute, a comprehensive study of the matter, comprising background papers, questionnaires, reports, and expert meetings. The final product, the "Interpretative Guidance on the Notion of Direct Participation in Hostilities Under International Humanitarian Law" (2008) 90 *International Review of the Red Cross* 872, 995–996 (adopted by the Assembly of the ICRC, 26.2.2009) offers a more restrictive interpretation than the one offered by the HCJ in the Targeted Killings judgment. The final document, however, failed to achieve consensus even amongst the experts who participated in the study, and some of them requested that their names be removed from it. See, e.g., W. H. Parks, "Part IX of the ICRC 'Direct Participation in Hostilities' Study: No Mandate, No Expertise, and Legally Incorrect" (2009–2010) 42 *NYU Journal of International Law & Politics* 769; K. Watkin, "Opportunity Lost: Organized Armed Groups and the ICRC 'Direct Participation in Hostilities' Interpretive Guidance" (2009–2010) 42 *NYU Journal of International Law & Politics* 641; B. Boothy, "'And for Such Time': The Time Dimension to DPH" (2009–2010) 42 *NYU Journal of International Law & Politics* 741. For a response to these critique and others, see N. Melzer, "Keeping the Balance Between Military Necessity and Humanity: A Response to Four Critiques of the ICRC's Interpretative Guidance on the Notion of DPH" (2009–2010) *NYU Journal of International Law & Politics* 831.

[65] Note that the *AP I* was designed to integrate the *Geneva* Law and the *Hague* Law, Nuclear Weapons Advisory Opinion.

defining the applicability of these two instruments in relation to the characterization of the conflict.

As noted earlier, the court defined the conflict as an international armed conflict, primarily on the ground that it "crosses the borders of the state."[66] In international law, however, it is not the *border* that determines the nature of a conflict, but rather the *identity* of the parties. Thus, the first paragraph of Common Article 2 of the 1949 Geneva Conventions defines an international armed conflict as "a conflict arising between two or more states." Consequently, all other conflicts are rendered noninternational. Arguably, the application of this provision should have generated the conclusion that the conflict is noninternational: later disputes about the statehood of the Palestinian Authority notwithstanding, at the relevant time it was not a state.[67]

A legal basis for the proposition that the conflict under discussion is of an international nature exists in Article 1(4) of *AP I*. This provision extends the applicability of the rules of international conflicts beyond the traditional interstate context to conflicts between states and other actors, such as national liberation movements. Given, however, that Israel is not a party to *AP I* and has persistently objected to this very expansion,[68] the court could not rely on it and chose to avoid referring to it altogether.

Given that the legal construction of war is closely related to the legal construction of combatants/civilians, this indeterminacy concerning the applicability of *GC IV* and *AP I* ultimately added further confusion, to the already eroded distinction between civilians and combatants: it accounts for the fact that the judgment, while denying that there is a third status of *unlawful combatants*, nevertheless de facto recognizes such a status, equating it with civilians who take a direct part in the hostilities. Such civilians/unlawful combatants are bereft of either immunity (of civilians) or privileges (of combatants).[69]

---

[66] Note, in this context, that the court opted to use the words "crosses the borders of the state" in lieu of using a more common international legal terminology, such as "cross-national" or "transnational."

[67] Cf. *Hamdan v. Rumsfeld* 548 US 557 (2006). See M. Sassòli, "The Role of Human Rights and International Humanitarian Law in New Types of Armed Conflicts," in O. Ben-Naftali (ed.), *International Human Rights and Humanitarian Law: Collected Courses of the Academy of European Law* (Oxford: Oxford University Press, 2011). Note further that had the court engaged in the discussion, it would have had to relate to Israel's position regarding the nonapplicability de jure of *GC IV* to the territories occupied since 1967, an issue it had always chosen to avoid. For a discussion on the latter issue, see entry G: Geneva Law.

[68] See note 13.

[69] The judgment further refers to civilians "who take direct part in hostilities" as "unlawful combatants," while at the same time denying that the latter exist as a status. See Targeted Killings, ¶ 26: "The result is that an unlawful combatant is not a combatant, rather a 'civilian.' However, he is a civilian who is not protected from attack as long as he is taking a direct part in

This result emanates from the court's blurring of the distinct logic informing the normative frameworks of GC IV and of AP I insofar as the definitions of combatants and civilians are concerned: GC IV stipulates strict qualifying conditions for combatants, which Palestinian fighters do not meet, primarily because "they have no fixed emblem recognizable at a distance, and they do not conduct their operations in accordance with the laws and customs of war."[70] This restrictive definition of combatants is directly related to the broad protection offered to civilians under the GC IV: there is no provision equivalent to Article 51(3) of AP I in the Geneva Conventions. While the purpose of AP I is identical to the purpose of the GC IV – i.e., to maximize humanitarian protection in terms of both immunities (to civilians) and privileges (to combatants) – its logic is different: recognizing that "there are situations in armed conflicts where, owing to the nature of the hostilities," an armed combatant cannot distinguish himself, it offers a less restrictive definition of combatants. This definition of combatants is, in turn, directly related to the lesser protection offered to civilians who take part in the hostilities under Article 51(3) of AP I. Palestinian fighters meet the flexible criteria for combatants stipulated in Article 44(3) of AP I. Israel, however, having objected persistently to this expansion of the definition, is not bound by it. Indeed, the court, by employing the restrictive definition of the GC IV to combatants, dismissed without much ado the notion that the Palestinian militants are combatants. This is a proper application of the relevant legal framework. At the same time, however, the court did not recognize them as civilians entitled to the broader protection offered by that framework, but rather applied to them the lesser protection offered to civilians under Article 51(3) of AP I. This is a problematic application of the law: applying simultaneously the framework of the Geneva Conventions to define combatants and the framework of AP I to define civilians, is formally valid, but substantively flawed.

Civilians who take direct part in hostilities lose their immunity for such time. This is prescribed both by Article 51(3) of the AP I and customary law. The interpretation of the scope of this provision cannot, however, be made in a normative vacuum and should be related to the relevant normative framework within which it is placed. Thus, a more expansive interpretation is called

---

the hostilities ... civilians who are unlawful combatants are legitimate targets for attack, and thus surely do not enjoy the rights of civilians who are not unlawful combatants, provided that they are taking a direct part in the hostilities at such time. Nor ... do they enjoy the rights granted to combatants. Thus, for example, the law of prisoners of war does not apply to them." See also the title of Section 6: "Civilians who are Unlawful Combatants," and related ¶¶ 29–31.

70 *Ibid.*, ¶ 24.

for within the context of *AP I*, but, outside its context, whenever the definition of combatants is applicable to a situation defined by the Geneva Conventions, the provision should be narrowly construed. Blurring the line between the frameworks of the Geneva Conventions and *AP I* (by denying, on the one hand, the broader definition of combatants, and by giving, on the other hand, a broad interpretation to the customary provision of Article 51(3)), results in the creation of a broad category of unlawful combatants: persons who are entitled to neither the privileges of combatants nor the immunities of civilians. This, however, is a category which neither instrument recognizes; indeed, it is a category which defies the humanitarian purpose of both and which the judgment itself otherwise rejects.[71]

The fate of unlawful combatants, a.k.a. "civilians who take direct part in the hostilities,"[72] is further worsened by the dynamic interpretation the court employs,[73] an interpretation that might complement the *AP I*'s framework, but not the Geneva Convention framework. Indeed, human rights law – an additional normative framework that the court refers to but refrains from applying[74] – could have been invoked in order to narrowly construe this situation, especially given the context of resistance to a long-term occupation, a context which the *AP I* was designed to address and which the judgment does not.[75]

---

[71] Note that in 2002, the Israeli parliament passed the Internment of Unlawful Combatants Law (2002) SH 1834. Article 2 of that law defines an "unlawful combatant" as "a person who has been engaged, either directly or indirectly, in hostile actions against the state of Israel or who is part of a force which engages in hostile action against the state of Israel, and who does not meet the conditions qualifying his for the status of a prisoner of war under international humanitarian law, as defined in Article 4 of the Third Geneva Convention." The Israeli supreme court, rejecting an appeal against the legality of the policy of administrative detention undertaken pursuant to this law, and referring to the Target Killings judgment, determined that the term "unlawful combatants" is a subcategory of the civilian category. See CrimA 6659/06 *A & B v. State of Israel* (March 5, 2007), http://elyon1.court.gov.il/files_eng/06/590/066/n04/06066590 .n04.pdf [Hebrew].

[72] Targeted Killings, ¶ 26.   [73] *Ibid.*, ¶ 28.   [74] *Ibid.*, ¶ 18.

[75] On the coapplication of IHL and IHRL in the context of targeted killings in situations of long-term occupations, see, e.g., O. Ben-Naftali and K. Michaeli, "'We Must not Make a Scarecrow of the Law': A Legal Analysis of the Israeli Policy of Targeted Killings" (2002– 2003) 36 *Cornell Journal of International Law* 233; D. Kretzmer, "Targeted Killing of Suspected Terrorists: Extra-Judicial Execution or Legitimate Means of Defense?" (2005) 16 *European Journal of International Law* 171; B. Medina, "Regulating Anti-Terror Warfare through the Individual Dangerousness Doctrine: Theory and the Israeli Supreme Court Jurisprudence" (May 1, 2013), http://papers.ssrn.com/sol3/papers.cfm?abstract_id=2259158; T. A. Keck, "Not all Civilians Are Created Equal: The Principle of Distinction, the Question of DPH and Evolving Restraints on the Use of Force in Warfare" (2012) 211 *Military Law Review* 115.

C.5 CONCLUSION: "INTERNATIONAL LAW PROGRESSES THROUGH ITS VIOLATIONS"

Civilians who directly participate in hostilities are, from a normative perspective, an exception to the rule that it is combatants who thus participate. The *AP I* – recognizing that, in reality, civilian participation in hostilities, far from being exceptional, has become a constant feature in recent armed conflicts – sought to regularize their otherwise irregular status.[76] Israel objected to this regularization. The *Targeted Killings* judgment, rather than containing the exception by advancing a narrow interpretation, employs a "selective" and "dynamic" interpretive methodology. The latter obfuscates the nature of the conflict and generates further erosion of the principle of distinction. Given that greater, not lesser, clarity is essential for meaningful distinction, the legal antinomy thus produced, acquires a particularly ironic poignancy.

That poignancy is underscored by the observation that the decision of the HCJ was not only unprecedented but itself set a global precedent: thus, in the United States the traditional prohibition on political assassination[77] gave way, in September 2001, to a worldwide license to kill suspected people who do not qualify as combatants.[78] Under the Obama administration, the practice has expanded meaningfully in terms of geographic, temporal, and personal scope.[79] The trigger for the American change of policy was 9/11.[80] Its legal foundations were supplied by the Israeli HCJ[81] in what has become the most successful (thus far) Israeli export of international legal doctrine. The point was succinctly, albeit somewhat boastfully, summarized by the legal architect of the legalization of this practice, Daniel Reisner, who at the relevant time served as the head of the International Law Division of the military advocate general's office, in these words:[82]

---

[76]   E. Crawford, "Regulating the Irregular: International Humanitarian Law and the Question of Civilian Participation in Armed Conflicts" (2010–2011) 18 *UC Davis Journal of International Law & Policy* 163.

[77]   See Hajjar, "Lawfare and Armed Conflict," text and note 46.

[78]   *Ibid.*, text and notes 48–52.

[79]   The USA even extended it to include American citizens amongst those who may be targeted because they pose an imminent threat and who cannot be arrested. *Ibid.*, text and note 57.

[80]   *Ibid.*

[81]   See, e.g., H. Koh "Keynote Speech," *Annual Meeting of the American Society of International Law: The Obama Administration and International Law* (Washington, DC, March 25, 2010), www.state.gov/documents/organization/179305.pdf www.state.gov/s/l/releases/remarks/139119.htm.

[82]   Y. Feldman and U. Blau, "Consent and Advise," *Haaretz* (January 29, 2009), www.haaretz.com.consent-and-advise-1.269127.

What we are seeing now is a revision of international law ... If you do something long enough, the world will accept it. The whole of international law is now based on the notion that an act that is forbidden today becomes permissible if executed by enough countries ... International law progresses through violations. We invented the targeted assassination thesis and we had to push it ... Eight years later it is in the center of the bounds of legitimacy.

The lasting effect of the judgment was thus the transformation of both the military imagination and the international legal terrains: exceptional operations hitherto conceived as extralegal were normalized. Henceforth, they will indeed be conducted routinely "inside" the law, eliminating people who, by "taking direct part in hostilities," have become, much like the "savages" of the colonial past, mere biological subjects.[83] There are no legal "black holes."[84] Law's reach has become all inclusive as law's protection has become ever more exclusive; interpretive constructions of law have become indistinct from law's violations, and the latter are construed as generating law's progress. The notion of the rule *of* law has given way to a rule *by* law – a rule indistinguishable from violence.[85]

It is thus not altogether surprising that if hitherto Israeli domestic law recognized the status of "unlawful combatants" for the purposes of regulating their imprisonment while denying them the privileges attached to POWs,[86] the current interpretation of international law regulates their death. Death is "inside" the law; life, "outside" the law.[87] The bureaucratization of the shadow-land between the rule and the exception, effected by the judgment, thus does more than merely facilitating the killing of Palestinians (and of others): in dispersing the power amongst the forces authorized to kill and the various experts authorizing and

---

[83] Mégret, "From 'Savages' to 'Unlawful Combats'."   [84] Targeted Killings, ¶ 61.

[85] W. Benjamin, "Critique of Violence," in P. Demetz (ed.), *Reflections: Essays, Aphorisms and Autobiographical Writings* (Berlin: Schoken, 1986), p. 277. For an analysis of "targeted killings" in the light of Walter Benjamin's reading of law and violence, see M. Gunneflo, *Targeted Killing: A Legal and Political History* (Cambridge: Cambridge University Press, 2016).

[86] The Internment of Unlawful Combatants Law, 5762–2002.

[87] Targeted Killings, ¶ 61: "The state determined that an essential measure from a military perspective is the preventative attack upon terrorists in the territories that causes their death. This sometimes causes innocent civilians to be injured or killed. This use of this preventative attack, notwithstanding its military importance, should be done within the law ... the struggle of the state against terrorism is not waged 'outside' the law. It is waged 'within' the law and with tools that the law makes available to a democracy." For further discussion, see entry L: Lawfare.

legitimizing the killing, it has transformed the space into a zone of "necropolitics."[88] Given that the space is inhabited by people whose lives have become but a biological fate and whose death has become a political experience, it also rationalized a new status – that of living dead.[89]

---

[88] See A. Mbembe, "Necropolitics" (2003) 15 *Public Culture* 11. The term "necropolitics" refers to contemporary forms of subjugation of life to death. It builds on Foucault's concept of biopower in the light of new technologies of destruction which confer upon vast numbers of people the status of "living dead" as the defining feature of their social existence. Mbembe regards the Israeli occupation of Palestine as the most proficient execution on necropolitics.

[89] *Ibid.* See also H. Ghanem, "Thanatos-Politics: A Dialectic of Life and Death in the Shade of the Occupation" (2005) 27 *Theory and Criticism* 181 [Hebrew]; N. Shalhoub-Kevorkian, "Necroplitics and the Economy of the Sacred and the Profane," in *Security Theology, Surveillance and the Politics of Fear*, 116–143 (Cambridge: Cambridge University Press, 2015) (focusing on the construction of Palestinian dead bodies as objects of security and fear, that must be evicted/erased).

D

Deportations

Michael Sfard

D.1 THE NORMATIVE FRAMEWORK

D.1.1 *Article 49 of the GC IV: The Prohibition on Deportation of Protected Persons*[1]

If Israel could rewrite the GC IV, it would surely have deleted Article 49 in its entirety. The prohibition on the occupying power to deport or transfer parts of its own civilian population to the occupied territory, a prohibition contained in paragraph 6 of Article 49, has attracted much attention in the context of the Israeli–Palestinian conflict: Israel indeed does not deport its citizens to the OPT, but it does encourage them to transfer there.[2] Less attention has been paid to the other prohibition on deportation contained in the first paragraph of Article 49 of the GC IV:

> Individual or mass forcible transfers, as well as deportations of protected persons from occupied territory to the territory of the Occupying Power or to that of any other country, occupied or not, are prohibited, regardless of their motive.

This prohibition is the focus of this entry.[3]

---

[1] Article 49 of the Geneva Convention Relative to the Treatment of Prisoners of War, Geneva, August 12, 1949, 75 UNTS 135; Article 33(1) of Geneva Convention Relative to the Protection of Civilian Persons in the Time of War, Geneva, August 12, 1949, 75 UNTS 287 [hereinafter: GC IV].

[2] See entry J: Jewish Settlements.

[3] IHL comprises three approaches to forced transfer: in situations of an international armed conflict, Article 45 of GC IV prohibits forcible transfer of protected persons to any state that does not respect the GC IV or may persecute them; in noninternational armed conflict, Article 3 of the GC IV is silent on the matter, but Article 17 of AP II forbids forcible transfer/deportations in a manner similar to Article 49 of GC IV. Protocol Additional to the Geneva Conventions of August 12, 1949, and relating to the Protection of Victims of Non-International

It is hard to find a clearer use of legal language: the drafters of this paragraph produced a categorical yet inclusive prohibition which covers all types of deportation and forced transfer[4] irrespective of their destination, the number of people affected, the actions with which they may have engaged, the threat they may present to public order or national security, and, indeed any other reason.[5]

The official ICRC Commentary suggests that this prohibition should be read in conjunction with Article 78 GC IV, which deals with the security measures the occupying power is permitted to take for imperative security reasons vis-à-vis protected persons who pose a security risk.[6] This provision allows subjecting protected persons both to internment and to assigned residence[7] within the occupied territory. It thus reaffirms the common understanding of the prohibition on deportation as being broad, inclusive, and categorical.

This prohibition is subject to only one qualification and one exception. The qualification is that the transfer or deportation has to be forced – that is, not voluntary.[8] The exception is contained in the second paragraph of Article 49, which refers to evacuations necessary for the security of the civilians involved or for imperative security military reasons. Even such evacuations, however, may not end in the displacement of the evacuees, who must be returned to their homes as soon as the hostilities in the evacuated area end.[9] The second

Armed Conflicts (Protocol II), Geneva, June 8, 1977, 1125 UNTS 609 [hereinafter: *AP II*]. Article 49, the focus of this entry, is applicable to situations of belligerent occupation.

[4] There has been some debate as to the distinction between forcible transfer and deportation, denoting that the former may take place within national boundaries and the latter across such boundaries; see, e.g., the *Stakić* case, Appeals Chamber Judgment, ICTY-97-24-A (March 22, 2006), ¶ 300. Note, however, that Article 7(2)(d) of the *ICC Statute* contains no such distinction. Given that both are prohibited, whether or not there is distinction seems quite immaterial. Rome Statute of the International Criminal Court, UN General Assembly, July 17, 1998, ISBN No. 92-9227-227-6 [hereinafter: *ICC Statute*].

[5] See generally, V. Chetail, "The Transfer and Deportation of Civilians," in A. Clapham, P. Gaeta, and M. Sassòli (eds.), *The 1949 Geneva Convention: A Commentary* (Oxford: Oxford University Press, 2015), pp. 1185-1213.

[6] J. S. Pictet (ed.), *The Geneva Conventions of 12 August 1949, Commentary – IV Geneva Convention Relative to the Protection of Civilian Persons in Time of War* (Geneva: International Committee of the Red Cross, 1958), p. 368 (hereinafter: Commentary on GC IV): "It will suffice to mention here that as we are dealing with occupied territory, the protected persons concerned will benefit by the provisions of Article 49 and cannot be deported; they can therefore only be interned, or placed in assigned residence, within the frontiers of the occupied country itself."

[7] See entry A: Assigned Residence.   [8] See e.g., *Stakić*, ¶ 279.

[9] Article 49 of GC IV, ¶ 2, reads: "Nevertheless, the Occupying Power may undertake total or partial evacuation of a given area if the security of the population or imperative military reasons so demand. Such evacuations may not involve the displacement of protected persons outside

paragraph has been interpreted as referring only to cases where the evacuation is in the interests of those evacuated – namely, when military operations endanger the safety of civilians in the evacuated area or when their presence hampers military operations.[10] The exceptionality and strict interpretation of the conditions where evacuation is allowed is supported by relevant jurisprudence.[11]

The object and purpose of this prohibition is clear: dislocation from one's home, homeland, and community is an affront to human dignity and identity. In the context of a belligerent occupation, the prohibition is also designed to ensure that the demographic composition of the territory remains intact, a rationale underscored by the corollary prohibition on the transfer of the population of the occupying power to the territory, contained in paragraph 6 of Article 49.[12]

The legislative history of the prohibition on deportations of protected persons from the occupied land dates back to the 1863 Lieber Code, which provided that "private citizens are no longer … carried off to distant parts."[13] In 1934, the Tokyo Draft of the International Convention on the Condition and Protection of Civilians of Enemy Nationality Who Are on Territory Belonging to or Occupied by a Belligerent, which preceded the GC IV in setting international law norms for occupied territories and contributed draft wordings to some of its clauses, prohibited "Deportations outside the territory of the occupied State." The Tokyo Draft also included an exception for evacuations needed to protect the evacuees[14] and was the basis for the wording of Article 49 paragraph 1.[15]

The prohibition on deportations and forcible transfers of protected persons from an occupied territory is considered a customary norm.[16]

---

the bounds of the occupied territory except when for material reasons it is impossible to avoid such displacement. Persons thus evacuated shall be transferred back to their homes as soon as hostilities in the area in question have ceased." ¶ 3 and ¶ 4 contain various requirements regulating evacuations.

[10] Pictet, Commentary on GC IV, pp. 280–281.
[11] See, e.g., the *Tadić* case, Trial Chamber Judgment, ICTY-95-9-T (October 17, 2003), ¶ 125.
[12] Chetail, "The Transfer and Deportation of Civilians," p. 1186.
[13] Article 23 of Instructions for the Government of Armies of The United States in the Field (Prepared by Francis Lieber, promulgated as General Orders No. 100 by President Lincoln, April 24, 1863).
[14] Article 19(b) of the Draft International Convention on the Condition and Protection of Civilians of Enemy Nationality Who Are on Territory Belonging to or Occupied by a Belligerent, Tokyo, 1934.
[15] See Pictet, Commentary on GC IV, p. 278: "Article 49 is derived from the Tokyo Draft which prohibited the deportation of the inhabitants of an occupied country."
[16] J.M Henckaerts and L. Doswald-Beck (eds.), *Customary International Humanitarian Law*, 2 vols. (Cambridge: Cambridge University Press, 2009), vol. I: Rules, pp. 457–462 (Rule 129A).

Its violation is a grave breach of the GC IV and constitutes a war crime.[17]

D.1.2 *Israel's Practice of Deportation of Palestinian Militants and Political Leaders*

Israel's means of exercising control over the OPT included the deportation of militants and political leaders out of the territory. During the first 15 years of the occupation, Israel deported Palestinians on a massive scale. According to official figures, during that time, 989 orders for the deportation of Palestinians from the OPT were signed.[18] Deportation of those perceived to be in a leadership position, alongside house demolitions,[19] and administrative detentions, was a major tool used to subdue opposition to the occupation. There were deportations of key figures (i.e., people who were perceived to be in a leading roles), and there were collective deportations, usually of Palestinian prisoners who met certain criteria. One example of collective deportation is an operation recorded in recently revealed documents that took place in Gaza in 1970–1971: Deteriorating security led IDF commanders to deport detainees, usually administrative detainees, over the Jordan River, in groups of 10 to 20 at a time. The criteria for deportation were the age of the detainees (relatively old) and the duration of their administrative detention (at least two years).[20] The operation, dubbed "Operation Patient," took place on January 4, 1971. This type of deportation was carried out without proper legal proceedings, without prior notice, and hence generated no legal challenge.[21]

---

[17]   Article 147 of GC IV; Article 85(4)(a) of Protocol Additional to the Geneva Conventions of August 12, 1949, and relating to the Protection of Victims of International Armed Conflicts (Additional Protocol I), Geneva, June 8, 1977, 1125 UNTS 3; Article 8(2)(b)(viii) of the ICC *Statute*.

[18]   B'Tselem, *Deportation of Palestinians from the Occupied Territories and the Mass Deportation of December 1992* (1993), p. 17. The figure is based on the response of Defense Minister Ariel Sharon to a parliamentary question submitted by M. K. Mordechai Virshuvsky, Knesset Record (1983), vol. 95, p. 1145. Another quote refers to 1,180 deportations; see D. Kretzmer, *The Occupation of Justice: The Supreme Court of Israel and the Occupied Territories* (Albany: State University of New York, 2002), p. 165.

[19]   See entry H: House Demolitions.

[20]   Letter from Yehoshua Almog, Foreign Ministry Delegate in the OPT, to Moshe Sasson, Foreign Ministry Deputy Executive Director, *Patient Operations* (August 28, 1970), The Conflict Records' Digital Repository (Akevot Institute for Israeli-Palestinian Conflict Research, hereinafter: Akevot Institute), Document no. 1004132. The document is stored in the National Archive, HZ 4470/05. The author is a member of the Akevot Institute's board of directors.

[21]   One exception was a proceeding challenging a deportation order issued under the Defence Regulations against a Palestinian resident of East Jerusalem. Since East Jerusalem had been

Deportations executed as a matter of fact devoid of judicial review of their legality ended in the late 1970s: In 1976, an attempt to subject a deportation order issued against a leading Hebron mayoral candidate for the position of mayor of Hebron for judicial review failed, as the order was executed hastily to frustrate the proceedings. Nevertheless, the court reprimanded the authorities, thereby making it difficult for them to escape future judicial review.[22] In 1979, a Palestinian administrative detainee who was about to be deported managed to notify his lawyer of the order issued against him before it was executed, and the petition that was filed halted the deportation, pending judgment.[23] The court eventually dismissed the petition, but in this and in subsequent rulings, enforced the deportees' procedural rights to a hearing, counsel, and judicial review prior to deportation.[24]

Having thus established itself as the institution determining the legality of deportation orders, the door was opened for considering the merits of their legality. Given the clear language of the prohibition on deporting protected persons from an occupied territory, on what basis could such a measure become legally permissible?

One such basis was found in the Defence (Emergency) Regulations 1945 (hereinafter: Defence Regulations), enacted in Mandatory Palestine pursuant to the supreme normative document of Mandatory law, the King's Order in Council.[25] The Defence Regulations empowered the Mandatory government to take draconian measures and suppress civil liberties "for securing the public safety, the defence of Palestine, the maintenance of public order and the suppression of mutiny, rebellion, and riot." The Defence Regulations, signed by the British High Commissioner, empowered him to order the "deportation of any person from Palestine" if he is "of the opinion" that such order is "necessary or expedient" for the goals set in the above King's order in Council.[26] Israel maintained that the Defence Regulations remained in force throughout Jordanian rule, and as

---

annexed and put under Israeli law, in terms of Israeli law this was not a case which involves international laws of occupation. See HCJ 17/71 *Mrar* v. *Minister of Defense* (1971) 28(1) PD 141.

[22] HCJ 159/76 *al-Natsheh* v. *Military Commander* (unreported).

[23] HCJ 97/79 *Abu Awad* v. *Commander of the Judea and Samaria Area* (1979) 33(3) PD 309.

[24] *Ibid.*; HCJ 320/80 *Qasem Qawasmeh* v. *Minister of Defense* (1980) 35(3) PD 113. For a complete overview of the deportations case-law, see Kretzmer, *The Occupation of Justice*, pp. 165–186.

[25] Memorandum on the Palestine (Defence) Order in Council, Supplement No. 2, 1937, p. 267. This 1937 Order in Council was preceded by the 1931 Order in Council which empowered the High Commissioner to issue emergency regulations (Palestine (Defence) Order in Council, 1931).

[26] Regulations 108 and 112 of the Defence Regulations, 1945.

such form part of the domestic law of the OPT which it has inherited and should indeed apply under the conservation principle of the laws of belligerent occupation.[27]

Article 49 provided another basis: The HCJ could not delete the first paragraph of Article 49, but it could and did interpret both its applicability and its substance in ways that turned it on its head. In doing so it ostensibly employed a variety of interpretative, and, at times, incommensurate, techniques which nevertheless had a common denominator: to legalize deportations. Section D.2 follows this judicial acrobatics employing a "before the law" perspective.[28] Section D.3 concludes.

D.2 A PURPOSEFUL COURT: FROM FORMALISM TO ORIGINALISM

D.2.1 *First Reading: Denying the International Norm a Domestic Entry Visa*

The first line of defense against constraints imposed by a norm is to deny that it applies at all. It is thus not surprising that, initially, the HCJ read the first paragraph of Article 49 as reflecting treaty law, rather than customary law. That reading, which the court indeed adopted with respect to the applicability of the GC IV generally,[29] is significant from a doctrinal perspective for two main reasons: First, customary norms are perceived as embedded in international society, reflecting as they advance an ethos of universally held values; second, such norms are considered enforceable in domestic law even in states which adopted the common-law rule that requires a legislative act of parliament to incorporate treaty law.

Israel follows the common-law rule requiring such incorporation for treaties to become part of the law of the land. Given that it did not incorporate the GC IV into its domestic legislation, the HCJ simply relied on the alleged conventional status of the first paragraph of Article 49 to conclude that it did not imbue individuals with rights enforceable by the state judiciary.[30]

---

[27] The argument that the Jordanians did not repeal the Defence Regulations was a matter for dispute in several cases. See Abu Awad; HCJ 698/80 *Daud Qawasmeh v. Minister of Defense* (1980) PD 35(1) 617.

[28] See Introduction, Section 2.2.   [29] See entry G: Geneva Law.

[30] *Daud Qawasmeh*, p. 627. See also, HCJ 629/82 *Mustafa v. The Military Commander of the West Bank* (1983) 37(1) PD 158; HCJ 500/72 *Al-Teen v. Minister of Defense* (1972) 27(1) PD 481. There was one exception at the time to this reading: in the Abu Awad case, then chief justice

This formalistic line of evasive defense proved to be quite tenuous: First, the very classification of this provision as reflecting treaty rather than customary law is dubious; second, the constraints imposed on the judiciary by domestic law do not exonerate the State from the charge that it violates international law.[31] This is a fortiori the case when the gap between the formality of the defense and the substantive harm to both human rights and to community political life is as glaring as it is in the practice of deportation. It is in light of these considerations that one should read Justice Haim Cohen's dissenting opinion in one of the most famous deportation cases, the 1980 *Qawasmeh* case.[32]

The *Qawasmeh* case concerned the deportation of three high-profile Palestinian leaders: two mayors of major Palestinian cities, Hebron and Halhul, and the Qadi (religious judge) of Hebron. Examining a large volume of legal literature, judgments, and state practice, Justice Cohen reached the conclusion that the prohibition on deportation in Article 49 reflects "a nucleus of customary international law that has been in effect, for all intent and purposes, since ancient times all over the world."[33] He ruled that the article represents customary law when it comes to treating the citizens of the country and treaty law regarding noncitizens, and found that the deportation orders against the mayors and the Qadi fell within the scope of the prohibition – a prohibition designed to outlaw exactly this sort of practice. As such, they were illegal and should be set aside.[34]

The majority, comprising two other judges, held that the prohibition had not yet attained the status of customary law and thus did not find it necessary to examine whether the Israeli practice was in any way at odds with it.[35] Still, the split in the court over what was already a highly controversial practice, and mounting international criticism, signified that the matter would not be put to rest for long. The 1980 *Qawasmeh* ruling begged for a review. The 1987 *Al-Affo* case provided it.[36]

Zussman concluded that Article 49 does not deal with deportations required for security reasons. This approach is discussed in the text at note 50.

[31] Note that under Article 27 of the Vienna Convention of the Law of Treaties, which itself reflects customary international law, a party to a treaty "may not invoke the provisions of its internal law as justification for its failure to perform a treaty." Vienna Convention on the Law of Treaties, May 23, 1969, 1155 UNTS 331 [hereinafter: VCLT].

[32] *Daud Qawasmeh*, pp. 646–648.   [33] *Ibid.*, p. 637.   [34] *Ibid.*, p. 647.   [35] *Ibid.*, p. 626.

[36] HCJ 785/87 *Al-Affo v. Commander of the IDF in the West Bank* (1988) 42(2) PD 4, http://elyon1.court.gov.il/files_eng/87/850/007/Z01/87007850.z01.pdf.

D.2.2 Second Reading: By Way of an Obiter Dictum

D.2.2.1. The Return of the Repressed: Setting the Stage for a Move from Formalism to Substance

Once the first Palestinian uprising ("Intifada") broke out, Israel stepped up its use of deportations of local and national leaders in an effort to crush it. A new wave of petitions, relying on justice Cohen's dissent in the *Qauassme* case, pressed for reopening the Article 49 argument. In 1987, then chief justice Meir Shamgar succumbed to the pressure. He joined several pending petitions, one of them filed by the Association for Civil Rights in Israel (ACRI), which challenged deportation orders issued against local operatives of Palestinian organizations, and convened an extended bench tasked with providing a conclusive ruling on the question. The judgment was rendered in April 1988 and covered 78 pages, 68 of them penned by Shamgar.

The court reaffirmed, this time unanimously, the conventional, noncustomary nature of Article 49. Hence, all members of the bench agreed that the petitioners could not rely on Article 49 in the domestic arena. This determination should have concluded the legal analysis of the petitioners' argument based on Article 49. It did not. This time, a new angle of the argument split the court: not the enforceability of the norm in a domestic court, but rather the (apparently theoretical) question of whether the Israeli practice of deportations was indeed prohibited by (the unenforceable) Article 49.

Justice Shamgar embroiled the court in an interpretive thesis that concluded that Israel's practice of deportation of Palestinians from the OPT is not prohibited by the (noncustomary) prohibition stipulated in the first paragraph of Article 49. If Shamgar had hoped that this would settle the legal controversy once and for all and would give the state a legal defense it could use in the international arena, he was bound for disappointment: A new dissent, this time written by justice Gavriel Bach, powerfully clashed with Shamgar's thesis. Since all justices agreed that the prohibition was not customary, most of the judgment dealt with a question that was not required for determining the case, and the blistering disagreement between the justices was waged entirely as an obiter dictum.

D.2.2.2 Intermezzo: Gate-keeping

As the hearing in the *Al-Affo* case began, counsels for ACRI, Prof. David Kretzmer and attorney Avigdor Feldman, raised a concern: Before joining the supreme court, chief justice Shamgar had served as the military advocate general and as Israel's attorney general. In both capacities he was the legal authority that gave its seal of approval for the deportation of Palestinians. But the main concern that they voiced in the courtroom was that he had also published his position on the inapplicability of the Geneva Convention in the OPT in a legal journal while serving as attorney general.[37] This was a key issue in the case, and apparently Shamgar had formed his opinion on the matter. ACRI's counsels argued that this was a case of a potential judicial bias. Shamgar treated the arguments as a recusal motion and dismissed them with apparent anger, ruling that expressing a legal view on a matter does not preclude subsequent participation in judicial proceedings in which the same legal issues arises as long as it involves a different set of facts. He further stated that if the criteria for recusal cited in the ACRI's arguments were always applied, any judge would be precluded from hearing "any matter that raises a theoretical issue to which he made reference in the past, whether as a lawyer appearing in court, in a lecture given in an academic context or in an opinion expressed as the Attorney General or the State Attorney."[38] This statement obfuscated the difference between expressing theoretical academic opinions, exercising executive authority, and exercising judicial review over the very same issue a judge had previously authorized in an executive capacity.

Indeed, justice Shamgar's reading of the prohibition on deportation stipulated in the first paragraph of Article 49, while no doubt original, was simultaneously anything but surprising. This reading is the focus of the following subsection.

D.2.2.3 Deporting the Text of Article 49 Paragraph 1

The language of the first paragraph of Article 49 indicates a clear and comprehensive prohibition on deportation. In order to read the prohibition as permission, the text has to give way. Justice Shamgar proposed a purposive or teleological reading of the text in order to turn the prohibition into permission.

This concoction of judicial alchemy comprised five ingredients. The first ingredient was an interpretive principle that limits the weight ascribed to the ordinary meaning of the text: It stipulates that, given the presumption that states do not wish to limit themselves, the preferred interpretation is the one

---

[37] E.g., M. Shamgar, "The Observance of International Law in the Administered Territories" (1971) 1 *Israel Yearbook of Human Rights* 262.

[38] *Al-Affo*, p. 3 [Hebrew; the paragraph containing this remark was omitted from the court's English translation].

least restrictive of the authority of the state.[39] The second ingredient was another interpretative principle which, equally designed to shy away from the ordinary meaning of the words used in the text, holds that provisions contained in an international convention must be interpreted bearing in mind the unique nature of the conventions: They, said Shamgar, are instruments that create an international order directed at their own authors and therefore preclude rigidity and formalism.[40]

The third ingredient was to invert the relationship between textual and teleological methods of interpretation: Beginning in the mid-1980s and lasting for almost three decades, teleological interpretation, and the judicial activism it entails, characterized the HCJ.[41] It is not, however, the preferred interpretative method of international law, probably because states are all too weary of judicial activism. Indeed, the rules of treaty interpretation, codified in Articles 31–33 of the Vienna Convention on the Law of Treaties, give clear primacy to a textual methodology of interpretation. Under the heading "General Rule of Interpretation," Article 31 (1) stipulates that "[A] treaty shall be interpreted in good faith in accordance with the ordinary meaning to be given to the terms of the treaty in their context and in the light of its object and purpose."[42] This provision provides the interpretive methodology: Words have an ordinary meaning; they matter as words which the context, and the object and purpose, help to elucidate. Ergo, interpretation proceeds from the textual to the contextual to the purposive. Justice Shamgar, while surely aware of this roadmap of treaty interpretation, decided nevertheless to take a shortcut: holding that the proviso of "object and purpose" provides a "bridge" from textual and to purposive interpretation,[43] he effectively crossed out the former.

The fourth ingredient required to inverse the methodology of the *VCLT* and to buttress the primacy of purpose over text was Article 32 of the *VCLT*. Under the heading "[S]upplementary means of interpretation," it authorizes recourse to such supplementary means, "including the preparatory work of the

---

[39]   *Al-Affo*, p. 18 [Hebrew], p. 15 [in the English translation]. Shamgar cited in this context J.G. Starke, *An Introduction to International Law* (8th edn, London: Butterworth-Heinemann, 1977), p. 510.

[40]   *Al-Affo*, pp. 19, 21 [Hebrew], pp. 15–17 [in the English translation].

[41]   Justice Aharon Barak, who succeeded Shamgar first as attorney general and eventually as chief justice, is most identified with this approach, which he employed in both judgments and academic writing; see, e.g., A. Barak, *Interpretation in Law* (Jerusalem: Nevo, 1993), vol. II: Legislative Interpretation (1993) and vol. III: Constitutional Interpretation (1994) [Hebrew]; A. Barak, *Purposive Interpretation in Law*, S. Bashi (trans.) (Princeton: Princeton University Press, 2005).

[42]   Article 31(2) of *VCLT*.   [43]   *Al-Affo*, p. 17 [Hebrew], p. 14 [in the English translation].

treaty and the circumstances of its conclusion," in order to confirm the meaning resulting from the application of Article 31, or when this application leaves the meaning ambiguous or obscure, or generates "a result which is manifestly absurd or unreasonable." The clear language of Article 49 paragraph 1 which easily lends itself to a textual interpretation that is neither ambiguous nor unreasonable, notwithstanding, the combination of these ingredients generated the conclusion that:

> [L]anguage does not govern the purpose, rather it serves it. The law is an instrument for realizing legal policy, and therefore interpretation needs to aim toward emancipating the wording from its semantic bonds, were these to distance it from the legislative purpose which the words are intended to realize.[44]

Having thus set aside the textual interpretation of the provision, the concoction just needed one more ingredient to deal the coup de grâce on the prohibition on deportation. That ingredient had to be ingenious. The reason is that normally an activist court resorts to purposive interpretation to advance a liberal reading of the law. This is true generally and certainly true of the jurisprudence of the Israeli HCJ. In order to meet this objective, the purpose is normally framed at a high level of abstraction and extracted from an entire system of legal and meta-legal sources, which encompass general principles and values that the legal system holds in the highest regard and wishes to promote or protect.

Article 49 paragraph 1 does have a purpose – one that can be inferred from its categorical language, and indeed one that coheres with and advances the general purpose of and the humanitarian sensibility underlying the *GC IV*. That purpose is, as noted earlier, to avoid the trauma of displacement, a purpose which, in the words of the International Criminal Tribunal for the former Yugoslavia (ICTY), "aims at safeguarding the right and aspiration of individuals to live in their communities and homes without outside interference."[45] So, how would a teleological reading of the provision generate an authorization to deport?

Chief justice Shamgar's found it under the dim lamppost of the original intent of the drafters' "plan of action."[46] According to this reading, the drafters intended merely to forbid mass deportations carried out by the Nazis and had no intention of limiting individual deportations required for

---

[44]   *Ibid.*, p. 14 [Hebrew], p. 11 [in the English translation].
[45]   The *Krnojelac* case, Appeals Chamber Judgment, ICTY-97–25-A (September 17, 2003), ¶ 218.
[46]   *Al-Affo*, p. 17 [Hebrew; the paragraph containing this remark was omitted from the court's English translation].

public order and security. This odd, not to say manipulative, reading had a history in the HCJ.

The first deportation case that reached judicial review in 1979 was not determined on the basis of Article 49.[47] Nevertheless, toward the conclusion of the judgment, then chief justice Zussman, devoted one paragraph to this provision:[48]

> [T]he purpose of said Article 49 is to prevent acts such as the heinous acts committed by the Germans during WWII, during which millions of civilians were expelled from their homes for various purposes, usually to Germany to perform forced labor for the enemy, and Jews and others were taken to concentration camps to be tortured and exterminated.

In light of this purpose, he concluded that the prohibition on deportation does not apply to nonarbitrary, personal deportation for security reasons, and that indeed the occupying power has the authority to do so in shouldering its responsibility under the Hague Regulation 43 to provide for safety and public order.

Shamgar reiterated this interpretation: The drafters, he noted, referencing the Convention's preparatory documents, spoke of deportations "such as those that took place during the last war."[49] Ergo, the deportations to which Article 49 refers are "arbitrary deportations of groups of nationals as were carried out during World War II for purposes of subjugation, extermination and for similarly cruel reasons."[50] The purpose of the provision was to prohibit neither the deportation of an individual suspected of threatening security, nor the deportation of a terrorist.

Having thus fastened the "legislative purpose" of Article 49 to the circumstances of the Holocaust, and in the process having ignored the Tokyo Draft of 1934, which contained a prohibition on deportations and was the basis for Article 49,[51] justice Shamgar proceeded to rewrite the otherwise clear text: Given that "Nazi methods of operation ... in which mass transfers were conducted, sometimes on the basis of common ethnic identity, or by rounding up people in Ghettos, in streets or houses, at times on the basis of individual summonses through lists of names,"[52] made it possible to cross out of Article 49

---

[47] *Abu Awad.*   [48] *Ibid.*, 315.
[49] *Al-Affo*, p. 24 [Hebrew; p. 23 in the English translation]. Shamgar references to *Actes de la Conference Diplomatique de Geneva de 1949* (tome II), pp. 648, 649, 743, 744, 810, 811.
[50] *Al-Affo*, p. 31 [Hebrew], pp. 31–32 [in the English translation].
[51] See Pictet, Commentary on GC IV, p. 278: "Article 49 is derived from the Tokyo Draft which prohibited the deportation of the inhabitants of an occupied country."
[52] *Ibid.*, p. 28 [Hebrew], p. 28 [in the English translation].

paragraph 1 the prohibition on individual deportation. It also made it possible to conclude that:[53]

> [T]he words "regardless of their motive" were intended to encompass all deportations of populations and mass evacuations for the purposes of labour, medical experiments or extermination, which were founded during the war on a variety of arguments and motives, including some which were but trickery and deceit (such as relocation, necessary work, evacuation for security purposes etc . . .).

Three justices concurred with chief justice Shamgar. Justice Gavriel Bach, a former state attorney and one of the prosecutors in the Eichmann trial, disagreed. He insisted that there is text in the *GC IV*:[54]

> The juxtaposition of the words individual or mass forcible transfers as well as deportation with the phrase "regardless of their motive" . . . admits, in my opinion, no room to doubt that the Article applies not only to mass deportations but to the deportation of individuals as well, and that the prohibition was intended to be total, sweeping and unconditional – "regardless of their motive."

Justice Bach did not deny that the historical background and the drafters' intent are relevant for interpretation, but he did deny that, in the case of Article 49, it precludes an interpretation of the prohibition which conforms to its clear language. In his view, Nazis' actions were the "trigger" for drafting the *GC IV*, but that did not contradict the thesis that the language chosen covered a broader range of actions. Indeed, he noted that the reading of Article 49 in conjunction with Article 78 of the *GC IV* – a provision which empowers the occupying power to assign the residence of a protected person who threatens security or to place him in administrative detention[55] – affirms that the prohibition in Article 49 paragraph 1 applies also to persons suspected or convicted of security offenses. Given, however, that the entire bench found that the provision is not part of customary international law and is thus unenforceable, both the majority and the dissent reading of Article 49 paragraph 1 remained an obiter dictum. The deportation was approved and executed.

D.3 CONCLUSION: FOR ALL (ORIGINAL) INTENT AND PURPOSES

Chief justice Shamgar's framed his rewriting of Article 49 paragraph 1 as grounded in a purposive legal philosophy, distinguishing it from the literal,

---

[53] *Ibid.*, p. 33 [Hebrew], p. 34 [in the English translation].
[54] *Ibid.*, p. 70 [Hebrew], p. 91 [in the English translation].
[55] See entry A: Assigned Residence.

narrow doctrinal approach of the petitioners and of justice Bach. His read-ing, deviating as it does from the ordinary meaning of the terms used in the provision in due regard to its object and purpose, attracted much criticism.[56] A full appreciation of this allegedly teleological reading requires that it be placed in the broader context of the HCJ's jurisprudence.

Teleological interpretation was undoubtedly the defining trademark of the Israeli supreme court under chief justice Shamgar and his successor, Aharon Barak. Seeking to uncover the purpose of an act of parliament became an exciting task that demands much more than just looking at the text itself and at the explanatory remarks of the legislators during the drafting process. "Every law, including that whose language is 'clear', requires interpretation," wrote Barak. "The law is 'clear' only after the interpretation has clarified it. It is not clear without interpretation. Words by themselves are not 'clear.' In fact, there is no less clear a statement than that words are 'clear.'"[57] Thus, finding the meaning of a norm, translating it from "human" or "semantic" language to "legal" language,[58] demands resorting to a wide range of interpretive benchmarks that create the force-field in which the norm floats. There are several such bench-marks, including literal meaning and legislative intent, but the most important are the fundamental principles and values of the legal system: The purpose of a singular norm is in synch with the purposes of the legal order. Purposive interpretation thus aspires to harmonize individual norms with other norms and with the normative system as a whole. As such, and given that the Israeli legal system is based on liberal and democratic values, the purposive approach, when applied by the court to Israeli legislation, enhanced the weight of universal values vis-à-vis particular legislative interests. It is this judicial philosophy that provided the court with a methodology for protecting freedoms and fundamental rights through interpretation, and eventually led it to declare that the 1992 Basic Laws[59] created a "constitutional revolution" which entrusted the judiciary with the power to vitiate legislation that breached the rights guaranteed therein.[60]

---

[56] See e.g., M. Jacques, *Armed Conflict and Displacement: The Protection of Refugees and Displaced Persons under International Humanitarian Law* (Cambridge: Cambridge University Press, 2012), p. 28; Kretzmer, *The Occupation of Justice*, pp. 48–51; J.-M. Henckaerts, "Deportation and Transfer of Civilians in Times of War" (1993) 26 *Vanderbilt Journal of Transnational Law* 469, 471.

[57] HCJ 47/83 *Tour Aviv (Israel) Ltd. v. Chairman of the Restrictive Trade Practices Control Board* (1985) 39(1) PD 169.

[58] Barak, *Purposive Interpretation in Law*, p. 6.

[59] Basic Law: Human Dignity and Liberty; Basic Law: Freedom of Occupation.

[60] HCJ 6821/93 *Bank Mizrachi Ltd. v. Givat Yoav Workers Village for Cooperative Agricultural Settlement Ltd.* (1995) 49(4) PD 221, http://elyon1.court.gov.il/files_eng/93/210/068/z01/93068 210.z01.pdf.

In this context, dubbing his interpretation of the prohibition on deportation as "purposive" thus appeared to offer not merely an elegant escape
from the *semantic sting* Article 49 presented for those who believed Israel's
security concerns allow it to deport protected people, but also to present the
court itself as dynamic and indeed liberal. Appearances, alas, are notoriously deceiving:[61] Identifying the purpose of Article 49 only with the
presumed *subjective* intent of the drafters, and thus with the concrete
historical context in which the GC IV was enacted is not purposive interpretation: rather, it is a conservative and formalistic interpretive method
that looks for the legislator's – in this case, representatives of scores of
countries, each possibly with their own "object" and "purpose" for supporting the language of the article – original intent. Rather than impregnating
the text with liberal values that harmonize this provision with other provisions, and indeed with the telos of the GC IV, this interpretation appears to
import American *originalism* into international law.[62] But this appearance
too is deceptive: Shamgar's construction of the drafters' original intent
reveals his own subjective sympathy and political preference, not theirs or
the GC IV's. It is indeed neither purposive nor originalist. It is merely
instrumental. Its only purpose is to legitimate and legalize the prohibited
practice of deportation.

It is thus not entirely surprising that as professor Kretzmer notes,[63] merely
six months after the *Al-Affo* judgment was delivered, chief justice Shamgar
adopted a textual, literal reading of the GC IV.[64] This time, it was GC IV
Article 76 that required interpretation. The petition challenged the practice
of holding administrative detainees who are residents of the OPT in facilities
inside Israel. One of the arguments the petitioners made was that Article 76,
which stipulates that "protected persons accused of offences shall be
detained in the occupied country, and if convicted they shall serve their
sentences therein," compels holding detainees in the occupied territory and
prohibits transferring them outside it. They further posited that this provision

---

[61] In reference to the language used by Judge Krylov in his dissenting opinion in Conditions of
      Admission of a State to Membership in The United Nations, Advisory Opinion, 1948 ICJ
      54, 107.

[62] On American originalism, see L. B. Solum, "What is Originalism? The Evolution of
      Contemporary Originalist Theory" (2011) *Georgetown University Law Center*, 6–17;
      H. J. Powell, "The Original Understanding of Original Intent" (1985) 98 *Harvard Law
      Review* 885; See also R. H. Fallon, Jr., "Judicially Manageable Standards and Constitutional
      Meaning" (1996) 119 *Harvard Law Review* 1275.

[63] Kretzmer, *The Occupation of Justice*, pp. 52–53.

[64] HCJ 253/88 *Sajdiya* v. *Minister of Defense* (1988) 42(3) PD 801.

coheres with Article 49's prohibition on deportation.[65] Chief justice Shamgar rejected the argument. In this case, too, he took the trouble to provide the reasons for his ruling, despite his principled position that the Convention was not customary to begin with and that there was, in this instance, a contradicting domestic law which explicitly allows the transfer of prisoners to incarceration facilities inside Israel. In stark contradiction to his interpretive approach in *Al-Affo*, in this case he employed a narrow, literal interpretation: Since administrative detainees are neither *accused* nor *convicted* of an offense, the article does not apply to them, and since Article 79, which lists which articles of the *GC IV* apply to administrative detainees, does not cite Article 76, the prohibition on transferring prisoners from the occupied territories should not be applied to administrative detainees.[66] Surely, a purposive interpretation of Article 76 would have concluded that the distinction between administrative and criminal detainees is immaterial to the location of their incarceration.

Deportation of Palestinian militants and leaders ended in 1992 with the largest collective deportation Israel had ever executed: In December of that year, after the brutal abduction and murder of a border police officer by a Hamas cell, the government of Israel decided to deport 415 members of Hamas and its sister organization, the Islamic Jihad. In an effort to evade judicial review which would delay the dramatic action, the deportees were rounded up in prisons or arrested in their homes and rapidly bussed to the Lebanese border, all under a veil of secrecy. News of this reached human rights lawyers from HaMoked: Center for the Defense of the Individual and ACRI, who rushed to file court petitions that same night. Justice Aharon Barak was on duty that night. He halted the deportation with a temporary order, and the buses stopped at the Lebanese border. What was meant to be a swift deportation turned into a legal fiasco. The HCJ, departing from its previous rulings regarding procedural guarantees in such matters, upheld the deportation.[67] The Lebanese authorities, however, refused to grant the deportees passage beyond the Israeli-controlled security zone, and the deportees were stranded in the no man's land between the Israeli-controlled area and the area controlled by the Lebanese army. The situation turned into a farce, and the deportee encampment generated huge media interest over the ensuing

---

[65] This position is supported by the official commentary: see Pictet, Commentary on GC IV, p. 368, according to which the Article 49 prohibition on deportation should be read into Article 78. See also entry A: Assigned Residence.

[66] *Sajdiya*, p. 812.

[67] HCJ 5973/92 *Association for Civil Rights in Israel v. Minister of Defense* (1993) PD 47(1) 267, http://elyon1.court.gov.il/files_eng/92/730/059/Z01/92059730.z01.pdf.

weeks and months, with mounting pressure on Israel. Israel was ultimately forced to allow the deportees to return to the OPT, and they did, as heroes. The political and diplomatic cost of deportation, not the legal prohibition, had stopped the practice, a prohibited practice which judicial verbal contortionism hitherto permitted.

E

Export of Knowledge

Hedi Viterbo

E.1 INTRODUCTION

Israel is the world's biggest weapons exporter per capita.[1] In absolute (non-per-capita) terms, the United States is unrivaled,[2] though Israel also ranks near the top of the list.[3] When it comes to drones, Israel's exports outweigh those of all other countries combined.[4] About a tenth of Israeli households are estimated to be directly economically dependent on the arms industry,[5] and public trust is highest for this sector.[6]

---

[1] A. Jackson, "Europe's Most Peace-Loving Countries Export a Huge Amount of the World's Weapons," *Business Insider* (May 23, 2014), www.businessinsider.com/sweden-and-switzerland-are-among-top-arms-exporters-in-the-world-2014–5. See also N. Gordon, "Israel's Emergence as a Homeland Security Capital," in E. Zureik, D. Lyon, and Y. Abu-Laban (eds.), *Surveillance and Control in Israel/Palestine: Population, Territory, and Power* (London: Routledge, 2011), p. 154. See also entry X: X-Ray.

[2] Al Jazeera News, "The 10 Countries that Export the Most Major Weapons," *Al Jazeera* (February 22, 2017), www.aljazeera.com/indepth/interactive/2017/02/10-countries-export-major-weapons-170220170539801.html; L. Doré, "These are the World's 10 Biggest Arms Exporters and the Countries they Send Weapons to," *The Independent* (February 23, 2016), www.indy100.com/article/these-are-the-worlds-10-biggest-arms-exporters-and-the-countries-they-send-weapons-to–b1b9WfJbu0e.

[3] R. Dagoni, "Israel – the World's Third Biggest Weapons Exporter," *Globes* (October 5, 2009) [Hebrew], www.globes.co.il/news/article.aspx?did=1000503033; News Agencies, "A Surge in Global Arms Trade: What Position Does Israel Occupy?," *Ynet News* (March 9, 2015) [Hebrew], www.ynet.co.il/articles/0,7340,L-4634809,00.html.

[4] G. Arnett, "The Numbers behind the Worldwide Trade in Drones," *Guardian* (March 16, 2015), www.theguardian.com/news/datablog/2015/mar/16/numbers-behind-worldwide-trade-in-drones-uk-israel (referring to the period from 1985 to 2014).

[5] J. Cook, "Israel's Thriving Arms Trade is a Setback to Peace Agreement," *The National – Opinion* (July 23, 2013), www.thenational.ae/thenationalconversation/comment/israels-thriving-arms-trade-is-a-setback-to-peace-agreement (quoting former Israeli prime minister and minister of defense Ehud Barak).

[6] N. Yefet, "Security Industry Receives Highest Public Trust – 61 percent," *Globes* (May 17, 2017) [Hebrew], www.globes.co.il/news/article.aspx?did=1001189001.

Yet, Israel and the United States are major exporters (and, as demonstrated in this entry, importers) not only of weapons but also of security knowledge.[7] This entry takes this sort of ideational export and import as a point of departure for exploring the circulation and sharing of, as well as the convergence and connections between, the security discourses and practices of these two countries.[8] Using a broad range of primary and secondary sources, the entry seeks to provide an empirically rich and uniquely close analysis of some of these processes. As this analysis will illustrate, Israel and the United States alike are unconfined to their borders, in two complementary respects. On the one hand, their security apparatuses reach far beyond the territories and populations under their control. On the other hand, these apparatuses relate to, resonate, and brim with supposedly external security discourses and practices.

There are two key reasons for centering on the United States. First, it is Israel's strongest ally and funder. According to the US Congressional Research Service, "Israel is the largest cumulative recipient of US foreign assistance since World War II. To date, the United States has provided Israel $127.4 billion ... in bilateral assistance ... [primarily] in the form of military assistance."[9] In 2014, for example, the United States donated more military funding to Israel than it did to all other countries combined.[10] In 2016, the US

---

[7] In this context, the term "export" can be used loosely, to designate a process that is not fully or necessarily intentional or preplanned. On the pitfalls of scholarly quests for intent or motivations, see H. Viterbo "Rights as a Divide-and-Rule Mechanism: Lessons from the Case of Palestinians in Israeli Custody" (forthcoming) *Law & Social Inquiry* (arguing that this approach "tends to resort to questionable structural and/or causal explanations," or "rests upon untenable assumptions about the transparency, knowability, and even existence of intentions," and adding that it "might inadvertently facilitate state attempts to legitimize its contentious actions by characterizing their consequences as 'unintended'").

[8] In political and policy studies, some of these phenomena are referred to as "policy convergence," "policy diffusion," "policy emulation," "policy transfer," and/or "policy translation." See, e.g., C. J. Bennett, "What is Policy Convergence and What Causes it?" (1991) 21 *British Journal of Political Science* 215; G. Boushey, "Punctuated Equilibrium Theory and the Diffusion of Innovations" (2012) 40 *Policy Studies Journal* 127; D. P. Dolowitz and D. Marsh, "Learning from Abroad: The Role of Policy Transfer in Contemporary Policy-Making" (2000) 13 *Governance* 5; B. Johnson and B. Hagström, "The Translation Perspective as an Alternative to the Policy Diffusion Paradigm: The Case of the Swedish Methadone Maintenance Treatment" (2005) 34 *Journal of Social Policy* 365; E. McCann and K. Ward, "Policy Assemblages, Mobilities and Mutations: Toward a Multidisciplinary Conversation" (2012) 10 *Political Studies Review* 325.

[9] J. M. Sharp, "US Foreign Aid to Israel, Congressional Research Service" (December 2016), https://fas.org/sgp/crs/mideast/RL33222.pdf.

[10] N. Thompson, "Seventy-Five Percent of US Foreign Military Financing Goes to Two Countries," *CNN News* (November 11, 2015), http://edition.cnn.com/2015/11/11/politics/us-foreign-aid-report/.

government pledged to give Israel a record $30 billion in military aid over ten years – the largest bilateral military aid package ever.[11] The funding primarily goes toward purchasing weaponry manufactured by US companies,[12] thereby ultimately subsidizing the US arms industry. Funding has come not only from the United States as a country but also from individuals who later became state officials. Prior to his appointment, the current US ambassador to Israel reportedly donated money to an illegal construction operation by Israeli settlers on privately owned Palestinian lands in the West Bank.[13] In 2003, future US president Donald Trump also made a donation to a West Bank settlement.[14]

Furthermore, the United States provides the Israeli government with other forms of material and diplomatic support. Among other things, it has used its veto power in the UN Security Council to block numerous resolutions on Palestine, starting with a 1973 resolution against the introduction of any "changes which may adversely affect the … fundamental rights of all the inhabitants" of the West Bank and Gaza Strip.[15] Support for Israel extends beyond political circles. While polls place Israel as the world's fourth most unpopular country, it is regarded highly favorably by the US public, and, conversely, the Israeli public holds an almost unparalleled positive view of the

---

[11] O. Dorrell, "US $38B Military Aid Package to Israel Sends a Message," *USA Today* (September 14, 2016), www.usatoday.com/story/news/world/2016/09/14/united-states-military-aid-israel/90358564/.

[12] E. Green, "Why Does the United States Give So Much Money to Israel?," *The Atlantic* (September 15, 2016), www.theatlantic.com/international/archive/2016/09/united-states-israel-memorandum-of-understanding-military-aid/500192/.

[13] J. Maltz, "Friedman Donated Money to Constructing a Building on Private Palestinian Land in Beit El," *Haaretz* (February 17, 2017) [Hebrew], www.haaretz.co.il/news/politics/.premium-1.3869095.

[14] J. Maltz, "Trump Donated $10,000 to West Bank Settlement," *Haaretz* (December 18, 2016), www.haaretz.com/israel-news/.premium-1.759738.

[15] S. Sarsar, "The Question of Palestine and United States Behavior at the United Nations" (2004) 17 *International Journal of Politics, Culture, and Society* 457. See also S. Zunes, "The United States and Israeli Violations of International Humanitarian Law," in A. T. Chase (ed.), *Routledge Handbook on Human Rights and the Middle East and North Africa* (London and New York: Routledge, 2017) (criticizing the United States' active role in defending Israeli violations of IHL and in discouraging the UN from addressing these violations). When the United States atypically abstained from vetoing a resolution demanding a halt to Israeli settlements, Israeli prime minister Benjamin Netanyahu called this an "absurd" and "shameful anti-Israel resolution," and added: "The Obama administration not only failed to protect Israel against this gang-up at the UN, it colluded with it behind the scenes." P. Beaumont, "US Abstention Allows UN to Demand End to Israeli Settlements," *Guardian* (December 23, 2016), www.theguardian.com/world/2016/dec/23/us-abstention-allows-un-to-demand-end-to-israeli-settlements. On this resolution, see entry N: Nomos.

United States.[16] In addition, the United States is Israel's largest trading partner, with bilateral commerce valued at $25.7 billion in 2016.[17]

A second reason for the focus on the United States in this entry is its enormous impact on Israeli law and politics. Since its early days, the Israeli supreme court has approvingly cited countless US court cases,[18] including – as shown in this entry – in matters concerning the West Bank and Gaza Strip. As also discussed in this entry, Israeli politicians have repeatedly cited the United States as a role model of so-called "national security" law and policy. In addition, notwithstanding their recent shift toward Europe and Asia, Israeli law schools have generally become increasingly similar to their US counterparts.[19] This trend, some have suggested, might incentivize Israeli legal scholars to concentrate on US law and universal theories at the expense of local issues and specificities.[20] There are, of course, countless other examples of these inextricable ties between the United States and Israel – for one, every fourth Israeli settler in the West Bank is a US citizen.[21] For these and many other reasons, what happens in Israel/Palestine concerns the United States, and vice versa.

This entry proceeds as follows. Section E.2 examines the movement of security knowledge between these countries, with a particular focus on

---

[16] BBC World Service, *Poll* (June 2014), pp. 10, 31–33, https://downloads.bbc.co.uk/mediacentre/country-rating-poll.pdf. In this poll, the only country holding a more favorable view of these countries than they have of each other was Ghana.

[17] S. Scheer and T. Cohen, "Investors Bet on Israel Tech Stock Windfall under Trump," *Reuters* (February 21, 2017), http://uk.reuters.com/article/us-usa-trump-israel-economy-idUKKBN1601KL.

[18] U. Gorney, "American Precedent in the Supreme Court of Israel" (1955) 68 *Harvard Law Review* 1194; E. Rivlin, "Thoughts on Referral to Foreign Law, Global Novel-Chain, and Novelty" (2009) 21 *Florida Journal of International Law* 1, 21–7; Z. Segal, "A Constitution Without a Constitution: The Israeli Experience and the American Impact" (1992) 21 *Capital University Law Review* 1. At the same time, in certain areas – such as freedom of speech – Israel's supreme court has shown ambivalence toward US law, possibly due, among other things, to cultural and political differences between the two countries. See P. Lahav, "American Influence on Israel's Jurisprudence of Free Speech" (1981) 9 *Hastings Constitutional Law Quarterly* 21.

[19] P. Lahav, "American Moment[s]: When, How, and Why Did Israeli Law Faculties Come to Resemble Elite US Law Schools?" (2009) 10 *Theoretical Inquiries in Law* 653.

[20] H. Sandberg, "Legal Colonialism – Americanization of Legal Education in Israel" (2010) 10 *Global Jurist* 1; see also O. Gazal-Ayal, "Economic Analysis of 'Law & Economics'" (2007) 35 *Capital University Law Review* 787, 792.

[21] E. Berlizon – Reuters, "Israeli Donald Trump Supporters Opened a Campaign Office in the West Bank to Get American Expats to Vote," *Business Insider UK* (September 5, 2016), http://uk.businessinsider.com/trump-israel-campaign-office-2016-9?r=US&IR=T. For a slightly lower estimate, see J. Maltz, "60,000 American Jews Live in the West Bank, New Study Reveals," *Haaretz* (August 27, 2015), www.haaretz.com/news/israel/.premium-1.673358.

US–Israeli military and police collaborations as well as the resort of the United States, both overseas and domestically, to counterterrorism and urban warfare tactics imported from Israel's Palestinian "laboratory." Section E.3 examines a longstanding dynamic that complements and reinforces this transfer of security knowledge: cross-references between US and Israeli legal and political discourses. Through a myriad of such cross-references, the two countries engage in a potentially self-perpetuating process of positioning one another as global security models, whose expertise and policies are universally applicable and therefore mobile. These cross-references, it will be shown, are often actually self-referential – for instance, a US reference to an Israeli source that, in turn, invokes the United States – thereby ultimately validating one's own laws and policies. Section E.4 turns to a related discursive phenomenon: the use of mutual language, imagery, and analogies by US and Israeli state officials. The concluding section summarizes key themes, considers them in view of the existing academic literature, and discusses their implications regarding the fluid political and legal borders of Israel and the United States alike.

E.2 TRANSFER OF SECURITY KNOWLEDGE

Recent years have witnessed the extensive export of Israeli security expertise, particularly regarding warfare in urban areas. According to some reports, during the battles of the second Intifada of 2002, US military observers, dressed in Israeli military uniform, accompanied Israeli soldiers.[22] A year later, ahead of the US invasion of Iraq, Israeli defense experts reportedly briefed US commanders on their experience in urban warfare.[23] Shortly after the beginning of the Iraq war, further reports appeared that the US military was seeking advice from its Israeli counterpart on the matter, with a particular interest in Israel's fighting in the West Bank city of Jenin during the second Intifada.[24] A few months into the war, the deputy chief of staff for doctrine and strategy at

---

[22] S. Graham, "Laboratories of War: Surveillance and US-Israeli Collaboration in War and Security," in E. Zureik, D. Lyon, and Y. Abu-Laban (eds.), *Surveillance and Control in Israel/Palestine: Population, Territory, and Power* (London: Routledge, 2011), pp. 133, 134 [hereinafter: "Laboratories of War"].

[23] D. Filkins, "A Region Inflamed: Strategy; Though New Tactics by US Tighten Grip on Iraq Towns," *New York Times* (December 7, 2003) [hereinafter: "A Region Inflamed"], www.nytimes.com/2003/12/07/world/a-region-inflamed-strategy-tough-new-tactics-by-us-tighten-grip-on-iraq-towns.html.

[24] J. Huggler, "Israelis Trained US Troops in Jenin-Style Urban Warfare," *Independent* (March 29, 2003), www.independent.co.uk/news/world/middle-east/israelis-trained-us-troops-in-jenin-style-urban-warfare-5352656.html.

the US Army Training and Doctrine Command wrote that Israel's experience "continues to teach us many lessons, and we continue to evaluate and address those lessons, embedding and incorporating them appropriately into our concepts, doctrine and training. For example, we recently traveled to Israel to glean lessons learned from their counterterrorist operations in urban areas."[25]

In 2006, the US Army War College also held a workshop designed to draw lessons from Israel's experience in managing Palestinian propaganda. In the workshop, the situation in the Palestinian Territory was used as a "proxy" for the US invasion of Iraq.[26]

Five years later, some 200 US Marines came to Israel for a month of training in counterterrorism and urban combat skills alongside Israeli soldiers. The Marines reportedly spent their time in several military locations, including the so-called Urban Warfare Training Center[27] – a large mock Palestinian village built as a training facility in an Israeli military base. This facility was largely funded by the United States, developed in collaboration with the US army, and, according to its director, designed to serve as "a valuable center of knowledge that will also benefit our American allies."[28] A senior US military official expressed interest in expanding such collaborations: "We are looking to increase relations [with the Israeli military] and to expand [joint] training . . . Israel came out of the intifada like we are coming out of the counter-insurgency environment."[29]

Not only the military but also other US state agencies have received counterterrorism training from Israel's security forces. US police officials, the Federal Bureau of Investigations (FBI), sheriffs, and the Department of Justice's Bureau of Alcohol, Tobacco, Firearms and Explosives have all been routinely traveling to Israel for such training.[30] Since 2012, the New York Police Department has even been operating a branch in Israel's police

[25] Filkins, "A Region Inflamed."   [26] Graham, "Laboratories of War," p. 138.
[27] J. Stahl, "US Marines Train in Israeli Warfare Camp," *CBN News* (August 17, 2011), www.cbn
     .com/tv/1396277129001; J. Colbert, "US-Israel Joint Training on the Increase, Missile Defense
     Cooperation Accelerates," *JINSA* (August 31, 2011), www.jinsa.org/publications/research-arti
     cles/us-israel-cooperation/us-israel-joint-training-increase-missile-defen.
[28] B. Opall, "Marines to Train at New Israeli Combat Center," *Marine Corps Times* (January 24,
     2007), www.deepjournal.com/p/2/a/en/807.html.
[29] Y. Katz, "US Army Seeks to Increase Joint Training with IDF," *Jerusalem Post* (August 11, 011),
     www.jpost.com/Defense/US-Army-seeks-to-increase-joint-training-with-IDF.
[30] S. Horwitz, "Israeli Experts Teach Police on Terrorism," *Washington Post* (June 12, 2005), www
     .washingtonpost.com/wp-dyn/content/article/2005/06/11/AR2005061100648.html; S. Kershaw,
     "Suicide Bombings Bring Urgency to Police in US," *New York Times* (July 25, 2005), www.nyt
     imes.com/2005/07/25/us/nationalspecial3/suicide-bombings-bring-urgency-to-police-in-us.html;
     D. Bagdy, "Brookhaven Police Deputy Chief Completes Counterterrorism Training in Israel,"

headquarters in the city of Kfar Saba to strengthen ties with Israeli security forces.[31] Meanwhile, Israeli security experts have been traveling across the United States to share counterterrorism techniques with local law-enforcement officials. One US police chief emphasized that "Israel is the Harvard of antiterrorism," and a former assistant FBI director likewise remarked that "Unfortunately for the Israelis, they have this down better than we do."[32]

Thus, in the words of Israel's former minister of interior security, Uzi Landau, "Israel is a laboratory for fighting terror."[33] The "laboratory"[34] – the West Bank and Gaza Strip – enables Israel to develop, test, and perfect combat-proven weapons, tactics, and theories that later end up in the hands of US state authorities and others. It is this laboratory that recently enabled an expo described as "the largest defense and security exhibition ever held in Israel"[35] to proudly advertise "Technologies and Tactics Deployed in Operation Protective Edge"[36] (Israel's 2014 offensive on Gaza).

The exported Israeli knowledge seems to have had a quick and visible influence on the abovementioned war in Iraq. Around the time of the 2003 US-led invasion of Iraq, an Israeli military strategy expert told reporters that, at his advice, the US military had bought some of the converted bulldozers Israel had used to demolish buildings in the West Bank during the second Intifada[37] (a tactic Israel also later used in Gaza in 2008–2009).[38] In the war that ensued,

Reporter Newspapers (July 4, 2016), www.reporternewspapers.net/2016/07/04/brookhaven-police-deputy-chief-completes-counterterrorism-training-israel/; S. Wilson, "LAPD Scopes out Israeli Drones, 'Big Data' Solutions," *Jewish Journal* (February 13, 2014), http://jewishjournal.com/m obile_20111212/126657/; P. M. O'Connell, "St. Louis County Chief Will Travel to Israel," *St. Louis Today* (March 24, 2011), www.stltoday.com/news/local/metro/st-louis-county-chief-will-tr avel-to-israel/article_9b614430-5679-11e0-999b-0017a4a78c22.html.

[31] Times of Israel Staff, "NYPD Opens Branch in Kfar Saba," *Times of Israel* (September 7, 2012), www.timesofisrael.com/nypd-opens-local-branch-in-kfar-saba/.

[32] Horwitz, Israeli Experts Teach Police on Terrorism.

[33] Washington Times, "US, Israel Discuss Joint Anti-Terror Office," *Washington Times* (June 29, 2002), www.washingtontimes.com/news/2002/jun/29/20020629-032632-7466r/.

[34] On the Palestinian Territory as such a laboratory, see Gordon, "Israel's emergence as a Homeland Security Capital," pp. 154, 162; Graham, "Laboratories of War"; D. Li, "The Gaza Strip as Laboratory: Notes in the Wake of Disengagement" (2006) 35 *Journal of Palestine Studies* 38; L. Khalili, "The Location of Palestine in Global Counterinsurgencies" (2010) 42 *International Journal of Middle East Studies* 413, 416, 418–419. Also see the documentary *The Lab* (Gum Films, 2013), director: Yotam Feldman, which deals with this subject matter.

[35] 8th International Defense and HLS Expo, "About Us," www.isdefexpo.com/home/about-isd ef-2/.

[36] 8th International Defense and HLS Expo, "Demonstrations and Workshops," www.isdefexpo .com/home/about-isdef-2/demonstrations-and-workshops/#1446667088294-8b68822f-f08c.

[37] Huggler, "Israelis Trained US Troops in Jenin-Style Urban Warfare."

[38] Khalili, "The Location of Palestine in Global Counterinsurgencies," p. 418.

the United States indeed bulldozed buildings it believed were harboring Iraqi guerrillas.[39]

More recently, 2014 – the year of one of Israel's military offensives on the Gaza Strip – saw the highest number of Palestinian casualties in recent history, most of whom are believed to have been civilians.[40] Yet, when asked about this, the US chairman of the joint chief of staff, Martin Dempsey, said "In this kind of conflict . . . you're going to be criticized for civilian casualties. . . . But they [i.e., the Israelis] did some extraordinary things to try and limit civilian casualties . . . [including] making it known that they were going to destroy a particular structure."[41]

Dempsey was alluding to "roof knocking" – Israel's tactic of firing so-called "warning" shots or rockets at civilian buildings, as discussed in other entries.[42] He added that the Pentagon (the headquarters of the US Department of Defense) had sent a team to Israel to learn lessons on "the measures they took to prevent civilian casualties."[43]

Two years later, the United States adopted Israel's controversial "roof knocking" practice in its fight against the so-called Islamic State, purportedly to evacuate Iraqi civilians before destroying buildings.[44] During joint training exercises conducted in Israel that same year (one of which was attended by more than 1,700 US service members), Israeli commanders reportedly demonstrated counterterrorism tactics to be used by the United States against the Islamic State.[45] The deputy commander for operations and intelligence for the US-led coalition in Iraq acknowledged Israel's influence in an interview: "That's exactly where we took the tactics and technique and procedure from.

[39]   Filkins, "A Region Inflamed."
[40]   United Nations Office for the Coordination of Humanitarian Affairs, Fragmented Lives: Humanitarian Overview 2014 (March 2015), pp. 3–6, www.ochaopt.org/sites/default/files/Annual_Humanitarian_Overview_2014_English_final.pdf.
[41]   D. Alexander, "Israel Tried to Limit Civil Casualties in Gaza: US Military Chief," *Reuters* (January 6, 2014), www.reuters.com/article/2014/11/06/us-israel-usa-gaza-idUSKBN0IQ2LH20141106.
[42]   See entries F: Future-Oriented Measures and X: X Rays.
[43]   Alexander, "Israel Tried to Limit Civil Casualties in Gaza: US Military Chief."
[44]   Y. Torbati and I. Ali, "US Military Used 'Roof Knock' Tactic in Iraq to try to Warn Civilians before Bombing," *Reuters* (April 26, 2016), www.reuters.com/article/us-mideast-crisis-usa-air strike-idUSKCN0XN2NK; C. Muñoz, "US Adopts Israeli 'Knock' Tactic to Reduce Civilian Deaths in ISIS Fight," *Washington Times* (April 26, 2016), www.washingtontimes.com/news/2016/apr/26/us-military-adopts-israeli-tactic-to-reduce-civili/; B. Starr, "Pentagon Adopts Israeli Tactic in Bombing ISIS," *CNN* (April 26, 2016), http://edition.cnn.com/2016/04/26/politics/u-s-uses-israeli-tactic-isis-bombing/index.html.
[45]   Times of Israel Staff, "IDF Commanders, US Marines Train Together Against Terror Threats," *Times of Israel* (July 28, 2016), www.timesofisrael.com/idf-commandos-us-marines-complete-joint-training/.

We've certainly watched and observed their procedure. As we formulated the way to get the civilians out of the house, this was brought forward from one of our experts."[46]

Some see this spread of Israeli warfare doctrines and tactics as an opportunity for steering international legal norms in a direction favorable to Israel's interests. The previously described warfare "laboratory" thus offers a platform for legal experimentation as well. As the author of the Israeli military's ethics code, Asa Kasher, once put it:

> We in Israel are in a key position in the development of the customary international law of war because we are on the front lines in the fight against terrorism. The more often Western states apply principles that originated in Israel to their own non-traditional conflicts in places like Afghanistan and Iraq, the greater the chance these principles have of becoming a valuable part of international law. ... In Gaza, the IDF employed a variety of effective efforts meant to minimize collateral damage, including ... the so-called "knock on the roof" [tactic] .... Customary international law accrues through an historic process. If [all] states ... involved in a certain type of military activity ... act quite similarly to each other, then there is a chance that it will become customary international law. ... My hope is that our doctrine ... will in this fashion be incorporated into customary international law.[47]

As mentioned elsewhere in this book, this attitude is shared by some of Israel's top military lawyers.[48]

Needless to say, security knowledge travels the other way around as well, from the United States to Israel,[49] informing Israel's rule over the West Bank and Gaza Strip since its inception. In 1966, for example, Israeli politician and former chief of general staff Moshe Dayan traveled to Vietnam, explaining his motivation as follows: "almost no one here [in Israel] had seen or participated in a war of such a scale ... I want to see and learn about the [US] war in Vietnam and its possible consequences in our region." In Vietnam, Dayan was issued a US uniform, joined a Marine company's patrols, and visited various units. Shortly after his return, he was appointed defense minister, a role he

---

[46]   Starr, "Pentagon Adopts Israeli Tactic in Bombing ISIS."

[47]   A. Kasher, "Analysis: A Moral Evaluation of the Gaza War," *Jerusalem Post* (February 7, 2010), www.jpost.com/Israel/Analysis-A-moral-evaluation-of-the-Gaza-War. For further analysis of Kasher's assertions regarding the "roof knocking" procedure, see entry F: Future-Oriented Measures.

[48]   See entry V: Violence, Section V.2 ("Law's Violence").

[49]   See also A. Siniver and J. Collins, "Airpower and Quagmire: Historical Analogies and the Second Lebanon War" (2015) 11 *Foreign Policy Analysis* 215, 220–222 (showing how the Israeli military's operational approach in the 2006 war in Lebanon drew inspiration from the experience of the United States in the two Gulf Wars in 1991 and 2003).

held during and after the 1967 war. When discussing the Palestinian territories, Dayan frequently mentioned the insights he had gained in Vietnam.
According to top military officials who worked with him, his policy on the
matter was heavily influenced by these insights.[50]

Thus, Israel and the United States have been mutually informing and
inspiring each other's security policies and practices. In so doing, they have,
in a sense, extended their security apparatuses far beyond the territories and
populations under their immediate control. This reciprocal transfer of security
knowledge has been reinforced and complemented by legal and political
cross-references between the two countries – a dynamic examined in the
following section.

E.3 THE CROSS/SELF-REFERENTIAL LOOP

Time and again, the United States and Israel have invoked each other as
counterterrorism exemplars. As will be now shown, such cross-referencing
complements and reinforces the transfer of security knowledge discussed in
the previous section. Through constant intercountry referencing, Israel and
the United States position themselves and one another as global security
models. Each country is thus portrayed as having experience, policies, and
methods that are relevant and useful not only to itself but also to others. An
important factor in enabling and reaffirming the circulation of these countries'
security approaches, then, is their depiction as somewhat universal and therefore mobile. This claim to universality can become a self-perpetuating process, wherein reference to Israeli or US policies supposedly provides evidence
of their presumed global applicability.[51]

In 2016, the then presidential candidate Donald Trump said on US television: "I think profiling is something that we're going to have to start thinking
about as a country. . . . You look at Israel and you look at others, and they do it
and they do it successfully."[52] During his presidency, Trump mentioned
Israel's "wall" – without specifying which wall he had in mind[53] – as a

---

[50] E. Shamir, "From Retaliation to Open Bridges: Moshe Dayan's Evolving Approach toward
       the Population in Counter Insurgency" (2012) 14 *Civil Wars* 63, 70–73.
[51] For a similar analysis of Israel's image as a global security leader, see R. Machold, "Mobility
       and the Model: Policy Mobility and the Becoming of Israeli Homeland Security Dominance"
       (2015) 47 *Environment and Planning A* 816, 817, 821–826.
[52] E. Stephenson, "Trump Says US should Consider Racial Profiling," *Reuters* (June 9, 2016),
       www.reuters.com/article/us-usa-election-trump-idUSKCN0Z50PV.
[53] See I. Kershner, "Trump Cites Israel's 'Wall' as Model. The Analogy Is Iffy," *New York Times*
       (January 27, 2017), www.nytimes.com/2017/01/27/world/middleeast/trump-mexico-wall-israel-
       west-bank.html ("It is not immediately clear which 'wall' Mr. Trump was referring to. Israel

model for the barrier he had vowed to build along the Mexican border: "a wall protects. All you have to do is ask Israel. They were having a total disaster coming across, and they had a wall. It's 99.9 percent stoppage."[54] Israel's prime minister, Benjamin Netanyahu, quickly responded online: "President Trump is right. I built a wall along Israel's southern border. . . . Great success. Great idea."[55]

Israeli politicians, including Netanyahu himself, have also long honed this practice of drawing on the other country's security record. In 2014, Netanyahu strongly supported a new law authorizing the force-feeding of Palestinian prisoners on hunger strike,[56] and told the Israeli media: "in Guantánamo, the Americans are using the method of force-feeding too."[57] The US military prison in Guantánamo also figured – without being mentioned by name – in a parliamentary debate on the revocation of Palestinian prisoners' right to enroll in academic studies. In 2013, the chair of the Interior and Environmental Affairs Committee of the Knesset objected to granting this right, and said: "Perhaps you should check . . . what [rights] Al-Qaeda terrorists get in the United States."[58]

Similar cross-references also pervade the legal discourses of both countries. Memos produced by US government lawyers have cited Israeli court rulings in an attempt to legally justify the use of contentious measures. Two months after the 9/11 terrorist attacks, a draft memo from the CIA's Office of General

---

has built fences along its borders with Egypt; along its northern border with Lebanon; and along its boundary with the Gaza Strip. But Israel's best-known barrier is the one built along and inside the West Bank"). On Israel's barrier in the West Bank, see entries B: Barrier and P: Proportionality.

54   S. Hannity, "Cable Exclusive: President Trump Sits Down with Sean Hannity at White House," *Fox News* (January 26, 2017), www.foxnews.com/transcript/2017/01/26/cable-exclu sive-president-trump-sits-down-with-sean-hannity-at-white-house.html. On various analogies and parallels between the US-Mexico border and Israel's West Bank barrier, see A. Lubin, "'We are all Israelis': The Politics of Colonial Comparisons" (2008) 107 *South Atlantic Quarterly* 671 [hereinafter: We are all Israelis].

55   Quoted in J. Gehrke, "Netanyahu: 'Trump is Right' about Border Wall," *Washington Examiner* (January 28, 2017), www.washingtonexaminer.com/netanyahu-trump-is-right-abou t-border-wall/article/2613257. Netanyahu's comment prompted harsh criticisms from Mexico's foreign ministry and Jewish community. See D. Graham, "Mexico Rebukes Israel over Netanyahu Wall Tweet," *Reuters* (January 29, 2017), www.reuters.com/article/us-usa-trump-mexico-israel-idUSKBN15D003.

56   On this law specifically, and on hunger strikes generally, see entry S: Security Prisoners.

57   Y. Even, "Netanyahu on the Hunger Strike of Administrative Detainees: We Will Find Doctors Willing to Force-Feed," *Channel 2 News* (June 2, 2014) [Hebrew], www.mako.co.il/news-military/security/Article-88d50fca86d5641004.htm.

58   Interior and Environmental Affairs Committee, 19th Knesset–Transcript (December 23, 2013), p. 160 [Hebrew], www.knesset.gov.il/protocols/data/rtf/pnim/2013-12-23.rtf. On this issue, see entry S: Security Prisoners.

Counsel cited the "Israeli example" as a basis for justifying torture.[59] Over the following years, CIA attorneys and the Department of Justice repeatedly invoked a 1999 Israeli supreme court ruling that granted impunity, under the "necessity defense," to interrogators who use torture.[60] For example, in 2005, one attorney who endeavored to garner legislative support for continued use of controversial interrogation methods mentioned that, following this ruling, the Israeli government "ultimately got limited legislative authority for . . . specific [interrogation] techniques." As he described it, the Israeli supreme court had

> ruled that several . . . techniques were possibly permissible . . . [and had] also specifically considered the "ticking time bomb" scenario[61] and said that enhanced techniques could not be pre-approved for such situations, but that if worse came to worse, an officer who engaged in such activities could assert a common-law necessity defense, if he were ever prosecuted.[62]

A 2007 memo issued by CIA lawyers analyzed the same Israeli court case in support of its eventual conclusion that the CIA's so-called "enhanced interrogation techniques" were "clearly authorized and justified by legislative authority."[63] Three years later, under president Obama, the Justice Department's Office of Legal Counsel authored a memo approving the extrajudicial drone killing of an American citizen in Yemen, which subsequently became the

59   Senate Select Committee on Intelligence, Committee Study of the Central Intelligence Agency's Detention and Interrogation Program (December 3, 2014), p. 19, note 51, http://i2 .cdn.turner.com/cnn/2014/images/12/09/sscistudy1.pdf. On the so-called "torture memos" – the infamous memos drafted by US administration lawyers to justify the administration's use of torture – see, e.g., A. W. Clarke, "Rendition to Torture: A Critical Legal History" (2009) 62 *Rutgers Law Review* 1; S. F. Kreimer, "'Torture Lite,' 'Full Bodied' Torture, and the Insulation of Legal Conscience" (2005) 1 *Journal National Security Law & Policy* 187 (2005); J. J. Paust, "Above the Law: Unlawful Executive Authorizations Regarding Detainee Treatment, Secret Renditions, Domestic Spying, and Claims to Unchecked Executive Power" (2007) 2 *Utah Law Review* 345; M. C. Bassiouni, "The Institutionalization of Torture under the Bush Administration" (2006) 37 *Case Western Reserve Journal of International Law* 389; J. D. Ohlin, "The Torture Lawyers" (2010) 51 *Harvard International Law Journal* 193.
60   *Ibid.*, p. 197, note 1155; D. Luban, "Liberalism, Torture, and the Ticking Bomb," in Karen Greenberg (ed.), *The Torture Debate in America* (New York: Cambridge University Press, 2006), pp. 35, 81, note 9. The Israeli case is HCJ 5100/94 *Public Committee Against Torture in Israel v. Israeli Government* (1999) 53(4) PD 817, http://elyon1.court.gov.il/files_eng/94/000/0 51/a09/94051000.a09.pdf. On this ruling and its implications, see entry V: Violence.
61   On the "ticking bomb" scenario, see entry V: Violence.
62   Senate Select Committee on Intelligence, Committee Study of the Central Intelligence Agency's Detention and Interrogation Program, pp. 196–197.
63   *Ibid.*, p. 197, note 1155.

subject of several lawsuits.[64] The memo cited a 2006 Israeli supreme court decision authorizing "targeted killings" under certain conditions.[65]

Numerous references to Israel also appear in the US Department of Defense's Law of War Manual – a lengthy legal guidebook for "commanders, legal practitioners, and other military and civilian personnel."[66] Among other things, the 2015 version of the manual (as amended in 2016) quotes, sometimes at length, from the same Israeli supreme court judgments on torture and "targeted killing" that were cited in the aforementioned memos.[67] Also cited in the manual is the Israeli statement to the UN Security Council, in 1981, about Israel's right to self-defense. This latter reference is meant to serve as a basis for the purported right of the United States to initiate military action on foreign territory without the territorial country's consent "when [that country] ... is unwilling or unable to prevent its territory from being used by non-State armed groups as a base for launching attacks."[68]

In Israel, the supreme court has likewise referred to the United States in many cases concerning noncitizen Palestinians.[69] In 1972, the Israeli court

---

[64] A US federal court ordered the release of a redacted version of this memo in response to a Freedom of Information Act lawsuit brought by the New York Times and the American Civil Liberties Union (ACLU). *New York Times Co v. DOJ*, 12–422, 12–442 WL 1569514 (2nd Cir. 2014). Another lawsuit, by the ACLU and the Center for Constitution Rights, charged that this killing violated the deceased US citizen's constitutional rights, but was dismissed. *Al-Aulaqui v. Panetta*, 12–1192 WL 1352452 (D.C, D.C 2012).

[65] US Department of Justice – Office of Legal Counsel, Memorandum for the Attorney General Re: Applicability of Federal Criminal Laws and the Constitution to Contemplated Lethal Operations Against Shaykh Anwar al-Aulaqi (July 16, 2010), pp. 20, 40, www.nytimes.com/in teractive/2014/06/23/us/23awlaki-memo.html. The Israeli case is HCJ 769/02 *Public Committee Against Torture in Israel v. Government of Israel* (December 13, 2006), http://elyo n1.court.gov.il/files_eng/02/690/007/a34/02007690.a34.pdf. For analysis of this case, see entry C: Combatants.

[66] US Department of Defense, Law of War Manual (June 2015, updated December 2016), p. iii www.defense.gov/Portals/1/Documents/pubs/DoD%20Law%20of%20War%20Manual%20-%20 June%202015%20Updated%20Dec%202016.pdf?ver=2016-12-13-172036-190 [hereinafter: Law of War Manual].

[67] *Ibid.*, pp. 85, 231, 234.   [68] *Ibid.*, pp. 1066–1067, note 219 and accompanying text.

[69] Other examples, in addition to the ones cited below, are: HCJ 591/88 *Taha v. Minister of Defence* (1991) 45(2) PD 45, ¶ 15 [Hebrew], www.nevo.co.il/psika_html/elyon/PADI-ND-2-0 45-L.htm; HCJ 2320/98 El-Amlah v. *IDF Commander* (1998) 52(3) PD 346, ¶ 2 [Hebrew], www.nevo.co.il/psika_html/elyon/98023200.htm; HCJ 769/02 *Public Committee Against Torture in Israel v. Government of Israel* (2006) 62(1) PD 507, ¶ 30 of justice Barak's majority opinion and ¶ 2 of justice Rivlin's concurring opinion, http://versa.cardozo.yu.edu/sites/defa ult/files/upload/opinions/Public%20Committee%20Against%20Torture%20in%20Israel%20v .%20Government%20of%20Israel.pdf; HCJ 7195/08 *Abu Rahma v. Military Advocate General* (2009) 63(2) PD 325, ¶ 8 of justice Melcer's opinion [Hebrew], www.nevo.co.il/psika_html/ elyon/08071950-r09.htm (see also analysis of this case in entry W: War Crimes). See also the cases cited in note 88, which cite the US Law of War Manual, as well as the cases discussed in

unanimously upheld the military's decision to assign electricity provision in an area of the West Bank to Israel's national electricity provider. Chief justice Moshe Landau conjured up the following quote from "an opinion of the US Attorney General in 1898, following the Spanish-American War": "in the granting of ... equitable rights, the succeeding sovereign is the absolute dictator. They [can only] ... be exercised ... by his grace."[70]

In another case, in 1988, the then chief justice Meir Shamgar cited at length US federal and state rulings to support Israel's denial of the applicability of GC IV:

> The question of the status of the Fourth Geneva Convention ... has also arisen in the United States: the federal courts have examined ... whether the ... Convention takes effect in US law ... even without legislation adopting it ..., and have explicitly replied in the negative. ... The California District Court subsequently reached a similar decision ... [regarding] the Third Geneva Convention. ... The position expressed in these rulings has also been adopted as the formal position of ... the US State Department ... [and] is all the more applicable [to Israel, where] ... not only is there no legislation adopting [the Convention] ..., but there is a statutory provision that contradicts it.[71]

A few years later, relying on US law, the Israeli supreme court dismissed a petition against Israel's settlement policy on grounds of over-generality and thus injusticiability. "The petition amounts to a general objection to Government policy," held chief justice Shamgar. "It is more general, by comparison, even than ... [a certain case in which] the US supreme court ... [refused to] ' ... decide abstract questions of wide public significance ....'." Shamgar proceeded to cite additional US supreme court cases, including one holding that "[t]he court does not deal with abstract problems, unless they are linked to a dispute with concrete implications; it will certainly not do so if the case is one of ... a predominantly political nature."[72]

L. Sheleff, "Activism Stops at the Green Line: The Margins and Routes of the HCJ Judgements Regarding the Territories" (1993) 17 *Iyunei Mishpat* [Tel Aviv University Law Review] 757 [Hebrew], www.sheleff.com/downloads/legalActivism_LSheleff.pdf (specifically the section "Five Foreign Cases").

[70] HCJ 256/72 *Jerusalem District Electricity Company Ltd* v. *Minister of Defense* (1972) 27(1) PD 124, pp. 136–137 [Hebrew], www.nevo.co.il/psika_html/elyon/KF-1–124-L.htm. On the attorney general's opinion and the principle expressed by it, see F. B. Sayre, "Change of Sovereignty and Concessions" (1918) 12 *American Journal of International Law* 705, 724.

[71] HCJ 253/88 *Sajadiyeh* v. *Minister of Defense* (November 8, 1988), ¶ 6 of chief justice Shamgar's opinion [Hebrew], www.hamoked.org.il/items/4060.pdf.

[72] HCJ 4481/91 *Bargil* v. *Government of Israel* (1993) 47(4) PD 210, ¶ 4 of chief justice Shamgar's opinion [Hebrew], http://elyon1.court.gov.il/files_eng/91/810/044/Z01/91044810.z01.pdf.

More recently, a 2016 ruling that authorized the force-feeding of Palestinian prisoners cited, among other sources, US laws that permit this practice in certain circumstances.[73] Other recent supreme court judgments, which upheld "administrative detentions"[74] of Palestinians, likewise cited US rulings concerning the detention and adjudication of foreign national terrorist suspects.[75] A large portion of one of these judgments was dedicated to describing how "[t]he United States ... has undergone a difficult legal process since the terror attacks of 11.9.01 ... [Initially, terrorist suspects] were incarcerated in Afghanistan ... [and] at the Guantánamo base outside the United States, with few rights, ... [and were] not subject to US judicial review."[76]

The events of 9/11 loomed large in another decision of the Israeli supreme court, which upheld a statute restricting "family unification" with Palestinians from the West Bank.[77] In his concurring opinion, justice Hanan Melcer remarked that "The relevant question ... is not how many 'marriage immigrants' have been involved in terrorism. ... Even a few terrorists might cause immeasurable harm. For example, the actions of the 19 aircraft hijackers in the attacks of September 11th in the United States resulted in over 3,000 casualties."[78]

Some Israeli state lawyers saw the events of 9/11 not only as a point of reference, but also as authorizing for greater Israeli legal and political leverage in the West Bank and Gaza Strip. When presented with the question "[d]id the attacks of September 11 influence your legal situation?," the former head of the Israeli military's international law department (a body examined in another entry)[79] replied:

> Absolutely. ... In April 2001 I met the American envoy ... and explained that above a certain level, fighting terrorism is armed combat and not law enforcement. His committee [which examined the circumstances of the

---

[73] HCJ 5304/15 *Israel Medical Association v. Israeli Knesset* (September 11, 2016) [Hebrew], ¶ 93 of justice Rubinstein's opinion, http://elyon1.court.gov.il/files/15/040/053/t11/15053040.t11.pdf. On this ruling, and the force-feeding issue more broadly, see entries S: Security Prisoners and F: Future-Oriented Measures.

[74] On the practice of so-called "administrative detention" – incarceration without charge or trial – see entries S: Security Prisoners and F: Future-Oriented Measures.

[75] HCJ 5303/08 *John Doe v. IDF Commander* (June 23, 2008), ¶ 6 [Hebrew], www.nevo.co.il/psika_html/elyon/08053030-t03.htm; HCJ 9441/07 *Abu Matar v. IDF Commander* (2007) 62 (4) PD 77, ¶ 10 [Hebrew], www.nevo.co.il/psika_html/elyon/07094410-t02-e.htm.

[76] *Ibid.*   [77] On the "family unification" issue, see entry K: Kinship.

[78] HCJ 466/07 *Gal'on v. Attorney General* (January 11, 2012), ¶ 35 of justice Melcer's opinion [Hebrew], www.nevo.co.il/psika_html/elyon/07004660-030.htm. Two of the other judges also referred to the United States: *ibid.*, ¶ 1 of justice Grunis' opinion, ¶¶ 4–9 of justice Rivlin's opinion.

[79] On the international law department, see entry L: Lawfare.

confrontation in the Palestinian Territory] rejected that approach. Its report called on the Israeli government to abandon the armed confrontation definition and revert to the concept of law enforcement. It took four months and four planes to change the opinion of the United States, and had it not been for those four planes I am not sure we would have been able to develop the thesis of the war against terrorism on the present scale.[80]

The cross-referencing between Israel and the United States is often circular or reciprocal. A case in point appears in the abovementioned US Law of War Manual, which stipulates that countries do not normally prosecute their own nationals for "war crimes as such," only "for offenses under ordinary domestic law or military law."[81] To substantiate this assertion, the manual quotes the 2013 report of the Israeli Turkel Commission (analyzed elsewhere in this book),[82] which was entrusted with inquiring whether Israel's investigation mechanisms comply with the country's obligations under international law. The Commission, headed by a former supreme court justice, was set up by the Israeli government in the aftermath of the 2010 Gaza flotilla raid.[83] Its report makes numerous references to US law and policy,[84] one of which is quoted in the US manual: "[I]n the US, the charging practice ... appears to be to prosecute violations of the law of armed conflict by members of the armed forces as general criminal law offenses or military offenses ... rather than as specific offenses relating to the law of armed conflict."[85]

Thus, rather than referring to Israeli law or policy per se, the US military's legal manual harnesses Israel as a means of what is – indirectly, but ultimately – self-referencing. Through this self-referential process, the United States builds on Israeli legal references to validate its own legal system. Israeli prime minister Netanyahu's reference to Trump's reference to the Israeli "wall" – quoted above[86] – is likewise self-referential and thus

---

[80]   Y. Feldman and U. Blau, "Consent and Advise," *Haaretz* (January 29, 2009), www.haaretz .com/consent-and-advise-1.269127.

[81]   Law of War Manual, p. 1118.   [82]   See entry I: Investigations.

[83]   On the flotilla incident, see entry Q: Quality of Life.

[84]   Public Commission to Examine the Maritime Incident of 31 May 2010, *Israel's Mechanisms for Examining and Investigating Complaints and Claims of Violations of the Laws of Armed Conflict According to International Law* (February 2013), pp. 55, 65, 68, 90, 100, 152, 159–161, 164, 167–172, 178–183, 204–216, 251–252, 257, 261, 263, 362–363, 367, 370–371, 375–376, 378–379, 390–391, 401, 419, 450 [hereinafter: The Turkel Report], www.turkel-committee.gov.il/files/n ewDoc3/The%20Turkel%20Report%20for%20website.pdf.

[85]   Law of War Manual, pp. 1118–1119, note 233. The Turkel report is also cited in *ibid.*, pp. 904– 905, note 156.

[86]   See text accompanying note 54.

self-validating. A similar form of cyclical referencing has also taken place between the US Law of War Manual and Israeli supreme court rulings: while the manual cites some of these rulings (as shown above),[87] the Israeli court has also, for decades, been citing the manual's position on various matters.[88]

There has also been reciprocal referencing specifically in relation to the terms "unlawful combatant" and "prisoner of war" (POW). As explained in detail in one of this book's other entries,[89] the international law of armed conflict distinguishes between civilians and combatants. Among other things, captives who meet the legal definition of "combatant" acquire POW status, and thus become shielded from prosecution for legally sanctioned fighting tactics. However, in 1969, an Israeli military court denied members of the Popular Front for the Liberation of Palestine POW status and classified them as neither civilians nor combatants in the legal sense, but, rather, as "unlawful combatants":[90]

> No International Law is possible without the maintenance of certain funda-
> mental principles regarding the conduct of war .... [C]ombatants who ... do
> not comply with the minimum qualifications of belligerents or are proved to
> have broken other rules of warfare, ... [are excluded from privileged

---

[87] See text accompanying note 67.

[88] HCJ 619/78 *E-Taliah Weekly* v. *Minister of Defense* (1979) 33(3) PD 505, ¶ 7 [Hebrew], www
.nevo.co.il/psika_html/elyon/78000619-HK.htm; HCJ 403/81 *Jabbar* v. *IDF Commander*
(1981) 35(4) PD 397 [Hebrew], www.nevo.co.il/psika_html/elyon/PADI-LD-4-397-L.htm;
HCJ 392/82 *Jama'iyat Iskan* v. *IDF Commander* (1982) 37(4) PD 785, ¶ 31 [Hebrew], www
.nevo.co.il/psika_html/elyon/PADI-LF-4-785-L.htm; HCJ 787/85 *Arjub* v. *IDF Commander*
(1988) 42(1) PD 353, ¶ 9 of Chief justice Shamgar's majority opinion [Hebrew], www.nevo.co
.il/psika_html/elyon/padi-na-1-353-l.htm; HCJ 270/88 *Kuttab* v. *IDF Commander* (1988) 42(3)
PD 260 [Hebrew], www.nevo.co.il/psika_html/elyon/PADI-NA-3-260-L.htm; HCJ 2164/09
Yesh Din v. *IDF Commander* (December 26, 2011), ¶ 8 [Hebrew], www.nevo.co.il/psi
ka_html/elyon/09021640-n14.htm. The 1956 version of the US Law of War Manual was
cited in MilC (Bethlehem Mil. Ct.) 1114/72 *Military Advocate General* v. *Scheinbaum*
(November 9, 1972), in General Military Corps, *Selected Rulings of the Military Court of
Appeals in the Administered Territories* (Military Advocate General's Office, 1974), vol. III, pp.
346, 357.

[89] See entry C: Combatants.

[90] More than two decades prior to this case, the US supreme court had already developed the
phrase "unlawful combatants" in a ruling that upheld US military courts' jurisdiction over
Nazi saboteurs: *Ex Parte Quirin* v. *Cox*, 317 US 1 (1942). For analysis of this case, and also of
earlier contexts in which the concept of "unlawful combatants" was implicitly recognized
(though not expressly used), see T. L. Lepri, "Safeguarding the Enemy Within: The Need for
Procedural Protections for US Citizens Detained as Enemy Combatants Under Ex Part
Quirin" (2003) 71 *Fordham Law Review* 2565, 2568–2575. For further historical context, see
S. Scheipers, *Unlawful Combatants: A Genealogy of the Irregular Fighter* (Oxford: Oxford
University Press, 2015).

treatment as POWs].[91] By [introducing] ... additional distinctions between lawful and unlawful combatants ... it becomes possible to give far-reaching protection to the overwhelming majority of the civilian population of occupied territories and captured members of the armed forces.[92]

The US Law of War Manual cites this case three times in support of the US military's legal stance on POWs.[93] Also quoting the case (four times) is a 2003 article on the topic of POWs and "unlawful combatants,"[94] one of whose authors was among the US government lawyers who wrote the abovementioned memos justifying the use of torture.[95] This article, in turn, was cited in a 2006 judgment of the Israeli supreme court that upheld Israel's use of "targeted killings."[96] But the back-and-forth referencing does not stop here. This Israeli supreme court judgment that cited the US government lawyer's article (an article that, in turn, quotes the Israeli military court case) was itself subsequently cited, as mentioned earlier, in another US legal memo that provided arguments supporting the use of torture.[97] This convoluted trail of cross-references concerning POWs and "unlawful combatants" continued thereafter. In 2009, a US army judge advocate published an article on the subject, discussing extensively Israel's so-called Internment of Unlawful Combatants Law[98] (which is used to detain without trial Palestinians from the Gaza Strip),[99] and recommending the modification of the US process for determining enemy combatant status in light of this Israeli statute.[100]

---

[91]   On the sociolegal proscription of "unlawful" resistance in and beyond the Israeli–Palestinian context, see entry V: Violence.

[92]   "Case 4/69 Military Prosecutor v Omar Mahmud Kassem and Others," in E. Lauterpacht (ed.), *International Law Reports* (Cambridge: Grotius Publications Limited, 1971), vol. 42, p. 470. Incidentally, the judgment quotes the US position on the scope of GC III. *Ibid.* For analysis of the Kassem case, see W. T. Mallison and S. V. Mallison, "The Juridical Status of Irregular Combatants under the International Humanitarian Law of Armed Conflict" (1977) 9 *Case Western Reserve Journal of International Law* 39, 71–72.

[93]   Law of War Manual, pp. 120–121, notes 157–158; p. 182, note 533.

[94]   J. C. Yoo and J. C. Ho, "The Status of Terrorists" (2003) 44 *Virginia Journal of International Law* 207.

[95]   On these memos, see note 59. On the role of the article's co-author, John Yoo, in producing these memos and his subsequent career, see L. Rosenthal, "Those Who Can't, Teach: What the Legal Career of John Yoo Tells Us About Who Should Be Teaching Law" (2011) 80 *Mississippi Law Journal* 1563 and the sources cited therein.

[96]   HCJ 769/02, ¶ 2 of Justice Rivlin's opinion.

[97]   See notes 64–65 and their accompanying text.

[98]   Internment of Unlawful Combatants Law, 2002.

[99]   For critical analysis, see B'Tselem and Hamoked, *Without Trial: Administrative Detention of Palestinians by Israel and the Internment of Unlawful Combatants Law* (2009), pp. 51–63, www.btselem.org/sites/default/files/publication/200910_without_trial_eng.pdf.

[100] T. J. Bogar, "Unlawful Combatants or Innocent Civilians? A Call to Change the Current Means for Determining Status of Prisoners in the Global War on Terror" (2009) 21 *Florida Journal of International Law* 29, 67–68, 84–85, 87.

E.4 COMMON TERMS

The intercountry transfer of knowledge is also evidenced by the language and imagery used by state agents. As discussed elsewhere in this book,[101] Israeli and US state officials and supporters are increasingly using the term "lawfare" to criticize the legal challenges their respective countries face from NGOs, international bodies, individuals, and other political entities. In 2012, Avichai Mendelblit, Israel's former military advocate general and now its attorney general, published an article on the subject, arguing that "every regular military in the West, not only the IDF, deals with this threat." Mendelblit proceeds to quote at length the definition and description of "lawfare" offered by "the former deputy judge advocate of the US Air Force, Charles Dunlap,"[102] who is commonly (and wrongly) credited with coining this term.[103]

Further illustrating this mutual or convergent discourse is the association between Israel/Palestine and some US torture methods. In his 2016 memoir, a former US interrogator in Iraq recalls having witnessed a torture device called "the Palestinian chair," which his colleagues said Israeli interrogators had taught them to build during a joint training exercise.[104] Similarly, detainees in US custody in Iraq were reportedly held in a high-stress position known as a "Palestinian hanging."[105]

Despite being called "Palestinian," however, these practices and instruments do not necessarily originate from Israel/Palestine. When asked in an interview about the name "Palestinian chair," the former US interrogator explicated: "I was never clear on the actual origin. The rumors ... were that Army interrogators had learned to use this chair by Israeli interrogators .... I certainly don't know if that's true."[106] Similarly, the so-called "Palestinian hanging" technique might not be Israeli in origin, and the adjective

---

[101] See entry L: Lawfare.

[102] A. Mendelblit, "Lawfare – the IDF's Next Legal Frontier" (2012) 4 *Military & Strategy* 47, 49 [Hebrew], http://i-hls.com/wp-content/uploads/2013/03/%D7%9C%D7%95%D7%97%D7%9E%D7%AA-%D7%9E%D7%A9%D7%A4%D7%98-%E2%80%94-%D7%94%D7%97%D7%96%D7%99%D7%AA-%D7%94%D7%9E%D7%A9%D7%A4%D7%98%D7%99%D7%AA-%D7%A9%D7%9C-%D7%A6%D7%94%D7%9C.pdf.

[103] See entry L: Lawfare.

[104] E. Fair, *Consequence: A Memoir* (New York: Henry Holt and Company, LLC, 2016), p. 112.

[105] D. Gregory, "Vanishing Points: Law, Violence, and Exception in the Global War Prison," in E. Boehmer and S. Morton (eds.), *Terror and the Postcolonial* (Chichester: Wiley-Blackwell, 2010), pp. 55, 58, 61, 79–81.

[106] A. Goodman and N. Shaikh, "Ex-Abu Ghraib Interrogator: Israelis Trained US to Use 'Palestinian Chair' Torture Device," *Democracy Now* (April 7, 2016), www.democracynow.org/2016/4/7/ex_abu_ghraib_interrogator_israelis_trained.

"Palestinian" could have simply been used to play on the fears evoked by mentioning Israeli torture.[107]

What matters, then, is not only the origin of such methods. Regardless of whether the United States directly adopted the "Palestinian chair" and "Palestinian hanging" techniques from Israel, the very conjuring up of Israel/Palestine illustrates its centrality in the US national security imagination. Moreover, the notion of an origin presupposes a linear movement from provenance to destination. Yet, as shown in the previous section,[108] the security discourses of the two countries often build upon one another through circular referencing, often without a clearly or accurately identified starting point.

A different form of discursive connection is security-related analogies.[109] Among other things, Israeli authorities and officials have used hypothetical analogies to garner US support. In 2014, during its offensive on the Gaza Strip, the Israeli military disseminated an image online, depicting rockets heading toward the Statue of Liberty in New York, with the caption "what would you do?"[110] Two decades earlier, Uri Shoham, currently an Israeli supreme court justice and at the time the military advocate general, published an article that opens with the following hypothetical analogy:

> [I]magine the United States being in control of an area of land a quarter its own size, located just scant miles away from major United States cities, and populated by no less than 120 million Iraqis. With a few minor adjustments, these are the circumstances Israel has had to face since [assuming control over the West Bank and Gaza Strip in] 1967.[111]

Analogies, comparisons, and cross-references are used not only by representatives and allies of Israel and the United States, but also, obviously, by their critics.[112] To mention but one example, a 2016 report by Israeli NGOs B'Tselem and HaMoked, examining Israel's abuse and torture of

[107] D. Rejali, *Torture and Democracy* (Princeton: Princeton University Press, 2007), pp. 355–356.
[108] See text accompanying notes 81–100.
[109] See also Lubin, "We are all Israelis," p. 685 (mentioning analogies Israeli advocates and opponents of an amendment preventing "family unifications" drew to the United States).
[110] See N. Gordon and N. Perugini, "The Politics of Human Shielding: On the Resignification of Space and the Constitution of Civilians as Shields in Liberal Wars" (2016) 34(1) *Environment & Planning D: Society and Space* 168.
[111] U. Shoham, "The Principle of Legality and the Israeli Military Government in the Territories" (1996) 153 *Military Law Review* 245, 245–246.
[112] On some of the ways in which state officials and critics alike use analogies between settler–Indigenous relations in Israel and the United States, see H. Viterbo, "Ties of Separation: Analogy and Generational Segregation in North America, Australia, and Israel/Palestine" (2017) 42 *Brooklyn Journal of International Law*, 686, 710–719.

Palestinians in the Shikma interrogation facility,[113] harnesses the US military prison in Guantánamo as a cautionary reference point.[114] In addition to accusing Israeli interrogation authorities of abuse and torture, the report describes them as indirectly participating in torture "by knowingly using information obtained by Palestinian Authority interrogators through use of torture ... against the ... same detainees."[115] The analogy to Guantánamo is fleshed out in the report as follows:

> [A]fter the 9/11 attacks, the CIA began holding detainees in incarceration facilities outside the United States, where it employed ... torture. The CIA was also authorized to ... transfer ... individuals to the custody of a foreign government ... for arrest and interrogation. .... The prohibition on torture is not limited by territory: a country must not ... use information obtained through torture, even if this is done outside its territory.[116]

Following the publication of the report, B'Tselem circulated a video online, titled "A day in the small Guantánamo," with the following accompanying text: "One need not travel all the way to Cuba [where the United States operates the Guantánamo facility]. Right here, next to the city of Ashkelon, lies a small Guantánamo – the Shikma Prison."[117]

E.5 CONCLUSION

By analyzing a broad range of sources and cases, this entry has sought to map some of the key interrelations and points of convergence between the security discourses and practices of Israel and the United States. Three mutually complementary processes, in particular, have been examined here. The first is the export and import of security knowledge, which takes place, among other things, through US–Israeli military and police collaborations, drawing lessons from each other's armed conflicts, and adopting one another's warfare and counterterrorism doctrines. The second process is the endless loop of

---

[113] B'Tselem and HaMoked, *Backed by the System: Abuse and Torture at the Shikma Interrogation Facility* (December 2015) [hereinafter: *Backed by the System*], www.btselem.or g/sites/default/files2/201512_backed_by_the_system_eng.pdf. On the related issue of "back to back" detention – the Palestinian Authority's political detention of individuals released from Israeli prison – see Addameer, *Stolen Hope: Political Detention in the West Bank* (2011), pp. 35–36, http://addameer.org/userfiles/EN%20PA%20Violations%20Report%202009-2010.pdf.

[114] On the invocation of the Guantánamo facility in statements of Israeli politicians, see text accompanying notes 56–58.

[115] B'Tselem and HaMoked, *Backed by the System*, p. 64.   [116] *Ibid.*, p. 47.

[117] B'Tselem, *A Day in Guantanamo Bay*, Facebook (February 23, 2016), www.facebook.com/btselemheb/videos/1041751702532861.

cross-references between US and Israeli legal and political discourses. This has been shown to enable the two countries to position themselves and one another as global security role models whose knowledge is deemed universally adoptable and mobile. Finally, each of these countries employs terms, images, and analogies that relate to, or share commonalities with, the other country, thus forging a common or convergent discourse.

A growing body of writing has juxtaposed, compared, or linked the security policies and practices of these two countries.[118] Rather than sketching parallels between Israel and the United States in broad strokes, this entry has aimed to make a unique and empirically rich contribution to this literature: a close analysis of varied cases and examples of the discursive and practical ties that give rise and credence to this intercountry commonality. In addition, some of these studies suggest that, in the post-9/11 era, the United States has increasingly endorsed control mechanisms akin to those used in Israel/Palestine – a so-called trend of "Israelization" or "Palestinization." Others argue that Israel/Palestine has undergone a comparable process of "Americanization." These terms, however, might be interpreted as suggesting that prior to 9/11, Israel and the United States were not already inextricably linked in their political and legal discourses and practices. In fact, as

---

[118] See, e.g., Y. Abu-Laban and A. B. Bakan, "The 'Israelization' of Social Sorting and the 'Palestinization' of the Racial Contract: Reframing Israel/Palestine and the War on Terror," in E. Zureik, D. Lyon, and Y. Abu-Laban (eds.), *Surveillance and Control in Israel/Palestine: Population, Territory, and Power* (London: Routledge, 2011), p. 276; J. Collins, *Global Palestine* (New York: Columbia University Press, 2011); Graham, "Laboratories of War"; D. Gregory, *The Colonial Present: Afghanistan, Palestine, Iraq* (Malden and Oxford: Blackwell, 2004); M. Gunneflo, *Targeted Killing: A Legal and Political History* (Cambridge: Cambridge University Press, 2016); L. Hajjar, "International Humanitarian Law and 'Wars on Terror': A Comparative Analysis of Israeli and American Doctrines and Policies" (2006) 36 *Journal of Palestine Studies* 21; R. Jones, *Border Walls: Security and the War on Terror in the United States, India and Israel* (New York: Zed Books, 2012); E. Kaufman, "Deference or Abdication: A Comparison of the Supreme Courts of Israel and the United States in Cases Involving Real or Perceived Threats to National Security" (2013) 12 *Washington University Global Studies Law Review* 95; E. N. Kurtulus, "The New Counterterrorism: Contemporary Counterterrorism Trends in the United States and Israel" (2012) 35 *Studies of Conflict and Terrorism* 37; N. Nilanovic, "Lessons for Human Rights and Humanitarian Law in the War on Terror: Comparing Hamdan and the Israeli Targeted Killings Case" (2007) 866 *International Review of the Red Cross* 373; S. Niva, "Walling Off Iraq: Israel's Imprint on US Counterinsurgency Doctrine" (2008) 15 *Middle East Policy* 67, www.mepc.org/walling-iraq-israels-imprint-us-counterinsurgency-doctrine; J. T. Parry, "Judicial Restraints on Illegal State Violence: Israel and the United States" (2002) 35 *Vanderbilt Journal of Transnational Law* 73; C. Toensing and I. Urbina, "Israel, the US and 'Targeted Killings'," *Middle East Report Online* (February 17, 2003), www.merip.org/mero/mero021703; H. Viterbo, "Seeing Torture Anew: A Transnational Reconceptualization of State Torture and Visual Evidence" (2014) 50 *Stanford Journal of International Law* 281.

other studies have indicated,[119] and as pre-9/11 examples in this entry further illustrate, the two countries have a much longer joint history.

One of this book's entries explains that Israel's rule over the Palestinian Territory has become potentially indefinite and thus transgresses its normative temporal boundaries.[120] Another entry examines the legal and political porosity of the borders between "Israel" and the "Palestinian territories."[121] By analyzing the movement of security discourses, techniques, and reference points from and into Israel/Palestine, the present entry lays bare two other, interrelated dimensions of this borderlessness: on the one hand, the Israeli security apparatus reaches far beyond the territory and population under its control; on the other hand, this apparatus relates to, resonates, and brims with supposedly external forces. The United States – Israel's chief political ally and sponsor – occupies a central place in this dynamic and is thus interconnected to Israel and also, like Israel, is politically and legally unconfined.

---

[119] See, e.g., K. P. Feldman, *Racing the Question: Israel/Palestine and US Imperial Culture* (Doctoral Dissertation, University of Washington, 2008), http://search.proquest.com/doc view/304439580; W. R. Mead, "The New Israel and the Old: Why Gentile Americans Back the Jewish State" (2008) 87 *Foreign Affairs* 28; J. H. Newman, "Tracing the Use of the Bible in Colonial Land Claims in North America," in F. Flannery and R.E. Werline (eds.), *The Bible in Political Debate: What Does It Really Say?* (London and New York: Bloomsbury, 2016), p. 127.

[120] See entry T: Temporary/Indefinite.

[121] See entry O: Outside/Inside, Section O.3 ("Israeli Law Does Not Stop at the Border").

F

Future-Oriented Measures

Hedi Viterbo

F.1 INTRODUCTION

Israel's entire control regime over the West Bank and Gaza Strip is future-oriented. It shapes the future and is also, in some cases, concerned with unwanted eventualities. Some of the practices and policies that make up this regime have a preventive, preemptive, or deterrent element, whether formally or effectively. Examples appear throughout this book. The restriction of Palestinian "family unifications,"[1] for instance, has been justified by Israeli authorities as a preemptive security measure. According to critics, however, the aim of this policy is to prevent another perceived danger: a demographic threat to Israel's Jewish majority.[2] Prosecution,[3] incarceration,[4] house demolitions,[5] and deportations[6] are all designed, among other things, to prevent and deter future Palestinian transgressions. Israel's control over planning and building permits in the West Bank[7] seeks to shape a desirable territorial future. The West Bank barrier,[8] Israel's surveillance apparatus, and the issuance of entry permits and IDs[9] are all meant, among other things, to prevent and deter unauthorized movement. Closed military zones[10] are often used in an attempt to prevent future demonstrations.[11] Israel presents its (oft-coerced) recruitment of Palestinian

---

[1]   See entry K: Kinship.
[2]   A. Gross, "In Love with the Enemy: Justice, Truth, Integrity and Common Sense Between Israel and Utopia in the Citizenship Law Case" (2009) 13 *Hamishpat* 141, 152–154 [Hebrew].
[3]   See entries M: Military Courts and Y: Youth.
[4]   See entries S: Security Prisoners and Y: Youth.   [5]   See entry H: House Demolitions.
[6]   See entry D: Deportations.   [7]   See entry Z: Zone.   [8]   See entry B: Barrier.
[9]   See entries P: Proportionality, V: Violence, and X: X-Ray.
[10]   See entry Z: Zone, Section Z.2.5.1 ("Military Zoning").
[11]   Association for Civil Rights in Israel, *The Status of the Right to Demonstrate in the Occupied Territories* (September 2014), p. 37, www.acri.org.il/en/protestright/the-right-to-demonstrate.

informants and collaborators,[12] as well as its use of undercover soldiers,[13] as means to gather necessary information for preempting proscribed activities. At the same time, by sowing suspicion among Palestinians, another future effect of the use of informants and undercover forces is to undermine Palestinian unity and collective resistance.[14] The recent separation of Palestinian children and adults in Israeli custody is likewise future-oriented: it hinders intergenerational Palestinian influences[15] in the hope of creating more docile future adults.[16]

Bringing this future-oriented element center stage, this entry investigates the role and consequences of prevention, preemption, and deterrence in two areas of Israeli policy and practice.[17] The first, examined in Section F.2, is preemptive attacks, with a focus on three issues: (a) purportedly preemptive military strikes, starting with the 1967 war that led to Israel's control over the West Bank and Gaza Strip; (b) extrajudicial assassinations, commonly referred to as "targeted killing" (in English) or "focused preemption" (in Hebrew); and (c) "warning" procedures, such as the "roof knocking" tactic of dropping low-impact munitions prior to bombing residential buildings. A second area, analyzed in Section F.3, is termed here "the penalty of potential threats."

---

[12] See entries V: Violence, X: X-Ray, and Y: Youth. On Israel's use of informants in the context of "preventive detention," see Section F.3.1.

[13] See entry X: X-Ray.

[14] T. Kelly, "In a Treacherous State: The Fear of Collaboration Among West Bank Palestinians," in S. Thiranagama and T. Kelly (eds.), *Traitors: Suspicion, Intimacy, and the Ethics of State-Building* (Philadelphia: University of Pennsylvania Press, 2010), p. 169; N. Gordon, *Israel's Occupation* (Berkeley and Los Angeles: University of California Press, 2008), pp. 42–43.

[15] See entry S: Security Prisoners.

[16] See H. Viterbo, "Rights as a Divide-and-Rule Mechanism: Lessons from the Case of Palestinians in Israeli Custody" *Law & Society Inquiry* (forthcoming) [hereinafter: Rights as a Divide-and-Rule Mechanism].

[17] Comparable practices are ubiquitous far beyond Israel/Palestine, and have been extensively studied. For representative examples, see R. V. Ericson and K. D. Haggerty, *Policing the Risk Society* (Oxford: Clarendon Press, 1997); B. E. Harcourt, *Against Prediction: Profiling, Policing, and Punishing in an Actuarial Age* (Chicago: University of Chicago Press, 2006); B. Anderson, "Preemption, Precaution, Preparedness: Anticipatory Action and Future Geographies" (2010) 34 *Progress in Human Geography* 777; C. Heath-Kelly, "Counter-Terrorism and the Counterfactual: Producing the 'Radicalisation' Discourse and the UK Prevent Strategy" (2013) 15 *British Journal of Politics & International Relations* 394; D. Kellner, "Preemptive Strikes and the War on Iraq: A Critique of Bush Administration Unilateralism and Militarism" (2004) 26 *New Political Science* 417; J. McCulloch and S. Pickering, "Pre-crime and Counter-terrorism" (2009) 49 *British Journal of Criminology* 628; G. Mythen and S. Walklate, "Terrorism, Risk and International Security: The Perils of Asking 'What If?'" (2008) 39 *Security Dialogue* 221. On the politics and culture of risk management, see, e.g., U. Beck, *Risk Society: Towards a New Modernity* (London: SAGE publications, 1992); A. Giddens, *Modernity and Self-Identity: Self and Society in the Late Modern Age* (Stanford: Stanford University Press, 1991).

Three components of this penalty will be examined: (a) "administrative detention" (also known as "preventive detention"): imprisonment without trial or charge on the basis of secret evidence; (b) the preemptive arrest of "potential offenders" for whom there is no evidence of an actual intent to break Israeli law; and (c) "mappings": house incursions to gather information about Palestinians who are considered innocent. The entry will analyze the stated objectives, the surrounding discourses, and the actual effects of each of these practices.

These two areas of future-oriented activity – preemptive attacks and the penalty of potential threats – align themselves differently with the different modes of control Israel exercises over the Gaza Strip and West Bank.[18] Following its unilateral pullout from the Gaza Strip in 2005, Israel has mostly been controlling this territory externally, including through closure and airstrikes.[19] Rather than being a permanent military presence on the ground, the Israeli military has conducted intermittent incursions. As a result, it is primarily toward the Gaza Strip that Israel has deployed its preemptive airstrikes and "warning" tactics in recent years, as is evident in Section F.2. In comparison, as described in Section F.3, the Israeli penalty of potential threats is now in use mainly (in the case of "administrative detentions") or almost exclusively (in the case of preemptive arrests and house "mappings") in the West Bank. It is primarily within this territory, which is also populated by hundreds of thousands of Jewish settlers, that Israeli security forces, legal institutions, and administrative authorities operate on a regular and extensive basis. Accordingly, the vast majority of Palestinians in Israeli custody are from the West Bank, whereas only a relatively small proportion are from the Gaza Strip.[20]

Social theorist Brian Massumi has put forward an insightful conceptualization of the three future-oriented modes of operation examined in this entry – prevention, deterrence, and preemption. As he articulates it, in prevention, the potential threat precedes the intervention. A successful prevention means that the threat never materializes. When prevention fails, the threat starts eventuating, and deterrence may take over. In order to maintain an immediate

---

[18]   For further discussion of the different modes and scales of Israeli control over the Gaza Strip and West Bank, see L. Allen, "The Scales of Occupation: 'Operation Cast Lead' and the Targeting of the Gaza Strip" (2012) 32 *Critique of Anthropology* 261; A. Cohen, "Israel's Control of the Territories – An Emerging Legal Paradigm" (2016) 21 *Palestine-Israel Journal* 102; D. Li, "The Gaza Strip as Laboratory: Notes in the Wake of Disengagement" (2006) 35 *Journal of Palestine Studies* 38.

[19]   See also entries Q: Quality of Life, V: Violence, and Z: Zone.

[20]   See entry S: Security Prisoners, Section S.1 ("Introduction: Terminology, Figures, and Context").

response capability to this unfolding threat, deterrence translates (or converts) it into a present danger. In other words, rather than preventing the threat altogether, deterrence contributes to its development. This creates a self-propelling process of advancing into the perilous future, even at the risk of self-annihilation. Alongside this difference, prevention and deterrence share a fundamental assumption: namely, that threats are empirically assessable, causes are identifiable, and there is a predictable causal link between them. In this logic, uncertainty about the nature of the threat is seen as simply the result of insufficient data. Preemption, in contrast, presumes that such uncertainty can never be overcome, because new and unpredictable threats are always bound to emerge, with potential terrorists or offenders whose identity and location are often unspecifiable. This requires state authorities to operate proactively – to make the first move – and in so doing contribute to the emergence and even proliferation of threats. The state's aim is to make these heretofore-unspecified threats emerge and proliferate on its own terms, so that now they can finally be managed. Like deterrence, preemption thus becomes a self-propelling process, but in a different manner: by bringing nonexistent threats into being (and, once these threats are materialized, invoking them to retroactively justify itself).[21]

While Massumi contrasts the three future-oriented modes of operation rather starkly and rigidly, in reality they overlap inextricably and defy clear-cut definitions. Yet, his analysis and others' earlier works[22] shed light on two key dimensions of Israel's future-oriented measures, both of which are illustrated throughout this entry. First, these measures are not only preclusive but also, no less importantly, productive in nature. In the process of supposedly thwarting eventualities that are deemed undesirable, they engender new and often greater threats and harms, intentionally or not, including the loss of civilian lives, mass suffering, and Palestinian animosity toward Israel. Second, as explained in this entry, Israel's future-oriented practices often evince a self-propelling or circular logic, according to which they are eternally necessary, regardless of the extent of actual threats and evidence.

---

[21] B. Massumi, "Potential Politics and the Primacy of Preemption" (2007) 10:2 *Theory & Event*, ¶¶ 5–24.

[22] See, e.g., S. Crook, "Ordering Risks," in D. Lupton (ed.), *Risk and Sociocultural Theory: New Directions and Perspectives* (Cambridge: Cambridge University Press, 1999), pp. 160, 171 ("In an organised regime the activities of scientific and technical experts, inspectorates and enforcement agencies, legislators and concerned citizens do not simply process risks that appear 'externally' over the horizon of the regimes in an ad hoc way. The apparatuses of surveillance and discipline … routinely produce the risks they assess and manage. The important corollary of this point is that only those risks are produced which are in principle 'manageable'"). See also the sources cited in note 17.

In addition to exploring the productive dimension and circular logic of the practices and policies under examination, this entry advances three other arguments. First, that some of these policies and practices potentially serve objectives that are entirely different from, or at least additional to, their stated ones. More specifically, they fulfill a function that is not directly concerned with prevention, deterrence, or preemption, or they target a different potential threat from their professed one. Second, this entry puts a spotlight on the sanitized terminology used to conceal and legitimize the harm and threats created by Israel's future-oriented measures. Finally, contrary to legalistic[23] criticisms of these measures as disregarding the law, the entry demonstrates their eager use of legal mechanisms, classifications, and arguments. The concluding section summarizes the key findings in relation to each of these aspects, and further delves into the close relationship between seemingly exceptional future-oriented practices and "normal" law.

F.2 PREEMPTIVE MILITARY ATTACKS

One of Israel's recurrent justifications for its violence toward Palestinians in the West Bank and Gaza Strip has been the management of future risks. Three key practices, in particular, have been presented as serving this objective: preemptive military strikes, extrajudicial assassinations, and "warning" procedures.

F.2.1 *Preemptive Strikes*

The 1967 war – the inception of Israel's rule in the West Bank and Gaza Strip – was presented by Israeli officials as preemptive self-defense against Arab aggression.[24] The Israeli government's official decision to wage this preemptive war proclaimed: "[T]he armies of Egypt, Syria, and Jordan are deployed for a multifront attack that *threatens Israel's existence*. It is therefore decided to *launch a military strike* aimed at liberating Israel from encirclement and *preventing assault by the United Arab Command*."[25]

---

[23] For a useful discussion the meaning(s) of "legalism," see K. McEvoy, "Beyond Legalism: Towards a Thicker Understanding of Transnational Justice" (2007) 34 *Journal of Law & Society* 411, 414–424. On the legalistic nature of the Israeli regime, see entries L: Lawfare and V: Violence.

[24] For an analysis challenging Israel's depiction of the war, see E. N. Kurtulus, "The Notion of a 'Pre-emptive War:' the Six Day War Revisited" (2007) 61 *Middle East Journal* 220.

[25] Quoted in M. B. Oren, *Six Days of War: June 1967 and the Making of the Modern Middle East* (London: Penguin Books, 2002), p. 158 (emphases added).

While depicted as meant to preempt future harms ("assault by the United Arab Command"), this war also brought about a different political and legal future, brimming with new harm and danger.

Since then, Israel has continued launching purportedly preventive or preemptive military strikes. As a case in point, in 2014, the Palestinian organization Hamas (which governs Gaza) signed a reconciliation agreement setting out plans to form a unity government with its rival, Fatah (which controls the Palestinian Authority in the West Bank). Minutes after the announcement, the Israeli air force fired two missiles into the Gaza Strip, injuring seven Palestinians. The Israeli authorities did not portray this as retaliation for firing from this territory. Instead, they described it as a "preventive attack ... designed to thwart terrorism," while admitting that the stated targets – rocket launchers – had not actually been hit. Shortly after the airstrike, two rockets were fired from the Gaza Strip into Israel (causing no Israeli casualties or damage to property).[26] The Israeli airstrike might have thus ended up triggering, or at least potentially legitimizing, the harm it supposedly sought to prevent – the firing of rockets from Gaza.

Further, aside from preventing such firing from the Gaza Strip, the Israeli attack may have been at least partly aimed at another perceived threat: Palestinian political unity. This is not entirely inconceivable given Israel's extensive attempts at politically fragmenting Palestinian society, as discussed elsewhere in this book.[27] Indeed, the Israeli government vocally censured and refused negotiation with the Palestinian unity government.[28] According to one Israeli commentator, Israel's prime minister, Benjamin Netanyahu, "viewed the reconciliation as a threat rather than an opportunity" because it "robbed him of the claim that in the absence of effective rule over Gaza, there is no point in striking a deal with [the Palestinian Authority]."[29] Like the preemptive war of 1967, then, this airstrike might have been concerned with governing the region's political future.

---

[26] G. Cohen, J. Khoury, and S. Seidler, "IDF Attacks in Gaza Minutes After the Announcement of the Unity Agreement," *Haaretz* (April 23, 2014) [Hebrew], www.haaretz.co.il/news/politics/1.2303190.

[27] See entry S: Security Prisoners, Section S.2, "Sociopolitical fragmentation." See also, e.g., Gisha, *The Separation Policy: List of References Prepared by Gisha* (2014), http://gisha.org/UserFiles/File/publications/separation_policy_2014.pdf; A. Korn, "The Ghettoization of the Palestinians," in R. Lentin (ed.), *Thinking Palestine* (London and New York: Zed Books, 2008), pp. 116–130; Viterbo, "Rights as a Divide-and-Rule Mechanism."

[28] B. Sobelman, "Israel Suspends Peace Talks with Palestinians," *Los Angeles Times* (April 24, 2014), www.latimes.com/world/middleeast/la-fg-israel-talks-20140425-story.html.

[29] A. Sharon, "Failure in Gaza," *New York Review of Books* (September 25, 2014), www.nybooks.com/articles/2014/09/25/failure-gaza/.

F.2.2 *Extrajudicial Assassinations*

Unlike the English term "targeted killing," its Hebrew equivalent *sikul memukad* (meaning "focused preemption/foiling/thwarting"), does not acknowledge the lethal nature of extrajudicial assassination.[30] Instead of the "killing" this practice entails, the Hebrew term emphasizes its future-orientedness – the alleged ability to preempt a future threat. It is thus not the precise outcome of this measure (killing) that is center stage but its temporal horizon.

Israeli authorities and officials have repeatedly emphasized this future-oriented dimension. In 2005, Moshe Ya'alon, the chief of staff at the time (and later the minister of defense), asserted that Israel's "targeted killings ... were intended to preempt ... terrorist attacks."[31] The state's response to a 2002 petition against Israel's so-called "focused preemption" policy characterized it as a "means of warfare used to preempt murderous attacks."[32] The supreme court's decision on the matter, in 2006, unanimously upheld the lawfulness of this policy (as analyzed in depth in another entry),[33] and reiterated the future-oriented language. The opinion of emeritus chief justice Aharon Barak described this as a "preventive strikes policy,"[34] and chief justice Beinisch concurred: "the function of 'focused preemption' is to prevent [Israeli] casualties as part of the state's duty to protect its soldiers and citizens."[35]

The judgment also touched on the potential uncertainty of the dreaded security threat. The state's response to the petition admitted the "uncertainty inherent to any belligerent act."[36] Chief justice Beinisch suggested managing this uncertainty as follows: "[I]n some circumstances, information about the terrorist's past activity can be used to assess the threat he poses. ... [T]his assessment should take into account the likelihood of the life-threatening

---

[30] "Extrajudicial assassination" and related phrases appear, inter alia, in Article 8 of the Rome Statute of the International Criminal Court, UN General Assembly, July 17, 1998, ISBN No 92–9227-227–6 (prohibiting "the carrying out of executions without previous judgement pronounced by a regularly constituted court"); Article 1 of the UN Principles on the Effective Prevention and Investigation of Extra-Legal, Arbitrary and Summary Executions, May 24, 1989, UN Doc E/RES/1989/65 ("Governments shall prohibit by law all extra-legal, arbitrary and summary executions").

[31] Quoted in A. Craig, *International Legitimacy and the Politics of Security* (Plymouth: Lexington Books, 2013), p. 141 [hereinafter: International Legitimacy]. The author adds that the military's international law department "constructed their advice to meet the Israeli understanding of ... [targeted killing] operations as 'anticipatory self-defence.'" *Ibid.*, p. 146. On the international law department, see entry L: Lawfare.

[32] HCJ 769/02 *Public Committee Against Torture in Israel* v. *Government of Israel* (December 13, 2006), ¶ 9 of Barak's opinion, http://elyon1.court.gov.il/files_eng/02/690/007/a34/02007690 .a34.pdf.

[33] See entry C: Combatants.   [34] HCJ 769/02, opening paragraph of Barak's opinion.

[35] *Ibid.*, Beinisch's concurring opinion.   [36] *Ibid.*, ¶ 13 of Barak's opinion.

terrorist activity. ... [S]ubstantial likelihood ... is required."[37] This contingency, the court ruled, should be weighed against another: the potential "military benefit" of the assassination. Only if the former is proportionate to the latter would the liquidation be regarded as lawful.[38] In the face of uncertainty, then, preemption rests on a calculation of probabilities.

What the Hebrew and English euphemisms "focused preemption" and "targeted killing" mask is that extrajudicial assassination is often neither focused nor targeted.[39] A relatively well-known example of this imprecision is Israel's assassination of Hamas military leader Salah Shehadeh in 2002, which killed not only Shehadeh himself and his guard, but also 14 other Palestinians, as well as injuring more than 80 others, and destroying 4 residential buildings.[40] In the name of thwarting one future harm or threat, such liquidations can thus end up creating other harms and threats: the loss of civilian lives, mass suffering, Palestinian animosity toward Israel, and, as a result, potentially, additional future threats. According to the supreme court, "there [must] be a proper proportionate relationship between the [Israeli] military objective and the [Palestinian] civilian damage"[41] – requiring the military, in this regard as well, to weigh uncertain contingencies against one another.

The alternative terms "extrajudicial assassinations" and "extrajudicial executions" convey the spatial and temporal deviation of this practice from the process of judicial review. Spatially, this procedure occurs outside the courtroom. Temporally, instead of subjecting evidence to judicial scrutiny before deciding how to handle the alleged terrorist, the order is reversed. The death of a Palestinian target is politically utilized as evidence of the existence and operation of terrorists. Rather than diminishing the threat of terrorism, extrajudicial assassinations and the harm they cause thus serve as evidence for the never-ending stream of future threats.[42]

---

[37] *Ibid.*, Beinisch's concurring opinion.

[38] *Ibid.*, ¶¶ 45–46, 58, 60 of Barak's opinion, ¶ 5 of deputy chief justice Rivlin's concurring opinion, Beinisch's concurring opinion.

[39] This is true even according to Israeli authorities' (debatable) standards: two out of every five Palestinian casualties of Israel's so-called "targeted killings" between September 29, 2000, and December 26, 2008, were not the formal object of the assassination. See B'Tselem, "Fatalities Before Operation 'Cast Lead'" (n.d.), www.btselem.org/statistics/fatalities/before-cast-lead/by-date-of-event.

[40] O. Ben-Naftali and K. Michaeli, "'We Must not Make a Scarecrow of the Law': A Legal Analysis of the Israeli Policy of Targeted Killings" (2002–2003) 36 *Cornell Journal of International Law* 233, 280.

[41] HCJ 769/02, ¶ 44 of Barak's opinion.

[42] S. Krasmann, "Targeted Killing and Its Law: On a Mutually Constitutive Relationship" (2012) 25 *Leiden Journal of International Law* 665, 681.

While upholding the lawfulness of Israel's "focused preemption" policy, the supreme court has ruled that "if a terrorist taking a direct part in hostilities can be arrested, interrogated, and tried, those are the means which should be employed ... Trial is preferable to use of [lethal] force."[43] Yet, classified documents leaked in 2008 suggest that the military has assassinated Palestinians who could have been arrested. The attorney general, however, refused to investigate this potential violation of the court's ruling. The only people prosecuted (and convicted) were the leaker and the Israeli journalist who published this information.[44] At the same time, the alternative this ruling proposes – arrest, interrogation, and trial – is far from perfect. As shown elsewhere in this book, trial in an Israeli court offers near-certain conviction.[45] And, as discussed in Section F.3.1, arrest often leads to "administrative detention": incarceration without trial on the basis of secret evidence.

F.2.3 *"Warning" Procedures*

Civil casualties, especially if documented and broadcast globally, can greatly erode the legitimacy of military attacks. Indeed, during its 2006 war against Hezbollah in Lebanon, Israel made frequent use of warnings to clear the battlefield of civilians: leaflets dropped from aircraft, radio broadcasts in Arabic, and telephone calls to local civic leaders. The military's international law department (examined in another entry)[46] was heavily involved in this endeavor. Yet, the warnings proved to be ineffective, as Israel's assumption that no civilians remained in the area turned out to be false.[47]

Drawing on its lessons from Lebanon, the Israeli military, advised by its international law department, refined this procedure in its assaults on the Gaza Strip from 2008 onward. For the military offensive of 2008–2009, the general staff issued an order with a legal annex stipulating that "as far as possible in the circumstances, the civilian population in the area of a legitimate target is to be warned," so long as such warning does not endanger Israeli forces or the military action. In addition to flyers and radio broadcasts, Israel began sending recorded warnings specifying evacuation locations to mobile phones of Palestinians in designated areas. The Israeli military also introduced the controversial "roof knocking" tactic, which has also been

---

[43] HCJ 769/02, ¶ 40 of Barak's opinion.
[44] See entry V: Violence, Section V.3 ("Invisible violence").
[45] See entry M: Military Courts.   [46] See entry L: Lawfare.
[47] Craig, *International Legitimacy*, pp. 165, 171, 185, 197.

employed in later offensives on the Gaza Strip: dropping low- or nonimpact explosives on residential buildings that allegedly house combatants or military infrastructure prior to bombing them with larger missiles.[48] In an address to the UN General Assembly, Israeli prime minister Netanyahu boasted: "Israel was doing everything to minimize Palestinian civilian casualties. . . . No other country and no other army in history have gone to greater lengths to avoid casualties among the civilian population of their enemies."[49]

However, the Israeli procedures have exposed to harm many of the Palestinians they purport to warn, in at least two ways. First, despite the soft tone of the name "roof knocking," the so-called "warning" munitions are hazardous and intimidating. They can damage or shake the targeted building, cause physical harm to the residents, induce great fear, and have even directly hit and killed civilians. In this sense, not only do they signal an impending attack, they are themselves a preliminary attack. Even Gazans who wished to evacuate were often unable to do so for various reasons: insufficient time; lack of clarity on which house was being targeted (due to simultaneous attacks nearby); uncertainty whether a bombing was a preliminary warning; the lack of nearby shelters; physical and health reasons; and a sense that there was no safe alternative given Israel's strikes throughout the Gaza Strip.[50] Some Palestinians did leave their buildings, but returned "too soon" (as the Israeli military later put it): though the Israeli pilot could see them running back to the house, the missile was already under way, resulting in their death.[51] Others were not in targeted houses themselves, but were injured as a result of bombings of nearby buildings. On other occasions, Israel's warning flyers designated

[48]   Y. Feldman and U. Blau, "Consent and Advise," *Haaretz* (January 9, 2009), www.haaretz.com /consent-and-advise-1.269127. See also Craig, *International Legitimacy*, pp. 185, 187, 196–219; E. Weizman, "Legislative Attack" (2010) 27 *Theory, Culture & Society* 11, 21–22; E. Weizman, "Gaza Attacks: Lethal Warnings," *Al Jazeera* (July 14, 2014), www.aljazeera.com/indepth/opi nion/2014/07/gaza-attacks-lethal-warnings-2014713162312604305.html. On the "roof knocking" tactic, see also entry X: X-Ray. On the subsequent adoption of this tactic by the US-led coalition forces in Iraq in 2016, see entry E: Export of Knowledge, Section E.2.

[49]   Haaretz, "Transcript of Benjamin Netanyahu's Address to the 2014 UN General Assembly," *Haaretz* (September 29, 2014), www.haaretz.com/israel-news/1.618308.

[50]   B'Tselem, *Black Flag: The Legal and Moral Implications of the Policy of Attacking Residential Buildings in the Gaza Strip, Summer 2014* (2015), pp. 54–57 [hereinafter: Black Flag], www .btselem.org/download/201501_black_flag_eng.pdf; Physicians for Human Rights – Israel et al., *Gaza, 2014: Findings of an Independent Medical Fact-Finding Mission* (2015), pp. 40–44, https://gazahealthattack.files.wordpress.com/2015/01/gazareport_eng.pdf; A. Iraqi, "The Humanitarian Myths of Israel's 'Roof-Knocking' Policy in Gaza," *World Post* (September 9, 2014), www.huffingtonpost.com/amjad-iraqi/the-humanitarian-myths-of_b_57 77364.html.

[51]   G. Cohen, "Israeli Army Says the Killing of 8 Gazan Family Members Was in Error," *Haaretz* (July 10, 2014), www.haaretz.com/israel-news/1.604128.

certain neighborhoods as safe, but Palestinians who fled there ended up perishing in an Israeli attack.[52]

Second, these measures have been utilized as a preemptive legal defense against potential accusations that Israel indiscriminately attacks populated areas in Gaza.[53] Under the international law of armed conflict, civilians, unlike combatants, are not considered legitimate military targets (as explained elsewhere in this book).[54] In a controversial application of this legal distinction, some Israeli officials have argued that warned civilians who remain in targeted buildings willingly become "human shields"[55] and thus relinquish their civilian status.

One senior military lawyer articulated this position as follows, in 2009:

> The people who go into a house despite a warning do not have to be taken into account in terms of injury to civilians, because they are voluntary human shields. From the legal point of view, I do not have to show consideration for them. In the case of people who return to their home in order to protect it, they are taking part in the fighting.[56]

Similarly, according to Israeli philosopher Asa Kasher, the author of the military's ethical code,

> there is no army in the world that will endanger its soldiers to avoid hitting the [already] well-warned neighbors of an enemy or terrorist. . . . Israel should favor the lives of its own soldiers over the lives of the well-warned neighbors of a terrorist when it is operating in a territory that it does not effectively control [referring to the Gaza Strip],[57] because in such territories it does not bear moral responsibility for properly separating between dangerous individuals and harmless ones, beyond warning them in an effective way.[58]

---

[52] B'Tselem, *Black Flag*, pp. 54–55.

[53] The description of these techniques as a "preemptive legal defense" is borrowed from: N. Gordon, "Using Human Shields as a Pretext to Kill Civilians," *Al Jazeera* (August 30, 2016), www.aljazeera.com/indepth/opinion/2016/08/human-shields-pretext-kill-civilians-1608 30102718866.html.

[54] See entry C: Combatants.

[55] For a critical analysis of Israel's use of the term "human shields," see N. Gordon and N. Perugini, "The Politics of Human Shielding: On the Resignification of Space and the Constitution of Civilians as Shields in Liberal Wars" (2016) 34 *Environment and Planning D: Society and Space* 168.

[56] Feldman and Blau, "Consent and Advise." This point is also touched upon in entry X: X-Ray, Section X.2.6.

[57] On the question of whether Israel has retained effective control after its 2005 unilateral from the Gaza Strip, see entries Z: Zone (specifically Section Z.2.2.1) and X: X Rays (specifically Section X.2.6).

[58] A. Kasher, "Analysis: A Moral Evaluation of the Gaza War," *Jerusalem Post* (February 7, 2010), www.jpost.com/Israel/Analysis-A-moral-evaluation-of-the-Gaza-War. For further analysis of Kasher's assertions on "roof knocking," see entry E: Export of Knowledge.

Initially justified as means to minimize collateral damage, these so-called "warning" measures can thus pave the way for destruction, suffering, and civilian casualties. They are therefore both a form of military offense in and of themselves and a preemptive legal defense, claiming to shift Palestinians who do not or cannot heed them from one legal category (legally protected civilians) to another (legitimate military targets).[59] The high proportion of Palestinian civilian casualties – between 73 and 77 percent in the 2014 Israeli military operation, according to some estimates[60] – demonstrates the broader context within which these supposedly cautionary measures potentially authorize killing civilians.

F.3 THE PENALITY OF POTENTIAL THREATS

In addition to military attacks, another context in which prevention, deterrence, and preemption occupy a central place is law enforcement. As explained in Section F.1, this context mostly pertains to the West Bank, whereas the preemptive military attacks analyzed in Section F.2 largely concern the Gaza Strip. The following discussion will focus on three specific practices: "administrative detentions," preemptive arrests, and "mappings." In different ways, the primary concern common to these future-focused practices is not past crimes but potential threats, specific or unspecifiable.

In general, criminal law has some future-oriented elements: sentencing, for example, incorporates deterrence considerations.[61] And yet, in certain key respects, criminal law usually insists on presenting itself as relying on the past – both as matter of principle (in drawing on precedent) and as a matter of fact (in inspecting evidence of defendants' past actions). "Administrative detention," preemptive arrest, and "mapping" make up a form of penalty that openly defies this mythical or ideal mode of criminal law: a penalty of potential threats, in which past-based decisions, though still in operation, become secondary and instrumental to the management of future and potential transgressions. Since the alleged threat is yet to materialize and is sometimes completely unknown, speculative evidence is produced, the basis of

---

[59] Weizman, "Legislative Attack," pp. 21–22.

[60] See, respectively, UN Office for the Coordination of Humanitarian Affairs, *Occupied Palestinian Territory: Gaza Emergency – Humanitarian Snapshot* (2014), www.ochaopt.org/content/gaza-emergency-humanitarian-snapshot-20-july-2014; Human Rights Watch, "Israel/Palestine: Unlawful Israeli Airstrikes Kill Civilians" (July 15, 2014), www.hrw.org/news/2014/07/15/israel/palestine-unlawful-israeli-airstrikes-kill-civilians.

[61] J. McCulloch and D. Wilson, "Before Pre-Crime: A History of the Future," in *Pre-Crime, Pre-Emption, Precaution and the Future* (London: Routledge, 2016), p. 17 [hereinafter: *Pre-Crime, Pre-Emption, Precaution*].

which is not past facts but a probability calculus.[62] After exploring this penality in this section, the entry will critically consider (in the concluding section) the extent to which it actually deviates from "normal" criminal law.

F.3.1 *"Administrative Detention"*

As discussed elsewhere in this book, Israel has placed thousands of Palestinians in so-called "administrative detention"[63] – imprisonment without charge or trial. This measure is also commonly referred to as "preventive detention,"[64] as its objective, officially at least, is to prevent potential risks rather than punish past actions. In the absence of specific charges, Palestinians are thus deprived of their liberty not due to actual offenses, but on grounds of allegedly posing a threat.

Usually, since such incarceration is based on secret evidence, neither the detainee nor the defense attorney are properly informed of the allegations, and therefore cannot effectively refute them. The incarceration can be extended every six months with no set limit, subject to military court review. This review, however, is not only based on secret evidence, but is also unbound by the regular rules of evidence and is held behind closed doors.[65] While

---

[62]   For a somewhat similar analysis, see L. Amoore, "Risk before Justice: When the Law Contests Its Own Suspension" (2008) 21 *Leiden Journal of International Law* 847, 850–851, 854–857 [hereinafter: "Risk before Justice"]. On speculative threats in the context of the legal principle of proportionality, see entry P: Proportionality, Section P.3 ("Values: Constants and Variables").

[63]   For further figures and analysis, see entry S: Security Prisoners, Section S.1.

[64]   See, e.g., H. Ludsin, *Preventive Detention and the Democratic State* (Cambridge: Cambridge University Press, 2016); C. V. Reicin, "Preventive Detention, Curfews, Demolition of Houses, and Deportations: An Analysis of Measures Employed by Israel in the Administered Territories" (1987) 8 *Cardozo Law Review* 515; T. Stahlberg and H. Lahmann, "A Paradigm of Prevention: Humpty Dumpty, the War on Terror, and the Power of Preventive Detention in the United States, Israel, and Europe" (2011) 59 *The American Journal of Comparative Law* 1051; D. Webber, *Preventive Detention of Terror Suspects: A New Legal Framework* (London: Routledge, 2016).

[65]   Articles 290–291 of Order No. 1651 Concerning Security Provisions (Integrated Version) (Judea and Samaria), 2009, www.law.idf.il/Templates/GetFile/GetFile.aspx?FileName=XG F5b3N0LWRvY3NdGFmcmloX2hha2lrYVxiaXRhaG9uXyZfcGxpbGGb2dkYW5faGFFraW thLnBkZg==&InfoCenterItem=true. For further discussion, see B'Tselem and Hamoked, *Without Trial: Administrative Detention of Palestinians by Israel and the Internment of Unlawful Combatants Law* (October 2009) [hereinafter: *Without Trial*], www.btselem.org/d ownload/200910_without_trial_eng.pdf; T. Pelleg-Sryck, "The Mysteries of Administrative Detention," in A. Baker and A. Matar (eds.), *Threat: Palestinian Political Prisoners in Israel* (London: Pluto Press, 2011), pp. 123–135. See also Amoore, "Risk before Justice," p. 855 ("Because the system … [deploys a risk] calculation that can never itself be made visible, people can never meaningfully access, challenge, or correct their risk category.").

review decisions of military courts can be appealed to the supreme court, none of the hundreds of appeals in the period 2000–2010 resulted in a release order or a rejection of the secret evidence.[66] Hence, the risk this mode of imprisonment professes to prevent remains incontestable throughout the review and appeal.

Often, the secret evidence is based on information provided by Palestinian informants, usually as a result of coercion (and sometimes payment) by the Israeli security authorities.[67] Rather than openly acknowledging the potential unreliability of such information, Israeli authorities invoke the need to protect informants' anonymity as a reason for not revealing the alleged evidence.[68] Military judges who review this evidence do not independently verify it. One former military judge, when asked in an interview whether he used to summon the informants to testify in such cases, replied: "Not the sources [i.e., the informants] themselves, but the [written] testimonies they provide," as presented by the Israeli security agencies. The interviewer sought clarification: "So what do you actually see?," to which the former judge answered "Documents, the source's code-name, I ask the GSS [General Security Service] agent to explain [these documents] … and whether the source is reliable. Of course I have to take as a given that all my information comes through the GSS agents. … [A]s a rule, I didn't doubt what they [i.e., the Israeli agents] said."[69]

---

[66] S. Krebs, "Lifting the Veil of Secrecy: Judicial Review of Administrative Detentions in the Israeli Supreme Court" (2012) 45 *Vanderbilt Journal Transnational Law* 639, 643 [hereinafter: "Lifting the Veil of Secrecy"]. The author adds that even if such an appeal were to succeed, the military court's unjustified extension of the "administrative detention" would unlikely be acknowledged, since the detention made it impossible for the presumed threat to materialize. *Ibid.*, pp. 648–649. On the near-certain outcome of such appeals and the way it fits into Israel's broader apparatus of "(un)certainty governance," see entry M: Military Courts.

[67] H. Cohen and R. Dudai, "Human Rights Dilemmas in Using Informers to Combat Terrorism: The Israeli-Palestinian Case" (2005) 17 *Terrorism and Political Violence* 229–243, 233–236. On Israel's use of Palestinian patients from Gaza as informants as a prerequisite for considering their applications for exiting Gaza for medical reasons, see entry V: Violence, Section V.3 ("Invisible Violence"). On the informants issue, see entries V: Violence, X: X-Ray, and Y: Youth.

[68] B'Tselem and Hamoked, *Without Trial*, pp. 27, 40. A former military judge voiced this rationale in the 2011 Israeli documentary *The Law in These Parts* (2013; Director: Ra'anan Alexandrowicz. American Documentary/POV): "The ['administrative'] detainee … isn't shown the material regarding what he allegedly did. That way we don't give away our sources." Some suggest that "administrative detention" is also sometimes used to recruit the detainees themselves as informants. Pelleg-Sryck, "The Mysteries of Administrative Detention," pp. 130–133.

[69] Former military judge Oded Pessenson's interview in *The Law in These Parts*. On this documentary, see entry M: Military Courts.

With the rise of social media, "administrative detentions" have also been increasingly targeted at Palestinians who write, share, or "like" allegedly suspicious posts on Facebook, blogs, and similar websites. This is part of the Israeli security agencies' growing use of "big data" – enormous sets of information analyzed by algorithms to reveal patterns of behavior.[70] A common way to trace these presumed patterns is to inspect the use of key words and phrases online. For example, reports suggest that Palestinians have been arrested after using the word *shahid* (Arabic for "martyr") online. In Israeli Jewish society, this term is usually understood as an expression of incitement, although for most Palestinians its meaning is different, showing respect for those who die in a political struggle.[71] One military officer has boasted that "if you get to their house a week before the attack, the [Palestinian] kid [who posted online] doesn't [even] know that he is a terrorist yet."[72] Put simply, this expresses a belief that Israeli authorities, equipped with advanced cyber technology, can predict unlawful actions that are unknown even to the would-be terrorists themselves.

[70]   Addameer, "Daring to Post: Arrests of Palestinians for Alleged Incitement" (August 24, 2016) [hereinafter: "Daring to Post"], www.addameer.org/publications/daring-post-arrests-palestinians-alleged-incitement; O. Hirschauge and H. Shezaf, "Revealed // How Israel Jails Palestinians Because They Fit the 'Terrorist Profile'," *Haaretz* (May 31, 2017) [hereinafter: "Revealed // How Israel Jails Palestinians"], www.haaretz.com/israel-news/.premium-1.792206; H. Shezaf, "The IDF is Putting Palestinians on Trial for Facebook Posts," +972 *Magazine* (March 17, 2016), http://972mag.com/the-idf-is-putting-palestinians-on-trial-for-facebook-posts/117910; A. Harel, "Israel Arrested 400 Palestinians Suspected of Planning Attacks After Monitoring Social Networks," *Haaretz* (April 18, 2017) [hereinafter: "Israel Arrested 400 Palestinians"], www.haaretz.com/israel-news/1.783672; A. Gibor, "'The Country Most Dangerous to Us in the Middle East is Facebook'," *Makor Rishon* (January 29, 2016) [Hebrew], www.nrg.co.il/online/1/ART2/751/369.html; A. Kane, "Post, Share, Arrest: Israel Targeting Palestinian Protesters on Facebook," *Intercept* (July 7, 2016), https://theintercept.com/2016/07/07/israel-targeting-palestinian-protesters-on-facebook/; Defence for Children International – Palestine, "Facebook Posts land Palestinian Teens in Administrative Detention" (October 17, 2016), www.dci-palestine.org/facebook_posts_land_palestinian_teens_in_administrative_detention; J. Brown, "'Minority Report': On What Grounds Does Israel Arrest Hundreds of Palestinians for Uncommitted Crimes?," *Haaretz* (April 19, 2017) [Hebrew] [hereinafter: "Minority Report"], www.haaretz.co.il/blogs/johnbrown/1.4035211. In some cases, the social media posts culminate not in "administrative detention" but in trials on charge of incitement. Addameer, "Daring to Post"; Hirschauge and Shezaf, "Revealed // How Israel Jails Palestinians"; Shezaf, "The IDF is Putting Palestinians on Trial for Facebook Posts."

[71]   Hirschauge and Shezaf, "Revealed // How Israel Jails Palestinians"; Shezaf, "The IDF is Putting Palestinians on Trial for Facebook Posts." See also Addameer, "Daring to Post"; Brown, "Minority Report"; G. Levy and A. Levac, "In 2016 Israel, a Palestinian Writer Is in Custody for Her Poetry," *Haaretz* (May 21, 2016), www.haaretz.com/israel-news/.premium-1.720418.

[72]   Hirschauge and Shezaf, "Revealed // How Israel Jails Palestinians."

Some critics suggest that by apprehending alleged "future criminals" before any crime actually occurs, "administrative detention," like other preventive measures, risks creating the very harm it formally seeks to thwart. As one Israeli human rights attorney observed in the late 1970s,

> the concept of preventive detention logically precludes a possibility of eventually charging the detainees with any offense. ... [Such Palestinian] detainees have been arrested by virtue of being "potential offenders" which means that they have committed no offence to which their arrest could be connected. No wonder, then, that ... [these] detainees can only reach one conclusion from their ordeal: "If I am busted and beaten when I have done nothing, then the next time I had better do something."[73]

At the same time, in some cases, the appeal of "administrative detention" for Israeli authorities may stem not from its preventive or predictive potential, but from its procedural laxity – the ability to rely on undisclosed secret evidence without having to undergo trial hearings. Possibly due to this reason, the military prosecution has been reported to resort to "administrative detention" after failing to get the detainee convicted in a military court trial.[74] Security agents have likewise occasionally justified using "administrative detention" as a way to avoid revealing classified evidence to the detainee.[75] Somewhat similarly, as discussed in one of this book's other entries, some Palestinian prisoners, having served their full sentences, have been placed in "administrative detention" immediately after their scheduled release.[76] In these and other respects, "administrative detention" can serve as a form of punishment without trial.

F.3.2 Preemptive Arrest

"Administrative detention" formally depends on evidence. This evidence is secret, potentially unreliable, and impossible to effectively contest – and yet, its existence allows Israeli authorities to claim reasonable suspicion. This, along with the judicial review in use, helps maintain a semblance of the rule of law.

---

[73] L. Tzemel, "Detention of Palestinian Youths in East Jerusalem" (1977) 6 *Journal of Palestine Studies* 206, 207.

[74] Shezaf, "The IDF is Putting Palestinians on Trial for Facebook Posts." See also Defence for Children International – Palestine, Facebook Posts Land Palestinian Teens in Administrative Detention.

[75] Krebs, "Lifting the Veil of Secrecy," p. 645, note 15.

[76] See entry S: Security Prisoners, Section S.1 ("Introduction: Terminology, Figures, and Context"). For a similar report, see Brown, "Minority Report."

In contrast, the Israeli military has also arrested numerous noncitizen Palestinians despite the absence of any evidence whatsoever of their intention to violate the law. Israeli authorities consider these Palestinians to be potential offenders who might end up breaking Israeli law in one way or another at some point in the future. Some of these Palestinians have a prior conviction. Others have no criminal record, and are reportedly targeted not due to their personal behavior but, rather, their age[77] and gender – typically, they are young men. On occasion, such arrests, instead of "administrative detention," have been the response of Israeli authorities to potentially inciteful social media posts.[78] Somewhat similarly to "administrative detention," but even more so, these speculative arrests seem to assess future risks as predetermined by past record and statistical factors.

In 2015, the military commander in charge of Israel's forces in the West Bank reportedly said: "We are looking for potential terrorists." His deputy concurred: "a ... terrorist can be traced and stopped before he makes the ultimate decision to stab or run over with a car." An Israeli reporter described this, sympathetically, as "a new, creative, and almost revolutionary approach" involving attempts "to deter ... and even persuade [potential offenders] ... during interrogation. Experience shows such persuasion, before the potential terrorist executes his plot, to be very effective."[79]

Preemptive arrest thus rests on a circular logic: its alleged "effectiveness" stems from non-offending by the arrested Palestinians after their release, although there was no evidence of their intent to offend to begin with. In fact, such evidence seems to be regarded as redundant, because it is precisely the lack of evidence – and, accordingly, the lack of offending – that supposedly serves as a sort of evidence of the success of preemptive arrests. Taking this logic to its ultimate conclusion, Israel's preemptive security measures can be nothing but necessary: if, after release, the Palestinian complies with Israeli law, then the preemptive arrest is deemed successful; if, on the other hand, s/he ends up breaking the law, this reinforces the call for ever-evolving preemptive tactics. In a sense, then, preemptive arrest bears resemblance to extrajudicial execution, which, as explained in Section F.2.2,

---

[77]   For a critical analysis of age-based Israeli measures, see entry Y: Youth, and entry S: Security
       Prisoners (Sections S.1.2 and S.4).
[78]   R. Ben Yishai, "Door Pounding, Ski Mask: Report from a Palestinian House – This is How the
       IDF is Trying to Stop the Next Terrorist," *Ynet News* (December 7, 2015) [Hebrew], www.ynet
       .co.il/articles/0,7340,L-4734559,00.html.
[79]   *Ibid*. For similar reports, see A. Harel, Israel Arrested 400 Palestinians; Hirschauge and Shezaf,
       Revealed // How Israel Jails Palestinians.

functions as evidence of the need for constant prevention in the face of a supposedly never-ending security threat.[80]

F.3.3 "Mapping"

The Israeli authorities have gone beyond allegedly proactive detentions and arrests. Another measure, apparently aimed to act as a deterrent (among other things), is so-called "mappings": military incursions into homes to take the details of Palestinians who are not suspected of any wrongdoing, actual or even potential. Soldiers usually raid houses in the West Bank at night, wake up the inhabitants, inspect their IDs, write down their details, sometimes photograph or videotape them, and on some occasions make a record of the layout of the house.[81] In East Jerusalem (which Israel controversially claims to have annexed), a similar practice has been repeatedly employed by the police[82] (exemplifying the commonality between Israel's conduct in East Jerusalem and the rest of the West Bank, despite the formal legal disparity between these regions).[83] The invisibility of Israeli state violence – an issue examined in another entry[84] – is vividly evidenced here by the masks the soldiers or police often wear.[85] At the same time, the hypervisibility of this

---

[80] See supra note 44 and its accompanying text.

[81] See, e.g., ACRI, "Searches in Residents' Homes ('mappings') – An Illegal Pattern in the Territories" (February 25, 2008) [Hebrew], www.acri.org.il/he/?p=1759; Breaking the Silence, "Mappings" (October 23, 2012), www.breakingthesilence.org.il/testimonies/videos/2 7830; B'Tselem, "In answer to B'Tselem, Israeli Military Confirms: Soldiers' Actions in Entering Palestinian Homes by Night for 'Mapping' Follow Procedures" (August 10, 2015) [hereinafter: "Israeli Military Confirms"], www.btselem.org/harrasment/20150809_night_in crusions_in_qusrah; B'Tselem, "Soldiers Enter 20 Palestinian Homes Near Nablus Late at Night, Unjustifiably Intimidating the Families and Disrupting their Lives" (June 24, 2015) [hereinafter: "Soldiers Enter 20 Palestinian Homes Near Nablus"], www.btselem.org/harass ment/20150624_night_incrusions_in_nablus_area.

[82] See, e.g., N. Hasson, "Rights Group: Police Collecting Intel by 'Visiting' E. J'lem Homes at 3 A.M.," *Haaretz* (May 23, 2016) [hereinafter: "Rights Group"], www.haaretz.com/israel-news/ .premium-1.720994; N. Hasson, "Police Raid East Jerusalem Houses Every Night," *Haaretz* (February 3, 2017) [Hebrew], www.haaretz.co.il/news/local/.premium-1.3626076.

[83] On further manifestation of this commonality, see entry Y: Youth, Section Y.3 ("The Rule of Exception beyond Israeli Military Law"). On continuities, connections, and parallels between Israel's formally disparate military and civil legal systems, see entry O: Outside/Inside, Section O.3 ("Israeli Law Does Not Stop at the Border").

[84] See entry V: Violence, Section V.3 ("Invisible Violence").

[85] See, e.g., B'Tselem, "Masked Soldiers Enter Palestinian Homes in Dead of Night, Order Residents to Wake their Children, and Photograph the Children" (March 24, 2015), www .btselem.org/hebron/20150324_night_search_in_hebron; B'Tselem, Soldiers enter 20 Palestinian homes near Nablus; Hasson, Rights Group; Hasson, Police Raid East Jerusalem Houses Every Night.

violence[86] manifests itself in the photographs and videos the Israeli forces take, as well as their desire to see up-close the inside of Palestinian homes.

Typically, "mappings" are conducted in houses or areas on which the military has little or no prior intelligence. The goal seems to be to proactively gather as much information as possible, in case it proves to be legally or operationally useful at some point in the future. As one former soldier who was frequently involved in "mappings" has described it, this practice

> wasn't focused on a specific place where there was intelligence about a fugitive hiding or about a terrorist. . . . When you set out to these mappings you are told in advance that they are . . . deliberately directed toward . . . people that are known to be innocent of any wrongdoing, known to have nothing to do with terrorists, and with the only objective of having informa-tion about everyone. And we, trained artillerymen . . . [who had no] high combat training in urban warfare, . . . knew right from the start that there's no way we were being sent to a dangerous house. . . . My commanders and the GSS believed that . . . everyone is a potential future terrorist, and that's why we have to know everything about them all.[87]

At the same time, other reports suggest that this practice serves another purpose: showing presence. An ex-soldier who was asked to take pictures of Palestinian inhabitants during "mappings" argues "The mappings were designed to make the Palestinians feel that we were there all the time. . . . I had the pictures [I had taken] for around a month. . . . [N]o commander asked about them, no intelligence officer took them. . . . At one point I deleted the pictures, I realized it was all a joke."[88]

Another former soldier similarly recalled, on a different occasion: "I don't think any mapping information ever went any higher [i.e., to the intelligence agencies]. I don't remember ever sending any photographs from the camera."[89] A possible interpretation of these accounts is that they illustrate Israel's "effective ineffectiveness," a mode of operation analyzed in another part of this book.[90] Alternatively, these testimonies may suggest that rather

---

[86]   On the hypervisibility of state violence, see, e.g., H. Viterbo, "Seeing Torture Anew: A Transnational Reconceptualization of State Torture and Visual Evidence" (2014) 50:2 *Stanford Journal of International Law* 281, 291–292, 295–297; N. Whitty, "Soldier Photography of Detainee Abuse in Iraq: Digital Technology, Human Rights and the Death of Baha Mousa" (2010) 10(4) *Human Rights Law Review* 689, 698–708.

[87]   Breaking the Silence, "Mappings."

[88]   Breaking the Silence, "Pictures at 3 AM," www.breakingthesilence.org.il/testimonies/videos/70540.

[89]   Breaking the Silence, "An element of overachievement" (May 6, 2011), www.breakingthesilence.org.il/testimonies/videos/14959.

[90]   See entry M: Military Courts, Section M.3 ("Un/certainty governance").

than being ineffective in collecting intelligence, "mappings" effectively fulfill a different function altogether: deterring Palestinian misdeeds through displays of constant and ubiquitous military presence.[91] Either way, whether for the purpose of preemptive information gathering or performative deterrence,[92] this future-oriented tactic humiliates, harasses, intimidates, and infringes on the privacy of blameless Palestinians.

"Mapping," preemptive arrest, and "administrative detention" are interrelated and mutually complementary. An Israeli colonel explains how they all fit into the military's preemptive strategy:

> We started … constructing a profile of [the potential terrorist] based on past attacks. Where does he live? How old is he? What is his motivation? We started [targeting] … those who met this profile. We … mapped risk groups of 15- to 25-year-olds … and started inspecting their Facebook pages. … Those we could [arrest], we arrested. Those we had no reason to arrest, we warned. For others, we mapped their home – arriving every night and searching it. We also exerted pressure on their families. … And the statistics started showing a decline [in terrorist attacks].[93]

This future-oriented strategy can provoke, and in some cases even initiate, the threats it purports to minimize, as explained thus far.

F.4 CONCLUSION

Prevention, deterrence, preemption, and the preoccupation with possible eventualities and risks have been central to Israel's control over the West Bank and Gaza Strip. This entry has shed critical light on two specific areas of such future-oriented policy and practice. The first – preemptive attacks – includes purportedly preemptive military strikes, extrajudicial assassinations, and "warning" tactics. The second – a penalty of potential threats – comprises "administrative detentions," preemptive arrests, and house "mappings."

---

[91] On the military's policy of deterrence through displays of presence, see also Breaking the Silence, *Occupation of the Territories: Israeli Soldier Testimonies 2000–2010* (2011), pp. 29, 36–38, www.breakingthesilence.org.il/wp-content/uploads/2011/02/Occupation_of_the_Territories_Eng.pdf; M. Zagor, "'I am the Law'! – Perspectives of Legality and Illegality in the Israeli Army" (2010) 43 *Israel Law Review* 551, 573–574.

[92] In a reply to a letter from the Israeli NGO B'Tselem, the military's spokesperson defined the objective of "mappings," vaguely, as serving "an operational need." See B'Tselem, Israeli Military Confirms.

[93] Y. Yehoshua, "Suddenly, A Regiment Commander Questions the Lack of IDF Backing for the Shooting Soldier. Once I Present the Facts, He Understands," *Yediot Aharonot* (April 28, 2016) [Hebrew], www.yediot.co.il/articles/0,7340,L-4796895,00.html.

In the process of tackling perceived threats, these measures have brought about additional and often greater harms and threats, wittingly or not. Israel's preemptive war in 1967 thus ultimately created decades of violence and suffering in Israel/Palestine. Extrajudicial assassinations and "warning" tactics have caused civilian casualties and injuries in the name of protecting civilians. "Administrative detention," preemptive arrests, and house "mappings" each, in different ways, deprive Palestinians of their liberty, or intimidate them, on the basis of either undisclosed evidence or no concrete evidence at all, and might therefore foster Palestinian animosity toward Israel. Israel's prevention, preemption, and deterrence practices, then, are no less productive than pre-clusive, consistently engendering new perilous futures.

Some of these practices also evince a circular logic, deeming them eternally necessary regardless of the extent of actual threats and evidence. In particular, in preemptive arrests, non-offending by the arrested Palestinians after their release is regarded as proof of the effectiveness of this measure, even though there was no evidence of their intent to offend to begin with. If, after release, the Palestinian ends up breaking Israeli law, this reinforces the call for ever-evolving preemption. Somewhat similarly, extrajudicial executions function as evidence of a supposedly never-ending security threat, which in turn is seen as requiring constant prevention. Prevention and preemption can thus become self-affirming and self-propelling.

Further, as this entry has demonstrated, some of Israel's future-oriented practices potentially serve objectives that are entirely different from, or additional to, their stated ones. Israeli military attacks on the Gaza Strip may seek to politically fragment Palestinian society. The Israeli military's "warning" tactics allegedly provide a legal defense against possible accusations of indiscriminate military attacks on populated areas. The procedural laxity of "administrative detention" makes it possible for Israeli security authorities to avoid the hassle of trial hearings. And "mappings" are a way for Israel to display a constant and ubiquitous military presence. In this regard, these practices achieve one of two things: either they fulfill a function that is not directly about prevention, deterrence, or preemption, or they target a different threat from their purported one.

Also apparent throughout this entry has been the sanitized terminology that conceals the future harm and threats brought about by these measures. The phrase "targeted killing" and its Hebrew equivalent "focused preemption" mask the often nontargeted and nonfocused nature of these political and extrajudicial assassinations. Similarly, behind the pleasant-sounding term "roof knocking" are dangerous bombings used to thwart accusations of civilian casualties. Though "detention" implies a temporary suspension of liberty due to a known suspicion, "administrative detention" actually refers to potentially indefinite imprisonment without charge or trial. "Mapping" likewise denotes the intimidation of innocent citizens. It is through this sanitized language, among other things, that the future-oriented practices to which Israeli authorities subject Palestinians in the West Bank and Gaza Strip claim legitimacy.

As touched upon in this entry, some critics lament what they describe as the illegality of Israel's future-oriented measures. Contrary to this legalistic criticism, and in line with the discussion of law's violence elsewhere in this book,[94] this entry has demonstrated that these measures eagerly utilize legal mechanisms, categories, and arguments. The invocation of Israel's "warning" tactics to retroactively justify indiscriminate military attacks (through a controversial application of the legal distinction between civilians and combatants) is one example. Other practices, such as so-called "targeted killing" and "administrative detention," have received the Israeli supreme court's stamp of approval.[95] As for Israel's penality of potential threats, while bypassing trial hearings, it conveniently remains under the auspices of law enforcement. In addition, rather than investigating alleged violations of the court's ruling on extrajudicial executions, the Israeli legal system has prosecuted and convicted those who revealed the potentially incriminating information.[96] Indeed, as the political geographer Louise Amoore has observed, "[i]t is not the case that 'law recedes' as risk advances, but rather that law itself authorizes a specific and particular mode of risk management."[97] This complicity of law in Israel's future-oriented practices warrants skepticism toward calls by some critics for a "return to law."

Moreover, prevention, preemption, and deterrence practices such as those deployed by Israeli authorities in the West Bank and Gaza Strip do not represent the abandonment of "normal" law. Rather, they resonate with, extend, and perfect longstanding legal mechanisms. With regard to the penality of potential threats in particular, criminal statutes since the very beginning of the nineteenth century have authorized indefinite preventive detention.[98] Numerous laws have also long attached criminal liability to status

---

[94]   See especially entry V: Violence, as well as entry L: Lawfare and Section 2.3. ("Critiquing Against/With the Law") in the Introduction.

[95]   In addition, "administrative detention" is legally enshrined in Article 78 of Geneva Convention Relative to the Protection of Civilian Persons in the Time of War, Geneva, August 12, 1949, 75 UNTS 287. For further discussion, see entry A: Assigned Residence, Section A.1. ("The Legal Parameters of 'Assigned Residence'").

[96]   See also Section V.3 ("Invisible Violence") of the entry V: Violence.

[97]   Amoore, "Risk before Justice," p. 850.

[98]   M. Finnane and S. Donkin, "Fighting Terror with Law? Some other Genealogies of Pre-emption" (2013) 2 *International Journal of Crime and Justice* 3, 5–7, 10–11.

or associations rather than specific individual actions. Further, the law of inchoate offenses criminalizes actions that are considered to have been undertaken toward a future offense.[99] Expert psychiatric opinion in criminal proceedings, as the social theorist Michel Foucault characterized it, "show[s] how the individual resembles his crime before he has committed it . . . [by] revealing what could be called a parapathological series [of past acts that are improper, albeit not unlawful]."[100] What practices such as those examined in this entry therefore do is not reverse or undermine "normal" law, but lay bare its myth. At the same time, the wide scope, frequency, and impact of these mechanisms in the West Bank and Gaza Strip, and Israel's ever-growing emphasis on nonspecific potential threats, are remarkable. The relation between Israel's future-oriented measures and supposedly "normal" law is thus best understood not as a dichotomy between exception and rule but, rather, as a continuity with a consequential difference in scope and depth.[101]

---

[99] McCulloch and Wilson, *Pre-Crime, Pre-Emption, Precaution.*
[100] M. Foucault, *Abnormal: Lectures at the Collège de France, 1974–1975*, V. Marchetti and A. Salomoni (eds.), A. I. Davidson (trans.) (London and New York: Verso, 2003), pp. 19–20.
[101] A similar observation is made in McCulloch and Wilson, *Pre-Crime, Pre-Emption, Precaution*, p. 18 (arguing that contemporary "pre-crime laws replicate and [at the same time] depart from" some "forward-looking aspects of traditional criminal law").

G

Geneva Law

Orna Ben-Naftali

G.1 THE NORMATIVE FRAMEWORK OF BELLIGERENT OCCUPATION

G.1.1 *General Overview: The Road from The Hague to Geneva*

The international law of belligerent occupation is part of international humanitarian law (IHL), setting out the rights and obligations of an occupying power vis-à-vis the occupied population. It comes into play once a foreign military force exercises effective control over a territory, despite having no sovereign title over that territory and without the sovereign's volition.[1]

The relevant normative framework governing belligerent occupation consists of the 1907 Hague Regulations, the Fourth Geneva Convention Relative to the Protection of Civilians Persons in Times of War,[2] and its 1977 Additional Protocol I.[3] These documents apply concurrently[4] and

---

[1] E. Benvenisti, *The International Law of Occupation*, 2nd edn. (Princeton: Princeton University Press, 2004), p. 4. The application of the law of belligerent occupation is triggered, in the language of Article 42 of the Hague Regulations, once a "territory is actually placed under the authority of a hostile army. The occupation extends only to the territory where such authority has been established and can be exercised." The Hague Convention (IV) Respecting the Laws and Customs of War on Land and its Annex: Regulations Concerning the Laws and Customs of War on Land, The Hague, October 18, 1907, 205 CTS 277; 36 Stat 2277 [hereinafter: The Hague Regulations].

[2] Geneva Convention Relative to the Protection of Civilian Persons in the Time of War, Geneva, August 12, 1949, 75 UNTS 287 [hereinafter: GC IV].

[3] Protocol Additional to the Geneva Conventions of 12 August 1949, and relating to the Protection of Victims of International Armed Conflicts (Additional Protocol I), Geneva, June 8, 1977, 1125 UNTS 3 [hereinafter: AP I].

[4] Article 154 of the GC IV provides that the Hague Regulations continue to apply. Article 3 of the AP I stipulates that it supplements the GC.

have gradually formed a single system[5] often referred to as the *Geneva Law*.[6] Over the past decades, it has been accepted that IHL provides the specific, but not the exclusive law governing occupation (*lex specialis*), and that it is complemented by international human rights law (IHRL).[7]

The amalgamation of the Hague Regulations and the Geneva Law, coupled with the confluence of IHL with IHRL, attest to continuity but also to change over time in both experience and legal consciousness. Continuity is evident mainly in two aspects: the need to balance between military needs and humanitarian concerns, and the privileged position sovereign states still retain, under these documents, in relation to other actors. Both aspects, however, have not been immune to change, reflected in two major and interrelated developments. The first development is the broadening of the qualifying conditions for combatant status to include fighters additional to those belonging to states' armies,[8] and the related expansion of the role of nonstate actors in the Geneva Law.[9] The second development is the shift in focus from preserving the interests of the ousted sovereign in the Hague Regulations, to protecting the rights of the occupied population in the GC IV. The latter are designated as *protected persons*, a designation which excludes nationals of the occupying power, and is absent from the Hague Regulations.[10]

The specific provisions of the documents comprising the Geneva Law, detail the three basic principles of the regime of belligerent occupation.[11] The first principle is that effective control by foreign military forces suspends,

---

[5] In The Nuclear Weapons Advisory Opinion, the ICJ noted that the Hague Regulations and the GCs "have become so closely interrelated that they have gradually formed a single complex system known today as international humanitarian law." See Legality of the Threat or Use of Nuclear Weapons, Advisory Opinion, 1996 ICJ 226, ¶ 75.

[6] Y. Dinstein, *The Conduct of Hostilities under the Law of Armed Conflict* (Cambridge: Cambridge University Press, 2004), pp. 9–13.

[7] See, e.g., Legality of Nuclear Weapons, ¶ 25; Consequences of the Construction of a Wall in the Occupied Palestinian Territory, Advisory Opinion, 2004 ICJ 136, ¶ 106; Armed Activities on the Territory of the Congo (Democratic Republic of the Congo v. Uganda), Judgment, 2005 ICJ Rep 168, ¶¶ 216–217. See generally, O. Ben-Naftali (ed.), *International Human Rights and Humanitarian Law* (Oxford: Oxford University Press, 2011).

[8] For a discussion of this expansion, see entry C: Combatants.

[9] Article 96(3) of the AP I allows national liberation movements to deposit a unilateral declaration indicating a willingness to abide by the GC. It should further be noted in this context that while States continue to enjoy a privileged position, various nonstate actors are increasingly playing a role in the implementation of the Geneva Law. See F. Mégret, "The Universality of the Geneva Conventions," in A. Clapham, P. Gaeta, and M. Sassoli (eds.), *The 1949 Geneva Conventions – A Commentary* (Oxford: Oxford University Press, 2015), pp. 669, 686.

[10] Article 4 of GC IV.

[11] Section 2.2 of the Introduction provides an exposé of these principles.

but does not transfer sovereignty.[12] Under current international law, and in view of the principle of self-determination, sovereignty remains vested in the occupied people. The prohibition on annexing an occupied territory is the normative consequence of this principle.[13] The second principle is that an occupation is a form of trust, the beneficiaries of which are the occupied people,[14] and which precludes the introduction of major systemic change.[15] The third principle is that an occupation is a temporary form of control, a principle implicit in both the principle that occupation does not confer title and in the conservation principle. The notion of limited duration further coheres with the presumed exceptionality of the regime, and highlights the need to resume as quickly as possible the normal international order.[16]

The customary character of the Hague Regulations has already been determined in the post–World War II trials of the major war criminals.[17] To the

---

[12] Article 43 of the Hague Regulations' reference to "the authority of the legitimate power having in fact passed into the hands of the occupant" expresses the distinction between a legitimate sovereign and a de facto occupying power. Despite the subtlety with which the distinction is made, it was already clear at the time that effective control does not transfer sovereignty. See Benvenisti, *International Law of Occupation*, 8 and references in note 9. Article 47 of the GC IV provides that "Protected persons ... shall not be deprived, in any case or in any manner whatsoever, of the benefits of the present Convention by any change introduced, as the result of the occupation of a territory, into the institutions or government of the said territory, nor by any agreement concluded between the authorities of the occupied territories and the Occupying Power, nor by any annexation by the latter of the whole or part of the occupied territory."

[13] S. P. Sharma, *Territorial Acquisition, Disputes and International Law* (Leiden: Kluwer Law International 1997) p. 148.

[14] Construction of a Wall, ¶ 88; Separate Opinion of Judge Koroma, ¶ 2, explicitly stated that occupied territories "constitute ... a sacred trust, which must be administered as a whole in the interests both of the inhabitants and the legitimate sovereign or the duly constituted successor in title"; cf. Separate Opinion of Judge Higgins, § 2; Separate Opinion of Judge Koojimans, ¶ 33.

[15] The basic rule regulating the occupant's governmental authority is articulated in Article 43 of the Hague Regulation and in Article 64 of the GC IV. Article 43 of the Hague Regulations delimits the occupant's authority "to restore and ensure, as far as possible, public order and safety/civil life, while respecting, unless absolutely prevented, the laws in force in the country." The authoritative French version uses the phrase "l'ordre et la vie publics." The English translation reads: "public order and safety." Since the authoritative text of the Hague Regulations is in the French language, the English text has no legal standing. For the discussion of the difference between the French and the English versions of Article 43 of the Hague Regulations, see Y. Dinstein, "Legislation under Article 43 of the Hague Regulations: Belligerent Occupation and Peace-Building," *Harvard Program on Humanitarian Policy and Conflict Research, Occasional Paper No.1* (2004) pp. 2–4. The language of Article 64 of the GC IV more permissively authorizes the occupying power to modify existing laws when such modification is necessary to enable it to fulfill its obligations. The latter are more specified and detailed in the GC IV than in the Hague Regulations.

[16] See entry T: Temporary/Indefinite.

[17] Trial of German Major War Criminals 1946 CMD 6964, Misc/No 12 at 65; In re Hirota (1948) 15 Ann. Digest, 356, 366.

extent that the *GC IV* contained new rules, in addition to those it had codified in 1949, it is now recognized that they have evolved into customary rules.[18] Most of the rules in the *AP I* are equally considered to reflect customary norms.[19] From a doctrinal perspective, the customary status of norms is significant for a variety of reasons: Such norms are perceived as embedded in the international society, reflecting, as they advance, an ethos of universally held values; it is commonly accepted that states cannot opt out of them unless they qualify as persistent objectors; and they are considered enforceable in domestic law, even in states which adopted the common-law rule that requires a legislative act of parliament to incorporate treaty law.[20]

G.1.2 *Israel and the Framing of the Law of Belligerent Occupation: Two Roads Diverged*[21]

From the perspective of the Geneva Law, Israeli control over the OPT had an auspicious beginning: on June 7, 1967, the military commander issued a proclamation that he had assumed all governmental powers in the area, and that the prevailing law would remain in force, subject to any orders he would promulgate. Attached to this proclamation was a security provisions order. Its detailed provisions for the military rule in the area, including the

---

[18]   Case concerning Military and Paramilitary Activities in and against Nicaragua (Nicaragua v. United States), ICJ Judgment on the Merits, June 27, 1986 ICJ Rep (1986), ¶ 218; Partial Award: Prisoners of War, Eritrea's Claim 17, Eritrea-Ethiopia Claims Commission (EECC) July 1, 2003, ¶ 39. The court based the customary nature of the Geneva Conventions on their universal ratification. See Legality of Nuclear Weapons, ¶ 79; Eritrea's Claim, ¶ 40; Prisoners of War, Ethiopia's Claim 4, ¶ 31. In Legality of Nuclear Weapons, ¶ 82, the ICJ further based the customary nature of the Conventions on the fact that the denunciation clauses had never been used. Ample practice, as extracted from military manuals, state legislations, and similar sources that correspond to the Conventions rules, further attest to their customary nature. For the sources comprising practice, see J.M. Hanckaerts and L. Doswald-Beck (eds.), *Customary International Humanitarian Law* (reprinted with corrections, Cambridge: Cambridge University Press, 2009), vol. I, p. xxxviii.

[19]   174 states are now parties to the *AP I*. Note further that Eritrea-Ethiopia Claims Commission decided to work on the assumption that both the GC and the *AP I* were customary, determining that in case of a dispute as to the customary status of a provision of the GC, the party who challenges the assumption would have the burden of proof and in the case of the *AP I*, the Commission would shoulder it. Partial Award: Prisoners of War, ¶ 41 re/ Eritrea's Claim and ¶ 32 re/ Ethiopia's claim.

[20]   Note that under Article 27 of the Vienna Convention of the Law of Treaties, which itself reflects customary international law, a party to a treaty "may not invoke the provisions of its internal law as justification for its failure to perform a treaty." Vienna Convention on the Law of Treaties, May 23, 1969, 1155 UNTS 331.

[21]   R. Frost, "The Road Not Taken," in *Collected Poems of Robert Frost* (Garden City: Halcyon House, 1942), p. 131.

establishment of military tribunals that "shall observe the provisions of the Geneva Convention of 12 August, 1949 Relative to the Protection of Civilian Persons in Time of War with respect to legal proceedings, and in the case of conflict between this Order and the said Convention, the provisions of the Convention shall prevail."[22]

The order, prepared well in advance of the actual occupation, reflected the legal assumption that the eventuality of an occupation will be regulated by the GC IV,[23] to which Israel is party.[24] Given that Israel did not incorporate it into its domestic legislation, that it follows the common-law rule requiring such incorporation for treaties to be part of the law of the land, and that, at the time, the customary character of the GC IV was less certain than in later years, the incorporation of the GC IV into the military legislation was designed to ensure its applicability and enforceability.[25]

Seemingly promising beginnings, much like seemingly benevolent intentions, do not necessarily pave the road to a happy end. This legal commitment to the application of the GC IV was short lived: Governmental references to the territories as being "liberated"[26] rather than occupied, and the revival of the biblical names "Judea and Samaria" to substitute the designation of the area otherwise known as the "West Bank," indicated a nascent "discursive annexation" of the OPT into Israel by virtue of historical rights,[27] and the emergence of the narrative of Jewish sovereignty over the area. The provision committing to the application of the GC IV was revoked in August 1967.[28]

---

[22] Security Provisions Order (West Bank – 1967), Article 35, in 1 *Proclamations, Orders and Appointments of the Judea and Samaria Command* 5. See D. Kretzmer, *The Occupation of Justice* (Albany: SUNY Press, 2002), p. 32.

[23] M. Shamgar, "Legal Concepts and Problems of the Israeli Military Government – The Initial Stage," in M. Shamgar (ed.) *Military Government in the Territories Administered by Israel 1967–1980, The Legal Aspects* (Jerusalem: Harry Sacher Institute for Legislative Research and Comparative Law, 1982), p. 13.

[24] Israel signed the Convention in 1949 and ratified it in 1951.

[25] Kretzmer, *The Occupation of Justice*, p. 32. Note that Israel originally adopted a monist approach to international law. See CrA 174/54 *Stampfer v. Attorney General* (1956) 23 *Israel Law Review* 284, 289. That approach was forsaken in favor of the common-law approach once security consideration came into play, see CA 148/55 *Custodian of Absentee Property v. Samra* (1956) 22 *Israel Law Review* 5.

[26] E.g., Minister of Justice Yaacov Shimshon Shapira relating to the territories as within Israel's sovereignty, 49 Divrei HaKnesset 2420 (June 27, 1967), cited in Kretzmer, *The Occupation of Justice*, p. 32 note 6.

[27] I. Zertal and A. Eldar, *The Lords of the Land*, V. Eden (trans.) (New York: Nation Books, 2007), p. 336. For an exposé of this narrative, see entry N: Nomos.

[28] See A. Rubinstein, "The Changing Status of the 'Territories' (West Bank and Gaza): from Escrow to Legal Mongrel" (1988) 8 *Tel Aviv Studies in Law* 59.

Legal mandarins, intent on arming political will with legal ammunition, were quick to overhaul their tool box: Already on June 22, 1967, Michael Comay, then political advisor to the minister of foreign affairs, recommended in a classified document that the term "occupation" be avoided. The reason given was to dodge discussions with the ICRC regarding the status of the territories, and to prevent its free access to the Palestinian inhabitants.[29] A secret cable written in 1968 by Michael Comay and Theodor Meron, then the legal advisor to the ministry of foreign affairs, and sent to the then Israeli Ambassador to the United States, Izhak Rabin, explains that "our consistent line is to evade discussing with foreign elements the situation in the administered territories on the basis of the Geneva Convention."[30] Two underlying considerations are explicitly stated. The first concerns violations of the GC IV by Israel: "express recognition on our part of the applicability of the Geneva Convention, will highlight serious issues with respect to the Convention in terms of blasting homes, deportation, settlements etc." The second consideration is that in order "to leave all options regarding borders open, we must not acknowledge that our status in the administered territories is simply that of an occupying power."

This was the genesis of Israel's legal thesis that the GC IV does not formally apply to the OPT, but that Israel would abide by its humanitarian provisions. This thesis is discussed and critiqued in Section G.2. The HCJ embraced this legal thesis. The interpretative horizon opened up by the coupling of the normative indeterminacy of the applicable law with the indefinite duration of the occupation, made it possible for the court not only to provide a legal basis for the authority of the military commander in the OPT, but also to expand it and facilitate its exercise. A critical review of the court's jurisprudence on the applicable law and its interpretation, substantiating this assessment, is the focus of Section G.3. Section G.4 concludes.

G.2 THE ROAD NOT TAKEN[31]

The thesis that the GC IV is inapplicable to the territories conquered in 1967 rests on a certain reading of Common Article 2 of the Geneva Conventions.

The first paragraph of Common Article 2 provides that "the present Convention shall apply to all cases of declared war or to any other armed conflict which may arise between two or more of the High Contracting Parties, even if the state of war is not recognized by one of them." The second

---

[29]   https://akevot.org.il/en/article/comay-memo-terminology/.
[30]   http://akevot.in/GCIVcable.   [31]   Frost, "The Road Not Taken."

paragraph provides that "the Convention shall also apply to all cases of partial or total occupation of the territory of a High Contracting Party, even if the said occupation meets with no armed resistance." In 1968, in a feat of legal ingenuity, Professor Yehuda Blum proposed a cumulative reading of these two paragraphs, positing that since Jordan was not a lawful sovereign in the West Bank (and that Egypt never claimed sovereign title over the Gaza Strip), the territories were not taken from "a High Contracting Party" and, ergo, Israel is not obligated to apply the GC IV.[32] Curiously, given that the Hague Regulations also refer to the territory of the "Hostile State" and to a "legitimate power,"[33] the same argument was not advanced in reference to them.

Israel's official position embraced this reading of Common Article 2. It has maintained since that it is under no obligation to apply the GC IV to the territories, but that it would unilaterally undertake to observe its humanitarian provisions.[34] No specification of these provisions was ever provided. The HCJ, as shall be discussed in the following section, reiterated the government's position, including its commitment to abide by the humanitarian provisions of the GC IV in innumerable decisions. It has applied its provisions routinely – including provisions devoid of any humanitarian content[35] – but it has never determined its applicability de jure, never required a strict standard of proof to determine the customary nature of specific provisions,[36] and never conceded that, whatever doubts may have existed in the past regarding the customary nature of the GC IV, they are widely considered to have been all put to rest.

To the extent that this unilateral undertaking was designed to convince both the world and the Palestinians that Israel is a humanitarian occupier concerned with the well-being of protected persons, and that its legal system merits trust, the recipients of this message failed to be impressed: the Israeli position was rejected by the relevant institutions of the international

---

[32] Y. Z. Blum, "The Missing Reversioner: Reflections on the Status of Judea and Samaria" (1968) 3 *Israel Law Review* 279; Shamgar, "Legal Concepts and Problems of the Israeli Military Government," pp. 33–34.

[33] N. Bar-Yaacov, "The Applicability of the Laws of War to Judea and Samaria (the West Bank) and the Gaza Strip" (1990) 24 *Israel Law Review* 485, 492–493.

[34] M. Shamgar, "The Observance of International Law in the Administered Territories" (1971) 1 *Israel Yearbook of Human Rights* 117, 266.

[35] E.g., Article 78 of the GC IV (authorizing the Occupying Power to assign the residence or intern protected persons for "imperative reasons of security") was applied by the HCJ in HCJ 7015/02 *Ajuri* v. *Commander of the IDF in Judea and Samaria* (2002) 56(6) PD 352 [Hebrew; English translation available at http://elyon1.court.gov.il/Files_ENG/02/150/070/A15/02070150 .A15.pdf]. For a discussion see entry A: Assigned Residence.

[36] HCJ 606/78 *Ayub* v. *The Minister of Defense* (1979) 33(2) PD 113 [Hebrew]; HCJ 69/81 *Abu Aita* v. *Commander of the Judea and Samaria Region* (1983) 37(2) PD 197, 238–239 [Hebrew].

community,[37] including the ICJ[38] and the ICRC,[39] as well as by the vast majority of international legal scholars.[40]

The major, though not the only reason for the less than splendid isolation of the Israeli position, is that the reading of the first two paragraphs of Common Article 2 as providing alternative rather than cumulative conditions for the Conventions' application, advances the humanitarian objectives of the Conventions. Given that the main impetus for the GC IV was to advance greater humanitarian protection than was hitherto provided, an interpretation which supports this objective is commonly considered as preferable to one that does not.

Israel's counterargument that the GC IV is designed to protect not only the humanitarian interests of the occupied population, but also the interests of the ousted sovereign[41] also failed to elicit enthusiasm: First, it does not distinguish between the primary and the secondary purposes of the law, let alone give preference to the former. Second, the genuineness of this rationale seemed dubious given that Israel did not make this argument with respect to the Hague Regulations, a document far more concerned with the interests of the ousted sovereign than with the protection of individuals.[42]

The official Israeli position since 1967 has thus been neither to deny that the Palestinian territories are under belligerent occupation nor to admit the application of the Geneva Law as a matter of a binding international obligation. In effect, it did deny that the territories were occupied and reject the de jure applicability of both the GC IV and the Hague Regulations, but simultaneously it never contested the application of the latter, and relied on it in its arguments before the HCJ.[43] After all, it had to retain a legal basis for the

---

[37]   E.g., GA Res 32/91 [A-C], UN Doc A/RES/32/91 [A-C] (December 13, 1977); SC Res 237, UN Doc S/RES/237 (June 14, 1967); SC Res 799, UN Doc S/RES/48 (1992).

[38]   Construction of a Wall, ¶ 101, states as follows: "Israel and Jordan were parties to the convention when the 1967 armed conflict broke out. The court accordingly finds that than convention is applicable in the Palestinian territories which before the conflict lay to the east of the Green Line and which, during that conflict, were occupied by Israel, there being no need for any enquiry into the precise prior status of those territories."

[39]   J. S. Pictet (ed.), *The Geneva Conventions of 12 August 1949, Commentary – IV Geneva Convention Relative to the Protection of Civilian Persons in Time of War* (Geneva: International Committee of the Red Cross, 1958), p. 22; ICRC, *Unresolved Problems Covered by the Fourth Geneva Convention, 1975 annual report*, p. 22.

[40]   See, e.g., A. Roberts, "Prolonged Military Occupations: The Israeli-Occupied Territories since 1967" (1990) 84 *American Journal of International Law* 44, 64; E. R. Cohen, *Human Rights in the Israeli-Occupied Territories 1967–1982* (Manchester: Manchester University Press, 1985), p. 53; G. E. Bisharat "Courting Justice? Legitimation in Lawyering under Israeli Occupation" (1995) 20 *Law and Social Inquiry* 349.

[41]   Shamgar, "Observance of International Law," pp. 265–266.

[42]   Benvenisti, *The International Law of Occupation*, p. 110.   [43]   *Ibid.*, p. 108.

exercise of authority by its long arm, the military commander, an authority grounded in the law of belligerent occupation.

This occupation/nonoccupation and de jure/de facto indeterminacies generated a normative obfuscation, which the jurisprudence of the HCJ did little to clear. Indeed, it enabled the court to assist the government in holding the rope at both ends, advancing the political vision of Greater Israel while ostensibly upholding the law of belligerent occupation, to minimize the wrath of the international community. The following section focuses on this jurisprudence relative to both the applicable law (G.3.1) and to its interpretation (G.3.2).

G.3 THE JURISPRUDENCE OF THE HCJ: I COULD TRAVEL BOTH[44]

G.3.1 *The Determination of the Applicable Law: The Road from Geneva to Jerusalem*

During the first decade of the occupation, there were relatively few petitions emanating from the OPT, and it was possible for the court to adjudge them without determining the applicable law. The reason was that the state declared in its responses that the military commander complied with the provisions of both The Hague Regulations and the *GC IV*, without specifying that he did that as a matter of binding law. In effect, the court was invited to evade determining the applicable law, an invitation it had accepted.[45]

The first time the court explicitly determined the applicability of the law of belligerent occupation to the OPT, occurred in the "landmark case"[46] known as *Elon Moreh*:[47] the petition concerned the authority of the military commander to requisition land in order to establish a settlement on grounds other

---

[44] Frost, "The Road Not Taken." Note that the original line is "I could not travel both."

[45] *Christian Society for the Holy Places* v. *Minister of Defense* (1971) 26(1) PD 574 [Hebrew; English summary available at (1972) 2 *Israel Yearbook of Human Rights* 354]. This was the first petition from the OPT that came before the HCJ. See Kretzmer, *The Occupation of Justice*, pp. 7–9.

[46] R. Shamir, "'Landmark Cases' and the Reproduction of Legitimacy: The Case of Israel's High Court of Justice" (1990) 24 *Law and Society Review* 781.

[47] HCJ 390/79 *Dweikat* v. *Government of Israel* (1979) 34(1) PD 1 [Hebrew] (the court ruled that confiscation of private Palestinian lands for the establishment of a settlement was illegal, as the military commander acted ultra vires by considering political considerations rather than military ones. The court reached its decision in the light of the settlers' argument – which was not repeated in later cases – that the raison d'etre of the settlement was the divine command to conquer the land of Israel).

than military requirements. One of the arguments presented to the court was that the law of belligerent occupation is inapplicable because the West Bank, having been promised by God to the Jewish people, is not occupied.[48] The court, in rejecting the authority of the military commander to requisition land in order to establish a settlement on grounds other than military requirements, refused to impregnate the law with this narrative. It determined that had the argument that the law of belligerent occupation does not apply been accepted, the inescapable conclusion would have to be that the military commander acted without authority.[49] In innumerable judgments since, the HCJ unequivocally held that the sole source of the legal authority of the military commander is the law of belligerent occupation.[50]

The applicability of the law of belligerent occupation does not, however, derive from a need to establish a source for the authority of the military commander. The latter is a consequence of, not a reason for its applicability. It was only about a decade later that the court provided another basis for the applicable normative framework. It had to decide whether the military administration ended once the 1979 peace agreement between Egypt and Israel was signed, thus rendering a deportation order issued by the military commander ultra vires. The court determined that the law of belligerent occupation applies because Israel exercises effective control over the area.[51] The application of a factual test for the applicability of the law of belligerent occupation, while grounded in legal doctrine, simultaneously implied that the issue was not a legal matter. In this manner, the thorny issue of sovereignty over the territory was extracted from the sphere of legal deliberations.[52]

The determination of a factual basis for the applicability of the normative framework is equally relevant to both The Hague Regulations and the GC IV. The court, however, decided not to take that road to Geneva.

[48] For a discussion of this case, see entry J: Jewish Settlements.
[49] *Dweikat*, p. 12. See also D. Kretzmer, "Bombshell for the Settlement Enterprise in Levy Report," *Haaretz* (July 10, 2012), www.haaretz.com/opinion/bombshell-for-the-settlement-enterprise-in-levy-report-1.450170.
[50] *Unprecedented: A Legal Analysis of the Report of the Committee to Examine the Status of Building in Judea and Samaria [the West Bank] ("The Levy Committee") – International and Administrative Aspects* (Tel Aviv: Yesh Din – Volunteers for Human Rights and The Emile Zola Chair for Human Rights, 2014) http://din-online.info/pdf/yd1e.pdf, annex A, lists more than 60 examples [Hebrew]. For the clearest pronouncement see HCJ 393/82 *Jam'iyyat Iskan* v. *IDF Commander in Judea and Samaria* (1982) 37(4) PD 785, 792 [Hebrew; hereinafter: Iskan II]. For a discussion of this judgment see Section G.3.2.
[51] HCJ 785/87 *Al-Affu* v. *Commander of the IDF forces in the West Bank* (1988) 42(2) PD 4, 49–50 [Hebrew; English translation available at (1990) 29 ILM 139].
[52] Zertal and Eldar, *Lords of the Land*, p. 339.

It determined that the Hague Regulations, which reflect customary international law, apply, but that the *GC IV*, which is treaty law, cannot apply
without incorporating legislation.[53] The court was cognizant of the fact that
while the Israeli legal system does follow the common-law tradition, there is
no requirement for the legislature to approve treaties because Israel's practice, a practice the court itself approved, is that legislative acquiescence is
sufficient for the determination of treaty ratification.[54] The court was further
well aware that the rationale behind the common-law rule requiring incorporation of international treaty law into domestic legislation is irrelevant to
situations of belligerent occupation: the rationale lies in the separation of
powers between the legislative and the executive branches of government;
such separation is irrelevant to situations, such as belligerent occupations,
where the legislative power is in the hands of the executive and where the
norms impact the rights and duties of persons who are not entitled to
participate in the democratic process. It simply rejected this position.[55]
More concerned with the relationship between the executive and the judicial branches, it chose to reiterate the formal position of the government, in
the process turning a blind eye to Israel's international obligations and
confusing applicability with domestic enforceability.[56]

It does not follow that the HCJ did not engage with the *GC IV*. Though it is
yet to determine that the *GC IV* in toto reflects customary law, it did consider
some of its provisions (as well as some provisions of the *AP I*) as customary and
therefore applicable;[57] a few of the judges regarded the unilateral undertaking
by the government to abide by the humanitarian provisions of the *GC IV* as

---

[53] E.g., *Ayub*; *Dweikat*, p. 29; *Al-Affu*, p. 67.
[54] CrA 131/67 *Kamiar* v. *the State of Israel* (1968) 22(2) PD 85 [Hebrew].
[55] *Al-Affu*, pp. 60–63.   [56] Kretzmer, *The Occupation of Justice*, pp. 40–41.
[57] E.g., *Dweikat* (determining that some of the provisions are customary, but not the provision of
   Article 49 which prohibits deportation). Note that one judge conceded that the *GC IV* applies,
   but "balanced" this deviation from the government's position by determining that the whole
   issue was nonjusticiable (Justice Witkon's opinion, ¶ 29). Interestingly, a few years earlier that
   same judge found that neither the Hague Regulations nor the *GC IV* are customary and
   therefore neither is applicable; see HCJ 302/72 *Hilou* v. *Government of Israel* (1972) 27(2) PD
   169 [Hebrew], pp. 179–182 (hereinafter: Rafia Approach case). His position changed pursuant
   to a critical article by professor Dinstein, positing that the Hague Regulations reflect customary international law and that the *GC IV* reflects what is accepted in enlightened nations. See
   Y. Dinstein, "The Ruling in the Matter of the Rafia Salient" (1973) 3 *Tel Aviv Law Review* 934;
   Zertal and Eldar, *Lords of the Land*, text and notes 346–347. *Ajuri* (applying Article 78 of the
   GC IV); HCJ 762/02 *Public Committee Against Torture* v. *Government of Israel* (2006) 2 IsrLR
   459 (applying Article 51 of *AP I*); HCJ 2150/07 *Abu Safiyeh* v. *Minister of Defense* (2009) 63(3)
   PD 331, ¶ 16 [Hebrew; English translation available at http://elyon1.court.gov.il/files_eng/07/
   500/021/m19/07021500.m19.pdf]. For a discussion on this case, see Section G.4 and notes
   101–111.

binding in view of Israeli administrative law;[58] some judges have chosen to resort to the *GC IV* in obiter dicta; and in other instances the court relied on provisions of the *GC IV* simply because the state claimed that its actions were in line with it. Indeed, the court even applied IHRL to the OPT.[59] In most of those instances, resort to the *GC IV* and to IHRL was undertaken to approve governmental action.[60] Quite tellingly, thus, the jurisprudence of the court which initially based the application of the law of belligerent occupation on the need to find a source for the authority of the military commander, remained concerned with facilitating and expanding, rather than limiting, this authority. The manner with which the HCJ interpreted the applicable law is the focus of Section G.3.2.

G.3.2 *Interpretation of the Applicable Law: The Road from Israel to Greater Israel*

Road 443 is a 28-kilometer route connecting Jerusalem with major cities in Israel. Half of the road passes through the West Bank. Its construction required expropriation of Palestinian-owned lands. The story of the physical road epitomizes the long and winding judicial road from Israel to Greater Israel, a state the effective sovereignty of which incorporates the West Bank.

The legal story begins in the late 1970s, when a Palestinian teachers' cooperative society purchased land north of Jerusalem with a view of establishing a teachers' housing complex. The cooperative society requested and received from the military administration building permits for the construction of 24 individual buildings. Work began. Shortly thereafter, a nearby industrial plant, owned by Jewish industrialists, brought to the attention of the military commander that construction began in their vicinity. In a move quite rare in Israeli construction practice once the arduous road to a permit ends successfully, the permits were suspended and then canceled altogether.[61]

---

[58] Initially, the court regarded this unilateral undertaking as a "political commitment" that is excluded from judicial purview, see HCJ 698/80 *Kawasme v. Minister of Defense* (1980) 35(1) PD 617 [Hebrew]. Subsequent decisions maintained that it carries a legal meaning. See Justice Barak's opinion, Iskan II, p. 794; Justice Bach's opinion, *Sajedia v. Minister of Defense* (1988) 42(3) PD 801, 830 (Keztiot case) [Hebrew; English Summary available at (1993) 23 *Israel Yearbook of Human Rights* 288].

[59] E.g., HCJ 7957/04 *Mara'abe v. Prime Minister of Israel* (2005) 60(2) PD 477, ¶ 19 [Hebrew; English translation available at http://elyon1.court.gov.il/files_eng/04/570/079/A14/04079570.a14.pdf]; *Abu Safiyeh*, ¶ 16.

[60] E.g., *Kawasme*, pp. 626–627; *Al-Affu* (deportation cases); *Ajuri* (assigned residence).

[61] On building permits in the OPT see entry Z: Zone, Section Z.2.2.3.2.

The cooperative society petitioned the HCJ, and the court rejected the petition. It determined that the permits were granted unlawfully in view of Mandatory and Jordanian planning laws and regulations relative to the construction of a complex. The court's concern for the number of parking spaces, schools, and accessible roads to and within the area is noteworthy for two reasons: first, because such concern has never been otherwise evident in relation to Palestinian dwellings; and second, because it was not the Palestinians who complained about the design of their projected neighborhood, but Israeli Jews who objected to its very construction. The sincerity of the concern is further belied by an additional development that found expression in this judgment: the cooperative society's submission to the planning authority of a detailed plan for the entire project was rejected. The rejection was based on two grounds: its proximity to an Israeli industrial zone and to security plantations in the OPT, and its location within an area destined for expropriation for the construction of traffic roads. At the time there were no plans approved for that construction. The court rejected the petitioners' appeal against this decision as well, on the grounds of relevant planning considerations.[62]

The spring of 1980 was not a balmy season for the cooperative society of teachers. Plans for the construction of the roads, requiring the expropriation of parts of their land, were approved. The cooperative society petitioned against the decision to seize the land. Its main argument was that the roads will serve the traffic needs of Israel, not of the occupied population, and that consequently the military commander is not authorized to construct them. The respondent submitted that the roads were designed to serve the traffic needs of the area, needs that the existing system cannot sustain and attending to them is thus within the authority of the military commander, to ensure the proper functioning of civil life.[63] In 1982, the HCJ determined that the expropriation of privately owned land undertaken to uphold the obligations of the military commander under the law of belligerent occupation is not only permissible, but indeed required under that law.[64]

The judgment has since become a milestone in the legal highway of the occupation. Three main reasons justify this assessment. The first reason is that the judgment set out the applicable legal framework, discussed in Section G.3.1 in a manner that has since been cited continuously: the source of the legal authority of the military commander derives from the international laws of belligerent occupation. Insofar as Israel is concerned, these laws exist in the

---

[62] HCJ 145/80 *Jamayit Iskan* v. *Minister of Defense* (1980) 35(2) PD 285 [Hebrew].
[63] Iskan II, ¶¶ 5–8.   [64] *Ibid.*, ¶ 36.

customary rules of the 1907 Hague Regulations. The question of whether the GC IV applies as well is highly contentious, but does not require a judicial determination since the GC IV is essentially constitutive and was not incorporated into Israel's domestic law. The court equally found no need to determine "the fine question" of whether the decision of the Israeli government to act in accordance with the humanitarian provisions of the GC IV, has rendered them applicable by virtue of Israeli administrative law.[65] Having thus set the framework, the court proceeded to apply the Hague Regulations to the question at hand.

The second reason why the judgment is significant is its interpretation of the authority of the military commander under Article 43 of the Hague Regulations. Noting that this authority extends to both the security needs of the occupying power and the needs of the occupied population, the court proceeded to offer a restrictive construction of the former and a permissive construction of the latter: military considerations are distinct from broad national security interests; they exclude national, economic or social considerations. An occupied area is not an open field for economic exploitation. Consequently, the military commander is not authorized to plan and construct "service roads" designed to serve the needs of the occupying state.[66] Insofar as the needs of the occupied population are concerned, the military commander is authorized – indeed, required – to take all measures necessary "to ensure the growth and development of the population; to develop industry, commerce, agriculture, education, health, welfare and like matters"[67] that a modern welfare state provides for the people under its authority. Such deviations from the 1907 conservation principle, drafted during the laissez faire era, are justified in view of the responsibility to attend to the well-being of the beneficiaries – the local population – especially in prolonged occupations. These judicial pronouncements read like the manifesto of an enlightened, albeit protracted belligerent occupation.

Applying the law to the facts, the court could find "no ground to doubt the veracity" of the respondent's assertion that the roads are to serve the needs of the inhabitants of the occupied area.[68] Curiously, though, having thus expressed its confidence in the truthfulness of the respondent's assertion, the court did proceed to voice some doubt as to whether the military commander's considerations, related exclusively to the well-being of the local population.[69] The reason for this judicial puzzlement, stems from the fact that the respondent did not even allude to the existence of a security consideration in the planning of the roads. Yet, in a previous case dealing with the general traffic

[65] *Ibid.*, ¶ 11.   [66] *Ibid.*, ¶ 13.   [67] *Ibid.*, ¶ 26.   [68] *Ibid.*, ¶ 14.   [69] *Ibid.*, ¶ 15.

plan for the area rather than with a particular road, the military commander added to his consideration relative to the welfare of the population, a consideration pointing to the need to allow swift military movement in the area in case of a war.[70] Shaking a finger at the inconsistency of the respondent,[71] and noting that its position would have been stronger had it been grounded in both civilian and military considerations, the court concluded that the consideration of the well-being of the civilian population suffices, and reiterated its "utter lack of doubt or qualm" that the traffic plan was not motivated by "Israel's considerations and its civilian needs."[72]

This "utter lack of doubt" merits a pause. The respondents presented no evidence that the needs of the local occupied population were motivating the planning of the road. In fact, documents dating back to the mid-1970s disclose the political motivation behind it: to enlarge Jerusalem and construct a wide Jewish strap cutting through the West Bank.[73] The state, thus, was misleading the court,[74] and the court allowed itself to be misled.

In light of the above it is therefore not surprising that, in hindsight, this judgment reads much like that Chekov's famous gun hanging on the wall in the first act. The petitioners' land was expropriated. No teachers' neighborhood was ever built. The judgment made it clear that this was a small sacrifice, initiated by a benevolent military commander and sanctioned by the law of belligerent occupation, which was required to safeguard the socioeconomic thriving of the petitioners' fellow Palestinians. Road 443 was constructed. During the 1990s it served tens of thousands of commuters on a daily basis – Israelis who reside in Israel, Israeli settlers in the West Bank, and Palestinians. In the early 2000s, the benevolent military commander decided to bar Palestinians from accessing the road, invoking the security needs of Israeli settlers and commuters, and maintaining that local Palestinians have an alternative transportation system available – the very system he had considered insufficient two decades earlier. The gap between the monumentally progressive judicial pronouncements in the Iskan II judgment and this reality, is the third reason for its significance. In late 2009, the HCJ addressed this gap in the Abu Safiyeh case.[75]

The decision to designate the road as Palestinian-free was made in response to several Palestinian attacks against Israeli commuters undertaken in the context

---

[70] *Ibid.* The court refers to HCJ 202/81 *Tabib* v. *Minister of Defense* (1981) 36(2) PD 622 [Hebrew].
[71] "How could it be that what is presented to one judicial panel of this court is not presented to us?," Iskan II, ¶ 15.
[72] *Ibid.,* ¶ 16.
[73] D. Kretzmer and G. Gorenberg, "Politics, Law and the Judicial Process: the Case of the HCJ and the Territories" (2015) 17 *Law and Government* 1, 65–79 [Hebrew].
[74] *Ibid.*   [75] Abu Safiyeh.

of the second Palestinian uprising (Intifada).[76] These attacks resulted in seven dead and numerous injured Israelis. The petitioners posited that the military order which imposed the ban on Palestinian traffic on the road, and adversely affected the fabric of their life, is illegal: insofar as road 443 has become an "internal" Israeli traffic artery, the military commander exceeded his authority; the order constitutes a form of apartheid; breaches the prohibition on collective punishment; is unreasonable and disproportionately prejudices Palestinian human rights; and runs counter to the original reason for the construction of the road, presented to the court in the Iskan II case. The respondents submitted that the ban is a temporary security measure undertaken by the military commander in a lawful exercise of his authority and obligation to preserve the life of Israeli civilians, and that a number of alternative "fabric of life" routes are being constructed for Palestinian use.[77] The court decided by a majority vote that the military commander exceeded his authority.[78] The judgment is exceptional for several reasons: first, the court rarely accepts petitions against decisions of the military commander, much less on the basis of lack of authority.[79] Second, the decision has been made, inter alia, in the light of the assurances made to the court in the Iskan II case (namely, that the road will serve mainly Palestinian traffic needs),[80] yet the judgment reads like a mirror image of the Iskan II case: in Iskan II, the decision was to reject the petition, but the jurisprudence offered a restrictive interpretation of the scope of authority of the military commander; in the Abu Safiyeh case, the petition was accepted but the jurisprudence significantly expanded the scope of the military commander authority. This change over time in the court's jurisprudence is evident in both the applicable law and in its interpretation, and therefore merits attention.[81]

---

[76] For a brief summary of the causes for the Itifada, primarily the opposition to the continuous occupation, see O. Ben-Baftali and A. Gross, "The Second Intifada" in Anthony Dworkin et al. (eds.) *Crimes of War (o.2): What the Public Should Know* (New York: W. W. Norton & Company, 2007). Note that while the HCJ routinely refers to Palestinian terrorist attacks, its narrative never contextualizes said attacks in the opposition to the continuous occupation.

[77] *Abu Safiyeh*, ¶ 9. On the transformation of "temporary" reasons of security to "indefinite" such reasons, see entry T: Temporary/Indefinite.

[78] The majority opinion, written by Justice Vogelman, with the concurring opinion of President Beinisch, further noted, in an obiter dictum, that the decision was also disproportionate. Justice Levy, in a minority opinion, determined that the military commander acted within the scope of his authority, that the complete ban was disproportionate, but that given the military commander's willingness to consider alternatives, there was no need to vitiate the order.

[79] The court has often used the doctrine of proportionality in lieu of, rather than as on the basis of, the issue of authority. See entry P: Proportionality.

[80] *Abu Safiyeh*, ¶¶ 25–26.

[81] For an excellent review of this change see, G. Harpaz and Y. Shany, "The Israeli Supreme Court and the Incremental Expansion of the Scope of Discretion under Belligerent Occupation Law" (2010) 43 *Israel Law Review* 514.

Beginning with the applicable normative framework, the judgment states that the military commander draws his authority from three sources: the law of belligerent occupation, the local law (consisting of both the law which existed prior to the occupation and new law enacted by the military government), and the principles of Israeli law.[82] The applicable law of belligerent occupation consists of the 1907 Hague Regulations, the customary provisions of the GC IV – including Article 4 which designates the category of "protected persons" – and the customary provisions of the AP I. In addition, wherever a lacuna exists, it may be filled by provisions of IHRL.[83] These laws determine the scope of authority of the military commander.

The authority *ratione personae* to safeguard public order and civil life in the West Bank extends not merely to "protected persons" but also to "residents living in Israeli settlements in the area ... although they are not protected persons," and indeed to "residents and citizens of Israel who do not live in the Area [i.e., the West Bank] (who) also use the Road primarily for travelling between the coastal road and Jerusalem." In short, it extends "to the entire population within the bounds of the Area at any given time."[84] The court proceeds to clarify that this authority over persons is relevant also to the military commander's duty to protect "the lives and the security of Israelis who reside within an area under belligerent occupation," a duty which extends "to anyone who is alleged to be present in the area unlawfully." Presumably cognizant of the contrary position of the ICJ regarding the relevance of the legality of the settlers' presence in the West Bank,[85] but without referring to it explicitly, the court grounds this duty not merely in Article 43 of the Hague Regulations, but also in internal Israeli law.[86]

This expansion in the scope of authority *ratione personae* of the military commander is coupled with an extension of the scope of his authority *ratione materiae*: the security interests he is authorized to consider are no longer confined to military needs of the West Bank as distinct from the national security needs of Israel.[87] He is "entitled to take into account considerations related to the security of the state of Israel," provided the threat originates in the West Bank subject to belligerent occupation.[88] In addition to the security consideration, the military commander is also authorized to take into account human rights considerations. Thus, while settlers and other Israelis are not "protected persons" under Article 4 of the GC IV, they too have human rights which need to be preserved under the Universal Declaration of Human

---

[82] Abu Safiyeh, ¶ 14.   [83] *Ibid.*, ¶ 16.   [84] *Ibid.*, ¶ 20.
[85] Construction of a Wall, ¶¶ 121–122.   [86] Abu Safiyeh, ¶ 21.
[87] Iskan II, ¶ 13; see also note 66.   [88] Abu Safiyeh, ¶ 23.

Rights,[89] and they too are entitled to the protection of their well-being and security under Article 43 of the Hague regulations.[90] These rights to well-being and safety – which include, by way of example, freedom of movement even if just for convenience purposes,[91] and access to Jewish worshiping sites[92] – are to be balanced with, and ergo compromise, Palestinian human rights, such as the right to private property, the right to freedom of movement, and the myriad of other human rights violated by its restriction.[93]

This mishmash of human rights and security considerations in effect subsumes human rights of Jews into the broadly construed security interests, that the military commander is to safeguard. In this manner, a horizontal balance is created between Palestinian and Israeli human rights,[94] emptying the category of "protected persons" of content, and reversing the proper relationship, which the HCJ otherwise acknowledges, between *lex specialis* and *lex generalis*.[95] Indeed, given the specific legal prohibition on settlements,[96] there is no lacuna in the laws of belligerent occupation that necessitated resort to human rights. The settlers' human rights could lawfully and effectively be protected in Israel, and the universality of human rights is not designed to camouflage, much less serve, a political agenda which defies this very universality. The judicial construction of an increasingly expansive scope of the military commander's authority, reflects the expansion of Israel and facilitates the translation of the political theology of "Greater Israel," which posits Israel's sovereignty over the OPT since time immemorial,[97] into a normative reality.[98]

An expansive scope of authority is not, however, synonymous with an unlimited authority. The order which completely barred Palestinian traffic on road 443 was found to have been issued ultra vires because it flew in the face

---

[89] Maar'abe, ¶ 19.   [90] *Abu Safiyeh,* ¶ 28.

[91] Such as the rights of commuters from "the coastal roads to Jerusalem"; Abu Safiyeh, ¶ 20.

[92] HCJ 1890/03 *Bethlechem Municipality* v. *Minister of Defense* (2005) 59(4) PD 736 [Hebrew].

[93] Freedom of movement is discussed in entries X: X-ray and Z: Zone.

[94] A. Gross, "Human Proportions: Are Human Rights the Emperor's New Clothes of the International Law of Occupation?" (2007) 18 *European Journal of International Law* 1. For an expanded and updated version, see A. Gross, *The Writing on the Wall: Rethinking the International Law of Occupation* (New York: Cambridge University Press, 2017), pp. 338–396.

[95] Harpaz and Shany, "Incremental Expansion of the Scope of Discretion," p. 548.

[96] See entry J: Jewish Settlements.

[97] *Report on the Legal Status of Building in Judea and Samaria* (2012), available at www.pmo.gov
.il/Documents/doch090712.pdf [Hebrew; English translation of the conclusions and recommendations is available at www.pmo.gov.il/English/MediaCenter/Spokesman/Documents/e
dmundENG100712.pdf, and at http://elderofziyon.blogspot.cz/2012/07/english-translation-of-
legal-arguments.html#.VjYsRvkrLIV].

[98] See entry N: Nomos.

of the original designation of the road, as presented to the court in Iskan II – that is, to serve Palestinian transportation needs, and because having thus transformed the road into a "service road" that benefits Israeli commuters, not the local population, it breached Article 43 of the Hague Regulations.[99] The judgment nevertheless left the order in force for five additional months to allow for a practical solution. The court refrained from specifying it. An open door, as is well known, may tempt a saint. It is thus not entirely shocking that this lack of specification enabled the military commander to ostensibly follow the letter of the decision while still discarding Palestinian needs: of the two entry points and four exit points connecting the road to Palestinian villages that were established following the judgment, only two exit points remained operational by 2015. They are not open at all hours, or at regular times, and passage through the checkpoints is both time consuming and humiliating. For all intent and purposes, the road remains virtually segregated.[100]

G.4 CONCLUSION: WHEN THE RUBBER HITS THE ROAD

The story of road 443 is the story the rule of law has played in the OPT writ small. The route itself attests to the inclusion of the OPT within – and to the exclusion of Palestinians from – metropolitan Israel. Built on expropriated private Palestinian land under the pretext of a benevolent occupying power, exercising lawful authority as a trustee responsible for the well-being of "protected persons" under the Geneva Law, it has become an Israeli service road which secures the freedom of safe and swift movement of Israeli residents and settlers, and their freedom only.

And yet, the OPT is not lawless. On the contrary, it overflows with laws (the Hague Regulations, the GC IV, the AP I, IHRL, Jordanian/Egyptian laws,[101] and Israeli laws, inclusive of Mandatory Emergency Regulations,[102] Ottoman

---

[99] *Abu Safiyeh*, ¶¶ 25–26. For a superb discussion, based on archival material disclosing the real, political grounds for the case (as well as two other cases), the gap between these grounds and the state's stated submissions to the HCJ, and the latter's role in this charade, see Kretzmer and Gurnberg, *Politics, Law and the Judicial Process*, pp. 65–80.

[100] See report of the Association for Civil Rights in Israel (July 5, 2015) at www.acri.org.il/he/2489 [Hebrew].

[101] See, e.g., CA 1432/03 *Yinon Food Products Manufacturing and Marketing Ltd v. Kara'an* (2004) 59(1) PD 345 (applying Jordanian law to the West Bank territory) [Hebrew]; *Labour Appeal* 207/08 *Az-Rom Steel Factories ltd v. Ashkanta* (January 13, 2012) (applying Egyptian law to the Gaza Strip territory) [Hebrew].

[102] See, e.g., HCJ 8091/14 *Hamoked v. Minister of Defense* (December 31, 2014) [Hebrew]; see also entry H: House Demolitions.

Land Laws,[103] and Israeli legislation applicable only to settlers on a personal
and territorial basis, thereby generating the application of different legal
systems to people who reside in the same area on an ethnic basis[104]), military
orders, and the exercise of authority by the military commander is subject to
judicial review.

Law, then, is part of the problem. Too much of it exacerbates the problem.
This may be explained by a variety of factors, including a deliberately obfuscated legal framework that conceals as it denies the reality of annexation,
inviting a "pick and choose" methodology and the substitution of rules for
standards in its application; a military commander who acts as a proxy for the
policies of his government; and a national court that tends, as such courts
traditionally do, to accommodate such policies.[105] Another factor which
merits attention is the nature of the judicial discourse itself. That discourse
is based on the fragmentation of reality into particles in a manner that
facilitates, as it denies, the construction of that very reality.

The Abu Safiyeh judgment is instructive here as well. Justice Vogelman's
judgment does determine that the military commander transformed a road
designed for Palestinian well-being, into an internal Israeli service road for
almost a decade. He acknowledges the breach of Palestinian rights to freedom
of movement and its impact on all aspects of their lives, and reaches the
proper, albeit rare conclusion in this specific case. He does so without reference to the petitioners' argument that the military ban on Palestinian traffic
represents a form of apartheid. Interestingly, President Beinisch's concurring
judgment chose to comment on "the argument raised by the petitioners in the
petition before us, and in additional petitions as well – to the effect that
segregation ... is in force," focusing on the "use of the word 'Apartheid' in this
context."[106] Noting that in previous judgments[107] the court at times accepted
and at others rejected the need for separation between Israelis and Palestinians

---

103 See, e.g., HCJ 5439/09 *Abdelkader v. Military Appeals Committee*, Offer Camp (March 20,
     2012) [Hebrew].
104 See *One Rule, Two Legal Systems: Israel's Regime of Laws in the West Bank* (Association for
     Civil Rights, October 2014).
105 E. Benvenisti, "Judicial Misgivings Regarding the Application on International Law:
     An Analysis of Attitudes of National Courts" (1993) 4 *European Journal of International
     Law* 159. In a later publication, Benvenisti notes that, as of the early 2000s, domestic courts
     have begun to engage seriously with international law, reacting as national agents to the forces
     of globalization, but that Israel (and the USA) is not thus engaged. See E. Benvenisti,
     "Reclaiming Democracy: the Strategic Uses of Foreign and International Law by National
     Courts" (2008) 102 *American Journal of International Law* 241.
106 Justice Beinisch's opinion, *Abu Safiyeh*, ¶ 1.
107 These judgments are specified *Ibid.*, ¶ 4.

on roads, and that ergo "there is no unequivocal answer to the question whether a security measure involving the segregation of travel on certain roads, for security reasons, is legal,"[108] she proceeded to acknowledge that security measures "which create a total segregation ... and prevent an entire population group from using the road, [give] rise to a sense of inequality and even the association of improper motives."[109] Total segregation, such association, and a sense of inequality notwithstanding, "we must be careful to refrain from definitions that ascribe a connotation of segregation, based on improper foundations of racist and ethnic discrimination, to the security means enacted."[110] The reason the comparison with apartheid "is not a worthy one," and one which "it is essential to avoid," is "the great distance between the security measures practiced by the state of Israel for the purpose of protection against terrorist attacks and the reprehensible practices of Apartheid policy."[111]

It is indeed possible to refute the comparison between apartheid policies and security practices against terrorist attacks by reiterating the habitual discourse, focusing on security measures in terms relative to terrorist attacks and the proper exercise of military authority in response. This discourse, however, is extracted from the broader context of opposition to occupation, annexation, and systematic discrimination. The "association with improper motives" and "the sense of inequality" are grounded in "reprehensible practices" of "total segregation" that characterize this contextual reality. The judicial discourse can and does render decisions, including those rare decisions that accepted Palestinian petitions, which ignore and deny this reality. In so doing, it participates in the making of this reality. *"And that has made all the difference."*[112]

---

[108]   *Ibid.,* ¶ 3.   [109]   *Ibid.,* ¶ 5.   [110]   *Ibid.,* ¶ 6.   [111]   *Ibid.*
[112]   Frost, "The Road Not Taken."

H

House Demolitions

Michael Sfard

H.1 INTRODUCTION: THE HOME FRONT

H.1.1 *The Sons Have Eaten Sour Grapes, and the Father's Teeth Are Set on Edge*

A house is not merely a physical structure. To the extent that a house is a building that functions as a home, its demolition signifies that the people who used to inhabit it have become homeless: both roofless and rootless. They have lost their ability to organize and to exercise control over their inner space, as well as their communal space. The destruction, thus, affects their material, emotional, and ontological sense of security – that is, their identity.[1]

Israel has inflicted such a loss on thousands on Palestinian families in the OPT (including East Jerusalem) in three major ways: first, houses demolished as a part of military operations during armed hostilities; second, administrative demolition of houses built without a building permit;[2] and third, houses demolished as a response to the engagement (suspected or affirmed) of one of the inhabitants in activities against Israel.[3] The jurisprudence of the Israeli HCJ concerning the latter type of house demolition,[4] commonly referred to as "punitive demolition," is the subject matter of this entry.

---

[1] See e.g., P. Somerville, "Homelessness and the Meaning of Home: Rooflessness or Rootlessness" (1992) 16(4) *Journal of Urban and Regional Research* 529; M. J. Radin, "Property and Personhood" (1981–1982) 34 *Stanford Law review* 957.

[2] Building without a permit results from Israel's refusal to issue zoning master plans. Without such a planning map to regulate building, it is impossible to get a building permit. See entry Z: Zone, Sections Z.2.2–3.

[3] See D. Simon, "The Demolition of Homes in the Israeli Occupied Territories" (1994) 19 *Yale Journal of International Law* 1, 7.

[4] The policy allows the IDF to impose one of two types of sanctions relating to the suspect's family home: a demolition order, and a sealing order. A demolition order is carried out by

Let us consider the otherwise unremarkable judgment in the Mahmoud al-Fasfous case. It is brief and provides very little information about him. All we know is that in May 1989, when he filed the petition, he was already quite old. We know that he lived at home with his son, Taha. We know Taha had been arrested and had confessed to throwing rocks and Molotov cocktails at laborers' cars to stop them from going to work and also at cars belonging to people he and his friends suspected as being Israeli collaborators. We do not know if anyone was hurt as a result of the son's actions, but it stands to reason that if they had, it would have been mentioned in the judgment. We know Taha, the son, was tried by a military court for his actions, and we know that the military commander decided to demolish their home.[5]

Al-Fasfous' lawyer filed a High Court petition against the demolition. He asked the panel, headed by then chief justice Meir Shamgar, to consider his client's old age, and the fact that he would remain homeless if the demolition order were carried out. He argued international law prohibits such harm to an elderly father who had done nothing wrong, and who was not even aware of his son's wrongful actions. Finally, he noted that it was the month of Ramadan, and that this, at the very least, should be taken into account and that a man (especially an old man) should not be made homeless during the holidays. The court rejected al-Fasfous' pleas in two short paragraphs. Determining that "given the proliferation of firebomb throwing, which, by its nature, is nothing short of an attempt to kill or injure people by burning them, we have seen no room to intervene in the discretion of the third respondent [the West Bank military commander]," the judgment further declined to order the demolition to be stayed until after the holiday.[6]

The lack of judicial empathy for the misery of old Mahmoud al-Fasfous is as chilling as it is common. Indeed, had he been a woman, his plight would have likely been worse, but would have encountered a similar indifference: In traditional Palestinian families, the demolition of a family house renders women more vulnerable than they already are, not only because they are expected to take care of the household without a house, but also because of physical, social, and emotional factors relative to their culture. They not only lose their security and their social anchor, they are thrown into a battlefield where they have to fend for themselves and for their dependents.[7] Almost none of the numerous judgments rendered by the HCJ on the matter has ever

---

bulldozing the structure or using explosives to destroy it. A sealing order is carried out by sealing the structure's doors and windows with cement. The latter is (at least theoretically) reversible.

[5]   HCJ 779/88 *al-Hadi Muhsin al-Fasfous* v. *Minister of Defense* (1989) 43(3) PD 576.   [6]   *Ibid.*

[7]   For research focusing on the importance of a house/home to women generally, see b. hooks, *Homeplace: A Site of Resistance* (London: Turnabout, 1991); I. M. Young, *House and Home:*

related to this dimension of the policy of house demolition. This judicial silence is worse than mere disinterest; it is a conscious endorsement of the policy's rationale. The thin, even anorectic judicial discourse on the legality of this policy, discussed in this entry, is equally designed to achieve this purpose.

H.1.2 Punitive House Demolitions: A Biography

A mere two days after the 1967 fighting ended, Israel demolished eight Palestinian houses.[8] Since then, the frequency with which this policy has been implemented has fluctuated, rising in times of high security tension and decreasing in times of relative quiet.

Hundreds of petitions challenging demolition orders were filed throughout the years. One research counted more than one hundred judicial rulings rendered by the HCJ in house demolition cases.[9] With the exception of five relatively recent cases in which the court had revoked demolition orders for reasons that are unrelated to whether or not the power to do so can at all be considered lawful,[10] all petitions against house demolitions were rejected.[11]

Feminist Variations on a Theme of Motherhood and Space (Palgrave: Macmillan, 2005). For studies focusing on the plight of Palestinian women in this and related contexts, see N. Shalhoub-Kevorkian, *Security Theology, Surveillance and the Politics of Fear* (Cambridge: Cambridge University Press, 2015); N. Shalhoub-Kevorkian, "Counter-Spaces as Resistance in Conflict Zones: Palestinian Women Recreating a Home" (2006) 17(3–4) *Journal of Feminist Family Therapy*, 109.

[8] A document uncovered by the *Akevot* research institute indicates that as early as July 13, 1967 – just two days after the fighting ended and a week before the military administration was put in place – IDF forces demolished eight homes in the Gaza Strip as the tracks left behind by people who had laid mines led to them. See Memorandum from Mr. Yaakov Avnun to Director General and Deputy Director General of the Ministry of Foreign Affairs, *Summary of Visit to Office of Military Governor of Gaza* (June 6, 1967), The Conflict Records' Digital Repository, Akevot Institute for Israeli-Palestinian Conflict Research, Document no. 1000576 (on file with author).

[9] G. Harpaz, "Being Unfaithful to One's Own Principles: The Israeli Supreme Court and House Demolitions in the Occupied Palestinian Territories" (2014) 47(3) *Israel Law Review* 401, 425.

[10] These demolition orders were revoked when it turned out that there had been a delay in implementing the order, that the house slated for demolition did not belong to the family of the assailant or that the assailant had not lived there, and when the family member's role in the attack was indirect. HCJ 7040/15 *Hamed* v. *Military Commander of the West Bank* (November 12, 2015), judgment of chief justice Naor, ¶¶ 45–46; HCJ 1125/16 *Mar'i* v. *Military Commander of the West Bank* (March 31, 2016) (unofficial translation available on the HaMoked website, www.hamoked.org/files/2015/HCJ%206754_15_judgment.pdf); HCJ 1336/16 *Atrash* v. *GOC Home Front Command* (April 3, 2016) (unofficial translation available on the HaMoked website, www.hamoked.org/Document.aspx?dID=Updates1701).

[11] There was, in fact, one exception in 1993, when a panel headed by then chief justice Ahraon Barak revoked a demolition order and replaced it with a partial sealing of the house given that

The power to issue demolition orders is a colonial legacy. It is stipulated in an emergency regulation enacted by the British High Commissioner for Palestine during the British mandate (1922–1947).[12] Israel maintains that these emergency regulations remained in force during the Jordanian and Egyptian rule over the West Bank and the Gaza Strip (respectively), and hence were part of the law of the land when Israeli troops entered them. One of those regulations, number 119, empowers the military commander to take possession of a house of a suspected terrorist and demolish it, regardless of whether others are living in it and whether or not they bear any responsibility for the acts of their family member. It actually permits much more. Regulation 119 allows the forfeiture and destruction of all the houses on the street where the suspect lives, and even, if the military commander so wishes, the entire neighborhood:

> A Military Commander may by order direct the forfeiture to the Government of Palestine of any house, structure, or land from which he has reason to suspect that any firearm has been illegally discharged, or any bomb, grenade or explosive or incendiary article illegally thrown, or of any house, structure or land situated in any area, town, village, quarter or street the inhabitants or some of the inhabitants of which he is satisfied have committed, or attempted to commit, or abetted the commission of, or been accessories after the fact of the commission of, any offence against the Regulations involving violence or intimidation or any Military Court offence; and when any house, structure or land is forfeited as aforesaid, the Military Commander may destroy the house or the structure or anything on growing on the land.

Since 1967, thousands of homes in the OPT have been demolished pursuant to Regulation 119. According to figures collected by Israeli human rights organizations, from the day the Gaza Strip and West Bank were occupied until the beginning of the first Intifada (Palestinian uprising) in 1987, the military demolished or sealed more than 1,300 homes pursuant to Regulation 119. Most of these actions took place in the dead of night with no real judicial process.[13] In the four years of the first Intifada, Israel demolished about 430 more homes,

---

a mother and seven sisters lived in the assailant's home. The court ruled in that case that although the military commander did have the power to order the house demolished, discretion requires a less drastic, more proportionate measure, HCJ 5510/92 *Turqman v. Minister of Defense* (1993) 48(1) PD 217.

[12]   Defence (Emergency Regulations), 1945.

[13]   HaMoked: Center for the Defence of the Individual, *Timeline – Punitive House Demolitions*, www.hamoked.org/timeline.aspx?pageID=timelinehousedemolitions; see also B'Tselem, *Demolition and Sealing of Houses in the West Bank and the Gaza Strip as a Punitive Measure During the* Intifada (1989), p. 10, www.btselem.org/download/198909_house_demo litions_eng.rtf.

and during the second Intifada (2001–2005), it demolished an additional 668 homes.[14] The policy was halted between 1998 and 2001, and again between 2005 and 2008. In late 2004 and early 2005, a committee headed by Maj. Gen. Ehud Shani examined the efficacy of house demolitions as a counterterrorism tool. When it completed its mission, the committee recommended a moratorium. Then Chief of the General Staff Moseh Ya'alon adopted the committee's recommendation, with a caveat that the military may depart from this new policy in "extreme cases."[15] After almost three years of moratorium, in 2008 the policy was resumed, first in isolated cases, but as the violence in the region escalated, the number of demolitions grew with it. Within two years, spanning the summer of 2014 to the summer of 2016, the military demolished or sealed a total of 39 homes belonging to families of Palestinians suspected of terrorism.[16]

Israel justifies its policy of Palestinian house demolition as a means for deterring future terrorists, and hence for saving lives.[17] Emergency Regulation 119 provides the legal basis for the implementation of this policy. This entry posits that (a) the implementation of this policy is a punitive measure – constituting collective punishment and destruction of private property – a measure that violates IHL and may well amount to a war crime; (b) the HCJ's discourse on the lawfulness of the policy, is an exercise in evasion; (c) the HCJ's consistent refusal to revisit its jurisprudence on the matter on the grounds that it is a court of justice, not of justices, defies justice; and (d) the HCJ's jurisprudence on house demolition substitutes violence for law. In order to substantiate this argument, Section H.2 presents, from a doctrinal perspective, the main legal issues the policy raises and narrates the history of attempts to have them adjudicated. Section H.3 examines the HCJ's jurisprudence on these issues and critiques them. Section H.4 concludes.

---

[14] *Ibid.*; see also B'Tselem, *Through No Fault of Their Own: Israel's Punitive House Demolitions in the al-Aqsa* Intifada (2004), www.btselem.org/publications/summaries/200411_punitive_house_demolitions.

[15] A presentation of the committee's recommendations which was provided to HaMoked: Center for the Defence of the Individual, states that while "the house demolition tool is part of the (small) tool box the IDF has for fighting terrorism," its negative effects, such as reinforcing the collective Palestinian national identity, the fact that house demolition is considered collective punishment which does not conform to the principle of human dignity and private property, and contradicts liberal values, and in fact reinforces the Palestinian refugee trauma, enhances the "occupation corrupts" argument and creates an unbridgeable gap. The presentation ends with an unequivocal statement: "The IDF, in a Jewish, democratic state, cannot walk the line of legality, let alone the line of legitimacy!!! [sic]."

[16] HaMoked: Center for the Defence of the Individual, *Updated Summary on Punitive Home Demolitions from July 2014 to August 31, 2016* (August 31, 2016), www.hamoked.org/Document.aspx?dID=Updates1783.

[17] See entry F: Future-Oriented Measures.

H.2 HOUSE OF CARDS: REGULATION 119 CASE-LAW

H.2.1 *The Legal Questions*

Regulation 119 empowers the military commander to demolish the family homes of individuals suspected of or convicted of violent actions. The text of the regulation is clear, and its legislative history,[18] as well as the purpose of the emergency regulations in toto,[19] leave no room for doubt. The British Mandate – in Palestine and elsewhere[20] – gave itself draconian powers to quell uprisings forcefully, even cruelly.

The major legal question concerns the relations between the mandatory emergency regulation and the international laws of belligerent occupation: Do the former contravene the latter? And, if so, should the emergency regulations be revoked? The answer to both questions, as discussed in this entry, is positive: Regulation 119 contradicts two prohibitions under both conventional and customary humanitarian law: the prohibition on collective punishment and the prohibition on destroying the property of protected persons.[21]

H.2.1.1 The Prohibition on Collective Punishment

Collective punishment is commonly understood as "a form of sanction imposed on persons or a group of persons in response to a crime committed

---

[18] In 1937, at the height of the Arab Revolt (a violent protest against colonial rule and increasing Jewish immigration), the king empowered the high commissioner to enact emergency regulations: The Palestine Gazette Extraordinary (No. 675), Memorandum on the Palestine (Defence) Order in Council, Supplement No. 2, 1937, p. 267. This 1937 Order in Council was preceded by the 1931 Order in Council which empowered the High Commissioner to issue emergency regulations (Palestine (Defence) Order in Council, 1931). The Regulations in force today are from 1945.

[19] The King's order in council empowered the High Commissioner to "make such regulations ... necessary or expedient for securing the public safety, the defence of Palestine, the maintenance of public order and the suppression of mutiny, rebellion and riot, and for maintaining supplies and services essential to the life of the community," Article 6 of the Memorandum on the Palestine (Defence).

[20] British legislation gave its colonial authorities the explicit power to impose collective punishment in Emergency Regulations and Ordinances in Cyprus, India, Kenya, Nigeria, Northern Rhodesia, Palestine, and elsewhere. See A. W. B. Simpson, *Human Rights and the End of Empire: Britain and the Genesis of the European Convention* (Oxford: Oxford University Press, 2001), pp. 82–89.

[21] The regulation in effect violates the notion of human dignity and contravenes a myriad of human rights enumerated in all the major human rights conventions. For the purposes of this entry, however, the discussion focuses only on the relationship between Regulation 119 and the prohibitions contained in IHL.

by one of them or a member of their group."[22] The notion that an individual is to be held accountable only for his or her own actions is a basic precept of justice, and it is thus not surprising that its roots date back to times immemorial.[23] The international legal prohibition on collective punishment was first incorporated into the 1907 Hague Regulations,[24] and was subsequently defined more precisely in the Geneva Conventions and their additional protocols.[25] The ICRC study concluded that it is a customary rule applicable in both international and noninternational armed conflicts.[26]

Article 50 of The Hague Regulations frames the prohibition using general language:

> No general penalty, pecuniary or otherwise, shall be inflicted upon the population on account of the acts of individuals for which they cannot be regarded as jointly and severally responsible.

Article 33(1) of the GC IV narrows the interpretation of the proviso in the Hague Regulation 50 to clarify that the population cannot be considered party to acts when individuals within it had no personal involvement in these acts:[27]

> No protected person may be punished for an offence he or she has not personally committed.

---

[22] P. Rabbat and S. Mehring, "Collective Punishment," in *Max Planck Encyclopedia of Public International Law*, http://opil.ouplaw.com/home/epil, ¶ 1.

[23] "That be far from thee to do after this manner, to slay the righteous with the wicked: and that the righteous should be as the wicked, that be far from thee: Shall not the Judge of all the earth do right?," Genesis 18:25 (King James version). See O. Ben-Naftali, "Human, All Too Human Rights: Humanitarian Ethics and the Annihilation of Sodom and Gomorrah," in U. Fastenrath, R. Geiger, D.-E. Khan, et al. (eds.), *From Bilateralism to Community Interest* (Oxford: Oxford University Press, 2011), pp. 424–427.

[24] Regulation 50 of The Hague Convention (IV) Respecting the Laws and Customs of War on Land and its annex: Regulations concerning the Laws and Customs of War on Land, The Hague, October 18, 1907, 205 CTS 277; 36 Stat 2277 [hereinafter: *HC IV*].

[25] Article 87 of the Geneva Convention Relative to the Treatment of Prisoners of War, Geneva, August 12, 1949, 75 UNTS 135; Article 33(1) of Geneva Convention Relative to the Protection of Civilian Persons in the Time of War, Geneva, August 12, 1949, 75 UNTS 287 [hereinafter: *GC IV*]; Article 75(2)(d) of Protocol Additional to the Geneva Conventions of August 12, 1949, and relating to the Protection of Victims of International Armed Conflicts (Additional Protocol I), Geneva, June 8, 1977, 1125 UNTS 3 [hereinafter: *AP I*]; Article 4(2)(b) of Protocol Additional to the Geneva Conventions of August 12, 1949, and relating to the Protection of Victims of Non-International Armed Conflicts (Protocol II), Geneva, June 8, 1977, 1125 UNTS 609 [hereinafter: *AP II*].

[26] J.M. Henckaerts and L. Doswald-Beck (eds.), *Customary International Humanitarian Law*, 2 vols. (Cambridge: Cambridge University Press, 2009), vol. I, pp. 374–375 (hereinafter: *CIHL*).

[27] J. S. Pictet (ed.), *The Geneva Conventions of 14 August 1949 – Commentary on Geneva Convention IV Relative to the Protection of Civilian Persons in Times of War* (Geneva: International Committee of the Red Cross, 1958), p. 225.

Collective penalties and likewise all measures of intimidation or of terrorism are prohibited.

Pillage is prohibited.

Reprisals against protected persons and their property are prohibited.

According to the official ICRC interpretation of the *GC IV*, the prohibition on collective punishment does not refer only to sentences handed down by a court in a criminal procedure, but also to "sanctions and harassment of any sort, administrative, by police action or otherwise," against an individual, or a group, for acts they did not personally commit.[28]

This interpretation is reinforced by subsequent development: reading the language of Article 33 of the *GC IV* in the light of Article 75(2)(d) and Article 4(2)(b) of the *AP I* and Article 6(2)(b) of the *AP II*, has generated the following formulation of the two components of the current customary rule prohibiting collective punishment:[29]

102. No one may be convicted of an offense except on the basis of individual criminal responsibility.

103. Collective punishment is prohibited.

The prohibition has no exceptions. In the context of belligerent occupations, it signifies that protected persons are not objects that may be used for achieving military or security-related objectives. Deterrence, posited by Israel as such an objective which justifies collective punishment, thus does not provide a lawful justification.[30]

The violation of the prohibition on collective punishment not only incurs state responsibility, it may also entail individual criminal responsibility. While opposition, attributed to occupying and annexing powers, prevented the inclusion of collective punishment in the list of war crimes in the Statute of the ICC,[31] its characterization as a war crime may well be grounded in custom: collective punishment was recognized as a war crime immediately after the first World War in the report of the *Commission on the Responsibility of the Authors of the War and on Enforcement of Penalties* established in the Paris

---

[28] *Ibid.* See also: Y. Sandoz, C. Swinarski, and B. Zimmermann (eds.), *Commentary on the Additional Protocols of 8 June 1977 to the Geneva Conventions of 12 August 1949* (Geneva: International Committee of the Red Cross, 1987), p. 874, ¶ 3055.

[29] Henckaerts and Doswald-Beck, *CIHL*, pp. 372–375.

[30] See S. Darcy, "The Prohibition of Collective Punishment," in A. Clapham, P. Gaeta, and M. Sassoli (eds.), *The 1949 Geneva Conventions: A Commentary* (Oxford: Oxford University Press, 2015), pp. 1155, 1162.

[31] *Ibid.*, p. 1167. Darcy notes (in note 95) that he had received this information in a conversation with Adriaan Bos, a chair of the Preparatory Committee.

Conference in 1919;[32] it is classified as a war crime in the statutes of both the ICTR[33] and the Statute of the SCSL;[34] and international jurisprudence, ranging from the classification of a violation of Article 50 of the Hague Regulations as a war crime by the Nuremberg Tribunal[35] to judgments rendered by the SCSL,[36] lend support to this proposition.[37] Collective punishment may also be construed as an "inhumane treatment" of protected persons, a crime under Article 8(2)(a)(ii) of the ICC Statute.[38]

H.2.1.2 The Prohibition on Destruction of Private Property not Justified by Military Necessity

The prohibition on the destruction of private property as part of an international conflict in general, and as part of a regime of occupation in particular, is set forth in both the Hague Regulations and the Geneva Convention. Article 23(g) of the Hague Regulations sets restrictions on combat methods and prohibits:

> To destroy or seize the enemy's property, unless such destruction or seizure be imperatively demanded by the necessities of war;

The prohibition on the destruction of private property belonging to protected persons in an occupied territory is enshrined in Article 53 of the GC IV, which stipulates that:

> Any destruction by the Occupying Power of real or personal property belonging individually or collectively to private persons, or to the State, or to other

32 Report Submitted to the Preliminary Conference of Versailles by the Commission on Responsibility of Authors of the War and on Enforcement of Penalties, Versailles, March 29, 1919, pp. 112–115.
33 Article 4(b) of the Statute of the International Criminal Tribunal for Rwanda, UN Security Council, November 8, 1994.
34 Article 3(b) of the Statute of the Special Court for Sierra Leone, UN Security Council, January 16, 2002.
35 See e.g., International Military Tribunal, *Trial of the Major War Criminals before the International Military Tribunal, Nuremberg, 14 November 1945 – 1 October 1946* (Nuremberg: 1947), vol. I, pp. 60–61.
36 Armed Forces Revolutionary Council (AFRC), Trial Chamber Judgment, SCSL-04-16-T, ¶¶ 673–675.
37 Darcy, "The Prohibition of Collective Punishment," pp. 1166–1169, offers further resources supporting the classification of collective punishment as a war crime.
38 *Akvidar v. Turkey*, Eur Ct HR, App. No. 57/1996/676/866 (1997) 23 EHRR 143. See also HaMoked: Center for the Defence of the Individual, *Expert Opinion: The Lawfulness of Israel's House Demolition Policy under International Law and Israeli Law*, www.hamoked.org /Document.aspx?dID=Documents2512.

public authorities, or to social or cooperative organizations, is prohibited, except where such destruction is rendered absolutely necessary by military operations.

The prohibition on arbitrary destruction of property as a form of deterrence or punishment is a well-established customary rule of international law,[39] and its violation constitutes a grave breach of the Geneva Conventions[40] and a war crime.[41] As stated in the final clause of Article 53 of the GC IV, the prohibition on the destruction of property applies unless it is "absolutely necessary by military operations." The term "military operations" has been interpreted by the ICRC as "movements, manoeuvres and actions of any sort, carried out by the armed forces *with a view to combat.*"[42] In other words, the military necessity exception is an *operational* exception relating to destruction that is warranted as part of military action.

Accordingly, the official ICRC interpretation of Article 53 requires the occupying power to interpret the "absolutely necessary by military operations" exception reasonably, while maintaining proportionality and balancing the expected military advantage against the anticipated harm. This is designed to ensure that the occupying power would not abuse the exception and render the rule meaningless.[43] Thus, there is a connection between the prohibition on destruction of property that is not absolutely required by military necessity, as stipulated in Article 53 and the prohibition on reprisals against property stipulated in Article 33(1):[44] destruction of property that does not constitute an absolutely necessary military operation (i.e., a violation of Article 53) and that is carried out as a sanction against a person or a group for acts they did not personally commit would be considered collective punishment in violation of

---

[39] Articles 15–16 of the Instructions for the Government of Armies of the United States in the Field (Prepared by Francis Lieber and promulgated as General Order No.100 by President Lincoln, 24.4.1863); Article 13(g) of the Project of an International Declaration concerning the Laws and Customs of War, Brussels, August 27, 1874; Rule 50 of the ICRC study: Henckaerts and Doswald-Beck, *CIHL*, pp. 175–177.

[40] Article 50 of Geneva Convention for the Amelioration of the Condition of the Wounded and Sick in Armed Forces in the Field, Geneva, August 12, 1949, 75 UNTS 31; Article 51 of Geneva Convention for the Amelioration of the Condition of Wounded, Sick and Shipwrecked Members of Armed Forces at Sea, Geneva, August 12, 1949, 75 UNTS 85; Article 147 of GC IV.

[41] Article 2(d) of the Statute of the International Criminal Tribunal for the Former Yugoslavia, UN Security Council, May 25, 1993; Articles 8(2)(a)(iv), 8(2)(b)(xiii) of the Rome Statute of the International Criminal Court, UN General Assembly, July 17, 1998, ISBN No. 92–9227-227–226.

[42] Sandoz, Swinarski, and Zimmermann, Commentary on *AP I*, p. 67, ¶ 152 (emphasis added). That was also the approach taken by the ICTY in Blaškić, Appeal Chamber Judgment, ICTY-95–14-T, ¶ 157.

[43] Pictet, Commentary on *GC IV*, p. 302.   [44] *Ibid.*, p. 301.

Article 33. There is also a broad consensus among scholars that the interpretation of the exception inserted into Article 53 of the *GC IV* is extremely
restrictive and does not apply to house demolitions for the purpose of deterrence or punishment, allowing them only if required for the purpose of
military operations.[45]

H.2.2 A Courthouse or a House of Justices? The Power
of Judicial Inertia

The question of the legality of house demolitions first made its way to the HCJ
in 1979. In a very short ruling, the court upheld the order issued for the sealing
of a room in a house in which a family member charged with membership in
an unlawful association and harboring a fugitive had lived. The ruling
acknowledged the order was a "punitive" measure, adding that "the main
purpose [of the sealing] was deterrence against the commission of similar
acts."[46] The court dismissed the argument that the power granted by
Regulation 119 contradicts the prohibitions stipulated in the *GC IV* on the
basis that the regulation formed part of the "local law" that preceded the
occupation[47] and therefore continued to apply regardless of whether or not it
violates the Convention. In other words, the justices avoided determining
whether house demolitions constituted collective punishment or prohibited
destruction of private property and ruled that a law that predates the occupation is impervious to international law.

The court, presided over by then President Shamgar, repeated this position
in another judgment in 1987.[48] In this second case, Shamgar went so far as to
say that it was the very laws of belligerent occupation that decreed the
application of domestic law, citing the conservation principle stipulated in
the Hague Regulation 43 and *GC IV* Article 64. Those were the first two cases

---

[45] Y. Dinstein, "The International Law of Belligerent Occupation and Human Rights" (1978) 8
    Israel Year Book of Human Rights 104, 128; D. Kretzmer, *The Occupation of Justice:
    The Supreme Court of Israel and the Occupied Territories* (Albany: State University of
    New York Press, 2002), p. 147; Simon, "The Demolition of Homes," p. 68; Harpaz, "Being
    Unfaithful to One's Own Principles."

[46] HCJ 434/79 *Sahweil v. Commander of the Area* (1979) 34(1) PD 464.

[47] "We need not address the question of whether the Respondent must comply with the
    provisions of the Geneva Convention, since, even if he does, no contradiction can be found
    between the provisions of said Convention, on which Ms. Tsemel relies, and the use the
    Respondent has made of the powers vested in him by statutory order valid in at the time the
    Judea and Samaria Area was under Jordanian rule, and the same statutory provision remains
    valid today," *Ibid.*

[48] HCJ 897/86 *Jaber v. GOC Central Command* (1987) 41(2) PD 522.

to discuss international law arguments and both included a very "thin" and short analysis of the subject. In fact, they were also the last to include some reference to the merits of arguments based on IHL.

As noted, in the 30 years since then, the HCJ revisited the issue of house demolitions dozens of times. Its interpretation greatly expanded the power to demolish. Thus, for instance, it authorized demolition orders issued with respect to houses of families of suspects not yet convicted;[49] houses in which the family of the suspected terrorist rents rather than owns the home;[50] an entire building even if the relevant family lives in only one unit in it;[51] cases in which the demolition takes place long after the terrorist attack attributed to the family member;[52] and even the homes of suicide bombers who were no longer alive at the time of the demolition.[53] In other judgments, most of them issued in later years, the HCJ scaled back the power to demolish homes on a number of planes: it outlined the considerations for issuing demolition orders and limited their use to cases in which they are a reaction to serious terrorist attacks,[54] and revoked an order issued with great delay,[55] an order for a structure that was not owned by the relevant family,[56] and an order issued because of a family member who had had indirect involvement in a terrorist attack.[57]

Despite the immense volume of HCJ jurisprudence on this issue, the court nevertheless, and astonishingly, never addressed – on its merits – the argument that the house demolition policy grounded in Regulation 119 contradicts international law, a law which governs the military's conduct in the area. Thus, no judicial answer was given to the question of whether the power granted by Regulation 119 should be considered collective punishment, as the term is understood in international law and whether it is a violation of the prohibition on destroying the property of protected persons without an operational military need.

Thus, in more than 100 judgments that upheld the practice, the dismissal of IHL arguments is based solely on the thin, technical reasoning of two original judgments from 1979 to 1987 that the regulation is local law predating the occupation, cannot be revoked by the laws of occupation, and, indeed, in

---

[49]   HCJ 361/82 *Hamri* v. *Military Commander of the Judea and Samaria Area* (1982) 36(3) PD 439.
[50]   HCJ 542/89 *al-Jamal* v. *IDF Commander in the Judea and Samaria Area* (1989) 89(2) PD 163.
[51]   HCJ 4772/91 *Hizran* v. *IDF Commander in the Judea and Samaria Area* (1992) 46(2) PD 150.
[52]   HCJ 1730/96 *Sabih* v. *IDF Commander in the Judea and Samaria Area* (1996) 50(1) PD 353.
[53]   HCJ 6026/94 *Nazal* v. *IDF Commander in the Judea and Samaria Area* (1984) 48(5) PD 338.
[54]   HCJ 2722/92 *al-Amarin* v. *IDF Commander in the Gaza Strip* (1992) 56(3) IsrSC 693.
[55]   HCJ 6745/15 *Abu Hashiyeh* v. *Military Commander of the West Bank* (December 1, 2015) (unofficial translation available on the HaMoked website, www.hamoked.org/Document.aspx ?dID=Documents2951).
[56]   HCJ 7040/15.   [57]   HCJ 1336/16.

conserving local law upholds the law of occupation. All subsequent judgments referred to these two judgments and to a growing number of later judgments that referred back to the two original ones. And so, through the dynamics of a self-referencing which characterizes the development of common-law rules – that is, by setting down a rule that gets reinforced from one decision to the next, gaining power and legitimacy with each additional ruling – a large, uniform, de and stable body of case-law was created on the issue of the legality of house demolition, affirming the validity of the power the regulation bestows to demolish the family homes of suspected terrorists.[58] A closer examination of this case-law reveals, however, that its impressive scope is inversely related to its meager substance.

In some of the rulings, however, the justices did feel the need to address, albeit only in obiter dicta, the argument regarding collective punishment. They handle the issue by generally labeling house demolitions a "deterrence" measure rather than a punitive one, usually without giving any reasoning or explaining why, even if it is a deterrent, it is not simultaneously a punitive act, and, as such, a prohibited collective punishment.[59]

Thus, an attempt made by eight Israeli human rights organizations to force the court to address the issues of principle, in a public interest petition that raised the issue directly and included an expert opinion from four of Israel's leading academic experts on humanitarian law and criminal law,[60] failed.[61] The panel decided there was no room to revisit the collective punishment and prohibited destruction of private property arguments, citing as grounds that two judgments,[62] delivered several months earlier, had addressed them.[63] A review of these two judgments reveals, alas, that like scores of judgments

---

[58] Eitan Diamond called it "an ancient error" which "rolls from one judicial ruling to the next": E. Diamonds, "On the Son's Sin and a Rolling Error" (January 2016) 51 *Insights in Judgments: The Law on Line, Human Rights* 43 [Hebrew], www.colman.ac.il/sites/default/files/diamond .pdf.

[59] HCJ 798/89 *Shukri v. Minister of Defense* (January 10, 1990); *Sabih*, ¶ 3; HCJ 8084/02 *Abbasi v. GOC Home Front Command* (January 5, 2003).

[60] See note 38, the experts were Prof. Ben-Naftali, Prof. Guy Harpaz, Prof. Mordechai Kremnitzer, and Prof. Yuval Shany.

[61] HCJ 8091/14 *HaMoked: Center for the Defence of the Individual v. Minister of Defense* (December 31, 2014) (unofficial translation available on the HaMoked website, www .hamoked.org/files/2014/1159007_eng.pdf). The petitioners were represented by the author of this entry, Michael Sfard.

[62] HCJ 4597/14 *Awawdeh v. West Bank Military Commander* (July 1, 2014), ¶ 15 (unofficial translation available on the HaMoked website, www.hamoked.org/images/1158437_eng.pdf), and HCJ 5290/14 *Qawasmeh v. Military Commander of the West Bank Area* (August 11, 2014) (unofficial translation available on the HaMoked website, www.hamoked.org/files/2014/1158 616_eng.pdf).

[63] HaMoked, justice Rubinstein, ¶ 16; remarks of justice Hayut, ¶¶ 1–4.

before them, they did not in any way address arguments regarding violations of the prohibition on collective punishment and the destruction of the property of protected persons. In fact, in those very cases, the state attorney's office pleaded with the justices not to address these questions because they had already been decided. When? Down the spiral of self-referencing judgments we go, all the way back to the 1970s.

Justice Hayut added another reason for her refusal to break with jurisprudence, a reason oft repeated in the judgments issued subsequently. Though she admitted that the "issues raised in the petition are difficult and troubling," and that "taking the line the path of case-law on this issue is not easy," she could not "agree to do that [i.e., revisiting the legality of house demolitions] without turning this court of justice into a court of justices."[64] Justice Hayut was alluding to the danger that, despite the existence of a clear case-law, each justice would make her or his own judgment, thus undermining the unified voice of the institution of which they are members. This position is an expression of a narrow personal-discretion approach to adjudication.[65] In fact, this very position deviates from the adjudicative approach of the court in almost all other issues.

An application for a further hearing before an extended panel was dismissed by the chief justice of the supreme court, determining that there was no room to hold a further hearing in a judgment that did not produce a new rule.[66]

Over the course of 2015 and 2016, seven supreme court justices – half the bench – expressed their opinion that an extended panel should, in fact, reconsider the case-law sanctioning the power to demolish the family homes of suspected terrorists.[67]

---

[64] *Ibid.*, opinion of Justice Hayut.

[65] For a critique of the narrow personal-discretion approach, see M. Sfard, "The Curse of the HCJ: Personal Responsibility for Collective Punishment" (January 2016) 51 *Insights in Judgments: The Law on Line, Human Rights* 6 [Hebrew], www.colman.ac.il/sites/default/file s/sfard.pdf.

[66] HCJFH 360/15 *HaMoked* v. *Minister of Defense* (November 12, 2015) (unofficial translation available on the HaMoked website, www.hamoked.org/files/2015/1159125_eng.pdf).

[67] Justice Vogelman in HCJ 5839/15 *Sidr* v. *IDF Commander of the West Bank* (October 15, 2015), ¶ 6 of his opinion (unofficial translation available on the HaMoked website, www.hamoked.org /files/2015/5839_15%20.pdf); justice Mazuz in HCJ 7220/15 *'Aliwa* v. *Commander of IDF Forces in the West Bank* (December 1, 2015), ¶ 17; Judgment of Justice Mazuz, ¶ 3 (unofficial translation available on the HaMoked website, www.hamoked.org/files/2015/1159935_eng.pdf). In addition, justices Barak-Erez, Jubran, Zilbertal, Baron, and Hayut all expressed doubt as to the legality of the policy but declared that as long as the court does not change its precedent they are bound by it. However, under Israeli Law the supreme court is not bound by its own precedents – Article 20 (b) Basic Law: The Judiciary: "A rule laid down by the Supreme Court shall bind any court other than the Supreme Court."

Justice Mazuz was the most forceful critic of the court's jurisprudence on the matter. He referred to the arguments regarding violations of international law as "weighty." He further bemoaned the fact that the discussion around these arguments in the case-law thus far had not been "exhaustive," "thorough," or "sufficiently comprehensive," and that the counterarguments were worthy of a "thorough examination."[68] In a rare dissenting opinion on the matter of house demolitions, he proposed the revocation of the demolition order in the case before him. Yet, subsequent attempts to secure reconsideration of the Regulation 119 precedents by an extended panel were all dismissed by chief justice Naor.[69]

H.3 HOUSE RULES: A CRITIQUE

The meager legal analysis contained in rulings on house demolitions precludes the identification of a methodical legal formulation used to ward off the substantive arguments that such demolitions violate IHL and entail criminal responsibility. The jurisprudence, however, does disclose two substantive positions: (a) first, Regulation 119 is pre-occupation local law and is therefore applicable even if it does contradict the laws of occupation; (b) the demolition is not collective punishment, but a measure meant to deter future potential terrorists.[70] Both these positions are rooted in fundamental legal errors.

H.3.1 Rule I: The First Floor Rests on the Ground Floor

The first argument ignores the basic rule that from an international legal perspective, international norms are of a higher normative order than local

---

[68] 'Aliwa, ¶ 17 of the judgment of justice Shoham; ¶ 3 of the judgment of justice Mazuz.

[69] HCJFH 2624/16 *Masudi* v. *Commander of IDF Forces in the West Bank* (March 31, 2016) (unofficial translation available on the HaMoked website, www.hamoked.org/files/2016/1160 399_eng.pdf); HCJ 2828/16 *Abu Zeid* v. *Commander of the Military Forces in the West Bank* (May 2, 2016) (unofficial translation available on the HaMoked website, www.hamoked.org /files/2016/1160463_eng.pdf). According to the law, the panel itself may decide to add members, but this power is rarely used and it is only available after deliberations begin, not ahead of time (Section 26(2) of the court law [incorporated version], 1984). An attempt to use this power also failed in HCJ 1336/16.

[70] Case-law has acknowledged that the efficacy of using house demolitions as a deterrent is, in fact, speculation. Justice Naor (as was her title at the time) ruled: "the impossibility to dismiss the view that some measure of deterrence exists, is sufficient in order not to intervene in the discretion of the military commander," HCJ 9353/08 *Abu Dheim* v. *GOC Central Command* (January 5, 2009), ¶ 8 of the opinion of Justice Naor; Justice Rubinstein put the logic behind deterrence at no more than "hope": "The impossibility to dismiss the view that some measure of deterrence exists, is sufficient in order not to intervene in the discretion of the military commander ... At the end of the day, before us is a hope for deterrence that would save human lives versus harm, albeit painful, to property," ¶¶ A and B of his opinion.

law. This is a fundamental rule of international law designed to ensure that a state would not rely on its domestic law to justify noncompliance with its international legal obligations.[71] This rule has been codified in the Vienna Convention on the Law of Treaties[72] and confirmed in the rulings of the ICJ.[73] When it comes to the laws of belligerent occupation, the situation is clearer still. The entire notion behind the legal framing of the situation of occupation is to create a constitution for the regime of occupation regulating the rights and obligations of civilians living under occupation, as well as the powers and obligations of the occupying power.[74] A position that allows the occupying power to eschew its obligations or respect for the rights of the occupied, by giving precedence to local laws that violate these rights and obligations, renders the legal framework international law created for occupation entirely redundant.

The position that local law is impervious to revocation under the laws of occupation is also rooted in error. Local law is protected from disregard by the occupier, and the Hague Regulation 43 does compel the occupier to respect it. However, the idea behind the duty of respect is to prevent the occupier from amending local law as it pleases, and this notion derives from the nature of occupation as a temporary trusteeship,[75] wherein the occupier is required to refrain from making systemic changes that are the sole purview of a sovereign. This norm, reflecting the "conservation principle" is subject to an exception, which allows changing local law if the occupier is "absolutely prevented" from upholding it.[76] A local law which blatantly violates a prohibition under the laws of belligerent occupation meets the exception. It is for this reason that "the Occupying Power was bound to repeal or suspend these Regulations and certainly it could not legitimately rely on them."[77] Moreover, in the case of house demolitions, local law does not compel the occupier or the occupying forces to demolish or seal homes, but rather gives them the discretionary power to do so. In this state of affairs, electing not to use the power cannot be said to be a violation of the duty to respect local law.[78]

---

[71] M. Shaw, *International Law* (4th edn, Cambridge: Cambridge University Press), p. 102.
[72] Article 27 of the Vienna Convention on the Law of Treaties, May 23, 1969, 1155 UNTS 331, reads: "A party may not invoke the provisions of its internal law as justification for its failure to perform a treaty."
[73] Applicability of the Obligation to Arbitrate Under Section 21 of the United Nations Headquarters Agreement of June 26, 1947, Advisory Opinion, 1988 ICJ 12, 34.
[74] See Introduction and entry G: Geneva Conventions.
[75] See entry T: Temporary/Indefinite.
[76] Regulation 43 of *HC IV*. See also the Pictet Commentary on *GC IV*, Article 64, pp. 335–336.
[77] Dinstein, "The International Law of Belligerent Occupation."
[78] O. Ben-Naftali and Y. Shany, *International Law between War and Peace* (Tel Aviv: Ramot, 2006), p. 180 [Hebrew].

Any other interpretation subverts the main object and purpose of the Hague Regulation 43 and of Article 64 of the GC IV. This is a fortiori the case when the so-called "local law" is Emergency Regulation 119: a foreign law enacted by a colonial power. Indeed, the logic behind courts preferring local law when it is diametrically opposed to international law, a principle many domestic legal systems follow, does not apply in this case: This principle originated in the deference domestic courts owe to their local legislatures and the constitutional principle of separation of powers. That logic is absent in the exercise of judicial review by the HCJ on the actions of the military commander on two levels: first, because Emergency Regulation 119 is the law of the occupied territory rather than of the Israeli parliament, and second, because it is not an enactment of the regime that preceded the occupation, but of the regime that preceded it, the Mandatory regime.

H.3.2 Rule II: Punitive Deterrence Exists. It Is Called "Punishment"

The unreasoned and unsubstantiated position of the judgments that house demolitions under Regulation 119 are a deterrent, and therefore not *punitive*, presumes that the difference between the two lies in the motivation for imposing the sanction. According to this reasoning, if the intent behind the decision is to deter future terrorists, the act is not punitive, and therefore does not constitute collective punishment; if the intent is to punish the family for the acts of one of its members, then it is collective punishment.

This, however, is not the test. The prohibition on collective punishment was not meant to abolish bad intentions, but to prevent injustice. Hence, in analyzing the issue, one must distinguish between the *motivation* and the *purpose* of the sanction imposed. Put differently, even if one accepts, for the sake of argument, Israel's assertion that its motive for house demolition is to deter potential future assailants, the method it has chosen for effecting such deterrence is harming innocents. These innocents are not incidental victims, a.k.a "collateral damage." They were not hurt by shrapnel from a missile targeted at something or someone else; they are the target. *Their suffering is a means for achieving the goal of deterrence* and they were selected out of the variety of potential victims because they are related to someone who is already suspected or convicted of having engaged in violent resistance. It follows that they are being punished for that person's actions. It is a classic case of punishing the innocent. It is worthwhile to recall that, as anyone who studies criminal law knows, one of the express purposes of punishment is, in fact, deterrence, and so even if we accept that the motivation for demolishing the homes of families of terrorists is to deter others, it does not rule out characterizing the practice as punishment. Given that it is a punishment for the actions of another, it is also a *collective punishment*.

From the dawn of history, armies have used cruel and barbaric practices of harming innocents because of the actions of a few in order to "teach a lesson" ("deter") and to scare those planning future "terrorist acts" from executing these plans. Israel's house demolition policy is no different.[79] The only difference is that over the past century such conduct is prohibited under the applicable law.

H.4 CONCLUSION: WHEN THE LAW IS UNREASONED, VIOLENCE IS UNVEILED

State violence destroyed Mr. al-Fasfous' home.

"Private" violence, attributed to his son, for which he was tried and sentenced, was presented as a legal justification for state violence and approved by the highest judicial authority in that state. The same fate befell thousands of Palestinian families, rendering them homeless.

The law is a mechanism for legitimizing one type of violence and delegitimizing another.[80] The presumed legitimacy of the very concept of "the rule of law" rests on the philosophical ethos behind it. It posits that any law is a general norm instituted through a veil of ignorance, without those participating in its enactment knowing on which side of the norm they might find themselves.[81] Acceptance of this liberal biography of law, and hence of the rule of law, gives it a halo of equality and lack of arbitrariness. Violence gets classified as legitimate or illegitimate in different ways, one of which is categorizing prohibitions, powers and rights as arbitrary or nonarbitrary. Use of arbitrary violence undermines the sense of justice and fairness; indeed, it undercuts the rule of law.

---

[79] House demolition is not the only means of collective punishment Israel uses. Other examples include closures of town and villages in the OPT, restrictions on electricity and water supplies, and the prolonged closure of Gaza, whereby "the whole of Gaza's civilian population is being punished for acts for which they bear no responsibility" is another example, characterized by the ICRC as "a collective punishment imposed in clear violation of Israel's obligations under international law." See "Gaza Closure: Not Another Year!", *ICRC News Release* (June 14, 2014). On this closure and its consequences, see entry Q: Quality of Life.

[80] In his famous *Politics as Vocation* (1919), Max Weber contends that the State claims monopoly over legitimate violence. Weber lists three "inner justifications" which legitimate state-sponsored violence, the third being *Legality*, and explained: "by virtue of the belief in the validity of legal statute and functional 'competence' based on rationally created rules." M. Waber, *Politics as Vocation* (New York: Oxford University Press, 1946), p. 4.

[81] J. Rawls, *A Theory of Justice* (Cambridge, MA: Harvard University Press, 1999), p. 118.

The presumption that legal norms are nonarbitrary means that legal norms have not just a *dictating* force but also a *justifying* force. We mostly accept a norm instituted through the normal constitutional process as justified. The legal norm describes proper conduct, and the conduct is proper because it was established through a legal norm. Therefore, a legal norm is at one and the same time what "is" and what "ought to be" – it both binds and educates.

This liberal, optimistic (some might say naïve) view of the law has been subject to a thoughtful critique.[82] Still, the conception of the law as nonarbitrary is tremendously powerful. Even in nondemocratic theaters, like a situation of occupation, where, in view of its exceptional nature, the presumptions that give law its nonarbitrary image clearly do not exist, a norm instituted as law still has a halo of legitimacy separating a state of civilization from a Hobbesian state of nature.[83] The mere existence of the normative framework signifies to the occupied population, to the occupying power, and to the world that the beast of arbitrary violence is kept at bay.

This is precisely why the Israeli regime of occupation took pains to drape all of its powers in law, particularly the draconian ones.[84] This is why the military, far from offering its weapons as justification for the violence it uses, relies on orders, proclamations, regulations, and laws of the occupied territory, and why the HCJ exercises judicial review over the latter. This review ostensibly protects the occupied people, but it also protects the very idea of the rule of law and protects the image of Israel as law-abiding. When this protection is as thin and brittle as it has been in respect of house demolitions and settlements,[85] the naked violence of law, arbitrariness, and injustice is exposed.[86]

---

[82]   See also, W. Benjamin, "Theses on the Philosophy of History," in H. Arendt (ed.), *Illuminations: Essays and Reflections*, H. Zohn (trans.) (Berlin: Schoken, 1969); W. Benjamin, "Critique of Violence," in P. Demetz (ed.) *Reflections: Essays, Aphorisms and Autobiographical Writing* (Berlin: Schoken, 1986); J. Derrida, "Force of Law: The Mystical Foundations of Authority" (1990) 11 *Cardozo Law Review* 919, 961. See entry V: Violence.

[83]   T. Hobbes, *Leviathan*, J. C. A. Gaskin (ed.) (Oxford: Oxford University Press, 2009).

[84]   Meir Shamngar, then attorney general, explained that legal advisors sought judicial review of the military administration's actions as a way of preventing arbitrary conduct and ensuring the rule of law. In: "Legal Concepts and Problems of the Israeli Military Government – The Initial Stage," in M. Shamgar (ed.), *Military Government in the Territories Administered by Israel 1967–1980, The Legal Aspects* (Jerusalem: Harry Sacher Institute for Legislative Research and Comparative Law, 1982), pp. 13, 43.

[85]   See entry J: Jewish Settlements.

[86]   It is in order to avoid this exposure that explains why, for instance, chief justice Shamgar took the trouble to address the legal challenge to deportation pursuant to Regulation 112, despite the fact that he could have simply restated his opinion that the GC IV was not customary law. See entry D: Deportations.

This is exactly what happened to the jurisprudence on house demolitions. It is not for nothing that when the court first outlined what considerations the military commander should take into account when deciding whether to use Regulation 119, it justified putting limits on the commander's discretion on the need to ensure that the act "is not clearly tainted by manifest unreasonableness."[87] The persistent refusal to address the arguments made against the house demolition policy over the decades which followed has, however, largely stripped the law of its reasonableness and exposed Palestinian families not to the rule of law but to law's violence.

---

[87] Justice Bach in HCJ 2722/92, p. 699.

I

Investigations

Michael Sfard

I.1 GENERAL: THE LEGAL BRICK ROAD TO THE OCCUPATION'S EMERALD CITY

The building blocks of the *rule of law* are comprised of substantive legislation and enforcement mechanisms. Relevant legislation, proper investigation of alleged offenses leading (when warranted) to prosecution, and judicial processes are required for the protection of civilians from abuse by other people, as well as by public officials. The role of law enforcement as a pillar of protection is especially crucial in an occupation regime, given the absence of alternative forms of protection and remedy, which stem from civil rights and political participation. This is a fortiori the case in indefinite occupations.[1] In this context, criminal legislation that defines certain acts as war crimes, investigations geared toward the exposure of the relevant facts, diligent prosecution of suspects, and a judicial system that renders a reasoned judgment and determines the appropriate punishment are crucial for a meaningful translation of the notion of the *rule of law* into reality. The role Israeli enforcement mechanisms have played in providing protection for "protected persons" in the OPT is the focus of this entry. This focus, in turn, allows for an appreciation of the role of the *rule of law* in these parts.[2]

To the naked eye, the law-enforcement agencies which Israel has set up in the OPT seem proper, capable, and even impressive: A military advocate

---

[1] See entry T: Temporary/Indefinite.

[2] The term "the law in these parts" refers to a documentary thus titled which focuses on the work of military courts sitting in judgment over Palestinians in the OPT, *The Law in These Parts* (2013), Director: Ra'anan Alexandrowicz; producer: Liran Atzmor. Note that this entry focuses only on law enforcement on Israeli civilians and soldiers in the OPT. This focus is complemented by a discussion on the operation of law enforcement on Palestinians in the OPT in entry M: Military Courts and by a discussion of the generation of a culture of impunity in entry W: War Crimes.

general corps (MAG) and a military police force have been set up to investigate and indict members of the IDF suspected of committing criminal offenses against Palestinians; a civilian prosecution apparatus and a full police district are in place to investigate and indict Israeli civilians who harass, intimidate, and abuse Palestinians or damage their property; military and civilian courts are empowered to try offenders; and a full body of laws, orders, regulations, and policies exists to direct the operation of those institutions. Oversight mechanisms in the form of the attorney general and the HCJ complete the picture.

This expansive system of enforcement, coupled with the reputation of the Israeli judiciary and the legal civil service as independent and professional institutions, allowed Israel to enjoy, both domestically and internationally, the trust that its procedures meet international standards. A close inspection discloses that there is less to it than meets the eye and that this trust may have been blind. The institutional density conceals the liquidity of law enforcement; the brick road to justice is as real as the royal palace of Oz.

In order to substantiate this proposition, the present entry follows the normative, procedural, and practical brick road leading to the Emerald City. Section I.2 discusses the relevant substantive legislation, which provides the framework for law enforcement in the OPT. Section I.3 describes the work of Israeli authorities invested with the task of investigations and prosecutions of civilians and members of security forces who are suspected of having abused Palestinians and provides an account of the record of their work. Section I.4 focuses on the oversight mechanisms and their effectiveness. Section I.5 concludes. A joint reading of this entry together with entry W: War Crimes and entry M: Military Courts invites reflection on the operational meaning of the rule of law in the OPT.

I.2 SUBSTANTIVE LEGISLATION

I.2.1 *Criminal Law*

The Nazi and Nazi Collaborators (Punishment) Law is the only Israeli enactment that includes war crimes as a criminal offense.[3] Substantively, the law

---

3   The Nazis and Nazi Collaborators (Punishment) Law, 1950. Israel also enacted the Crime of Genocide (Prevention and Punishment) Law, 1950, incorporating the Convention on the Prevention and Punishment of the Crime of Genocide, New York, December 9, 1948, 78 UNTS 277. In 1966, the Crimes Against Humanity (Abolition of Prescription) Law, 1966 was enacted, establishing that there would be no statute of limitations on crimes under this law and under the Nazi and Nazi Collaborators (Punishment) Law.

defines *war crimes* in a manner that is almost identical to its definition in the
Nuremberg Principles.[4] That law is chronologically and geographically
delimited to the period of the Nazi regime – that is, to crimes that were
committed before Israel was established and outside of its territory. Subject
to this exceptional enactment, some of the crimes classified under the Statute
of the International Criminal Court (ICCSt)[5] as *war crimes* are thus indistinguishable from other crimes in the Israeli penal legislation.

Section 16(a) of the Israeli Penal Code provides that

> Israel's penal laws will apply to foreign offenses, which Israel has, under
> multilateral conventions that are open to accession, committed itself to
> punish, even if they are perpetrated by a person who is neither a citizen nor
> a resident of Israel, and irrespective of the place in which the offense was
> committed.

This section thus provides the source of universal jurisdiction in Israeli law,
but does not establish offenses additional to those listed in the Israeli Penal
Code for Israeli citizens.[6] The Penal Code, however, does not list war crimes
offenses, nor is there any legislation that incorporates war crimes into Israeli
criminal law through reference to relevant provisions of international law.[7]

Israel thus refrained from enacting any dedicated legislation to meet its
obligation under Article 146 of the GC IV "to enact any legislation necessary to
provide effective penal sanctions for persons committing, or ordering to be
committed any of the grave breaches of the present Convention."[8] Indeed, it

---

[4] Principles of International Law Recognized in the Charter of the Nuremberg Tribunal and in
the Judgment of the Tribunal, 1950, legal.un.org/ilc/texts/instruments/english/draft_articles/7
_1_1950.pdf.

[5] Rome Statute of the International Criminal Court, UN General Assembly, July 17, 1998, ISBN
No. 92–9227-227–6 [hereinafter: ICCSt].

[6] Y. Shany and A. Cohen, *The IDF Investigates Itself: The Investigation of Suspected Breaches of
the Laws of War* (Jerusalem: Israeli Democracy Institute, 2011), pp. 29–32 [Hebrew].

[7] Legislation by reference to international law may follow the static referral, or "cut and paste"
approach (a model followed by e.g., the UK) or the dynamic approach, which refers generally
to the laws of war or to customary international law (a model followed by e.g., the USA). Some
follow a mixed approach employing both models model (e.g., Finland). See generally, K.
Dormann and R. Geiss, "The Implementation of Grave Breaches into Domestic Legal Order"
(2009) 7 *Journal of International Criminal Law* 703; S. J. Hankins, "Overview of Ways to Import
Core International Crimes into National Criminal Law," in M. Bergsmo, M. Harlem, and N.
Hayashi (eds.), *Importing Core International Crimes into National Law* (Oslo: FICHL, 2010),
p. 7; L. Yavne, *Lacuna: War Crimes in Israeli Law and Court Martial Rulings* (Tel Aviv: Yesh
Din, 2013), pp. 18–22, files.yesh-din.org/userfiles/file/Reports-English/Yesh%20Din%20-%20L
acuna%20Web%20-%20English.pdf.

[8] Geneva Convention Relative to the Protection of Civilian Persons in the Time of War,
Geneva, August 12, 1949, 75 UNTS 287 [hereinafter: GC IV], Article 146.

did not even establish an "aggravated circumstances" clause in its criminal legislation signifying the distinction between a domestic crime and an international crime. Israel thus maintains that the regular provisions of its Penal Code correspond to war crimes in a manner that responds adequately to its international obligations.[9] A comparative reading of the provisions of the Penal Code and the 50 crimes listed in Article 8 of the ICCTs generates the conclusion that only eight forms of conduct that amount to war crimes exist under Israeli law.[10]

I.2.2 *Military Law*

Israel Defence Forces soldiers are subject, like all Israeli citizens, to the Israeli Penal Code, but also to the Military Justice Act 1955 (MJA).

The MJA, much like the Penal Code, contains no reference to international law generally, or to grave breaches under the *GC IV* specifically. The drafting history reveals that such inclusion was contemplated but rejected because the IDF, in the words of then attorney general Shapira, "is not an occupying army but an army that defends the country's borders and, therefore, there are no provisions here on how to treat the 'natives'."[11] The fact that the IDF has been an occupying army for the last 50 years is yet to be reflected in the MJA.

The Chief Military Prosecutor's Directives that guide military prosecutors on the prevailing policy concerning indictments neither make such reference nor otherwise emphasize the gravity of offenses that may amount to war crimes in general and in the context of dealing with *protected persons* in particular.[12]

---

[9] This was the position taken by then attorney general Weinstein in a letter dated September 27, 2011, to Justice (ret.) Jacob Turkel, Chairman of The Public Commission to Examine the Maritime Incident of 31 May 2010. See The Public Commission to Examine the Maritime Incident of 31 May 2010, *Israel's Mechanisms for Examining and Investigating Complaints and Claims of Violations of the Laws of Armed Conflict According to International Law* (February 2013), p. 364, www.turkel-committee.gov.il/files/newDoc3/The%20Turkel%20Report%20for%20website.pdf [hereinafter: The Turkel Commission Second Report].

[10] These are: willful killing; conducting biological experiments; willfully causing great suffering, or serious injury to body or health; extensive destruction and appropriation of property, not justified by military necessity; unlawful deportation or transfer; taking of hostages; rape and other acts of sexual violence; and looting. See Y. Vaki and N. Wiener, *The Rome Statute of the International Criminal Court and Israeli Criminal Law: Complementarity and Compatibility* (Rishon Lezion: The Concord Research Center for Integration of International Law in Israel, 2011).

[11] Quoted in Z. Inbar, "Military Justice Act Draft Law, 5709-1949" (1988) 8 *Law and the Military* 139; cited in Yavne, *Lacuna*, p. 55, note 149.

[12] Yavne, *Lacuna*, pp. 33–37.

Indictments thus must "translate" the alleged violation of the laws of war to a criminal offense under the Penal Code or the MJA.[13]

Two other documents contain directives of conduct for IDF soldiers, but none of them provide a normative source for indictment. The first document is General Staff Order 33.0133, "Conduct in accordance with international conventions to which Israel is a party," which was issued in the 1980s. It stipulates the duty of IDF soldiers to act in accordance with the provisions of the *GC IV* and in accordance with the Hague Convention for the Protection of Cultural Property in the Event of Armed Conflict. It further provides that soldiers be briefed on the provisions of the Conventions prior to each exercise of military power in relevant circumstances. As a general directive, the Order may help prosecute soldiers for criminal offenses of a disciplinary nature, such as "conduct unbecoming" or "exceeding authority" as set forth in the MJA.

The second document is an ethical code titled "The IDF spirit."[14] Written in the 1990s and updated in 2000, it refers to "universal moral values based on the value and dignity of human life" as one of its sources, the others being the IDF tradition and its military heritage; the tradition of the State of Israel, its democratic principles, laws, and institutions; and the tradition of the Jewish People throughout their history. Its values include "purity of arms," the principle of distinction, and the assertion that blatantly illegal orders are not to be obeyed. While the document has no binding legal force, it occasionally carries weight in sentencing.

Two further points should be noted in this context; first, neither the Israeli Penal Code nor the MJA include the principle of "command responsibility" requiring military commanders and other superiors to ensure that their subordinates are acting lawfully and to take effective measures in response to any

---

[13] The Military Advocate General, *The accordance of Israel's mechanisms for examining and investigating complaints and claims of violations of the laws of armed conflict with Israel's duties under international law, and the Implementation of that mechanism in relation to the maritime incident on May 31, 2010* (Position paper, December 2010), p. 6, note 10, submitted to the Turkel Commission.

[14] The document is accessible at the IDF website www.idfblog.com/about-the-idf/idf-code-of-e thics/. See Yavne, *Lacuna*, p. 26. Note that a third document, titled "The Ethical Code for Fighting Terrorism," and written in 2004 upon the initiative of Maj. Gen. Amos Yadlin and Prof. Asa Kasher, has not been officially adopted by the IDF. It draws on various principles of international law, and in some instances, such as the principle of distinction, does so in a most controversial manner. On the controversy see A. Kasher, "Israel & the Rules of War': An Exchange," *The New York Review of Books* (June 11, 2009), www.nybooks.com/articles/2009/ 06/11/israel-the-rules-of-war-an-exchange/; A. Margalit and M. Walzer, "'Israel: Civilians & Combatants': An Exchange," *The New York Review of Books* (August 13, 2009), www.nybooks .com/articles/2009/08/13/israel-civilians-combatants-an-exchange/.

suspicion that they have committed international crimes.[15] Consequently, a commander or civilian cannot be prosecuted in Israel for crimes committed by his or her subordinates unless he or she personally ordered them to be committed, had direct involvement in their commission, or aided and abetted.[16] Second, a 2011 amendment to the MJA[17] has retroactively reduced both the period of the criminal record of defendants convicted of a misdemeanor[18] in courts-martial and the number of public bodies to which the record may be disclosed. One of the justifications for this amendment was to spare the convicts the criminal stain that may otherwise hamper their post-service employment opportunities.[19]

Israeli legislation thus does not include any explicit reference to war crimes in its legislation, and the offenses to which war crimes could be "translated" are quite few. The HCJ, however, in the context of dismissing a petition submitted by three human rights organizations to order criminal investigations against people suspected of being responsible for acts of killing and destruction in the Gaza Strip during the 2004 military operations, found that:[20]

> even without applying international law as an independent part of the Israeli criminal code, Israel meets its obligations under article 146 of the GC IV because it allows effective criminal sanctions to be imposed on violators of material articles [of the GC IV] ... as long as the indictment reflects the criminality of the action ... and the punishment imposed in case of conviction reflects the aggravated circumstances of committing the crime against protected persons under the laws of war.

A report by the Public Commission appointed by the Israeli government to examine the Maritime Incident of 31 May 2010[21] reached a different

---

[15] Article 28 of ICCSt.   [16] Vaki and Wiener, *Complementarity and Compatibility*, p. 46.

[17] Military Justice Act (amendment No. 63), 2011.

[18] A misdemeanor in Israeli law is defined as an offense which carries a maximum penalty of more than 3 months' and not more than 3 years' imprisonment.

[19] Yavne, *Lacuna*, pp. 53–54.

[20] HCJ 3292/07 *Adalah v. The Attorney General* (December 8, 2011), ¶ 10.

[21] The Turkel Commission Second Report. The Commission issued two reports: the first, issued in 2011, examined whether the Israeli blockade of Gaza and its action in taking over the flotilla which attempted to break the blockade (which resulted in the killing of 9 and the wounding of 20 passengers and with 10 IDF soldiers wounded) complied with international law. The second report, issued in 2013, focused on whether Israel's mechanisms for examining and investigating claims raised in relation to violations of the laws of armed conflict, as conducted in Israel generally and implemented with respect to the flotilla incidents specifically, conform with Israel's obligations under international law. The second report from 2013 is of relevance to the present discussion.

conclusion. Having noted that the explicit adoption of international norms relating to war crimes into Israeli domestic legislation serves not only practical needs but also normative purposes of education and deterrence, and that such adoption is the preferred approach internationally, the core of its first recommendation was that:

> The Ministry of Justice should initiate legislation wherever there is a deficiency regarding international prohibitions that do not have a "regular" equivalent in the Israeli Penal Code, and rectify that deficiency through Israeli criminal legislation. Furthermore, the Commission sees importance in the explicit adoption of the international norms relating to war crimes into Israeli domestic legislation. From the trend reflected in the survey of the six countries it appears that the accepted approach is to incorporate the international criminal offenses into domestic legislation.[22]

Its second recommendation was to amend Israeli law to impose direct criminal liability on commanders and superiors who do not take reasonable measures to prevent offenses by their subordinates.[23]

A subsequent report, issued in 2015 by another commission appointed by the government to review and implement the recommendations contained in the 2013 Turkel Report,[24] in effect diluted the implementation of the first recommendation and circumvented the implementation of the second: in relation to the recommendation to incorporate international crimes into Israeli legislation, it advised the preparation of draft bills on the incorporation of the crime of torture and crimes against humanity into Israeli law when they are committed as part of systematic and widespread policy, but it remained silent on the incorporation of war crimes into Israeli domestic legislation.[25] Its recommendation regarding the incorporation of command and superior responsibility into Israeli legislation was that the matter should continue to be examined, rather than implemented. Israel's position that its legal system meets the requirements of the complementarity principle, at least insofar as its legislation is concerned, seems thus to have been weakened. Legislative

---

[22]   The Turkel Commission Second Report, pp. 362–366.
[23]   The Turkel Commission Second Report, pp. 366–369.
[24]   This commission, known as the Ciechanover Commission, was established pursuant to recommendation 18 of The Turkel Commission Second Report. For its report, see Report of the *Team for the Review and Implementation of the second Report of the Public Commission for the Examination of the Maritime Incident of May 31st 2010 Regarding Israel's Mechanisms for Examining and Investigating Complaints and Claims of Violations of the Law of Armed Conflicts According to International Law* (August 2015), www.pmo.gov.il/Documents/Report Eng.pdf.
[25]   Yesh Din, *The Ciechanover Report: Dodging the Criminalization of War Crimes and Practical Steps Towards Implementation* (2015), files.yesh-din.org/userfiles/Ciechanover%20Eng.pdf.

silence on the very possibility of the commission of war crimes is echoed in the functioning of investigation and prosecution processes.

I.3 INVESTIGATION AND PROSECUTION IN PRACTICE

The proper functioning of the rule of law requires that the law be enforced through crime prevention, investigation of offenses, and prosecution. The IDF is responsible for law enforcement in the West Bank (excluding East Jerusalem). This responsibility consists of military law enforcement that applies to IDF soldiers and of police law enforcement that applies to civilians, including settlers. The latter has been delegated by the IDF to the Israeli police by a military order that grants police officers the same powers given to any soldier under security legislation, as well as the powers that were granted to any police officer under the law in force on the day the occupation began.[26]

Noting that "[I]nvestigations and, if appropriate prosecutions of those suspected of serious violations are necessary if respect for human rights and humanitarian law is to be ensured and to prevent the development of a climate of impunity,"[27] the Report of the United Nations Fact-Finding Mission on the Gaza Conflict proceeded to review the Israeli system of investigations and prosecution in order to assess whether Israel meets its international duty in this respect.[28] It concluded, in relation to the Israeli system of investigations of its armed forces, that it does not comply with the universal principles of independence, effectiveness, promptness, and impartiality;[29] that "there are serious doubts about the willingness of Israel to carry out genuine investigations in an impartial, independent, prompt and effective way, as required by international law"; and that Israel's system "presents inherently discriminatory features that have proven to make the pursuit of justice for Palestinian victims very difficult."[30]

A study of the operation of the military law-enforcement system conducted by B'Tselem – The Israeli Information Center for Human Rights in the Occupied Territories, found that from 2000 to 2015, more than 96 percent of complaints regarding hundreds of incidents involving fatalities, injuries,

---

[26] In 1967, the military commander issued an order giving the Israeli police the same law-enforcement powers soldiers have: Order Concerning Police Forces Acting In cooperation With the IDF (Judea and Samaria) (No. 52), 1967. See also: Order Concerning Security Provisions (Consolidated Version) (Judea and Samaria) (No.1651), 2009.

[27] UN Human Rights Council, Report of the United Nations Fact-Finding Mission on the Gaza Conflict, UN Doc A/HRC/12/48 (September 25, 2009), ¶ 1773.

[28] *Ibid.*, ¶¶ 1586–1600, 1789–1803.   [29] *Ibid.*, ¶¶ 1831.   [30] *Ibid.*, ¶ 1832.

beating, property damage, and the use of human shields were closed without indicting soldiers suspected of violating the laws of war (in 30 percent of cases no criminal investigation was carried out at all).[31] Other studies corroborate these findings,[32] with the most recent indicating that only 3.1 percent of criminal complaints processed by the army in 2015 ended with an indictment.[33]

The record of the law-enforcement agencies regarding offenses committed by Israeli civilians, usually settlers, against Palestinians does not fare much better. These offenses are ideologically motivated. A study by Yesh Din – Volunteers for Human Rights, of the operation of police investigations following complaints from Palestinian victims of offenses committed by Israeli civilians reveals that only 7.4 percent of more than a thousand such complaints made to the Samaria and Judea District Police from 2005 to 2014 led to indictments.[34] A review of investigation files generating no charges discloses that 85 percent of all investigations were closed in circumstances indicating failure on the part of the police to secure enough evidence against the perpetrators.[35] A staggering figure related to cases of willful damage to groves, mainly olive groves, owned by Palestinians, usually in the form of uprooting or sawing trees, setting fire to crops, etc., deserves special attention: since 2005, 260 such cases that led to police investigations were documented. Indictments, however, were served in just six cases. Thus, 95 percent of the cases were closed due to police investigative failure, making it the highest failure rate for investigations of ideologically motivated crimes.[36]

[31]   B'Tselem, *The Occupation's Fig Leaf: Israel's Military Law Enforcement System as a Whitewash Mechanism* (2016), www.btselem.org/download/201605_occupations_fig_le af_eng.pdf.

[32]   L. Yavne, *Alleged Investigations: The Failure of Investigations into Offenses Committed by IDF Soldiers against Palestinians* (Tel Aviv: Yesh Din, 2011), www.yesh-din.org/en/alleged-investi gation-the-failure-of-investigations-into-offenses-committed-by-idf-soldiers-against-palesti nians/.

[33]   Yesh Din, *Law Enforcement on Israeli Soldiers Suspected of Harming Palestinians: Figures for 2015* (2017), www.yesh-din.org/en/december-2016-data-sheet-law-enforcement-idf-soldiers-sus pected-harming-palestinians-summary-2015-data/

[34]   Z. Stahl, *Mock Enforcement: The Failure to Enforce the Law on Israeli Civilians in the West Bank* (Tel Aviv: Yesh Din, 2015), files.yesh-din.org/userfiles/Yesh%20Din_Akifat%20Hok_%2 0English.pdf. The author of this entry serves as legal advisor to Yesh Din.

[35]   *Ibid.*, pp. 31–32.

[36]   Yesh Din, *Law Enforcement on Israeli Citizens Who Harm Palestinians and Their Property in the West Bank* (2015), www.yesh-din.org/en/data-sheet-october-2015-law-enforcement-on-isra eli-citizens-who-harm-palestinians-and-their-property-in-the-west-bank/.

Even in the very few cases in which Israeli civilians are indicted, the chances of securing a remedy for the victim in the form of conviction and penalty for the perpetrator are not high: The Yesh Din study shows that only one-third of the legal proceedings resulted in a full or partial conviction of the defendants. Nearly a quarter of the legal proceedings were eventually canceled or vacated, and another quarter resulted in a judicial decision not to convict the defendants, despite a finding that they did commit the offenses for which they were tried.[37]

While mere statistics do not necessarily generate the conclusion that the enforcement systems are at fault, the analysis substantiates that these results are due to a significant gap between the legal system described in the books and the law in action – a gap attesting to a myriad of systemic failures in law enforcement: most of these failures exist in both military and police investigations. These include, for instance, negligence and lack of professionalism in the conduct of investigations, most noticeable in military pre-investigation field inquiries (which, in most cases, are a condition and a basis for a decision on whether to launch a criminal investigation) which almost exclusively rely on testimonies of soldiers and Palestinians involved with no effort to reach other witnesses; significant delays in taking testimonies and taking them at face value even in cases of clear contradictory statements; difficulties in locating both the soldiers and the Palestinians; material inaccessibility of the systems to Palestinians, who have to get a special permit to reach the relevant investigative units, a permit that may not be given, and who thus have to rely on human rights organizations or private lawyers to launch a claim and otherwise engage in a process the responsibility for which rests with the IDF or the police; lack of transparency in the working of the criminal and military authorities, etc.

In addition, each of these systems has its own shortcomings: thus, for instance, within the military, since the outbreak of the second Intifada, in all cases of Palestinian fatalities, and in some cases of other violence, an operational inquiry is conducted before a decision regarding on the opening of a criminal investigation is made.[38] The two functions are quite different in terms of their purpose and procedure: An operational inquiry is a mechanism

---

[37] Yesh Din, *Prosecution of Israeli civilians suspected of Harming Palestinians in the West Bank* (2015), www.yesh-din.org/en/data-sheet-may-2015-prosecution-of-israeli-civilians-suspected-of-harming-palestinians-in-the-west-bank/.

[38] In 2011, IDF investigation policy was amended, mandating automatic investigations in cases of civilian fatalities in the OPT caused by military use of force (the Military Advocate General announced the amendment in a notice to the high court in a case that focused on the IDF

dedicated to studying operational failures with an aim to improving future military performance, whereas a criminal investigation seeks to uncover the truth and make findings regarding individual accountability and is conducted by trained investigators. Given this difference, the priority given to the operational inquiry undermines the subsequent criminal investigation: The inquiry is classified and its findings, which serve also as the basis for the decision on the opening of a criminal investigation, are inadmissible by law and are not disclosed to the military police unit. The soldiers, aware of this sequence, may well coordinate their stories and refrain from giving true accounts in an effort to evade incrimination. Further, the effects of the passage of time between the ending of an operational inquiry and the beginning of a criminal investigation (which can amount to months and in extreme cases even years[39]) in terms of physical evidence and memory are not conducive to a rigorous investigation.[40] Enforcing the law on Israeli civilians, especially for ideologically motivated crimes committed by settlers, suffers from a sense that both the political echelons and significant segments of the public do not regard the offenders as criminals, but rather as true patriots.[41] Such sensibility does not provide a great incentive for a rigorous investigation.[42]

Prosecution, before either a court martial or a criminal court, in the relatively few cases that it is generated after an investigation, does not, as a general rule, make any reference to obligations under international law, including war crimes or the special responsibility owed to protected persons.[43] This is not surprising given that the normative framework within which the enforcement system operates, as discussed in Section I.2, is equally silent on these obligations.

---

investigation policy, see HCJ 9594/03 *B'Tselem v. Military Advocate General* (August 21, 2011)). However, an exception to the new policy provided that if the death was caused in "pure combat" circumstances the regular investigatory decision-making mechanism would be in effect. Consequently, an operational inquiry would be held prior to a decision on whether a criminal investigation is merited. The exception has since generated several refusals to investigate killings of Palestinians on the basis that they occurred during combat (see for example Y. Gurvitz, "A Life Cut Short – 'By Accident'," *Yesh Din* (January 22, 2017), www .yesh-din.org/en/life-cut-short/.

39   Yavne, *Alleged Investigations*, p. 28.

40   B'Tselem, *The Occupation's Fig Leaf*, pp. 17, 23; see generally, A. Cohen and Y. Shany, *The IDF and Alleged International Law Violations: Reforming Policies for Self-Investigation*, policy paper 93 (Jerusalem: Israeli Democracy Institute, 2011). An abstract in English is accessible in www.idi.org.il/media/3460/takzir_e_93.pdf.

41   On the public discourse see entry W: War Crimes, Section W.3.

42   Stahl, Mock Enforcement, p. 138.   43   Yavne, *Lacuna*, pp. 11, 34.

I.4 OVERSIGHT MECHANISMS

Two civilian institutions, the attorney general and the HCJ,[44] are entrusted with the exercise of oversight over law enforcement, both military and police, in the West Bank. Additionally, ad hoc committees of experts and governmental commissions of inquiry may be formed by the government to exercise such functions.

The attorney general first exercised this mandate over police investigations in the West Bank in 1981 pursuant to criticism made by both academics and the HCJ of lack of proper investigations of settlers' harassment of Palestinians.[45] He appointed a monitoring team headed by his then deputy, attorney Yehudit Karp. The ensuing 1982 Karp Report determined that investigations were seriously flawed, related this finding, inter alia, to the ideological motivation of the offenders, and concluded that police failures were but a symptom of "a much deeper process" that required the formulation of "an official government position ... in order to prevent matters from deteriorating and eroding the foundations of the rule of law."[46] Twelve years and no meaningful implementation later, the Hebron Massacre, perpetrated by the settler Baruch Goldstein,[47] led to the establishment of the Shamgar Commission of Inquiry. Its 1994 report, having noted the failure to implement the Karp Report, recommended a clearer division of responsibilities between the military and the police and related structural and procedural changes.[48] These recommendations were implemented, but no meaningful amelioration of police investigations ensued, as was disclosed in the 2005 Sasson Report. Talia Sasson was appointed by then prime minister Sharon to inquire into the issue of unauthorized outposts in the West Bank.[49] Her report identified various problems which impede police investigations including reluctance of IDF soldiers and settlers on the one hand, and Palestinians on the other hand, to cooperate with the police, and, most importantly, a message from the high political echelons that "no one seriously intends to enforce the law" and that the institutional system is but

---

[44] The oversight role of the HCJ is discussed in entry W: War Crimes, Section W.2.2.
[45] HCJ 175/81 *Anabi a-Natsheh v. Minister of Defense* (1981) 35(4) PD 361.
[46] Y. Karp, *The Investigating of Suspicions against Israelis in Judea and Samaria – Report of the Monitoring Team*, Ministry of Justice (Jerusalem, 1982), p. 31, media.wix.com/ugd/cdb1 a7_3342db25459b43ff8dab68d9ee20e32e.pdf [Hebrew], quoted in Stahl, Mock Enforcement, p. 21.
[47] See entry Z: Zone, Section Z.2.2.2.1.
[48] *Report of the Commission of Inquiry into the Massacre at the Tomb of the Patriarchs in Hebron* (Jerusalem, 1994), pp. 246–252 [Hebrew].
[49] On "outposts," see entry R: Regularization.

"false pretense."[50] Given that over the years this message became ever more explicit, as is attested to, inter alia, by the governmental move to legalize the outposts rather than enforce the law,[51] it is little wonder that the quality of police investigations has not improved.

The attorney general, as head of the prosecutorial system and legal advisor to all government bodies, oversees the military advocate general (MAG). The 2015 guidelines relative to this oversight function clarify that only in exceptional cases, the implications of which exceed the military context, will the attorney general intervene in the MAG's discretion.[52] The guidelines establish a right to an administrative appeal process before the attorney general on a MAG's decision relating to the investigation and prosecution of a civilian fatality caused by military use of force. In practice, apart from this relatively new and narrow appeal process in cases of fatalities, which are too recent to assess, the attorney general has not carried out significant oversight of the MAG's policies. Given that the MAG's authority extends to military legislation, the executive direction of the military's operative legal counseling, and his quasi-judicial authority to decide to launch an investigation and to prosecute, there is a built-in conflict of interest in his function.[53] The likelihood that he would order an investigation into a policy he authored and authorized is thereby minimized.[54]

The Turkel Commissions made several recommendations with respect to the functioning of the MAG. These included streamlining the military's examination and investigative procedures;[55] rendering the proceedings more transparent;[56] institutionalizing the MAG's independence in a manner designed to ameliorate the conflict of interest inherent in his function;[57]

---

[50] T. Sasson, *Opinion Concerning Unauthorized Outposts* (2005), pp. 43–47; Stahl, Mock Enforcement, pp. 23–24.

[51] Z. Stahl, *Under the Radar: Israel's silent policy of transforming illegal outposts into official settlements* (Tel Aviv: Yesh Din, 2015) reveals that at the time of publication more than a quarter of the unauthorized outposts in the West Bank (25 out of 100) had been retroactively authorized or were in the process of being authorized. The number subsequently grew to a third (34); see Yesh Din, *Settlement Blocs that Sever the West Bank – the Shilo Valley as a Case study* (2016), www.yesh-din.org/en/settlement-blocs-sever-west-bank-shilo-valley-case-study/. See also entry R: Regularization.

[52] "Military Advocate General" Attorney General Guidelines No. 4.5003, 2015.

[53] E. Benvenisti, *The Duty of the State of Israel to Investigate Violations of the Law of Armed Conflict*, Expert Opinion submitted to the Turkel Commission (April 13, 2011), p. 24 [Hebrew]; Cohen and Shany, *The IDF and Alleged International Law Violations*.

[54] B'Tselem, *The Occupation's Fig Leaf*, pp. 22–23, 27–28; Cohen and Shany, *The IDF and Alleged International Law Violations*, pp. 86–117.

[55] The Turkel Commission Second Report, Recommendations 3–10.

[56] *Ibid.*, Recommendation 11.   [57] *Ibid.*, Recommendation 8.

implementing measures designed to improve oversight of the MAG corps comprising enhanced expertise in IHL in the ministry of justice and adding to the possibility of appealing the MAG's decisions to the HCJ, an appeal to the attorney general, delimiting the duration of the process;[58] setting durations for investigations and prosecutorial decision making;[59] improving the working procedures of the complaints controller;[60] and establishing mechanisms for inquiring into complaints against the civil authorities.[61]

While these recommendations still fail to solve the situation of the military investigating itself, especially with respect to illegal commands which the MAG authorized and which do not tackle the issue of examining the legality of governmental responsibility for policies that contravene IHL, they nevertheless had potential for ameliorating the process.[62] That potential seems to have been minimized by the Ciechanover Commission: established to make practical recommendations for implementing the recommendations of the Turkel Report, its report does not address such practicalities related to human resources, budgeting, and time-tables. This failure may well suggest the eventual fate of the implementation process.[63]

Finally, it should be noted that in the legislative debates leading to the establishment of an agency authorized to review complaints against legal representatives of the state before judicial bodies,[64] the legislators have declined to include the MAG corps in the definition of legal representatives of the state and explicitly excluded the MAG corps from the commission's purview. The proposal to include them was submitted by the minister of justice who explained that it would strengthen Israel's position vis-à-vis international legal processes.[65]

The failure of the military justice system to discharge justice and the loss of faith in its efforts to do so have led B'tselem, following a quarter of a century of

---

[58] *Ibid.*, Recommendations 12–13.   [59] *Ibid.*, Recommendation 10.

[60] *Ibid.*, Recommendation 14.   [61] *Ibid.*, Recommendation 17.

[62] A proposal made by Shany and Cohen to establish a permanent independent committee authorized to examine legality of directives given by both civilian and military policymakers was presented to the Turkel Commission but not included in its recommendations. See Shany and Cohen, *The IDF and Alleged International Law Violations*; Y. Stein, *Promoting Accountability: The Turkel Commission Report on Israel's Addressing Alleged Violations of International Humanitarian Law* (Jerusalem: B'Tselem, 2013), www.btselem.org/download/position_paper_on_turkel_report_eng.pdf.

[63] Yesh Din, *The Ciechanover Report*, pp. 3–4.

[64] Commissionership for Public Complaints on Legal Representatives of the State Before Judicial Bodies Act, 2016.

[65] The Minister of Justice was quoted in the Knesset website: main.knesset.gov.il/Activity/committees/Huka/News/Pages/01082016.aspx.

experience of working together with the military justice system, to decide to end its cooperation with the system. This decision conveys more than lack of trust in the justice that the system produces; it conveys a belief that the very act of cooperation with it assists the system in its major role: not to enhance a culture of accountability, but to cover up for a culture of impunity; to pretend to advance the rule of law, while in effect emptying it of meaning.[66] In this, it no longer wishes to be complicit.

This position is controversial within the Israeli human rights community. While it is true that over the years, there has been a decline of some 30 percent in Palestinian crime victims who feel there is a point in putting the time and energy into filing a complaint with the Israeli police,[67] there are others who still seek remedy, ask for their complaints to be recorded and processed, and require assistance. Further, some NGOs, like Yesh Din, see value in monitoring the justice system and thus choose to continue their cooperation with the MAG corps and the military police, simultaneously monitoring and critiquing their operation.[68]

I.5 CONCLUSION: DON'T BE SILLY, TOTO. SCARECROWS DON'T TALK[69]

The Palestinian village of Bil'in is located west of Ramallah. Since 2005, when the separation barrier walled off more than half of its lands, rendering them inaccessible, its residents have waged a struggle against its construction.[70] In tandem with weekly demonstrations and marches, they have filed a petition to the HCJ claiming the route is illegal. In 2007, the HCJ ordered a rerouting of the barrier in a manner which would restore about half of the lands to the

---

[66] B'Tselem's decision was made public in its *The Occupation's Fig Leaf* report, p. 5.

[67] Yesh Din, *Avoiding Complaining to Police: Facts and Figures on Palestinian Victims of Offenses Who Decide Not to File Complaints with the Police* (2016), www.yesh-din.org/en/av oiding-complaining/. About half of the Palestinians stated mistrust in the system as the reason for avoiding complaints.

[68] A fascinating analogous fierce debate on the question of whether liberal judges in Apartheid South Africa should resign, and whether human rights lawyers should litigate in its courts, was waged between South African law professors Reymond Wacks and John Dugard in the mid-80s. See R. Wacks, "Judges and Injustice" (1984) 101 *South African Law Journal* 266; J. Dugrad, "Should Judges Resign? A Reply to Professor Wacks" (1984) 101 *South African Law Journal* 286; R. Wacks, "Judging Judges: A Brief Rejoinder to Professor Dugard" (1984) *South African Law Journal* 295.

[69] *The Wizard of Oz* (Metro-Goldwyn-Mayer, 1939); director: Victor Fleming (based on the novel *The Wonderful Wizard of Oz* by L. Frank Baum (Chicago: George M. Hill Company, 1900).

[70] See entry B: Border/Barrier.

Palestinian farmers.[71] Over the following four years, the village was forced to embark on yet another struggle, this time aimed at compelling the state of Israel to adhere to the HCJ ruling. It was during the weekly demonstrations of those years that two of the Bil'in Abu Rahme family siblings were killed, and a third injured, all by IDF fire.

First was Ashraf Abu Rahme. While detained during a demonstration in July 2008, handcuffed and blindfolded, he was shot point blank in the leg with a rubber-coated bullet. The incident was videotaped by a B'Tselem volunteer, and upon release instantly became viral. The soldier who shot Abu Rahme was ordered to do so by his commanding officer who later claimed he had only wanted to scare the detainee and never meant for it to be carried out literally by his subordinate.

Nine months later, Ashraf's brother, Bassem, was fatally hit in the chest while participating in a small, quiet protest near the then yet to be removed fence. A gas canister was fired directly at him, in clear violation of IDF regulations, and killed him.

A year and a half later, at a protest in December 2010, the military dispersed a massive quantity of tear gas, and Bassem and Ashraf's sister, Jawaher Abu Rahmah, suffered from severe tear gas inhalation. She died several hours later.

The scandalous mishandling of the subsequent inquiries into the killing and injuring of the Abu Rahmes is sadly an apt representation of Israel's failure to adhere to basic professional standards when Palestinians are victims of alleged criminal actions by Israelis.

In the case of Ashraf's shooting, the MAG has decided not to charge the soldier and the officer of injury. Instead, the indictment served against them alleged conduct unbecoming, an offense designed to protect the image and reputation of the army, rather than protect life and limb. The HCJ intervened, albeit reluctantly, and ordered the MAG to change the indictment so as to reflect the seriousness of the incident.[72] Still, the defendants were eventually charged and convicted for relatively minor offenses: attempted intimidation (the officer) and illegal use of a weapon (the soldier). The sentences were accordingly lenient: a two-year delay in promotions (the officer) and a drop to the rank of private (the soldier).

---

[71] HCJ 8414/05 *Ahmad Issa Abdallah Yassin, Bil'in Village Council Chairman v. The Government of Israel* (2007) TakSC 2007(3) 3557. The author of this entry represented the petitioners.

[72] HCJ 7195/06 *Ashraf Abu Rahme v. Brigadier General Avichay Mandelblitt the MAG* (unpublished). The case is discussed and critiqued in entry W: War Crimes.

Although Bassem's killing was documented by three different cameras,[73] initially the MAG dismissed the demand to launch a criminal investigation, arguing that, though tragic, the incident did not raise any suspicion of illegal use of weapons. After the family and B'Tselem secured a spatial-ballistic expert report analyzing the video documentation of the event and concluding the canister was shot at a direct angle,[74] MAG changed its position and ordered an investigation. The investigation and the subsequent decision to close the case without charges took three years. Administrative and judicial reviews pursued by the family, and assisted by B'Tselem and Yesh Din, took four more years.[75] In dismissing the appeal against MAG's decision, the state attorney[76] has finally conceded that the lethal shot was indeed fired directly at Bassem, thus in violation of IDF regulations.[77] However, he concluded there was not enough evidence to establish the identity of the killer. Eight years of probes, investigations, and prosecutorial oversight culminated in a file that was lacking the most basic feature such an inquiry must include: a thorough examination of the positions and type of ammunition used by the handful of soldiers involved. Finally, the state attorney also disclosed that the original investigation file was lost and only a partial copy of it remains at the authority's disposal.

As for Jawaher, following a command inquiry which the MAG believed did not raise suspicion of any criminal actions, it was decided not to launch a criminal investigation. The HCJ has upheld the MAG's decision.[78]

It is safe to assume that the military police and the MAG corps devoted thousands of hours to the Abu Rahme cases. Two administrative appeals were heard, and five High Court petitions adjudicated. Justice was administered in the Abu Rahme cases – administered intensively, but not served.[79]

[73] The story of the killing of Bassem Abu Rahme was narrated in a documentary *Five Broken Cameras* by village resident Emad Burnat and Israeli director Guy Davidi. The film was nominated for an Academy Award for best documentary in 2013.
[74] Summary of Findings on the April 17, 2009 Death of Bassem Ibrahim Abu Rahma, Bil'in, *Forensic Architecture team lead by Eyal Weizman and by SITU Studio*, www.forensic-architecture.org/case/bilin/.
[75] At the time of writing, an HCJ petition demanding that charges are brought against the shooting soldier and his commanding officers is pending: HCJ 9850/16 *Subhiyya Moussa Abu Rahme v. The Attorney General*. Author of this entry represents the petitioners.
[76] Since the attorney general at the time of filing the appeal was Avichai Mandelblit, who served as MAG when the incident occurred and was involved in the case in its first years, the appeal was considered and decided by state attorney, Shai Nitzan.
[77] Decision in the appeal regarding the death of Bassem Abu Rahme (March 5, 2017), unpublished, copy with author's archive.
[78] HCJ 6547/11 *Subhiyya Moussa Abu Rahme v. The Attorney General* (2014) *Takdin Elyon* 2014 (3)8798. Author of this entry represents the petitioners.
[79] On law as violence see entry V: Violence.

Israel has established, and maintains, two sets of law-enforcement agencies in the West Bank. These systems are ostensibly designed to uphold Israel's obligation under the law of belligerent occupation to protect the Palestinian civilians subject to its effective control. The extensive research human rights organizations have conducted on these systems, the vast data that they have collected regarding their functioning, and indeed numerous governmental-commissioned reports and international reports all generate the conclusion that Israel has failed to enforce the law in the OPT. The fact that the recommendations made by its own government commissions were essentially shelved and left to collect dust over the years underscores the point.

In the main, Israel's enforcement agencies in the West Bank are not engaged in law enforcement; they are engaged in make-believe, in a photo-op: There are police stations (both military and civilian), interrogation rooms, cruisers, and an array of officers and commanders who manage interrogation files, but their materiality is akin to a cardboard theater set. The set is a set-up. It has internalized the advice Tiger whispered to the girl from Kansas: "'[H]ush Dorothy' ... 'You'll ruin my reputation if you are not more discreet. It isn't what we are, but what folks think we are, that counts in this world.'"[80] In the process, it has made a scarecrow of the law[81] and paved the brick road to a culture of impunity.[82]

---

[80] L. F. Baum, *The Road to Oz* (Fairfield: 1st World Library – Literary Society, 2004), p. 138 (originally published in 1909).

[81] W. Shakespeare, Measure for Measure, Act II Scene II: "We must not make a scarecrow of the law, setting it up to fear the birds of prey."

[82] See entry W: War Crimes.

J

Jewish Settlements

Michael Sfard

J.1 INTRODUCTION: THE LEGAL PROHIBITION ON SETTLING AN OCCUPIED TERRITORY

The prohibition on establishing settlements in an occupied territory, legally phrased as the prohibition against transferring parts of the occupying power's civilian population into the occupied territory,[1] is one of those prohibitions the purpose of which permeates IHL. Unlike, for example, the prohibitions and restrictions on damaging private property in the occupied territory, which are meant specifically to protect the property of protected persons,[2] the prohibition on establishing settlements is aimed at protecting not just one value, but the entire gamut of values the laws of occupation set out to protect. The prohibition on settling occupied territory is also pivotal to ensuring that the main principles of occupation are upheld: that it is temporary, that the occupied territory is held and managed as a trusteeship, and that the occupying power does not gain sovereignty over the occupied land.[3]

Human history teaches us that colonization of an occupied territory and the changes it brings to the area's demographic makeup is a crucial step toward eliminating the temporary nature of the occupation and significantly reduces the occupying power's readiness to serve as the protected persons' trustee and act in their best interests. It is also a big step toward bringing the status of the occupying power on par with that of a sovereign. Such developments, in turn, lead to systemic, multidimensional violations of the fundamental rights

---

[1] Article 49 paragraph 6 of the Geneva Convention Relative to the Protection of Civilian Persons in the Time of War, Geneva, August 12, 1949, 75 UNTS 287 [hereinafter: *GC IV*].

[2] Regulation 23(g) of The Hague Convention (IV) Respecting the Laws and Customs of War on Land and its annex: Regulations concerning the Laws and Customs of War on Land, The Hague, October 18, 1907, 205 CTS 277; 36 Stat 2277 [hereinafter: *HC IV*]; Article 53 of the *GC IV*; see also entry H: House Demolitions.

[3] See Introduction and entry T: Temporary/Indefinite.

granted to protected persons under the international laws of occupation and international human rights law: their rights to property, livelihood, freedom of movement, enjoyment of their land's natural resources, equality, and dignity. An occupation which forces protected persons to have their land settled with citizens of the occupying power is, by definition, antithetical to the type of regime international law sought to secure through the laws of occupation.

The prohibition on settling occupied territory is to the law of occupation what the prohibition on coercion and extortion is to contract law and what the prohibition on abolishing elections is to constitutional law: All prohibit a practice that threatens the overarching goal, the raison d'être, of the legal branch that produced it.

The ban on settling occupied territory is anchored in the rule prohibiting the transfer of citizens of the occupying power into the occupied territory. It is articulated in the sixth paragraph of Article 49 of the GC IV: "The Occupying Power shall not deport or transfer parts of its own civilian population into the territory it occupies."

The language is concise and clear: The prohibition makes no exceptions and covers both "deportation" and "transfer." Some have claimed that the paragraph refers only to forcible transfers,[4] but there is scant support for this position.[5] First, the difference between the wording of this paragraph and the wording of the first paragraph of Article 49, which concerns the deportation of protected persons from an occupied territory ("forcible transfers, as well as deportation"), ostensibly indicates that where the authors of the Convention wished to refer to *forcible* transfer, they did so explicitly. Second, when breach of this ban was listed as an offense in the Rome Statute of the International Criminal Court, the words "directly or indirectly" were added (the Rome Statue reads: "The transfer, directly or indirectly, by the Occupying Power of parts of its own civilian population into the territory it

[4]   See, e.g., HCJ 785/87 *Al-Affu v. Commander of the IDF Forces in the West Bank* (1988) 42(2) PD 4, chief justice Shamgar, pp. 21–33; A. Baker, *The Settlements Issue: Distorting the Geneva Convention and the Oslo Accords* (Jerusalem Center for Public Affairs, January 5, 2011), jcpa.org /article/the-settlements-issue-distorting-the-geneva-convention-and-the-oslo-accords/. This was also the position of the *Report on the Legal Status of Building in Judea and Samaria* (2012), www .pmo.gov.il/Documents/doch090712.pdf [Hebrew]. For an analysis of the position of the Levy Commission, see entry N: Nomos.

[5]   See, e.g., D. Kretzmer, *The Occupation of Justice: The Supreme Court of Israel and the Occupied Territories* (Albany: State University of New York Press, 2002), p. 77; Y. Dinstein, "Settlements and Expulsion in Occupied Territories" (1979) 7 *Iyunei Mishpat* 188 [Hebrew]; E. Benvenisti, *The International Law of Occupation* (Princeton: Princeton University Press, 1993), p. 140; Consequences of the Construction of a Wall in the Occupied Palestinian Territory, Advisory Opinion, 2004 ICJ 136. For references to the authorities comprising the wide consensus on the matter, see entry N: Nomos, Section N.3, text and notes 55–81.

occupies"),[6] to underscore that the ban also applies to cases in which the transfer of the occupying power's population is not forcible.

The official commentary of the International Committee of the Red Cross supports the above analysis regarding the purpose of the prohibition. According to the commentary, the prohibition was meant to prevent a practice adopted by some powers during the Second World War, of transferring parts of their civilian population to territories they occupied for political and demographic reasons: "Such transfers worsened the economic situation of the native population and endangered their separate existence as a race."[7]

Israel began settling the OPT shortly after the 1967 war, and the Israeli HCJ was asked to adjudicate on the project's legality early on. The unique character and magnitude of the Israeli settlement process have transformed the occupation into a project of settler – colonialism. This transformation is discussed in Section J.2. The Israeli HCJ played a pivotal role in this transformation by forcing an exception on a rule; carving an exception on a rule; and ignoring the absence of an exception to a rule. This position is substantiated in Sections J.3 and J.4. Section J.5 concludes.

J.2 CONTEXT: THE ISRAELI SETTLER-COLONIAL PROJECT

Occupation, under international law, comes into being when a territory "is actually placed under the authority of the hostile army."[8] Hence, occupation is both a military act and a military regime, created and maintained by combatants. Simply put, occupation is a military takeover and control of a foreign territory. Colonization, on the other hand, is a process of inhabitation of an area by foreign civilians.[9] Settler-colonialism is a land-focused project, the driving logic of which is to permanently eliminate the native as native, in effect replacing them with settlers.[10] The observation that it is

---

[6]   Article 8(2)(b)(viii) of the Rome Statute of the International Criminal Court, UN General Assembly, July 17, 1998, ISBN No. 92–9227-227–6.

[7]   J. S. Pictet (ed.), *The Geneva Conventions of 12 August 1949, Commentary – IV Geneva Convention* (Geneva: International Committee of the Red Cross, 1958), p. 283.

[8]   Regulation 42 of *HC IV*.

[9]   The term "colonization" is also used to describe the inhabitation of new types of plants or animals in an area. In the human context, "colonization" is a process of human migration into an area and it is related to "colonialism," which very broadly means the practice of subjugation of a country or an area to another through the transfer of population to the dominated country. See M. Kohn, *The Stanford Encyclopedia of Philosophy*, E. N. Zalta (ed.) (Stanford: Stanford University, 2014), plato.stanford.edu/entries/colonialism/.

[10] E. Cavanagh and L. Veracini, "Editors Statement" (2013) 3(1) *Settler-colonial Studies* 1.

a project denotes that it is not an event, but a systemic process of such replacement.[11] Colonization may theoretically occur in an area that was empty of human habitation. Settler colonization occurs when a new socially distinct group settles in an already inhabited place. In both cases, colonization is a process conducted by civilians, but the latter type involves the sharing or taking over of the colonized area from its Indigenous dwellers and their dispossession. Thus, occupation can – and many times does – take the sole form of military control, while colonization is the creation of a civil presence in the controlled territory. From an international legal perspective, the former operates *intra-legem*; the latter, *contra-legelm*. These two distinct phenomena may coincide; they do so in the OPT.

The first settlement of Israeli civilians in the West Bank was established shortly after the area was occupied in the 1967 war. The settlement, Kfar Etzion, had existed until 1948 when it was destroyed during the war. In the summer of 1967, it was re-established in the Gush Etzion area. Kfar Etzion was followed by more settlements in that area, in the Jordan Valley, and in the Judean Hills. By the time the occupation reached its tenth anniversary, 24 Israeli settlements had been established.[12]

Israeli colonization expanded in the decades that followed, and settlements were established in every part of the OPT. Most Israeli governments encouraged Israeli migration into the West Bank, providing funding for infrastructure and offering settlers subsidies and other financial benefits. Israel's entire government administration was mobilized to help plan, fund, and build dozens of urban and rural Israeli communities in the occupied territory. At the time of writing (summer 2016), there are 120 official settlements in the West Bank and about 100 unofficial ones (established without formal approval by the government of Israel, and known as "outposts").[13] According to the Israeli Central Bureau of Statistics, as of 2015, these settlements were home to 386,000 Israelis, excluding East Jerusalem where a further 190,000 settlers

---

[11] See P. Wolfe, "Settler Colonialism and the Elimination of the Native" (2006) 8(4) *Journal of Genocide Research* 387; M. Rodinson, *Israel: A Colonial-Settler State?* (New York: Monad Press for the Anchor Foundation, 1973).

[12] I. Zertal and A. Eldar, *Lords of the Land: The Settlers and the State of Israel, 1967–2004* (Or Yehudah: Kineret Zmora-Bitan & Dvir, 2004), p. 568.

[13] The distinction between *settlements* – that is, Israeli communities established officially by the government of Israel in the OPT – and *outposts* – that is, communities created without an official Israeli governmental approval and thus illegal under domestic law – is irrelevant from an international law perspective. Both are violations of the prohibition on transfer of civilians. Since 2012, the Israeli government has attempted to legalize the hitherto illegal outposts. This in entry R: Regularization.

live.[14] In other words, Israel has settled more than half a million Israelis in the occupied West Bank.

Israeli settler colonization has changed the OPT beyond recognition. Hundreds of thousands of dunums of land, most of which in use by Palestinians, were confiscated and allocated for the settlements; road, water, and sewage networks meant to serve the settlements were built throughout the West Bank; water sources and other natural resources which had been used by the Palestinian population were subjugated, on a staggering scale, to serve the settlements; rings of legal and physical restrictions on movement, applicable to Palestinians only, were drawn around the settlements; a separate, modern legal system was applied to the Israeli settlers on a personal basis as well as to the settlements' administration. The IDF was largely transformed into a body that serves and protects the settlements and the settlers. This task motivates and influences a very large portion of the military commanders' decisions, diverting their attention away from the safety and welfare of the protected persons and toward a consideration foreign to the laws of occupation: serving and protecting the colonization project. Furthermore, daily friction between Israeli settlers and Palestinian residents within the same territory has resulted – and continues to result – in death, serious physical injury, and, of course, property damage.[15] Research by human rights groups shows that Israeli authorities fail almost entirely to provide the Palestinian civilian population with the protection it needs against settler violence.[16]

The Israeli colonization of the OPT has led to extensive violations of the entire array of fundamental rights of Palestinian West Bank residents. It has also caused a demographic change that endangers their existence as a separate community and prevents the realization of their right to self-determination. In fact, the Israeli colonization project has brought to fruition of the entire spectrum of risks meant to be mitigated by the prohibition on population transfers into the occupied territory.[17]

---

[14]   Israeli Bureau of Statistics table is available at www.cbs.gov.il/shnaton67/st02_15x.pdf. For the figure on East Jerusalem, see the Peace Now website, peacenow.org.il/node/297. East Jerusalem was annexed by Israel and Israeli law was applied to it, but due to the international law principle prohibiting annexation of land by force, the annexation is not acknowledged by most of the international community. See entry Z: Zone, Section Z.2.2.3.

[15]   Z. Stahl, *Mock Enforcement: The Failure to Enforce the Law on Israeli Civilians in the West Bank* (Tel Aviv: Yesh Din, 2015). See more in entry I: Investigations.

[16]   L. Yavne, *A Semblance of Law: Law Enforcement on Israeli Civilians in the West Bank* (Tel Aviv: Yesh Din, 2006).

[17]   Entry Z: Zone offers an analysis of the impact of the settlements on Palestinian space and life.

J.3 THE HCJ JURISPRUDENCE ON SETTLEMENT CONSTRUCTION IN THE OPT: PHASING IN AND PHASING OUT

J.3.1 Phase One: Settlement as a Private Property Issue

The first case challenging the legality of settlement activity on occupied land brought before the HCJ dealt with a settlement block planned in the beginning of the 1970s to be erected in the Rafah Approach area of the Sinai Peninsula.[18] Thousands of Bedouins who dwelled in the area were forcibly removed by the army and seizure orders were issued for their lands. In the judgment, published in May of 1973, two of the three judges presiding over the case evaded the question of the legality of the establishment of settlements in occupied lands, holding the legality of the seizure orders to be a purely proprietary question: Was the military entitled to seize possession of private property? Given that the state toned down the colonizing motivation behind the seizure orders and argued that the land is needed for security purposes regardless of whether it will be settled in the future,[19] the panel saw it fit to evade the major legal question posed to it: "It appears from the affidavit [supporting the State's submission] that of the measures that could be taken, the IDF has, at least for the time being, taken only the first, that is, sealing the area and turning it into a buffer zone," justice Landau wrote in his judgment. "I shall therefore focus on reviewing matters in this light and shall not address the question of settlement for security purposes outside the jurisdiction of the state – a question that has its own legal aspects and was not addressed in the arguments before us."[20] The court ruled that land seizure, a temporary forcible takeover of usage rights of land, was permissible if it was necessary for security purposes:[21]

> In the case at hand, ownership of the property has not been confiscated, but rather possession of the land has been seized. In any event, this case comes

---

[18] HCJ 302/72 *Abu Hilo v. Government of Israel* (1973) 27(2) PD 169.

[19] In a legal-historical pioneering research, law professor David Kretzmer and journalist Gershom Gorenberg reveal that the notion of building settlements in the Rafah Approach had been on the agendas of the Defense Minister Moshe Dayan, the Israeli government, and Israeli settling authorities ever since the fall of 1968. Based on archival documents, they argue that the state's arguments and affidavits included explanations that, though maybe not outright lies, were phrased in a very misleading manner, both with respect to the motives for the expulsion and the description of the conclusions of the various inquiry committees. D. Kretzmer and G. Gorenberg, "Politics, Law and the Judicial Process: the case of the High Court of Justice and the Territories" (2015) 17 *Mishpat uMimshal* 1, 24–34, 50 [Hebrew].

[20] HCJ 302/72 *Abu Hilo v. Government of Israel* (1973) 27(2) PD 169, 176.   [21] *Ibid.*, p. 178.

under the exclusion included in Article 23(g) of the Hague Regulations which prohibits the destruction or seizure of the enemy's property, unless such destruction or seizure is imperatively demanded by the necessities of war.

Unlike justice Landau, justice Witkon was ready to take the bull by the horns and confront the plan, which the state did not deny existed, to build settlements in the area that had been cleared of Bedouins. He, however, was willing to uphold the displacement, even if it had been done for the purpose of building a Jewish settlement. His view about this possibility went on to set the legal foundation for the Israeli settlement project throughout the 1970s:[22]

> It is clear that the fact that the same lands, in whole or in part, are designated for Jewish settlement does not negate the security nature of the action as a whole. The security considerations that had been raised and reviewed in the judgment of my honorable colleague, were not refuted nor revealed to be fictional or camouflage for other considerations, when it was learnt from General Tal himself that the area (or part thereof) was designated for settlement of Jews, which in itself, in this case, is a security measure.

In other words, justice Witkon was ready to accept the idea that a *civilian* settlement serves a *military* purpose.

As for the normative framework, the HCJ ruled that the GC IV, which sets forth the prohibition on population transfer, was binding only on the international level and could not be relied on in a domestic litigation. It was seen as conferring rights and duties between states, not enforceable by individuals. Since the Rafah judgment, the approach to the status of the GC IV in the HCJ has changed and Palestinians have been allowed to base their petitions to the HCJ on the violations of rights stipulated in the convention.[23] However, as shall become clear, by the time the change occurred, the colonization project had reached dimensions far beyond the reach that a court of law could annul.

A direct discussion of the legality of establishing civilian settlements in the occupied territory and transferring civilians to them took place in the Beth El case in 1978, a settlement established on privately owned Palestinian land seized by military order.[24]

True to its position that the GC IV did not constitute customary law, the court once again focused on the prohibition against violating property rights and damaging the property of residents of an occupied territory. This prohibition also appears in the Hague Regulations, the customary status of which was

---

[22] *Ibid.*, p. 181.
[23] On the court's jurisprudence on the relevance and status of the GC IV, see entry G: Geneva Law.
[24] HCJ 606/78 *Ayub v. Minister of Defense* (1979) 33(2) PD 113.

undisputed. Following the Witkon analysis, the state advanced an argument that in historical hindsight seems ironic: Establishing a civilian settlement in the midst of a hostile population is necessary for protecting the State of Israel. Hence, settlements are needed for security purposes. A military thesis was developed to support the argument, and an affidavit by a major general affirmed that civilian settlements in strategic locations in the occupied territory reinforce "regional defense" and act as a support for military action in the area. This is why Kiryat Arba, Kfar Etzion, Beth El, and Yamit had to be established.

The HCJ, having reduced the discussion to the property issue, accepted the argument that the security exception to the prohibition on destroying or seizing enemy property applies to the establishment of a Jewish–Israeli settlement:[25]

> In terms of the pure security consideration, there is no doubt that the presence of settlements, even "civilian," of citizens of the holding power makes a significant contribution to security in the area and helps the military carry out its mission. It does not take a security or military expert to see that terrorist elements operate more easily in an area where the entire population is either apathetic or sympathetic to the enemy, than in an area where there are also those who may follow their actions and inform the authorities of any suspicious movement. Terrorists will not find shelter, assistance and equipment among them. The matter is simple and there is no need to elaborate. We simply recall that according to the affidavits of the Respondents, the settlers answer to the military, whether formally or as a matter of circumstances. Their presence in the area is permitted and made possible by the military. Therefore, I believe, as I did in the Rafiah Approach case, that Jewish settlement in the held territories – as long as there is a state of belligerence – answers concrete security needs.

Once military officials declared that, in their professional opinion, the establishment of civilian settlements was required for security reasons, the court accepted their position without much ado. It rejected Palestinian claims that the security argument was merely a cover-up for an ideologically motivated colonization. However, as in the Rafah Approach case, here too the court did not rule out the possibility that there was *another* purpose for the seizure: that the specific location chosen for Beth El was determined by a Jewish romantic belief which maintained that it was the place where the patriarch Jacob dreamed of a ladder with angels ascending and descending, where God promised him the land and changed his name to Israel.[26]

---

[25] *Ibid.*, p. 118.   [26] See the Beth El council website: www.bet-el.info/history.asp [Hebrew].

The court found that this purpose, when it exists *alongside* the military imperative, does not render the seizure of land unlawful:[27]

> Where the law empowers an authority to carry out an act for a specific purpose and such act is, in fact, really and truly carried out for this purpose, the fact that there may have been another purpose, in addition to the purpose defined by law, does not render the action unlawful. The additional purpose may raise doubt as to whether the action was taken for the purpose defined by law, but it does not necessarily mean that the additional purpose was the only one that motivated the authority to exercise its powers and that the purpose defined in law was argued simply as camouflage.

Both cases raised the issue of the temporary nature of the settlements. As stated, the laws of occupation assume that an occupation will be temporary[28] and decree the conservation principle prohibiting the making of long-term systemic changes in the occupied territory. These laws explicitly and absolutely prohibit the confiscation of private land (i.e., transfer of ownership, as opposed to "seizure," which is a temporary capture of possession).[29] How, then, can the appropriation of the land required to establish the Rafah Approach settlement block or Beth El be reconciled with this prohibition?

It seems that where there is a political will, there is judicial way. In the Rafah Approach case, the HCJ accepted the position of the military and the state attorney's office that the land had not been confiscated, but rather "seized for security purposes," without batting an eyelid. Given that the HCJ had found this explanation plausible in the past, petitioners' counsel in the Beth El case posed a new question: The Beth El plan did not look temporary. It involved the construction of private and public buildings, the settlement of entire families whose children would grow up in the place, the establishment of a local council, and the total transformation of the landscape. All this begged the question: If it looks permanent and smells permanent, can it really be temporary? The HCJ, however, accepted the state's thesis that once the security needs no longer existed, the land would be returned to its owners:[30]

> Mr. Khoury asks: How can a permanent settlement be erected on land seized for temporary use only? That is a serious question. Yet, I do see the merit in

[27] HCJ 606/78 *Ayub v. Minister of Defense* (1979) 33(2) PD 113, pp. 117–118.
[28] On the temporary nature of occupation see entry T: Temporary/Indefinite.
[29] Regulation 46 of *HC IV* reads: "Private property cannot be confiscated." See entry R: Regularization.
[30] HCJ 606/78 *Ayub v. Minister of Defense* (1979) 33(2) PD 113, 130. (Gabriel Bach, then the state attorney and later a justice of the supreme court.)

the response of Mr. Bach that the civilian settlement will be able to exist in that location only as long as the IDF holds the land on the strength of a requisition order. This possession itself may one day come to an end, as a result of international negotiations that will gain force under international law and determine the fate of this settlement, like all the other settlements that exist in the Occupied Territories.

It appears, then, that while confiscation is permanent, seizure is temporary, just like the occupation itself, and therefore entirely compatible with its governing principles. The HCJ accepted the state attorney's subterfuge that a lengthy period of time could, nevertheless, still be temporary. The justices must not have been familiar with the observation made by French philosopher and author, Albert Camus, that: "[I]f tyranny, even progressive, outlasts a generation, for millions of people it means a life of slavery and nothing more. When the temporary coincides with a person's lifespan, for that person, it is final."[31]

Twelve families – nine from al-Bira near Ramallah and three from Beit Hannina in East Jerusalem – tried to stop the establishment of Beth El on their land. They doubtlessly still have their title deeds, as they patiently wait, almost four decades after the judgment was delivered, for the temporary to come to end, so that they might have their land back.

A few months after the Beth El judgment, a petition was filed against the establishment of another settlement, Elon Moreh. The petitioners, 17 residents of the small Palestinian village of Rujeib, near Nablus, whose small plots of land had been seized for the establishment of the settlement, challenged the security argument. They too were represented by Adv. Elias Khoury, now joined by veteran lawyer Amnon Zichroni and another lawyer from his office who went on to become the leading lawyer representing Palestinians in the HCJ, Avigdor Feldman. Their position was that Elon Moreh had been established for ideological, political reasons, not for security ones.

In court, the military's counsel protested strongly: Political considerations? Certainly not! But, the petitioners from Rujeib found unlikely support for their position: The settlers, members of the Elon Moreh founding group, asked to join the petition so that they might present their own position. The court granted their request. Their position was straightforward: First, the initiative to establish the settlement was political/ideological; and second, on the issue of the temporary nature of the occupation, the Elon Moreh settlers

---

[31]   In the original French: "Si la tyrannie, même progressiste, dure plus d'une génération, elle signifie pour des millions d'hommes une vie d'esclave, et rien de plus." A. Camus *Actuelles, Tome 1: Chroniques 1944–1948* (Paris: Editions Gallimard, 1950), p. 192.

unequivocally exclaimed that the duration of their settlement was nothing short of eternal. We are here in the name of Zionism and Jewish Law, they said, and we have no intention of ever leaving.[32]

The court also learned that the exact location of the settlement was chosen by the settlers for religious reasons, based on the biblical verse: "Abram traveled through the land as far as the site of the great tree of Moreh at Shechem"[33] (Genesis 12:6). The military did not choose the spot for security reasons, but rather acceded to the settlers' choice.

The litigation further revealed a fierce disagreement between the chief of staff, who supported the establishment of the settlement and was willing to confirm it served security needs, and the minister of defense, a former decorated major general himself, who objected and did not believe that an Israeli community in that location would contribute to security.[34]

The court, willing to go a long way in the name of security, had no choice but to reject the argument that the settlement had been established for security reasons, and strike down the seizure orders.

Following the judgment, the government of Israel, with Menachem Begin at the helm, decided that settlements would no longer be built on private land, but on public land (often referred to by Israeli bodies as "state land"), thus eliminating the need to use the legal tool of seizure orders for security purposes. To increase the reserve of public land (which stood at approximately 520,000 dunams when the IDF entered the West Bank), the justice ministry developed an entire system for declaring land considered private as public land.[35] During the 1980s and the 1990s, more than 900,000 dunams of land were declared "state land" using this system.[36]

The Elon Moreh case was the first judgment in which the HCJ struck down the establishment of a settlement, but it was also the last time it agreed to review the question of the legality of the settlements. With the establishment of settlements on security grounds approved, the prohibition on the transfer of population into the occupied territory ignored, and the issue turned into nothing more than a question of property rights (as opposed to a question of the limits to be imposed upon an occupying power in an occupied territory), Likud-led

---

[32] For description of their submission see in the court's ruling in the case: HCJ 390/79 *Dweikat v. Government of Israel* (1979) 34(1) PD 1, 9.
[33] Genesis 12:6.   [34] *Dweikat*, pp. 8, 22.
[35] The authority to issue such declarations is based on a military order (Order Regarding Government Property (Judea and Samaria) (No. 59), 1967), and the substantive normative basis governing the declaration is the Ottoman Land Code, 1858, which provides, among other things, the transfer of full title over private uncultivated agricultural land to the ruler.
[36] N. Shalev, *Under the Guise of Legality: Israel's Declarations of State Land in the West Bank* (Jerusalem: B'Tselem, 2012), p. 15.

governments were able to significantly expand the settler-colonization project. In the late 1980s and early 1990s, the HCJ realized that the *Golem* it had created had grown wild and was completely out of its control. Ever since the Elon Moreh case (with the exception of claims that settlements had spilled over onto privately owned land), the HCJ has declined to address the legality of the settlements on grounds of nonjusticiablity, meaning that the issue was inherently political rather than legal, and therefore inappropriate for the court to review and decide. This position is discussed in Section J.3.2.

J.3.2 Phase Two: Settlements as a Nonjusticiable Issue

Shifting the focus of the colonization project onto public land left little opportunity for challenging its legality based on claims that private property rights had been violated, but it highlighted the permanency of the settlements and made it impossible to talk about them in temporary terms befitting a temporary seizure for security purposes. The HCJ, however, steadfastly refused to consider the legality of the settlements through the prism of the prohibition on population transfers. This stance was first anchored in a 1993 judgment in a case brought by Israel's largest and oldest peace group, Peace Now. Peace Now had filed the first petition that focused on issues of principle, relying mostly on the prohibition prescribed in Article 49 paragraph 6 of the GC IV rather than on claims regarding interference with private property. The petition sought a ruling that the establishment of settlements – be it on private or public land – was unlawful due to the prohibition on transferring the occupying power's population into the occupied territory. In the judgment,[37] the HCJ found that although the issue raised in the petition had a legal dimension, it was predominantly political and therefore "in the jurisdiction of another branch of Government."[38] One of the justices called the petition a "legal mine," which the court must be careful not to step on. In other words, the HCJ found that the doctrine of institutional nonjusticiability applied.[39] This finding was aided by the fact that the petition sought a general remedy

---

[37] HCJ 4481/91 *Bargil* v. *Government of Israel* (1993) 47 PD 210.   [38] *Ibid.*, p. 215.

[39] The passive approach the HCJ expressed in the Peace Now case stood in stark contrast to the HCJ's image at the time as an ultra-activist, indeed "imperialist" court. The same court, with the same president, just two weeks after rejecting the Peace Now petition for nonjusticiability, infuriated prime minister Yitzhak Rabin by ruling that he had to fire minister of interior Aryeh Deri because he had been indicted on charges of bribery, though no law requires firing an accused minister (HCJ 3094/93 *The Movement for Quality Government in Israel* v. *Government of Israel* (1993) 47(5) PD 404). Two years later, the same court declared that it had the power to repeal laws it thought contradicted the protection afforded to fundamental rights in two recently enacted basic laws. The judgment declaring this new power expressed

rather than focused on a specific settlement, which allowed the court to rule that the issue was political:[40]

> The petition amounts to a general objection to Government policy. It is more general, by comparison, even than the case heard in the United States Supreme Court, Warth v. Seldin (1975) (a petition claiming that the planning and building legislation in a certain city prevented persons with medium or low incomes from living in that city). In that case, the petition was denied, inter alia, because it violated the rule that the judiciary, by virtue of its judicial self-governance, does not consider abstract matters of sweeping public significance that are merely general objections on matters of policy, best considered by the legislature or the executive.

The court, however, repeated its finding of nonjusticiability even when asked to rule on the legality of a plan for expansion of a specific settlement, when the petitioners' argument was based on the prohibition on transferring the population of the occupying power to the occupied territory and the prohibition on subjugating the occupied territory's natural resources to the occupying power.[41] In the petition which challenged the plans to expand the Maaleh Edomim settlement, the HCJ even recruited the Israeli–Palestinian peace process as a justification to avoid adjudication:[42]

> The issue of Israeli settlement is one of the issues on the negotiating table in talks between Israel and the PLO about a permanent settlement. The status of Israeli communities in the Area will be determined in diplomatic agreements. This court is not meant to address this issue while diplomatic negotiations are taking place, thus indirectly intervening in how maps are drawn. This is clearly the work of the Government and its various branches.

Since these judgments, the court has repeatedly refused to address the legality of the settlements.[43]

J.4 ANALYSIS: MASTERING THE ART OF EXCEPTIONS

When the Rafah case was litigated, the total number of settlers did not exceed a couple of hundred, but when the Peace Now petition was deliberated, the settler community numbered well past 100,000. As stated, it now exceeds half

---

Barak's view that the two basic laws in question had brought a "constitutional revolution" (CivA 6821/93 *United Mizrahi Bank Ltd.* v. *Migdal Cooperative Village* (1995) 49(4) PD 221).

[40] HCJ 4481/91 *Bargil* v. *Government of Israel* (1993) 47 PD 210, pp. 215–216.

[41] HCJ 3125/98 *Ayad* v. *Commander of the IDF Forces in Judea and Samaria Area* (1999) 55(1) PD 913. The author represented the petitioners in this case.

[42] *Ibid.*, p. 918.   [43] HCJ 7957/04 *Mara'abe* v. *Prime Minister of Israel* (2005) 60(2) PD 477.

a million settlers. None of the conditions stipulated by the HCJ had been fulfilled – there was no security justification for the settlements; in fact, the opposite is true: they are a security liability; they are certainly not planned to be temporary. The creature the court godfathered has turned into Frankstein's monster, too wild for the court to rein in.

During the colonization judicial journey, the court exploited an exception to a prohibition, carved an exception to a judicial trend, and ignored the absence of an exception to a fundamental rule – all in an effort to accommodate political will, and, especially, enable advancing the core vision of consecutive governments of Israel to establish the fait accompli of a "Greater Israel." This effort seems to come with a price tag insofar as the vision of the rule of law is concerned.

J.4.1 *Forcing an Exception*

In its first rulings on the matter during the 1970s, the HCJ applied the military imperative necessity exception to the rule prohibiting the destruction or seizure of property of protected persons. It did so like a child realizing that "technically" omitting a truth is not lying.

The court ignored the clear and strict language of the exception set out in Article 23(g) of the Hague Regulations which, decrees that destruction or seizure of property is permissible only when "imperatively demanded by the necessities of war."[44] Dismissing the textual meaning of the phrase, it widened it to include a very general and speculative contribution to security.

The court also ignored the fact that the regulation it relied upon was intended to apply in the battlefield, in actual fighting which takes place within the framework of an international armed conflict:[45] Regulation 23 is located in section II of the regulations annexed to Hague Convention IV, titled "Hostilities" in chapter I titled "Means of injuring the enemy, Siege and Bombardments." The court was not impressed by the fact that this location (rather than section III, which deals with occupation and is titled "Military Authority over The Territory of The Hostile State"), strongly supports the view

---

[44] The language of the exception to the prohibition on destruction of property contained in Article 53 of GC IV is no less narrow: "except where such destruction is rendered absolutely necessary by military operations."

[45] The term "military operations" which forms the exception in Article 53 of GC IV has been interpreted by the ICRC as "movements, manoeuvres and actions of any sort, carried out by the armed forces *with a view to combat*" (Emphasis added). See J. Pictet, *Commentary on the Additional Protocols of 8 June 1977 to the Geneva Conventions of 12 August 1949* (Geneva: International Committee of the Red Cross, 1987), pp. 67–68, 152. That was also the approach taken by the ICTY in ICTY, Blaškić, Trial Judgement, ICTY-95–14-T (March 3, 2000).

that it was meant to regulate the fighting. It overlooked the fact that Regulation 46, which stipulates that "[F]amily honour and rights, the lives of persons, *and private property*, as well as religious convictions and practice, must be respected," is the regulation which governs the protection of private property in an occupation regime.[46]

Lastly, until the Elon Moreh judgment of 1979, the court lent a hand to the fictitious thesis that Jewish civilian communities are serving a military purpose rather than an ideological one. By doing so, it not only shied away from the political reality known to every toddler at the time, but also breached the most fundamental principle of IHL, its raison d'etre: the principle of distinction, which obliges parties to a conflict to distinguish at all times between civilians and combatants and between civilian and military objects.[47] It accepted that civilians have a military role in the conflict, hence risking reclassifying them as a legitimate target of attack.[48]

J.4.2 Carving an Exception

The late 1970s brought a generational change to the HCJ and with it a dramatic transformation in the judicial character of the institution. The new court, led by chief justice Shamgar opened its doors and expanded the right of standing, minimized the nonjusticiability doctrine, and boldly shaped a new interventionist model. In the Peace Now judgment, nonjusticiability of the prohibition on population transfer became a lone exception to its judicial philosophy as an interventionist court, one that believes that "all is justiciable."[49] The judicial institution known for its unprecedented broad right of standing,[50] its judicial activism, and its broad purposive interpretation theory, hid behind the nonjusticiability doctrine, associated with conservatism and judicial restraint, in order to avoid ruling on the legality of Israel's settlement policy in the Occupied Palestinian Territories.

The exceptionality of this position is underscored by the fact that during the '80s and '90s the court did not evade handling questions that divided the Israeli public to the point that it became a central factor in Israeli politics: It

---

[46]   Regulation 46 of *HC IV*. Emphasis added.

[47]   Articles 48, 51(2), and 52(2) of Protocol Additional to the Geneva Conventions of August 12, 1949, and relating to the Protection of Victims of International Armed Conflicts (Additional Protocol I), Geneva, June 8, 1977, 1125 UNTS 3; see entry C: Combatants.

[48]   Dinstein, "Settlements and Expulsion." 191.

[49]   The phrase "everything is justiciable" is attributed to justice Aharon Barak, who served as a supreme court justice from 1978, and as its chief justice between 1992 and 2006.

[50]   E. Shraga and R. Shahar, *Administrative Law*, 6 vols. (Bnei Brak: Bursi, 2009), vol. E, pp. 31–35 [Hebrew].

dismissed the flat exemption ultra-orthodox Jews received from mandatory military service prescribed by law,[51] it outlawed governmental policies which coerced religious practices on seculars,[52] and it was even ready to judicially review the army's open-fire regulations.[53] The court flatly rejected any application of the doctrine of normative nonjusticiability[54] and went as far as ruling that "there is no application of the institutional nonjusticiability doctrine where recognition of it might prevent the examination of impingement upon human rights."[55] Yet, this very court abandoned one of its hallmarks as a judicial institution when it came to the legality of the settlements. It made an exception to the justiciability doctrine it had created. And what an exception this is. It is difficult to imagine an issue whose avoidance has had a greater impact on the State of Israel and on the human rights of Palestinians.

J.4.3 *Ignoring the Absence of an Exception*

Finally, the court had to ignore the important fact that the prohibition on transfer of civilians from the occupying power to the occupied territory is one of the rare prohibitions of IHL that knows no exception (next to the prohibition on confiscation of private property[56]). At first, the court used the distinction between customary and conventional international law to justify its reluctance to apply Article 49 paragraph 6 of GC IV. Once the notion that the prohibition on population transfer to an occupied territory is not customary became too difficult – probably impossible – to defend,[57] the court resorted to the nonjusticiability doctrine like a passenger in a sea vessel clinging to a life vest when the waves get high.

Among legal principles, those who have no exception are an exclusive club. Legal orders need exceptions since every norm is by definition a restriction of other norms, just like the rights of one are a restriction to the freedom of others.

---

[51] HCJ 910/86 *Ressler v. Minister of Defense* (1988) 42(2) PD 441.
[52] See, e.g., HCJ 217/80 *Segal v. Minister of Interior* (1980) 34(4) PD 429 (the Daylight Savings Time case); HCJ 5016/96 *Horev v. Minister of Transportation* (1997) 51(4) PD 1 (Saturday Bar Ilan Street Closure case).
[53] HCJFH 4110/92 *Hess v. Minister of Defense* (1994) 48(2) PD 811.
[54] HCJ 910/86 *Ressler v. Minister of Defense* (1988) 42(2) PD 441.
[55] HCJ 769/02 *The Public Committee against Torture in Israel v. Government of Israel* (2006) 62(1) PD 507 (the Targeted Killings case).
[56] Regulation 46 of HC IV.
[57] Especially in the light of the consensual opposite position of the international community on the matter, e.g., "Legal Consequences of the Construction of a Wall in the Occupied Palestinian Territory." For a detailed discussion of the international community's consensus on the status of the OPT as occupied and the illegality of the settlements, see entry N: Nomos.

Without exceptions, norms would constantly collide. Exceptions allow a complex interlacing of rules to create legal harmony. Hence, exceptionless prohibitions, like absolute rights, are a superior class of norms. Bending to no other norm, they define the borders of the legal field and its object and purpose.[58] Failing to apply them, therefore, jeopardizes not only the specific value they directly protect, but the legal order in its entirety.

No wonder, then, that by overlooking the prohibition on population transfer to an occupied territory, the policy in question created the complete opposite of what occupation law envisaged: a permanent colony that serves the occupying power and its citizens at the expense of the protected individuals and the occupied nation. It is hard to imagine a subject on which refusing to adjudicate is so equivalent to an active ruling.

J.5 CONCLUSION: LAW'S PROVINCE

The HCJ jurisprudence on settlements facilitated the colonization project, but it has not cemented it. In 2005, when settlers from the Gaza Strip and from the north of the West Bank faced evacuation as part of the disengagement plan,[59] they petitioned the court and asked it to acknowledge their right to reside in their settlements. The court, resurrecting the temporary nature of the occupation and thus of the settlers' communities from the ashes of the law of belligerent occupation, dismissed their petition without much ado:[60]

> The petitioners deny the claim that the area is under temporary belligerent occupation. They argue that the Israeli settlement in the area relied on a continuous representation of the Israeli governments, that it is a permanent settlement in one of the grounds of the land of Israel ... [However,] the normative reality is eviction from an area of belligerent occupation. The nature of such an area is that Israelis' presence in it is temporary ... the possibility of eviction occurring one day hangs over the Israeli's head at all times.

When the executive pursues a colonization policy, the court has found ways to allow it even at the expense of artificially forcing it into a narrow exception, or exceptionally resorting to a legal philosophy of restraint. It has done so even

---

[58] Object and purpose, next to "ordinary meaning," is the primary interpretive principle for international treaties; see Article 31(1) of the Vienna Convention on the Law of Treaties, May 23, 1969, 1155 UNTS 331.

[59] Disengagement Plan Implementation Law, 2005.

[60] HCJ 1661/05 *Gaza Coast Regional Council v. The Israeli Knesset* (2005) 59(2) PD 481, ¶ 28 and ¶ 115.

at the cost of frustrating of the most basic principles of the relevant legal field. When the executive wishes to evacuate settlements, however, the court pulls out the fundamentals of occupation law from the attic. It reminds the settlers that occupation and land seizure are all temporary.

Judicial power has thus followed and enabled politics; it has not constrained it. In this sense, while the HCJ has generally espoused the Dworkian notion of *Law's Empire*,[61] in the context of the settlements enterprise its jurisprudence was but an instrument of Israel's Empire. Human rights ceased to be a trump.

It may well be that the reason for the bent of the bench is that in certain core political issues the majoritarian democratic process has to determine the direction. This respect for the democratic process is not ipso facto without merits, were it not for one obstacle: The Palestinians, the occupied people, the legally defined *protected persons*, are not part of that process; they have no voice in the making of decisions that affect their lives and livelihoods. The only place where they allegedly do have a voice is in a court of law.

---

[61]   R. Dworkin, *Law's Empire* (Cambridge, MA: Harvard University Press, 1988).

K

Kinship

Orna Ben-Naftali

K.1 INTRODUCTION

K.1.1 Of Kith and Kin

Kinship connotes human affinity related to the social construction of the basic facts of lives of most people: mating, gestation, breeding, and nourishing are conceptualized and structured to achieve a variety of social ends, ranging from the socialization of children to the forming of economic, political, and cultural communities.[1] Given that the family, denoting a group of people affiliated by blood, marriage, or co-residence, is designed to achieve a wide array of these ends, it is commonly considered the basic institution of kinship. Kinship generally, and family specifically, thus constitute the world where most of us are initiated into the familiar and the familial; the practical, the intimate, and the performative aspects of our relational existence. This initiation, the happy and unhappy experience within family life, marks us. We will carry that mixed bag of anxieties and pleasures in which we will invariably find fault and to which we will pay tribute throughout our lives. It is an experience that forms us. This significance attached to the institution of the family explains the right to respect for family life, a right recognized in peacetime and in wartime, both internationally and domestically.

In the case of tens of thousands of Palestinian, the very condition of possibility for the formative experience, and the relative certainty associated with living with one's family and within one's community, has ceased to exist. For them, separation and the dissolution of the family, and indeed of kinship, has been and continues to be the determining influence of their lives. This

[1] See e.g., R. Fox, *Kinship and Marriage: An Anthropological Perspective* (Cambridge: Cambridge University Press, 1967), p 30.

entry focuses on the legal dimension of the disintegration of these Palestinian families. As background for this discussion, Section K.1.2 presents the legal concept of the family; the substance and scope of the universal recognition of the right to family life; and, proceeding to focus on family unification, presents the argument relative to Palestinian families subject to Israel's effective control.

K.1.2 *The International Right to Respect for Family Life and Family Unity*

K.1.2.1 The Legal Concept of the Family

Both change over time in the notion of the family and cultural, social, and legal diversity in its construction, explain why the obligation to protect the family as the "natural and fundamental group in society"[2] is stipulated without subjecting the notions of "family," "family group," or "next of kin" to any standard definition.

Thus, the UN Human Rights Committee concluded that "the concept of the family may differ in some respects from State to State, and even from region to region within a State, and that it is therefore not possible to give the concept a standard definition."[3] Accordingly, its General Comment on Article 17 of the *ICCPR* stated that for the purposes of this provision, "family" should be interpreted to include "all those comprising the family as understood in the society of the State party concerned."[4] The European Court of Human Rights includes the relationship between husband and wife and the children

---

[2]   Article 23(1) of the International Convent on Civil and Political Rights, opened for signature December 19, 1966, 999 UNTS 171 (entered into force March 23, 1976) [hereinafter: *ICCPR*]; Article 10(1) of the International Covenant on Economic, Social and Cultural Rights, opened for signature December 16, 1966, 993 UNTS 3 (entered into force June 3, 1976) [hereinafter: *ICESCR*]; Article 17(1) of the American Convention on Human Rights, opened for signature January 22, 1969 (entered into force 18 July 1978) [hereinafter: *ACHR*]; Article 15(1) of the Additional Protocol to the American Convention on Human Rights in the Area of Economic, Social and Cultural Rights, November 16, 1999, A-52 ("Protocol of San Salvador"); Article 18 of the African Charter on Human and Peoples' Rights, opened for signature June 27, 1981, CAB/LEG/67/3 rev. 5 (entered into force October 21, 1986); Article 16 of the European Social Charter, May 3, 1996, CETS 163.

[3]   UN Human Rights Committee (HRC), CCPR General Comment No 19, Article 23 (The Family) Protection of the Family, the Right to Marriage and Equality of the Spouses, July 27, 1990, § 2.

[4]   HRC, CCPR General Comment No 16: Article 17 (Right to Privacy), The Right to Respect of Privacy, Family, Home and Correspondence, and Protection of Honour and Reputation, April 8, 1988, § 5.

dependent on them within the notion of family.[5] When children are involved, it has expanded this definition to include siblings, persons living together outside marriage, and grandparents.[6]

In the context of humanitarian law, Pictet's Commentary on the GC IV does define the "family" rather thinly as "people who are related or connected by marriage,"[7] but over time this definition has broadened. Thus, for instance, the ICRC tracing services understand the term "family" "to include all those who consider themselves and are considered by each other to be part of the family."[8]

K.1.2.2 The Substance of the Right to Respect Family Life

Under IHRL, the right to respect for family life entails an obligation to protect the family "by society and the State,"[9] providing that "the widest possible protection and assistance should be accorded to the family, which is the natural and fundamental group unit of society, particularly of its establishment."[10]

IHL too attaches a deep-seated social and humanitarian value to the family from its early days,[11] and the obligation to respect family life "as far as

---

[5] H. and B. v. UK, Eur Ct HR, App No 70073/10, 44539/11 (April 9, 2013) (the court stated that "the mutual enjoyment by parent and child of each other's company constitutes a fundamental element of family life").

[6] Johnston and Others v. Ireland, Eur Ct HR, App No 9697/82 (December 18, 1986); Moustaquim v. Belgium, Eur Ct HR, App No 12313/8 (February 18, 1991); Vermeire v. Belgium, Eur Ct HR, App No 12849/87 (November 29, 1991).

[7] J. S. Pictet (ed.), The Geneva Conventions of 14 August 1949: Commentary on Geneva Convention IV Relative to the Protection of Civilian Persons in Times of War (Geneva: ICRC, 1958), p. 192.

[8] Resolution 4 of the Council of Delegates of the International Red Cross and Red Crescent Movement, Restoring Family Links Strategy (and Implementation Plan) for the international Red Cross and Red Crescent Movement (2008–2018), November 23–24, 2007, www.icrc.org /eng/assets/files/other/icrc_002_1108.pdf. The service further uses the terms "relatives" and "loved ones" interchangeably. ICRC, Restoring Family Links Strategy: Including Legal References (2009), www.icrc.org/eng/assets/files/other/icrc_002_0967.pdf, pp. 11–37.

[9] Article 23(1) of ICCPR; Article 17(1) of ICCPR specifies that arbitrary or unlawful interference with the family is prohibited, and Article 17(2) provides that "everyone has the right to protection of law against such interference." This reiterates the language of Article 12 of the Universal Declaration of Human Rights, General Assembly, December 10, 1948, 217 A (III).

[10] Article 10(1) of ICESCR. Article 10(3) provides that special measures of assistance should be taken on behalf of children and young persons.

[11] The obligation to respect the family rights of persons in occupied territory appears already in Article 37 of the Lieber Code, Instructions for the Government of armies of the United States in the Field (Prepared by Francis Lieber and promulgated as General Order No 100 by President Lincoln, April 24, 1863), reproduced in D. Schindler and J. Toman (eds.),

possible" is a customary norm in both international and noninternational armed conflicts.[12] This obligation is codified in Article 46 of the Hague Regulations.[13] Focusing specifically on civilians under an occupation regime, the first paragraph of Article 27 of the GC IV, on which the "whole of 'Geneva Law' is founded,"[14] extends it to all protected civilians, providing that "protected persons are entitled, in all circumstances, to respect for ... their family rights." Other provisions obligate the occupying power to ensure, to the greatest possible extent, that "members of the same family are not separated"; to provide for the maintenance and re-establishment of family links and transmission of information; and that interned families must be given "facilities for leading a proper family life."[15]

Both IHRL and IHL consider that the maintenance of family unity is a sine qua non condition for meeting the obligation to respect family life. Under IHRL, this unity encompasses the ability of family members to be together free from arbitrary, unlawful, or abusive interference in their family life;[16] to

The Laws of Armed Conflict. A Collection of Conventions, Resolutions and Other Documents (The Hague: Brill, 1988); in the Brussels Declaration, Article 38 of the Project of an International Declaration concerning the Laws and Customs of War, Brussels (August 27, 1874), https://ihl-databases.icrc.org/ihl/INTRO/135; and in the Oxford Manual, Article 49 of The Laws of War on Land, adopted by the Institute of International Law, Oxford (September 9, 1880), https://ihl-databases.icrc.org/ihl/INTRO/140?OpenDocument.

[12] J.M. Henckaerts and L. Doswald-Beck (eds.), *Customary International Humanitarian Law, Volume 1: Rules* (reprinted with corrections, Cambridge: Cambridge University Press, 2009) – Rule 105, pp. 379–383 and *Volume 2: Practice – Respect for Family Life* (practice relating to Rule 105), pp. 2525–2536 [hereinafter: *CIHL*].

[13] Hague Convention (IV) Respecting the Laws and Customs of War on Land and its annex: Regulations concerning the Laws and Customs of War on Land, The Hague, October 18, 1907, 205 CTS 277; 36 Stat 2277.

[14] Article 27 of the Geneva Convention Relative to the Protection of Civilian Persons in the Time of War, Geneva, August 12, 1949, 75 UNTS 287 [hereinafter: GC IV]; Pictet, *Geneva Conventions*, pp. 199–205.

[15] See, e.g., Articles 24, 49(3), 82(3) of GC IV. The latter is the basis for specific rules relative to family unity, in Article 4(3)(b) of Protocol Additional to the Geneva Conventions of August 12, 1949, and relating to the Protection of Victims of Non-International Armed Conflicts (Protocol II), Geneva, June 8, 1977, 1125 UNTS 609 [hereinafter: AP II] (reunion of families temporarily separated); Article 5(2)(a) of AP II (accommodation of men and women of the same family in detention or internment); Article 37(c) of the Convention on the Rights of the Child, General Assembly, November 20, 1989, 1577 UNTS 3 [hereinafter: CRC] (accommodation of children with their parents during deprivation of liberty). The CIHL study lists 18 military manuals that include the duty to respect family rights; see *CIHL Volume 2*, pp. 2529–2531.

[16] Article 17(1) of ICCPR ("arbitrary or unlawful interference") (cited in *CIHL Volume 2*, p. 2526, § 3909); Article 16(1) CRC ("arbitrary or unlawful interference") (*ibid.*, p. 2527, § 3920); Article 11 of ACHR ("arbitrary or abusive interference") (*ibid.*, p. 2526, § 3912). The UN Human Rights Committee's General Comment on Article 17 of the *ICCPR* states that interference with family life will be "arbitrary" if the interference is not in accordance with the provisions, aims and objectives of the Covenant and if it is not "reasonable in the particular circumstances"; see

reunite[17] and to have contact with each other, including, when required, to obtain information on the whereabouts of family members.[18] Maintenance of family unity is also of prime concern to the *GC IV*: it includes a duty to avoid, as far as possible, separating family members in the context of transfers or evacuations of civilians by an occupying power;[19] to facilitate the reunion of dispersed families;[20] to maintain family unity during internment of family members;[21] and to give and receive personal news amongst themselves.[22]

Israel's domestic law and jurisprudence recognize the importance of the family, and protect the right to family life and derivative rights, such as the right to parenthood; the right to family unification; and the right of a child to have and maintain contact with both parents. Indeed, the Israeli *nomos*[23] does not settle merely for a negative duty of noninterference in family life, but actively encourages it.

Numerous laws and regulations guarantee a wide variety of social and health benefits, related to procreation, pregnancy, birth benefits, and social security payments assisting families with numerous children. Such regulation, coupled with deeper cultural reasons encompassing religious decrees, memories of the Holocaust, and the national/ethnic wish to ensure the thriving of a Jewish state,[24] help explain the datum that the birthrate in Israel far exceeds

HRC, General Comment No 16 (*ibid.*, pp. 3533–3534, § 3972); see also Inter-American Commission on Human Rights, Report on Terrorism and Human Rights, Doc OEA/Ser.L/V/II.116, Doc 5 rev 1 corr (October 22, 2002), § 55. The right to respect for "private and family life," enshrined in the European Convention on Human Rights, stipulates that no public authority may interfere with it except in accordance with the law and as is necessary in a democratic society in the interests of national security, public safety, or the economic well-being of the country, for the prevention of disorder or crime, for the protection of health or morals, or for the protection of the rights and freedoms of others. See Article 8(2) of the European Convention for the Protection of Human Rights and Fundamental Freedoms, Council of Europe, November 4, 1950, ETS 5.

[17] On the importance of family reunification in human rights law, see, e.g., Articles 1, 22(2) of CRC; the European Council Directive 2003/86/EC (September 22, 2003) on the right to family reunification.

[18] On the right of detainees to communicate with their families through correspondence and receiving visits, subject to reasonable restrictions concerning timing and censorship of mail, see, e.g., *Brannigan and McBride v. UK*, Eur Ct HR, App No 5/1992/350/423–424 (April 22, 1996), ¶ 64; Inter-American Commission on Human Rights, Report on the Situation of Human Rights in Peru (March 12, 1993), p. 29.

[19] Article 49(3) of GC IV.

[20] Article 26 of GC IV; Article 4(3)(b) of AP II; Article 74 of Protocol Additional to the Geneva Conventions of August 12, 1949, and relating to the Protection of Victims of International Armed Conflicts (Additional Protocol I), Geneva, June 8, 1977, 1125 UNTS 3.

[21] Article 82(3) of GC IV.　　[22] Article 25(1) of GC IV.　　[23] See entry N: Nomos.

[24] See e.g., D. Sperling, "Commanding the 'Be Fruitful and Multiply' Directive: Reproductive Ethics, Law and Policy in Israel" (2010) 19 *Cambridge Quarterly Healthcare and Ethics* 363.

the average of other OECD states.[25] These reasons all point to the role demographic considerations play in the regularization of family life. From this perspective, it is thus not entirely surprising that in Israel, to paraphrase Tolstoy, all Jewish families are alike; each non-Jewish family is unhappy in its own way. This distinction is sanctioned by law. In cases where the recognition of the various rights to family life collides with immigration laws pertaining to a non-Jewish spouse, child, or sibling of an Israeli citizen, the latter take precedence. Family life and the universal respect bestowed on it, speak the language of inclusion. National immigration laws normally speak the language of exclusion. There is, however, a distinction between exclusion and discrimination. In Israel, as the present entry clarifies, this distinction has been blurred.

K.1.2.3 Family Reunification

Traditionally, international law did not guarantee the right of an alien to enter or reside in a particular state.[26] Such a right has been considered a matter for the immigration policy of the state concerned. It is in the light of this traditional approach that one should read the rather feeble language of Article 10(1) of the CRC: it does not obligate state parties to allow for family reunification, but merely urges that "application by a child or his or her parents to enter or leave a state party for the purpose of family reunification shall be dealt with by States in a positive, humane and expeditious manner."[27]

Over time, and in view of globalization processes, ensuing migration, and the development of IHRL, this deference to states' sovereignty has ceased to be the exclusive factor in respect of family reunification.[28] The realization that a state that does not allow entry or exit for family reunification empties its obligation to respect and protect the right to family life of content, has led

---

[25] See Central Bureau of Statistics, Population of Israel, www.cbs.gov.il/publications17/yar hono217/pdf/b1.pdf; OECD (Organisation for Economic Co-operation and Development) data, Fertility rates, https://data.oecd.org/pop/fertility-rates.htm.

[26] See Nationality Decrees Issued in Tunis and Morocco, Advisory Opinion, 1921 PCIJ (ser. B) No 4.

[27] Article 10(1) of CRC.

[28] On this evolution in relation to migrants, see A. Kemp, "Managing Migration, Reprioritizing National Citizenship: Undocumented Migrant Workers' Children and Policy Reforms in Israel" (2007) 8 *Theoretical Inquiries in Law* 24; V. Kattan, "The Nationality of Denationalized Palestinians" (2005) 74 *Nordic Journal of International Law* 64. On the relevant factors delineating a state's discretion regarding collective attribution of nationality and residency rights, see A. Peters, "Les Changements Collectifs de Nationalité," in *Societé Française pour le Droit International* (Paris: Editions Pedone 2012), p. 175 [French].

Europe to take a bolder approach: The European Directive on the Right to
Family Reunification provides that "[m]easures concerning family reunification should be adopted in conformity with the obligation to protect the family
and respect family life."²⁹ The European court of justice seems to have taken
a further step, determining that "the removal of a person from a country where
close members of his family are living may amount to an infringement of the
rights to respect for family life as guaranteed by Article 8(1) of the ECHR."³⁰
Both the directive and the judgment allow for exceptions on the basis of
national security considerations, provided they are justified and proportionate.
In essence, thus, the presumption is that states are obligated to permit family
reunification, but this presumption can be refuted on grounds of justified
security concerns.

Indeed, any other presumption would not merely result in the infringement
of the right to respect for family life, but would also, in cases where a citizen
would be effectively compelled to leave his or her state of citizenship in order
to unite with his or her family, violate that state's obligation to allow its citizens
to live in their state of citizenship.³¹

Finally, given that the principle of equality before the law and nondiscrimination permeates every state act, and may well be considered a peremptory
norm of international law,³² it is unlawful for a state to prevent family unification in a discriminatory manner that rests on racial or ethnic grounds, with
respect to both foreigners and its own ethnic minority.

In the light of these considerations, most states allow family unification
which entails the admission of a noncitizen, at least for spouses and
their children.³³ In matters related to family unifications of Palestinian
families subject to Israel's control, be they its own citizens, permanent
residents of East Jerusalem or "protected persons" residing in the
OPT, Israel has ceased to be amongst such states: in 2003, the Israeli
parliament amended the Citizenship and Entry into Israel Law

---

²⁹ European Council Directive, preamble § 2. See also, Expert Opinion on the Right to Family
    Life and Non-discrimination, A Submission by the Open Society for Justice Initiative
    November 2008, ¶ 22 (attached to Adalah's petition to the HCJ challenging the Citizenship
    and Entry into Israel Law (Temporary Order), 2003, www.opensocietyfoundations.org/sites/
    default/files/expert-opinion-20081124.pdf).
³⁰ *European Parliament v. Council of the European Union*, CJEU (Grand Chamber), App
    No C-540/03 (June 27, 2006), Summary of Judgment, ¶ 2.
³¹ Article 12 of *ICCPR*.
³² See, e.g., Juridical Condition and Rights of the Undocumented Migrant, Advisory Opinion,
    OC-18/03, 2003 IACrtHR (Ser. A) No 18, ¶ 101.
³³ ICRC Restoring Family Links, "Reuniting Families," https://familylinks.icrc.org/en/Pages/
    HowWeWork/reuniting-families.aspx.

(Temporary Order).[34] The temporary nature of the law, much like the temporary nature of the occupation,[35] has been extended, with a few amendments, since then (on an annual basis). The law effectively forbids Israeli citizens and permanent residents who marry women under the age of 25 or men under the age of 35[36] from the OPT, Iran, Iraq, Lebanon, and Syria[37] from bringing their spouses to Israel. The HCJ rejected, first in 2006 and again in 2012, petitions which challenged the constitutionality of the law on both domestic and international legal grounds.[38]

The stated objective of the policy of family separation – indeed, disintegration and displacement – was the need to secure the Israeli public from terrorist attacks. Its real objective was, and remains, the wish to secure the Jewish majority in Israel. The law was conceived of, and operates as, the means to achieve this purpose. Its procedure rests on ethnic profiling. The HCJ's judgments enabled the realization of the policy. Its impact on the status of Palestinians has been devastating: uncertainty regarding status, generates material and emotional consequences on kinship and families generally, and on women and children particularly. In order to substantiate this proposition, Section K.2 discusses the legal situation prior to the law and proceeds to discuss the 2003 change and its rationale. Section K.3 presents a critical review of the two judgments which upheld the law. The impact of the law is the focus of Section K.4. Section K.5 concludes by highlighting the manner in which the law reflects, as it advances, the logic of Israel's indefinite control over the OPT and complements other ways and means by which this control is exercised.

K.2 ENEMIES, A LAW STORY: THE LAW OF FAMILY SEPARATION

K.2.1 *Uncertain Status – First Phase: Policy and Law 1967–2002*

Status matters. The Palestinian residents of the OPT are not Israeli citizens. They are "protected people" under the GC IV, and as such have a right to

---

[34] The Citizenship and Entry into Israel Law (Temporary Order), 2003, www.knesset.gov.il/laws/special/eng/citizenship_law.htm.

[35] See entry T: Temporary/Indefinite.

[36] Article 3 of the Citizenship and Entry into Israel Law (add 2005).

[37] The extension of the law to citizens of "enemy states" was enacted in 2007. See The Citizenship and Entry into Israel Law (Amendment No 2) (add 2007).

[38] HCJ 03/7052 *Adalah Legal Centre for Arab Minority Rights in Israel* v. *Minister of Interior* (May 14, 2006), http://elyon1.court.gov.il/Files_ENG%5C03%5C520%5C070%5Ca47/03070520.a47.htm [Hebrew]; HCJ 466/07 *MK Zahava Galon – Meretz-Yahad* v. *Attorney General* (January 11, 2012) [Hebrew].

reside in their occupied homeland.[39] To the extent that a home is a place where, to paraphrase Robert Frost, one can be certain that s/he cannot be turned away from, that certainty was denied to the Palestinian residents from the very beginning of the occupation: they could be, and were indeed, deported under Emergency Regulation 112 of the Defense Regulations;[40] and their residency could be, and has been, revoked by a determination, left to the absolute discretion of the military commander, that they had established residence elsewhere.[41] The absolute discretion of the military commander was extended to situations of family unifications as well. Indeed, the very framing of this discretion attests to its underlying presumption: family unification is not a right; it is not even generally permissible unless there are legitimate reasons to prevent it, but rather the other way around.[42] That presumption withstood change over time in the policy driving the exercise of discretion,[43] and even

[39] The situation of the Palestinian residents of East Jerusalem was different: following a 1967 census conducted by Israel in the OPT, those who were physically present within the Jerusalem municipality boundaries were granted permanent residency, a status entitling them to participate in municipal, but not in national elections. This status incurred under Articles 11 and 12 of the Citizenship and Entry into Israel Law. That status can be revoked by the Interior Minister, upon determination that Jerusalem is no longer the "center of life" of the person, whether s/he lived in the OPT or in another state. See HCJ 282/88 *Awad v. Yizthak Shamir, Prime Minister of Israel* (1988) 41(2) PD 424 [Hebrew]. In 2017, the supreme court intervened to limit this discretion: In AA 14/3268 *Al Huq v. Ministry of the Interior* (March 14, 2017) [Hebrew], a panel of three justices (Naor, Vogelman, and Mazuz) determined unanimously that there is a distinction to be maintained between people who received permanent residency status as immigrants and people who had permanent residency because they were born in Israel, or in a territory that became part of Israel (i.e., East Jerusalem). In the latter case, the minister of the interior has to take account of the unique situation of these residents who have a strong link to the place of their birth – and at times also the place where their parents and grandparents were born, and where they maintain family and community life. See justice Vogelman, ¶ 19. Under such circumstances, people requesting the renewal of their permanent residency, and "taking into consideration the special status of residents of East Jerusalem as indigenous residents," should receive a temporary residence for two years and thereafter receive their permanent residency; see justice Mazuz, ¶ 3.

[40] This issue is discussed in entry D: Deportation.

[41] That absolute discretion was nevertheless subject to proof of bad faith or corruption on the part of the military commander. See, HCJ 209/73 *La'afi v. Minister of the Interior* (1973) 28 PD 13 [Hebrew]; D. Kretzmer *The Occupation of Justice: The Israeli Supreme Court and the Occupied Territories* (Albany: SUNY Press, 2002), pp. 101–102.

[42] See Krezmer, *ibid.*, p. 111; Y. Dinstein, "Family Unification in the Occupied Territories" (1988) 13 *Tel Aviv Law Review* 221 [Hebrew].

[43] During the 1970s, requests made by minor children and spouses of local residents for family unification were normally granted; see, e.g., *La'afi*; HCJ 466/73 *Garbia v. Minister of the Interior* (1974) 28(2) PD 104 [Hebrew]. During the following decade, they were generally denied; see, e.g., HCJ 724/85 *Khalil v. IDF Commander in Judea and Samaria* (1986) 42(3) PD 324 [Hebrew]; HCJ 31/87 *Sharab v. Head of Civil Administration in Gaza* (1987) 41(4) PD 670 [Hebrew].

eventual judicial intervention: the latter, originating in the 1986 *Samara* case, generated the subjection of the discretionary authority of the military commander to substantive judicial review of the propriety of his reasoning on a case-by-case basis, but did not change the underlying presumption.[44]

A review of the case-law discloses the following:[45]

(a) The determination that a person born and raised in the OPT, who lived abroad for a time and upon wishing to return discovered that s/he has been transformed into a tourist wishing to settle there,[46] was ostensibly objective: it was based on various factors that determine one's "center of life" such as length of time spent elsewhere, acquiring citizenship and raising a family there.

(b) Laws and orders of the military commander exercising his authority to provide for the security of the area supersede local Jordanian law, under which Jordanian citizens could choose their place of residence without losing their status.[47]

(c) The absolute discretion of the military commander extends to situations of family unifications between Palestinians from the OPT and other Palestinians who were not citizens of Israel.

(d) The internationally recognized human right to family life does not entail the right to have a nonresident spouse living with a resident. International law does not impose a legal obligation on states to allow entry of noncitizens, even if they are married to residents or to citizens of that state. Indeed, even if it did, that obligation would have been inapplicable to situations of belligerent occupation.[48]

(e) The discretion of the military commander extends beyond security reasons to unspecified "political considerations" and "vital state interests."[49] Thus, as a general rule, it is within his authority to implement a restrictive policy, permitting family unification only for his "own reasons,"[50] and in cases of severe humanitarian concerns. The question is not whether to give effect to marriage, but whether

---

[44] HCJ 802/79 *Samara v. IDF Commander in Judea and Samaria* (1979) 34(4) PD 1 [Hebrew].
[45] For a comprehensive and detailed review and analysis of the case-law, see Kretzmer, *The Occupation of Justice*, pp. 101–111 and accompanying references.
[46] HCJ 500/72 *Al-Teen v. Minister of Defense* (1972) 27(1) PD 481, 484 [Hebrew].
[47] *Ibid.*, p. 486.
[48] HCJ 13/86 *Shahin v. IDF Commander in Judea and Samaria* (1987) 41(1) 197 [Hebrew].
[49] *Al-Teen*, p. 486.
[50] *Shahin*, p. 213. Note that the military commander's "own reasons" concern the recruitment of collaborators within the occupied population. In this manner Palestinian kinship is jeopardized twice: first, because they are deprived of the right to family life, and second because their communities, rather than providing support, are torn by poisonous internal suspicion.

"the authorities have a duty to permit wide-scale movement that encompasses thousands of people." The court determined that they do not.[51]

The presumption in cases where an Israeli citizen requested to establish and maintain family life with a non-Israeli was different. It was that absent exceptional reasons, such as fake marriage and substantial evidence that the non-Israeli presents a real security threat, s/he would be able to immigrate to Israel and eventually become an Israeli citizen. Both domestic law[52] and jurisprudence[53] recognized that right, and it was equally applicable to family unification between an Israeli citizen, usually of Palestinian origin, and a spouse and/or children residing in the OPT. As of 2002, that right has been eliminated for the latter category of people.

K.2.2 Phase 2: The 2002 Freeze on Palestinian Family Unification

At the height of the second Palestinian uprising against the continuous occupation of the OPT (Intifada) in late March 2002, the then minister of the interior, Eli Yishai, issued an emergency regulation. It stipulated a freeze on family unification processes between an Israeli citizen or an Israeli resident and his or her Palestinian spouse who resides in the OPT.[54] It is commonly assumed that its immediate context was the need for greater security: a suicide terrorist attack, killing 16 people, in a restaurant in Haifa was committed by a Palestinian who, being a son of an Israeli citizen, had an Israeli ID. This assumption is not supported by evidence: the minister of the interior established a professional team to "reduce the nationalization of non-Jews" before the suicide attack. The team produced a document, which the minister presented to the cabinet in a meeting which took place after the suicide attack. The presentation refers to security only once. Its main thrust is the portrayal of Palestinian families seeking unification as being driven by two objectives: to

---

[51] *Shahin*, p. 217.
[52] Up to the 2003 amendment to the Citizenship and Entry into Israel, Israeli law recognized three categories of people: (a) Jews are granted the right to immigrate to Israel and become citizens upon entry. That right extends to the spouses, children, grandchildren, and to their non-Jewish partners. See Law of Return, 1950, www.knesset.gov.il/laws/special/eng/return.htm; (b) foreigners do not have a right to immigrate to Israel and become citizens. The minister of the interior has wide discretion in matters pertaining to their status. See Articles 5 and 6 of the Entry Into Israel Law, 1952; (c) the foreign partner of an Israeli citizen has a right to immigrate to Israel and, following a transition period, become an Israeli citizen. See Article 7 of the Entry into Israel Law.
[53] HCJ 3648/97 *Stamka v. Minister of the Interior* 53(2) PD 728 [Hebrew].
[54] The Citizenship and Entry into Israel Law.

undermine the Jewish majority in Israel, and to receive social security benefits for their numerous children and wives. Convinced that Palestinian family unification presents a "clear and present danger" to the Jewish and democratic (!) character of Israel, the presentation's meshing of overt racism with demographic considerations ends with a call for the enactment of a law prohibiting this phenomenon.[55] In May 2002, the Israeli government resolved to reject family unification requests between a citizen or resident of Israel and a nonresident spouse of Palestinian origin.[56]

Petitions to the HCJ for an *order nisi* allowing the temporary residence of such couples in Israel, pending a decision on the legality of the decision, were rejected.[57] The petitions argued, inter alia, that such a decision requires primary legislation. The 2003 amendment to the Citizenship and Entry into Israel Law did just that.

K.2.3 Phase 3: The 2003 Amendment to the Citizenship and Entry into Israel Law (Temporary Order)

In July 2003, the Israeli parliament enacted the amendment to the Citizenship and Entry into Israel Law (Temporary Order).[58] The law put an end to the possibility of family unification in Israel between an Israeli citizen (or a Palestinian resident of Jerusalem) and his or her Palestinian spouse, who is a resident of the OPT. Article 2 provides that the minister of the interior would not grant a resident of the area (the definition of which, in Article 7, comprises Judea and Samaria and the Gaza Strip, and excludes residents of Israeli settlements) citizenship or residency in Israel, and that the military commander would not grant such a resident a permit to stay in Israel. Article 3 allows for some exceptions to this prohibition: (a) The minister of the interior still retains discretion to grant residency or citizenship to a Palestinian resident of the area who "identifies with the State of Israel and its objectives" and who (or a member of his family) contributed actively to Israel's security, economy, or

---

55 For the presentation, see Ministry of Interior, Immigration and Settlement of Foreigners in Israel (May 2002), www.hamoked.org.il/items/5760.pdf [Hebrew]. During the meeting the minister further said that "through Israel's back door, the Palestinians are realizing their right of return," and that it was "surprising and worrisome." See N. Kadman and A. Szlecsan, *Temporary Order? Life in East Jerusalem under the Shadow of the Citizenship and Entry into Israel Law* (Jerusalem: Hamoked: Center for the Defense of the Individual, 2014), www .hamoked.org/files/2014/1158910_eng.pdf, p. 16.

56 Government Resolution No 1813, www.hamoked.org.il/items/2960.pdf [Hebrew].

57 HCJ 4022/02 ACRI – *The Association for Civil Rights in Israel* v. *Minister of Interior* (January 11, 2007) [Hebrew]; HCJ 4608/02 *Awad* v. *the Prime Minister* (January 11, 2007) [Hebrew].

58 The Citizenship and Entry into Israel Law 2003.

other significant interests; (b) The minister or the military commander may grant permission to reside in Israel or to stay there temporarily for a cumulative period that would not exceed six months to a Palestinian resident of the OPT for work, medical treatment, or another temporary purpose; and (c) Permission to reside or stay in Israel may also be granted in order to prevent the separation of a child under the age of 12 (since 2005, 14[59]) from a parent who resides lawfully in Israel. In a 2007Amendment, the minister of the interior was further authorized to grant permission to reside or stay for exceptional humanitarian reasons, and for this purpose to establish a humanitarian committee.[60]

The amended law, like the administrative freeze which preceded it, applied retroactively to Palestinian spouses who married Israeli citizens and were in the process of receiving their full residency.[61] The preparatory work for the legislation discloses the same demographic purpose that motivated the administrative freeze.[62]

Petitions to the HCJ, challenging the constitutionality of the law in 2003, were rejected in 2006 by a majority of 6 to 5.[63] In 2012, the HCJ dismissed yet again (by a majority of 6 to 5) a 2007 petition against the constitutionality of the law.[64] These decisions enabled, inter alia, the transformation of the law into an indefinite "temporary order": since 2003, the provisional amendment has been renewed on an annual basis with only minor changes. It seems that the interplay between the provisional and the permanent applies not only to the duration of the occupation, but also to domestic legislation. The following section focuses on these decisions.

K.3 TRIALS OF LOVE: THE HCJ JUDGMENTS AND THEIR CRITIQUE

The HCJ concluded, in both the 2006 and the 2012 judgments, that the law is justified in view of security considerations, reflects the prerogative of states to shape their immigration policies, and meets the proportionality requirement

---

[59] In reality, that 2005 amendment was erased by administrative means: the interior ministry issued thereafter a new procedure according to which a child over 12 but under 14 would not get permanent residency but merely a two-year temporary residency.

[60] Article 3A of the Citizenship and Entry into Israel Law (Amendment No. 2) 2007.

[61] Article 4 of the Citizenship and Entry into Israel Law.

[62] See, e.g., Protocol of the Interior and Environment Committee meeting 63 of the Knesset (July 29, 2003) [Hebrew]. This motivation was also noted by some of the justices in the first appeal against the law; see Adalah, Justice Joubran, ¶ 24; justice Procaccia, ¶ 14.

[63] Adalah.   [64] Galon.

included in the Israeli Basic Law: Human Dignity and Liberty. It therefore rejected the petitions against the law's constitutionality.

These decisions were reached despite the fact that data provided by the state indicated that a miniscule percentage of the tens of thousands of Palestinians who hitherto received status by virtue of marriage, were suspected of having been engaged in acts of terror. The coupling of these data with the fact that the law upheld the discretionary authority of the minister of the interior to allow Palestinians to enter Israel for work[65] and with the Knesset's discussions, suggests that the decisive objective of the law was not to enhance Israel's security – it was demographic.

There is an inverse relationship between the length of the judgments and the clarity of their reasoning.[66] For the purposes of the present discussion,

---

[65] Article 3(b)(2) of The Citizenship and Entry into Israel Law, and as noted by then chief justice Barak's dissenting opinion in *Adalah*, ¶ 112.

[66] The 2006 judgment (*Adalah*) is 281 pages long; the 2012 judgment (*Galon*) is 288 pages long. In *Adalah*, 5 justices (chief justice Barak and justices Beinisch, Procaccia, Joubran, and Hayut) found that the law was unconstitutional; 5 justices (deputy chief justice Cheshin and justices Rivlin, Grunis, Naor, and Adiel) found that it was constitutional, and justice Levy found that the law was unconstitutional but refrained from vitiating it on the grounds that the Israeli parliament should be given time to amend it so as to render it proportional. Substantively, then, in 2006 six justices found the violation of the right to family life and the sweeping prohibition on family unification to be unconstitutional. In the 2012 decision, a majority of six justices (deputy chief justice Rivlin and justices Grunis, Naor, Rubinstein, Melcer, and Hendel) found the law constitutional. Five justices comprising the minority (chief justice Beinisch and justices Levy, Arbel, Joubran, and Hayut) found it unconstitutional. This time, justice Levy was part of the minority, but differed from his colleagues in determining that it was not even necessary to subject the law to the test of proportionality since its purpose was discriminatory and therefore unconstitutional. See Justice Levy opinion, ¶¶ 32–34. Both the law and the judgments received scholarly attention. For scholarship supporting the law and/or the judgments, see, e.g., A. Bakshi and G. Sapir, "For the Right of a Nation State – on the Absence of the National Consideration in the Judgments concerning the Citizenship and Entry into Israel Law (Temporary Order) 2003" (2013) 36 *Tel Aviv Law Review* 509 [Hebrew]; A. Rubinstein and L. Orgad, "Human Rights, State Security and a Jewish Majority" (2006) 48 *Hapraklit* 315, 340 [Hebrew]; L. Orgad, "Immigration, Terror and Human Rights: the Policy of Entry into Israel in Times of Emergency" (2009) 25 *Mehkerey Mishapt* 485 [Hebrew]; Y. Zilberschatz, "On Immigration of Non-Jewish Foreigners to Israel – Opening a Discussion" (2006) 10 *Mishapt u'Mimshal* 87 [Hebrew]. For less unequivocal support, see, e.g., D. Barak-Erez, "Israel: Citizenship and Immigration Law in the Vise of Security, Nationality and Human Rights" (2008) 6 *International Journal of Constitutional Law* 184; N. Carmi, "The Nationality and Entry to Israel Case Before the Supreme Court of Israel" (2007) 22 *Israel Studies Forum* 26. Critical scholarship includes N. H. Aviad, "Liberty and Higher Risk-Taking: The Nationality Law Case and the Supreme Court of Israel's Jurisprudence of Risk" (2006) *University of California, Berkeley – From the Selected Works of Nimrod Haim Aviad*, https://works.bepress.com/nimrod_aviad/3; Y. Ben-Shemesh, "Constitutional Rights, Immigration and Demography" (2006) 10 *Mishpat u'Mimshal* 27 [Hebrew]; G. Davidov, Y. Yovel, I. Saban, and A. Reichman, "A Family or a State? Citizenship and Entry into Israel Law (Temporary Order) 2003" (2005) 8 *Mishpat*

however, three ostensibly distinct yet nevertheless related points should be elucidated:

K.3.1 *The Conspicuous Absence of an Analysis in the Light of International Law*

In both the 2006 and the 2012 judgments, the issue of family unification was analyzed mostly as a domestic constitutional matter in the light of Israel's Basic Law: Human Liberty and Dignity. References to international law were few and far between: The 2006 minority opinion of chief justice Barak stated that the focus should be on the Israeli spouse whom the amended Citizenship and Entry into Israel Law prevents from uniting with his family in Israel. There is thus no need to determine whether IHRL and even IHL are violated by this amendment because even if they were, the amended law is a specific Israeli enactment which, from an internal Israeli point of view, takes precedence over international law. Consequently, the validity of the amended law depends solely on whether or not it contravenes the Basic Law: Human Dignity and Liberty.[67] The opinions of the minority justices in the 2012 judgment made no reference to international law.

The majority opinion in both judgments accepted the respondents' position that the "temporary amendment" does not prevent the formation of family relations; it simply does not permit its implementation in Israel.[68] Thus, while there is no denying that international law (and domestic law) recognizes the right to family life, this recognition does not entail "an explicit and concrete right, which creates a positive obligation upon the state to allow immigration into its territory for marriage purposes even in times of peace."[69] Immigration policies, left to the sovereign discretion of states, are designed to ensure that the entry of immigrants would not generate

---

u'*Mimshal* 643 [Hebrew]; A. Gross, "From Lover to Enemy: Justice, Truth, Integrity and Common Sense between Israel and Utopia in the HCJ judgment on the Citizenship Law" (2008) 13 *Hamishpat* 141 [Hebrew]; M. Masri, "Love Suspended: Demography, Comparative Law and Palestinian Couples in the Israeli Supreme Court" (2013) 22(3) *Social and Legal Studies* 309; B. Medina and I. Saban, "Human Rights and Risk Taking: 'Ethnic Profiling' and the Tests of the Limitation Clause" (2007) 39 *Mishaptim* 47 [Hebrew]; Y. Peled, "Citizenship Betrayed: Israel's Emerging Immigration and Citizenship Regime" (2007) 8 *Theoretical Inquiries in Law* 603.

[67] *Adalah*, justice Barak opinion, ¶ 17.

[68] *Ibid.*, ¶ 14 (referring to ¶ 35 of the respondents' brief of 3.11.2005).

[69] *Ibid.*, justice Cheshin opinion, ¶ 53 (citing Rubinstein and Orgad, "Human Rights, State Security and a Jewish Majority," p. 340); *Galon*, justice Rivlin opinion, ¶ 12.

security, economic, cultural, and demographic burdens on their citizens.[70] As a matter of policy, wrote justice Cheshin in the 2006 judgment, Israel, like other advanced, liberal states, recognizes the right to family life, including the right of foreign spouses of Israeli citizens to maintain it in Israel.[71] At present, however, given the continuous violent conflict between Israel and the Palestinians, that right extends neither to the Palestinian residents of the OPT – construed as "enemy residents" – who married Israeli citizens, nor indeed to the Israeli citizens who marry Palestinian residents of the OPT.[72] This construction of protected persons as "enemy residents" creates the nexus to the second point.

K.3.2 *The Construction of All Palestinians as an Enemy Population*

The notion that during war time, including the twilight zone of "quasi-war,"[73] every state is permitted to ban entry of enemy aliens even if they are married to its own citizens, and that the Palestinian residents of the OPT are such enemies of Israel, has a context. That context, according to justice Cheshin, is the armed conflict which erupted in 2000 (the second Intifada), comprising murderous terrorist attacks that the Palestinian launched against Israelis.[74] These attacks, in turn, render Israel's relations with the Palestinian Authority similar to those between states fighting each other.[75] Significantly absent from the narrative are, the occupation in general, and the specific events leading to the outbreak of the second Intifada in particular.[76] This absence allows for the presentation of Israel as an innocent victim of Palestinian violence, and thus as a defensive democracy. In this manner, this narrative strengthens Israel's right to ban the family unification of its Palestinian enemies (with their Palestinian spouses who are Israeli citizens/residents), as a measure a democracy is lawfully entitled to take to defend itself against security threats. This very narrative has led

---

[70] Galon, justice Rivlin opinion, ¶ 12; justice Levy opinion, ¶¶ 16, 22.
[71] *Adalah*, justice Cheshin opinion, ¶¶ 68–69.   [72] *Ibid.*, ¶¶ 2, 12, 27.   [73] *Ibid.*, ¶ 73.
[74] *Ibid.*, ¶¶ 7–8.
[75] "In our times – unlike in the past ... wars – again, unlike in the past – are not necessarily between states. But the rules and principles that were intended to protect the citizens and residents of the state are valid and logical even where an armed conflict is being waged not between states, but between a state and an entity, like the Palestinian Authority, which is not a state. In such circumstances, and in other similar ones, the presumption of hostility exists in full strength," *Ibid.*, ¶¶ 12, 79–80.
[76] On these events and the general context of the occupation, see O. Ben-Naftali and A. Gross, "The Second Intifada," in Anthony Dworkin et al. (eds.) *Crimes of War (0.2): What the Public Should Know* (New York: W. W. Norton & Company, 2007).

justice Grunis, dismissing the second petition in 2012, to state that "human rights are not a recipe for national suicide."[77]

Worse still, as noted by Aeyal Gross, the elimination of the occupation from the narrative obfuscates the reality in which, for the purposes of Jewish settlements in the OPT, Israel acts as a sovereign in the area, but for the purposes of allowing entry into Israel of Palestinian residents of the OPT who are family members of Israelis, the OPT is equated with an enemy state. For the Jewish settlers there is no border; for the Palestinian spouses of Palestinians who are Israeli citizens and residents, there is an impenetrable border.[78] In this manner, the judgments embrace the biopolitical profiling of the Palestinian population in toto – both in the OPT and in Israel – as the enemy.[79] This point brings us to the third significant issue.

K.3.3 *Profiling the Palestinian Family*

The judgments construe the entire Palestinian population under Israeli control as enemies not because of an action attributed to an individual, but because of their collective affiliation, and even though the statistical methodology employed for the assessment of the risk suggested that it is negligible.[80]

This construction is premised on a few problematic assumptions: First, the assumption that the basic right to family life of an individual could properly be balanced against the public right to security. This assumption, reiterating judicial decisions relative to profiling in airports,[81] confuses a human right with a public interest in a manner that defies the very logic of human rights and fails to take them seriously.[82] It thus subjects deontological considerations

---

[77] *Galon*, Justice Grunis opinion, ¶ 10.

[78] A. Gross, "From Lover to Enemy: Justice, Truth, Integrity and Common Sense between Israel and Utopia in the HCJ judgment on the Citizenship Law" (2008) 13 *Hamishpat* 141, 151 [Hebrew].

[79] It is worthwhile to note in this context that a 2017 amendment to the law forbids the entrance into Israel of foreigners who support boycotting of settlements. This amendment, equating Israel's enemies with peaceful criticism designed to affect its settlement "enterprise," affects Jews and non-Jews alike and may also affect Palestinian family unification. See The Citizenship and Entry into Israel Law (Amendment No 28) (add 2017).

[80] Medina and Saban, "Human Rights and Risk Taking," pp. 55–63.

[81] See entry X: X-Ray, Section X.3.

[82] See R. Dworkin, *Taking Rights Seriously* (New York: Bloomsbury, 1977), p. xi: "Individual rights are political trumps held by the individuals. Individuals have rights when, for some reason, a collective goal is not a sufficient justification for denying them what they wish, as individuals, to have or to do, or not a sufficient justification for imposing some loss or injury upon them."

to the calculus of proportionality. Second, the assumption that Palestinians residing in the OPT are "enemy aliens" rather than "protected persons," an assumption rejected in the post–World War II international legal order,[83] and an assumption which turns a blind eye to the special obligations Israel shoulders toward protected persons who have been under its control for decades. And third, the assumption, echoing the long-discredited decisions of American courts which concerned the treatment of American citizens of Japanese origins during WWII,[84] that Palestinian citizens of Israel are also enemies by affiliation and association. In this manner it blurs the distinction between Israel's own citizens, protected persons, and foreigners, alienating the former and discriminating against them on the basis of their ethnic and religious affiliation. Such discrimination is legally prohibited even in times of emergency "that threaten the life of the nation."[85] The HCJ nevertheless found it proportionate.

Israel's territorial expansion into the OPT, coupled with its demographic angst and with its security cult,[86] generates the perception that Palestinians are carriers of an infectious risk virus: they cease to be conceived of as citizens or protected persons endowed with rights; they are construed as an "objective enemy."[87] Such enmity is not grounded in either a concrete action or a concrete threat assessment, which defines "real enemies"; it is grounded in racism.[88] Profiling is its methodological procedure.

---

[83]   E.g., Article 44 of the GC IV provides that "In applying the measures of control mentioned in the present Convention, the Detaining Power shall not treat as enemy aliens exclusively on the basis of their nationality 'de jure' of an enemy State, refugees who do not, in fact, enjoy the protection of any government." See also Pictet, *Geneva Conventions*, pp. 262–265.

[84]   *United States* v. *Korematsu*, 323 US 214 (1944); *Hirabayashi* v. *United States*, 320 US 81 (1943). This similarity was noted by Justice Proccacia in her minority opinion in *Adalah*, ¶ 21. See also Medina and Saban, "Human Rights and Risk Taking," pp. 54–55, 107–112.

[85]   Article 4 of the ICCPR: "In time of public emergency which threatens the life of the nation and the existence of which is officially proclaimed, the States Parties . . . may take measures derogating from their obligations under the present Covenant to the extent strictly required by the exigencies of the situation, provided that such measures are not inconsistent with their other obligations under international law and do not involve discrimination solely on the ground of race, colour, sex, language, religion or social origin."

[86]   A. Kemp, "Dangerous Populations, State Territoriality and the Constitution of National Minorities," in J. Migdal (ed.) *Boundaries and Belonging* (Cambridge: Cambridge University Press, 2004), pp. 73–98.

[87]   H. Arendt, *On Revolution* (Harmondsworth: Penguin, 1965), p. 548; Y. Berda "The Security Risk as a Security Risk: Notes on the Classification Practices of the Israeli Security Services," in A. Beker and A. Matar (eds.) *Threat: The Palestinian Prisoners in Israeli Jails* (London: Pluto Press, 2009), pp. 50–51.

[88]   Z. Bauman, *Modernity and Holocaust* (Cambridge: Polity, 1989), p. 60.

It is illuminating to compare the bent of the Israeli bench and the stand of US courts faced with challenges to Executive Order 13769 of January 27, 2017,[89] and 13780 of March 6, 2017,[90] issued by president Trump: the former suspended issuance of visas to nationals of certain countries listed by the Department of Homeland Security (Iran, Iraq, Libya, Somalia, Sudan, Syria, and Yemen), decreased the number of refugees to be admitted in 2017, and banned the entry of Syrian refugees altogether. Following judicial interventions which noted, inter alia, that "the public had an interest in free flow of travel, in avoiding separation of families, and in freedom from discrimination,"[91] the Order was revoked and replaced by Order 13870. The latter, seeking "to protect its [US] citizens from terrorist attacks," imposed a "temporary suspension of entry" of nationals of the same countries for 90 days, subject to categorical exceptions and case-by-case waivers. In respect to this order too, the veil of security hiding the ugly face of religious profiling was lifted by a federal court. Issuing a temporary restraining order which suspended the Order's main provisions, the court found that the plaintiffs are likely to succeed on the merits of their claim concerning the Establishment Clause of the First Amendment to the Constitution, since "[a] reasonable, objective observer – enlightened by the specific historical context, contemporaneous public statements [made by the president], and specific sequence of events leading to its issuance – would conclude that the Executive Order was issued with a purpose to disfavor a particular religion, in spite of its stated, religiously-neutral purpose."[92] The Israeli HCJ, by contrast, sanctioned profiling. The latter signifies the classification of population into those who are risk carriers and those who are not according to race, ethnicity, class, religion, or national origin. The enemy may well be within and enmity resides in his being; not in his action.[93] These threats, thus, do not abide by the peace/war dichotomy

---

[89] Executive Order No 13769, "Protecting the Nation from Foreign Terrorist Entry into the United States" 82 Federal Register 8977 (February 1, 2017), www.federalregister.gov/documents/2017/02/01/2017-02281/protecting-the-nation-from-foreign-terrorist-entry-into-the-united-states.

[90] Executive Order no 13780, "Protecting the Nation from Foreign Terrorist Entry into the United States" 82 Federal Register 13209 (March 9, 2017), www.federalregister.gov/documents/2017/03/09/2017-04837/protecting-the-nation-from-foreign-terrorist-entry-into-the-united-states.

[91] *State of Washington* v. *Trump*, Case No C17-0141JLR (W.D. Wash. February 3, 2017); *State of Washington* v. *Trump*, No 17–35105 (9th Cir. February 9, 2017) https://cdn.ca9.uscourts.gov/datastore/opinions/2017/02/09/17-35105.pdf, pp. 28–29.

[92] *State of Hawai'i* v. *Trump*, CV No 17–00050 DKW-KSC (D. Haw. March 15, 2017), available at www.vox.com/2017/3/15/14940946/read-full-text-hawaii-court-order-trump-refugee-travel-ban, pp. 28–29. The suspension of Executive Order 13780 was extended by the court in a following decision (March 29, 2017). Both decisions were appealed by the government to the US Court of Appeals for the 9th circuit; at the time of writing this chapter, the appeal is yet to be heard.

[93] Arendt, *On Revolution*, p. 100. Note that while Foucault does not refer to Arendt, his biopolitical reading of enmity is clearly influenced by her notion of the "objective enemy."

any more than they abide by an external/internal dichotomy. From the perspective of the legal order, they blur the norm/exception relations and generate a permanent state of emergency[94] which "threatens the life of the (Jewish) nation."[95]

In Israel, a state of emergency has been the defining matrix of the normative order since its establishment; the threat within was perceived to emanate from the Arab/Palestinian minority in Israel, conceived of as potential enemies; it was then expanded to Palestinians classified as de facto enemies – that is, those who attempted to return to Israel from neighboring countries pursuant to the 1949 Armistice agreements[96] – and eventually to the Palestinian residents of the OPT, including East Jerusalem. The amendments to the Citizenship and Entry into Israel Law have indeed merged the various categories of Palestinians under Israel's control together with citizens of Israel's "Enemy States," and extended the "temporary order" indefinitely. The impact of the indefinite suspension of Palestinian family unification on Palestinian intimate and social space is briefly discussed in Section K.4.

K.4 SUSPENDED FAMILIES: THE IMPACT OF THE LAW

Scholarly attention bestowed on the "temporary order" suspending indefinitely the unification of Palestinian families hardly ever related to its impact on their lives.[97] That impact has received some media[98] and social media

---

[94] G. Agamben, *State of Exception*, K. Attell (trans.) (Chicago: University of Chicago Press, 2005).

[95] See e.g., ICCPR, art. 4(1).

[96] Hashemite Jordan Kingdom-Israel: General Armistice Agreement, UN Doc S/1302/Rev1 (April 3, 1949), adopted by the Security Council in Resolution No 72, UN Doc S/RES/72 (August 11, 1949).

[97] Two notable exceptions are the analysis offered by Leora Bilsky of the views of Citizenship in Palestinian literature as contrasted with the those of the HCJ justices: see L. Blisky, "Citizenship as a Mask: Between the Impostor and the Refugee" (2008) 15 *Constellations* 72; L. Bilsky, "Speaking through the Mask: Israeli Arabs and the Changing Faces of Israeli Citizenship" (2009) 1 *Middle East Law and Governance* 166; and a qualitative research by Yael Plitmann, comprising discussions with six Palestinian women, citizens of Israel who have been separated from their husbands pursuant to the law, which, following Robert Cover's notion of the nomos, analyzes their reactions to the law as a crisis in their normative universe. See Y. Plitmann, "The Story of Six Women: Different Faces of the Family Unification Issue," in R. Zarik and A. Saban (eds.) *Law, Minority and National Conflict* (Tel Aviv: Tel Aviv University – Law Society and Culture, 2017), pp. 335–374 [Hebrew].

[98] Haaretz journalist Nir Hasson has been covering the issue, normally in the context of the occasion of the annual renewal of the "temporary order"; see, e.g., N. Hasson, "About 250 minors lack a status due to the prohibition on family unification," *Haaretz* (June 16, 2016), www.haaretz.co.il/news/politics/.premium-1.2977513 [Hebrew]; N. Hasson, "15 Years to the

attention,[99] and was the focus of various reports by human rights organizations.[100] The information retrieved from these reports and analyses allows for some assessment of the major effects of the law on the Palestinian families.

Uncertainty with respect to one's status is the first major effect of the ban on Palestinian family unification. The uncertainty does not derive merely from the fact that the temporary duration of the law has been transformed into the indefinite (which, by definition, may or may not have an end), but also from the administrative process through which the Palestinians requesting family unification may or may not get residency status in Israel.

This administrative via dolorosa – characterized by de-humanizing bureau-cracy, even in the working of the "humanitarian committee" entrusted with dealing with exceptionally difficult humanitarian cases[101] – begins when a qualified Palestinian citizen or permanent resident of Israel requests to be unified with a spouse or a child who lacks status. The qualification requires, first, meeting the age specification (over 35 in case of a man, over 25 in case of a woman, and nominally less than 14 in case of a child[102]), and second, proof that Israel has been the "center of life" during the two years preceding the request. The latter requires innumerable documents comprising, inter alia,

---

law prohibiting family Unification, thousands Without a status," *Haaretz* (February 27, 2017), www.haaretz.co.il/news/politics/.premium-1.3886089 [Hebrew].

[99] See e.g., I. Landau, "Inside the Entrails of Israel's Most Racist Law," *Don't Die a Fool* (January 29, 2015), https://idanlandau.com/2015/01/29/inside-israels-most-racist-law/ [Hebrew] (the blog of Idan Landau, linguistics Professor at Ben-Gurion University).

[100] For NGOs' reports see, e.g., Y. Stein, *Forbidden Families – Family Unification and Child Registration in East Jerusalem* (Jerusalem: B'Tselem and Hamoked, 2004); A. Ashkar, *Frozen Families – the Prohibition Israel Imposes on Family Unification in the Territories* (Jerusalem: B'Tselem and Hamoked, 2006); The Society of St. Yves, Catholic Center for Human Rights, *Palestinian Families Under Threat: 10 Years of Family Unification Freeze in Jerusalem* (2013), www.saintyves.org/uploads/files/10_years_freeze_of_family_unification_in_jerusalem.pdf; N. Baumgarten-Sharon, *So Near Yet so Far – Implications of Israeli-Imposed Seclusion of Gaza Strip on Palestinians' Right to Family Life* (Jerusalem: B'Tselem and Hamoked, 2014).

[101] As mentioned in above text and note 60, the humanitarian committee was established in Art. 3A of the Law. Reflecting on its working has led justice Daphne Barak-Erez of the supreme court to wonder "[H]ow nasty and brutish must a person's life be for its case to be recognized as 'humanitarian' in a way that justifies the grant of a status in Israel?" See HCJ 4380/11 *Anonymous v. the Minister of the Interior*, https://supremedecisions.court.gov.il/Home/Dow nload?path=HebrewVerdicts\11\800\043\a57&fileName=11043800_a57.txt&type=4 (March 26, 17).

[102] In the case of a child the real determining age is 12; see above text and note 59. Note further that the 2005 amendment to the law stipulated that a person registered in the Palestinian registry would be considered a resident of the OPT, even if s/he was born in Israel or has always lived there. Such registrations were due to long delays in registering children born in East Jerusalem even prior to the 2003 enactment of the "Temporary Order."

property deeds or a rental contract for an apartment; bills, bank accounts, and records; children's school certificates; social security payments; and clear criminal and security records.

The process may take months, during which time the OPT spouse does not even have a temporary permit to stay and is thus exposed to deportation. If a permit is granted, it is granted only for one year. Its renewal requires the resubmission of updated documents proving the "center of life." The request for renewal may be submitted three months before the expiry of the current temporary residence, but that period does not always suffice for the administrative process to complete. In this case, the spouse may become yet again an illegal resident facing deportation, and, if caught, a criminal record would ensue, disqualifying the request.

Proof of a clear security record sounds reasonable enough. It is not: The 2005 amendment to the Citizenship and Entry into Israel Law provided that even if a resident of the OPT does not present a security threat, if one of his/her relatives – even if they maintain no contact – presents such a threat, it is enough to deny the request. A 2007 amendment went even further, stipulating that it was enough to show that activity threatening the security of Israel or its citizens takes place, either in an area of the OPT or in a state where the Palestinian requesting residence is registered, even if s/he has never lived there, to reject the request.[103] The security services are not required to present evidence of the security threat.

Gaza is, of course, an area that ipso facto presents a threat.[104] Consequently, spouses from Gaza who have not previously obtained permanent residency status cannot obtain it, even if they had been married for many years.[105] The annulment of family unification between Israeli citizens, Israeli permanent residents, and residents of the West Bank with their spouses in Gaza effectively compels them to either live in Gaza or separate. Given that, subject to few exceptional humanitarian circumstances, all passage between the West Bank and Gaza and between Israel and Gaza is prohibited, maintaining any semblance of family contact is virtually impossible. The Separation Wall, checkpoints, and the permit regime within the West Bank and between the West Bank and Israel, including East Jerusalem, also render the maintenance of such contact quite difficult.[106]

---

[103] Article 3(d) of the Citizenship and Entry into Israel Law.
[104] See entry Z: Zone Section Z.2.2.1.
[105] Pursuant to HCJ 4019/10 *Hamoked* v. *IDF Commander in the West Bank* (April 21, 2013) [Hebrew], the authorities no longer expel to Gaza a spouse who had moved to the West Bank prior to 2005.
[106] See entry B: Border/Barrier; entry Z: Zone.

A temporary status and uncertainty as to its duration generate both economic and emotional hardships. From an economic perspective, up to an
HCJ intervention in 2013, temporary status did not allow for a work permit.[107]
Until 2015, such status also did not entail social security and health benefits,
a denial that applied to both spouses, even if one of them is an Israeli citizen or
a permanent resident. This policy was changed pursuant to a petition to the
HCJ, but the new policy still discriminates against Palestinians in terms of
health insurance costs, this time with judicial approval.[108]

The emotional costs of the ban on family unification are as evident as they
are heart-breaking. Uncertainty, blatant discrimination, fear of deportation
and actual deportation, years of unemployment and economic devastation,
different statuses within a nuclear family, and legal and material difficulties in
maintaining contacts with the extended family have generated the disintegration of marriage, resentment within families, and the dissolution of kinship.
The plight of women in these circumstances has been most dreadful.

Women are doubly jeopardized due to the coupling of Israel's ban with the
traditionally patriarchic structure of Palestinian society.[109] The latter includes
the expectation that a wife would move in with her husband's family. Thus, if
she is a resident or citizen of Israel who married a man from Gaza and wishes
to live with him, she must relocate to Gaza, and her visits to Israel entail
a lengthy bureaucratic process, during which she is separated from her husband and children. If she is a resident of the West Bank who married a man
from Gaza or a resident from Gaza who married a man from the West Bank,
the difficulty of leaving her own family and kin behind is augmented by the
near impossibility of visits. Deprived of her social network, she becomes
completely dependent on her husband, thus accentuating the gender-gap
between them. A woman who is an Israeli citizen or permanent resident
who marries a man from the OPT also risks the revocation of her status, as it
may well be determined that she has relocated "the center of her life," even if
in fact she has not.

If the woman is from the OPT and lives with her husband who is an Israeli
citizen or resident in Israel, including East Jerusalem, she is under threat from

---

[107] HCJ 6615/11 *Salhab v. The Minister of Interior*, state's response to the petition, www.hamoked
       .org/files/2012/114822_eng.pdf [Hebrew].
[108] HCJ 2649/09 *ACRI – The Association for Civil Rights in Israel v. Minister of Health*
       (November 4, 2015) [Hebrew].
[109] See e.g., S. Abu-Rabiah-Quider and N. Wiener-Levi (eds.), *Palestinian Women in Israel:
       Identity, Power Relations and Coping* (Jerusalem: The Van Leer Jerusalem Institute and
       Hakibbutz Hameuchad, 2010) [Hebrew]; L. Abu-Tabich, "On Collective National Rights,
       Civil Equality and Women's Rights: Palestinian women in Israel and the Denial of their
       Right to Chose their Place of Residence" (2009) 34 *Theory and Criticism* 43 [Hebrew].

both the state and her husband: lacking status, fearing deportation, and otherwise restricted from the public sphere, she is practically placed under house arrest and may not feel safe enough to attend even religious or family events. If she is the victim of domestic violence, fear of deportation would prevent her from complaining. If her husband decides to divorce her, she faces deportation, a loss of whatever status she has had, including the social benefits attached to it, as well as loss of the rights attached to divorce. If they have children, the father will retain custody of them. Once back with her original family, she becomes both an economic and a social liability. If the woman is an Israeli citizen/permanent resident and the husband is from the West Bank, during the years he could not work, in addition to her household duties she would have to be employed, often at low-level jobs in an unwelcoming environment. If she is the victim of domestic violence, but wishes to remain with her husband and regularize his status, the need for him to have a clear criminal record would prevent her from complaining to the authorities.

The impact of the 2003 Citizenship and Entry into Israel (Temporary Order) is an effect of the continuous control of Israel over Palestinian lives in both Israel and the OPT. This impact is nothing short of an affront to human dignity. It should have been a shock to democratic sensibilities. Instead, much like the occupation itself, its indefinite continuation has contributed to the numbing of these sensibilities.

K.5 CONCLUSION: LOVE, AN ENEMY STORY

Palestinian kinship has always existed between the Mediterranean and the Jordan River. The Citizenship and Entry into Israel Law (Temporary Order) of 2003 represents an Israeli attempt to limit Palestinian presence in parts of the land. The major and interrelated trait-marks of this attempt include the following:

(a) It is coherent with other measures Israel has undertaken to achieve this objective. These include the slicing of the Palestinian land; the expansion of Jewish settlements; the construction of the Wall and the checkpoints; and the myriad of administrative barriers which accompany these material constructions. They too are designed to transform the Palestinian place into a no-place.[110]

---

[110]　See entries Z: Zone; J: Jewish Settlements; B: Border/Barrier; D: Deportation; H: House Demolitions; X: X-Ray.

(b) Much like the occupation itself, the "temporary" duration of the law is a fiction. It is indefinite.[111] This is not the only fictitious element of the law: the consciously false confusion of correlation (most suspects of engagement in terrorism are men under the age of 35) and causal link (ergo, most Palestinian men under the age of 35 are engaged in terrorism) is another. The real objective is to be understood in terms of the correlation between territory and demography. Consequently, justifying the law and the ethnic profiling its implementation entails in security considerations is yet another fiction. Such fictions are to be found in a multitude of other measures undertaken to achieve as much territory with as few Palestinians as possible.[112]

(c) The attempt receives the blessing of the highest judicial authority in Israel. The court collaborates with this objective, and indeed advances its underlying fictitious narratives, and finds that a discriminatory law and the ethnic profiling its implementation requires – a law that violates a myriad of human rights protected by both IHRL and IHL and otherwise recognized under Israeli law – meets the proportionality requirement of the Basic Law: Human Dignity and Liberty. In this manner, the commonly accepted distinction between law and violence becomes meaningless.[113] Attempting to assist the state in fortifying its ever-expanding "villa in the jungle,"[114] the court introduced a constitutional jungle into the villa. It too inhabits the sui generis nomos developed by successive Israeli governments to justify Israel's control over the OPT.[115]

Yet, the commonality between this measure and others notwithstanding, the Citizenship and Entry into Israel Law is singularly offensive to democratic sensibilities. This may well be due to the uncanny violent nature of the interference with the most intimate sphere of human existence, to engaging in a demographic war, and to the presentation to Palestinians with a variation of a "Sophie's choice" between love and home, between a home and a homeland.

---

[111] See entry T: Temporary/Indefinite.   [112] See entry G: Geneva Law, Section G.3.2.
[113] See entries V: Violence; P: Proportionality.
[114] The colonial metaphor of a "villa in the jungle" to explain Israel's position vis-à-vis the Arab world was first used by then Israeli prime minister Ehud Barak and has become quite common since. See, e.g., A. Benn, "The Jewish Majority in Israel still see their Ccountry as 'a villa in the jungle'," *The Guardian* (August 20, 2013), www.theguardian.com/commentis free/2013/aug/20/jewish-majority-israel-villa-in-the-jungle; "Israel's Villa in the Jungle," *The Economist* (May 14, 2016), www.economist.com/news/special-report/21698439-israels-foes-have-weakened-palestinians-are-winning-battle-womb-israels.
[115] See entry N: Nomos.

L

Lawfare

Hedi Viterbo

L.1 INTRODUCTION

The term "lawfare" – an amalgamation of "law" and "warfare" – is traceable to at least the 1950s.[1] It reappeared at the turn of the century, first in a 2001 article by the anthropologist John Comaroff, who employed it to denote "the effort to conquer and control indigenous peoples by the coercive use of legal means."[2] In his later work with Jean Comaroff, the definition of the concept was broadened to encompass, more generally, "the resort to legal instruments, to the violence inherent in the law, to commit acts of political coercion, even erasure. . . . Lawfare," they add, "always seeks to launder brute power in a wash of legitimacy, ethics, propriety."[3]

Yet, it is a former deputy judge advocate of the US Air Force, Charles Dunlap, who is commonly credited with coining the term in reference to military warfare. In late 2001, Dunlap defined "lawfare" as "the use of law as a weapon of war" and "a method of warfare where law is used as a means of realizing a military objective."[4] Dunlap's definition was later quoted at length in an article Avichai Mendelblit (currently Israel's attorney general) published on lawfare[5] in 2012, shortly after he had completed his quarter-century-long

---

[1] L. N. Sadat and J. Geng, "On Legal Subterfuge and the So-Called 'Lawfare' Debate" (2010) 43 *Case Western Reserve Journal of International Law* 153, 157.

[2] J. L. Comaroff, "Colonialism, Culture, and the Law: A Foreword" (2001) 26 *Law & Social Inquiry* 305, 306.

[3] J. L. Comaroff and J. Comaroff, "Law and Disorder in the Postcolony: An Introduction," in J. Comaroff and J. L. Comaroff (eds.), *Law and Disorder in the Postcolony* (Chicago: The University of Chicago, 2006), p. 1.

[4] C. J. Dunlap Jr., *Law and Military Interventions: Preserving Humanitarian Values in 21st Century Conflicts* (Carr Center for Human Rights, John F. Kennedy School of Government, Harvard University, Working Paper, 2001), p. 4.

[5] While using the phrase "legal warfare" in Hebrew, Mendelbit explicitly translated it into English, in the first instance, as "lawfare." Hence my use of this word in this translated excerpt.

service in the Israeli military legal system (including as a military prosecutor, a military judge, and the military advocate general). After discussing Dunlap's definition,[6] Mendelblit's article proceeds to criticize what he describes as

> the increasing attempts to fundamentally change the law of war while manipulatively accusing the IDF of not following this law. ... [In] this legal frontier, there is an ongoing worldwide battle over the law of war. ... For example, following ... [Israel's] attack on the UNRWA's Al-Fakhura School [in Gaza in 2009] ... a UN committee sought to establish a new principle in the law of war, which would have prohibited retaliating to fire coming from UN facilities.[7] The greatest threat, however, is the attempt to import human rights law norms into ... warfare. ... [The] IDF's answer ... to ... [this] lawfare ... [has included the] operational legal advice the Military Advocate General's Office [provides] ... to commanders ... In addition, the [military's] orders and operational plans incorporate international law obligations. ... During combat, legal advice is provided at all ... relevant military levels ... If necessary, legal information is disseminated domestically and globally to clarify the IDF's compliance with its obligations under the law of war.[8]

Like the article written by his Israeli counterpart, Dunlap's initial definition of lawfare aimed to criticize the growing recourse of nonstate actors to international law and the resultant erosion of public support for his country's involvement in warfare. In 2008, however, Dunlap slightly changed his tone, remarking that

> concern from the public, NGOs, academics, [and others] ... about the behavior of militaries is ... a legitimate and serious activity ... [Lawfare] is much like a tool or weapon that can be used properly in accordance with the

---

[6] The transfer of security knowledge between the United States and Israel, as exemplified by Mendelblit's quotation of Dunlap, is examined in depth in entry E: Export of Knowledge.

[7] Contrary to Israel's claim that its attack was merely a response to gunfire coming from the Gazan school, a UN Board of Inquiry found that there had been "no firing from within the compound and no explosives in the school." United Nations General Assembly Security Council, Summary by the Secretary-General of the Report of the United Nations Headquarters Board of Inquiry into certain incidents in the Gaza Strip between December 27, 2008 and January 19, 2009 (May 2009), A/63/855, S/2009/250, ¶ 22 https://unispal.un.org/DPA/DPR/unispal.nsf/0/3800655E522591FD852575CB004CA773.

[8] A. Mendelblit, "Lawfare – the IDF's Next Legal Frontier" (2012) 4 *Military & Strategy* 47, 48–51 [Hebrew], http://i-hls.com/wp-content/uploads/2013/03/%D7%9C%D7%95%D7%97%D7%9 E%D7%AA-%D7%9E%D7%A9%D7%A4%D7%98-%E2%80%94-%D7%94%D7%97%D7%9 6%D7%99%D7%AA-%D7%94%D7%9E%D7%A9%D7%A4%D7%98%D7%99%D7%AA-% D7%A9%D7%9C-%D7%A6%D7%94%D7%9C.pdf.

higher virtues of the rule of law – or not. It all depends on who is wielding it, how they do it, and why.[9]

Over time, the concept of lawfare has continued to evolve in public and academic discourses, assuming various and sometimes competing definitions.[10] Notwithstanding their disparity, most understandings of this term revolve around two themes: state and nonstate lawfare.[11] The former, explored in critical scholarship on the subject (such as the Comaroffs'), designates the deployment of law by states in planning, executing, and legitimizing their contentious military objectives. The latter, as expressed by state allies and representatives (such as Mendelblit), denounces attempts of individuals, liberal human rights organizations, and other political entities at harnessing law to curtail or rebuke state policies and practices. Lawfare thus embodies some of the competing uses and interpretations to which law lends itself in the hands of the state on the one hand, which seeks to monopolize violence,[12] as well as those who, on the other hand, pose a direct or indirect challenge to this monopoly. Further, "lawfare" not only represents these various phenomena, it is also part of the vocabulary through which political players address each other: to characterize another party as engaging in "lawfare" is to attach a certain normative judgment to their actions. Lawfare thus operates at once as the object and the framework of inquiry.[13]

---

[9] C. J. Dunlap Jr., "Lawfare Today: A Perspective" (2008) 3(1) *Yale Journal of International Affairs* 146, 148. See also C. J. Dunlap Jr., "Lawfare Today … and Tomorrow" (2011) 87 *International Law Studies Series US Naval War College* 315, 315 (redefining lawfare as "the strategy of using – or misusing – law as a substitute for traditional military means to achieve a warfighting objective").

[10] D. Hughes, "What Does Lawfare Mean?" (2016) 40 *Fordham International Law Journal* 1; W. Tiefenbrun, "Semiotic Definition of Lawfare" (2011) 43 *Case Western Reserve Journal of International Law* 29, 51–57; W. G. Werner, "The Curious Career of Lawfare" (2010) 43 *Case Western Reserve Journal of International Law* 61.

[11] Cf. L. Hajjar, *Lawfare and Armed Conflict: Comparing Israeli and US Targeted Killing Policies and Challenges Against Them* (Issam Fares Institute for Public Policy and International Affairs, January 2013), p. 4 [hereinafter: *Lawfare and Armed Conflict*], www.aub.edu.lb/ifi/int ernational_affairs/Documents/20130129ifi_pc_IA_research_report_lawfarc.pdf (distinguishing between "state lawfare" and simply "lawfare," with the latter category designating legal contestations over state warfare policies and practices).

[12] M. Weber, "Religious Rejections of the World and Their Directions," in H. H. Gerth and C. Wright Mills (eds. and trans.), *From Max Weber: Essays in Sociology* (New York: Oxford University Press, 2009), pp. 323, 334. See also W. Benjamin, "Critique of Violence," in M. Bullock and M. Jennings (eds.), *Selected Writings*, E. Jephcott (trans.) (London: Harvard University Press, 1999), vol. I, pp. 1237, 1239.

[13] On the use of conceptual tools as both the mode and object of inquiry, see H. Viterbo, "Ties of Separation: Analogy and Generational Segregation in North America, Australia, and Israel/Palestine" 42 *Brooklyn Journal of International Law* 686 (2017).

This entry examines these various meanings and uses of lawfare in the Israeli/Palestinian context, using "lawfare" critically, descriptively, or both. While law has long had close ties with warfare, this dynamic and its surrounding discourses have evolved in recent years, as evidenced by the actions of political and social players in Israel/Palestine. Demonstrating this in relation to Israel's lawfare, Section L.2 investigates the growing involvement of military lawyers in operational matters – a development also mentioned in the above excerpt from Mendelblit's article. Section L.3 turns to the legal challenges Israel's critics and victims have pursued through three key avenues: Israeli courts, including both the military court system[14] and the High Court of Justice (HCJ); foreign national courts, on the basis of the universal jurisdiction doctrine; and, more recently, international tribunals, namely the International Criminal Court (ICC) in Rome and the International Court of Justice (ICJ) in The Hague. The pitfalls and potential of each of these courses of action are discussed. Tying together these two areas of lawfare, Section L.4 examines how Israel and its NGO allies have used law as a weapon against the above legal challenges. This has included accusing Israel's critics and victims of perpetrating "legal terrorism"; exploring lawsuits against Palestinian leaders overseas; utilizing military lawyers to prevent prosecutions against Israelis; passing laws that clamp down on liberal human rights NGOs; and, at the same time, continuing to maintain that Israel cherishes law and human rights. As this entry explains, Israel's legal struggle against unwanted legal proceedings stands not in contrast to, but in continuation of its insistence on a rhetoric of law and of human rights, as both aim to preserve its reliance on law to achieve and legitimize its political objectives. The concluding section highlights key issues and themes from these different contexts.

L.2 ISRAELI STATE LAWFARE

Despite a common assumption to the contrary, lawfare is by no means an entirely novel phenomenon, even if its manifestations have transformed over history. In premodern times, belligerents created and recognized war codes and costumes, which required, among other things, avoiding undue harm, distinguishing between combatants and civilians, and sparing war prisoners. The nineteenth and twentieth centuries ushered in modern codifications of the laws of war, notably including the Lieber Code, the so-called Saint Petersburg Declaration, the Brussels Declaration, the Hague Regulations,

---

[14]   See entry M: Military Courts.

and the Geneva Conventions. In a testament to law's violence, these legal tools have served no less to legitimate than to limit state violence.[15]

Depending on one's definitions of lawfare and warfare, state lawfare can be understood either as a specific aspect of, or as synonymous with, Israel's reliance on law in devising, operating, and justifying its rule over the West Bank and Gaza Strip. This cozy relationship between law and state violence[16] is a common thread across much of this book, with specific entries shedding light on its implications in a wide range of practices – from mass incarceration[17] through Israel's West Bank barrier[18] to house demolitions[19] (to mention but three examples). To complement these entries, this section focuses on another site of state lawfare: the legal expertise the Israeli military obtains from its lawyers, and the functions this expertise fulfills.

With the establishment of the State of Israel in 1948, the legal services of the Hagana (a Jewish paramilitary organization from the British Mandate period) were formalized into the Israeli military as the military advocate general corps.[20] When Israel took over the West Bank and Gaza Strip in 1967, specially trained units of the corps entered these territories with the Israeli brigades, and were subsequently attached to the military's different regional headquarters.[21] Since then, the military advocate general corps has grown to 1,000 personnel, including 300 active-duty soldiers. Among its responsibilities are the drafting of military legislation and policy, as well as the enforcement of military justice and disciplinary issues.[22] It is within these areas of activity that one finds the military legislation Israel applies to Palestinians in the West Bank, the military legal system that prosecutes and tries these Palestinians, and also Israel's investigations of soldiers accused of violating Palestinians' rights – issues examined in other parts of this book.[23] The Corps is also entrusted with

---

[15]   C. Jochnick and R. Normand, "The Legitimation of Violence: A Critical History of the Laws of War" (1994) 35 *Harvard International Law Journal* 49.

[16]   On law's complicity in state violence, see entry V: Violence.

[17]   See entries M: Military Courts, S: Security Prisoners, and Y: Youth.

[18]   See entries B: Border/Barrier and P: Proportionality.   [19]   See entry H: House Demolitions.

[20]   C. A. Jones, "Frames of Law: Targeting Advice and Operational Law in the Israeli Military" (2015) 33 *Environment and Planning D: Society and Space* 676, 678 [hereinafter: "Frames of Law"].

[21]   M. Shamgar, "Legal Concepts and Problems of the Israeli Military Government – the Initial Stage," in M. Shamgar (ed.), *Military Government in the Territories Administered by Israel, 1967–1980: The Legal Aspects* (Jerusalem: Hebrew University, 1982), pp. 13, 24–25.

[22]   M. N. Schmitt and J. J. Merriam, "The Tyranny of Context: Israeli Targeting Practices in Legal Perspective" (2015) 37 *University of Pennsylvania Journal of International Law* 53, 82.

[23]   On the military legislation and courts, see entries M: Military Courts and Y: Youth. On investigations, see entries I: Investigations and W: War Crimes.

providing legal advice and education, with the latter currently including some training in international humanitarian law for all commanders.[24]

Within the military advocate general corps operates the military's international law department, known until the 1990s as the international law branch.[25] Its task, according to a former top official in the department, "is not to tie down the army, but to give it the tools to win in a way that is legal."[26] One of the department's former heads has reiterated the point, describing their role as attempting to "find legal ways to achieve the goals of the army. . . . I am not there only to say what they can't do. I am also there to say what they can do and how to do what they want to do in a legal way."[27] Another former head of the department has added: "We defended policy that is on the edge," such as "the 'neighbor procedure' [making Palestinians knock on the door of their potentially dangerous neighbors], house demolitions, deportation, [and] targeted assassination."[28] According to reports in the Israeli media, department personnel also authorized an easing of the rules of engagement during military operations in the Gaza Strip, which increased Palestinian civilian casualties.[29] One senior military lawyer indeed described in an interview how, during the Israeli offensive on the Gaza Strip in 2008–2009, commanders "thought it is not allowed to attack mosques, but I, the legal practitioner, tell them that it is allowed. You can attack, no problem." Another military lawyer, when asked whether law protected Palestinian civilians, admitted: "I'm not sure it lessens harm ... The opposite is sometimes true."[30]

Formal statements by the military have been more cautious in their choice of words when describing the department's work. Thus, in line with Israel's long tradition of seeking legitimacy by invoking law, the military asserts on its website:

---

[24] Jones, "Frames of Law," pp. 678, 684; A. Pfeffer, "IDF to Seek Legal Advice During Future Conflicts," *Haaretz* (January 1, 2010), www.haaretz.com/idf-to-seek-legal-advice-during-future-conflicts-1.265596. On the military advocate general corps, see also M. Geva, *Law, Politics and Violence in Israel/Palestine* (Cham: Springer International Publishing, 2016), pp. 115–136.

[25] Y. Feldman and U. Blau, "Consent and Advise," *Haaretz* (January 9, 2009), www.haaretz.com /consent-and-advise-1.269127.

[26] U. Blau and Y. Feldman, "How IDF Legal Experts Legitimized Strikes Involving Gaza Civilians," *Haaretz* (January 22, 2009), www.haaretz.com/how-idf-legal-experts-legitimized-strikes-involving-gaza-civilians-1.268598.

[27] A. Craig, *International Legitimacy and the Politics of Security: The Strategic Deployment of Lawyers in the Israeli Military* (Lanham: Lexington Books, 2013), p. 185 [hereinafter: *I'ntl Legitimacy & Politics of Security*].

[28] Feldman and Blau, "Consent and Advise."   [29] *Ibid.*

[30] Quoted in Geva, *Law, Politics and Violence in Israel/Palestine*, p. 175.

The impact of military actions upon the civilian population is of critical concern for the IDF. As a democratic society subscribing to the principles of human rights and respect of dignity, Israel seeks to mitigate the adverse effects of such activities upon non-combatants. As an example, the unit [i.e., the international law department] continuously reviews and advises the IDF regarding the impact of the economic embargo upon the inhabitants of Gaza.[31]

Former heads of the international law department, when interviewed about their service, have recalled an expansion of the department's role over time. In the past, they recount, the department's involvement in operational matters was limited, primarily concerned policing matters, and normally took place before the fact – a case in point is the department's participation in drafting the military's rules of engagement. Only on exceptional occasions would a department lawyer be asked to accompany a military operation in real time, such as when the Israeli navy sent a flotilla to intercept a Palestinian refugee ship in 1988. With the advent of the twenty-first century, however, Israel's growing use of so-called "targeted killings" necessitated quick legal advice on the conformity of a future assassination to international legal principles such as proportionality, distinction, and necessity.[32]

This shift was particularly apparent in 2007, with the establishment of an operational advice team within the department,[33] as well as in Israel's subsequent attacks on the Gaza Strip. Military lawyers, including those from the department, were involved both in advance planning and in real-time legal advice to commanders on the ground.[34] For "Operation Cast Lead" in 2008–2009, the general staff reportedly issued an order with a legal annex spelling out key principles of international law and directing commanders as follows: "Before using … [incendiary] weapons, the Military Advocate General or [the military's] International Law Department must be consulted in each specific case."[35] In 2010, the chief of staff issued an order likewise

---

[31] "International Law," *IDF MAG Corps*, www.law.idf.il/589-en/Patzar.aspx. On the closure of the Gaza Strip and its consequences, see entries Q: Quality of Life, V: Violence, and Z: Zone.

[32] Craig, *I'ntl Legitimacy & Politics of Security*, pp. 145–46; Feldman and Blau, "Consent and Advise." On "targeted killings" see entries C: Combatants and F: Future-Oriented Measures. On the principles of proportionality, distinction, and necessity, see entries P: Proportionality, C: Combatants, and G: Geneva Law; on the malleability of such legal principles to competing interpretations, including those that serve state violence, see entry V: Violence.

[33] "International Law Department," *IDF MAG Corps*, www.law.idf.il/456-he/Patzar.aspx.

[34] Craig, *I'ntl Legitimacy & Politics of Security*, p. 183; Feldman and Blau, "Consent and Advise"; Geva, *Law, Politics and Violence in Israel/Palestine*, pp. 137–166; "International Law," *IDF MAG Corps*, www.law.idf.il/589-en/Patzar.aspx.

[35] Feldman and Blau, "Consent and Advise."

requiring consultation with the military's legal advisors at the divisional level, not just when military operations are being planned but also while they are underway.[36] The military advocate general corps, with the international law department as "the focal point of much of [its] ... operational activities,"[37] has thus been incorporated into the decision-making process before and during each warfare activity, even if the lawyers are not formally the decision-makers.

The military's strategy document, which was made public in 2015, makes evident the legitimating function[38] of this ever-expanding reliance on lawyers:

> [O]ffensive force [against the enemy] ... shall be deployed ... while *following the rules of international law, with an emphasis on the laws of warfare and preserving Israel's legitimacy.* ... The enemy's force deployment characteristics have changed ... [and now include] *legal efforts* .... The [IDF's] primary efforts and capabilities [include] ... carrying out effective *legal and public diplomacy efforts* during and following combat in order to generate *legitimacy for operation.* The diplomatic, perception-shaping, and *legal effort to preserve and enhance the operation's legitimacy* shall begin in the preparations stage, and continue throughout the campaign. This, in order to *generate, preserve, and improve operation legitimacy* in both Israel itself and the international community. Internal and external perception-shaping efforts and diplomatic efforts in the international, media, and *legal arenas* shall be employed. ... Achieving and preserving *legitimacy* [requires using] intelligence, public diplomacy, press service, psychological warfare, diplomatic and political channels, *legal processes*, and so forth.[39]

Israel's reliance on law to shape and justify its political aims is, in itself, anything but new. And yet, as evidenced by the increasingly institutionalized and strategic resort to military lawyers in operational and other decisions, the role of legal expertise and mechanisms in Israel's control over the West Bank and Gaza Strip continually evolves and expands.

---

[36]   Pfeffer, "IDF to Seek Legal Advice During Future Conflicts." In addition, a year later, an Israeli Special Inquiry Commission recommended: "The legal advice accompanying deliberations by the security echelons prior to making a substantive decision regarding the carrying out of a targeted killing must be expanded and institutionalized." Quoted in Craig, *I'ntl Legitimacy & Politics of Security*, p. 153.

[37]   "International Law," *IDF MAG Corps*, http://www.law.idf.il/589-en/Patzar.aspx.

[38]   On the relationship between legitimacy and legality, see entry V: Violence.

[39]   Israel Defense Forces – Office of the Chief of the General Staff, *The IDF Strategy* (August 2015), pp. 9, 12, 17, 19, 21 [Hebrew], http://go.ynet.co.il/pic/news/16919.pdf (emphases added and modified). An English translation, as well as analysis, is available in: A. S. Khalidi, "Introduction: On the Limitations of Military Doctrine" (2016) 45 *Journal of Palestine Studies* 127.

L.3 LAWFARE IN THE HANDS OF ISRAEL'S CRITICS

As explained earlier, the term "lawfare" has been attached not only to such state policies and practices, but also to the legal challenges the state faces from NGOs, international bodies, individuals, and other political entities. Critics of Israel, victims of Israeli actions, and those subjected to Israel's rule have all mounted this sort of lawfare through three key forums that will now be discussed: Israel's own legal system, foreign national courts, and international tribunals.

NGOs and lawyers representing Palestinian petitioners or defendants routinely avail themselves of the first of these avenues: the Israeli legal system. Trying to maneuver between the pitfalls and potential benefits of this course of action, they are presented with a dilemma.[40] On the one hand, as is evident throughout this book, the Israeli judiciary has shown great deference to the security authorities (and their lawyers). The very rare decisions in favor of Palestinian petitioners or defendants have had no substantial long-term effect on Israel's conduct. They have had two other consequences, however. First, these judgments have served Israel's efforts at presenting itself as a law-abiding democracy and thus garnering domestic and international legitimacy. To this end, they have been translated into English and repeatedly cited in the media, in court decisions, and in government statements. Second, these judgments have often authorized – and thus "legalized" and institutionalized – abusive and discriminatory state practices, or at best have driven Israeli authorities to seek alternative legal justifications for their actions. Not only has litigation in Israeli courts thus failed to bring about structural and significant changes, it also risks entrenching and legitimizing Israel's actions. Hence, so-called NGO

---

[40] The discussion of this dilemma in this entry draws primarily on the following sources: D. Kretzmer, *The Occupation of Justice: The Supreme Court of Israel and the Occupied Territories* (Albany: State University of New York Press, 2002); G. E. Bisharat, "Courting Justice? Legitimation in Lawyering under Israeli Occupation" (1995) 20(2) *Law & Social Inquiry* 349; H. Jabareen, "Transnational Lawyering and Legal Resistance Before National Courts: Palestinian Cases Before the Israeli Supreme Court" (2010) 13 *Yale Human Rights & Development Journal* 65 [hereinafter: "Transnational Lawyering"]; M. Sfard, "The Price of Internal Legal Opposition to Human Rights Abuses" (2009) 1:1 *Journal of Human Rights Practice* 37; R. Shamir, "'Landmark Cases' and the Reproduction of Legitimacy: The Case of Israel's High Court of Justice" (1990) 24 *Law & Society Review* 781; E. Weizman, "Cause Lawyering and Resistance in Israel: The Legal Strategies of Adalah" (2016) 25:1 *Social & Legal Studies* 43. Some arguments presented here are adopted, with the necessary changes, from analyses of litigation dilemmas in other contexts: M. Cheh, "Should Lawyers Participate in Rigged Systems? The Case of the Military Commissions" (2005) 1:2 *Journal of National Security Law & Policy* 375; A. D. Lahav, "Portraits of Resistance: Lawyer Responses to Unjust Proceedings" (2010) 57:3 *UCLA Law Review* 725.

lawfare, when carried out internally through Israeli legal channels, can unwittingly play into the hands of Israeli state lawfare, rather than effectively challenging it.

On the other hand, participation in Israel's legal system enables liberal human rights NGOs and lawyers to attain some modest gains. Petitions to the HCJ can help stimulate public debate about Israel's conduct and policies, in addition to producing a potentially valuable historical record for future generations. Further, in order to avoid a judgment, Israeli authorities occasionally agree to reconsider decisions regarding individual Palestinians, grant specific remedies, or impose slightly more lenient sanctions. If none of these are accomplished, then a petition can, at the very least, "buy" Palestinians time until Israeli authorities execute the policy or decision in question. Along similar lines, by representing Palestinian detainees in the Israeli military court system, lawyers are sometimes able to provide them with moral support, and can also inform their families about their condition. In addition, providing legal counsel to interested Palestinian detainees respects their desire to try fighting for their interests, beliefs, or reputation in the Israeli court. Through the legal process, NGOs are also able to acquire information about the shortcomings of Israeli law and policy, which can be of value outside the courtroom, in various public platforms locally and abroad.

Such effects and considerations may seem mostly palliative or symbolic. And yet, from the point of view of many of the Palestinian detainees or petitioners concerned, they are valuable, as evidenced by the continued demand for such legal representation. Moreover, the assumption that engagement with Israel's courts necessarily lends legitimacy to Israel overlooks two key issues. The first is that this course of action can potentially accomplish quite the opposite, by exposing the hollowness of the Israeli legal system. And second, Israel's rule-of-law rhetoric has little to no currency among the many audiences, globally and in Palestine/Israel, who do not view Israel's laws, policies, or courts as legitimate in the first place.[41]

A related dilemma is whether or not to file complaints on behalf of Palestinian individuals with Israel's self-investigation mechanisms, as some NGOs have done for years. As detailed in other entries, only a fraction of complaints concerning violence by Israeli soldiers or settlers has led to

---

[41] A recent poll found a nearly 40 percent disapproval rate for Israel's court system even within Israel itself. See H. Ma'anit, "Poll: Low Point in Public Trust in the Legal System, the Knesset, and the Police," *Globes* (October 26, 2015) [Hebrew], www.globes.co.il/news/article.aspx?did=1001076264. This may lead to the conclusion that for many Israelis, their country's rule over the West Bank and Gaza Strip is legitimate regardless of the Israeli courts' actions on the matter.

indictments (usually ending without conviction).[42] Even worse, though more than 800 complaints of abuse or torture by Israeli general security service interrogators were submitted to the Israeli state attorney's office between 2001 and 2014, none of them resulted in a criminal investigation.[43] More recent data, obtained from the Israeli authorities, suggests the persistence of this trend.[44] Filing complaints with Israeli authorities despite their poor record therefore risks unwittingly lending credence to them and to the state lawfare in which they are involved. Possibly in order to avoid this risk, in 2014 the prominent Israeli NGO B'Tselem announced its decision to "break with its practice" of collaborating with the military's investigations of alleged offenses by soldiers against Palestinians. As the NGO has put it, the "military law enforcement system … is marred by severe structural flaws that render it incapable of conducting professional investigations," hence amounting to no more than "whitewashing mechanisms."[45]

There have also been attempts to utilize legal channels overseas: national and international courts. The doctrine of universal jurisdiction – which, among other things, formed the basis for the Eichman trial in Israel[46] – opens the door for foreign states and international organizations to prosecute Israeli state agents for grave violations of international law. On this legal basis, for example, Palestinian survivors brought a case in Belgium in 2001, requesting that Israel's then prime minister, Ariel Sharon, be prosecuted for his role in the 1982 massacres of Sabra and Shatilla in Lebanon. But, two years later, the

---

[42]   See entries I: Investigations (specifically Section I.3, "Investigation and Prosecution in Practice") and W: War Crimes (specifically Section W.2.1. "Courts-Martial").

[43]   Public Committee Against Torture in Israel, *Prosecutorial Indifference: Systematic Failures in the Investigation of Soldier Violence Against Detainees in the Occupied Palestinian Territories* (2014), p. 5, http://stoptorture.org.il/wp-content/uploads/2015/10/%D7%91%D7%9E%D7%A6 %D7%97-%D7%9C%D7%90-%D7%A0%D7%97%D7%95%D7%A9%D7%94-%D7%92%D 7%A8%D7%A1%D7%94-%D7%91%D7%90%D7%A0%D7%92%D7%9C%D7%99%D7%AA Prosecutorial-Indifference.pdf. On the related issue of the overall unaccountability of Israeli soldiers and settlers accused of violence toward Palestinians, see entry I: Investigations (specifically the section "Investigation and Prosecution in Practice").

[44]   Y. Berger, "Hundreds of Interrogees Have Complained, Yet the Ministry of Justice Has Not Opened a Single Investigation Against GSS Personnel," *Haaretz* (December 7, 2016) [Hebrew], www.haaretz.co.il/news/politics/.premium-1.3145349 (reporting on complaints submitted between the years 2009 and 2016).

[45]   B'Tselem and Yesh Din, *Israeli Human Rights Organizations B'Tselem and Yesh Din: Israel is Unwilling to Investigate Harm Caused to Palestinians* (September 2014), www.btselem.org/p ress_releases/20140905_failure_to_investigate. See also B'Tselem, *The Occupation's Fig Leaf: Israel's Military Law Enforcement System as a Whitewash Mechanism* (May 2016), www .btselem.org/sites/default/files2/201605_occupations_fig_leaf_eng.pdf.

[46]   For further discussion of the doctrine, see C. M. Bassiouni, "Universal Jurisdiction for International Crimes: Historical Perspectives and Contemporary Practice" (2001) 42 *Virginia Journal of International Law* 81.

Belgian parliament repealed the country's universal jurisdiction law, leading the supreme court to drop the case. In the United States, in 2005 the NGO the Center for Constitutional Rights filed a class action against the former head of the Israeli general security service, Avraham Dichter. The plaintiffs – 150 Palestinians who had been injured in an Israeli "targeted killing" in 2002, as well as several others who had lost their close relatives – alleged Dichter's responsibility for the military operation, and sought compensatory and punitive damages. The courts, however, adopted the US executive branch's claim of nonjusticiability, and therefore dismissed the case, as well as the plaintiffs' appeal. Attempts to hold former Israeli officials accountable for this attack were similarly unsuccessful in other countries. In 2005, political interference by the British government enabled a former Israeli military official to leave the country without disembarking from his plane, leading to the cancelation of an arrest warrant against him; six years later, parliament granted the UK's director of public prosecutions veto power over such warrants. When a similar warrant was issued against Israel's former chief of staff in New Zealand, in 2006, the country's attorney general immediately quashed it.[47]

Another potential legal forum, alongside foreign national courts, is international tribunals: specifically, the ICC and the ICJ.[48] In 2012, the previous prosecutor of the ICC rejected an application by the Palestinian Authority (PA) to recognize the court's jurisdiction over the West Bank and Gaza Strip, pending clarification from the United Nations on Palestine's legal status. Later that year, the UN General Assembly granted Palestine the status of a nonmember observer state,[49] and in 2015 the newly recognized state acceded to the Rome Statute of the ICC.[50] Subsequently, at the time of writing, Palestine is awaiting the outcome of a preliminary investigation by the ICC prosecutor into some of Israel's alleged war

---

[47] This account draws on: Craig, *I'ntl Legitimacy & Politics of Security*, pp. 122–128, 153–154; N. Erakat, "Litigating the Arab-Israeli Conflict: The Politicization of US Foreign Courtrooms" (2009) 2 *Berkeley Journal of Middle East and Islamic Law* 27; Hajjar, *Lawfare and Armed Conflict*, pp. 21–22; Human Rights Watch, Israel: Ariel Sharon's Troubling Legacy (January 11, 2014), www.hrw.org/news/2014/01/11/israel-ariel-sharons-troubling-legacy; Jabareen, "Transnational Lawyering." See also Center for Constitutional Rights, "Matar et al v. Dichter," https://ccrjustice.org/home/what-we-do/our-cases/matar-et-al-v-dichter.

[48] See also J. Dugard, "Lifting the Guise of Occupation and Recourse to Action before the ICJ and ICC" (2014) 17 *Palestine Yearbook of International Law* 9.

[49] A. Zimmerman, "Palestine and the International Criminal Court Quo Vadis?: Reach and Limits of Declarations under Article 12(3)" (2013) 11 *Journal of International Criminal Justice* 303.

[50] "The State of Palestine Accedes to the Rome Statute," *ICC Press Release* (January 7, 2015), www.icc-cpi.int//Pages/item.aspx?name=pr1082_2.

crimes.[51] Whether this amounts to much remains to be seen, and in any event could take quite a long time. Additionally, in 2004, at the request of the UN General Assembly, the ICJ issued an advisory opinion, finding Israel's West Bank barrier to be in breach of international humanitarian law as well as various human rights treaties.[52]

Like human rights litigation within Israeli courts, then, the resort to overseas legal forums is by no means free from pitfalls. Its failure to bring about its professed legal objectives should come as no surprise: all courts are inherently political,[53] even if each national or international court is political in its own unique way.[54] Legal challenges abroad may not be entirely ineffectual, as evidenced by reports that Israeli former officials have had to cancel travels for fear of prosecution.[55] And yet, legal amendments such as those enacted in Belgium and the United Kingdom mitigate this concern.[56] Moreover, it is doubtful that the prospect of overseas prosecution alone would have a significant deterrent effect on Israel's current armed forces, given the highly potent denial and self-justification mechanisms in play in Israeli society.[57]

---

[51] "The Prosecutor of the International Criminal Court, Fatou Bensouda, Opens a Preliminary Examination of the Situation in Palestine," *ICC Press Release* (January 16, 2015), www.icc-cpi .int/Pages/item.aspx?name=pr1083. For further discussion of these developments specifically, and of the ICC and war crimes in general, see entry W: War Crimes.

[52] Legal Consequences of the Construction of a Wall in the Occupied Palestinian Territory, Advisory Opinion, 2004 ICJ 136. For further discussion of the ICJ's advisory opinion, see entries B: Border/Barrier, N: Nomos, P: Proportionality, and T: Temporary/Indefinite. See also A. M. Gross, "The Construction of a Wall Between The Hague and Jerusalem: Humanitarian Law or a Fata Morgana of Humanitarian Law," in his *The Writing on the Wall: Rethinking the International Law of Occupation* (Cambridge: Cambridge University Press, 2017).

[53] See also entry V: Violence, as well as Section 2.3 ("Critiquing Against/With the Law") in the Introduction.

[54] This is a paraphrasing of Leo Tolstoy's famous remark in *Anna Karenina*: "Happy families are all alike; every unhappy family is unhappy in its own way."

[55] See, e.g., R. McCarthy, "Israeli Minister Cancels UK Trip in Fear of Arrest," *The Guardian* (December 7, 2007), www.theguardian.com/world/2007/dec/07/israelandthepalestinians .foreignpolicy; BBC, "Israel Minister Feared UK Arrest," *BBC News* (October 5, 2009), http://news.bbc.co.uk/1/hi/world/middle_east/8290554.stm; B. McKernan, "Former Israeli Foreign Minister Cancels Brussels Trip After Threat of Arrest for 'War Crimes'," *Independent* (January 23, 2017), www.independent.co.uk/news/world/middle-east/israel-belgium-brussels-war-crimes-foreign-minster-tzipi-livni-benjamin-netanyahu-ehud-olmert-ar rest-a7541401.html.

[56] See, e.g., B. Quinn, "Former Israeli Minister Tzipi Livni to Visit UK After Change in Arrest Law," *The Guardian* (October 4, 2011), www.theguardian.com/world/2011/oct/04/tzipi-livni-arrest-warrant.

[57] On such social mechanisms, see generally S. Cohen, *States of Denial: Knowing About Atrocities and Suffering* (Cambridge and Malden: Polity Press, 2001); S. Sontag, *Regarding the Pain of Others* (London and New York: Penguin, 2004). For discussion in the

The ICJ's opinion was merely advisory, and its reasoning was not without blind spots, as some academic critics of Israel's West Bank barrier have pointed out.[58] One can only speculate on how big an impact these legal developments have had on Israel's image or on Israeli society, as compared with the impact of other, possibly more influential social arenas, such as the media.

L.4 ISRAEL'S DEPLOYMENT OF LAW AS A WEAPON AGAINST CRITICAL LAWFARE

For all its above limitations, the resort of Israel's critics and victims to domestic and international legal forums has certainly not gone unnoticed by Israeli authorities. In fact, it has evoked repeated denunciations by Israeli officials, who, by terming it "lawfare" often characterize it as a threat to national security and to Israel's legitimacy.[59] A former head of the military's international law department thus described Palestine's accession to the Rome Statute as "lawfare [that] will push us ever closer to a multiple-front conflict."[60] Sympathizers with the Israeli government have criticized the ICJ's opinion on the legality of the West Bank barrier as "perhaps the most prominent" campaign by "Palestinians and their supporters ... of what many Israelis term 'lawfare,' judicial 'warfare' through the use of legal

---

Israeli–Palestinian context, see, e.g., D. Dor, *The Suppression of Guilt – The Israeli Media and the Reoccupation of the West Bank* (London and Ann Arbor: Pluto Press, 2005); Z. Orr and D. Golan, "Human Rights NGOs in Israel: Collective Memory and Denial" (2014) 18 *International Journal of Human Rights* 68; N. Peled-Elhanan, "Legitimation of Massacres in Israeli School History Books" (2010) 21 *Discourse & Society* 377. On the role of invisibility and denial in Israel's control over the West Bank and Gaza Strip, see entry V: Violence.

[58] See, e.g., I. Scobbie, "Words My Mother Never Taught Me: 'In Defense of the International Court'" (2005) 99 *American Journal of International Law* 76; A. Imseis, "Critical Reflections on the International Humanitarian Law Aspects of the ICJ Wall Advisory Opinion" (2005) 99 *American Journal of International Law* 102; D. Kretzmer, "The Advisory Opinion: The Light Treatment of International Humanitarian Law" (2005) 99 *American Journal of International Law* 88; Y. Shany, "Capacities and Inadequacies: A Look at the Two Separation Barrier Cases" (2005) 38 *Israel Law Review* 230; O. Ben-Naftali, "'A la Recherche du Temps Perdu': Rethinking Article 6 of the Fourth Geneva Convention in Light of the Legal Consequences of the Construction of a Wall in the Occupied Palestinian Territory Advisory Opinion" (2005) 38 *Israel Law Review* 211.

[59] On Israel's use of the term "lawfare" to portray liberal human rights NGOs as a national security threat, see N. Gordon, "Human Rights as a Security Threat: Lawfare and the Campaign against Human Rights NGOs" (2014) 48 *Law & Society Review* 311, 331 [hereinafter: "Human Rights as a Security Threat"].

[60] Quoted in L. Brayman, "Palestinian 'Lawfare': Toward Brinkmanship or Progress?," +972 *Magazine* (January 10, 2015), http://972mag.com/palestinian-lawfare-toward-brinkmanship-or-progress/101170/.

forums."[61] At one point, Israel's deputy foreign minister used a "lawfare" metaphor: "today the trenches are in Geneva in the Council of Human Rights, or in New York in the General Assembly, or in the Security Council, or in the Hague, the ICJ."[62] Along similar lines, in his abovementioned article on lawfare, Israel's former military advocate general, Avichai Mendelblit, cautioned of

> lawfare [accusations] ... that [the Israeli military] ... is committing war crimes, is intentionally (or at least "disproportionately") harming civilians, and that [its] "war criminals" [should therefore be punished]. ... [The Israeli] answer [to this lawfare has been] ... to prove [that Israel has] ... acted in accordance with the law of war and international norms.[63]

Others went further, associating these legal challenges with terrorism. One senior military official called the threat of universal jurisdiction no less than "legal terrorism."[64] The exact same phrase was used a few years later by the deputy speaker of the Knesset, this time in relation to the activity of local liberal human rights NGOs.[65] In 2010, the Israeli ministry of foreign affairs published a lengthy report, painting a similar picture:

> The number of lawsuits that have been filed against Israeli officials has grown exponentially in recent years. ... This form of lawfare does not simply impede Israeli travel plans ... [but aims] to intimidate officials from acting out of fear of prosecution, and in fact ... strains international ties, and serves to delegitimize the Jewish state ... It must be recognized that ... lawfare is a continuation of terrorist activity by other means.[66]

---

[61] Y. Ben Meir and O. Alterman, The Delegitimization Threat: Roots, Manifestations, and Containment, Strategic Survey for Israel 130 (Institute for National Security Studies, Tel Aviv University, 2011), www.inss.org.il/uploadimages/Import/(FILE)1316602658.pdf (also cited in www.ngo-monitor.org/academic-publications/the_delegitimization_threat_roots_manifestations_and_containment).

[62] Quoted in Gordon, "Human Rights as a Security Threat," p. 331.

[63] Mendelblit, "Lawfare – the IDF's Next Legal Frontier," pp. 49–50.

[64] T. Zarchin, "IDF: War Crime Charges Over Gaza Offensive Are 'Legal Terror'," *Haaretz* (February 19, 2009), www.haaretz.com/print-edition/news/idf-war-crime-charges-over-gaza-offensive-are-legal-terror-1.270460.

[65] C. Levinson and Y. Berger, "The Knesset Preliminarily Approves Act Expropriating Private Palestinian Land," *Haaretz* (December 5, 2016) [Hebrew], www.haaretz.co.il/news/politi/1.3143802.

[66] Quoted in Gordon, "Human Rights as a Security Threat," pp. 331–332.

Israeli authorities and their supporters have sought to tackle such legal challenges in a characteristically legalistic manner.[67] As one neoconservative academic in Israel has written, the weapon used by the enemy "was created by our own hands – that is the rule of law";[68] thus, this would also be the weapon of Israeli authorities and their supporters against what they denounce as "lawfare." One arena for deploying this weapon is civil litigation in the United States, Israel's closest ally. Ever since the 1980s, lawsuits have been filed in the United States, first against the Palestine Liberation Organization (PLO) and later against members or leaders of the PA or Hamas.[69] The Israeli government has also recently explored ways to bring war crimes prosecutions against Palestinian leaders in retaliation for Palestine's accession to the Rome Statute.[70] In the words of a high-ranking military officer: "our objective is to put Palestinians on the defense, to demonstrate to the world that they are the ones violating international legal rules."[71]

NGOs that self-identify as allies of the Israeli government have also sought to make use of these and other legal platforms. A notable example is Shurat HaDin, which boasts, on its website: "As a non-governmental organization . . . [we can] undertake actions that the Israeli government is unable to formally engage in. We are not constrained by political pressures, diplomatic relations, nor international treaties."[72] Yet, reports suggest the NGO has received assistance from the Israeli prime minister's office for some of its actions,[73] and, in addition, the NGO's website quotes praise for its activity from Israel's former defense minister and a former head of the Israeli military's international law department.[74] Moreover, according to a classified cable from the US embassy in Israel, which has been published by Wikileaks, the NGO's director "said that in many of her cases she receives evidence from . . . [Israeli government] officials, and added that in its early years . . . [her NGO] took direction from

---

[67] For a useful discussion the meaning(s) of "legalism," see K. McEvoy, "Beyond Legalism: Towards a Thicker Understanding of Transnational Justice" (2007) 34 *Journal of Law & Society* 411, 414–24.

[68] Quoted in Gordon, "Human Rights as a Security Threat," p. 324.

[69] See A. N. Schupack, "The Arab-Israeli Conflict and Civil Litigation against Terrorism" (2010) 60 *Duke Law Journal* 207, 210–221.

[70] A. Fisher-Ilan, "Israel Withholds Funds, Weighs Lawsuits Against Palestinians," *Reuters* (January 3, 2015), www.reuters.com/article/us-mideast-palestinians-israel-idUSKBN 0KC07Q20150103.

[71] A. Gibor, "The Country Most Dangerous to Us in the Middle East is Facebook," *Makor Rishon* (January 29, 2016) [Hebrew], www.nrg.co.il/online/1/ART2/751/369.html.

[72] Shurat HaDin, "About Us," http://israellawcenter.org/about/.

[73] A. Goodman, "Meet the Legal Wonks Who Brought Down the Flotilla," *Commentary* (August 22, 2011), www.commentarymagazine.com/culture-civilization/shurat-hadin-flotilla/.

[74] Shurat HaDin, "About Us," http://israellawcenter.org/about/.

the [the Israeli government] . . . on which cases to pursue." At the same time, the leaked cable suggests that "[w]hile the [NGO's] . . . mission dovetails with . . . [Israel's] objectives . . . the often uncompromising approach of . . . [Shurat HaDin] attorneys seems to overreach . . . official . . . policy goals [of the Israeli government]."[75]

The activities and objectives of Shurat HaDin, as it describes them, include:

> [D]efending against lawfare suits [and] . . . utilizing court systems around the world to go on the legal offensive against Israel's enemies. . . . In their attempt to delegitimize Israel, advance their cause internationally, and pressure Israel to make concessions in the "peace process," the Palestinians have stepped up their efforts to bring condemnation upon Israel in national and international tribunals. . . . Among other things . . . Shurat HaDin has . . . submitted several complaints to the ICC documenting international crimes committed by the Palestinian Authority and Palestinian leaders. . . . Israel [also continues] . . . to be confronted by . . . various "lawfare" tactics to attack Israel and Israelis with baseless legal actions. Shurat HaDin has taken a lead in combatting these efforts . . . using legal procedures to foil attempts to weaken Israel's security, such as the Gaza Flotilla that sought to breach Israel's . . . blockade of the . . . Gaza Strip.[76]

In addition, Israeli state lawyers, including the military's abovementioned international law department, have been involved in defending former or incumbent Israeli officials facing possible arrest or prosecution abroad. A special office, bringing together lawyers from the military advocate general and other state experts, was also established within the Israeli Ministry of Justice in 2009, tasked with "handling all international legal proceedings against Israel, Israeli soldiers or officials."[77] In fact, according to a former head of the military's international law department, Israel's ever-growing reliance on lawyers was largely designed to shield soldiers from precisely this

---

[75] US Embassy in Tel Aviv, "Israeli NGO Sues Terrorists, Ties Up PA Money," *Wikileaks* (August 30, 2007), https://search.wikileaks.org/plusd/cables/07TELAVIV2636_a.html. Shurat Hadin, "About Us," http://israellawcenter.org/about/.

[76] Shurat HaDin, "About Us," http://israellawcenter.org/about/. The flotilla was planned to travel from Greece in 2011, a year after Israel violently blocked another flotilla arriving from Turkey. In response, Shurat HaDin approached the US attorney general, arguing that American flotilla activists were in violation of a US statute that prohibits acts against allied countries. The NGO also warned maritime insurance companies that if they insure the flotilla they could be charged with "aiding and abetting" a terrorist organization. Goodman, "Meet the Legal Wonks Who Brought Down the Flotilla."

[77] I. Rozenzweig and Y. Shany, "Establishment of a Legal Department by the Israeli Security Cabinet to Deal with Issues of International Jurisdiction" (2009) 12 *Terrorism & Democracy*; Craig, *I'ntl Legitimacy & Politics of Security*, pp. 153–154.

legal risk. "The commanders," he told Israeli journalists, "hear about this and say, 'I might find myself in that court; where is my lawyer?' So it becomes natural for the military to put lawyers in places where they have never been before."[78] The Israeli minister of foreign affairs, Tzipi Livni, reiterated this point in the aftermath of the destructive assault on Gaza in 2014, writing on her Facebook page that Israel had "used our understanding of the law to its full extent, so that IDF soldiers would be able to protect Israeli citizens while being furnished with a legal flak jacket and with a legal Iron Dome over their heads."[79] The issue was close to home for Livni, whose own travel plans have been affected by the possibility of being prosecuted abroad for her ministerial responsibility for war crimes.[80]

Within the domestic arena, Israeli authorities have clamped down on individuals and organizations that report, criticize, or legally challenge Israel's violations of Palestinian rights. Government officials, as well as right-wing organizations and academics, have also accused liberal human rights NGOs of publishing reports that end up being cited in lawsuits against Israelis, critical UN reports, and international condemnations.[81] Recent legal initiatives to curtail such unwanted activities include, for instance, a new statute requiring organizations whose primary funding comes from "foreign government entities" to note this on their websites and in their publications, reports, and correspondence with state officials. Included within the "foreign government entities" category are not only governments, but also international unions such as the United Nations and the European Union, as well as foreign charities funded by such political entities.[82] As critics have pointed out, this piece of legislation primarily stigmatizes liberal human rights organizations, since the existing law already requires transparency about funding from so-called "foreign government entities," and since the statute makes no reference to donations from private sources – a substantial source of funding for right-wing organizations.[83] Other legislative initiatives are under discussion in the Knesset.[84]

---

[78] Feldman and Blau, "Consent and Advise."   [79] Quoted in Jones, "Frames of Law," p. 689.
[80] McKernan, "Former Israeli Foreign Minister Cancels Brussels Trip After Threat of Arrest for 'War Crimes'"; Quinn, "Former Israeli Minister Tzipi Livni to Visit UK After Change in Arrest Law."
[81] Gordon, "Human Rights as a Security Threat," pp. 322–336.
[82] Disclosure Obligations of Recipients of Support from Foreign Government Entities Law, 2011.
[83] Association for Civil Rights in Israel, *Overview of Anti-Democratic Legislation in the 20th Knesset* (March 2017), pp. 2–4, www.acri.org.il/en/wp-content/uploads/2016/09/Overview-of-Anti-Democratic-Legislation-March-2017–1.pdf; Association for Civil Rights in Israel, *Law Requiring Disclosure by NGOs Supported by Foreign Governmental Entities (Amended) –* 2016 (July 2016), www.acri.org.il/en/wp-content/uploads/2016/07/Summary-of-NGO-Law.pdf.
[84] ACRI, Overview of Anti-Democratic Legislation in the 20th Knesset.

Insofar as the above responses of Israeli officials and their self-proclaimed allies are to be taken at face value, they evince a deep anxiety over the dreaded consequences of the "legal terrorism" that is allegedly being waged against Israel: the erosion of Israel's legitimacy, damage to its international relations, and obstacles to the travel plans of Israelis for fear of prosecution abroad.[85] If, however, Israeli authorities are more concerned with public opinion and politics within Israel than with global implications,[86] their combative actions may largely have to do with pointing fingers at purported enemies and scapegoats – be they NGOs, the United Nations, Palestinian claimants, or others. The added benefit, from this point of view, is the diversion of attention away from Israel's half-century-long control over the West Bank and Gaza Strip. Presumably, both of these elements – genuine concern and political manipulation – are in operation.

While seeking to suppress liberal human rights NGOs and accusing them of misusing the law, Israel continues to use them, as it long has, to maintain its self-image as a law-abiding state respectful of human rights. Its 2015 periodic report to the UN Committee against Torture, for instance, asserts:

> When preparing its periodic reports to the CAT and other UN Human Rights Committees, Israel makes a concerted effort to involve civil society in the process, to every extent possible. . . . [The] relevant and leading NGOs [have been invited] . . . to submit comments prior to the compilation of the report . . . Civil Society contributions are given substantial consideration during the drafting of the Report. In addition, the Ministry of Justice actively seeks data and information on the relevant NGOs' websites . . . [Israel makes] an honest attempt . . . [to adhere] to the rule of law and [respect] . . . the human rights of all individuals in its territory.[87]

Israel's vehement opposition to unwanted legal proceedings on the one hand, and its fondness for a rhetoric of law and human rights on the other, are in fact two sides of the same coin: Israel's desire to ensure its continued reliance on law as a means of achieving and legitimizing its military and

---

[85] See text accompanying notes 55, 56.

[86] Former US secretary of state, Henry Kissinger, is reported to have said that Israel has no foreign policy, only domestic politics. See, e.g., H. A. Barari, *Israeli Politics and the Middle East Peace Process, 1988–2002* (London: Routledge, 2004), pp. 6–7.

[87] UN Committee Against Torture, Consideration of reports submitted by States Parties under Article 19 of the Convention Pursuant to the Optional Reporting Procedure: Fifth Periodic Reports of States Parties due in 2013 – Israel (February 2015), ¶¶ 450–451, 103, http://docstore .ohchr.org/SelfServices/FilesHandler.ashx?enc=6QkG1d%2FPPRiCAqhKb7yhsmEKqNhdz bzr4kqou1ZPE787pA64z90a%2FZN18JHW%2Bkxawxyoig%2FWuoddnyM% 2BN7PHmuASmEY6ojM6VX3krxvNSVxPuoqb1FlsbvTHqntEyOT5.

political objectives. This dynamic is far from new, as exemplified by recently revealed classified documents from the 1960s and 1970s, which show that Israeli authorities had people in local human rights organizations secretly reporting to them on their activities and contacts.[88] Current relations between liberal human rights NGOs and the Israeli authorities are profoundly different in some respects, but something about Israel's approach to human rights and law nonetheless seems all too similar.

L.5 CONCLUSION

"Lawfare" simultaneously denotes and provides a language for criticizing the various uses of law in relation to military warfare. While law's close relationship with warfare goes back a long way, it has evolved in recent years, as evidenced by the actions of different political and social agents in Israel/ Palestine. In recent years, Israel's extensive record of lawfare has been further expanded, as the military advocate general corps, and particularly its international law department, have assumed a growing place in operational decisions. Israeli commanders, who would previously encounter these military lawyers either during their legal training or when drafting military policies, are now also legally required to consult with them on the legality of each operation, both in advance and in real time. This, according to Israeli statements, aims to preserve Israel's legitimacy and shield its soldiers from possible legal proceedings abroad.

Critics and victims have turned to legal avenues outside and within Israel in the hope of bringing an end to, or some accountability for, Israel's treatment of Palestinians. Each legal forum, however, presents serious pitfalls alongside some potential gains for those who seek to use it in this manner. Israelis who are responsible for gross violations of international law could, in principle, be arrested and prosecuted in foreign countries through the doctrine of universal jurisdiction. In practice, however, political pressures and considerations have prevented this outcome, and some countries have even amended their legislation to limit or prevent future prosecutions. The prospect of proceedings at the ICC is currently unclear, and the ICJ's opinion regarding Israel's West Bank barrier, despite its political impact, was merely advisory, and brimming with blind spots.

---

[88] L. Yavne and N. Hofstadter, "Appropriate Tools: Israeli Ministry of Foreign Affairs and Amnesty's Israel Section, 1969-1977," *Akevot* (March 17, 2017), http://akevot.org.il/en/article/appropriate-tools/.

Litigation within Israel's own courts likewise risks lending them credence without substantially changing Israel's practices and policies, thus unwittingly playing into the hands of Israeli state lawfare. Filing complaints to Israel's self-investigation bodies faces a similar risk, given the structural flaws and poor record of these mechanisms. At the same time, petitions to the Israeli HCJ can stimulate public debate, create an important historical record, and in some cases even drive Israeli authorities to reconsider their decisions in order to avoid a judgment. Somewhat similarly, representation of Palestinians in the Israeli military courts, though largely hopeless in terms of the eventual legal outcome, respects these Palestinians' wish to have legal counsel, and can sometimes provide them and their families with support or helpful information. Further, rather than legitimizing the Israeli legal system, engagement with it can expose its shortcomings and hollow rhetoric, especially for audiences, in Israel/Palestine and overseas, who are already open to questioning Israel's rule over the West Bank and Gaza Strip.

Israeli authorities and their NGO allies have responded to these legal challenges – especially those pursued overseas (and to a lesser extent those undertaken in the HCJ) – in several complementary ways: making accusations of "legal terrorism"; exploring lawsuits against Palestinian leaders overseas; using military lawyers to prevent future prosecutions against Israelis; advancing legislative initiatives targeted at liberal human rights NGOs; and, at the same time, continuing to insist on Israel's self-image as a law-abiding country respectful of human rights. While the rhetoric of Israeli officials suggests genuine concern over the potential damage to Israel's legitimacy and foreign relations, this response may also serve as a distraction tactic, shifting attention from Israel's contentious conduct to its alleged enemies at home and abroad. Here, as in many other areas examined in this book, the strong ties between law and state violence are in plain view.

M

Military Courts

Hedi Viterbo

M.1 INTRODUCTION

Military courts, which have been in use throughout modern times, are often described as an "exceptional" or "extraordinary" legal institution.[1] However, not only is this characterization generally debatable,[2] it is certainly inapplicable to the military courts in which Israel brings Palestinians to trial. As the judicial arm of a control regime that has been deemed the longest military occupation in modern history,[3] at the time of writing these courts have been operating uninterrupted for half a century, trying thousands of Palestinians

---

[1] For historical and comparative overviews of military courts, including some examples of the language of "exceptionality" and "extraordinariness," see, e.g., F. Ní Aoláin and O. Gross (eds.), *Guantánamo and Beyond: Exceptional Courts and Military Commissions in Comparative Perspective* (Cambridge: Cambridge University Press, 2013); P. Richards, *Extraordinary Justice: Military Tribunals in Historical and International Context* (New York: NYU Press, 2007). See also A. W. Pereira, "Virtual Legality: Authoritarian Legacies and the Reform of Military Justice in Brazil, the Southern Cone, and Mexico" (2001) 34 *Comparative Political Studies* 555. The type of military courts discussed here should be distinguished from courts-martial, which try the state's own soldiers and are subject to different sets of laws.

[2] See, e.g., N. Hussain, "Beyond Norm and Exception: Guantánamo" (2007) 33 *Critical Inquiry* 734, 737–750; F. Johns, "Guantánamo Bay and the Annihilation of the Exception" (2005) 16 *European Journal of International Law* 613; J. Krishman and V. Sharma, "Exceptional or Not? An Examination of India's Special Courts in the National Security Context," in Ní Aoláin and Gross, *Guantánamo and Beyond*, p. 283. On the normality of (seeming) exceptions under Israeli rule, see entry Y: Youth; D. Filc and H. Ziv, "Exception as the Norm and the Fiction of Sovereignty: The Lack of the Right to Health Care in the Occupied Territories," in J. T. Parry (ed.), *Evil, Law and the State: Perspectives on State Power and Violence* (Amsterdam: Rodopi Press, 2006), p. 71; R. Zreik, "The Persistence of the Exception: Some Remarks on the Story of Israeli Constitutionalism," in R. Lentin (ed.), *Thinking Palestine* (London: Zed Books, 2008), p. 131. On the untenability of the exception/norm dichotomy more broadly, see the Introduction, Section 2.3 ("Critiquing Against/With the Law"), and entry O: Outside/Inside.

[3] On the duration of the so-designated Israeli military "occupation" as unparalleled in modern history, see, e.g., D. Kretzmer, "The Law of Belligerent Occupation in the Supreme Court of Israel" (2012) 94 *International Review of the Red Cross* 207, 208.

each year. In 2006, for example, first-instance military courts held about 42,000 hearings,[4] and the military court of appeals heard 267 appeals.[5] Not all charges are framed as relating to security:[6] traffic violations, for instance, have made up between as much as a third and nearly half of indictments in recent years.[7] Yet, usually, noncitizen Palestinians find themselves in Israeli courts and prisons for charges classified as "security offenses" – a legal category discussed in one of this book's other entries.[8]

Israeli military judges are military officers and the prosecutors are Israeli soldiers.[9] Either a three-judge panel or a single judge hears first-instance court proceedings, as compared with a three-judge panel in the appeals court proceedings (with the notable exception of remand appeals, which are heard by a single judge).[10] Since the early 2000s, all military judges have been lawyers, whereas previously two judges in the three-judge panels had no legal training.[11] The military courts' number and distribution have changed considerably

[4] IDF Spokesperson's Unit, "Response to the Yesh Din report Draft: 'Backyard Proceedings'," *Yesh Din* (November 12, 2007), ¶ 14, www.yesh-din.org/en/backyard-proceedings.

[5] IDF Military Advocate General, *Annual Activity Report – 2010* (2011), p. 71, www.mag.idf.il /sip_storage/FILES/7/967.pdf [Hebrew].

[6] K. Cavanaugh, "The Israeli Military Court System in the West Bank and Gaza" (2007) 12 *Journal of Conflict and Security Law* 197, 206; L. Hajjar, *Courting Conflict: The Israeli Military Court System in the West Bank and Gaza* (Oakland: University of California Press, 2005), p. 255; S. Weill, "The Judicial Arm of the Occupation: The Israeli Military Courts in the Occupied Territories" (2007) 89 *International Review of the Red Cross* 395, 405–406.

[7] N. Baumgarten-Sharon and Y. Stein, *Presumed Guilty: Remand in Custody by Military Courts in the West Bank* (2015), p. 12, www.btselem.org/download/201506_presumed_guilty_eng.pdf (citing data published by the military court system regarding the years 2008–2013); L. Yavne, *Backyard Proceedings: The Implementation of Due Process Rights in the Military Courts in the Occupied Territories* (2007), pp. 42–44, www.yesh-din.org/en/backyard-proceedings (citing information provided by the military in reference to the years 2002–2006).

[8] See entry S: Security Prisoners.

[9] The military prosecutors have a Bachelor's degree in law, and are either officers or not. For further information on the military prosecutors, see Hajjar, *Courting Conflict*, pp. 11, 96–97, 118–119, 222, 254; L. Yavne, "Backyard Proceedings," pp. 51–53. There are also defense attorneys, Israelis and Palestinians, of whom Palestinian defendants may avail themselves under the current military law. Articles 74 and 76 of Order Concerning Security Provisions (Judea and Samaria) (No. 1651), 2009. The military law also requires the courts to appoint attorneys for unrepresented defendants charged with an offense that is punishable by ten years or more, subject to the defendants' consent. Order No. 1651, Article 77(a). On defense attorneys' views of the military court system, see Hajjar, *Courting Conflict*, pp. 11, 92, 232. For an earlier study of Palestinian defense lawyers in the Israeli military courts, see G. Bisharat, *Palestinian Lawyers and Israeli Rule: Law and Disorder in the West Bank* (Austin: University of Texas Press, 1989).

[10] Cases can be transferred from a single judge to three judges, and vice versa. The main difference between these two panels is that a court sitting as a single judge cannot impose prison sentences of more than 10 years. Order No. 1651, Articles 15, 17–19.

[11] N. Benichou, "Criminal Law in the Regions of Judea, Samaria, and Gaza" (2004) 18 *Mishpat Ve-Tsava (Law & Military)* 293, 305–306 [Hebrew]; L. Yavne, "Backyard Proceedings,"

throughout Israel's rule in the Palestinian Territory, and in recent years these courts have mainly operated in two military bases in the West Bank: Ofer, next to the Palestinian city of Ramallah, and Salem, on the West Bank's northern border.[12] The military court of appeals, which hears appeals against first-instance military court decisions, was established in 1989.[13]

With the exception of East Jerusalem (which Israel controversially purports to have annexed),[14] these courts currently assume jurisdiction over the entire West Bank, including Area A, which is supposedly under Palestinian Authority control.[15] In inter-Palestinian civil and criminal matters, the Israeli military generally allows the Palestinian Authority to try Palestinians in its own courts.[16] In contrast, the military denies these Palestinian courts jurisdiction over Israeli settlers' offenses within Palestinian Authority territory. Instead, domestic Israeli law is extraterritorially applied to all settlers, and they are tried in Israeli civil courts.[17] There have also been cases in which Palestinians in

pp. 50–51. A single-judge panel, however, would be a lawyer. In practice, the change took place in 2001, but only in 2004 was it enshrined in the military legislation. See also E. Rozin, "The Silent Revolution in the Courts in the Occupied Territories" (2004) 48 *Ha-Praklit* 58 [Hebrew].

[12]   Weill, "The Judicial Arm of the Occupation," p. 396. In addition, a few other courts in Israel deal with remands of Palestinians interrogated by the Israeli general security service. For criticism of these courts' location inside Israel, see L. Yavne, "Backyard Proceedings," pp. 40–41; HCJ 1958/10 *Palestinian Prisoners Office* v. *Israeli Defense Forces Commander in the Region* (March 9, 2010), www.humanrights.org.il/articles/בתיה%20משפט%20צבאיים.doc.

[13]   Benichou, "Criminal Law in the Regions of Judea, Samaria, and Gaza," p. 296; Yavne, "Backyard Proceedings," pp. 37–38.

[14]   As part of this purported annexation, Palestinian residents of East Jerusalem are usually tried in Israeli civil courts under domestic Israeli law. On the status of East Jerusalem under Israeli law, see entries B: Border/Barrier, J: Jewish Settlements, and Z: Zone.

[15]   Order No. 1651, Articles 10(d)–10(e); MilC (Mil. Ct. App.) 2016/07 *Issa* v. *Military Prosecutor* (May 16, 2007); MilC (Mil. Ct. App.) 3924/06 *Sa'adi* v. *Military Prosecutor* (October 17, 2007). For critical discussion, see Weill, "The Judicial Arm of the Occupation," pp. 407–409.

[16]   Catherine Cook, A. Hanieh, and A. Kay (in association with DCI – Palestine), *Stolen Youth: The Politics of Israel's Detention of Palestinian Children* (London: Pluto Press, 2004), p. 25; A. Khalil, "Formal and Informal Justice in Palestine: Dealing with the Legacy of Tribal Law" (2009) 184 *Etudes Rurales* 169; Y. Shany, "Binary Law Meets Complex Reality: The Occupation of Gaza Debate" (2008) 41 *Israeli Law Review* 68, 78. For further information on the Palestinian Authority's court system, operating since the 1990s, see F. Milhem and J. Salem, "Building the rule of law in Palestine: Rule of law without freedom" in S. M. Akram et al. (eds.), *International Law and the Israeli-Palestinian Conflict: A Rights-Based Approach to Middle East Peace* (London; New York: Routledge, 2011), p. 253. For an English translation of the Palestinian criminal legislation, see R. Friedrich et al. (eds.), *The Security Sector Legislation of the Palestinian National Authority* (Geneva; Ramallah: DCAF, 2008), pp. 405–504.

[17]   T. Kelly, "'Jurisdictional Politics' in the Occupied West Bank: Territory, Community, and Economic Dependency in the Formation of Legal Subjects," 31 *Law & Social Inquiry* 39 (2006), pp. 47–49; I. Zertal and A. Eldar, *Lords of the Land: The War Over Israel's Settlements*

areas under military jurisdiction have been tried, exceptionally, in Israeli civil courts.[18] These issues illustrate the intricate relationship between Israeli military law and domestic law, a relationship examined elsewhere in this book.[19] Further, until Israel's unilateral pullout from the Gaza Strip in 2005, the military courts had jurisdiction over this territory as well. Since then, Israel has tried the Gazans arrested in its military incursions to this territory in Israeli civil courts,[20] or has held them without trial in "administrative detention" (a form of incarceration discussed in Section M.3).

The following sections shed light on two intertwined, and so far largely overlooked, facets of Israel's military courts: discrepancy and (un)certainty. Section M.2 examines these courts' long record of diverging not only from international legal norms, as their critics argue,[21] but also from the Israeli law and policies that supposedly bind them. Section M.3 explains the significance of such legal discrepancies, as evidenced by the uncertainty to which they subject Palestinians and their attorneys. After examining additional uncertainties, but also near-certainties, produced by the military courts, these courts are characterized as an epitome of Israel's "un/certainty governance" – a wider mode of control characterized by a manipulable interplay of uncertainties and near-certainties. Section M.4 summarizes this analysis, and critically reflects on the interrelation between Israeli military courts' un/certainty governance and these courts' relative marginality in academic and public debates.

[ ] *in the Occupied Territories, 1967–2007* (New York: Nation Books, 2007), pp. 372–373. See also entry J: Jewish Settlements.

[18] See Cavanaugh, "The Israeli Military Court System," pp. 199–200; Hajjar, *Courting Conflict*, p. 234; CrimC 4506/08 *Ajaj v. The State of Israel* (May 1, 2008) (Jerusalem Dist. Ct.).

[19] See entry O: Outside/Inside, Section O.3 ("Israeli Law Does Not Stop at the Border"), and entry Y: Youth, Section Y.3 ("The Rule of Exception Beyond Israeli Military Law").

[20] On the current legal status of the Gaza Strip, see entry Q: Quality of Life.

[21] Some have called into question Israel's compliance with, for example, Article 66 of the Geneva Convention Relative to the Protection of Civilian Persons in the Time of War, Geneva, August 12, 1949, 75 UNTS 287 [hereinafter: GC IV], which requires military courts to be "properly constituted" and "non-political." See Cavanaugh, "The Israeli Military Court System," p. 219; Weill, "The Judicial Arm of the Occupation," pp. 398–399. In this context, it is worth quoting, on the one hand, the words of former military court judge Jonathan Livni, appearing in the 2011 Israeli documentary *The Law in These Parts*: "You [the military court judge] serve a system . . . . You're in uniform, you represent the IDF [the Israeli military]. You represent a significant part of Israeli society, which has very set opinions about 'us' and 'them.' It's hard to shake that off. . . . As a military judge you don't just represent justice. I think that a civilian judge represents justice . . . As a military judge you represent the authorities of the occupation . . . You're conducting a trial against your enemy." On this documentary, see also note 58 in this entry. On the other hand, a basic tenet of critical thinking about law is that no judge or court is ever apolitical; therefore, criticism of Israeli military courts should focus not on their political nature per se, but on its concrete consequences in the rather unique context in which these courts operate.

M.2 LAW'S DISCREPANCIES

The very day the Israeli military took over the West Bank and the Gaza Strip, it issued the first of thousands of military orders to be enacted in these territories: Order Concerning Security Provisions.[22] Article 5 of this preprepared[23] order declared the establishment of "military courts ... authorized to try offenses defined in ... [military] orders," while Article 35 added that these courts and their staff "shall observe the provisions of the Geneva Convention of August 12, 1949 Relative to the Protection of Civilian Persons in Time of War with respect to legal proceedings, and in the event of conflict between this Order and the said Convention, the provisions of the Conventions shall prevail."[24]

A narrative shared by many international law scholars is that Israel quickly reversed its position on the applicability and primacy of *GC IV*. Indeed, within four months of its enactment, the above reference to the Convention was removed from the statutory military law,[25] though this did not prevent Israeli military lawyers from repeatedly referring to the Convention as a justification for Israel's operation of military courts in the Palestinian Territory.[26] Over the years, Israeli governments have persistently claimed that they are not bound by the Convention, a highly controversial stance formulated comprehensively by some Israeli jurists since at least 1968.[27]

This, however, is only part of the story. A far less known but equally significant fact is that the military courts, despite being formally bound by Israel's statutory military law, continued reasserting the applicability of *GC IV*

---

[22] Articles 5, 7, 12 of Order Concerning Security Provisions (West Bank), 1967. The Israeli military has issued more than 2,500 orders in the West Bank and more than 2,400 orders in the Gaza Strip. Milhem and Salem, "Rule of Law without Freedom." References throughout this entry are to orders applicable to the West Bank, but similar orders were issued in the Gaza Strip. Z. Hadar, "The Military Courts," in M. Shamgar (ed.) *Military Government in the Territories Administered by Israel – 1967–1980: The Legal Aspects* (Jerusalem: The Hebrew University of Jerusalem, 1982), vol. I, p. 171.

[23] For discussion of the advance preparation of this military order, see entry O: Outside/Inside, Section O.2 ("Before 1967").

[24] Security Provisions Order, Articles 5 and 35.

[25] Articles 1, 8 of Order Concerning Security Provisions (Amendment No. 9) (No. 144), 1967, in IDF, *Proclamations, Orders and Appointments of Judea and Samaria Command* (1967) p. 303, www.nevo.co.il/law_html/law70/zava-0008.pdf.

[26] See, e.g., Benichou, "Criminal Law in the Regions of Judea, Samaria, and Gaza," p. 295; Hadar, "The Military Courts," pp. 173–175; A. Strashnov, *Justice Under Fire* (Tel Aviv: Yedioth Ahronoth, 1994), p. 37 [Hebrew].

[27] Two early and influential examples are: Y. Z. Blum, "The Missing Reversioner: Reflections on the Status of Judea and Samaria" (1968) 3 *Israel Law Review* 279; M. Shamgar, "The Observance of International Law in the Administered Territories" (1971) 1 *Israeli Yearbook on Human Rights* 262. For further discussion, see entry G: Geneva Conventions.

to the Palestinian Territory, as well as its primacy over Israeli military law, for two whole years after the above amendment removed the statutory reference to GC IV.[28] Only since the early 1970s have these courts fallen into line, for the most part, with Israel's formal position.[29] "For the most part" is the operative phrase, because the courts have not been entirely consistent. In at least one case, in 2002, a military court held that the customary international law of occupation – including provisions of GC IV – prevails over Israeli military law,[30] thereby deviating yet again from the formal position of Israeli authorities.

This has not been the military courts' only divergence from the letter of Israel's statutory military law. In 2009, the statutory military law, which up to that point included no clear definition of the age of criminal majority (the age under which a person is considered a "minor"),[31] was amended to set that age at 16 years.[32] Formally, this statutory amendment eliminated judicial discretion in classifying minors, unlike other issues, such as sentencing or remand,

---

[28] MilC (Ramallah) 144/68 *Military Prosecutor* v. *Bakis* (1968), in Military Attorney General's Office, *Selected Rulings of the Military Courts in the Administered Territories* (Tel Aviv: 1970), vol. I, p. 371 (holding that the GC IV overrides the Israeli military law when there is conflict between the two); MilC (Gaza) 1238/69 *Military Prosecutor* v. *Abu Janas* (1969), in Military Attorney General's Office, "Selected Rulings," vol. I, p. 130 (holding that the GC IV applies to the occupied territories).

[29] MilC (Bethlehem) 48/69 *Military Prosecutor* v. *Harufa* (1970), in Military Attorney General's Office, "Selected Rulings," vol. I, p. 565 (holding that the GC IV does not override the Israeli military law); MilC (Bethlehem) 1114/72 *Military Prosecutor* v. *Scheinbeum* (1972), in Military Attorney General's Office, "Selected Rulings," vol. III, pp. 346, 354–357 (holding that the Israeli military, though purportedly respecting international treaty law in the West Bank and Gaza Strip, is not bound by this law). See also MilC (Nablus) 348/69 *Military Prosecutor* v. *Al-Nasser* (1969), in Military Attorney General's Office, "Selected Rulings," vol. I, p. 272 (holding that the GC IV does not constrain an occupying force's legislation regarding evidence and procedure).

[30] MilC (Samaria) 5708/01 *Military Prosecutor* v. *Udda* (2002), in Military Attorney General's Office, "Selected Rulings," vol. XIII, pp. 269, 277. For some related analysis, see Y. Ronen, "Blind in Their Own Cause: The Military Courts in the West Bank" (2013) 2 *Cambridge Journal of International and Comparative Law* 738, 746–748.

[31] A definition of "minor" was introduced into the statutory military law in 1975, but it applies only in the particular context of release on bail. Article 7a(e) of Order Concerning the Adjudication of Juvenile Delinquents (No. 132). In 1988, a military order that has since then been annulled defined "minor" as "anyone who cannot be criminally prosecuted due to his [sic] age." Article 1 of Order Concerning the Supervision of Minors" Behavior (Imposition of Bond) (Temporary Order) (Judea and Samaria) (No.1235), 1988.

[32] Article 1 of Order Concerning Security Provisions (Temporary Order) (Amendment No. 109) (No. 1644), 2009. Two years later, the statutory age of criminal majority was raised from 16 to 18 years. Article 3 of Order Concerning Security Provisions (Judea and Samaria) (Amendment No. 10) (No. 1676), 2011. On Palestinian minors' legal status, and on reasons why amendments such as the raising of the age of majority are merely token reforms, see entry Y: Youth.

where such discretion remained. But in practice, even after this amendment, some military judges defined 16- and 17-year-old defendants as minors, thereby effectively raising the age of criminal majority above the unequivocal statutory age.[33]

The military courts have been similarly inconsistent in enforcing the legislation enacted by the military to regulate Palestinian protest. In some cases, the courts have cited this legislation to the letter in determining whether the demonstration in which the defendant had participated was illegal. On other occasions, however, they have completely ignored this legislation and, instead, employed their own (different) tests to determine the legality of the demonstration.[34]

M.3 UN/CERTAINTY GOVERNANCE

Discrepancies such as these, between military court practice and the letter of the military law, carry important implications that go beyond the tired "law in the books" versus "law in action" distinction.[35] In terms of their ramifications for Palestinian defendants, such legal discrepancies operate at two different levels. At the individual defendant's level, they can produce more favorable outcomes, at least in some circumstances. In the above examples, reference to *GC IV*, the raising of the age of majority, and the disregard for the military legislation regarding demonstrations could, in principle at least,[36] provide a military judge with a justification for a relatively lenient sentence. Yet, at a broader (collective or institutional) level, increased uncertainty ensues when defense lawyers are prevented from anticipating matters as basic as their clients' classification as minors/adults, the criteria for determining a demonstration's legality, or the validity of referring to *GC IV*. This situation can also be described in terms of rule and exception. When basic legal issues such as the applicable law or statutory age thresholds are rendered fluid, it becomes impossible to identify and distinguish between the operating rule and its exception.[37]

---

[33] H. Viterbo, "The Age of Conflict: Rethinking Childhood, Law, and Age Through the Israeli-Palestinian Case," in M. Freeman (ed.), *Law and Childhood Studies – Current Legal Issues* (Oxford: Oxford University Press, 2012) vol. 14, pp. 133, 139–142.

[34] Association for Civil Rights in Israel, *The Status of the Right to Demonstrate in the Occupied Territories* (September 2014), pp. 38–39, www.acri.org.il/en/protestright/the-right-to-demonstrate.

[35] R. Pound, "Law in Books and Law in Action" (1910) 44 *American Law Review* 12.

[36] In practice, the courts' consideration of defendants' young age is more complex. See Viterbo, "The Age of Conflict," pp. 142–147.

[37] On the related phenomenon of statutory exceptions operating as the de facto rule, see entry Y: Youth.

Contrary to the instincts of many lawyers, uncertainty is not necessarily a problem; as jurist James Boyd White has aptly suggested, lawyers should be given "a training ... in the ways one can live with an increased awareness of the limits of one's knowledge and mind, accepting ambiguity and uncertainty as the condition of life."[38] Therefore, rather than an abstract debate about uncertainty, a critical analysis of Israel's rule over the Palestinian Territory warrants a nuanced investigation of the ways in which uncertainty functions in the context in question.

At the military courts' hands, Palestinians are subjected to a myriad of additional uncertainties, exemplified vividly by these courts' review of "administrative detention" (detention without trial). Military courts review "administrative detentions" behind closed doors, usually on the basis of secret evidence not disclosed to the defense, and without being bound by the regular rules of evidence. As a result, Palestinian "administrative detainees" are condemned to uncertainty about the alleged reasons for their incarceration. Furthermore, in the absence of a fixed sentence, such detainees are kept in a stressful cycle of hope toward each judicial review, despair following continued detention, and, subsequently, inability to anticipate their release from prison and plan their lives accordingly.[39]

Other forms of uncertainty await detainees who, in contrast, are brought to trial. First, uncertainty about their sentence is greater than in some other court systems. The substantial disparity between the sentences Israeli military courts issue for similar charges[40] is a reality acknowledged even by the military court of appeals.[41] Second, Palestinian defendants are likely to be uncertain about, and incapable of comprehending, the course of their proceedings. A central reason for this, aside from the familiar issue of unintelligible legalese, is that while Palestinian defendants usually speak Arabic, it is Hebrew in which their hearings are conducted. There are soldiers, mostly Druze,[42] serving as court

---

[38]   J. B. White, *The Legal Imagination*, abridged edition (Chicago: University of Chicago Press 1985), p. xv.

[39]   On "administrative detention," see entries F: Future-Oriented Measures, Section F.3.1, ("Administrative Detention") and S: Security Prisoners, Section S.1 ("Introduction: Terminology, Figures, and Context").

[40]   Hajjar, *Courting Conflict*, p. 256.

[41]   For judicial criticism of the inconsistency of military court rulings in relation to Palestinian minors' penalties and detention periods, see MilC (Mil. Ct. App.) 355/03 *Abiyat v. Military Prosecutor* (August 11, 2004); MilC (Mil. Ct. App.) 4497/08 *Military Prosecution v. Hawajah* (September 25, 2008). One military judge further described the military prosecution as inconsistent in relation to the sentences it pursues for minors. MilC (Judea) 1261/09 *Military Prosecution v. Al-Farukh* (February 23, 2009).

[42]   The Druze are a religious community that emerged from Islamism. On their participation in Israel's security forces (unlike most Palestinian citizens of Israel), see H. Frisch, "The Druze Minority in the Israeli Military: Traditionalizing an Ethnic Policing Role" (1993) 20 *Armed*

interpreters, but their professional training is often partial and unsystematic, and a considerable part of their function is to ensure order and proper conduct in the proceedings.[43] Further aggravating defendants' uncertainty and incomprehension is the unusual brevity of their hearings. According to Israeli NGO Yesh Din, military court hearings for authorizing continued remand until completion of trial, for example, last a minute and 54 seconds on average[44] – a reversal of the "justice delayed is justice denied" maxim, illustrating that justice hastened is justice equally denied. Add to this two other issues – the rarity of evidentiary trials (in which witnesses give testimony, evidence is examined, and closing arguments are made),[45] and the prevalence of plea bargains (meaning that many trials are concluded outside the court)[46] – and it becomes clear why some Palestinian ex-detainees, when interviewed about their encounter with the Israeli legal system, described their interrogation, rather than their courtroom trial, as their "real" trial.[47]

Though largely overlooked, uncertainty is a useful prism for gaining a better understanding of the military court system. Among other things, this prism helps bring to light the military courts' otherwise overlooked connections to other Israeli institutions and practices that produce comparable effects. Among these uncertainty-inducing mechanisms are: the constantly changing

    Forces & Society 51; R. Halabi, "Invention of a Nation: The Druze in Israel" (2014) 49 *Journal of Asian and African Studies* 267, 275–279.

[43] Hajjar, *Courting Conflict*, pp. 133, 135–137; S. L. Lipkin, "Norms and Ethics Among Military Court Interpreters: the Unique Case of the Judea Court," Master's thesis, Department of Translation and Interpreting Studies – Bar Ilan University (2006), pp. 63–72, 81–91 [Hebrew]; L. Yavne, "Backyard Proceedings," pp. 146–148. These soldiers' role is defined in Order No. 1651, Article 116. For further discussion of the perspectives and position of Druze interpreters, see Hajjar, *Courting Conflict*, pp. 132–153.

[44] L. Yavne, "Backyard Proceedings," pp. 13, 71–72 (based on observations of 118 detention hearings, conducted between the years 2006 and 2007). On the brevity of Israeli military court hearings, see also Hajjar, "Courting Conflict," p. 93; S. Ben-Natan, *All Guilty! Observations in the Military Juvenile Court* (2011), pp. 27–28, nolegalfrontiers.org/images/stories/report_2011/report_en.pdf.

[45] In 2010, of over 9,500 military court cases, only 82 (0.86 percent) reportedly included evidentiary trials. B'Tselem, *13 Dec. '11: Military Court Partially Acquits Palestinian due to Forced Confession* (2011), www.btselem.org/torture/20111213_hamidah_verdict.

[46] On plea bargains in the military court system and the reasons for their prevalence, see also N. Baumgarten-Sharon, *No Minor Matter: Violation of the Rights of Palestinian Minors Arrested by Israel on Suspicion of Stone-Throwing* (Jerusalem: B'Tselem, 2011), pp. 55–57, www.btselem.org/download/201107_no_minor_matter_eng.pdf; Hajjar, "Courting Conflict," pp. 83, 218–219, 220–226, 234; L. Yavne, "Backyard Proceedings," pp. 138–141. The exact plea bargain rate is in dispute. L. Yavne, "Backyard Proceedings," pp. 28, 136–137.

[47] Hajjar, "Courting Conflict," pp. 188–190. See also J. Collins, *Occupied by Memory: The Intifada Generation and the Palestinian State of Emergency* (New York and London: New York University Press, 2004), pp. 136–137.

statutory military law;[48] the recurrently vague and sometimes conflicting instructions and orders guiding the Israeli security authorities; and the changing rules determining eligibility for permits to enter Israel or move within the West Bank. Such mechanisms generate "control through uncertainty," or "effective ineffectiveness"[49] – a mode of governance that, while not always fulfilling Israeli authorities' intentions,[50] nonetheless uniquely expands these authorities' possibilities for ad hoc discretion and on-the-spot, flexible interpretations.

But again, this is only part of the story. Alongside such uncertainties, the Israeli rule in the Palestinian Territory, and the military courts specifically, are rife with near-certainties, which from Palestinians' standpoint can be no less burdensome. The military courts' 99.76 percent conviction rate,[51] for instance, makes the outcome of each military court trial near-certain in advance. The uniqueness of this situation derives not from the high figure per se – after all, there are some other jurisdictions with high conviction rates – but from the unusual legal process leading up to it: arrest by a belligerent power's soldiers, indictment by that power's military prosecution, and adjudication by its military judges according to military laws. Similarly, it is nearly certain that,

---

[48] See, e.g., Ben-Natan, "All Guilty!," p. 10 (reporting that the military amended its main piece of criminal legislation, Order Concerning Security Provisions (Judea and Samaria) (No. 378), more than 120 times since enacting it in 1970).

[49] N. Gordon and D. Filc, "Hamas and the Destruction of Risk Society" (2005) 12 *Constellations* 542, 551–552; A. Hendel, "Exclusionary Surveillance and Spatial Uncertainty in the Occupied Palestinian Territories," in E. Zureik, D. Lyon, and Y. Abu-Laban (eds.), *Surveillance and Control in Israel/Palestine: Population, Territory, and Power*, Routledge Studies in Middle Eastern Politics 33 (London; New York: Routledge, 2011), p. 260; Y. Shenhav and Y. Berda, "The Colonial Foundations of the State of Exception: Juxtaposing the Israeli Occupation of the Palestinian Territories with Colonial Bureaucratic History," in A. Ophir, M. Givoni, and S. Hanafi (eds.) *The Power of Inclusive Exclusion: Anatomy of Israeli Rule in the Occupied Palestinian Territories* (New York: Zone Books, 2009), pp. 337, 339–340, 355–360. See also T. Kelly, "Documented Lives: Fear and the Uncertainties of Law During the Second Palestinian Intifada" (2006) 12 *Journal of the Royal Anthropological Institute* 89 (discussing the unpredictability characterizing Israel's inspection of Palestinians' identity papers); N. Gordon, *Israel's Occupation* (Berkeley, Los Angeles, and London: University of California Press, 2008), p. 43 (discussing the uncertainty in Palestinian society caused by Israel's recruitment of Palestinian informants and collaborators). See also entry G: Geneva Law, on the nonspecification of the "humanitarian provisions" Israel has vowed to observe in the Palestinian Territory.

[50] On the incoherence and unintended consequences of state practices, see, e.g., Gordon, "Israel's Occupation," pp. 12, 15–17; R. Shamir, "'Landmark Cases' and the Reproduction of Legitimacy: The Case of Israel's High Court of Justice" (1990) 24 *Law & Society* 781, 783.

[51] C. Levinson, "Nearly 100% of All Military Court Cases in West Bank End in Conviction, Haaretz Learns," *Haaretz* (November 29, 2011), www.haaretz.com/nearly-100-of-all-military-court-cases-in-west-bank-end-in-conviction-haaretz-learns-1.398369 (the data, provided by the Israeli military, refers to the year 2010).

despite abundant reports of coerced confessions,[52] a military judge will not exclude a confession obtained from a Palestinian during interrogation.[53] The outcome of an appeal to Israel's supreme court against a military court review of "administrative detention" is, likewise, almost certain: of more than 300 such appeals heard by the supreme court between the years 2000 and 2010, not a single one resulted in a release order or in a rejection of the secret evidence.[54] Again, various elements of the Israeli rule in the Palestinian Territory, other than the military courts, have similar effects.[55]

The "near" in "near-certainty" is of importance and relevance even for outcomes that seem absolutely certain, because, despite past experience, hope for a different outcome often prevails. As a case in point, appeals against military court decisions on "administrative detentions" persist, in spite of the bleak statistics mentioned earlier. The Israeli legal system in the Palestinian territories owes much of its potency to "un/certainty governance" – the maintenance of the manipulable interplay of uncertainties and near-certainties described so far. There are, of course, military court actions whose outcomes are neither entirely uncertain nor near-certain. But here, too, odds are often not favorable to Palestinians. For instance, according to information provided by the Israeli military, in 2010, the military court of appeals was twice as likely to accept appeals by the military prosecution (against the leniency of the sentence) as defendants' appeals.[56]

---

[52] On the prevalence of interrogational abuse and torture, see, e.g., Y. Lein, *Absolute Prohibition: The Torture and Ill-treatment of Palestinian Detainees* (Jerusalem: B'Tselem & Hamoked, 2007), www.btselem.org/download/200705_utterly_forbidden_eng.pdf; B. Shoughry-Badarne, "A Decade After the High Court of Justice 'Torture' Ruling, What's Changed?," in A. Baker and A. Matar (eds.), *Threat: Palestinian Political Prisoners in Israel* (London: Pluto Press, 2011), p. 114. See also entry V: Violence.

[53] Hajjar, *Courting Conflict*, p. 109 (reporting that none of the interviewed military court judges recalled ever having excluded a confession, and that defense attorneys working in the military court system considered challenging a confession ineffective and even potentially harmful in terms of the eventual sentence).

[54] S. Krebs, "Lifting the Veil of Secrecy: Judicial Review of Administrative Detentions in the Israeli Supreme Court" (2012) 45 *Vanderbilt Journal Transnational Law* 639, 643. On the supreme court's record of deference to the military's decisions, see, e.g., D. Kretzmer, *The Occupation of Justice: The Supreme Court of Israel and the Occupied Territories* (Albany: State University of New York Press, 2002); G. Harpaz and Y. Shany, "The Israeli Supreme Court and the Incremental Expansion of the Scope of Discretion under Belligerent Occupation Law" (2010) 43 *Israel Law Review* 514.

[55] A. Korn, "The Ghettoization of the Palestinians," in Lentin, *Thinking Palestine*, pp. 123–124 (detailing how "the situation prevailing in the Territories is by no means anarchy. . . . Very clear rules operate . . . as almost every aspect of Palestinian life is regulated through permits and licenses. . . . Palestinians know very well what is allowed and what is forbidden").

[56] Levinson, "Nearly 100% of All Military Court Cases in West Bank End in Conviction."

M.4 CONCLUSION

The military court system epitomizes a broader issue examined in greater depth elsewhere in this book:[57] Israel's longstanding reliance on law – on legal institutions, arguments, and professionals – for designing, operating, and justifying its control over the West Bank and Gaza Strip. As shown, these courts also derive much of their potency from subjecting Palestinians to various uncertainties on the one hand, and near-certainties on the other hand. These include – to reiterate but three of the abovementioned examples – Palestinians' uncertainty when faced with Israeli military courts' divergence from statutory Israeli law, or when awaiting military court review of their "administrative detention," but also the near-uncertain outcomes of many military court proceedings. This manipulable interplay of un/certainties, termed here "un/certainty governance," is indeed another important, though largely under-examined, sense in which the military courts both facilitate and exemplify the workings of Israel's control over Palestinians' lives.

Much of this dynamic has gone unexamined, in large part, due to the military courts' relative peripherality in legal literature and public discourse on Israel's rule in the Palestinian Territory. International law has attracted considerably greater attention than the immensely important Israeli law on the ground.[58] To date, there has been no systematic study of military court judgments, and writing on military legislation has been very limited. Much of the existing legal literature on Israeli military law is out of date and/or written by members, past or present, of the military legal system.[59] Possible reasons for the academic neglect of this pivotal legal system include: the relative difficulty

---

[57] See entries L: Lawfare and V: Violence.

[58] The situation has slightly changed in recent years following some NGO and media reports, and also, notably, following the release of the 2011 Israeli documentary *The Law in These Parts*, the winner of the 2012 Sundance Film Festival best documentary award, which presents interviews with former high-ranking members of the Israeli military legal system. For further discussion of this film, see L. Lambert, "Law as a Colonial Weapon: Review of 'The Law in These Parts' by Ra'anan Alexandrowicz," *Critical Legal Thinking* (November 2, 2013), criti callegalthinking.com/2013/10/02/palestine-law-colonial-weapon/.

[59] See, e.g., Benichou, "Criminal Law in the Regions of Judea, Samaria, and Gaza"; M. Drori, *The Legislation in the Judea and Samaria Region* (Jerusalem: The Hebrew University of Jerusalem, Faculty of Law, 1975) [Hebrew]; Z. Hadar, "The Military Courts"; D. Yahav et al. (eds.) *Israel, the "Intifada" and the Rule of Law* (Tel Aviv: Israel Ministry of Defense Publications, 1993); T. Lekah and A. Dahan, "A Conviction Rate of 99.9 percent in Israel: Is the Law Distorted or is Only the Statistics Distorted?" (2010) 5 *Din U-Dvarim* 185 [Hebrew]; Rozin, "The Silent Revolution"; Shamgar, "The Observance of International Law"; Strashnov, *Justice Under Fire*.

of accessing most military court judgments;[60] the restrictions imposed on those wishing to observe military court hearings or interview military officials;[61] the overall difficulty of obtaining clear information from the Israeli security forces;[62] and other hurdles placed by the military.[63] The absence of courses in Israeli law schools on the military law applied to Palestinians,[64] and the lack of anything close to a textbook on this body of law, further perpetuate this situation.

Inadvertently or not, the general academic and public neglect of the Israeli military court system helps shield the military courts from scrutiny, thereby maintaining these courts' un/certainty governance. Moreover, the reasons for the current state of academic and public knowledge on the military legal system are part and parcel of these courts' un/certainty governance. The inaccessibility of military legal documents, for example, not only hinders research and informed debate, but also makes it difficult for defense lawyers to effectively defend their Palestinian clients.[65] For those interested in the military legal system's decisive role in Israel/Palestine, the Israeli military courts' un/certainty governance is thus both a potential object of inquiry and a knowledge-governing force.

---

[60] In 2008, the military began sending Israeli online legal database Nevo copies of new decisions of the military court of appeals. Yet, first-instance military court decisions – the majority of military court decisions – often remain unpublished, as do almost all military court rulings from previous years.

[61] On the above issues, see also Hajjar, *Courting Conflict*, pp. 16–17, 59; Yavne, "Backyard Proceedings," pp. 14, 25–26, 82–88.

[62] For example, on the difficulty of obtaining precise and clear information from the Israeli security forces on their handling of Palestinian children, see H. Viterbo, "Rights as a Divide-and-Rule Mechanism: Lessons from the Case of Palestinians in Israeli Custody" (forthcoming) *Law & Social Inquiry*.

[63] See, e.g., Gisha, *Military Changes Procedure in Order to Justify its Refusal to allow a British Student to enter the Gaza Strip* (2014), gisha.org/updates/2690.

[64] The few elective courses defined as dealing with "military law" focus on the law applicable to Israeli soldiers in courts-martial.

[65] On this issue, see Cook, Hanieh, and Kay, "Stolen Youth," p. 25; Hajjar, "Courting Conflict," p. 225; L. Yavne, "Backyard Proceedings," p. 17.

N

Nomos

Orna Ben-Naftali

N.1 A TALE OF TWO NOMOI: ISRAEL AND THE INTERNATIONAL LEGAL COMMUNITY

N.1.1 *Robert Cover's Nomos*

We all inhabit at least one *nomos*, a normative universe, posits Robert Cover in his seminal article *Nomos and Narrative*, "a world of right and wrong, of lawful and unlawful, of valid and void."[1] This universe consists of law and of "the narratives that locate it and give it meaning."[2] The nomos provides us with a common discourse or community where these shared narratives render our world legible and give our life a sense of direction.[3]

Pluralistic societies encompass divergent nomoi, each subscribing to different interpretations of the founding legal texts of the society. Each of these nomoi is equally valid, and minority communities are not obligated to accept the worldview espoused by the dominant community; they may preserve their own nomos and retain "nomic insularity,"[4] and may indeed attempt to change the sociopolitical order and have their nomos prevail. Communities that strive to transform the existing order are "redemptive communities":[5] their normative universe, however, must contain a way to reconcile the world as it is and

---

[1] R. M. Cover, "The Supreme Court 1982 term – Foreword: Nomos and Narrative" (1983) 97 *Harvard Law Review* 4.

[2] *Ibid.*, p. 4.

[3] *Ibid.*, pp. 12–13. Note that Cover distinguished two types of nomoi comprising each nomos: the paideic and the imperial. The former is a world-creating normative universe; the latter, a world-maintaining such universe. The paideic nomos denotes a common body of precepts and narrative; a common and personal way of being educated into this corpus; and "a sense of direction or growth that is constituted as the individual and his community work out the implications of their law." The imperial universe is constituted by enforcement, effectiveness, and weak interpersonal commitments. *Ibid.*, p. 13.

[4] *Ibid.*, pp. 28–29.   [5] *Ibid.*, pp. 33–44.

the world as they think it should be. Since the advancement of their vision requires their engagement in negotiations with other normative communities, they cannot retain their nomic insularity.

Israel inhabits a sui generis nomos with respect to its control over the OPT. The relationship between the nomos inhabited by the international community and the nomos inhabited by Israel is the focus of this entry.[6]

The text which succinctly exemplifies the Israeli nomos is contained in a report of an expert committee, established by the Israeli prime minister and the then minister of justice in 2012, to examine the legal status of Israeli construction in the Judea and Samaria[7] [hereinafter: the Levy Committee].[8] This report concluded that from an international legal perspective, the West Bank is not occupied territory; the law of belligerent occupation is not applicable to the area; the "prevailing view" in international law is that Jewish settlements are lawful; and that Israel has a valid claim to sovereignty over the territory.

N.1.2 *The Levy Committee Report and the International Legal Discourse*

The decision to establish the Levy Committee was made on February 13, 2012, in response to both legal and public pressures: in the legal arena, numerous petitions requesting the HCJ to order the state to demolish, or implement demolition orders against illegal construction by Israeli settlers in outposts in the West Bank, or otherwise order the evacuation of unauthorized such outposts, were pending.[9] In the public arena, the settlers' lobby wanted to establish a legal foundation for existing and planned Jewish constructions in the

---

[6] Cover's pluralistic jurisprudence is of particular relevance to international law; see P. S. Berman, "A Pluralist Approach to International Law" (2007) 32 *Yale Journal of International Law* 301.

[7] Power resorts Orwellian "newspeak": the territory known as "the West Bank" in international legal language, is referred to in official Israeli language as "Judea and Samaria," connoting the link between the State of Israel and the Biblical Promised Land.

[8] *Report on the Legal Status of Building in Judea and Samaria* (June 21, 2012) [hereinafter: the LCR], www.pmo.gov.il/Documents/docho9o712.pdf [Hebrew; an English translation of the conclusions and recommendations is available at http://elderofziyon.blogspot.com/2012/07/english-translation-of-legal-arguments.html#.vjysrvkrliv].

[9] "Outposts" is a term denoting unauthorized settlements, i.e., settlements established without government authorization. These are communities that do not comply with one or more of the following conditions: (a) governmental authorization to build the settlement; (2) the land is state land or owned by Jews; (3) the settlement is built according to a master plan, pursuant to which building permits may be issued; (4) the community's jurisdiction is determined by order of the commander of the area. See T. Sasson, *Interim Report on the Subject of Unauthorized Outposts* (Jerusalem: 2005), pp. 20–21. [Hebrew; an English summary of the report is available at www.mfa.gov.il/mfa/aboutisrael/state/law/pages/summary%20of%20opinion%20concerning %20unauthorized%20outposts%20-%20talya%20sason%20adv.aspx]. The report was presented

West Bank and, in the process, refute a 2005 report commissioned, and subsequently approved, by then prime minister Sharon and then attorney general Mazuz, which concluded that the construction of unauthorized Jewish outposts in the West Bank was illegal under domestic law.[10]

The members the Levy Committee submitted their report on June 21, 2012, [hereinafter: the LCR].[11] The essence of their conclusion is twofold: first, from an international legal perspective, there is no belligerent occupation of the West Bank. Ergo, the law of occupation does not apply and, accordingly, there is "no doubt" that Jewish settlements are not illegal.[12] Second, from the perspective of Israeli public law, the establishment of the outposts has enjoyed implied governmental consent and is thus legal. This entry focuses solely on the first conclusion.[13]

---

to late prime minister Sharon in February 2005. Government Resolution No 3376, www.pmo .gov.il/Secretary/GovDecisions/2005/Pages/des3376.aspx [Hebrew], endorsed the report's findings and recommendations on March 13, 2005. The term "unauthorized outposts" is designed to differentiate them from the settlements. Note that from an international legal perspective there is no difference between an "unauthorized outpost" and a settlement: both are equally unauthorized as they violate Article 49(6) of the Geneva Convention Relative to the Protection of Civilian Persons in the Time of War, Geneva, August 12, 1949, 75 UNTS 287 [hereinafter: GC IV]. On February 6, 2017, the Israeli parliament passed a law, applicable directly to the OPT, which provides for "the regularization" of outposts: see The Settlement Regularization in Judea and Samaria Law, 2017. This law is the focus of entry R: Regularization.

[10] Sasson, *Interim Report*. On the backdrop of the establishment of the Levy Committee, see generally *Unprecedented: A Legal Analysis of the Report of the Committee to Examine the Status of Building in Judea and Samaria [the West Bank] ("The Levy Committee") – International and Administrative Aspects* (Tel Aviv: Yesh Din – Volunteers for Human Rights and The Emile Zola Chair for Human Rights, 2014).

[11] The Committee was chaired by justice Levy (ret.), the only judge in a panel of 11 judges who accepted a petition submitted by the Gaza Coast Regional Planning against the government's decision to withdraw troops from the Gaza Strip and evacuate the settlers from the area. In this context, he determined that: "the State of Israel, which now holds these territories, does so not by virtue of being an 'occupying power,' but by virtue of the fact that on the one hand it replaced the Mandate government, and on the other hand, it is the representative of the Jewish people. As such it enjoys not only the historical right to hold and settle in these areas, about which it is not necessary to speak at length but simply to study the Bible, but also a right enshrined in international law." See HCJ 1661/05 *Gaza Coast Regional Council v. The Israeli Knesset* (2005) 59(2) PD 481 [Hebrew], ¶ 14 of the dissenting judgment. The two other members were judge (ret.) Tchia Shapira, who served in the Tel Aviv district court, and Alan Baker, former Israeli ambassador to Canada, who had previously served as the legal advisor to the Israeli foreign ministry.

[12] The LCR, ¶ 9.

[13] The substance of the present critique of the LCR is based on O. Ben-Naftali and R. Reznik, "The Astro-Nomos: On International Legal Paradigms and the Legal Status of the West Bank" (2015) 14 *Washington University Global Studies Law Review* 399. Note that other than this article, the LCR received immediately upon publication only brief, albeit overwhelmingly critical, reaction. See, e.g., J. H. H. Weiler, "Editorial – Differentiated Statehood? 'Pre-States'?

The proposition advanced in this entry is threefold: first, given that there is an overwhelming (and rare) international legal consensus that the territories are occupied, that the law of belligerent occupation applies, and that the settlements are illegal and indeed constitute a grave breach of the GC IV, the LCR's construction of the law of belligerent occupation proposes a different nomos for the international community and indeed purports to advance a paradigmatic revolution.[14] Second, the arguments advanced by the LCR reflect a colonialist/Orientalist paradigm that has been discarded to the garbage can of history and replaced with a paradigm that rests on the right of peoples to self-determination. In that sense, the LCR attempts to initiate a backward-looking revolution. Third, the LCR's rejection of the nomos inhabited by the international community also explains why it does not advance international legal arguments as an apology for power. The latter operates within the structure of the international legal discourse, not outside it.[15] The LCR advances a particularly idiosyncratic type of a utopian vision, one that is simultaneously hegemonic and insular: its politics are hegemonic and reflect the political position of the Israeli government; its "nomic insularity" does not.

In order to substantiate this proposition, Section N.2 presents the thesis advanced by the LCR. Section N.3 offers a detailed critique of this thesis and proceeds to assess it in the light of the interpretative commitments of the nomos inhabited by the international community. Section N.4 concludes.

Palestine@the UN" (2013) 24 *European Journal of International Law* 1, 1; I. Scobbie, "Justice Levy's Legal Tinsel: The Recent Israeli Report on the Status of the West Bank and Legality of the Settlements," *EJIL: Talk! – Blog of the European Journal of International Law* (September 9, 2012), www.ejiltalk.org/justice-levys-legal-tinsel-the-recent-israeli-report-on-the-status-of-the-west-bank-and-legality-of-the-settlements; D. Kretzmer, "Bombshell for the settlement enterprise in Levy report," *Haaretz* (July 10, 2012), www.haaretz.com/opinion/bombshell-for-the-settlement-enterprise-in-levy-report-1.450170; D. Kretzmer, "Undoing the State of Israel," *Jerusalem Report* (July 24, 2012), www.jpost.com/Jerusalem-Report/Israel/Undoing-the-State-of-Israel; A. Gross, "If there are no Palestinians, there's no Israeli occupation," *Haaretz* (July 10, 2012), www.haaretz.com/news/diplomacy-defense/if-there-are-no-palestinians-there-s-no-israeli-occupation-1.449988; Y. Shany and I. Rosenzweig, "Groundless" (October 2012) 17 *Orech Hadin (The Attorney)* 18 [Hebrew]; E. Lieblich and S. Krebs, "The Outposts Report: War is Peace, Occupation is Freedom," *The Israel Democracy Institute* (July 25, 2012) [Hebrew]. For a rare positive reaction to the LCR, see A. Bell, "Paper no. 176: The Levy Report: Reinvigorating the Discussion of Israel's Rights in the West Bank," *The Begin-Sadat Center for Strategic Studies, Perspectives* (July 31, 2012), https://besacenter.org/perspectives-papers/the-levy-report-reinvigorating-the-discussion-of-israels-rights-in-the-west-bank/.

[14] T. S. Kuhn, *The Structure of Scientific Revolutions*, 3rd edn (Chicago: University of Chicago Press, 1996).

[15] M. Koskenniemi, *From Apology to Utopia: The Structure of International Legal Argument* (Cambridge: Cambridge University Press, 2006).

N.2 THE NOMOS THE LEVY COMMITTEE INHABITS

"[T]he status of the Judea and Samaria Areas from the perspective of interna-tional law" is the focus of the paragraphs 3–9 of the LCR.[16] The discussion generates the following interrelated assertions: first, Israel is not a belligerent occupying power in these areas.[17] Second, and alternatively, even if its control over the territories were subject to the law of belligerent occupation, Article 49 paragraph 6 of the GC IV is irrelevant to the Jewish settlements in the area.[18] Third, there is a legal basis for Israel's sovereignty over the territory.[19] The inevitable conclusion is that there is "no doubt that from the perspective of international law, the establishment of Jewish settlements in the Judea and Samaria area is not illegal."[20] What are the substantive and methodological bases for this threefold thesis?

The assertion that the West Bank is not occupied territory is based on the following two propositions: (a) the law of belligerent occupation is premised on a relatively short duration. Israel's presence in and hold over the territories, however, has lasted for decades and "no one can predict its ending, if at all";[21] and (b) the laws of belligerent occupation are applicable only to territories taken from a sovereign state. Given that the annexation of the area by Jordan lacked a legal basis, and given further that it since withdrew its claim to sovereignty over the area, the West Bank does not qualify as a territory taken from a sovereign state.[22] The LCR provides no legal authorities in support of either of these propositions.

The above assertion obviates the need to consider the application of Article 49 paragraph 6 of the GC IV, which provides that "the Occupying Power shall not deport or transfer parts of its civilian population into the territory it occupies."[23] The LCR nevertheless decided to posit as an alternative ground for the legality of the Jewish settlements in the West Bank, what it considers to be "the prevailing view" regarding the interpretation of this provision.[24] This interpretation holds that the prohibition on the settlements of citizens of the occupying power in occupied territories "was intended to respond to the

---

[16] In paragraph 3 the LCR presents the views on the matter submitted to it by representatives of various peace and human rights organizations. In paragraph 4 it presents the views of representatives of settlers. Paragraphs 5–9 consist of the Levy Committee's analysis, essentially embracing the latter.

[17] *Ibid.*, ¶ 5.   [18] *Ibid.*, ¶¶ 5–6.   [19] *Ibid.*, ¶ 5.

[20] *Ibid.*, ¶ 9. Cf the translation of the conclusions to English, above note 8, which reads: "Therefore, according to International law, Israelis have the legal right to settle in Judea and Samaria and the establishment of settlements cannot, in and of itself, be considered to be illegal."

[21] *Ibid.*, ¶ 5.   [22] *Ibid.*   [23] Article 49(6) of GC IV.   [24] The LCR, ¶ 5.

difficult reality imposed on some of the nations during the Second World War, when some of their residents were deported and forcibly transferred to the territories they had conquered."[25] Read in this light, the LCR concludes that the provision is inapplicable to "persons who sought to settle in Judea and Samaria not because they were 'deported' or 'exiled' thereto by force, but because of their worldview – the settlement of the Land of Israel."[26] Methodologically, five sources are cited in support of the assertion that this interpretation constitutes "the prevailing view": the ICRC Commentary to the *GC IV*; a short communication published by Eugene Rostow in the "Notes and Comments" section of the 1990 *American Journal of International Law*;[27] a 2009 piece in the *Commentary*, written by David Phillips and citing Julius Stone, albeit without a reference;[28] a 2012 piece written by Alan Baker, a member of the Levy Committee, and published on the website of the Jerusalem Center for Public Affairs;[29] and a 1987 decision of the Israeli HCJ.[30]

The third leg of the LCR's conclusion relative to the status of the territories under international law grounds Israel's claim to sovereign rights therein in an historical narrative unfolding along the following milestones: (a) the 1917 Balfour Declaration; (b) the reiteration, mutatis mutandis, of the Balfour Declaration in the 1920 San Remo Conference; and (c) Articles 2 and 6 of the 1922 Mandate for Palestine granted to Great Britain by the League of Nations. Methodologically, the LCR assigns no legal significance to the first two documents other than as precursors to the Mandate. The latter, concludes the LCR, established that Palestine is the national home of the Jewish people and granted only civil and religious rights to non-Jewish communities in the area.[31]

The subsequent milestones comprising the narrative include: (a) the 1947 General Assembly Resolution 181 (i.e., the resolution which contained "the partition plan": it partitioned Mandatory Palestine between the Arab and

---

[25] *Ibid.*   [26] *Ibid.*, ¶ 6.

[27] Responding to A. Roberts, "Prolonged Military Occupations: The Israeli-Occupied Territories since 1967" (1990) 84 *American Journal of International Law* 44.

[28] D. M. Phillips, "The Illegal Settlements Myth" (December 2009) 128 *Commentary* 32, 36–37, www.commentarymagazine.com/article/the-illegal-settlements-myth. Note that the LCR cites the year as 2010.

[29] A. Baker, "The Settlements Issue: Distorting the Geneva Convention and the Oslo Accords," *Jerusalem Center for Public Affairs* (January 5, 2011), http://jcpa.org/article/the-settlements-issue-distorting-the-geneva-convention-and-the-oslo-accords.

[30] HCJ 785/87 *Al-Affu v. Commander of the IDF forces in the West Bank* (1988) 42(2) PD 4 [Hebrew; English translation available at (1990) 29 ILM 139].

[31] The LCR, ¶ 7.

Jewish communities in the area, and approved the establishment of two states with economic union within these borders and with Jerusalem and Bethlehem as *corpus seperatum*[32]). This Resolution, posits the LCR, lacks validity on two grounds: first, it was taken ultra vires in the light of Article 80 of the UN Charter, which provides that nothing in the Charter shall alter the rights of states and peoples as recognized under mandates.[33] Second, it was rejected by the Arab States and subsequently overwhelmed by the reality of the 1948 war, and the occupation of the Gaza Strip by Egypt and of the West Bank by Jordan; (b) the 1949 Armistice lines which, according to the LCR, were not intended to constitute boundaries given the standing of the Arab states; and (c) the 1950 illegal annexation of the West Bank by Jordan which, when coupled with its subsequent waiver of any claim to sovereign rights over the area, has restored, asserts the LCR, "the original legal status of the territory": the Jews, who had a "right of possession," which they could not exercise in view of the result of a war imposed on them and Jordanian rule, have returned to their land.[34]

This narrative leads to the conclusion that Israel has a valid claim to sovereignty over the area; that this indeed has been the position of all Israeli governments; and that the only reason Israel refrained from annexing the area was "to enable peace negotiations with the representatives of the Palestinian people and the Arab States."[35] Indeed, asserts the LCR, Israel never regarded itself as an occupying power "in the classical sense of the term," and ergo never committed itself to apply the GC IV, settling merely for a declaration that it would voluntarily apply its humanitarian provisions. The inescapable conclusion is that its policy has been to allow its citizens to reside in the area of their free will, subjecting their continuous presence to the result of the political negotiations process.[36]

The Levy Committee inhabits a normative universe: its understanding of international law is inseparable from a narrative.[37] That narrative unfolds a deep conviction in the exclusive right of the Jewish people to sovereignty over the land of Mandatory Palestine. This conviction – indeed, vision – informs its construction of international law. Transported to the normative world, this vision posits a revision of international law.

Given that alternative visions do exist and that the normative world provides the bridge between vision and reality, any attempt to advance a revisionist interpretation requires an engagement with alternative visions and the meaning they invest in the normative world. Such engagement, as tense and

---

[32]   The Partition Plan, GA Res 181 (II), UN Doc A/RES/181(II) (November 29, 1947).
[33]   The LCR, ¶ 8.   [34]   *Ibid.*   [35]   *Ibid.,* ¶ 9.   [36]   *Ibid.*
[37]   Cover, "Nomos and Narrative," p. 5.

wrought with conflicts as it surely is, is nevertheless a sine qua non condition for transforming a nomos. An insular vision that fails to be thus engaged and insists on living "an entirely idiosyncratic normative life, would be quite mad."[38] This is not a fruitful vantage point from which to advance a revision of our normative universe. It does not follow that change is impossible. It simply requires that its introduction relates to the "'disciplinary matrix' of concepts, assumptions, basic laws, proven methods and other objects of commitment common to the practitioners of a particular discipline or specialty."[39] In the case at hand, this requirement should have led the members of the Levy Committee to pay a visit to the nomos the international legal community actually inhabits. Their failure to do so is discussed in Section N.3.

N.3 THE NOMOS THE INTERNATIONAL LEGAL COMMUNITY ACTUALLY INHABITS

The mandate of the Levy Committee did not require it to visit the international legal terrain. It chose to travel that road. This choice is meritorious: international law provides the relevant normative framework for the determination of the status of a territory and the means and methods by which it may be lawfully acquired. The LCR's application of that normative framework to the status of the West Bank, however, defies as it ignores the disciplinary matrix it ostensibly employs.

The first leg on which the LCR's proposition that the West Bank does not qualify as a territory under belligerent occupation rested, is that the international legal regime of belligerent occupation is premised on a short duration, whereas the Israeli control over the area has no end in sight.[40] Neither doctrine nor principle support this line of reasoning.

It is no doubt true that the regime is premised on a relatively short duration. It is equally true that the indefinite duration of the Israeli control over the territory defies that premise.[41] It does not follow, however, that the mere duration of a regime (a political phenomenon) transforms its normative classification and affects the applicable legal framework.[42]

---

[38] *Ibid.*, p. 10.
[39] C. G. A. Bryant, "Kuhn, Paradigms and Sociology" (1975) 26 *The British Journal of Sociology* 354.
[40] See above text and note 21.   [41] See entry T: Temporary/Indefinite.
[42] Even if it were determined that the occupation is illegal, the applicable legal framework would continue to apply. See Continued Presence of South Africa in Namibia (South West Africa) Notwithstanding Security Council Resolution, 276 (1970), Advisory Opinion, 1971 ICJ 16.

Prolonged belligerent occupations are rare. They are an anomaly which attests to the failure of political processes. A political anomaly is not to be confused with a legal anomaly. Prolonged occupations do not vitiate the relevant normative paradigm, and indeed call for extra vigilance in its application.[43] The suggestion that they do, belongs to the alchemy of law and falls outside the matrix of the discipline. It is thus little wonder that no legal authority was advanced by the LCR to support it. There is none: indeed, the applicability of the law of belligerent occupation to prolonged occupations has never been questioned by any known primary or secondary source of international law. It is perhaps particularly instructive that it is not only international judicial, quasi-judicial, and political institutions that resort to this legal framework as a matter of course,[44] but so do Israeli authorities as well: till now, the argument of the LCR was never made by any Israeli authority responding to petitions emanating from the OPT. It was advanced by Jewish settlers in the petition of the Gaza Coast Regional Council and unequivocally rejected by the court:

> The petitioners deny the claim that the area is under temporary belligerent occupation. They argue that the Israeli settlement in the area relied on a continuous representation of the Israeli governments, that it is a permanent settlement in one of the grounds of the land of Israel ... [However,] the normative reality is eviction from an area of belligerent occupation. The nature of such an area is that Israelis' presence in it is temporary ... the possibility of eviction occurring one day hangs over the Israeli's head at all times.[45]

The notion that a prolonged occupation vitiates the law of belligerent occupation is not merely unfounded in terms of doctrine, it also turns the principle on its head: in attempting to transform a political anomaly into a legal justification, the LCR posits that a wrong can and does make a right.[46]

The second leg on which the LCR's proposition that the West Bank does not qualify as a territory under belligerent occupation rests is based on a cumulative reading of the two paragraphs comprising Common Article 2

---

[43]   If anything, prolonged occupation underscores the need to interpret specific provisions in a manner that would ensure that the rights of the occupied population provided for within the normative framework are not further jeopardized. See Roberts, "Prolonged Military Occupations," pp. 53–56.

[44]   See, e.g., Legal Consequences of the Construction of a Wall in the Occupied Palestinian Territory, Advisory Opinion, 2004 ICJ 136 [hereinafter: Construction of a Wall]; GA Res 55/132, UN Doc A/RES/55/132 (December 8, 2000).

[45]   *Gaza Coast*, ¶ 115.

[46]   R. Dworkin, *Taking Rights Seriously* (Cambridge, MA: Harvard University Press, 1978), p. 29.

of the Geneva Conventions. It posits, in essence, that since Jordan was not
a lawful sovereign in the West Bank (and that Egypt never claimed sovereign
title over the Gaza Strip), the territories were not taken from "a High
Contracting Party" and ergo, Israel is not obligated to apply the GC IV.[47]
This reading, discussed and critiqued in entry G: Geneva Law,[48] is inspired by
a narrative that posits Jewish ownership of the land since time immemorial
and attempts to turn the vision into a normative reality. Said attempt has long
been rejected by the international legal community.[49] The LCR is silent about
the very rejection of its position, the grounds on which it is based, and the
scope and nature of its sources.

Indeed, had the LCR's argument that the territory is not subject to the law of
belligerent occupation been accepted, the question of from where the authority of the military commander, representing the occupying power, is derived
would have to be addressed. There are two possible answers to this question:
either he has been acting *ultra vires*, or Israel is the lawful sovereign. In the
nomos inhabited by the members of the Levy Committee, the latter is the
answer.[50] This reading of the law is informed by a strong narrative grounded in
the divine promise of the land to the Jewish people. That very narrative was
presented to the HCJ in the 1979 landmark case[51] known as *Elon Moreh*.[52]
The court, in rejecting the authority of the military commander to requisite
land in order to establish a settlement on grounds other than military needs,

---

[47] Y. Z. Blum, "The Missing Reversioner: Reflections on the Status of Judea and Samaria" (1968)
       3 *Israel Law Review* 279; M. Shamgar, "Legal Concepts and Problems of the Israeli Military
       Government – The Initial Stage," in M. Shamgar (ed.) *Military Government in the Territories
       Administered by Israel 1967–1980* 13 (Jerusalem: Sacher Institute, 1982), pp. 33–34. The LCR
       fails to refer to these authorities.
[48] See entry G: Geneva Law, Section G.2.
[49] E.g., GA Res 32/91 [A-C], UN Doc A/RES/32/91 [A-C] (December 13, 1977); SC Res 237, UN
       Doc S/RES/237 (June 14, 1967); Construction of a Wall, ¶ 101, states as follows: "Israel and
       Jordan were parties to that convention when the 1967 armed conflict broke out. The Court
       accordingly finds that than convention is applicable in the Palestinian territories which before
       the conflict lay to the east of the Green Line and which, during that conflict, were occupied by
       Israel, there being no need for any enquiry into the precise prior status of those territories";
       J. S. Pictet (ed.), *The Geneva Conventions of 12 August 1949, Commentary – IV Geneva
       Convention Relative to the Protection of Civilian Persons in Time of War* (Geneva:
       International Committee of the Red Cross, 1958), p. 22.
[50] The Judea and Samaria Settlement Regulation Law 2017 underscores this proposition: the
       Israeli parliament, not the military commander, enacted a law that applies directly to the
       territory and to its Palestinian inhabitants. This is a paradigmatic sovereign act. The law is
       discussed in entry R: Regularization.
[51] R. Shamir, "'Landmark Cases' and the Reproduction of Legitimacy: The Case of Israel's High
       Court of Justice" (1990) 24 *Law and Society Review* 781.
[52] HCJ 390/79 *Dweikat* v. *Government of Israel* (1979) 34(1) PD 1 [Hebrew]. For an analysis of the
       case see entry J: Jewish Settlements.

refused to impregnate the law with this narrative. It determined that had the argument that the law of belligerent occupation does not apply been accepted, the inescapable conclusion would have to be that the military commander acted without authority and the land would have had to be returned to its lawful Palestinian owners.[53] In hundreds of judgments since, the HCJ unequivocally held that the sole source of the legal authority of the military commander is the law of belligerent occupation.[54] In the nomos inhabited by the international community, inclusive of the HCJ, the applicable legal paradigm is the law of belligerent occupation. The Levy Committee had to step into this paradigm[55] in its quest for the holy grail that would put to rest any legal challenge to the Jewish settlements in the West Bank.

Even if the GC IV were to apply, posits the LCR, the "prevailing view" is that Article 49 paragraph 6 providing that "the Occupying shall not deport or transfer parts of its own civilian population into the territory it occupies,"[56] is inapplicable to the Jewish settlers in the West Bank.[57] This is so because the latter are "persons who sought to settle in Judea and Samaria not because they were 'deported' or 'exiled' thereto by force, but because of their worldview – the settlement of the Land of Israel."[58] The leap from this "worldview" to the "prevailing view" in international law reflects little more than wishful thinking. The "prevailing view" of the Security Council;[59] the General Assembly;[60] the International Court of Justice;[61] all of the United Nations Expert Committees, including the Human Rights Committee,[62] the Committee on Economic, Social and Cultural Rights,[63] and the Committee on the

---

[53] *Ibid.*, p. 12; HCJ 2056/04 *Beit Sourik Village Council v. Government of Israel* (2004) 58(5) PD 807, 828 [Hebrew; English translation available at http://elyon1.court.gov.il/Files_ENG/04/5 60/020/A28/04020560.A28.pdf].

[54] *Unprecedented*, annex A, lists more than 60 examples [Hebrew].

[55] As noted at above text and notes 22–30, the LCR offers an interpretation of Article 49(6) of the GC IV, as an alternative to its main proposition regarding the inapplicability of the entire law of belligerent occupation.

[56] Article 49(6) of the GC IV.   [57] See above text and notes 22–30.   [58] The LCR, ¶ 6.

[59] See, e.g., SC Res 465, UN Doc S/RES/465 (March 1, 1980); SC Res 2334, UN Doc S/RES/2334 (December 23, 2016).

[60] See, e.g., GA Res 2253 (ES–V), UN Doc A/RES/2253 (ES–V) (July 4, 1967) from 1967, through GA Res 67/229, UN Doc A/RES/67/229 (April 9, 2013) of 2013. A full list of over 200 decisions is provided in *Unprecedented*, appendix B.

[61] *Construction of a Wall*, ¶ 120.

[62] UN Doc CCPR/C/79/Add.93 (August 18, 1998); UN Doc CCPR/CO/78/ISR (August 5, 2003); UN Doc CCPR/C/ISR/CO/3 (September 10, 2010).

[63] UN Doc E/C.12/1/Add.27 (December 4, 1998); UN Doc E/C.12/1/Add.90 (May 25, 2003); UN Doc E/C.12/ISR/CO/3 (December 16, 2011).

Elimination of Racial Discrimination;[64] and the overwhelming majority of international legal experts[65] is that the settlements signify the transfer of residents of the occupying power to the occupied territory, a transfer which the provision prohibits regardless of its motive. This prohibition is customary[66] and is thus applicable even if the international legal community were to accept, miraculously, the LCR's position concerning the inapplicability of the *GC IV*.

The LCR, alas, fails to mention, let alone engage with any of these sources. It does cite the ICRC Commentary as a source supporting its interpretation of Article 49.[67] The commentary, however, offers no such support, and indeed, in light of the conservation principle, regards any demographic changes as prohibited.[68]

In this context, too, the LCR weaves a self-serving temporal web: in tracing the roots of the prohibition to Nazi *Judenrein* policies it seeks to suggest the audacity of a comparison between the latter and Jewish settlements in the OPT.[69] The commentary, however, clarifies that the prohibition on such practices predates the Second World War, and indeed was considered customary before the coming into force of the Geneva Conventions.[70] It further sheds light on its meaning and scope: its

---

[64] UN Doc A/49/18, ¶¶ 73–91 (August 19, 1994); UN Doc CERD/C/304/Add.45 (March 30, 1998); UN Doc CERD/C/ISR/CO/13 (June 14, 2007); UN Doc CERD/C/ISR/CO/14–16 (March 9, 2012).

[65] See e.g., A. Cassese, "Legal Considerations on the International Status of Jerusalem" (1986) 3 *Palestine Yearbook of International Law* 13; Roberts, "Prolonged Military Occupations"; J. H. H. Weiler, "Israel, the Territories and International Law: When Doves are Hawks," in A. E. Kellermann, K. Siehr, and T. Einhorn (eds.), *Israel Among the Nations* (Leiden: Kluwer Law International, 1998), p. 381; J. Crawford, "Opinion: Third Party Obligations with respect to Israeli Settlements in the Occupied Palestinian Territories," *TUC* (January 2012), www.tuc .org.uk/tucfiles/342/LegalOpinionIsraeliSettlements.pdf; E. Benvenisti, *The International Law of Occupation*, 2nd edn (Princeton: Princeton University Press, 2004); Y. Dinstein, "The International Legal Status of the West Bank and the Gaza Strip – 1998" (1999) 28 *Israel Yearbook of Human Rights* 37; O. Ben-Naftali and Y. Shany, *International Law between War and Peace* (Tel Aviv: Ramot, 2006) [Hebrew]; D. Kretzmer, *The Occupation of Justice: the Supreme Court of Israel and the Occupied Territories* (New York: State University of New York Press, 2002).

[66] Rule 130 of the ICRC's guide to customary IHL states that "States may not deport or transfer parts of their own civilian population into a territory they occupy," J. M. Henckaerts & L. Doswald-Beck, *Customary International Humanitarian Law, Volume 1: Rules* (reprinted with corrections, Cambridge: Cambridge University Press, 2009), p. 462.

[67] The LCR, ¶ 5.   [68] Pictet, *The Geneva Conventions*, p. 283.

[69] See the LCR's reference to Julius Stone, at ¶ 5.

[70] Pictet, *The Geneva Conventions*, p. 279. See also J. M. Henckaerts, "Deportation and Transfer of Civilians in Time of War" (1993–1994) 26 *Vanderbilt Journal of Transnational Law* 469, 480, 482–485, 500.

application is not restricted to forced transfer or deportation; the words "transfer" and "deport" "do not refer to the movement of protected persons but to the nationals of the occupying power," and the paragraph "provides protected persons with a valuable safeguard."[71]

A proper reading of the provision in the light of the commentary generated already in 1967, the advice given by the then legal advisor to the Israeli ministry of foreign affairs, Theodore Meron, that "civilian settlement in the administered territories contravenes explicit provisions of the Fourth Geneva Convention"; that the prohibition on such settlement is "categorical," that is, "not conditional upon the motives for the transfer or its objectives"; and that "its purpose is to prevent settlement in occupied territory of citizens of the occupying state."[72] This position was hushed and ignored.

Two later legislative developments signify the importance the international community attaches to the prohibition, in the process shedding a dim light on both the Jewish settlement in the OPT and on the LCR's interpretation: the first is reflected in Article 85(4)(a) of *AP I*,[73] which has transformed a violation of this prohibition from a breach of the *GC IV* into a "grave breach" thereof. This transformation was deemed necessary, according the ICRC Commentary, "because of the possible consequences for the population of the territory concerned from a humanitarian point of view."[74] The second development is articulated in Article 8(2)(b)(viii) of the Statute of the International Criminal Court (ICCSt). It designates as a war crime "the transfer, directly or indirectly, by the Occupying Power of parts of its own civilian population into the territory it occupies, or the deportation or transfer of all or parts of the population of the occupied territory within or outside this territory."[75] While concerned with individual responsibility, it does not, as noted by the International Law Commission, "relieve a state of any

---

[71] Pictet, *The Geneva Conventions*, p. 283.

[72] Memorandum from Theodore Meron to Mr. Adi Yafeh, Political Secretary to the Prime Minister, *Settlement in the Administered Territories* (classified as "top secret," September 18, 1967), www.soas.ac.uk/lawpeacemideast/resources/file48485.pdf.

[73] Protocol Additional to the Geneva Conventions of 12 August 1949, and relating to the Protection of Victims of International Armed Conflicts (Additional Protocol I), Geneva, June 8, 1977, 1125 UNTS 3 [hereinafter: *AP I*].

[74] C. Pilloud, J. de Preux, Y. Sandoz, B. Zimmermann, P. Eberlin, H. P. Gasser, and C. F. Wenger, *Commentary on the Additional Protocols of 8 June 1977 to the Geneva Conventions of 12 August 1949*, Y. Sandoz, C. Swinarski, and B. Zimmermann (eds.) (Geneva: Martinus Nijhof, 1987), p. 1000.

[75] Article 8(2)(b)(viii) of the Rome Statute of the International Criminal Court, UN Doc A/CONF. 183/9, 2187 UNTS 90 (July 17, 1998).

responsibilities under international law for an act or omission attributed to it."[76] The words "directly or indirectly" were inserted,

> to clearly express that indirect transfer policies are also covered ... such as confiscation laws, military or other protection of unlawful settlements, as well as economic and financial measures such as incentives, subsidies, exoneration of taxes and permits issued on a discriminatory basis ... the perpetrator does not need any particular motive or special intent other than the intent of transferring parts of the population of the occupying power into the occupied territory.[77]

Israel is neither a party to the *AP I* nor to the *ICCSt*, in large measure due to these provisions.[78] The latter, however, clearly indicates the "prevailing view" of international law. The LCR could have engaged with this view from a critical position.[79] Instead, it chose to reverse it.

It is in this light that one should read the concluding paragraph of the LCR's exposé of the international legal perspective. The Committee, reiterating Israel's unilateral commitment to apply the humanitarian provisions of the *GC IV* without thereby admitting any legal obligation to do so, stated that "consequently Israel had adopted a policy that allows Israelis to live in the area out of their own free will according to the rules established by the Israeli government and subject to the review of the Israeli legal system."[80] This conclusion alludes to the prohibition imposed on the occupying power to "transfer directly or indirectly" parts of its population to the occupied area, and appears to posit that the case of the settlements involves neither kinds: from

---

[76] Henckaerts, "Deportation and Transfer," p. 488, citing the Draft Code of Crimes Against the Peace and Security of Mankind, GA Res 95(I), UN Doc A/RES/95(I) (December 11, 1946).

[77] M. Cottier, "Article 8(2)(b)(viii)," in O. Triffterer (ed.), *Commentary on the Rome Statute of the International Criminal Court* (2nd edn., Baden-Baden: Nomos, 2008), p. 369.

[78] Israel's opposition to, inter-alia, Article 85(4)(a) of *AP I*, should probably be construed as a persistent objection. See C. Greenwood, "Terrorism and Humanitarian Law: The Debate Over Additional Protocol I" (1989) 19 *Israel Yearbook of Human Rights* 187. On its position regarding the ICCSt, see D. Benoliel and R. Perry, "Israel, Palestine, and the ICC" (2010–2011) 32 *Michigan Journal of International Law* 73; Y. Ronen, "ICC Jurisdiction over Acts Committed in the Gaza Strip: Article 12(3) of the ICC Statute and Non-state Entities" (2010) 8 *Journal of International Criminal Justice* 3; Y. Shany, "In Defence of Functional Interpretation of Article 12(3) of the Rome Statute: A Response to Yaël Ronen" (2010) 8 *Journal of International Criminal Justice* 329.

[79] See, e.g., M. Bothe, "War Crimes," in A. Cassese (ed.), *The Rome Statute of the International Criminal Court: A Commentary* (Oxford: Oxford University Press, 2002), p. 413; A. Levy, "Comments: Israel Rejects Its Own Offspring: The International Criminal Court" (1999–2000) 22 *Loyola L.A. International and Comparative Law Review* 207.

[80] The LCR, ¶ 9. This point resonates with the LCR's dismissal of the relevance of Article 49(6) of the *GC IV*, inter-alia on the grounds that the settlers were motivated to settle there "because of their world-view – the settlement of the land of Israel." The LCR, ¶ 6.

each settler's point of view, the decision to reside in a settlement is but an expression of free will.

There is no dispute that Israel did not force its citizens to settle in the West Bank. Yet, the dialectical relationship between consciousness and experience tends to draw a very thin line between being coerced and being coaxed. In the case at hand, the text of "individual free will" is to be read in the context of material governmental intervention.

There are currently more than 600,000 settlers living in the West Bank (including East Jerusalem).[81] Some of them surely gravitated to the territory on ideological grounds and would probably have done that without governmental incentives. The latter, however, explain the attraction of the area to the vast majority of Jews residing in the West Bank: coming from a lower socioeconomic strata,[82] the lure of subsidized housing located not too far from urban centers, new infrastructure, public education, health and welfare services that in Israel proper are undergoing privatization, and lower taxes is not to be dismissed.[83] These data suggest that where the LCR sees free will in pure form, a critical examination discloses a disciplinary matrix of law, ideology, and political economy.

The construction of a legal status for the settlements is the raison d'être of the Levy Committee. It explains not only its reading of Article 46 paragraph 6 of the GC IV, but also its determination regarding the irrelevance of the international law of belligerent occupation to the West Bank. Lurking behind the LCR's reading of the law is a vision. The vision is of an international law that vindicates Israel's exclusive sovereignty over the area. That international law, which ostensibly recognized the Jewish people's right to self-determination in Palestine, and only its right, is found in quasi-legal and legal documents from the early 1920s, primarily the 1922 Mandate for Palestine.[84] The clock, it would seem, has not just stopped ticking for the Palestinians; from the LCR's perspective of international law, it has actually

---

[81] According to the American Central Intelligence Agency, Central Intelligence Agency (CIA), *The World Factbook – Middle East: The West Bank*, https://www.cia.gov/library/publications/the-world-factbook/geos/we.html.

[82] D. Gutwien, "Comments on the Class Foundations of the Occupation" (2004) 24 *Theory and Criticism* 203 [Hebrew].

[83] *Ibid.*, p. 206. Various mechanisms facilitate these economic benefits, including the classification of numerous settlements as "national high priority area," a category traditionally intended for the socioeconomic periphery within the green line in numbers. See e.g., The Association for Civil Rights in Israel, *Situation Report: The State of Human Rights in Israel and the OPT 2012* (December 2012), pp. 77–83, www.acri.org.il/en/wp-content/uploads/2012/12/ACRI-Situation-Report-2012-ENG.pdf.

[84] See text between notes 30–33.

turned back to the era of colonialism, and, given the specificity of the chronotope,[85] of Orientalism.[86] This is the context which illuminates the third leg on which the legal position of the LCR rests:[87] the text of the Balfour Declaration, the San Remo Resolution, and the British Mandate.

Nobless oblige: The Balfour Declaration was made in a letter written by one nobleman, Lord Balfour, then foreign secretary of Great Britain, to another, Lord Rothschild, son of the first Jewish peer in England. It is perhaps no coincidence that the paradigmatic example Edward Said uses to explain the specific juxtaposition of knowledge and power that constitutes the Orientalist nomon in a lecture given by the very same Lord Balfour to justify the need for Britain to continue to exercise control over Egypt.[88] The then dominant international legal paradigm provided the colonialist enterprise with a seemingly objective, scientific apology for "the continuing subjugation of various regions of the world."[89] Within the Orientalist paradigm, the Indigenous population of Palestine, not European Jewry, was construed as the "other." The recognition of the Jews' right to build "a national home in Palestine," simultaneously preserving their political rights in Europe,[90] was not perceived as an anomaly.

Yet, even then, there was a whiff of change. The demise of the colonial project is attributable to a myriad of factors, including unease with the gap between self-proclaimed Western values of self-determination and equality and the dispossession and subjugation of the rest of the world. Europe remained the center of gravity, but it could no longer retain the identification of the European order with the international one. Membership in the League of Nations, which for the first time included non-European states on a footing of equality with European states, is one indicator that an alternative paradigm was emerging. In this context, the success of the Zionist movement to secure recognition in "the historical *connection* of the Jewish People in Palestine"

---

85   For the term "chronotope" see entry T: Temporary/Indefinite.
86   E. W. Said, *Orientalism* (London: Penguin Classics, 2003).
87   See above text and note 31.   88   Said, *Orientalism*, p. 32.
89   J. Allain, "Orientalism and International Law" (2004) 17 *Leiden Journal of International Law* 391, 391.
90   The Balfour Declaration, San Remo Resolution, and Mandate for Palestine all incorporate the phrase: "it being clearly understood that nothing should be done which might prejudice the civil and religious rights of existing non-Jewish communities in Palestine." See *Mandate for Palestine*, League of Nations Doc C.529M.314 1922 VI (August 12, 1922); A photographed copy of The Balfour Declaration, November 2, 1917, is reproduced in J. N. Moore (ed.), *The Arab-Israeli Conflict, Volume 3: Documents* (New Jersey: Princeton, 1974), p. 885. The text of the declaration is available at www.jewishvirtuallibrary.org/text-of-the-balfour-declaration; The text of The San Remo Resolution, April 25, 1920, is available at www.mideastweb.org/san_remo_palestine_1920.htm.

and in the "establishment *in* Palestine of *a* national home for the Jewish people,"[91] should be read against its failure to substitute the term "title" for "connection" and to secure Palestine *as the* national home of the Jewish people.[92] The interpretation offered by then secretary of state for the colonies, Winston Churchill, in his White Paper further signifies this change: the Balfour Declaration, he clarified, never contemplated that "Palestine as a whole should be converted into a Jewish National Home, but that such a Home should be founded in Palestine."[93] This 1922 reading of the meaning of the Mandate and its antecedent documents, as understood by the Mandatory Power, should have caused the members of the Levy Committee to at least pause before marshaling Article 80 of the UN Charter as a ground for invalidating the Partition Plan.[94] Later developments relative to the colonialist paradigm should have propelled them to rethink the validity of their own nomos. In such rethinking, alas, they have not engaged.

The noble of a by-gone nomos often becomes the ignoble of later years. Loss of faith in the colonialist paradigm led to the consideration of alternatives, and eventually to its denunciation. The current membership in the United Nations attests to the overwhelming normative acceptance of the new paradigm, revolving around the core principles of sovereign equality, self-determination, and nonintervention.[95] It is not without significance to recall that given that these principles have not been inscribed on a tabula rasa, "alien occupation" echoes the soggy saga of the discarded colonialist paradigm. It is for this reason that the disciplinary matrix of international law groups belligerent occupation together with colonial domination, racist regimes[96] and related practices of subjugation, domination, and

---

[91]   *Mandate for Palestine* (emphasis added).
[92]   See Proposals for Palestine Mandate, March 20, 1919, UK National Archives FO 608/100 (emphasis added).
[93]   See House of Commons, 23 *Sessional Papers*, 1922, Cmd 1700 (UK), pp. 17–21. See generally, V. Kattan, "Palestine and International Law: An Historical Overview," in V. Kattan (ed.), *The Palestine Question in International Law* (London: British Institute of International and Comparative Law, 2008), p. xxv.
[94]   See above text between notes 31–33. Article 80 of the UN Charter, ¶ 1 provides: "Except as may be agreed upon in individual trusteeship agreements … nothing in this Chapter shall be construed in or of itself to alter in any manner the rights whatsoever of any states or any peoples or the terms of existing international instruments to which Members of the United Nations may respectively be parties."
[95]   Article 2 of the UN Charter, ¶¶ 1, 2, and 55; Article 1, ¶ 1 of the International Covenant on Civil and Political Rights, opened for signature December 19, 1966, 999 UNTS 171 (entered into force March 23, 1976).
[96]   Article 4 of AP I.

exploitation.[97] A new international legal order has replaced the Eurocentric legal order. The LCR remains deeply rooted in the latter.

The LCR's anachronistic reading of the international legal matrix, in terms of both the epistemic method used and its ontological consequences, is the Ariadne's thread that is woven into its construction of the invalidity of the 1947 Partition Plan, the indeterminacy of the 1949 armistice lines, and the 1988 Jordan's waiver of a claim to sovereignty over the West Bank,[98] in a manner that generates the foregone conclusion that Israel has a valid claim to sovereignty over the area. This claim, asserts the LCR, has been upheld by successive Israeli governments which refrained from realizing it through annexation only because of their wish to "enable peace negotiations."[99]

The legal validity of General Assembly Resolution 181 (the partition plan), was subject to some debate at the time, but not for the reasons advanced in the LCR. The debate focused on the competence of the General Assembly: on the one hand, it is not a legislative body, and is therefore empowered merely to make recommendations;[100] on the other hand, the General Assembly succeeded the Council of the League of Nations, and the latter was competent to make binding decisions regarding Mandate territories.[101] The rejection of the Resolution by Arab States, posited in the LCR as a ground for its invalidity, reflected their sense that the partition was inequitable and that the proposed Arab state would not be economically viable. This stand was surely significant politically, but not legally. By contrast, Israel's embrace of the Resolution, which the LCR is silent about, carries a legal impact: given that in 1948 the government of Israel saw fit to ground Israel's statehood in this Resolution and indeed incorporated a paragraph therefrom into its Declaration of Independence,[102] it is estopped from arguing against the Resolution's validity.[103]

---

[97]   See the Declaration on Principles of International Law Concerning Friendly Relations and Co-operation Among States in Accordance with the Charter of the United Nations, GA Res 2625 (XXV), UN Doc A/RES/25/2625 (October 24, 1970).

[98]   The LCR, ¶ 8.   [99]   The LCR, ¶ 9.   [100]   Articles 10–14 of the UN Charter.

[101]   This was the position of then Secretary-General Trygve Lie; see A. W. Cordier and W. Foote (eds.), *Public Papers of the Secretaries-General of the United Nations, vol. 1: Trygve Lie, 1946–1953* (New York: Columbia University Press, 1969), pp. 106–115. See also, R. J. Tyner, "Wars of National Liberation in Africa and Palestine: Self-Determination for Peoples or for Territories" (1978–1979) 5 *Yale Studies in World Public Order* 234, 265.

[102]   Declaration of Establishment of State of Israel from May 14, 1948, www.mfa.gov.il/mfa/forei gnpolicy/peace/guide/pages/declaration%20of%20establishment%20of%20state%20of%20isr ael.aspx. The Declaration refers to the Partition Plan as "calling for the establishment of a Jewish State in Eretz-Israel ... This recognition by the United Nations of the right of the Jewish people to establish their State is irrevocable."

[103]   On estoppel under international law, see The Temple of Preah Vihear (Cambodia v. Thailand), 1962 ICJ Rep 6, ¶¶ 22–26; P. C. W. Chan, "Acquiescence/Estoppel in

The LCR is equally silent about the 1988 Palestinian Declaration of Independence which also accepted the Resolution as providing international legitimacy to the "right of the Palestinian Arab people to sovereignty."[104]

Finally, in the words of the ICJ, "the responsibility of the United Nations" in matters relative to the Israeli–Palestinian conflict, "has its origin in the Mandate and the Partition Resolution concerning Palestine."[105] Having been referred to in numerous later resolutions, including the resolution which requested the ICJ to render an advisory opinion on the legality of the construction of the wall in the OPT,[106] GA Resolution 181 reflects the universally accepted basis for the establishment in the land of Mandatory Palestine of "two independent States, one Arab, the other Jewish."[107]

The road leading the Levy Committee to its destination regarding exclusive Jewish sovereignty over Mandatory Palestine passes through two additional signposts: the 1949 armistice lines and the 1988 Jordanian waiver of sovereignty over the West Bank. The armistice lines were drawn in various agreements, pursuant to Security Council Resolution 62 (1948).[108] The Rhodes Agreement of April 1949 between Israel and Jordan fixed the demarcation line known as the "Green Line."[109] The latter was never officially designated as a final boundary and indeed the agreement itself allows for revisions by mutual consent.[110] It does not, however, follow that the Green Line is devoid of legal meaning, let alone that Israel has a sovereign right in the OPT. Quite the opposite: so long as such consent has not been reached, and given the principle of nonacquisition of territory by force, "the Palestinian territories east of the Green Line," in the words of the ICJ, "are occupied."[111] By the same token, Jordan's waiver of its claim to sovereignty over the West Bank does not generate the LCR's conclusion that said waiver "has restored the original legal

---

International Boundaries: Temple of Preah Vihear Revisited" (2004) 3 *Chinese Journal of International Law* 421. The ICJ revisited the case in 2013, following the Request for Interpretation of the Judgment of 15 June 1962 in the Case Concerning the Temple of Preah Vihear (Cambodia v. Thailad), Judgment, 2013 ICJ Rep 281 (November 11, 2013), www.icj-cij .org/docket/files/151/17704.pdf. See S. Chesterman, "The International Court of Justice in Asia: Interpreting the Temple of Preah Vihear Case" (2015) 5 *Asian Journal of International Law* 1.

[104] Palestine National Council, November 15, 1988; See Y. Lukacs, *The Israeli-Palestinian Conflict: a documentary record, 1967–1990*, 2nd edn (Cambridge: Cambridge University Press, 1992).

[105] Construction of a Wall, ¶ 49.

[106] *Ibid.*, ¶ 1; GA Res ES-10/14, UN Doc A/RES/ES-10/14 (December 12, 2003).

[107] Construction of a Wall, ¶ 76.   [108] SC Res 62, UN Doc S/1080 (November 16, 1948).

[109] Hashemite Jordan Kingdom – Israel: General Armistice Agreement, UN Doc S/1302/Rev.1 (April 3, 1949), adopted by the Security Council in SC Res 72, UN Doc S/RES/72 (August 11, 1949).

[110] Armistice Agreement, *ibid.*, Article IX.   [111] Construction of a Wall, ¶¶ 78, 101.

status of the territory," that is, Jewish sovereignty.[112] It does not because the original legal status of the territory was not, and was not intended to be, under Jewish sovereignty.

The nomos inhabited by the members of the Levy Committee consists of entirely different terrains and shades of visibility. There, there is no Palestinian people vested with a right to self-determination; the West Bank is *terra nullius*,[113] an empty space; "a land without people" still awaiting to be restored "to a people without a land";[114] a land over which Jews have always had a right of possession; a land promised once by the good Lord and once again by another Lord representing the British Empire; indeed, a land impregnated with Jewish sovereignty. In the nomos inhabited by the rest of the international community, there is a right to self-determination. That right exists *erga omnes*.[115] That right "was the ultimate objective of the mandate system."[116] That right stems from a principle enshrined in the UN Charter. The Palestinian people enjoy this right, and thus have a claim to sovereignty over the territory. Israel is under an obligation to respect this right.[117] The admission of Palestine as a member state to various international governmental organizations has not settled the debate on whether or not it meets the criteria of statehood,[118] but it surely attests to the overwhelming view of the international community on the right of the Palestinians to exercise self-determination in the form of a Palestinian state in the OPT.

There can be little doubt that Israel's actual display of respect for the Palestinian claim to sovereignty over the OPT leaves a lot to be desired. From a normative perspective, however, and contrary to the assertion of the

---

[112] Above text between notes 34–36.
[113] See Western Sahara, Advisory Opinion, 1975 ICJ 12, ¶¶ 79–80 ("[T]he State practice of the relevant period indicates that territories inhabited by tribes or peoples having a social and political organization were not regarded as *terrae nullius* . . . the acquisition of sovereignty was not generally considered as effected unilaterally through 'occupation' of *terra nullius* by original title but through agreements concluded with local rulers").
[114] This phrase, attributed to British writer Israel Zangwill, was first used in the writings of nineteenth-century Evangelical writers. On its genesis see D. Muir, "A Land Without People for a People Without a Land" (2008) XV *Middle East Quarterly* 55.
[115] Construction of a Wall, ¶ 155; Continued Presence of South Africa in Namibia (South West Africa) Notwithstanding Security Council Resolution, 276 (1970), Advisory Opinion, 1971 ICJ 16, ¶ 126; East Timor (Portugal v. Australia), 1995 ICJ Rep 90, ¶ 29.
[116] Construction of a Wall, ¶ 88.   [117] *Ibid.*
[118] See, e.g., F. A. Boyle, "The Creation of the State of Palestine" (1990) 1 *European Journal of International Law* 301; J. Crawford, "The Creation of the State of Palestine: Too Much Too Soon?" (1990) 1 *European Journal of International Law* 307.

LCR, from the early 1990s successive Israeli governments did recognize this claim.[119]

The odyssey undertaken by the Levy Committee requires it to explain why Israel, as the lawful sovereign of the West Bank, did not simply annex it. The explanation, according to the LCR, is Israel's wish "to enable peace negotiations."[120] This policy assessment may well qualify as an apology for power, but it is neither a legal argument nor is it convincing in view of the de jure annexation of Jerusalem,[121] surely a major issue in the peace negotiations. Indeed, it serves to obfuscate rather than illuminate the puzzle. Could it not be that Israel did not annex the territories because it has, at least thus far, gained more than it lost by keeping its current form of control over the OPT? The ontology of this occupation suggests that legal indeterminacy has thus far been its determinate feature, and offers an alternative explanation: it has allowed Israel to act as a sovereign in the OPT, settle its citizens there, and extend to them its laws, yet avoid international accountability for having illegally annexed the territories; it has allowed Israel to pursue the policies of "Greater Israel" in the West Bank without jeopardizing its Jewish majority.[122]

These policies advance a hegemonic vision. The structural indeterminacy inherent in the application of the international legal paradigm of the law of

---

[119]   For an Israeli recognition of the reciprocal political rights of both people see e.g., the agreements constituting the Oslo Accord, see Declaration of Principles on Interim Self-Government Arrangements (September 13, 1993), www.knesset.gov.il/process/asp/event_frame.asp?id=37; Agreement on the Gaza Strip and the Jericho Area (May 4, 1994), www .knesset.gov.il/process/asp/event_frame.asp?id=38; the Israeli-Palestinian Interim Agreement on the West Bank and the Gaza Strip (September 28, 1995), www.mfa.gov.il/mfa/foreign policy/peace/guide/pages/the%20israeli-palestinian%20interim%20agreement.aspx; Protocol Concerning the Redeployment in Hebron (January 15, 1997), www.knesset.gov.il/process/asp/ event_frame.asp?id=45; and the Wye River Memorandum (October 23, 1998), http://mfa.gov .il/MFA/ForeignPolicy/Peace/Guide/Pages/The%20Wye%20River%20Memorandum.aspx. Even Prime Minister Netanyahu in his 2009 Bar Ilan speech recognized the two-state solution. The full text of the speech is available at www.haaretz.com/news/full-text-of-netanyahu-s-foreign-policy-speech-at-bar-ilan-1.277922.

[120]   The LCR, ¶ 9.

[121]   Israel initially objected to the use of the term "annexation" to describe its imposing of Israeli law and administration on East Jerusalem, claiming it was done for purely municipal and administrative reasons. The Basic Law: Jerusalem, The Capital of Israel, 34 LSI 209 (1980), put this objection to rest. From an international legal perspective the annexation of East Jerusalem (expanding gradually its boundaries from 6.5 to 71 square kilometers) is illegal. This illegality was affirmed by both the Security Council and the General Assembly and the ICJ. See SC Res 478, UN Doc S/RES/478 (August 20, 1980); GA Res 35/169E, UN Doc A/RES/35/ 169E (December 15, 1980); SC Res 673, UN Doc S/INF/46 (October 24, 1990); Construction of a Wall, ¶¶ 74–75, 120–122.

[122]   O. Ben-Naftali, A. M. Gross, and K. Michaeli, "Illegal Occupation: Framing the Occupied Palestinian Territory" (2005) 23 *Berkeley Journal of International Law* 551, 609–12 (2005).

belligerent occupation by Israeli governmental and judicial authorities to the
territory has served as an apology for power which has facilitated the piecemeal
realization of this vision. The LCR steps out of the structural confinements of
the discipline. It does not present an argument *intra-legem*. It is, quite simply,
contra-legem. It reflects an insular yet hegemonic vision of power and destiny
that requires no apology.

N.4 CONCLUDING THOUGHTS

Looking at life through the wrong end of the telescope, much like being
nostalgic for the future, may well have its rewards. At times, it may even
transcend individual self-deception and become a political force driving
a backward-looking revolution. Scientific/disciplinary revolutions, however,
do not develop anachronistically.

The profession of faith is not to be confused with a profession. The deep
conviction shared by the members of the Levy Committee in the sovereign
right of the Jewish people to the entire land of Mandatory Palestine is not
shared by the international community. The failing of the LCR is not, however, to be attributed to the mere fact that its reading of the relevant international legal paradigm differs from the prevailing view. The position
maintained by a majority is not necessarily closer to the truth than the position
espoused by the few. It is not a quantitative, but a qualitative blemish that
stains the LCR.

In epistemic terms, inhabiting a nomos in an engaged, productive way,
much like working creatively within a disciplinary matrix, may well require
the poetic imagination of Don Quixote, but it also necessitates the prag-
matic bookkeeping of Sancho Panza. The disciplinary straitjacket is the
mantle of the creative scientist.[123] The members of the Levy Committee,
alas, did not merely offer an interpretation of the prevailing international
legal paradigm different from that shared by the majority of experts; they
ignored the latter and advanced a paradigm they had discarded, indeed
discredited. It does not follow that at times, an out-of-date paradigm cannot
be resurrected "as a special case of its up-do-date successor," as Kuhn
acknowledges, but "it must be transformed for the purpose."[124] No trace
of such transformation can be detected in any of the stale arguments of
the LCR.

The offering of an organizing principle for a community to adopt is the
essence of utopian thinking. Insofar as a real place is experienced by

---

[123] Kuhn, *Scientific Revolutions*, pp. 144–145.   [124] *Ibid.*, p. 103.

a community as no place (outopia), generating a wish to reach a good place (eutopia),[125] there is nothing wrong with such thinking. There is also nothing wrong in impregnating legal texts with a meaning that reflects a particular vision shared by a minority. Indeed, in pluralistic communities such as the international community, a majority is not ipso facto right. The question of right or wrong depends on the nature of the utopian vision, as determined by the relevant community in a discursive process. A nomic insularity that does not engage in this process, renounces it.

The relevant community is the international community.[126] The nomos inhabited by that community was clearly expressed by Security Council Resolution 2334 of December 23, 2016: reaffirming a string of previous resolutions, the purposes and principles of the Charter, most specifically the inadmissibility of the acquisition of territory by force, and Israel's obligation as the occupying power "to abide scrupulously by its legal obligations" under the GC IV, it condemned "all measures aimed at altering the demographic composition, character and status of the Palestinian Territory occupied since 1967, including East Jerusalem." Such measures "include, *inter alia*, the construction and expansion of settlements, transfer of Israeli settlers, confiscation of land, demolition of homes and displacement of Palestinian civilians, in violation of international humanitarian law and relevant resolutions." Having expressed "grave concern that continuing Israeli settlement activities are dangerously imperiling the viability of the two-State solution based on the 1967 lines," the operative paragraphs of the resolution state that "the establishment by Israel of settlements in the Palestinian Territory occupied since 1967, including East Jerusalem, has no legal validity and constitutes a flagrant violation under international law and a major obstacle to the achievement of the two-State solution and a just, lasting and comprehensive peace"; demand that Israel immediately and completely cease all settlement activities in the OPT, including East Jerusalem; underline that "it will not recognize any changes to the 4 June 1967 lines, including with regard to Jerusalem, other than those agreed by the parties through negotiations"; and call on "all States to distinguish, in their relevant dealings, between the territory of the State of Israel and the territories occupied since 1967."[127]

---

[125]   Thomas More's "Utopia" is a pun of the original Greek terms "outopia" and "eutopia." T. More, *Utopia*, P. Turner (trans.) (London: Penguin Books, 1965) (1516); M. Parker, "Utopia and the Organizational Imagination: Eutopia," in M. Parker (ed.), *Utopia and Organization* (Oxford: Blackwell, 2002), p. 217.

[126]   See Construction of a Wall, ¶ 49.   [127]   SC Res 2334, preamble and ¶¶ 1–3, 5.

This, then, is the "prevailing view," the nomos, of the international community.[128] Read in the light of this response, the LCR's coupling of nomian insularity with a hegemonic vision seems senseless, indeed "quite mad,"[129] at least insofar as our current normative universe is concerned.

---

[128] Cf. the LCR ¶ 5.   [129] Cover, "Nomos and Narrative," p. 10.

O

Outside/Inside

Hedi Viterbo

O.1 INTRODUCTION: ISRAEL'S DUALITY TOWARD THE WEST BANK AND GAZA STRIP

Israel/Palestine is a political regime whose different territories are all effectively subject, as shown throughout this book, to varying forms and degrees of Israeli control. The slash in "Israel/Palestine" intimates a duality in Israel's relation toward both Palestinians and the West Bank and Gaza Strip.

On the one hand, this slash denotes the separation and exclusion, desired and/or actual, of certain Palestinian territories and populations from "Israel proper." This side of the duality – explored in other entries in this book[1] – manifests itself in Israeli legal discourse in a myriad of ways. For example, the supreme court has referred to prisoners from the West Bank – including residents of Area C, where Israel retains full authority over security and civil matters according to the Oslo Accords[2] – as "foreign prisoners" residing "outside the borders of the State of Israel."[3] The Israeli judiciary has also tended to distinguish "Israeli law" (referring exclusively to what can be called the "domestic law"[4]) from the "military law," as if the former does not include the latter. The supreme court has thus spoken of "the differences between penalties under Israeli law and those under security legislation in the [West Bank] area,"[5] and

---

[1] See especially entries A: Assigned Residence, B: Border/Barrier, K: Kinship, P: Proportionality, Q: Quality of Life, V: Violence, X: X Rays, and Z: Zone.

[2] See entry Z: Zone, Section Z.2.2.2.1 ("The Partition of the West Bank Into Areas A, B, and C").

[3] HCJ 4644/15 *Ra'ee* v. *Prison Service* (June 15, 2016), ¶ 1 of justice Vogelman's opinion. For a publication of Israel's national prison authority using the same terminology, see D. Valk, "We and the World – Incarceration Figures in Israel and Other Countries" (2012) 33 *Seeing Shabas* 27 [Hebrew], http://shabas.millenium.org.il/Items/04434/33.pdf.

[4] The phrase "domestic law" is in inverted commas given the legal porosity between the outside and the (supposedly domestic) inside of Israel.

[5] HCJ 1073/06 *Masalme* v. *Military Court of Appeals in the Judea and Samaria* Area (March 26, 2006), ¶ 2 of justice Rubinstein's opinion.

302 Outside/Inside

has also described, similarly, how "the military courts have dedicated large portions of their judgments to the question of the weight they should give to Israeli law."[6] Military courts themselves have likewise considered their "connection to Israeli law," given, among other things, that sometimes cases are simultaneously adjudicated "both in Israeli courts and in the military courts."[7] Such distinctions between "Israeli" and "military" law have also appeared in reports of human rights NGOs.[8] The perception of the military law that Israel applies to noncitizen Palestinians as somehow external to Israeli law may also explain why the military law is very rarely taught and researched in Israeli law schools – an issue discussed in one of this book's other entries.[9]

On the other hand, "Israel proper" is also closely connected to, and deeply influenced and informed by, the Israeli practices, laws, and policies toward the Palestinian populations and territories conquered in 1967. This entry examines how this side of the duality – namely, the inseparability of "Israel proper" from these territories – precludes a demarcation between Israel's professed "inside" and "outside," between the seeming legal–political "norm" and its "exception." Other entries demonstrate, relatedly, that Israel's control over these territories is far from temporary;[10] that the West Bank has been increasingly annexed to Israel, formally or effectively;[11] that the Gaza Strip remains under considerable Israeli control despite the unilateral pullout in 2005;[12] and that Israel's practices and policies toward noncitizen Palestinians have traversed and impacted far beyond Israel/Palestine.[13] All of this further highlights the failure of the term "occupation" to convey Israel's actual control regime – a conceptual issue tackled elsewhere, in this book[14] and beyond.[15]

Israel's duality toward the West Bank and Gaza cuts across Israeli discourse and practice. For example, a recent poll found that 44.3 percent of Israeli Jews support the annexation of the entire West Bank, whereas 38 percent oppose it. When further asked whether Palestinians in the annexed territory should be granted full and equal civil rights, 48 percent of Israeli Jews replied in the

---

6 HCJ 7932/08 *Elharub* v. *Military Commander in the Judea and Samaria Area* (December 29, 2009), ¶ 12 of Justice Rubinstein's opinion.
7 MilC (Judea Mil. Ct.) 353/03 *Military Advocate General* v. *Abu Snine* (April 4, 2004).
8 See, e.g., B'Tselem – The Israeli Information Center for Human Rights in the Occupied Territories, *No Minor Matter: Violation of the Rights of Palestinian Minors Arrested by Israel on Suspicion of Stone-Throwing* (2011), pp. 8–16, www.btselem.org/download/201107_no_minor_matter_eng.pdf (dedicating separate sections to analyzing "Israeli law" and "military law").
9 See entry M: Military Courts.   10 See entry T: Temporary/Indefinite.
11 See entries B: Border/Barrier, N: Nomos, R: Regularization, and Z: Zone.
12 See entries Q: Quality of Life, V: Violence, and Z: Zone.
13 See entry E: Export of Knowledge.   14 See Introduction, Section 1.1 ("Subject Matters").
15 See Y. Shenhav, "Why Not 'The Occupation'" (2007) 31 *Theory & Criticism* 5, 5–9 [Hebrew].

negative and 42 percent in the positive.[16] A similar duality characterizes Israeli legal discourse. In a 2016 supreme court judgment, for instance, justice Shoham remarked that "the law, adjudication, and administration of the State of Israel do not apply in [the West Bank] . . . This area has not been annexed to Israel [and] . . . the state's laws have not been applied to it." Justice Amit, however, noted: "I concur with [justice Shoham's] . . . conclusion, but . . . I shall not consider issues concerning the applicability of Israeli law [in the West Bank]."[17] A list of similar examples could go on endlessly.[18]

A growing body of academic writing has sought to analyze this duality.[19] In the late 1980s, Israeli jurist Amnon Rubinstein (who has also served as a minister in two governments) noted that the partition between "Israel proper" and the West Bank and Gaza Strip had gradually eroded, both legally and economically. Israel, he suggested, had shifted from perceiving these territories as an "escrow" under international law to incorporating them into the realm of its rule as a sort of "legal mongrel."[20] A decade later, Israeli sociologist Adriana Kemp pointed out that a separation–inclusion duality characterizes Israel's relation not only to the West Bank and Gaza Strip, but also to its Palestinian citizens. Since 1948, she argued, Israel had incorporated this population as citizens and subjects while at the same time excluding and separating them as "dangerous" others, spatially and discursively.[21]

Israeli sociologist Yehuda Shenhav, cultural theorist Ariella Azoulay, and philosopher Adi Ophir have provided further insights on the subject.

16 Channel 2 News, "48% of Israeli Jews: The Left is Disloyal to the Country," *Channel 2 News* (December 6, 2016) [Hebrew], www.mako.co.il/news-israel/education-q4_2016/Article-7d2 c28c4bf2d851004.htm.
17 CivA 2050/16 *Angel* v. *Civil Administration in Judea and Samaria* (December 22, 2016), ¶ 28 of justice Shoham's opinion and the opening (unnumbered) paragraph of justice Amit's opinion [Hebrew].
18 See, e.g., entry R: Regularization.
19 In addition to the references that follow, see also, e.g., A. Arnon, "Between 'Two' and 'One': Economics Between the Sea and Jordan Since 1967" (2007) 31 *Theory and Criticism* 45 [Hebrew]; M. Benvenisti, "In Favor of a Binational Solution of the Conflict" (2009) 20 *Mita'am* [Hebrew]; I. Schnell, "Geographical Ramifications of the Occupation on Israeli Society," in D. Bar-Tal and I. Schnell (eds.), *The Impacts of Lasting Occupation: Lessons from Israeli Society* (Oxford: Oxford University Press, 2013), pp. 93–121.
20 A. Rubinstein, "The Changing Status of the 'Territories' (West Bank and Gaza): From Escrow to Legal Mongrel" (1988) 8 *Tel Aviv University Studies in Law* 59. See also O. Ben-Naftali, A. M. Gross, and K. Michaeli, "Illegal Occupation: Framing the Occupied Palestinian Territory" (2005) 23 *Berkeley Journal of International Law* 551 (revisiting Rubinstein's thesis and assessing the legality of the Israeli "occupation" in light of the blurring of the "rule"/ "exception" distinction).
21 A. Kemp, "The Mirror Language of the Borders: Territorial Borders and the Establishment of a National Minority in Israel" (1999) 2 *Israeli Sociology* 319 [Hebrew] [hereinafter: "The Mirror Language of the Borders"].

According to Shenhav, the 1967 conquest enabled the Israeli Zionist left –
which up to that point had struggled to reconcile its idealistic self-image with
its complicity in the harm and injustice done to Palestinians – to easily
distinguish "here" from "there," "normal Israel" from the West Bank and
Gaza Strip, and, eventually, good Israelis from "bad settlers." What this false
divide obfuscates, he contends, is that Israel's rule over these territories is
deeply woven into, produced by, and facing toward Israeli society itself.[22]
Along similar lines, Azoulay and Ophir have jointly argued that the conception of the control over these territories as temporary and external to the Israeli
regime, and of noncitizen Palestinians as outside enemies, helps maintain
Israel's self-image as a democratic state. As they note, however, Israeli Jews
who are less concerned with the democratic image or elements of their
country accept, more willingly and openly, the Israeli regime for what it really
is: an apparatus of permanent and inclusive separation designed to preserve
Israel's Jewish character.[23]

This entry sheds light on two key, interrelated aspects of the legal and
political inseparability of "Israel proper" from the "Palestinian territories."
The first, analyzed in Section O.2, is the continuity between the post-1967
Israeli control regime and pre-1967 practices and policies. In particular, the
analysis engages with Israel's military rule over its Palestinian citizens from
1948 to 1966, with the Israeli occupation of the Gaza Strip from 1956 to 1957,
with the devising of the legal infrastructure for a belligerent occupation of the
West Bank in the early 1960s, and with various legacies of British Mandate and
Ottoman law. The second aspect, examined in Section O.3, is the legal and
political porosity of the 1949 Armistice border (Israel's pre-1967 delimitation,
known in Israel as the "Green Line").[24] Three key elements of this porosity will
be analyzed: the expansion of domestic and military jurisdiction into both
sides of this border; the growing convergence of Israeli military and domestic
laws, with a focus on developments in the area of youth justice during the first
two decades of the twenty-first century; and, finally, parallels and connections

---

[22]   Y. Shenhav, "The Red Line of the Green Line: The Left and the Al-Aqsa Intifada," in A. Ophir
       (ed.), *Real Time* (Ben Shemen: Keter, 2001) [Hebrew]; Y. Shenhav, "The Occupation Does
       Not Stop at the Checkpoint," in Y. Menuchin (ed.), *Occupation and Refusal* (Tel Aviv:
       November Books, 2006) [Hebrew]. See also Y. Shenhav, *Beyond the Two-State Solution:
       A Jewish Political Essay*, D. Reider (trans.) (Cambridge: Polity Press, 2012), p. 5 (arguing that
       the border supposedly separating Israel from the West Bank and Gaza Strip is a "cultural
       myth," whose power as such grows the more it becomes blurred in actuality).
[23]   A. Azoulay and A. Ophir, *The One-State Condition: Occupation and Democracy in the State of
       Israel/Palestine* (Stanford: Stanford University Press, 2012), pp. 12, 18–19, 183, 221–225 [herein-
       after: *The One-State Condition*].
[24]   On the 1949 Armistice lines, or the "Green Line," see also entry Z: Zone.

between Israel's treatment of two groups of non-Jewish noncitizens: Palestinians outside the country's pre-1967 borders, and African asylum seekers. The concluding section summarizes the entry's key findings and argues, additionally, that the ambiguity of the "outside"/"inside" (and "exception"/ "rule") distinctions is by no means entirely unique to Israel/Palestine. This suggests that these seemingly opposite concepts are, in fact, neither historically nor structurally antithetical.

O.2 BEFORE 1967

The legal and political infrastructure for Israel's rule over the West Bank and Gaza Strip was in place long before Israel actually gained control of these territories in 1967. Notwithstanding important differences between the pre- and post-1967 contexts, and despite the absence of a simple linear connection between them, this historical continuity is crucial for understanding the Israeli control regime.

With the establishment of the state of Israel in 1948, emergency regulations enacted during the British Mandate period were absorbed, with some modification, into Israeli legislation, despite the Jewish community's earlier outrage when the British were the ones imposing these regulations on them.[25] To this day, the country remains under a state of emergency.[26] The emergency regulations and the measures they authorized were enforced almost exclusively against Palestinians, even though in principle they could apply to Jews as well.[27]

In particular, emergency regulations provided the legal basis for the military government[28] that was established in 1948 in zones inhabited by the vast

[25] A. Korn, "Political Control and Crime: The Use of Defense (Emergency) Regulations During the Military Government" (2004) 4 *Adalah's Review* 23, 23–24 [hereinafter: "Political Control and Crime"]; S. Robinson, *Citizen Strangers: Palestinians and the Birth of Israel's Liberal Settler State* (Stanford: Stanford University Press, 2013), pp. 41–42 [hereinafter: *Citizen Strangers*].

[26] For analysis, see Y. Mehozay, *Between the Rule of Law and States of Emergency: The Fluid Jurisprudence of the Israeli Regime* (Albany: State University of New York Press, 2016).

[27] I. Abu-Saad, "Palestinian Education in Israel: The Legacy of the Military Government" (2006) 5 *Holy Land Studies* 21, 22–23 [hereinafter: "Palestinian Education in Israel"]; Robinson, *Citizen Strangers*, pp. 47–48; M. Sabri, "The Legal Status of Israeli Arabs" (1973) 3 *Iyunei Mishpat* 568, 569–571 [Hebrew] [hereinafter: "The Legal Status of Israeli Arabs"].

[28] Y. Bäuml, "The Military Government," in N. N. Rouhana and A. Sabbagh-Khoury (eds.), *The Palestinians in Israel: Readings in History, Politics and Society* (Haifa: Mada al-Carmel, 2011), p. 49 [hereinafter: "The Military Government"]; Korn, "Political Control and Crime," pp. 24–25; D. Kretzmer, *The Legal Status of the Arabs in Israel* (Boulder: Westview Press, 1990), p. 54; I. Lustick, *Arabs in the Jewish State: Israel's Control of a National Minority* (Austin: University of Texas Press, 1980), pp. 177–178 [hereinafter: *Arabs in the Jewish State*]; Y. Mehozay, "The Fluid Jurisprudence of Israel's Emergency Powers: Legal Patchwork as

majority of the Palestinians who remained within the new state after the war.[29] For the first two years, the military referred to these areas as "Administered Territories,"[30] the same term Israel would later apply to the West Bank and Gaza Strip. Central elements of Israel's rule in the West Bank and Gaza, as discussed throughout this book, were developed or honed during this nearly 20-year-long military rule: travel permits, checkpoints, and other restrictions of movement;[31] military courts;[32] "administrative detention";[33] preemptive measures;[34] land expropriation;[35] Jewish settlement;[36] the proscription of unwanted political activity;[37] the recruitment of informants;[38] and attempts at socially and politically fragmenting Palestinians.[39]

Among other things, the military regime – Palestinians' main contact with the state[40] – controlled and restricted movement between the different regions under its authority. This was done by issuing travel and work permits and IDs, declaring closed military zones and curfews, and operating checkpoints.[41] For this and other reasons, left-wing members of the Knesset who opposed the military rule described it as creating "ghettos for Arab citizens in Israel."[42] This ghettoization, in turn, fragmented the Palestinian community, spatially and socially.[43]

---

a Governing Norm" (2012) 46 *Law & Society Review* 137, 151 [hereinafter: "The Fluid Jurisprudence of Israel's Emergency Powers"]; Robinson, *Citizen Strangers*, pp. 33, 39, 42.

[29] Robinson, *Citizen Strangers*, p. 39.   [30] *Ibid.*, pp. 58–59.

[31] See entries A: Assigned Residence, B: Border/Barrier, P: Proportionality, V: Violence, X: X-Ray, and Z: Zone.

[32] See entry M: Military Courts.

[33] See entries F: Future-Oriented Measures and S: Security Prisoners.

[34] See entry F: Future-Oriented Measures.

[35] See entries G: Geneva Law, J: Jewish Settlements, and Z: Zone.

[36] See entries G: Geneva Law and J: Jewish Settlements.

[37] See entries S: Security Prisoners, V: Violence, W: War Crimes, and Y: Youth.

[38] See entries F: Future-Oriented Measures, V: Violence, X: X-Ray, and Y: Youth.

[39] See entry S: Security Prisoners.

[40] Bäuml, "The Military Government," pp. 48–49; A. Korn, "Military Government, Political Control and Crime: The Case of Israeli Arabs" (2000) 34 *Crime, Law & Social Change* 159, 159, 171 [hereinafter: "Military Government, Political Control and Crime"]. On Palestinians' resistance to the military rule system, see M. Nasasra, *The Politics of Non-Cooperation and Lobbying: The Naqab Bedouin and Israeli Military Rule, 1948–67*, in M. Nasasra et al. (eds.), *The Naqab Bedouin and Colonialism: New Perspectives* (London and New York: Routledge, 2015), p. 123; A. H. Sa'di, "The Incorporation of the Palestinian Minority by the Israeli State, 1948–1970: On the Nature, Transformation, and Constraints of Collaboration" (2003) 75 *Social Text* 75, 86–89 [hereinafter: "The Incorporation of the Palestinian Minority"].

[41] Abu-Saad, "Palestinian Education in Israel," p. 22; Kemp, "The Mirror Language of the Borders," pp. 342–345; Korn, "Military Government, Political Control and Crime," pp. 142, 164–167; Lustick, *Arabs in the Jewish State*, pp. 123–129; Robinson, *Citizen Strangers*, p. 42.

[42] Quoted in Kemp, "The Mirror Language of the Borders," p. 341.

[43] E. Zureik, "Strategies of Surveillance: The Israeli Gaze" (2016) 66 *Jerusalem Quarterly* 12, 24 [hereinafter: "Strategies of Surveillance"].

Using emergency regulations, military governors and their staff outlawed political organizations, censored the media, placed political activists in so-called "administrative detention" or under house arrest, and confiscated lands on a massive scale.[44] The latter practice went hand in hand with efforts to "Judaize" the country, as prime minister Ben-Gurion intimated: "The military government came into existence to protect the right of the Jewish settlement in all parts of the state."[45] Shimon Peres, the deputy defense minister at the time and Israel's future prime minister and president, similarly asserted: "It is by making use of mandatory regulation 125, on which the military government is to a great extent based, that we can directly continue the struggle for Jewish settlements and Jewish immigration."[46]

Undercover security agents were deployed. Palestinian individuals, including dignitaries, were also recruited as informants and collaborators through a combination of incentives and disincentives, the former including store licenses, travel permits, payment, jobs, university admissions, and favors, and the latter including the denial of permits and licenses, blacklisting, and other forms of pressure.[47] Thousands of Palestinians were tried and convicted in military courts for violations of the emergency regulations, primarily for failing to carry proper permits or exceeding travel restrictions.[48] In 1957, the prime minister's advisor on Arab affairs justified this military regime through a preemptive rationale akin to the one Israel currently employs regarding the West Bank and Gaza Strip (as discussed in another entry):[49]

> Ben-Gurion always reminds us that we cannot be guided by the subversion the Arab minority has not engaged in. We must be guided by what they *might* have done if they had been given the chance ... If we cancelled the restrictions [enforced by the military government, the Arabs might] ... squat on

---

[44] Kemp, "The Mirror Language of the Borders," p. 345; Korn, "Military Government, Political Control and Crime," pp. 165, 168, 173; Robinson, *Citizen Strangers*, p. 44; Sabri, "The Legal Status of Israeli Arabs," p. 572.

[45] Quoted in Mehozay, "The Fluid Jurisprudence of Israel's Emergency Powers," pp. 151–152.

[46] Quoted in *ibid.*, p. 152.

[47] Abu-Saad, "Palestinian Education in Israel," p. 25; Korn, "Military Government, Political Control and Crime," pp. 161, 168–169; J. Lockard, "Somewhere Between Arab and Jew: Ethnic Re-Identification in Modern Hebrew Literature" (2002) 5 *Middle Eastern Literatures* 49, 58–59; Robinson, *Citizen Strangers*, p. 44; Sa'di, 'The Incorporation of the Palestinian Minority,' pp. 76–81; Zureik, *Strategies of Surveillance*, pp. 24–25. On Israel's use of collaborators and informants, see also H. Cohen, *Good Arabs: The Israeli Security Agencies and the Israeli Arabs – Agents and Operators, Collaborators and Insurgents, Objectives and Methods* (Ben Shemen: Keter and Ivrit, 2006) [Hebrew].

[48] Korn, "Military Government, Political Control and Crime," pp. 167, 176; Korn, "Political Control and Crime," pp. 23, 29–30; Robinson, *Citizen Strangers*, p. 42.

[49] See entry F: Future-Oriented Measures.

their ruins, demand their lands back . . . [and] the return of the refugees. They
will form organizations, parties, fronts, anything to make trouble.[50]

From late 1959 onward, the travel restrictions were gradually eased, the
presence of military personnel was reduced, and powers were transferred from
the military to the police.[51] Though the military apparatus was formally
dismantled in December 1966[52] (six months before Israel took over the West
Bank and Gaza Strip), the police continued enforcing the permit regime on
the basis of the emergency regulations until 1968. In fact, in the first few
months of 1967, permit restrictions actually became more stringent than
previously.[53]

The nearly two-decade-long military government over Palestinian citizens
informed Israel's rule over the West Bank and Gaza Strip.[54] In 1967, former
military government professionals were recruited to serve in these territories.[55]
Moshe Dayan, the defense minister from 1967 to 1974, was influenced in his
policy toward these territories by lessons learned from this earlier form of
military rule.[56] Decades later, in 2015, the former minister of foreign affairs,
Avigdor Lieberman (currently the defense minister), stated publicly that Israel
should once again "begin using emergency law and institute a military government everywhere it is necessary to eradicate terrorism."[57]

While the military government was imposed on Palestinian citizens of
Israel, the Israeli military also got to control the lives of noncitizen
Palestinians outside the 1949 Armistice border a decade before 1967. In 1955,
the director of the Mossad (Israel's national intelligence agency) proposed

[50]   Quoted in Robinson, *Citizen Strangers*, p. 45.
[51]   Bäuml, "The Military Government," pp. 52–54; Korn, "Military Government, Political
       Control and Crime," p. 166; Korn, "Political Control and Crime," p. 27; Robinson, *Citizen
       Strangers*, pp. 190–192.
[52]   Korn, "Political Control and Crime," p. 23; Robinson, *Citizen Strangers*, p. 195.
[53]   Bäuml, "The Military Government," pp. 49, 55. See also Korn, "Political Control and
       Crime," p. 28.
[54]   In addition, the military rule's legacy is evident in some of Israel's current policies toward its
       Palestinian citizens. See, e.g., Abu-Saad, "Palestinian Education in Israel"; A. H. Sa'di,
       *Thorough Surveillance: The Genesis of Israeli Policies of Population Management,
       Surveillance and Political Control Towards the Palestinian Minority* (Manchester:
       Manchester University Press, 2013).
[55]   A. Korn, *Crime and Law Enforcement in the Israeli Arab Population Under the Military
       Government* (Doctoral Dissertation, Jerusalem: Hebrew University, 1996), pp. 194–196; cited
       in Azoulay and Ophir, *The One-State Condition*, p. 275.
[56]   E. Shamir, "From Retaliation to Open Bridges: Moshe Dayan's Evolving Approach toward
       the Population in Counter Insurgency" (2012) 14 *Civil Wars* 63, 73.
[57]   Jerusalem Post Staff, "Liberman: Israel Should Revert to a Military Government to Eradicate
       Terror," *Jerusalem Post* (October 13, 2015), www.jpost.com/Breaking-News/Liberman-Israel-
       should-revert-to-a-military-government-to-eradicate-terror-423814.

conquering the Egyptian-held Gaza Strip, and this is precisely what Israel did the following year, during its war against Egypt. Shortly thereafter, foreign minister Golda Meir stated that "the Gaza Strip was an integral part of Israel," and Prime Minister Ben-Gurion likewise spoke of the "liberation of homeland." Partly resonating with the stance it would adopt after 1967, the Israeli government tried arguing that the Gaza Strip was never part of Egypt and that, therefore, the Egyptians had no legal claim over it. Intense international pressure eventually forced Israel to evacuate the occupied territory after several months, but this left enough time for Israel to experiment for the first time with military rule in Gaza. Having declared the newly occupied territory under a military governor, Israeli authorities seized the local land registry, listed Gazan landowners, instituted a military tribunal, replaced the local police with hundreds of Israeli police officers, disqualified unwanted teachers and school books, and started introducing additional administrative, monetary, and infrastructural reforms with the aim of permanent Israeli presence. Two agricultural army settlements were established in areas that had been declared closed military zones, to which Moshe Dayan – the chief of staff at the time – advocated adding an array of other settlements. In the 1970s, some of the settlers and their children resettled in the Gaza Strip. The Israeli security authorities also closely monitored political expressions in Gaza, confiscated printing presses and posters, deployed covert intelligence agents, recruited local informants, and detained political activists.[58] According to declassified military documents, information was used regarding the homosexuality of at least one of these detainees,[59] bringing to mind the military's much more recent practice of targeting closeted gay Palestinians for recruitment as informants.[60]

---

[58] N. Masalha, "The 1956–57 Occupation of the Gaza Strip: Israeli Proposals to Resettle the Palestinian Refugees" (1996) 23 *British Journal of Middle Eastern Studies* 55, 56–57, 60, 62; M. O. Jorgensen, *Revisiting the First United Nations Peacekeeping Intervention in Egypt and the Gaza Strip, 1956–1967: A Case of Imperial Multilateralism?* (Doctoral Dissertation in History, Gent University, 2016), pp. 188–191, https://biblio.ugent.be/publication/7242947/file/8074778; Classified minutes of January 13, 1957 meeting with the General Officer Commander at the Gaza headquarters (January 16, 1957) [Hebrew], http://akevot.org.il/wp-content/uploads/2016/12/CRDR-7495.pdf; Classified Report of the Head of the Special Police Unit, M. Novik, Concerning An Attempted General Strike in Gaza (January 20, 1957) [Hebrew], http://akevot.org.il/wp-content/uploads/2016/12/CRDR-07497-redacted.pdf [hereinafter: Report Concerning an Attempted General Strike in Gaza]; Classified Report by the Head of Unit 50 of the General Security Service Concerning Subversive Activity in the Gaza Region (January 27, 1957) [Hebrew], http://akevot.org.il/wp-content/uploads/2016/12/CRDR-07503.pdf; M. Rapoport, "Revelation: The Settlement Project Was Already Born In Moshe Dayan's Mind in 1956," *Haaretz* (July 10, 2010) [Hebrew], www.haaretz.co.il/misc/1.1211253.

[59] Report Concerning an Attempted General Strike in Gaza.

[60] P. Beaumont, "Israeli Intelligence Veterans Refuse to Serve in Palestinian Territories," *The Guardian* (September 12, 2014), www.theguardian.com/world/2014/sep/12/israeli-

Further, as early as 1963 – three years before the military relinquished control over Israel's Palestinian citizens – Israel started preparing for a possible belligerent occupation of the West Bank. Senior officers from the military advocate general corps (discussed elsewhere in this book)[61] conducted a series of meetings on the subject with the chief of general staff and other top military officials. Among the issues under discussion were the establishment of military courts in the West Bank, the Jordanian law in force in this territory, and the adaptation of the emergency regulations inherited from the British Mandate for a future Israeli military occupation. Drawing on its accumulated knowhow and experience in military rule over Palestinian citizens and noncitizens, the military advocate general corps also started providing its officers with a special month-long course on the subject. The first course, in 1963, covered theories of military government, lessons from Israel's military occupation of the Gaza Strip in 1956–1957, a scenario involving the occupation of the old city of Jerusalem, and issues surrounding Jordan and Islam. An attempt was also made to involve Israel's former military governor in the second course, the following year, but he declined, saying that the world's superpowers would never allow Israel to occupy territories again.[62]

As part of the contingency plan, all military lawyers were also equipped with what the military advocate general at the time, Meir Shamgar (who would later become attorney general and eventually chief justice) described as "emergency kits including basic legal textbooks and other material . . . [including] a large set of precedents of military government proclamations and order, vital at the initial stages of military government as well as detailed legal and organisational instructions and guidelines."[63]

---

intelligence-reservists-refuse-serve-palestinian-territories. After the 1948 war, Ben-Gurion also voiced dissatisfaction with Israel's "unnatural" borders, and suggested, on several occasions, conquering the West Bank. From 1948 to 1955, together with Dayan, he advocated expanding Israel's borders through various military operations. B. Morris, *Israel's Border Wars, 1949–1956* (Oxford: Clarendon Press, 1993), pp. 242–243. Cited in G. Laron, "'Logic Dictates that They May Attack When They Feel They Can Win': The 1955 Czech-Egyptian Arms Deal, the Egyptian Army, and Israeli Intelligence" (2009) 63 *Middles East Journal* 69, 81. See also *ibid.*, pp. 82–84.

61   See entry L: Lawfare.

62   Z. Inbar, "The MAG and the Administered Territories" (2002) 16 *Mishpat Ve-Tsava* 149, 151–155 [Hebrew].

63   M. Shamgar, "Legal Concepts and Problems of the Israeli Military Government – the Initial Stage," in M. Shamgar (ed.), *Military Government in the Territories Administered by Israel, 1967–1980: The Legal Aspects* (Jerusalem: Hebrew University, 1982), pp. 13, 25 [hereinafter: "Legal Concepts and Problems of the Israeli Military Government"]. See also Inbar, "The MAG and the Administered Territories," pp. 155–156.

A key legal document published by the corps at the time was the lengthy *Manual for the Military Advocate General in Military Government*. Among other things, the manual provided guidelines on the forms and modes of military legislation in occupied territories, an overview of the municipal law in force in Israel's different neighboring countries, and the full text of the first military enactments Israel would later promulgate in the West Bank and Gaza Strip – including enactments concerning the establishment of military courts and the handling of security offenders.[64] In 1965, the GSS (General Security Service), too, started training its agents for a possible occupation of the West Bank and Gaza Strip.[65]

As already evident from Israel's repeated use of the British Mandate's emergency legislation, the practices and policies that informed the Israeli rule over the West Bank and Gaza Strip partly predate not only 1967 but also 1948, the year of Israel's establishment. Examples are numerous, and a few will suffice here. Israel's use of Palestinian informants and undercover military units, a practice discussed in some of this book's other entries,[66] dates back to the British Mandate over Palestine.[67] In fact, the current Hebrew name for undercover units – "mista'arvim" (meaning "Arabized" forces) – originally referred to the special undercover unit within the Palmach, the armed force of the Jewish community during the British Mandate period.[68] Britain's authorities in Palestine also used identity cards and mappings for surveillance purposes, as well as punitive detention laws on which the "administrative detention" used by Israel is largely based.[69]

Further, more than 60 years before Israel established "military youth courts" for Palestinian children (as discussed elsewhere in this book and also in Section O.3.2),[70] an amendment to the British emergency regulations

---

[64] Shamgar, "Legal Concepts and Problems of the Israeli Military Government," pp. 25, 27, 29–31. On the two latter issues, see, respectively, entries M: Military Courts and S: Security Prisoners. On the military's contingency plan for a possible occupation of the West Bank, see also S. Gazit, *The Carrot and the Stick: Israel's Government in Judea and Samaria* (Tel Aviv: Zmora-Bitan, 1985), pp. 23–38 [Hebrew]; S. Teveth, *The Cursed Blessing: The Story of Israel's Occupation of the West Bank*, M. Bank (trans.) (London: Weidenfeld & Nicolson, 1970), pp. 29–34; both cited in Azoulay and Ophir, *The One-State Condition*, p. 3.

[65] Azoulay and Ophir, *The One-State Condition*, p. 3, citing D. Ronen, *The GSS Year* (Tel Aviv: Ministry of Defense, 1989), pp. 17–20 [Hebrew].

[66] See entries F: Future-Oriented Measures, V: Violence, X: X-Ray, and Y: Youth.

[67] Robinson, *Citizen Strangers*, pp. 20, 57–58.

[68] N. Ben-Yehuda, *Political Assassinations by Jews: A Rhetorical Device for Justice* (Albany: State University of New York, 1993), p. 255; cited in M. Gunneflo, *Targeted Killing: A Legal and Political History* (Cambridge: Cambridge University Press, 2016), p. 62.

[69] L. Khalili, "The Location of Palestine in Global Counterinsurgencies" (2010) 42 *International Journal of Middle East Studies* 413, 421, 424.

[70] See Section Y.3 ("Token Reforms Beyond the Rule of Exception") of entry Y: Youth, as well as Section O.3.2 ("Youth Justice") of this entry.

authorized military courts in Palestine to act as juvenile courts.[71] The statutory age categories Israeli military law has used for Palestinian child detainees since 1967 (specified in another entry)[72] also originated in British Mandate legislation.[73] Similarly, some of the laws through which Israel has expropriated Palestinian land[74] are a legacy of the British Mandate, which, in turn, inherited and modified them from the Ottomans in Palestine.[75]

O.3 ISRAELI LAW DOES NOT STOP AT THE BORDER

The blurring of the distinction between Israel's "inside" and "outside" is of both a temporal and a spatial nature. Temporally, as shown thus far, the Israeli rule in the West Bank and Gaza Strip is not entirely an exception to, but rather, largely, a continuation of the pre-1967 history of Israel/Palestine. Spatially, the 1949 Armistice lines that supposedly separate "Israel proper" from these territories are porous, both legally and politically. This section analyzes three key manifestations of this porosity: the expansion of the jurisdiction of each of the two Israeli legal systems – the military and the domestic – across the different territories and populations of Israel/Palestine; the growing convergence of Israeli military and domestic laws, with a particular focus on developments concerning youth justice; and connections between Israel's treatment of noncitizen Palestinians and African asylum seekers.

O.3.1 *Jurisdiction Beyond the Border*

During the first years following Israel's conquest of the West Bank and Gaza Strip, not only were numerous noncitizen Palestinians brought to military trial[76] on criminal charges, but also several Israeli citizens who had entered these territories. In October 1967, four months after Israel assumed control, the Gaza military court sentenced a Jewish citizen of Israel to two years' imprisonment for stealing a Gazan Palestinian's wallet. The conviction was made under a 1936 ordinance enacted by the British Mandate

---

[71]   H. Viterbo, "Ties of Separation: Analogy and Generational Segregation in North America, Australia, and Israel/Palestine" (2017) 42 *Brooklyn Journal of International Law*, 686, 730 [hereinafter: "Ties of Separation"].

[72]   See entry Y: Youth, Section Y.1 ("Introduction").   [73]   Viterbo, "Ties of Separation," p. 730.

[74]   On land expropriation, see entries G: Geneva Law, J: Jewish Settlements, and Z: Zone.

[75]   A. Kedar, "The Legal Transformation of Ethnic Geography: Israeli Law and the Palestinian Landholder 1948-1967" (2001) 33 *International Law and Politics* 923; R. Home, "An 'Irreversible Conquest'? Colonial and Postcolonial Land Law in Israel/Palestine" (2003) 12 *Social Legal Studies* 291.

[76]   On the military court system, see entry M: Military Courts.

government[77] – yet another testament to the influence of pre-1967 laws and practices, examined earlier.

Two years later, another Israeli – a Palestinian citizen – was tried in the Gaza military court for making a false statement to Israeli authorities in the Gaza Strip and thereby violating Israel's statutory military law. The court held:

> The occupying power's right under public international law to enact its laws in the occupied territory is general and unqualified ... [T]his right [applies not only to] ... the population of the occupied territory ... [but also to] others, visiting or staying in ... [this] territory. The law does not distinguish between Israeli citizens or residents and other [i.e., non-Israeli] residents.[78]

In the West Bank, in 1972, four Jewish–Israeli left-wing activists were given a three-month suspended sentence by the Bethlehem military court. Their crime: disseminating a poster in the West Bank that stated, among other things, "peace and security will be attained by: recognizing Palestinians' right of self-determination alongside the state of Israel; [and] a [political] deal without annexations and settlements." This time, the charges were based both on military legislation and the above British Mandate enactment. In an uncharacteristically long judgment, the court reiterated the military law's applicability to anyone residing or visiting the West Bank – Palestinian, Israeli, or other.[79] Cited in the judgment, along with the previous military case, was a 1967 supreme court ruling upholding the jurisdiction of the Israeli military court in the Golan Heights over offenses committed there by Israelis.[80]

In 1975, Israeli emergency regulations regarding the West Bank and Gaza were amended to authorize civil courts to try, under the domestic law, anyone whose actions in these territories would have been unlawful if committed within the jurisdiction of these courts.[81] The main consequence was applying the domestic law to Israeli settlers on a personal rather than

---

[77] MilC (Gaza Mil. Ct.) 349/67 *Military Advocate General v. Zion* (October 30, 1967), in General Military Corps, *Selected Rulings of the Military Court of Appeals in the Administered Territories* (Military Advocate General's Office, 1970), vol. I, pp. 18–19 [hereinafter: Selected Military Rulings vol. I].

[78] MilC (Gaza Mil. Ct.) 1238/69 *Military Advocate General v. Ghanem* (1969), in Selected Military Rulings vol. I, pp. 130–131.

[79] MilC (Bethlehem Mil. Ct.) 1114/72 *Military Advocate General v. Scheinbaum* (November 9, 1972, 5.12.1972), in General Military Corps, *Selected Rulings of the Military Court of Appeals in the Administered Territories* (Military Advocate General's Office, 1974), vol. III, pp. 346–373.

[80] HCJ 210/67 *Levi v. Commander in Chief of the Israeli Defense Forces* (1967) 21(2) PD 21, 165.

[81] Article 1 of Law Amending Emergency Regulations (Territories Administered by the Israel Defense Forces – Adjudication and Legal Aid), 1975 [Hebrew], www.nevo.co.il/Law_word/law14/LAW-0779.pdf.

territorial basis[82] and thus entrenching Israel's ethnically based legal structure. In principle, military courts have also retained jurisdiction over Israelis, including settlers, but in practice they usually exercise this power only to review administrative restraining orders issued by the military against certain settlers.[83] In 2011, the military advocate general's office objected to proposals to try right-wing Jewish rioters in military courts, invoking what they described as the negative experience of military trials of Israelis in the 1970s.[84]

Further expanding the domestic legal system's reach into the West Bank and Gaza Strip was the supreme court's earlier decision, in 1972, to hear petitions concerning these territories.[85] In addition, in some cases, Palestinians from areas under military jurisdiction have been tried in Israeli civil courts.[86] Furthermore, in civil disputes between Israeli citizens and Palestinian noncitizens, Israeli courts have often either prioritized the domestic law over the military law or even considered only the domestic law.[87] Moreover, as discussed in another entry, a government-appointed commission controversially concluded, in 2012, that Israel had a valid claim for sovereignty over the West Bank and that this territory was not occupied.[88]

Whereas the domestic law has expanded into the territories under Israeli military control, the military courts, conversely, assume jurisdiction not only in the West Bank – including areas supposedly under the Palestinian Authority's control[89] – but also anywhere else. According to the military legislation,

---

[82]   T. Kelly, "Jurisdictional Politics" in the Occupied West Bank: Territory, Community, and Economic Dependency in the Formation of Legal Subjects" (2006) 31 *Law & Social Inquiry* 39, 47–49; I. Zertal and A. Eldar, *Lords of the Land: The War Over Israel's Settlements in the Occupied Territories, 1967–2007* (New York: Nation Books, 2007), pp. 372–373. See also entry J: Jewish Settlements.

[83]   See, e.g., Y. Berger, "Restraining Order Against a Right-Wing Activity Defined as an 'Immediate Security Threat' Has Been Vacated," *Haaretz* (November 25, 2016) [Hebrew], w ww.haaretz.co.il/news/politics/.premium-1.3133087.

[84]   C. Levinson and T. Zarhi, "Military Prosecution: Do Not Prosecute Right-Wing Rioters Under Military Law," *Haaretz* (December 27, 2011) [Hebrew], www.haaretz.co.il/news/poli tics/1.1601831.

[85]   HCJ 337/71 *Christian Society for the Holy Places* v. *Minister of Defence* (1972) 26(1) PD 574.

[86]   See entry M: Military Courts, Section M.1 ("Introduction").

[87]   I. Canor, "Israel and the Territories: Private International Law, Public International Law, and Their Relationship" (2005) 8 *Mishpat U-Mimshal* 551 [Hebrew].

[88]   See entry N: Nomos.

[89]   Article 10(f) of Order 1651 Concerning Security Provisions (Judea and Samaria), 2009. The military's jurisdiction in Palestinian Authority territories has been upheld by the supreme court in CrimC 4343/08 *Ajaj* v. *State of Israel* (June 29, 2008) [Hebrew], www.hamoked.org.il /files/2011/114401.pdf. For further discussion, see entry M: Military Courts, Section M.1 ("Introduction").

A military court is authorized to try any offense defined in military legislation and in law. . . . [It is also] authorized to try . . . a person who commits, outside the [West Bank] area,[90] an act that would have been unlawful if committed in the area and that harmed or was meant to harm the security of the area or public order.[91]

In a 2016 case concerning a Palestinian citizen of Israel, the supreme court held that this statutory provision also grants the military jurisdiction over citizens residing within Israel's pre-1967 borders.[92] In 2014, eight Palestinian citizens of Israel who were arrested during a political demonstration inside Israel "proper" and dealt with by civil courts were reportedly initially charged with an offense enshrined only in the military law.[93]

In addition to this unbound jurisdiction in terms of the location of the offense or the offender, legal institutions located within Israel "proper" regularly deal with matters concerning noncitizen Palestinians. This includes a few military courts that handle remands of Palestinians interrogated by the GSS[94] and also Israel's detention and prison facilities. The supreme court has approved the jurisdiction of the former over Palestinians from the West Bank and Gaza[95] as well as the transfer of such Palestinians into the latter, issues examined in another entry.[96] The border's porosity thus concerns both adjudication and incarceration.[97]

O.3.2 *The Growing Overlap Between Military and Domestic Law: The Test Case of Youth Justice*

A different, albeit related, manifestation of the legal porosity of the 1949 Armistice borders is the growing overlap between Israel's military and domestic laws. Among other things, the military law has increasingly adopted

---

[90]   The statutory term "the Area" designates the West Bank according to Article 1(9) of Order 1729 Concerning Interpretation [Integrated Version] (Judea and Samaria), 2013.

[91]   Articles 10(a) and 10(e) of Order 1651.

[92]   CrimC 9102/16 *Eyad v. State of Israel* (December 4, 2016) [Hebrew], http://elyon1.court.gov.il /files/16/020/091/g02/16091020.g02.htm, ¶ 5.

[93]   R. Hovel, "Police Arrested Eight Israelis Using a Statutory Military Provision Applicable Only to the Territories," *Haaretz* (July 14, 2014) [Hebrew], www.haaretz.co.il/news/law/1.2376341.

[94]   L. Yavne, *Backyard Proceedings: The Implementation of Due Process Rights in the Military Courts in the Occupied Territories* (2007), pp. 40–41, www.yesh-din.org/en/backyard- proceedings; HCJ 1958/10 *Palestinian Prisoners Office v. Israeli Defense Forces Commander in the Region* (March 9, 2010), www.humanrights.org.il/articles/בתיר%20משפט%20צבאיים.doc.

[95]   HCJ 6504/95 *Wajiyeh v. State of Israel* (November 4, 1995) [Hebrew], www.hamoked.org.il /files/2011/2350.pdf.

[96]   See entry S: Security Prisoners, Section S.2.1 ("Removal, Distancing, and Isolation").

[97]   See *ibid.*

elements from the domestic law. Thus, the military courts were once required by law to follow the rules of evidence applied in courts-martial (which try Israeli soldiers), but a 1992 amendment to the military legislation subjected them to the evidentiary rules applicable in criminal proceedings within Israel's domestic legal system.[98] More recently, in 2015, some key concepts of the domestic criminal law were incorporated into the central military order concerning "security offenses," including definitions of the elements of an offense (the *mens rea* and *actus reus*), definitions of the legal terms "negligence" and "strict liability," an explanation of "reasonable doubt," and a prohibition on retroactive liability (ex post facto laws).[99] A 2017 amendment also rendered judgments of military courts in the West Bank admissible evidence in trials within the domestic legal system.[100] The bill's sponsor explained that it would "help Israeli terror victims claim compensation [in a civil proceeding] from [Palestinian] terrorists" who have been convicted by military courts, whereas critics of the bill warned of "creeping annexation."[101]

One area where the alignment of the military law with the domestic law has been particularly visible is youth justice. During the first two decades of the twenty-first century, this legal field underwent two complementary processes: elements from the domestic law were incorporated into the military law, and measures were introduced under the domestic law with a striking resemblance to military law.

The first process – the incorporation of domestic youth justice elements into the military law concerning Palestinian children – was marked by three central reforms. First, whereas previously Israel incarcerated most Palestinian children with adults, a series of amendments and developments nearly eliminated joint incarceration. Second, in 2009, "military youth courts" were established to adjudicate cases involving Palestinian child defendants separately from those involving adults. And third, in 2011, the age of criminal majority under statutory military law was raised from 16 to 18 years.

However, despite the much greater rights and protections granted to Israelis under the domestic law than to Palestinians under the military law, the

---

[98] N. Benichou, "Criminal Law in the Judea, Samaria, and Gaza Regions" (2004) 18 *Mishpat Ve-Tsava* 293, 300–301 [Hebrew]. This provision currently appears as Article 86 of Order 1651.

[99] Order 1754 Concerning Security Provisions (Amendment No. 45) (Principles of Criminal Responsibility) (Judea and Samaria), 2015. The term "negligence" previously appeared in the statutory military law but was not defined; while there was also no explicit definition of *mens rea*, the terms "intent" and "motive" were defined. See 2014 version of Order 1651.

[100] Law Amending the Evidence Ordinance (No. 18), 2017.

[101] 20th Knesset, "Passed: The Findings and Conclusions of a Military Court Ruling Shall Be Admissible Evidence in Civil Law" (January 16, 2017) [Hebrew], http://main.knesset.gov .il/News/PressReleases/Pages/press160117l.aspx.

growing confluence between the two legal systems has not necessarily been to Palestinians' benefit.[102] For reasons described in another entry, increased separation in Israeli custody could disempower and even endanger Palestinian children.[103] Further, as shown in yet another entry, the reforms in 2009 (establishing "military youth courts") and 2011 (raising the age of majority) have been designed and enforced in ways that largely prevent any actual improvement to Israel's treatment of young Palestinians.[104] Moreover, as shown elsewhere in this book, the military courts have a record of inconsistent rulings (including with regard to the age of criminal majority), and this creates an uncertainty that further disempowers Palestinians who encounter the military legal system.[105]

A second and somewhat converse process to this incorporation of domestic law elements into the military law has been the appearance, in the domestic law, of provisions similar to those of the military law. These provisions were introduced through three amendments to the domestic law in 2015 and 2016, which were passed following riots and a surge in stone-throwing in East Jerusalem (where Israel applies its domestic law).[106] First, under the military law, "throwing an object, including a stone" has long been an offense punishable by up to 20 years' imprisonment.[107] The domestic law previously made no reference to such an offense, but in 2015 it was amended to likewise criminalize stone-throwing specifically, with a maximum penalty of 20 years' imprisonment.[108] Second, whereas the military law allows sentencing Palestinian children as young as 12 years to prison, the domestic law used to authorize custodial sentences only for children aged 14 years and above.[109] Another 2015 amendment to the

---

[102] In addition, such reforms might increase the power imbalance between the Israeli military prosecution and Palestinian defense attorneys, as explained in S. Ben-Natan, "The Application of Israeli Law in the Military Courts of the OPT" (2014) 43 *Theory & Criticism* 143, 164–165 [Hebrew].

[103] See entry S: Security Prisoners, Section S.2.2 ("Division"). For a more comprehensive analysis, see H. Viterbo, "Rights as a Divide-and-Rule Mechanism: Lessons from the Case of Palestinians in Israeli Custody" (forthcoming) *Law & Society Inquiry* [hereinafter: "Rights as a Divide-and-Rule Mechanism"].

[104] See entry Y: Youth. See also Viterbo, "Rights as a Divide-and-Rule Mechanism."

[105] See entry M: Military Courts.

[106] On the status of East Jerusalem under Israeli law, see entries B: Border/Barrier, J: Jewish Settlements, M: Military Courts, and Z: Zone.

[107] For further analysis, see entry Y: Youth, Section II ("The Rule of Exception in Israeli Military Law").

[108] Articles 1, 3 of Penal Code (Amendment No. 119), 2015.

[109] See, respectively, Article 168(b) of Order 1651; Article 25(d) of Youth Law (Adjudication, Punishment, and Modes of Treatment), 1971. For discussion of this legal disparity, see H. Viterbo, "The Age of Conflict: Rethinking Childhood, Law, and Age Through the Israeli-

domestic law, however, now enables incarcerating children under the age of 14 years in security juvenile facilities.[110]

Finally, in 1988, during the first Intifada, a military order was enacted to effectively authorize imposing a financial sanction on Palestinian parents in the West Bank and Gaza Strip due to their child's suspected behavior. Though the military order did not speak of fines but of "financial guarantees," these were imposed on parents merely due to suspicions of their child's wrongdoing (as opposed to an actual conviction). A Palestinian parent unable to provide such a guarantee could be sentenced to a year's imprisonment.[111] Following a petition, the supreme court upheld this order in 1991,[112] but eventually, after the Intifada, it was revoked, and the military law now only authorizes imposing financial guarantees on parents following their child's conviction.[113] About two decades later, in 2014, the Israeli state prosecution started implementing an identical measure in East Jerusalem (where the domestic law is applied), while publicly acknowledging both the past use of this measure under the military law and its approval by the supreme court.[114] The following year, the domestic law was also amended to deny state benefits to parents of convicted child "security prisoners."[115]

Technically, the amendments to the domestic law are applicable to all Israeli children and parents, regardless of ethnicity. In practice, prime minister Netanyahu made it no secret that their chief objective was to "act[] aggressively against … stone-throwers" and "return quiet and security to every part of Jerusalem."[116] Further, the amendments are likely to disproportionately affect Palestinians in Israel, given that the vast majority of Israeli "security prisoners" are Palestinian citizens or

Palestinian Case," in M. Freeman (ed.), *Law and Childhood Studies* (Oxford: Oxford University Press, 2012), pp. 136–138.

[110] Article 1 of Youth Law (Adjudication, Punishment, and Modes of Treatment) (Amendment 22 – Temporary Order), 2016.

[111] Articles 2, 5 of Order 1235 Concerning Supervision Over Minors' Behavior (Imposition of Financial Guarantees) (Temporary Order), 1988.

[112] HCJ 591/88 *Taha v. Minister of Defense* (January 21, 1991).   [113] Article 177 of Order 1651.

[114] N. Hasson, "Prosecution Imposes Fines on Rioters' Parents," *Haaretz* (October 31, 2014) [Hebrew], www.haaretz.co.il/news/politics/.premium-1.2472769.

[115] Article 3 of Penal Code (Amendment No. 120), 2015. At the time of writing, a petition against this amendment is pending before the supreme court: petition in HCJ 3390/16 *Adalah v. Knesset* (April 21, 2016) [Hebrew], www.adalah.org/uploads/Children_Allowances_Sawsa n_April_2016.pdf.

[116] B. Ravid and J. Lis, "Netanyahu's Cabinet Backs Bill to Jail Stone-Throwers Up to 10–20 Years," *Haaretz* (November 2, 2014), www.haaretz.com/news/national/.premium-1.624039; Jerusalem Post Staff, "In Move to Restore Order to Jerusalem: Up to 20 Years in Jail for Stone-Throwers," *Jerusalem Post* (November 2, 2014), www.jpost.com/Israel-News/In-move-to-restore-order-to-Jerusalem-Up-to-20-years-in-jail-for-stone-throwers-380528.

residents;[117] that Israeli authorities usually classify stone-throwing by Palestinians as a "security offense";[118] and that more than half of the children sentenced to imprisonment or community service in Israel's domestic legal system are Muslim (despite Muslims constituting less than a fifth of Israel's population).[119] The impact on East Jerusalem Palestinians is likely to be particularly harsh, considering their relatively difficult socioeconomic background.[120] Relatedly, as another entry demonstrates in detail, Israel's handling of Palestinian children in East Jerusalem shares another parallel with the military law: in both contexts, Israeli authorities have relied heavily on statutory exceptions, thereby denying Palestinian children their formal protections.[121]

O.3.3 *African Asylum Seekers: Connections and Parallels*

Israel's discourses and practices regarding noncitizen Palestinians have also come to closely resemble and converge with those concerning another group of non-Jewish noncitizens: African asylum seekers. At the time of writing, Israel is home to around 40,000 asylum seekers, mostly Eritrean and Sudanese.[122] Both groups are considered protected from forcible repatriation[123] under the Refugee

---

[117] For figures, see entry S: Security Prisoners, Section S.1 ("Introduction: Terminology, Figures, and Context").

[118] See entry Y: Youth. See also Viterbo, "Rights as a Divide-and-Rule Mechanism."

[119] Addendum: Written Replies of Israel to the Committee on the Rights of the Child (CRC/C/ISR/Q/2–4/Add.1) (May 22, 2013), http://docstore.ohchr.org/SelfServices/FilesHandler.ashx?enc=6QkG1d%2fPPRiCAqhKb7yhsv1txuQys3LgW6ocwoE2%2bBXBtcHR0EqMe%2fr%2brOnXoCgDdc5oAuNRpBZ4vz6iUeu6l4igUcn2FviseAtJMJG%2b7UkbD1kkphZTrDKJffTDpVIh9c2dsdAdjZANisqnh6W9Mg%3d%3d (see specifically Part II, Table 22). According to a recent study by the Israeli court system, Arab defendants are more likely to be convicted, and are sentenced to longer periods, than their Jewish counterparts. T. Zarchin and Y. Lis, "Court Study: Arabs Are Discriminated Against in Punishment," *Haaretz* (August 2, 2011) [Hebrew], www.haaretz.co.il/news/law/1.1371246.

[120] Association for Civil Rights in Israel, *Arrested Childhood: The Ramifications of Israel's New Strict Policy Toward Minors Suspected of Involvement in Stone Throwing, Security Offenses and Disturbances* (2016), p. 19, www.acri.org.il/en/wp-content/uploads/2016/02/Arrested-Childhood0216-en.pdf.

[121] See entry Y: Youth, Section Y.3 ("The Rule of Exception Beyond Israeli Military Law").

[122] Hotline for Refugees and Migrants, "Refugees and Asylum Seekers," http://hotline.org.il/en/refugees-and-asylum-seekers-en/.

[123] Refugees' Rights Forum, *The Principle of Non-Refoulement of a Person to a Place in Which He Is Expected to Suffer Danger to Life, Liberty, Persecution or Torture* (2008), http://hotline.org.il/wp-content/uploads/202513842-Non-Refoulement-Paper.pdf. See also Hotline for Refugees and Migrants, *No Safe Haven: Israeli Asylum Policy as Applied to Eritrean and Sudanese Citizens* (2014), http://hotline.org.il/wp-content/uploads/No-Safe-Haven.pdf.

Convention.[124] Between July 2009 and August 2013, Israel recognized 0.15 percent of asylum seekers as refugees,[125] compared with global recognition rates of
82 and 68 percent for Eritrean and Sudanese asylum seekers respectively.[126]
As discussed throughout this book, Israeli authorities have framed and treated
Palestinians as a security and demographic threat;[127] as this section will demonstrate, African asylum seekers, whose movement Israel heavily restricts, have
been perceived and treated in a similar manner.

  The Israeli authorities and mainstream media refer to asylum seekers as
"infiltrators." Originally, this term was applied primarily to Palestinian refugees who crossed the border into Israel from their countries of exile in the years
following the 1948 war. The refugees' motivations for entering Israel varied:
visiting or reuniting with their families, returning to their homes and property,
finding jobs, or, in a small albeit nontrivial minority of cases, committing
terrorist attacks.[128] A 1954 Israeli statute enacted in response to this phenomenon – the Prevention of Infiltration Law – criminalizes "infiltrators," whom it
defines as unlawful entrants who are either Palestinian refugees or nationals,
residents, or visitors of neighboring countries.[129] Though the statute avoids
using the term "refugee,"[130] internal military correspondence in the 1950s

---

[124] Article 33 of Convention Relating to the Status of Refugees, UN General Assembly,
28 July 1951, 189 UNTS 137 (ratified by Israel in 1954).

[125] Human Rights Watch, *"Make Their Lives Miserable": Israel's Coercion of Eritrean and
Sudanese Asylum Seekers to Leave Israel* (2014), p. 72, www.hrw.org/sites/default/files/report
s/israel0914_ForUpload_0.pdf.

[126] UN High Commissioner for Refugees, *Statistical Yearbook 2012* (2013), pp. 102, 104, https://
reliefweb.int/sites/reliefweb.int/files/resources/2012-12%20SYB12_FULLBOOK_low.pdf.

[127] On the perception, prevalent in Israeli Jewish society, of Palestinians as a demographic threat,
see, in particular, entries F: Future-Oriented Measures (Section F.1, "Introduction"), K:
Kinship, and X: X Rays. On their equally prevalent image as a security threat, see, e.g., entries
A: Assigned Residence (Section A.3.1, "The Narrative Framework"), F: Future-Oriented
Measures (Section F.3, "The Penality of Potential Threats"), S: Security Prisoners, and Z:
Zone (Section Z.2.3.2, "Control Over Movement"). On Israel's restriction of Palestinian
movement, see entries B: Barrier, P: Proportionality, V: Violence, and X: X Rays.

[128] According to some estimates, "violent infiltrators constitute[d] less than 10% of all infiltrators"
in the early 1950s. O. Bracha, "Unfortunate or Perilous: The Infiltrators, the Law, and the
Supreme Court 1948-1954" (1998) 21 *Iyunei Mishpat* 345, 340–341 [Hebrew] [hereinafter:
"Unfortunate or Perilous"]. The author also cites another source that reaches a similar
conclusion: B. Morris, *Israel's Border Wars 1949–1956* (Tel Aviv: Am Oved, 1996), pp. 61–70
[Hebrew] [hereinafter: *Israel's Border Wars*].

[129] Article 1 of Prevention of Infiltration (Offenses and Jurisdiction) Law, 1954.

[130] Instead of this term, the statute refers to "a Palestinian citizen or a Palestinian without
nationality or citizenship or whose nationality was doubtful and who … left his ordinary
place of residence of residence in the area which has become part of Israel for a place outside
Israel." *Ibid.*

expressly noted the close overlap of the Palestinian refugee and "infiltrator" issues.[131]

Having entered Israel without permission through the Egyptian border, Eritrean and Sudanese asylum seekers are hence labeled as "infiltrators" under Israeli law. The perception of African asylum seekers as a threat may stem not only from racism – though this certainly seems to play a central role regarding both them and Palestinians – but also, in part, from the fear that granting them refugee status would somehow serve the claim of Palestinians refugees for the right of return.[132] Another term in frequent use with regard to African asylum seekers, "illegal aliens," has also traditionally denoted unauthorized Palestinian entrants.[133]

Senior Israeli state officials have been unapologetic in portraying asylum seekers as a demographic and security threat. In 2012, for instance, prime minister Benjamin Netanyahu described them as a threat to "the national security and [to] our national identity. The country," he added, "is flooded [with infiltrators] and our identity as a Jewish and democratic state is being eliminated . . . ." The interior minister at the time, Eli Yishai, similarly called for deporting asylum seekers in the interest of "maintaining the Jewish identity if we don't want War of Independence II, and I'm not exaggerating." On another occasion, Yishai made explicit the analogy to Palestinians: "The infiltrators, along with the Palestinians, will quickly bring us to the end of the Zionist dream. . . . We must prepare military bases for incarcerating all of them [i.e., infiltrators] without exception. . . . Most of the people coming here are Muslim who think that this country doesn't belong to us, the white man."

The then deputy Knesset speaker, Danny Danon (currently Israel's ambassador to the United Nations), likewise alerted: "We see that an enemy state is being established in Israel. The state of infiltrators, who come here from Muslim countries." On a similar note, internal security minister Yitzhak Aharonovitch characterized asylum seekers as "a ticking time bomb . . . due

---

[131] Morris, *Israel's Border Wars*, p. 45, cited in Bracha, "Unfortunate or Perilous," p. 337.

[132] Y. Raz, *Ordered Disorder: African Asylum Seekers in Israel and Discursive Challenges to an Emerging Refugee Regime* (UN High Commissioner for Refugees research paper no. 205, March 2011), pp. 9–10, [hereinafter: *Ordered Disorder*], www.refworld.org/pdfid/4d7e19ab2 .pdf.

[133] Hotline for Refugees and Migrants, *"Cancer in Our Body": On Racial Incitement, Discrimination and Hate Crimes against African Asylum Seekers in Israel* (2012), pp. 4–5, http://hotline.org.il/wp-content/uploads/IncitementReport_English.pdf [hereinafter: *"Cancer in Our Body"*]. See also entries B: Border/Barrier and P: Proportionality, as well as B'Tselem, *Crossing the Line: Violation of the Rights of Palestinians in Israel Without a Permit* (March 2007), www.btselem.org/down load/200703_crossing_the_line_eng.doc.

to fears they might join terror organizations."[134] Supreme court justices have also repeatedly framed asylum seekers as a security threat in relevant judgments.[135] Justice Amit voiced the demographic anxiety as well: "What is the 'red line' [of 'infiltrators'] that a country can accommodate without substantially risking its … character, its national identity, its cultural-social features, the composition of its population, and the entirety of its unique traits … ?"[136]

Not only the rhetoric but also the actions of Israeli authorities show parallels and connections with those concerning Palestinians. Somewhat akin to the "administrative detention" without trial of Palestinians,[137] Israeli law currently provides for incarcerating asylum seekers without trial. Initially, after entering the country, the asylum seekers are held for three months in prisons near the Egyptian border, one of which (Ktzi'ot Prison) was previously primarily designated for Palestinian "security prisoners."[138] Subsequently, they are detained for an additional year in the nearby Holot camp, whose current warden previously supervised a facility for Palestinian "security prisoners" in the West Bank.[139] All of this is done under an amended version[140] of the 1954 statue that, as explained earlier, was originally enacted against re-entry into Israel by Palestinian refugees. The amended law maintains the term "infiltrator," as do the recent supreme court judgments in petitions against some recent amendments to the law.[141] During a parliamentary discussion of one of these amendments, the representative of the justice ministry remarked that the

[134] All quoted in Hotline for Refugees and Migrants, *"Cancer in Our Body,"* pp. 19–20, 23–24, 29. Contrary to some of these statements, most of the asylum seekers in Israel are Christian. *Ibid.*, p. 13.
[135] HCJ 7146/12 *Adam* v. *Knesset* (September 16, 2013), ¶¶ 3, 114, 120 of justice Arbel's opinion, ¶ 2 of justice Hendel's opinion, and ¶ 2 of justice Amit's opinion [Hebrew], http://elyon1.court .gov.il/files/12/460/071/B24/12071460.B24.htm; HCJ 8425/13 *Gebrselassie* v. *Knesset* (September 22, 2014), ¶¶ 29, 68 of justice Vogleman's opinion and ¶ 10 of justice Amit's opinion [Hebrew], http://elyon1.court.gov.il/files/13/850/073/M19/13073850.M19.htm; HCJ 8665/14 *Desta* v. *Knesset* (August 11, 2015), ¶ 3 of justice Amit's opinion [Hebrew], http://elyon1 .court.gov.il/files/14/650/086/c15/14086650.c15.htm.
[136] HCJ 7146/12, ¶ 2 of justice Amit's opinion.
[137] On "administrative detention," see entries F: Future-Oriented Measures and S: Security Prisoners.
[138] Addameer, "Negev Desert (Ketziot) Prison," www.addameer.org/content/ketziot-prison. On the so-called "security prisoners" in general, see entry S: Security Prisoners.
[139] Y. Kubovich, "A Detainee Was Mistakenly Released from Ofer Prison, the Warden Has Been Dismissed – and Will Supervise Holot," *Haaretz* (March 21, 2014) [Hebrew], www.haaretz.co .il/news/politics/.premium-1.2276124.
[140] Prevention of Infiltration and Ensuring the Departure of Infiltrators Law (Amendments and Temporary Orders), 2014.
[141] HCJ 7146/12; HCJ 8425/13; HCJ 8665/14.

government's reliance on the 1954 statute was intentional, since the statute entrusts the defense minister with its enforcement, and since "infiltration" connotes a serious threat.[142]

Further, a recent amendment bill emphasized that the prolonged detention without trial aims to deter potential "infiltrators."[143] This approach parallels another future-looking practice, examined elsewhere in this book: the pre-emptive detention of Palestinians in the West Bank.[144] The desire to discourage potential "infiltrators" has been informed not only by the events of the 1950s but also by Israel's ongoing battle against Palestinian entry from the West Bank and Gaza Strip. In 2013, during a parliamentary debate over an amendment to the counter-"infiltration" statute, the then interior minister, Gideon Sa'ar, stated: "The fence [with Egypt] alone is not enough [to stop African asylum seekers]. There is also a fence within the Land of Israel and illegal Palestinian residents do cross it. … Without … [detention] facilities … asylum seekers will [still] come."[145]

The parallels do not end here. Part of what can deter unwanted entry, or at least renders unsustainable the claims of asylum seekers, is not just Israel's measures in and of themselves, but also their ever-changing trial-and-error nature, which has been described as "ordered disorder."[146] In addition, an Israeli court has criticized the country's refugee determination mechanism for "taking … an unreasonably long time, with no clear end date," adding: "the asylum seeker [finds herself/himself] … operating on the basis of uncertainty."[147] Accusations have also been made that the information Israeli authorities publish about African asylum seekers is incomplete and inaccurate.[148] These issues bring to mind the unpredictability inherent to Israel's manipulable "un/certainty governance" over noncitizen Palestinians,

---

[142] HCJ 7146/12, ¶ 13 of justice Vogleman's opinion.
[143] Prevention of Infiltration (Offenses and Jurisdiction) Bill (Amendment No. 4 and Temporary Order), 2013, in 817 *Government Bills*, p. 121 (November 20, 2013) [Hebrew], www.nevo.co.il /Law_word/law15/memshala-817.pdf.
[144] See entry F: Future-Oriented Measures, Section F.3 ("The Penality of Potential Threats").
[145] Quoted in S. Weinblum, "The Management of African Asylum Seekers and the Imaginary of the Border in Israel," in M. Leese and S. Wittendorp (eds.), *Security/Mobility: Politics of Movement* (Manchester: Manchester University Press, 2017) pp. 114, 121.
[146] Raz, *Ordered Disorder*, p. 5.
[147] AdminC 49098–10-14 *John Doe v. Ministry of the Interior* (January 26, 2015), p. 8 [Hebrew], www.nevo.co.il/psika_html/mechozi/ME-14-10-49098–44.htm.
[148] I. Lior, "How Many African Immigrants Reside in Israel? It Depends in What Month You Ask," *Haaretz* (August 4, 2013) [Hebrew], www.haaretz.co.il/news/education/.premium-1 .2088238; I. Lior, "Aid Organizations Accuse the State of Opacity," *Haaretz* (August 4, 2013) [Hebrew], www.haaretz.co.il/news/education/.premium-1.2088316.

as analyzed in another entry.[149] In addition, somewhat reminiscent of the recruitment of Palestinian informants[150] has been Israeli authorities' payment to asylum seekers to secretly provide information on other asylum seekers. A petition to reveal the sums and incentives given or promised to these informants was rejected in 2008.[151]

Furthermore, in line with the centrality of security in the public discourse over African asylum seekers, the military has played a key role in shaping and carrying out Israel's counter-"infiltration" policies. Though Egypt is not considered an enemy state, it is the military, rather than the border police, that handles unauthorized entrants from the Egyptian border and transfers them to the Israeli prison authorities.[152] The military's involvement in this context resonates not only with its ongoing control over noncitizen Palestinians, but also with its efforts to prevent the return of Palestinian refugees during the first years of Israel's statehood. The military government over Palestinian citizens, discussed in Section O.2, was tasked with blocking the return of refugees to their prewar homes and property by various means, including through a census in the areas under its jurisdiction in the hope of monitoring changes to the Palestinian population.[153] Moreover, the military's international law department, whose activity regarding the West Bank and Gaza Strip is examined in another entry,[154] has been particularly active in relation to African asylum seekers. As the military advocate general's office put it in its 2012 annual report, "The construction of the fence [along the Egyptian border] . . . has helped deal with infiltration from Egypt . . . Officers of the [international law] department provided continuous legal advice on the matter . . . assisted in . . . implementing the [amended] counter-infiltration statute . . . and handled legal proceedings concerning the prevention of infiltration by IDF forces."[155]

---

[149] See entry M: Military Courts.
[150] See entries F: Future-Oriented Measures, V: Violence, X: X-Ray, and Y: Youth. See also Section O.2 ("Before 1967") in this entry.
[151] AdminC 558/07 *Movement for Freedom of Information v. Administration of Immigration* (September 16, 2008) [Hebrew], www.nevo.co.il/psika_html/minhali/mm07000558-16.htm. For further details, see Y. Livnat, "The Arrest and Release of the Foreigner Who Refused to Identify Himself" (2010) 15 *Hamishpat* 227, 262 [Hebrew].
[152] G. Cohen, "IDF Reduces Preparations for Receiving African Immigrants," *Haaretz* (September 27, 2013) [Hebrew], www.haaretz.co.il/news/politics/.premium-1.2126954.
[153] Korn, "Military Government, Political Control and Crime," pp. 162–163.
[154] See entry L: Lawfare.
[155] Office of the Military Advocate General, *Annual Activity Report – 2012* (2013), pp. 25–26 [Hebrew], www.mag.idf.il/sip_storage/FILES/2/1422.pdf.

O.4 CONCLUSION

The distinctions between Israel's "inside" and "outside," between the "norm" and its legal–political "exception," are blurry. Temporally, Israel's rule over the West Bank and Gaza Strip has, in large measure, been a continuation of, rather than an exception to, the pre-1967 history of Israel/Palestine. This entry has investigated the following manifestations of this continuity: the military government over Palestinian citizens during the first two decades of Israeli statehood, which informed and developed key elements of the post-1967 military rule; Israel's experience of military rule over noncitizen Palestinians during the occupation of the Gaza Strip in the 1950s; the preparation, in the early 1960s, of contingency plans and legal tools for a military occupation of the West Bank; and various laws and practices dating back to the days of British and Ottoman rule in Palestine.

Spatially, the 1949 Armistice lines that supposedly separate "Israel proper" from the West Bank and Gaza Strip are, in fact, porous, legally and politically. This entry has investigated three central manifestations of this porosity: the expansion of both military and domestic jurisdiction across the different territories and populations of Israel/Palestine; the increased convergence of Israeli domestic and military laws, a trend especially visible in the area of youth justice; and, finally, connections between the Israeli discourses and practices concerning two groups of non-Jewish noncitizens: Palestinians outside the 1949 Armistice line, and African asylum seekers. Though a distinction between "temporal" and "spatial" may be of some analytical use, the two dimensions are inseparable, as evidenced, among other things, by the influence of earlier policies from one side of the border on later policies on the other side.

While these continuities and parallels are crucial for understanding the Israeli control regime, they are neither linear nor clear-cut. There are weighty differences, both between the pre- and post-1967 modes of governance and between the various territories and population under Israeli control. Israel/Palestine is thus governed by and through a duality between "outside" and "inside": while separating, excluding, and differentiating unwanted Palestinian populations and territories, Israel has maintained an ever-evolving, inextricable connection to the West Bank and Gaza Strip. Whereas the separation, exclusion, and differentiation side of this duality is explored in other parts of this book, the present entry has tackled its other side: the legal and political overlap, similarity, and continuity between Israel's "inside" and "outside."

Despite the focus of this entry on Israel/Palestine, the ambiguity of the divide between "inside" and "outside," between "norm" and "exception," is anything but unique to the Israeli–Palestinian context. Historical continuity and spatial porosity comparable to those examined in this entry can be found in various contexts outside Israel/Palestine.[156] In the words of the philosopher Giorgio Agamben, whose writing on the rule–exception relation is discussed elsewhere in this book,[157] "together with the process by which the exception everywhere becomes the rule, the realm ... originally situated at the margins of the political order ... gradually begins to coincide with the political realm, and exclusion and inclusion, outside and inside, ... enter into a zone of irreducible indistinction."[158]

Notwithstanding the endless specificity of each particular context and place, it would therefore be naïve to envisage Israel/Palestine as unparalleled in its duality regarding the "outside–inside" relation.[159] This entry thus suggests the need to deconstruct not only simplistic oppositions between "Israel" and the West Bank and Gaza Strip, but also, more broadly, the relationship between "outside" and "inside," between "norm" and "exception."

---

[156] See, e.g., M. Neocleous, "From Martial Law to the War on Terror" (2007) 10 *New Criminal Law Review* 489; J. M. Chacón, "The Security Myth: Punishing Immigrants in the Name of National Security," in J. A. Dowling and J. X. Inda (eds.), *Governing Immigration Through Crime: A Reader* (Stanford: Stanford University Press, 2013); F. Cochrane, "Not So Extraordinary: The Democratisation of UK Counterinsurgency Strategy" (2013) 6 *Critical Studies on Terrorism* 29; M. I. Ahmad, "Guantánamo is Here: The Military Commissions Act and Noncitizen Vulnerability" (2007) 2007 *University of Chicago Legal Forum* 1; N. T. Saito, "Interning the 'Non-Alien' Other: The Illusory Protections of Citizenship" (2005) 68 *Law & Contemporary Problems* 173; E. Hernández-López, "Guantánamo as Outside and Inside the US: Why is a Base a Legal Anomaly?" (2010) 18 *Journal of Gender, Social Policy & Law* 471; F. Laguardia, "Special Administrative Measures: An Example of Counterterror Excesses and Their Roots in US Criminal Justice" (2015) 51 *Criminal Law Review* 157; N. Hussain, "Beyond Norm and Exception: Guantánamo" (2007) 33 *Critical Inquiry* 734; N. Hussain, "Hyperlegality" (2007) 10 *New Criminal Law Review* 514; A. N. Paik, "Carceral Quarantine at Guantánamo: Legacies of US Imprisonment of Haitian Refugees, 1991-1994" (2013) 115 *Radical History Review* 142; P. Fitzpatrick and R. Joyce, "The Normality of the Exception in Democracy's Empire" (2007) 34 *Journal of Law & Society* 65; M. Neocleous, *War Power, Police Power* (Edinburgh: Edinburgh University Press, 2015); L. Volpp, "The Indigenous as Alien" (2015) 5 *UC Irvine Law Review* 289.

[157] See Section 2 ("The Law–Rule–Exception Relationship") of the Introduction.

[158] G. Agamben, *Homo Sacer: Sovereign Power and Bare Life*, D. Heller-Roazen (trans.) (Stanford: Stanford University Press, 1998), p. 9. On the dissolving of borders between outside and inside in emergency regimes, see O. Gross and F. Ni Aolain, *Law in Times of Crisis* (Cambridge: Cambridge University Press, 2006), p. 18.

[159] For further explanation of why the rule and the exception are neither historically nor structurally antithetical, see the Introduction, Section 2.3 ("Critiquing Against/With the Law").

P

Proportionality

Michael Sfard

P.1 WEIGHING EVILS

International humanitarian law exists in the realm of the lesser evil: It accepts the reality of armed conflicts and attempts to reduce the suffering it invariably causes, particularly, though not solely, the harm it causes to the civilian population. This is its raison d'être as manifested in the principle of distinction.[1] Simultaneously, however, IHL accepts that eliminating all forms of harm to civilians would frustrate war efforts and, given that military necessity is a parallel governing principle of IHL,[2] it does not outlaw all attacks or all acts that might, or are even likely to cause incidental harm to civilians and civilian objects. While some forms of attack are considered inherently indiscriminate and thus illegal, others may be legal or illegal depending on the degree of harm they are anticipated to inflict on civilians. Adherence to a certain balance between the harm to civilians and civilian objects caused by the attack and the military advantage secured by it is required under the principle of proportionality, another general principle of IHL. This principle is the focus of this entry.

Article 51(5)(b) of Additional Protocol I of the Geneva Conventions codifies the principle of proportionality. It defines a disproportionate attack as one "which may be expected to cause incidental loss of civilian life, injury to civilians, damage to civilian objects, or a combination thereof, which would be excessive in relation to the concrete and direct military advantage anticipated"[3] and decrees the illegality of such an attack. The definition,

---

[1] See entry C: Combatants; J.M. Henckaerts and L. Doswald-Beck (eds.), *Customary International Humanitarian Law*, 2 vols. (Cambridge: Cambridge University Press, 2009), vol. I, pp. 3–79.

[2] See entry G: Geneva Law, Section G.1.1.

[3] The definition is repeated in Article 57(2)(a)(iii) of Protocol Additional to the Geneva Conventions of August 12, 1949, and relating to the Protection of Victims of International Armed Conflicts (Additional Protocol I), Geneva, June 8, 1977, 1125 UNTS 3 [hereinafter:

thus, demands weighing the *expected* incidental civilian casualties (as opposed to *intentional* casualties, which are always illegal) against the *anticipated* concrete military advantage,[4] and considers disproportionate any attack that, on balance, is *excessive*.

The principle of proportionality carries the footprint of the old moral concept of "the lesser evil."[5] Grounded in theological thought aimed at explaining divine acts and omissions and rationalizing natural and human catastrophes, this concept has been transformed by moralists into a claim about the ethical behavior required of humans faced with two or more bad options.[6] If the lesser evil is better than the greater evil, then it is the relative good, so the argument goes, and thus the path to follow. The IHL version of this can be accepted as a faithful translation of the moral dictum only if we agree that alongside the well-being of civilians and the integrity of civilian objects, military necessity is also a *good* to be pursued. This is quite a leap, given that the principle of proportionality is part of the laws of war (*jus in bello*) which are designed to govern hostilities regardless of whether the original decision to use force was just or even legal (an issue regulated by the laws of war regulating the initial use of force, the *jus ad bellum*). It is only under a premise that attaches value to war efforts (regardless of their legality or justness) that military need at any expense of civilian interests could ever be considered the lesser evil, or, in the language of the proportionality principle, "not excessive." The result is an axiom which serves as the cornerstone of proportionality: that victory in hostilities (a military triumph, regardless of the lawfulness of legitimacy of war's motivations and the initial use of force – *jus in bello*) – is a *good*. It follows that military advantage can be measured on the same meter of goodness as the well-being of civilians.

AP I]; Article 3(3) and Article 3(8)(c) of Protocol Additional to the Convention on Prohibitions or Restrictions on the Use of Certain Conventional Weapons Which may be deemed to be Excessively Injurious or to have Indiscriminate Effects of October 10, 1980, on Prohibitions or Restrictions on the Use of Mines, Booby-Traps and Other Devices (Additional Protocol II), Geneva, May 3, 1996, 1342 UNTS 137; Article 8(2)(b)(iv) of the Rome Statute of the International Criminal Court, UN General Assembly, July 17, 1998, ISBN No. 92-9227-227-6 [hereinafter: *ICC Statute*] incriminates an intentional disproportionate attack.

4   The crime defined in Article 8(2)(b)(iv) of the *ICC Statute* deviates from the *AP I* definition by adding the word "overall" ("in relation to the concrete and direct *overall* military advantage anticipated"). The ICRC saw this change as changing existing law (e.g., Henckaerts and Doswald-Beck, *Customary International Humanitarian Law*, p. 50).

5   For an excellent account of the relationship between the ancient concept of the "lesser evil" and the modern concept of "proportionality," see E. Weizman, *The Least of All Possible Evils: Humanitarian Violence from Arendt to Gaza* (London: Verso, 2011).

6   *Ibid.*, pp. 1–6.

Being a general rather than a specific principle, proportionality's providence in IHL commands not only classic attacks using firearms that might physically kill, injure, or damage, but also the application of noncombative military powers over enemy combatants and civilians that may delay, limit, or deny rights. This is particularly relevant to belligerent occupations where armies perform the roles of all branches of government and regulate life in the occupied territory. The task of balancing competing interests or rights, which is a central element in any exercise of public powers, is in essence also a type of economy of lesser and greater evils.

The moral judgment that is at the core of the proportionality principle sets it apart from normative principles that lack such judgment. Of course, the classification of questions as moral or factual is not an exact science. Moral judgments involve factual assessments and what appear to be "purely" factual questions inevitably often involve moral assertions. Assessed by their dominant trait, however, proportionality – with its metric of evils – is essentially different from, for example, the principle of distinction: the latter is easily applied once an answer is provided to the question of whether the target in question is military or civilian, a result of fact-dominant analysis. The main implication of the difference between *moral-judgment driven norms* and *fact-judgment-driven norms* is the breadth of the spectrum of opinions the norm is likely to generate for a given question, with judgment-driven norms generating a much more diverse array of results. Nothing demonstrates this better than the results yielded by an *excessive* formula for proportionate attacks.[7]

The principle of proportionality thus creates a unique, unstable kind of normative space where the border between the legal and the illegal is subject to a greater disagreement than that generated by fact-dominant norms. In simple terms: The deferral to a moral calculation of *excessiveness of harm* invites subjective judgments.

---

[7] On assessing proportionality, see J. Dill, "Joint series on international law and armed conflict," *ICRC –Inter Cross Blog* (October 11, 2016), http://intercrossblog.icrc.org/blog/r19aesa7v1kylc c5a4hbcwvfx8imus. Empirical investigation quoted in the article demonstrates how varied opinions on proportionality are. Asked about the number of collateral civilian casualties caused by an attack expected to eliminate Taliban fighters in an Afghan village, 20–27 percent of lay American and British interviewees rejected the notion that any number of casualties could be proportionate, 17–21 percent held any number as justified, and the rest ranged between 1 casualty to 10,000. Interviews Dill held with Israeli, American, and Afghan military commanders similarly "led to the inescapable conclusion that even individuals with military expertise have widely diverging reactions to most attacks that cause some incidental harm and yield some military advantage." See also R. Sulitzeanu-Kenan, M. Kremnitzer, and S. Alon, "Facts, Preferences, and Doctrine: An Empirical Analysis of Proportionality Judgment" (2016) 50 *Law and Society Review* 348, www.idi.org.il/media/9298/facts-preferences-and-doctrine-an-empirical.pdf.

This feature has made proportionality extremely attractive to Israeli judges who applied it extensively to rule on exceptions to the rights of protected persons, exceptions that are scattered throughout the laws of belligerent occupation. The Israeli HCJ of the '80s and '90s was especially ripe for a proportionality era of jurisprudence and the value-based analysis it involves. The generational change of the bench that took place in the late '70s replaced what had been a fairly formalistic judicial approach to adjudication with a purposive philosophy of law that did not shy away from values as a key legal interpretive principle.[8] Proportionality – rather than authority – thus became the legal battleground for almost every public policy or practice challenged in the court as abusive to human rights, including reviews of Israel's policies and actions in the OPT.[9] While petitioners argued that certain policies were incompatible with IHL, and ergo ultra vires, the High Court almost routinely shifted the focus of analysis toward the arithmetic of competing rights or interests. Such was the case in the litigation on assigned residence,[10] encirclement of towns and cities and movement restrictions,[11] restrictions on worship in holy places,[12] house demolitions during operations,[13] punitive house demolitions,[14] Palestinian incarceration conditions,[15] targeted killings,[16] and many more.

The implications of stretching proportionality to serve as the main, if not the only, standard for determining the legality of acts carried out by Israel's occupation forces are addressed in this entry through an analysis of two cases. The first concerns a judicial review of Israel's construction of the

---

[8] M. Mautner, *The Decline of Formalism and the Rise of Values in Israeli Law* (Tel Aviv: Maagaley Daat, 1993) [Hebrew]; E. Shraga and R. Shahar, *Administrative Law*, 6 vols. (Bnei Brak: Bursi, 2009), vol. V, pp. 30–33 [Hebrew]. On the interpretative turn of the bench, see entry D: Deportations.

[9] Proportionality, in its different manifestations, including the doctrine which vitiated administrative acts on ground of "radical unreasonableness," has been at the core of numerous challenges.

[10] HCJ 7015/02 *Ajuri v. Commander of the IDF in Judea and Samaria* (2002) 56(6) PD 352, http://elyon1.court.gov.il/Files_ENG/02/150/070/A15/02070150.A15.pdf); See entry A: Assigned Residence.

[11] HCJ 2847/03 *Alawneh v. IDF Commander in Judea and Samaria* (July 14, 2003); HCJ 2410/03 *al-Arja v. IDF Commander in Judea and Samaria* (July 8, 2003).

[12] HCJ 10356/02 *Hass v. Commander of the IDF forces in the West Bank* (2004) 58(3) PD 443.

[13] HCJ 4219/02 *Ghosin v. IDF Commander in Gaza* (2002) 56(4) PD 608.

[14] HCJ 5510/92 *Turqman v. Minister of Defense* (1993) 48(1) PD 217, 219; HCJ 1730/96 *Sabih v. IDF Commander in the Judea and Samaria Area* (1996) 50(1) PD 353, 364; HCJ 893/04 *Faraj v. IDF Commander in the West Bank* (April 4, 2004).

[15] HCJ 9437/05 *HaMoked – Center for the Defence of the Individual v. IDF Commander in the West Bank* (January 17, 2006); HCJ 5591/02 *Yassin v. Commander of Kziot Military Camp – Kziot Detention Facility* (2002) 57(1) PD 403.

[16] HCJ 769/02 *The Public Committee Against Torture in Israel v. The Government of the State of Israel* (2006) 62(1) PD 507.

separation fence in the occupied territory, and the second relates to a challenge against the application of the fence's associated permit regime. Section P.2 discusses these cases. Section P.3 analyses the methodology of applying proportionality at the expense of authority-based rules, followed, in Section P.4, by a critical discussion of the predicament of the very rule of law once proportionality is blown out of proportion. Section P.5 concludes.

P.2 AUTHORITY ON THE BALANCE

P.2.1 Israel's Separation Fences and Walls Project

In 2002, in the face of a wave of suicide terrorism that washed over the country, and under tremendous public pressure, the government of Israel decided to install a physical barrier for the official purpose of denying unmonitored movement of Palestinians into Israel. In the three and a half decades leading up to this decision, Israel's actions had been geared toward amalgamating the West Bank and Israel, though, for political reasons, it stopped short of formal annexation (with the exception of East Jerusalem).[17] As part of these actions, the 1949 Armistice border between Israel and the West Bank, known as the Green Line, had been effectively erased. Israel and the West Bank shared a road system, the electricity grid, and the water network, and travel between the two areas was unobstructed. The separation fence, which is, in fact, a system of different types of fences, walls, ditches, and patrol roads running several dozen meters across, with a three-meter high detection fence in the center, was poised to bring the Green Line back to life. Under pressure from the powerful settler lobby, which objected to building a fence on the armistice line for fear this would cement it as the future border, the Israeli government exploited the public demand for physical separation and the understandable fear of vicious terrorist attacks and drew a new line which embraced, to the west of it (i.e., on the side that is not physically separated from Israel's sovereign territory), the major settlement blocs along with as much land as possible for future development.[18] This is why the route selected for the fence intruded deeply into the West Bank and redivided the land to the west of the Jordan River into two contiguous areas: from the Jordan River to the fence and

---

[17] On the fragmentation of the West Bank, see entry Z: Zone.
[18] For an historical account of the politics which led to the design of the separation fence, see S. Arieli and M. Sfard, *Homa Ve-Mehdal: Geder Ha-Frada – Bitahon o Hamdanut (The Wall of Folly)* (Tel Aviv: Sifrey Aliyat Ha-Gag, 2008) [Hebrew]. Order Regarding Defense Regulations (Judea and Samaria) (No. 378), 1970, Declaration Regarding Closure of Area No s/2/03 (Seam Area). See also entry B: Border/Barrier.

from the fence to the Mediterranean. Under this new division, more than 16 percent of the West Bank (920 km²) were to remain on the so-called Israeli side of the fence, and with them hundreds of thousands of dunams of land owned and used by Palestinians, as well as several Palestinian communities that were to remain trapped between the State of Israel to the west and the fence to the east. The route itself was to twist and wind its way through valleys and mountains, running a course of 720 km, twice the length of the Green Line – all in order to encircle as many Israeli settlements and as much yet-to-be-settled land as possible.

The fence created what Israel calls "the seam zone," a space that is still within the West Bank, and hence, ostensibly permitted for Palestinian entry.[19] In order to prevent their entry into Israel, a legal fence had to be erected. The latter, made up of military declarations and orders coupled with a bureaucratic permit system, was tasked with doing what the physical fence is not smart enough to do: selection. To use the fence as a filter, the military had to cast a complicated legal net around it, impenetrable to Palestinians but open to everyone else. The legal fence is known as the "permit regime": It is predicated on a declaration of the seam zone as a military zone entry into which is prohibited without a military-issued permit.[20] The permit regime was designed in such a way as to absolve Israelis[21] – defined as Israeli citizens and permanent residents, people eligible under Israel's Law of Return, that is, anyone who is Jewish[22] – as well as tourists[23] of the need to obtain a permit. The permit regime is thus clearly a legal regime of separation and discrimination based on nationality/ethnicity.

A decade of litigation in the HCJ, with more than 100 petitions filed against different segments of the fence, has ultimately led to some changes in its route, and the area trapped to the west of it was reduced to encompass slightly less than 9 percent of the West Bank. The notion that an occupying power may, for security reasons, put up a physical barrier that divides the occupied territory,

---

[19] See entry Z: Zone, Section Z.2.2.4.
[20] Order Regarding Defense Regulations (Judea and Samaria) (No. 378), 1970, Declaration Regarding Closure of Area No s/2/03 (Seam Area); See also entry B: Border/Barrier.
[21] *Ibid.*, Article 4(a)(1) stipulates that the proclamation is not applicable to any "Israeli." "Israeli" is defined in Article 1.
[22] In May 2004, the Proclamation was amended: the exemption of Israelis was vacated, and a general permit was issued for them instead.
[23] Article 4(a)(2) empower the military commander to issue individual or general permits for entry and presence in the seam zone. Accordingly, the military commander has signed on October 2, 2003. A General Permit to Enter the Seam Zone (Judeah and Samaria) which provided a general permit to people with a valid foreign passport and visa to enter the State of Israel.

was, however, upheld by the court. The court also declared the permit regime legal. On both planes, as is discussed in Sections P.2.2 and P.2.3, the HCJ shifted the focus of the legal analysis from the question of authority to the question of proportionality.

P.2.2 *The Beit Surik Case*

The principled arguments against the construction of the fence were first thoroughly examined in the petition filed by the village council of Beit Surik, together with seven neighboring villages, against plans to build the separation fence on their land.[24] The HCJ in Jerusalem engaged with this case and discussed the legality of the separation fence at the same time that the ICJ in The Hague was reviewing the same issue in response to a request for an advisory opinion on the matter from the UN General Assembly.[25] The crucial point of distinction between the two instances appears to be located in perspective: The ICJ focused on the legality of the entire fence on the grounds that the decision to build it exceeded the powers of the military commander in the occupied territory; the HCJ refused to rule in a petition filed before the Beit Surik case, in which the same argument had been made.[26] The ICJ's opinion is, thus, authority-based; the HCJ's judgments substituted authority for proportionality: then chief justice Aharon Barak believed that the legality of the fence should be reviewed one section at a time, given that each section of the fence had different implications for life around it. Barak's decision to employ a segmented perspective could help reveal factual patterns that would be undetectable from a wider angle, but, at the same time, dictated blindness to many other facts only the bigger picture could reveal – e.g., the existence of patterns in the route such as the fact that the fence invades areas where no

---

[24] The Beit Surik case was preceded by two petitions that were dismissed without substantive reasoning, HCJ 3325/02 *al-Rahman Rashid Hassan Khatab (Qar'us)* v. *Judea and Samaria Area Military Commander* (April 24, 2002); see also, HCJ 8172/02 *Ibtisam Muhammad Ibrahim* v. *IDF Commander in the West Bank* (October 14, 2002). In this case grounds were provided, but given the state's position that an immediate decision was necessary, the reasoning was extremely brief and did not address all the legal arguments challenging the legality of the fence.

[25] GA Res 10/14E, UN Doc A/RES/35/169E (December 15, 1980) Illegal Israeli actions in Occupied East Jerusalem and the rest of the Occupied Palestinian Territory; Consequences of the Construction of a Wall in the Occupied Palestinian Territory, Advisory Opinion, 2004 ICJ 136, ¶¶ 74–75, 120–122.

[26] A petition by HaMoked – Center for the Defence of the Individual, discussed later in this section (A translation of the petition is available on HaMoked's website www.hamoked.org /Case.aspx?cID=Cases0099. Author of this entry Michael Sfard represented the petitioner in this case).

Palestinians live, or that it keeps areas earmarked for future development of the settlements to its west. Barak later wrote that the immense discrepancy between the conclusions of the HCJ and the ICJ could be explained by these different perspectives or judicial techniques.[27] There is, however, another, perhaps more plausible possibility: that the difference between the judgments was not the result of the different techniques used to examine the route, but rather that the techniques were selected in advance to serve different judicial outcomes.[28]

The legal basis Israel presented for building the fence was military necessity, and the exceptions set in IHL for the prohibition on interference with private property. Those exceptions determine that such interference is permissible only when it is "imperatively demanded by the necessities of war"[29] or "absolutely necessary by military operations."[30] The argument was that the fence was meant to prevent terrorists from crossing into Israel and entering some of the settlements. The petitioners argued that the building of the fence created de facto annexation of the area trapped between it and the Green Line and that its route was selected to serve the needs of the settlements in the area, a purpose that cannot be considered as meeting the military necessity exception.

In its ruling, the HCJ accepted the argument that security considerations – as distinct from political considerations, which it deemed to be extraneous and wrongful – may justify building the fence. The fragmentation of the discussion, however – that is, the focus on one segment of the fence – precluded the petitioners from presenting the route's overall patterns as evidence that settlement interests; in other words, political considerations determined its route. The net result was that the decision to split judicial review into segments was tantamount to turning a blind eye to the issue of authority. In this situation, the affidavits given by the military commander, affirming that the route had been

---

[27] HCJ 7957/04 *Mara'abe* v. *Prime Minister of Israel* (2005) 60(2) PD 477, http://elyon1.court.gov
      .il/files_eng/04/570/079/A14/04079570.a14.pdf.

[28] On the differences between the advisory opinion and the judgment, see, e.g., the articles
      collected in the Special Double Issue: Domestic and International Judicial Review of the
      Construction of the Separation Barrier, (2005) 38(1–2) *Israel Law Review*; A. M. Gross,
      "The Construction of the Wall between The Hague and Jerusalem: The Enforcement and
      Limits of Humanitarian Law and the Structure of Occupation" (2006) 19 *Leiden Journal of
      International Law* 393 (for a revised and updated version see A. Gross, *The Writing on the Wall*
      (Cambridge: Cambridge University Press, 2017), pp. 265–337).

[29] Article 23(g) of The Hague Convention (IV) Respecting the Laws and Customs of War on
      Land and its annex: Regulations concerning the Laws and Customs of War on Land,
      The Hague, October 18, 1907, 205 CTS 277; 36 Stat 2277.

[30] Article 53 of Geneva Convention Relative to the Protection of Civilian Persons in the Time of
      War, Geneva, August 12, 1949, 75 UNTS 287.

selected for security reasons, went unchallenged. The coupling of this tactic with the HCJ's traditional refusal to determine the legality of the settlements[31] impeded the petitioners from arguing that the deviation of the fence from the Green Line cannot be considered a legitimate security necessity. And so, once the court positioned the legal question within the confines of the military necessity exclusion, it shifted the focus from the question of authority to the question of proportionality.

The court concluded that 30 of the 40 km of the fence considered in this case were disproportionate, while the remaining 10 km did meet the proportionality requirement. It refrained, however, from articulating an operative standard for assessing proportionality. The judgment lists the damage residents of the villages would suffer, and though there was a great difference in the petitioners' and the respondents' assessment of its extent, makes no principled reasoned choice.[32] It simply ruled that military necessity would be compromised should the route of the fence be altered, but refrained from assessing the scope of this necessity and the extent to which it would be compromised were the route changed, absolving itself of the need to create a tool for assessment of the military need, on the grounds that judges are not "military experts." Without clear values to insert into the proportionality equation, the judicial conclusion appears to be entirely subjective.

P.2.3 *The Seam Zone Permit Regime Case*

Two petitions filed by HaMoked – Center for the Defence of the Individual and the Association for Civil Rights in Israel challenged the permit regime associated with the separation fence. These petitions argued that the permit regime defies prohibitions on discrimination and collective punishment and violates fundamental rights allowing no exception. These arguments thus related to authority. The HaMoked petition further compared the permit regime to the Pass Laws imposed on blacks in Apartheid South Africa, requiring them to obtain passes to enter "white"

---

[31] See entry J: Jewish Settlements.
[32] The differences in the anticipated damage assessed by the parties is indeed staggering: For example, for the village of Beit Annan, petitioners argued that 600 dunams of their lands will be severely damaged by the construction of the fence and that 6,500 dunams of cultivated land will remain on the other side, and will be inaccessible to them. The respondents argued that only 410 dunams will be used for the erecting of the fence and that eventually only 1,200 dunams of cultivated land would remain on the other side. The parties also diverged on the question of the degree of access to their lands on the other side of the fence the villagers will enjoy.

areas,[33] and explicitly argued that the permit regime meets the terms of the crime of apartheid, as defined in international law. Responding to comments made by the judges during the oral hearing, HaMoked's counsel[34] clarified that the argument was that with respect to breaches of some legal prohibitions, the question of proportionality does not even arise, as the policy under review is deemed unacceptable at a stage of the deliberation that precedes the more advanced stage of examining its proportionality. The fact that the permit regime is based on group affiliation (nationality/ ethnicity) where one group must obtain a permit in order to exercise fundamental rights and the other does not, without any individual parameters, makes the regime one of these policies.

The court dismissed this position. It is worthwhile to cite its reasoning at some length:

> Indeed, it is difficult to disagree that the declaration of the areas of the seam zone as closed areas, as well as the mere erection of the security fence, severely encumber the Palestinian inhabitants, and in particular, severely injure innocent inhabitants who happen to be in the seam zone against their will due to the fact that they live or work in the area, as their businesses or fields and agricultural lands remained locked within the zone. The application of the permit regime, and the need to obtain a permit in order to enter and leave the zone, imposes a clear restriction on the freedom of movement of the inhabitants of the Area within this zone, and restricts the accessibility of the inhabitants – to their homes, lands and businesses located within the seam zone. As further specified below, this state of affairs creates a reality, which makes it difficult to maintain routine family life, social life, commerce, and work both for the inhabitants who live in the seam zone and for those who have connections to such inhabitants but do not live therein.
>
> However, as is known, the rights with which we are concerned are relative rights, which may be restricted in light of additional considerations and interests, such as considerations of national security, public order and the rights of others ... Therefore, one should examine, with utmost care, the second aspect which is required for the purpose of determining whether the authority to close the area was lawfully exercised, which is the question of

[33] See J. Dugard, *Human Rights and the South African Legal Order* (Princeton: Princeton University Press, 1978), pp. 75–77; M. Horrell, *The Pass Laws* (Johannesburg: South African Institute of Race Relations, 1960). The pass laws was a system which regulated movement of black persons by a requirement of permits for legal entrance, exit or movement inside specified areas. The laws were consolidated in 1952 by the misleadingly titled Bantu (Abolition of Passes and Co-ordination of Documents Act No67, 1952) which requires every black person above the age of 16 will carry a reference book with his/her passes and made a failure to produce it an offense.

[34] Hamoked counsel was the author of this entry, Michael Sfard.

whether, in making his decision to close the area, the military commander had properly balanced the various considerations.[35]

There is very little direct reference to the Apartheid and discrimination arguments in the judgment. "There is no escape from prohibiting unsupervised entry of Palestinians into the seam zone," Dorit Beinisch, then chief justice of the HCJ, wrote, proceeding to reprimand the petitioner for the "careless manner by which this term [Apartheid] was used."[36] And so, even faced with a policy that is clearly based on discrimination by group affiliation, the court steered the legal analysis toward the realm of balancing interests and ruled that the legality of this policy should be determined according to a cost–benefit analysis of rights versus security.

The petitioners did not merely contest the authority to establish the permit regime. They suggested an alternative: an individual vetting process, including physical security checks at the separation fence crossings. The respondents vigorously objected, raising the concern that a terrorist might cross the fence unarmed and then be armed on the other side.[37] The court refrained from embarking on an investigation of the extent of the loss of security that will be suffered by selecting the individual vetting option, making any concretization of the proportionality formula impossible. Instead, the court repeated its· assertion that the expertise on security matters is vested with the respondents, and declined to review it.

The result was that while approving the general policy as balanced and legal, the bench dove into the complex task of examining its inner workings, procedures, and forms, recommending changes, and expanding some of the grounds for obtaining permits.

P.3 VALUES: CONSTANTS AND VARIABLES

Neither the petitioners nor the respondents found in the judgments the precise exchange rate between security interests and humanitarian concerns. This is neither surprising, nor is it indeed reasonable to expect an exact formula. Even if one accepts at face value the court's turning a blind eye to the political motivations behind the route of the fence and proceeds from the supposition that it was determined according to security considerations, the trouble with shifting the focus to the question of proportionality is that it pits

---

[35] HCJ 9961/03 *HaMoked – Center for the Defence of the Individual* v. *Government of Israel* (April 5, 2011), ¶¶ 22–23 (English translation available on the website of HaMoked – Center for the Defence of the Individual, www.hamoked.org/files/2013/114260_eng.pdf).
[36] *Ibid.*, ¶ 44.   [37] *Ibid.*, ¶¶ 31–30.

the security of the occupiers against the fundamental rights of protected persons. This contest is forever vertical because security is translated into a life-threat and in the economy of evils the right to life is positioned above life's quality – that is, above making a living, property rights, and dignity.[38]

Indeed, skipping over the issue of authority is problematic not only because of the political nature of the route, but also, and perhaps mainly, because it fragments the law of occupation in a manner that defies its fundamental principles and forever works to the detriment of the occupied population: The fence creates profound demographic, cultural, and economic changes in the occupied territory. It severs the ties between the seam zone and the rest of the West Bank and weaves new ones with Israel. This is a breach of the conservation principle, the trust principle, and the temporariness of occupation. All this is possible only when the focus shifts to an examination of proportionality, which obscures the outer limits the laws of occupation set for the occupier's powers. The difficulty with this methodology is chillingly expressed in the approval of the permit system.

It is, in fact, a methodology akin to racial profiling: An entire group of people is labeled dangerous and the rights of its members are denied (or "merely" circumscribed) because of their group affiliation – that is, because of who they are rather than because of what they did.[39] To make matters worse, while racial profiling is limited to security checks, the permit regime is an entire legal regime that denies rights and creates duties. Looking at it from the proportionality perspective essentially dilutes the very status of the fundamental prohibition on discrimination. If everything is relative, nothing is constant.

There is yet another problem with the focus on proportionality, deriving from the secularization of the theological notion of *the lesser evil*: The divine economy of evils is precise; it is always right. God is, after all, omniscient, and therefore able to insert exact values into the proportionality equation. Humans, on the other hand, must rely on estimation, speculation, and guess-work: How many people will be hurt in terrorist attacks that are not foiled if the fence is placed south of the hill rather than north of it? How will the number of olive oil barrels decrease if farmers are allowed to access their land only twice a year rather than daily? The uncertainty that goes hand in hand with assessing proportionality makes sacrificing the fundamental principles that should function as constants particularly egregious. The conservation principle

---

[38]   On the security theology, see entry X: X-Ray: Surveillance and Profiling Technologies. On the impact of the security considerations on the peoples' welfare, see entry Q: Quality of Life.
[39]   On profiling, see entries X: X-Ray and K: Kinship.

within the laws of occupation and the prohibition on discrimination according to group affiliation (i.e., the notion of the shared humanity inherent to us all) are banished in favor of a speculative balance of the lesser evil.

The danger of using proportionality in this manner is far reaching. The notion of the lesser evil derives its powerful, at times lethal, attraction from a rational moral intuition: Less evil is better than more evil, and more good is better than less good. This apparently simple mathematics is, alas, slippery, providing not certainty but uncertainty: When it is enlisted for use such as the one made in the fence cases, it is manipulated, because the level of uncertainty is so high that what is at stake is no longer the "lesser evil," but the "anticipated lesser evil," and the transition from necessary evil to anticipated evil is a threat to the most fundamental values of society. One example of the anticipated lesser evil is the ticking-bomb scenario, which theoretically justifies torturing a suspect who has information about the location of this bomb. The trouble with this thesis, like the trouble with the issue of what evil will result from replacing the permit system with security checks, is the *certain* sacrifice of fundamental values for the sake of what is, by definition, *potential* harm to security, values, or rights.

Abandoning constants in favor of variables that are subject to estimation and guesswork also serves an institutional purpose: It augments the status of the judiciary. Since the debate over whether a certain set of circumstances meets the test of proportionality is almost never exhausted, given its inherent subjectivity, the shift of focus from authority to balance of interests boosts the judiciary's power to affect the policy. In practice, it invites legal challenges to every executive act carried out within the framework of the policy, under the premise that not only is there nothing to lose, but there is always a chance of securing some degree of success. In other words, by its very nature, proportionality-based jurisprudence generates less judicial clarity and certainty and therefore encourages litigation on a case-by-case basis. This, in turn, allows the court to micromanage executive practice rather than regulate it. This is best demonstrated in the Israeli separation fence jurisprudence: Following the *Beit Surik* judgment, rather than being channeled into clear attributes of what constitutes a "legal" route, thus avoiding litigation, rivals in later fence legal battles were encouraged to make their own (very different) proportionality calculations. The unsurprising result was that the court docket was flooded with petitions against every segment of planned fence. The Beit Surik proportionality-based methodology of reviewing the legality of the route cemented the court's high-resolution involvement in sketching it, to the degree that

Israeli commentators concluded that the HCJ is in fact drafting the future border of the State of Israel.[40]

P.4 PROPORTIONALITY BLOWN OUT OF PROPORTION

Proportionality is a doctrine that is helpful for deciphering the boundaries of executive power in cases that are not subject to a more primary limitation. It thus comes into play only once the primary issue of the very existence of the executive authority to act in a certain manner has been determined, not in lieu of this determination. Once proportionality becomes an all-encompassing doctrine, one that applies to all acts and all policies and determines their legality, it cannot be guaranteed that any prohibition is absolute or that an exception will not become the rule.

Indeed, the economy of anticipated evils may be understood to generate, in clear cases, total bans. In reality, however, due to the nature of the judgment that is in its core – one that includes moral valuations and factual specula-tions – it is impregnated with the seed that is prone to generate, at one point or another, a negative balance for the prohibition. Given the right circum-stances, proportionality as a mega-doctrine will allow a range of practices that are abusive to the most fundamental principles of the law of belligerent occupation. It allows racial profiling,[41] it allows internment of citizens accord-ing to a certain group affiliation,[42] and it may justify or provide a defense for torture. Indeed, it might even justify a nuclear attack.[43] The staggering fact is that the decimation of these prohibitions is made in the name of none other

---

[40]   Then minister of justice, Tzipi Livni said in a conference that "in practice the High Court is drawing in its rulings the borders of the State [of Israel]." See Y. Yoaz, "Livni: The Separation Fence is the Future Border of the State [of Israel]," *Haaretz* (November 30, 2005), www .haaretz.co.il/misc/1.1062723.

[41]   See entry X: X-Ray.   [42]   *Korematsu v. United States*, 323 US 214 (1944).

[43]   For an analysis of a lesser-evil justification of dropping the atomic bombs on Hiroshima and Nagasaki in World War II, see G. Blum, "The Laws of War and the 'Lesser Evil'" (2010) 35 *The Yale Journal of International Law* 1, 28; see, e.g., Legality of the Threat or Use of Nuclear Weapons, Advisory Opinion, 1996 ICJ 226, the ICJ concluded that "the threat or use of nuclear weapons would generally be contrary to the rules of international law applicable in armed conflict, and in particular the principles and rules of humanitarian law. *However, in view of the current state of international law, and of the elements of fact at its disposal, the Court cannot conclude definitively whether the threat or use of nuclear weapons would be lawful or unlawful in an extreme circumstance of self-defence, in which the very survival of a State would be at stake*" (Reply (e), p. 266, emphasis added, the justices were split 7–7, the determination upheld by the president Bedjaoui's casting vote). This determination alludes to proportionality as governing the question of threat or even use of nuclear weapons. For a critique, see D. Kennedy, *The Dark Side of Virtue: Reassessing International Humanitarianism* (Princeton: Princeton University Press, 2004), pp. 316–323.

than human rights. This is the most subversive feature of the proportionality calculation.

The replacement of authority-based prohibitions with an assessment of proportionality may be compared to a shift in evidence law from admissibility to weight. Once this is accepted, no evidence exclusion rule is safe. Indeed, why not call into question the absoluteness of the principle of distinction? Maybe, as suggested by the proponents of the Hiroshima and Nagasaki nuclear attacks, more civilians would have died and more damage would have been inflicted on humanity if the allied forces had invaded Japan rather than dropped the bomb on the two cities?[44]

P.5 CONCLUSION: WEIGHTLESS WORLD?

The adoption of a mega-doctrine of proportionality, in its evil-guessing-game form, while shrinking the domain of simple authority rules, unavoidably creates a slippery slope that allows the gradual erosion of prohibitions formerly considered absolute, or the injection of elasticity into exceptions which then become rules. The judicial sanctioning of the permit system serving the Israeli separation fence, with its associated suspect-classification criteria, is an obvious example. This, in turn, uncovers the most abusive aspect of the proportionality-gone-wild treatment of rights: While on the face of it, proportionality with its value-based judgment is attractive to jurists who subscribe to Dworkin's interpretive methodology in *Taking Rights Seriously*,[45] its expansive application in a manner that obviates recourse to the antecedent question of authority fails to take rights seriously as it replaces or reformulates strict prohibitions that govern the most basic do's-and-don'ts of the applicable legal system. Instead of asking what acts the Israeli army could carry out to secure the lives of Israelis given the limits imposed by the laws of occupation, the proportionality-led analysis calls into question these very limits. In effect, rather than construing methodically the permissible scope of exceptions to the protection of rights, it breaks them up and allows the use of power that is otherwise legally impermissible. The way proportionality is used to dilute restrictions on public power warrants special attention: Rather than conceding a (permissible) violation of normative limitations, it masquerades as a new reading of them, one that finds an ostensible necessary deviation from a prohibition to be permissible in the first place.

---

[44]   Kennedy, *ibid.*
[45]   R. Dworkin, *Taking Rights Seriously* (Cambridge, MA: Harvard University Press, 1977).

Proportionality appears like an invitation to give more weight to moral values. Appearances, alas, are deceiving:[46] Due to its abovementioned short-comings, uncertain factors, and subjective assessments, applying it as a primary rather than as a secondary principle carries the danger of severely impairing, if not altogether destroying, the very fundamental values its rhetoric ostensibly protects. This is a proportionality gone out of proportion.

---

[46] In reference to the language used by Judge Krylov in his dissenting opinion in Conditions of Admission of a State to Membership in The United Nations, Advisory Opinion, 1948 ICJ 54, 107.

Q

Quality of Life

Orna Ben-Naftali

Q.1 GENERAL: *AMUSE BOUCHE*

Q.1.1 *The Concept of Quality of Life*

"Quality of Life" is a concept so common as to seem self-evident. Its content, however, is not self-explanatory. Indeed, given that it is dynamic, encompasses both objective and subjective elements, and relates to a variety of spheres of life, it is little wonder that it has been researched from a wide range of disciplinary perspectives and methodologies.

Four main approaches have been employed to the study of quality of life: first, an objective approach, seeking to analyze it through external variables from the perspectives of the social sciences, economics, health sciences, environmental studies, etc.; second, a normative approach which employs various variables derived from philosophy and theology relative to the notion of the good or meaningful life; third, a utilitarian approach, based on economics, which seeks to define quality of life by focusing on the degree of fulfillment of needs/desires of the individuals comprising a society; and fourth, a subjective approach which, grounded in behavioral studies and psychology, focuses on the way individual members of society define their well-being – that is, on the gap between a person's expectations and experiences.[1]

These various approaches have further generated a multitude of methodologies employing various indicators for measuring quality of life. Beginning in the 1960s, research focusing on data collection of numerous economic indicators has resulted in detailed international reports comparing and grading quality of life in various states. Later research employed other objective social

---

[1] G. Bognar, "The Concept of Quality of Life" (2005) 31 *Social Theory and Practice* 561; E. Diener and E. Suh, "Measuring Quality of Life: Economic, Social, and Subjective Indicators" (1997) 40 *Social Indicators Research* 189.

parameters (e.g., life span, infant mortality, number of medical doctors per capita, rate of criminal activity), and, eventually, qualitative empirical research was undertaken to generate subjective understanding of well-being. Currently, it is generally accepted that a proper study should combine objective and subjective methodologies and cross-refer social indicators with indicators relative to a sense of life satisfaction. Such correlations disclose a strong link between subjective well-being and income, human rights, societal equality, and a certain level (albeit culturally differentiated) of autonomy that allows for the pursuit of personal goals.[2] The underlying assumption of the research is that policymakers care about the quality of life of members of their respective societies and strive to secure it. It is thus designed primarily to assist them in assessing their policies and related allocation of resources.[3]

Law and legal institutions do not directly conduct quality of life research. They do, however, relate to and have a direct impact on both objective and subjective quality of life indicators in numerous areas, ranging from labor and social welfare to criminal enforcement, equality and nondiscrimination, civic participation, and political culture. Legal issues such as governance and human rights are thus commonly included in social indicators measuring quality of life,[4] and empirical subjective research has found a direct correlation between the scope of protection of human rights and the level of personal well-being.[5]

Explicit references to "quality of life" or to the somewhat narrower, more objective and quantifiable, yet interchangeably used "standard of living," appear both in the Universal Declaration of Human Rights and in various international and regional human rights treaties,[6] as well as in various

---

[2]   Diener and Suh, "Measuring Quality of Life."

[3]   The leading quality of life research, the Human Development Index, is undertaken annually by UNDP (United Nations Development Programme), http://hdr.undp.org/en/content/hum an-development-index-hdi; a complementary UN research, The World Happiness Report, is undertaken annually by the UNSDSN (United Nations Sustainable Development Solutions Network), http://worldhappiness.report. See also the OECD (Organisation for Economic Co-operation and Development) Better Life Index, www.oecdbetterlifeindex.org.

[4]   See, e.g., http://ec.europa.eu/eurostat/statistics-explained/index.php/Quality_of_life_ indicators.

[5]   See, e.g., R. Veenhoven, "Quality of Life and Happiness: Not Quite the Same," in G. De Girolamo, P. Becchi, F. S. Coppa, D. De Leo, G. Neri, P. Rucci, and P. Scocco (eds.), *Salute e Qualità dell Vida* (Torino: Centro Scientifico Editore, 2001), p. 67 scheme 5 [Italian; English translation available at https://personal.eur.nl/veenhoven/Pub2000s/2001e-full.pdf].

[6]   See, e.g., Article 25 of the Universal Declaration of Human Rights, GA Res 217A (III), UN Doc A/810 71 (1948) [hereinafter: UDHR]; Article 11 of the International Convention on Economic Social and Cultural Rights, December 16, 1966, 993 UNTS 3; Article 2 of European Union, Treaty on European Union (Consolidated Version), Treaty of Maastricht, February 7, 1992, Official Journal of the European Communities C 325/5; Preamble to the Charter of the Indian

judgments and judicial opinions.[7] In essence, the various elements comprising "quality of life" in these documents signify and pour content into the idea of human dignity, the assumption that the individual is never to be treated as a means to an end, and states' obligations to protect, respect, and advance the conditions of possibility to lead a dignified life.

Q.1.2 *Quality of Life Under Occupation*

International legal obligations designed to secure not merely the very right to life but also a certain quality of life, extend to territories that are not sovereign, including those under belligerent occupation. Thus, Article 43 of the Hague Regulations shoulders the occupying power with the responsibility to ensure "l'ordre et la vie publics."[8] The legislative history suggests that "la vie publics" or "civil life" encompasses "social functions, ordinary transactions which constitute daily life."[9] This reading reflects the basic premise, confirmed in the introductory sentence of Article 43, that in order to guarantee normal life for the civilian population, all functions of government must be provisionally

Ocean RIM association for regional cooperation (IOR-ARC) Concluded at Mauritius, March 7, 1997, Entered into force, March 7, 1997, IOR-ARC/ MIN97/1/CH, 36 ILM 807 (1997); The Durban Declaration in Tribute to the Organization of African Unity and the Launching of the African Union, AU Doc ASS/AU/Decl 2(1), Assembly of the AU, 1st Ord Sess, Durban, South Africa, July 9–10, 2002; Article 10, Inter-American Democratic Charter, September 11, 2001, OAS Doc OEA/Ser.P/AG/RES.1 (XXVIII-E/01), 40 ILM (2001) 1289.

[7] See e.g., Legality of the Threat or Use of Nuclear Weapons, Advisory Opinion, 1996 ICJ 226, ¶ 29; Gabcicovo-Nagymaros Project (Hungary/Slovenia), Judgment, 1997 ICJ Rep 7, ¶ 140; *Kozacioglu* v. *Turkey*, Eur Ct HR, App No 2334/03 (February 19, 2009); UNHCR/OSCE Assessment of the Situation of Ethnic Minorities in Kosovo (October 23, 2000), www.osce .org/kosovo/13304?download=true

[8] The authoritative French version uses the phrase "l'ordre et la vie publics." The English translation reads: "public order and safety." Since the authoritative text of The Hague Convention (IV) Respecting the Laws and Customs of War on Land and its annex, Regulations concerning the Laws and Customs of War on Land, The Hague, October 18, 1907, 205 CTS 277; 36 Stat 2277 [hereinafter: the Hague Regulations], is in the French language, the English text has no legal standing. For a discussion of the difference between the French and the English versions of Article 43 of the Hague Regulations, see Y. Dinstein, "Legislation under Article 43 of the Hague Regulations: Belligerent Occupation and Peace-Building," *Harvard Program on Humanitarian Policy and Conflict Research, Occasional Paper* No.1 (2004), pp. 2–4.

[9] This explanation has been proposed by Baron Lambermont, the Belgian representative at the negotiations for the Brussels Convention of 1874, which never entered into force, but is known as the "Brussels Declaration," considered to codify many old rules of IHL. Article 43 of the Hague Regulations combines Articles 2 and 3 of the Brussels Declaration. See Ministère des Affaires Etrangères de Belgique, Actes de la Conférence de Bruxelles de 1874, p. 23, reproduced in E. Schwenk "Legislative Power of the Military Occupant Under Article 43, Hague Regulations" (1945) 54 *Yale Law Journal* 393.

assumed by the occupying power. This premise signifies the principle that an occupation regime is a form of trust, the beneficiaries of which are the protected persons.[10] Numerous aspects of what constitutes "civil life" and the measures an occupying power must, may, or may not take to restore or maintain it are detailed in specific provisions of the Hague Regulations themselves,[11] and are further expanded in the GC IV.[12]

The obligation of the occupying power to provide for the well-being of the occupied population has also been recognized by the Israeli HCJ since the early days of the occupation.[13] What this obligation entails is, however, a matter of debate. The debate is habitually framed in terms of the dialectical tension between this obligation and security concerns. This tension – and the position commonly taken by the HCJ in this respect – is well exemplified in the following excerpt from a judgment in which the HCJ rejected a petition made on behalf of a Palestinian from Gaza to enter Israel for medical treatment:[14]

> As for the type of cases – "saving of life" and "quality of life" – there is no disagreement among the parties with respect to cases which, in the humanitarian context, refer to saving life. As for cases which refer to "quality of life" – we find it difficult to define this very notion. Thus, for instance, a person who loses his eyesight or limbs but remains alive, the injury is so severe that saving his eyesight or limbs is highly significant. Some of these people are also neutralized from causing direct terrorist damage due to their medical situation. On the other hand, neither we nor the petitioners, stand at the Erez crossing [the gate for the passage of persons between Israel and Gaza] exposed to the danger of terror each time it opens, and therefore, it would be unfair to expose, with a stroke of a pen, IDF soldiers and civilians at the crossing to its opening beyond that which is necessary ... Having said that, we nevertheless assume that the respondents would exercise a humane approach, so that the

---

[10] See Introduction, Section 2.2.

[11] See, e.g., Article 46 on family rights, property, and religious practice, Articles 48–52 on taxation, contributions, and requisitions, and Articles 53, 55, and 56 on public property, of the Hague Regulations.

[12] E.g., Article 56 of Geneva Convention Relative to the Protection of Civilian Persons in the Time of War, Geneva, 12 August 1949, 75 UNTS 287 [hereinafter: GC IV] is concerned with hygiene and public health, Article 55 with medical and food supplies, Articles 59–62 with relief, Article 57 with hospitals, Article 58 with spiritual assistance, Articles 51 and 52 with labor, working conditions and labor market measures and Article 50 (3) with some aspects of education.

[13] HCJ 337/71 *The Christian Society for the Holy Places* v. *The Minister of Defence* (1972) 26(1) PD 574 [Hebrew; for an English summary, see (1972) 2 *Israel Yearbook of Human Rights* 354–357].

[14] HCJ 5429/07 *Physicians for Human Rights* v. *Minister of Defense* (June 28, 2007), ¶ 6(5)(B) [Hebrew].

very difficult cases, where the quality of life changes dramatically and no medical care is accessible, would not go unheeded. We do not think, however, that we should be engaged with each of these cases individually but rather leave it (to the respondents) to assess and determine the merits of each case.

These words convey more than the bent of the bench, and more than the indeterminate and elastic meaning of the notion of "quality of life." They signify that it is possible to draw a very thin, almost imperceptible line between bare life and livable life and between humanitarian and military considerations. That thin line, as it was penciled in red in the context of the supply of food to the Gaza Strip between 2007 and 2010, is the focus of this entry.

Q.1.3 *Israel's Red Lines Policy: Humanitarian Minimum and Quality of Life and of Law*

A military document, titled "Food Consumption in the Gaza Strip – Red Lines,"[15] was conceived in early 2008 and its existence and content revealed by journalists Yotam Feldman and Uri Blau in *Haaretz* in 2009.[16] A 2012 judicial decision made pursuant to a petition submitted by Gisha – the Center for Freedom of Movement, on the basis of the Freedom of Information Act, ordered the disclosure of this and two related documents (hereinafter: the Red Lines documents).[17] The Red Lines documents outlined the minimum number of calories required to sustain Gaza's population of (then) 1.5 million at the level of just above the UN definition of hunger and thus to posit not only that "there is no hunger in Gaza," but also that the supply of food Israel permits international agencies to deliver is part of a humanitarian enterprise.

The Red Lines documents were based on a mathematical formula which, as explained by Eyal Wiezman, meant that "If you divide food in the Strip by the daily consumption needs of residents you will get the number of days it will take before people run out of basic provisions and start dying."[18] They

---

[15] An unofficial translation of the document is available at www.gisha.org/UserFiles/File/publi cations/redlines/red-lines-presentation-eng.pdf.

[16] U. Blau and Y. Feldman, "Gaza Bonanza," *Haaretz* (June 15, 2009), www.haaretz.com/gaza-bonanza-1.277760.

[17] AdminC (TA) 2744/09 *Gisha v. Ministry of Defense* (March 22, 2011) [Hebrew]; The state's appeal on the judgment was rejected by the supreme court, AdminA 3300/11 *State of Israel – Ministry of Defense v. Gisha* (September 5, 2012) [Hebrew]. The two additional documents were "Permission to Transfer goods into the Gaza Strip" and "Procedure for Monitoring and assessing Inventories in the Gaza strip."

[18] E. Weizman, *The Least of All Possible Evils* (New York: Verso, 2011), p. 83.

enumerated the calories an adult male (2,279, which is 179 calories above the minimum defined by the World Health Organization), a female, and a child (varying, depending on age and the child's gender) would require; calculated the quantity of local production and the number of residents in the Strip; and divided the total number of calories into cereals, fruits, vegetables, meat, milk, and oil. Certain foods were forbidden (e.g., coriander), others classified as essentials (e.g., rice) and some as luxury (e.g., plums). These classifications were subject to change. This change was neither explained nor known in advance. When it was anything other than a whim, it could be traced to domestic economic interests and to foreign pressure.[19] On the basis of these indicators, a calculation was made on the tonnage (2,575) and the number of trucks (88.8 a day, 5 days a week) allowed into Gaza.

This policy had a context: in 2005 Israel dismantled its settlements in the Gaza Strip, withdrew its ground forces, and transferred its authority to the PA. This process, labeled "disengagement," transformed Gaza into an enclave: Israel controls the airspace and the territorial water. The land is delimited by a perimeter fence. Crossing points, other than the Egyptian-controlled Rafah crossing between Gaza and Egypt, are situated in and controlled by Israel. In June 2006, Hamas won the elections in Gaza, ousted the PA Government, and took control over the territory.[20] Shortly thereafter, Israel devised a policy, the objective of which was to force Hamas out of power. Hunger pangs – or, in the words attributed to attorney Dov Weisglass, advisor to the then prime minister Ehud Olmert, "The idea is to put the Palestinians on a diet but not to make them die of hunger" – were the means.[21] In 2007, in response to Hamas rocket fire on Israel's towns, Israel's cabinet declared Gaza a "hostile territory" and imposed a naval and a territorial blockade. The declaration further articulated its objectives: to limit the movement of people to and from the Gaza Strip and reduce the movement of goods and the supply of fuel and electricity. It also indicated that these restrictions would be implemented systematically, "following a legal examination, taking into account the humanitarian situation and with the intention of preventing a humanitarian

---

[19]   Economic interests of Israeli producers were domestic, see Blau and Feldman, "Gaza Bonanza." Senator John Kerry's dismay at having discovered that pasta is not allowed into Gaza generated the lifting of this particular restriction. See A. Issacharoff and B. Ravid, "Clinton Warns Israel over Delays in Gaza Aid," *Haaretz* (February 25, 2009), www.haaretz .com/print-edition/news/clinton-warns-israel-over-delays-in-gaza-aid-1.270882.

[20]   For more detailed information on Gaza see entry Z: Zone, Section Z.2.2.1; see also I. Scobie, "Gaza," in E. Wilnshurst (ed.), *International Law and the Classification of Conflicts* 280 (Oxford: Oxford University Press, 2012).

[21]   Cited in C. Urquhart, "Gaza on Brink of Implosion as Aid Cut-Off Starts to Bite," *The Guardian* (April 16, 2006), www.theguardian.com/world/2006/apr/16/israel.

crisis."[22] The Red Lines documents reflect the system that received legal approval. While the blockade is yet to be lifted and Hamas is still in power, the implementation of the food restrictions was significantly halted, following international criticism of Israel in the wake of the 2010 flotilla incident.[23] Israel continues to interrupt provisions of goods and electricity, but is ever careful not to cross the red line.[24] The translation of this carefulness into but one indicator for measuring quality of life is that at present (2016) more than 70 percent of the Gazan population is dependent on humanitarian relief.[25]

Placing a whole population under siege, the substance of which was to keep it on the verge of starvation, was framed as a humanitarian project, echoing in some respects the sanction regime imposed on Iraq after the first Gulf war.[26] This humanitarian project received judicial approval upon assurances from the state that it has not crossed the red line of the humanitarian minimum, and that responsible monitoring in coordination with international agencies and the Palestinian health ministry would ensure that it would not.[27]

It is surely true that the situation could have been, and could become, worse. Indeed, given that the humanitarian project of supplying food and other basic necessities to the people of Gaza was framed as an economic warfare undertaken to pressurize them into overthrowing their government and co-opted international agencies, the message that it could get worse was calculated into it.[28]

[22] Israel Ministry of Foreign Affairs Press Release, Security Cabinet Declares Gaza Hostile Territory (September 19, 2007), http://mfa.gov.il/MFA/ForeignPolicy/Terrorism/Pages/Security%20Cabinet%20declares%20Gaza%20hostile%20territory%2019-Sep-2007.aspx, cited in HCJ 9132/07 *Al-Bassiouni v. Prime Minister* (January 30, 2008), ¶ 2 [Hebrew].

[23] The "flotilla incident" was a military operation undertaken on May 31, 2010, by Israel against six civilian ships of the "Gaza Freedom Flotilla," organized by the Free Gaza Movement and the Turkish Foundation for Human Rights and designed as a symbolic act against the blockade of the Gaza Strip. Nine activists were killed in the raid. It drew widespread international condemnation, generated domestic and international committees of inquiry, discussed below at text and notes 40–46, and eventually to the shelving of the Red Lines policy.

[24] For the updated policy, see the Coordination of Government Activities in the Territories unit, Restricted Import List: Gaza Strip 2013 (2013), www.cogat.idf.il/Sip_Storage/FILES/4/4014.pdf.

[25] Gisha, The Gaza Cheat Sheet: Real Data on the Gaza Closure (August 10, 2016), www.gisha.org/userfiles/file/publications/Info_Gaza_Eng.pdf.

[26] The sanction regime, equally based on the advice and complicity of nutrition and health experts, resulted in the death of hundreds of thousands of Iraqi children. See J. Gordon, *Invisible War: The United States and the Iraq Sanctions* (Cambridge, MA: Harvard University Press, 2010).

[27] *Al-Bassiouni.*

[28] See A. Ophir, "The Politics of Catastrophization: Emergency and Exception," in D. Fassin and M. Pnadolfi (eds.) *Contemporary States of Emergency: The Politics of Military and Humanitarian Interventions* 40 (Cambridge, MA: MIT Press, 2010).

It is equally true, however, that the "humanitarian project" inflicting scarcity, pain, and humiliation on the civilian population could have been averted altogether. The fact that such an option was not part of the legal discourse suggests that it accepts the notion that a state may legally exercise maximum control over, with minimum responsibility toward, people subject to said control.[29] This entry posits that it may not: there is a difference between ensuring minimal humanitarian provisions sufficient to sustain bare life, and ensuring the conditions of possibility for a certain quality of life, or a certain standard of living. The former is a brute exercise in biopolitics that treats people as a means to other ends.[30] Israel has been engaged in this exercise. Section Q.2 substantiates this position from a doctrinal position, engaging an analysis of the policy in the light of the law of armed conflicts, the law of belligerent occupation, and IHRL. The obfuscation of the difference between sustaining bare life providing for a quality of life in the legal discourse over the siege and its attendant "minimum humanitarian" project is, as proposed in Section Q.3, a form of Orwelian newspeak, an engagement in lawfare.[31]

Q.2 THE "HUNGER GAMES"[32] IN GAZA 2007–2010: MAIN COURSE

Israel's Red Lines policy had, as noted, two official objectives: first, to prevent a humanitarian crisis in Gaza; and, second, to engage in economic warfare designed to put political pressure on the Hamas government. The legality of this policy is the focus of this section. Section Q.2.1 presents the normative framework that Israel believes applies to this policy and analyzes its legality

---

[29] D. Li, "The Gaza Strip as Laboratory: Notes in the Wake of Disengagement" (2006) 35 *Journal of Palestine Studies* 38.
[30] M. Foucault, *Society Must Be Defended: Lectures at the Collège de France, 1975–76*, M. Bertani and A. Fontana (eds.), D. Macey (trans.) (London: Penguin Books, 2004), p. 256; for an analysis of the situation in Gaza in these terms, see Y. Feldman, "Kavim Adimum (Red Lines)" (2010) 22 *Mita'am* 132 [Hebrew].
[31] See entry L: Lawfare.
[32] S. Collins, *The Hunger Games* (New York: Scholastic Press, 2008). This is the first book of a trilogy which takes place in Panem, a postapocalyptic America governed by an authoritarian central government set in "the Capitol." The Capitol's inhabitants enjoy a high quality of life whereas the rest of the citizens – controlled by extensive electronic surveillance and by a brutal police force – struggle to fend off starvation in 12 slave colonies, or "Districts." Once a year the Capitol televises a spectacle where two teenagers, selected by lottery from each district, are brought to the Capitol, and following training are transported to an arena for a battle where only one of them can survive.

within that framework. Section Q.2.2 presents alternative normative frameworks and proceeds to analyze the legality of the policy in their light.

Q.2.1 A Red Line Normative Framework: The Laws of Armed Conflict

Q.2.1.1 Israel's Position

The normative framework within which Israel claims that its Red Lines policy is lawful is the international law of armed conflict (ILAC). In this reading, pursuant to Israel's disengagement from the Gaza Strip, the latter is no longer an occupied territory and Israel is not burdened with the responsibilities attached to an occupying power.[33] Gaza is "a hostile territory," "an enemy entity," "a danger zone," or "an area controlled by a terrorist organization," which engages in an armed conflict with Israel.[34] Its civilian population no longer qualifies as "protected persons" under the law of belligerent occupation, though they do enjoy the protection afforded to noncombatants in an armed conflict. This position, based on a narrow interpretation of "effective control," has been embraced by the HCJ in numerous decisions.[35] It is also supported by some leading international jurists.[36]

Within this framework, Article 23 of the GC IV obligates a party to an armed conflict to allow the free passage of all consignments of essential foodstuffs intended for the civilians of its adversary, and Article 54 of the AP I prohibits

---

[33]   The State of Israel, The 2014 Gaza Conflict: Factual and Legal Aspects (2015), http://mfa.gov.il /ProtectiveEdge/Documents/2014GazaConflictFullReport.pdf, §§ 45, 374.

[34]   Note that the common denominator of all these names is that they are devoid of a legally recognized meaning. See, e.g., S. Darcy and J. Reynolds, "An Enduring Occupation: The Status of the Gaza Strip from the Perspective of International Humanitarian Law" (2010) 15 *Journal of Conflict & Security Law* 211, 240–241; C. James, "Mere Words: the Enemy Entity Designation of the Gaza Strip" (2009) 32 *Hastings International And Comparative Law Review* 643, 653–655.

[35]   The leading precedent is Al-Bassiouni, discussed in text and notes 38–39.

[36]   E.g., E. Benvenisti, *The International Law of Occupation*, 2nd edn (Princeton: Princeton University Press, 2004), pp. 211–212; A. Roberts, "The Termination of Military Occupations," in *Occupation and Other Forms of Administration of Foreign Territory: Expert Meeting* (Geneva: ICRC, 2012), p. 41, www.icrc.org/eng/assets/files/publications/icrc-002-4094.pdf; Y. Shany, "Binary Law Meets Complex Reality: the Occupation of Gaza Debate" (2008) 41 *Israel Law Review* 68. The notion that "boots on the ground" is a sine qua non condition for "effective control" has found judicial support in Armed Activities on the Territory of the Congo (*Democratic Republic of the Congo v. Uganda*), Judgment, 2005 ICJ Rep 168, ¶ 173; *Banković v. Belgium*, Eur Ct HR, App no 52207/99 (December 19, 2001); *Chiragov v. Armenia*, Eur Ct HR, App No 13216/05 (June 16, 2015); *Sargsyan v. Azerbaijan*, Eur Ct HR, App No 40167/06 (June 16, 2015).

the starvation of civilians as a method of warfare. Israel accepts these obligations: it allows for the passage of the required humanitarian minimum of foodstuff. In this manner, the first objective of its Red Lines policy, the prevention of a humanitarian crisis in the Gaza Strip, is lawfully achieved. Given further that the applicable law contains no prohibition on economic warfare, provided it meets the minimum humanitarian standard, the second objective of the policy is equally lawful. Reports of the World Food Program (WFP) support the assertion that there was neither starvation nor continuous – as distinct from sporadic – shortage of essential foodstuffs in Gaza.[37]

Israel presented this position in court in 2007 in its response to the Al-Bassiouni petition. The petition argued that the closure and the related restrictions on the passage of fuel and electricity are a form of prohibited collective punishment.[38] The HCJ rejected the petition. The court noted that the laws of war do not provide the only relevant normative framework due to Israel's control over land crossings and borders, and to Gaza's dependence on Israel for its supply which was generated by the long-term occupation as well as by the state of belligerency.[39] Yet, the court refrained from specifying what other normative frameworks may be relevant and authorized the restrictions.

Israel's position regarding both the applicable normative framework and the consequential lawfulness of the minimum humanitarian standard received even stronger support in the reports of two commissions entrusted with the examination the flotilla incident. The first, the "Public Commission to Examine the Maritime Incident of 31 May 2010" (The Turkel Commission) was appointed by the Israeli government.[40] Its report embraced the position that, pursuant to its disengagement from Gaza, Israel exercises no effective control over the Gaza Strip, and that between Israel and Hamas there is an international armed conflict. The ILAC is applicable and, within its framework, the relevant rules are specified in the San Remo Manual on International Law Applicable to Armed Conflicts at

---

[37] Gisha, Position Paper: Keys to the "Red Lines" documents, www.gisha.org/userfiles/file/pub
      lications/redlines/redlines-position-paper-heb.pdf, p. 2.

[38] Al-Bassiouni Petition, www.hamoked.org.il/items/9220.pdf, pp, 18–21 [Hebrew].

[39] *Ibid.*, p. 12; See also Y. Shany, "The Law Applicable to Non-Occupied Gaza: A Comment on
      Al-Bassiouni v. Prime Minister of Israel" (2009) 42 *Israel Law Review* 10; A. Gross and
      T. Feldman, "'We Didn't Want to Hear the Word "Calories"': Rethinking Food Security,
      Food Power, and Food Sovereignty – Lessons from the Gaza Closure" (2015), 33 *Berkeley
      Journal of International Law* 379, 411–413.

[40] Government Resolution No 1796 (June 14, 2010) [Hebrew], www.pmo.gov.il/Secretary/Gov
      Decisions/2010/Pages/des1796.aspx.

Sea.[41] This document is the *lex specialis*, and ergo international human rights law (IHRL) is inapplicable.[42]

The Manual prohibits a naval blockade only if its sole purpose is the starvation of the civilian population, if the suffering to the latter is disproportionate to the direct military advantage expected from the blockade,[43] and if it has no end date. Applying the law to the facts, the commission's report, while noting that the blockade had a dual purpose, one military and the other "indirect economic warfare," and that it had no expiry date, nevertheless concluded that the blockade was legal;[44] that no data supported the allegation that Israel's policy intended to cause, or resulted in, starvation in Gaza; and that, in fact, its policy was designed to prevent such starvation.[45]

The second inquiry was undertaken by the UN Secretary-General appointed "Panel of Inquiry on the 31 May 2010 Flotilla Incident" (Palmer Panel). Its report, noting that there is a separation between a naval blockade and a land blockade, determined that the former was legal on grounds similar to those of the Turkel Report.[46]

Q.2.1.1.1 CRITIQUE The above analysis is problematic on both doctrinal and conceptual grounds. It is problematic even if one accepts both the factual assertion that there was no humanitarian crisis in Gaza – an assertion disputed by various international governmental and nongovernmental sources[47] – and the normative assumption regarding the exclusive applicability of the ILAC to the determination of the legality of the Red Lines policy. It is also problematic because it generates the conclusion that the thin line that arguably exists between law and violence has been crossed.

---

[41] San Remo Manual on International Law Applicable to Armed Conflicts at Sea, June 12, 1994, www.icrc.org/applic/ihl/ihl.nsf/xsp/.ibmmodres/domino/OpenAttachment/applic/ihl/ihl.nsf/ 5B310CC97F166BE3C12563F6005E3E09/FULLTEXT/IHL-89-EN.pdf [hereinafter: the San Remo Manual].

[42] The Public Commission to Examine the Maritime Incident of 31 May 2010 – The Turkel Commission, Part One (January 2011), www.turkel-committee.gov.il/files/wordocs//87072002 11english.pdf [hereinafter: the Turkel Report], § 100.

[43] The San Remo Manual, Article 102.   [44] The Turkel Report, §§ 36–68, 91.

[45] The Turkel Report, §§ 72–78.

[46] G. Palmer, A. Uribe, J. Ciechanover Itzhar, and S. Özdem Sanderk, Report of the Secretary-General's Panel of Inquiry on the 31 May 2010 Flotilla Incident (September 2011), www.un.org /News/dh/infocus/middle_east/Gaza_Flotilla_Panel_Report.pdf [hereinafter: the Palmer Report], § 70.

[47] See, e.g., Gisha, "Towards an independent Palestinian economy in the Gaza Strip – Obstacles and options," in *The Palestinian Economy in the Gaza Strip – a Path to Long-Term Development* (Physicians for Human Rights-Israel, 2012), www.gisha.org/UserFiles/File/pub lications/potential-2012/gisha_chapter_eng.pdf.

From a doctrinal perspective, it is unclear in what way a naval blockade which (a) carries no expiry date, and (b) the objective of which is economic warfare, meets the requirements specified in the San Remo Manual that it be proportionate to the concrete and direct military advantage expected of it.[48]

From a conceptual perspective, as proposed convincingly by Aeyal Gross and Tamar Feldman, the notion of "food security," rather than the concepts of "humanitarian crisis" or "hunger," provides a sharper lens through which to analyze the Red Lines policy. Food security exists when "all people, at all times, have physical, social and economic access to sufficient, safe and nutritious food which meets their dietary needs and food preferences for an active and healthy life."[49] Food security – a corollary of the right to food – turns the focus from the availability of food to economic access to food.[50] Analyzing the naval and land blockade from this perspective indicates that the Red Lines policy has generated a sharp increase in the cost of food, in unemployment, and in poverty rates; impaired dramatically the buying power of the population; and created an extreme dependence on aid agencies, aid without which they would not merely have survived on the brink of a humanitarian crisis but would have succumbed to it. The fact that the concept of food security does not figure in the ILAC suggests that even if it is accepted that it is the *lex specialis* governing the situation, it has to be complemented by other normative sources.

Finally, the political objective of the blockade – that is, engaging in economic warfare in a manner that uses the civilian population as a means to put political pressure on its leadership, an objective noted only to be glossed over by the judicial and quasi-judicial institutions that were engaged in determining the legality of the Israeli policy – should give us pause. Its meaning is not merely that a person becomes a means to another end with the attendant implications on her or his quality of life, but that s/he becomes a weapon; that the routine harm to civilians thereby caused, far from being an

---

[48]   See A. Cohen and Y. Shany, "The Turkel's Commission Flotilla Report (Part One): Some Critical Remarks," *EJIL: Talk! – Blog of the European Journal of International Law* (January 28, 2011), www.ejiltalk.org/the-turkel-commissions-flotilla-report-part-one-some-critical-remarks; Gross and Feldman, "'We Didn't Want to Hear the Word "Calories"'," pp. 410–413.

[49]   The definition of the Food and Agriculture Organization, see World Food Summit, Plan of Action (November 1996), www.fao.org/docrep/003/w3613e/w3613e00.htm, § 1. For the argument that the Red Lines policy violated the right to food security, with an emphasis on the population buying power, see Gross and Feldman, "'We Didn't Want to Hear the Word "Calories"'," p. 399.

[50]   Gross and Feldman, "'We Didn't Want to Hear the Word "Calories"'," p. 418.

unfortunate "collateral damage" of warfare, becomes its very objective. A determination that such a policy meets the standards of the ILAC means that law not merely professes to regulate warfare, it is also an integral part thereof.[51]

Q.2.1.2 Alternative Normative Frameworks: "One If by Land, and Two If by Sea"[52]

Israel controls access to and from Gaza by land, by sea, and by air. It has done so since 1967. The imposition of the naval and territorial blockade – a blockade that enabled the implementation of the Red Lines policy – is but a manifestation of this continuous control. This reality suggests that the legality of the policy is not to be determined only within the framework of the laws of war. Both the law of belligerent occupation and IHRL are alternative normative frameworks within which the Red Lines policy can be evaluated.

Q.2.1.2.1 THE LAW OF BELLIGERENT OCCUPATION The applicability of the law of belligerent occupation to the postdisengagement Gaza Strip rests on a broad reading of the notion of "effective control," asserting that its existence is not to be determined exclusively by boots on the grounds. The fact that Israel retains and routinely exercises such control over a wide array of matters relative to daily life in Gaza – including access of foreign visitors and goods, Gaza's population registry, family unification with Palestinians from the West Bank, transfer of money, and supply of water, electricity, and other essential materials – indicates that it is still the occupying power in the area, and ergo that the law of belligerent occupation still applies. This position enjoys strong institutional and scholarly support.[53]

---

[51] E. Weizman, "Legislative Attack" (2010) 27 *Theory, Culture & Society* 11, 16. See also entry L: Lawfare.

[52] These words, from Longfellow's poem, *Paul Revere's Ride*, describe the signal used to guide the "midnight ride of Paul Revere" at the start of the American revolutionary war. H. W. Longfellow, "Paul Revere's Ride," *The Atlantic* (January 1861), www.theatlantic.com /magazine/archive/1861/01/paul-revere-s-ride/308349.

[53] E.g., UN Security Council Resolution 1860, UN Doc S/RES/1860 (January 8, 2009); UN General Assembly Resolution 63/96, UN Doc A/RES/63/96 (December 18, 2008); UN General Assembly Resolution 64/92, UN Doc A/Res/64/92 (December 10, 2009); UN Human Rights Council, Report of the United Nations Fact-Finding Mission on the Gaza Conflict, UN Doc A/HRC/12/48 (September 25, 2009), §§ 276–280; Report of the International Fact-Finding Mission to Investigate Violations of International Law, Including International Humanitarian and Human Rights Law, Resulting from the Israeli Attacks on the Flotilla of

In between the position that excludes the applicability of the law of belligerent occupation and the position that it applies in toto is the functional approach to occupation, positing a correlation between the level of responsibility to be shouldered and the actual power exercised.[54] The HCJ acceptance in the Al-Bassiouni judgment of the argument that laws of war do not provide the only relevant normative framework, in view of both Israel's long-term occupation of Gaza and of its continuous control over Gaza's land crossings and borders, seems to lend support to this reading.[55]

The application of either the position that the law of belligerent occupation applies in full or of the functional approach to the actual control Israel exercises in implementing the Red Lines policy, generates the conclusion that Israel breaches Articles 55 and 59 of the *GC IV*. Article 55 obligates the occupying power to ensure "[T]o the fullest extent of the means available to it ... the food and medical supplies of the population; it should, in particular, bring in the necessary foodstuffs, medical stores and other articles if the resources of the occupied territory are inadequate." Article 59 supplements this provision by shouldering the occupying power with the responsibility to allow and facilitate consignments in cases where the occupied population is

Ships Carrying Humanitarian Assistance, UN Doc A/HRC/15/21 (September 27, 2010), §§ 63–64; Report of the Detailed Findings of the Independent Commission of Inquiry Established Pursuant to Human Rights Council Resolution S-21/1, UN Doc A/HRC/29/ CPR.4 (June 24, 2015), §§ 26–30; T. Ferraro, "Determining the Beginning and End of an Occupation Under International Humanitarian Law" (2012) 94 *International Review of the Red Cross* 133; P. Maurer, "Challenges to International Humanitarian Law: Israel's Occupation Policy" (2012) 94 *International Review of the Red Cross* 1508; Y. Dinstein, *The International Law of Belligerent Occupation* (Cambridge: Cambridge University Press, 2009), pp. 277–280; I. Scobbie, "An Intimate Disengagement: Israel's Withdrawal from Gaza, the Law of Occupation and of Self-Determination" (2006) 11 *Yearbook of Islamic and Middle Eastern Law* 3; N. Stephanopoulos, "Israel's Legal Obligations to Gaza After the Pullout" (2006) 31 *Yale Journal of International Law* 524; S. Darcy and J. Reynolds, "An Enduring Occupation: the Status of the Gaza Strip from the Perspective of International Humanitarian Law" (2010) 15 *Journal of Conflict and Security Law* 215, 235. This position too finds support in determination of various international tribunals, e.g., *Nuremberg Tribunal, US v. List* (1949) VIII *Law Reports of Trials of War Criminals* 38, 55–56; ICTY, *Prosecutor v. Naletilic and Martinovic*, IT-98–34-T (March 31, 2003) ¶¶ 214–217.

54   E.g., A. Gross, "The Binary Approach to Occupation: A Double Bind?," *Opinion Juris* (April 26, 2012), http://opiniojuris.org/2012/04/26/the-binary-approach-to-occupation-a-double-bind; A. Gross, *The Writing on the Wall: Rethinking the International Law of Occupation* (Cambridge: Cambridge University Press, 2017), pp. 4–6, 52–135. For a similar reading, see Reports of International Arbitral Awards, Ethiopia-Eritrea Claims Commission – Partial Award: Western Front, Aerial Bombardment and Related Claims – Eritrea's Claims 1, 3, 5, 9–13, 14, 21, 25 & 26, § 27 (December 19, 2005), http://legal.un.org/riaa/cases/vol_XXVI/291–349.pdf.

55   See above text and note 39.

"inadequately supplied."[56] Adequate supply is a standard which exceeds the minimum humanitarian benchmark of the Red Lines policy.

International Human Rights Law (IHRL) Both the extraterritorial application of IHRL and its coapplication with IHL are positions that enjoy solid international legal support.[57] The application of IHRL to the implementation of the Red Lines policy generates the conclusion that Israel violates the right of the people of Gaza to an adequate standard of living, of which the right to food and related rights are constitutive elements. At the very least, these rights should have informed the interpretation of the ILAC.

The right to an adequate standard of living, including food, has already been recognized in the UDHR.[58] The ICESCR, to which Israel is a party, states in Article 11(1) that the right to "an adequate standard of living" includes "adequate food," and obligates state parties to take appropriate steps to ensure its realization. Paragraph 2 relates to the minimum threshold of that right in a manner that echoes the basic IHL standard, specifying that states parties, "recognizing the fundamental right of everyone to be free from hunger, shall take, individually and through international co-operation," various specific measures, means and programs to "improve methods of production, conservation and distribution of food."

General Comment No.12 details the constitutive elements and the scope of protection of the right to food.[59] Stating that "[T]he right to adequate food shall ... not be interpreted in a narrow or restrictive sense,"[60] it proceeds to

---

[56] Articles 55 and 59 of the GC IV.
[57] See e.g., Legality of Nuclear Weapons, ¶ 25; Consequences of the Construction of a Wall in the Occupied Palestinian Territory, Advisory Opinion, 2004 ICJ 136, ¶ 106; Armed Activities on the Territory of the Congo, ¶¶ 216–217. See generally, O. Ben-Naftali and Y. Shany, "Living in Denial: The Application of Human Rights in the Occupied Territories" (2004) 37 *Israel Law Review* 17; N. Lubell, "Human Rights in Military Occupations" (2012) 94 *International Review of the Red Cross* 317; Y. Arai-Takahashi, *The Law of Occupation: Continuity and Change of International Humanitarian Law, and its Interaction with International Human Rights Law* (Leiden: Martinus Nijhoff Publishers, 2009), pp. 399–547; A. Gross, "Human Proportions: Are Human Rights the Emperor's New Clothes of the International Law of Occupation?" (2007) 18 *European Journal of International Law* 1; O. Ben-Naftali (ed.), *International Human Rights and Humanitarian Law* (Oxford: Oxford University Press, 2011). Y. Shany, "The Law Applicable to Non-Occupied Gaza: A Comment on Bassiouni v. Prime Minister of Israel" (2009) 42 *Israel Law Review* 101.
[58] Article 25 of UDHR.
[59] UN Committee on Economic, Social and Cultural Rights (CESCR), General Comment 12: The Right to Adequate Food (art. 11), UN Doc E/C.12/1999/5 (May 12, 1999), http://tbinternet.ohchr.org/_layouts/treatybodyexternal/Download.aspx?symbolno=E%2fC.12%2f1999%2f5&Lang.
[60] Ibid., § 6.

specify that the right includes (a) physical and economic access at all times to adequate food or means for its procurement.[61] The accessibility is further specified to include sustainability;[62] (b) availability of food in a quantity and quality sufficient to satisfy the dietary needs of individuals.[63] Said availability requires "the possibilities either for feeding oneself directly from productive land or other natural resources, or for well functioning distribution, processing and market systems that can move food from the site of production to where it is needed in accordance with demand";[64] (c) the nutritional value of the food which should not be equated "with a minimum package of calories, protein and other specific nutrients,"[65] but rather satisfies, in quantitative and qualitative terms, "the dietary needs of individuals." The latter implies a diet that "contains a mix of nutrients for physical and mental growth, development and maintenance, and physical activity that are in compliance with human physiological needs at all stages throughout the life cycle and according to gender and occupation";[66] and (d) "cultural or consumer acceptability," implying the need to "take into account perceived non nutrient-based values attached to food."[67]

Focusing on the scope of the protection of the right to adequate food, General Comment 12 details what is entailed in the obligations to respect, to protect, and to fulfill it:[68]

> The obligation to respect existing access to adequate food requires States parties not to take any measures that result in preventing such access. The obligation to protect requires measures by the State to ensure that enterprises or individuals do not deprive individuals of their access to adequate food. The obligation to fulfill (facilitate) means the State must proactively engage in activities intended to strengthen people's access to and utilization of resources and means to ensure their livelihood, including food security ...

Finally, General Comment 12 specifies that each state party is obligated to "refrain at all times from food embargoes or similar measures which endanger conditions for food production and access to food in other countries. Food should never be used as an instrument of political and economic pressure."[69]

---

[61] *Ibid.* [62] *Ibid.*, § 8. [63] *Ibid.* [64] *Ibid.*, § 12. [65] *Ibid.*, § 6. [66] *Ibid.*, §§ 8–9.
[67] *Ibid.*, § 11. [68] *Ibid.*, § 15.
[69] *Ibid.*, § 37. In this context, the Committee referred to its General Comment No 8, on the relationship between economic sanctions and respect for economic, social, and cultural rights.

Given that the explicit objective of Israel's Red Lines policy was to use food as an instrument of political and economic pressure, it is little wonder that the implementation of the policy presents, in every aspect, a mirror image of the obligations to respect, protect, and ensure the right to adequate food.

The right to adequate food is not the only right that the Red Lines policy violated. It also breached the right to culture in both its narrow and broad sense. In its narrow sense, one of the constitutive elements of the right to adequate food, as clarified in General Comment 12, is its "cultural or consumer acceptability."[70] Indeed, that consideration does appear in the Red Lines documents, which include a guideline referring to the suitability of the foodstuff to the local culture and experience. These words might as well have been eaten: the implementation of the policy ignored that guideline and at different, often arbitrary points in time, prohibited the passage of foodstuffs that are part of the daily local kitchen in Gaza. The prohibitions on the passage of coriander,[71] or of sesame seeds used for the making of locally distinctive tahini,[72] are examples.

In its broader sense, human engagement with food is not merely material. It is cultural. To the extent that the story of civilization is to no small extent the story of how meats, grains, seeds, and leaves, and the ways of cooking them, migrated from place to place, food and the rituals associated with food represent both who we are and how we perceive ourselves individually and collectively: our self-knowledge.[73] From this perspective, the Red Lines policy breached the right of the Gazans to take part in cultural life, a right enshrined in Article 15(1) of the ICSECR,[74] and indeed tore the very fabric of communal life.

The policy also signifies the inverse relationship between the penetrating, even intimate reach of Israel's control over Gaza and its claim that it has no effective control, and that ergo that a policy that conveys utter contempt and disregard for the human dignity and autonomy of its inhabitants is lawful.

---

[70]   See note 67.

[71]   A. Hass, "Why Won't Israel Allow Gazans to Import Coriander," *Haaretz* (May 7, 2010), www .haaretz.com/why-won-t-israel-allow-gazans-to-import-coriander-1.288824.

[72]   Gross and Feldman, "'We Didn't Want to Hear the Word "Calories"'," p. 392. They also note in this context that this prohibition was motivated by economic interests: the ban made the purchase of such seeds that were smuggled into Gaza through the tunnels too costly, and the Gazans had to buy Israeli produced Tahini.

[73]   A. Gopnik, *The Table Comes First* (New York: Vintage Books, 2012), pp. 3–10.

[74]   See G. Harpaz, "How the Policy of Restricting the Passage of Food to Gaza Between 2007-2010 Affected the Quality of Life of the Local Population – an International Law Analysis" (LL.M. Seminar paper on file with authors) [Hebrew].

Q.3 FOOD FOR THOUGHT – DIGESTIVE

The quality of life of people under belligerent occupation is tenuous even under the best of circumstances, if only because they do not participate in the political processes wherein decisions affecting their lives are made. The duration and the various forms the exercise of control by Israel over Palestinian lives have taken suggest that Palestinians would score rather low on the various objective and subjective indicators used for measuring this quality.[75] Numerous entries in this volume substantiate and explain this self-evident truth.[76] Yet, the diet imposed on the people of Gaza, keeping them under siege at the minimum level of physical subsistence, merits special attention in a study of the role law has played in its making.

In one of the earlier modern meditations on the human meaning of food, Brillat-Savrin wrote *"[D]is-moi ce que tu manges, je te dirai ce que tu es"* [Tell me what you eat and I will tell you what you are].[77] The red line policy told the people of Gaza that they are who Israel determines they are; that Israel has the power to determine their identity at will and whim; that they are but means at the service of Israel's political goals; and that Israel could, if it so wished, reduce their lives below the red line.[78] At the same time, Israel also claimed that it has no effective control over the Gaza Strip, and that consequently its policy is perfectly lawful and indeed qualifies as a humanitarian project. This claim was endorsed by its highest judicial institution and by domestic and international committees of experts.[79] The meaning of this endorsement is

---

[75] Quantitative and qualitative research supports this assessment. For a study of quality of life in Gaza during the period under consideration see N. M. E. Abu-Rmeileh et al, "Health-Related Quality of Life of Gaza Palestinians in the Aftermath of the Winter 2008-09 Israeli Attack on the Strip" (2011) 22 *European Journal of Public Health* 732, http://eurpub.oxfordjournals.org /content/eurpub/22/5/732.full.pdf; for studies relative to the quality of life in Palestine (including Gaza) in later years see, e.g., J. Helliwell, R. Layard, and J. Sachs, World Happiness Report 2016, volume 1, http://worldhappiness.report/wp-content/uploads/sites/2/2016/03/HR-V1_web .pdf; UNDP, Human Development Indicators, http://hdr.undp.org/en/countries/pro files/PSE.

[76] See entries H: House Demolitions, K: Kinship, M: Military Courts, V: Violence, X: X Ray, and Z: Zone.

[77] A. Brillat-Savarin, *Physiologie du Gout, ou Meditations de Gastronomie Transcendante* (1826); see also L. A. Feuerbach, *Concerning Spiritualism and Materialism* (1863/4), "Der Mensch ist, was er ißt" ("Man is what he eats").

[78] And at times, it did; see Gisha, "Keys to the 'Red Lines' documents." On catastrophization, understood as a process by which catastrophe is imminent yet suspended, a suspension creating the conditions for collaboration between those who are the agents of the impeding catastrophe and those who actually oppose them but who have an interest in preventing the catastrophe from actually happening, see Ophir, "The Politics of Catastrophization," pp. 40–45.

[79] As discussed in Section Q.2.1.

that it is legally permissible to turn people from subjects whose well-being is a matter of concern to those with the power to protect, respect, and advance it,[80] into weapons. The equation thus produced between warfare and lawfare signifies that the presumed red line that exists between law and violence has become imperceptible.[81]

The potential for legalized violence has not been exhausted. In fact, as noted, while the maritime and territorial closure of the Gaza Strip still persists, the Red Lines policy has been shelved. The story, however, gives us, well, a taste of what the unleashing of this potential may mean for war and for law. Given that the "disengagement" from Gaza is, in reality, a new method of exercising maximum control with minimum responsibility over minimum land with maximum people, this story is less unique and less confined in terms of time and space than is commonly assumed. Indeed, the main matrix governing Israeli policies toward the OPT in its entirety since 1967 concerns the ratio between the land and the Palestinians,[82] and devising methods to effect a relationship of maximum control (over Palestinian land) and minimum responsibility (toward the Palestinians). This is the matrix that explains the severing of the Gaza Strip from the rest of the OPT, just as it explains land slicing within the OPT.[83] In Gaza, it translates into minimum land, maximum people; for the rest of the OPT, it is maximum land, minimum people. The power matrix governing both is maximum control, minimum responsibility.[84] How law digests this matrix has, and continues to have, a devastating impact on the quality of life of the people, and may well have an impact on the potential for violence that is yet to be unleashed.[85]

---

[80] As discussed in Section Q.2.2.   [81] Weizman, "Legislative Attack," p. 26.

[82] A protocol of the Israeli cabinet of August 20, 1967, focusing on the Israeli policy toward the West Bank, reveals that the issue was defined in these terms. Thus, for instance, then minister of commerce and industry, Zeev Scherf, says: "I want to deal with the dilemma of the maximum and the minimum. The question is should we have maximum Arabs and minimum land or minimum Arabs and maximum land, or ... minimum land with minimum Arabs or maximum land with maximum Arabs. The decision is difficult." State of Israel Archive, file g-18718/6 (August 20, 1967), http://akevot.org.il/article/question-of-arabs-and-question-of-jews/?full# [Hebrew].

[83] This logic is discussed in entry Z: Zone.

[84] Li, "The Gaza Strip as Laboratory," pp. 38–40.

[85] For further discussion, see entry L: Lawfare.

R

Regularization Law

Michael Sfard

R.1 INTRODUCTION: ON RULE OF LAW AND RULE BY LAW

Regularization commonly denotes the establishment of an official basis in law for an exceptional situation that hitherto existed in reality but without such a basis and was thus either unregulated or blatantly illegal. A common example of the use of the process involves the regularization of immigrants' status. A less common use of the process involves the regularization of the status of Jewish settlements, known as "outposts," that were established in the West Bank on privately owned Palestinian land, without governmental authorization and thus not only in grave breach of international law, but also in violation of domestic law. The Law for the Regularization of Settlement in Judea and Samaria 2017 (hereinafter: the Regularization Law),[1] passed by the Israeli parliament (Knesset) on February 6, 2017, is such an uncommon, well, irregular regularizing law. This law is the focus of the present entry.

In essence, the Regularization Law addresses property rights, construction, and planning in the occupied West Bank. This is not the first instance in which the Israeli legislature has acted to apply norms extraterritorially in the OPT. Throughout the years, the Knesset applied various laws to Israelis living in the West Bank on a personal, as well as on a semipersonal, semiterritorial

---

[1] The Judea and Samaria Settlement Regulation Law, 2016. Note that in translating the name of the enactment into English, both the words *regulation* and *regularization* may be used. The original title in Hebrew misleadingly suggests that the law *regulates* the establishment of settlements, technically setting a regulatory basis for them. In fact, as will be detailed in this entry, the law *legalizes* settlements otherwise illegal even under the very narrow Israeli understanding of what makes settlements illegal. Hence, we prefer *Regularization* – a term connoting the process whereby the irregular and the illegal are rendered regular and formally legal, if not substantively lawful.

basis.[2] The Regularization Law is nevertheless distinct and unprecedented, because therein, for the first time, the Knesset sought to change the substantive laws of the occupied territory and apply its legislation to the Palestinian residents of these territories. The law institutes a mechanism for large-scale confiscation of privately owned Palestinian land, its transfer for use by Israeli Jewish settlers, and the approval of master plans that would retroactively sanction the hitherto illegal construction the settlers had carried out. This is the illegality that the law regularizes. A legislative act passed by the parliament of the occupying power thus alters both property laws and building and planning laws in the occupied territory, as well as breaches the fundamental rights of the occupied population, a population that is neither represented nor participates in the elections of that parliament.

The main proposition advanced in this entry is threefold: first, in enacting the cynically yet aptly named "Regularization Law," Israel has asserted itself as the sovereign of the OPT. Second, this assertion ends the 50-year-old masked ball during which Israel has managed to act in the territories as a de facto sovereign, without admitting that it is thus engaged. Third, while honesty is preferable to deceit, not all truths are created equal: The Regularization Law purports to legalize actions considered criminal under the applicable international law. To the extent that the notion of the rule of law encompasses rules that are just, applied equally, and protect fundamental human rights, the Regularization Law transforms the rule of law into a rule by law – that is, a law that is de jure indistinguishable from violence.[3]

In order to substantiate this proposition, Section R.2 presents the background to the Regularization Law and its substance. Section R.3 offers a critical assessment of the law from the perspective of the currently applicable international normative framework of belligerent occupation and from the

---

[2]   Most notably it applied Israeli criminal law extraterritorially to Israelis when they are present in the OPT, Defense (Emergency) Regulations (Judea and Samaria – Adjudication of Offenses and Legal Assistance), 1967. See Association for Civil Rights in Israel (ACRI), *One Rule, Two Legal Systems: Israel's Regime of Laws in the West Bank* (October 2014), www.acri.org.il/en/wp-content/uploads/2015/02/Two-Systems-of-Law-English-FINAL.pdf;   A.   Rubinstein,   "The Changing Status of the Territories (West Bank and Gaza): From Escrow to Legal Mongrel" (1988) 8 *Tel Aviv University Studies in Law* 59; O. Ben-Naftali, A. Gross, and K. Michaeli, "Illegal Occupation: Framing the Occupied Palestinian Territory" (2005) 23 *Berkeley Journal of International Law* 551, 583–588.

[3]   This entry advances a "before the law" analysis of the relations between law and violence. For a discussion proceeding of this relation from an "against the law" perspective, see entry V: Violence. On the differences between this approaches see P. Ewick and S. S. Silbey, "The Social Construction of Legality," in *The Common Place of Law: Stories from Everyday Life* (Chicago: University of Chicago Press, 1998), pp. 48–49 and the brief exposé in the Introduction to his book, Section 2.

perspective of international criminal law. Section R.4 concludes by tracing the
main junctions where the Regularization Law transforms the hitherto indeterminate nature of Israel's control over the OPT, otherwise known as "belligerent occupation," into sovereignty, and the notion of the rule of law into a
rule by law. The latter bridges the gap between word and deed and, in the
process, exposes the face of violence.

R.2 THE REGULARIZATION LAW: BACKGROUND AND SUBSTANCE

R.2.1 *Why Was the Regularization Law Enacted?*

The Regularization Law came into being to avert a political crisis emanating
from the settlers' strong lobby and significant representation in parliament and
in the government. Its immediate purpose is to satisfy the settlers' appetite for
Palestinian land. Its deeper purpose is the realization of the vision of "Greater
Israel." In this sense it reflects the *nomos* of Israel's sovereignty over ever-
greater portions of Mandatory Palestine.[4] A brief exposé of its specific background is required.

Jewish settlements in the West Bank were built over the past five decades
with governmental support and the blessing-through-nonintervention of
Israel's HCJ. The former's authorization, based on a peculiar reading of
prohibition of Article 49 paragraph 6 of the *GC IV* on the transfer of the
occupying power's population to the occupied territory, was rejected in toto
by the international community. The latter's nonintervention, based on
determination of political nonjusticiability, was, however, subject to some
limitations: The construction of Jewish settlements had to advance a security
need, otherwise it could not be undertaken on privately owned Palestinian
land.[5]

The adverse effects of the very existence of the settlements on Palestinian
space, everyday life, and human rights are well known. Some of the most
disturbing effects are detailed in various entries in this volume.[6] One
such effect, particularly pertinent to the present entry, concerns extensive
settler violence directed at Palestinians and their property. Israel did not
deny – and, indeed, acknowledged – that it shoulders a legal obligation to
protect Palestinians from settler violence. It simply failed to enforce the law

---

[4] See entry N: Nomos.   [5] See entry J: Jewish Settlements.
[6] See entries B: Border/Barrier; I: Investigations; J: Jewish Settlements; P: Proportionality; T:
Temporary/Indefinite; U: Usufruct; W: War Crimes; Z: Zone.

in this respect.[7] The gap between its law-abiding rhetoric and law-mocking deeds has been generally sustained internationally as well as by its domestic legal institutions, with one significant exception: the establishment of unauthorized outposts.

Outposts are settlements established without governmental official author-ization and, to a large extent, on privately owned Palestinian land. They violate the rights of the landowners who are robbed of their property.[8] Their construction expresses the response of the settlers' movement to the morator-ium on building new settlements instituted by the Rabin government and entrenched in the agreements between Israel and the PLO.[9] Between 1995 and 2005 more than one hundred outposts were erected in the West Bank.[10]

The outposts appear to be a private initiative: They have been established without permission from the Israeli government, with no master plans approved by the planning authorities and no building permits for construction in them. Appearances, alas, are notoriously deceiving: In many cases, they enjoyed the cooperation of the Israeli leadership, which prevented enforcement of stop-work and demolition orders issued for construction therein. They also received active assistance from various government ministries, mostly the ministry of construc-tion and housing, both for laying infrastructure and for funding and planning.[11]

---

7   See e.g., L. Yavne, *A Semblance of Law: Law Enforcement on Israeli Civilians in the West Bank* (Tel Aviv: Yesh Din, 2006); L. Yavne, *Alleged Investigations: The Failure of Investigations into Offenses Committed by IDF Soldiers against Palestinians* (Tel Aviv: Yesh Din, 2011), www.ye sh-din.org/en/alleged-investigation-the-failure-of-investigations-into-offenses-committed-by-id f-soldiers-against-palestinians/; Z. Stahl, *Mock Enforcement: The Failure to Enforce the Law on Israeli Civilians in the West Bank* (Tel Aviv: Yesh Din, 2015), files.yesh-din.org/userfiles/Yesh% 20Din_Akifat%20Hok_%20English.pdf. The issue is discussed in entry I: Investigations.

8   According to Peace Now data, 80 of the 100 or so outposts are located partially or entirely on private Palestinian land, http://peacenow.org.il/outposts.

9   Article XXXI(7) of The Israeli-Palestinian Interim Agreement on the West Bank and the Gaza Strip Oslo II (September 28, 1995), 36 ILM 551, stipulates a prohibition on either party initiating or taking "any step that will change the status of the West Bank and the Gaza Strip pending the outcome of the permanent status negotiations"; the Performance Based Roadmap to a Permanent Two-State Solution to the Israeli-Palestinian Conflict (April 30, 2003) [hereinafter: Road Map] states that Israel undertakes to freeze all settlement activity (including natural growth); and in the Annapolis Conference of November 2007, Prime Minister Ehud Olmert repeated the commitment to the roadmap.

10 *Opinion Concerning Unauthorized Outposts* (2005) [hereinafter: The Sasson report]. The Sasson report was submitted to Prime Minister Ariel Sharon in March 2005. A summary of the report can be found on the Israeli MFA site: www.mfa.gov.il/mfa/aboutisrael/state/law/pages/ summary%20of%20opinion%20concerning%20unauthorized%20outposts%20-%20talya%20s ason%20adv.aspx.

11 T. Sasson, *Interim Report on the Subject of Unauthorized Outposts* (Jerusalem, 2005), pp. 20–21. [Hebrew; an English summary of the report is available at www.mfa.gov.il/mfa/aboutisrael/ state/law/pages/summary%20of%20opinion%20concerning%20unauthorized%20outposts%20

The international community was not oblivious to this development, and Israel pledged on various occasions that it would evacuate the unauthorized outposts.[12] In this, as in other instances, this undertaking merely widened the gap between word and deed. The outposts remained in place and construction in them continued. It was, however, in the domestic legal arena that law was beginning to be enforced: Given the HCJ's previous jurisprudence relative to the prohibition on the construction of settlements on privately owned Palestinian land, and in the face of a wave of petitions to the HCJ filed by Palestinian landowners through Israeli NGOs, government officials pledged enforcement and binding demolition and evacuation orders were issued and executed in various instances.[13]

Each of these evacuations or demolitions sparked a political storm in Israel. The pro-settler lobby, which had gained massive political power over these years, campaigned to prevent each of the evacuations. Consequently, each such law-enforcement sent the coalition government into crisis. The knowledge that hundreds, maybe thousands, of structures were built on privately owned Palestinian land,[14] and the realization that given Israel's official legal

-%20talya%20sason%20adv.aspx]. The report was presented to late prime minister Sharon in February 2005. Government Resolution No 3376, www.pmo.gov.il/Secretary/GovDecisions/2005/Pages/des3376.aspx [Hebrew], endorsed the report's findings and recommendations on March 13, 2005.

[12] The most concrete commitment was embedded in the Road Map which prescribed that the Government of the State of Israel "immediately dismantles settlement outposts erected since March 2001." This commitment to the principles of the Road Map was reiterated in the Joint Statement which concluded the Annapolis Conference was a Middle East peace conference (held on November 27, 2007).

[13] In 2006, Israel had to demolish nine homes built in the outpost of Amona, an event that resulted in violent altercations between security forces and hundreds of settlers, see HCJ 851/06 *Amona Farmer's Cooperative for communal settlements Ltd.* v. *Minister of Defense* (January 29, 2006). Between 2012 and 2017, the Government of Israel had to evacuate several outposts: Ulpana Hill (Jabal Artis) (2012), see HCJ 9060/08 *Abdallah* v. *the Minister of Defense* (May 7, 2012); Migron (on land belonging to the Palestinian village of Burqah) (2012), see HCJ 8887/06 *el-Nabut* v. *The Minister of Defense* (August 2, 2011); Beit El South (on land belonging to the village of Dura al-Qar') (2015) see HCJ 6528/13 *al-Rahman* v. *the Minister of Defense* (September 8, 2014), Amona (on land belonging to the villages of Silwad, Ein Yabrud, and Taybah) (2017), see HCJ 9949/08 *Hamad* v. *the Minister of Defense* (December 25, 2014), and nine homes in the settlement of Ofra (on land belonging to Silwad) (2017), see HCJ 4457/09 *Manaa* v. *The Minister of Defense* (July 27, 2011). In all cases mentioned in this note the landowners and/or the Human Rights NGOs were represented by the author of this entry, Michael Sfard.

[14] A report issued by settler NGO Regavim concluded that 2,026 housing units in the West Bank were found by a civil administration commission entrusted with demarcation of public land, as located on private land. The report was not published but only reported in the rightist press. See H. Baruch, "Right Wing Sources Warn: 2026 Structures Slated for Demolition in Judea and Samaria," *Channel 7* (May 2, 2015), www.inn.co.il/News/News.aspx/297654 [Hebrew].

position that it must protect Palestinian property, and given the HCJ's past jurisprudence on the matter, the court is likely to authorize more evacuations and demolitions, sent politicians looking for a solution.

That search led first to the appointment in 2012 of the Levy Committee "to examine the legal status of Israeli construction in the Judea and Samaria."[15] Its report contained two major recommendations: first, that the government should adopt an official position according to which international law sanctions the sovereignty of Israel over the territory of the West Bank; and, second, that it should authorize retroactively all outposts built on public as well as on some private land.[16] The Israeli government refrained from adopting officially the Levy report precisely because it was diametrically opposed to its official positions, but proceeded to nevertheless implement effectively its recommendation relative to the outposts.[17] In this case, too, it thus walked the tightrope stretching across the gap between word and deed and sustaining the de jure/de facto, occupation/nonoccupation, annexation/nonannexation indeterminacies. By 2016, 13 outposts were fully regularized and 19 more were in various stages of regularization.[18] Retroactive authorization efforts included approval of master plans for outposts built on public land and widespread use of the controversial practice of "state land declarations."[19] Such declarations change the status of a piece of land from privately to publicly owned while still enabling the state to argue that the change is declarative rather than constitutive, and therefore does not amount to confiscation.

---

[15] The Levy Committee was appointed by the prime minister and the minister of justice, circumventing the attorney general. *Report on the Legal Status of Building in Judea and Samaria* (2012), www.pmo.gov.il/Documents/doch090712.pdf [Hebrew]; an English translation of the conclusions and recommendations is available at http://israelipalestinian.procon .org/sourcefiles/The-Levy-Commission-Report-on-the-Legal-Status-of-Building-in-Judea-and-Samaria.pdf.

[16] The text of the report as it pertains to international law is presented, contextualized, and analyzed in Entry N: Nomos; For an analysis of its recommendation relative to the regularization of outposts, see also: *Unprecedented: A Legal Analysis of the Report of the Committee to Examine the Status of Building in Judea and Samaria [the West Bank] ("The Levy Committee") – International and Administrative Aspects* (Tel Aviv: Yesh Din – Volunteers for Human Rights and The Emile Zola Chair for Human Rights, 2014).

[17] Z. Stahl, *From Occupation to Annexation: the silent adoption of the Levy report on retroactive authorization of illegal construction in the West Bank* (Tel Aviv: Yesh Din – Volunteers for Human Rights, 2016), https://s3-eu-west-1.amazonaws.com/files.yesh-din.org/%D7%9E%D7% 9B%D7%99%D7%91%D7%95%D7%A9+%D7%9C%D7%A1%D7%99%D7%A4%D7%95% D7%97/From+Occupation+to+Annexation+English+Yesh+Din.pdf.

[18] *Ibid.*

[19] During the 1980s and the 1990s, more than 900,000 dunams of land were declared "state land" using a controversial interpretation of the Ottoman Land Code, 1858, which provides, among other things, the transfer of full title over private uncultivated agricultural land to the ruler. See entry J: Jewish Settlements.

The regularization process did not satisfy the gargantuan appetite of the settlers: It was slow; even as it was underway, judicial orders continued to result in the removal of illegal construction; and, worse still from their perspective, the methods employed failed to "regulate" construction on privately registered land which was therefore not subject to the "declaration" procedure. A more radical and decisive step was necessary. That step was the enactment of the Regularization Law.

R.2.2 How Does the Law Regularize the Outposts?

The Regularization Law begins with a declaration of purpose. Article 1 states that: "[T]he purpose of this law is to regularize and enable the continued establishment and development Israeli settlements in Judea and Samaria."[20] In these unequivocal, simple, and straightforward terms it pulls the fifty-year-old rug from under the feet of Israeli diplomacy.

In order to achieve its stated purpose, the law's provisions are tailored to cover the entire gamut of Israeli settler takeover of Palestinian land. Below is a brief summary of these provisions.

Jurisdiction *ratione personae* – the law authorizes, indeed instructs the supervisor of government property in the civil administration in the West Bank to appropriate the "usage and possession rights" in lands on which Israeli settlements were built,[21] on the condition that said construction was carried out in good faith *or* with the state's consent.[22]

Three points merit a special emphasis. First, the very notion that Jewish settlements in the OPT could have ever been established in good faith is an oxymoron from an international legal perspective. The fact that Israeli domestic law has thus far distinguished between the legality of settlements built on public or so-called "state land" and the illegality of settlements built on private Palestinian land, and therefore regards the former as having been established in good faith, normalizes not merely an illegality but also a grave breach of the GC IV. Second, the consent of the state is defined very broadly, encompassing, for example, any government involvement in construction, however minute, as well as government involvement carried out in excess of authority or in breach of the law.[23] Second, the state itself is defined broadly to encompass (a) entities that otherwise do not form part of Israel's executive branch, such as Israeli local

---

[20] Article 1 of the Regularization Law.   [21] Article 3(2) of the Regularization Law.
[22] Article 3 of the Regularization Law.
[23] Article 2 defines state consent as: "Explicit or implicit, advance or retroactive, including assistance in laying infrastructure, providing incentives, issuing publications that encourage construction or development, or participating in money or in kind contributions."

authorities in the West Bank; (b) nonstatutory entities handling settlement, most notably the two main institutions of the Zionist movement – the World Zionist Organization and the Jewish Agency; and (c) private institutions recognized by the minister of agriculture as "settling bodies."[24] Jewish communities or settlements are defined as including not just the built-up portion of the community, but also farmland used by the inhabitants, access roads and water, and sewage and electricity infrastructure.[25]

Jurisdiction ratione materiae – the law instructs the confiscation of Palestinian land for the purposes of Jewish settlements. Indeed, it "regularizes" the takeover of Palestinian land in situations as far removed from "good faith" as one's imagination allows: Thus, when state consent is established, the land can be confiscated even in cases where settlers forcibly and violently have taken it over, uprooted the olive trees that had been planted there, and replaced them with a vineyard. For the "consent" to be established, it is sufficient to show, for instance, that the Israeli local council to which these settlers belong had (illegally) invested money in the vineyard. Given that over the years, as established by the Sasson report, (a) multiple local councils in the West Bank supported, helped, encouraged, and funded invasions into land outside their jurisdiction; (b) the World Zionist Organization allocated land it never had rights to for use by settlers; (c) government ministries also improperly assisted the establishment of outposts; and (d) the engagement of all these entities qualifies under the law as "state consent," the net result would be that, subject to rare exceptions, the law would enable the confiscation of virtually all private land Israelis had taken over. A study conducted by Peace Now[26] estimates that, if implemented, the law would result in the confiscation of 11,000 dunams of privately owned Palestinian land where settler construction had been undertaken.[27] Studies on Israeli takeover of land for farming purposes adds 27,000 dunams to this estimate.[28]

---

[24] The definition of "the state" in Article 2 includes a "settling body" which, in turn, is defined in the Candidates for Agricultural Communities Law, 1953 as "The Government, the World Zionist Organization, the Jewish Agency and any other body engaged in settling people on land and which has been recognized by the Minister of Agriculture, through registry announcement, as a settling body for purposes of this law."

[25] Article 2 of the Regularization Law, definition of "settlement."

[26] Peace Now, *The Grand Land Robbery: Another Step toward Annexation* (November 2016).

[27] Accounting for 8,138 dunums of land invaded and built on by settlers and an additional 3,174 dunums of land currently under a military seizure order – the system in place for building settlements until the late 1970s. On the latter, see entry: J: Jewish Settlements.

[28] Naboth's Vineyard, *Israeli Settler Agriculture as a Means of Land Takeover in the West Bank* (October 2013), p. 73: http://rhr.org.il/heb/wp-content/uploads/Kerem-Navot.pdf.

Jurisdiction ratione temporis – the law establishes that the expropriation of usage and possession rights of privately owned Palestinian land shall remain in effect "until such time as a political resolution is reached as to the status of the Area and Israeli settlements therein."[29] This caveat, which ostensibly retains the temporary/indefinite indeterminacy in referring to the future resolution of the conflict through political processes, is the only mask still placed on the fact of Israel's sovereignty over the area.[30] Since the authorities have the power to return title over confiscated properties to their robbed owners anyway, and parties to conflicts have power to make significant changes to status of lands, this reservation does not have real effect on the postconfiscation legal status of the lands. It is therefore a transparent camouflage.

The law instructs the supervisor to register the rights to the confiscated lands in its name in the land registry[31] and allocate them for use by the settlement already built on it.[32] It further instructs the Israeli authorities of the West Bank to take action toward completing planning procedures that would retroactively approve existing construction on the land.[33] The law proceeds to establish a moratorium on all enforcement proceedings regarding illegal construction on OPT lands which are covered by the law, pending the completion of planning procedures.[34] Once the latter are complete, the law decrees the expiration of administrative orders issued against the construction.[35] Indeed, the law goes so far as to list specific settlements where enforcement procedures are to be suspended for one year during which the authorities would determine whether the law applies to them.[36]

The law offers landowners a choice of compensation at a rate of 125 percent of the land's worth, as determined by an assessment committee or alternative land "to the extent possible in the circumstances of the matter."[37]

R.3 HOW MANY INTERNATIONALLY WRONGFUL ACTS CAN ONE FIT IN ONE LAW?

From a strictly legal perspective, in 11 not too lengthy articles, the Regularization Law produces a long list of breaches of the international law of belligerent occupation and facilitates the large-scale commission of war

[29] Article 3(2)(b) of the Regularization Law. [30] See entry T: Temporary/Indefinite.
[31] Article 4 of the Regularization Law. [32] Article 5 of the Regularization Law.
[33] Article 6 of the Regularization Law. [34] Article 7(a) of the Regularization Law.
[35] Article 7(b) of the Regularization Law.
[36] Article 11 of the Regularization Law and the Annex list.
[37] Articles 8–10 of the Regularization Law.

crimes.[38] Section R.3.1 details the most fundamental of such breaches, and Section R.3.2 focuses on war crimes.

R.3.1 Breaches of the Law of Belligerent Occupation

R.3.1.1 Annexation

The Regularization Law is designed to implement in the occupied territory a norm enacted by the parliament of the occupying power. As such, the law is primarily a clear manifestation of de jure annexation.

The laws of occupation obligate the occupying power "unless absolutely prevented"[39] to respect local law in the occupied territory. The term "absolutely prevented" has been interpreted as pertaining to two types of cases: first, instances where a pre-existing local law must be changed because it contradicts the principles of international law in general, and the laws of belligerent occupation in particular;[40] second, when the occupier's duties in terms of maintaining security and/or order and civil life necessitate changing local laws.[41] Legalizing settlements, which are illegal under international law and indeed constitute a grave breach of that law, is not a case that meets the "absolutely prevented" clause. In normative terms, the occupying power is indeed absolutely prevented from enacting it.

Furthermore, even when local laws must be changed, the power to do so rests with the *occupying forces* – that is, the military commander of the occupied territory,[42] not the parliament of the occupying power. The reason

---

[38] The law further infringes numerous fundamental human rights under IHRL. The present section focuses, however, only on the violation of IHL, the *lex specialis*. On the applicable normative framework see Introduction, Section 2.2.

[39] Regulation 43 of The Hague Convention (IV) Respecting the Laws and Customs of War on Land and its annex: Regulations concerning the Laws and Customs of War on Land, The Hague, October 18, 1907, 205 CTS 277; 36 Stat 2277 [hereinafter: *HC IV*]; see also Article 64 of Geneva Convention Relative to the Protection of Civilian Persons in the Time of War, Geneva, August 12, 1949, 75 UNTS 287 [hereinafter: *GC IV*].

[40] The ICRC commentary on Article 64 states, regarding the occupying power's obligation to respect the penal legislation of the occupied country, that: "when the penal legislation of the occupied territory conflicts with the provisions of the Convention, the Convention must prevail," J. S. Pictet (ed.), *The Geneva Conventions of 12 August 1949, Commentary – IV Geneva Convention Relative to the Protection of Civilian Persons in Time of War* (Geneva: International Committee of the Red Cross, 1958), pp. 335–336 [hereinafter: Commentary on GC IV].

[41] HCJ 393/82 *Ascan v. IDF Commander in Judea and Samaria* (1983) 37(4) PD 785, 797; Y. Dinstein, "The Power to Legislate in the Administered Territories" (1971–1972) 2 *Iyuney Mishpat* 505, 509 [Hebrew].

[42] As was acknowledged by the Israeli HCJ see *Ascan*, ¶ 17; HCJ 10/5324 *Malka v. the Civil Administration in Judea and Samaria* (December 28, 2011), ¶¶ 12–17.

for this lies at the very core of the regime of belligerent occupation as reflected in its basic tenets[43] and detailed in the various provisions comprising the Geneva Law:[44] The laws of occupation form a temporary regime wherein sovereignty is suspended *not replaced*.[45] The military commander of the occupied territory, not the legislature of the occupying power, fills in for the sovereign on a temporary basis only, and administers the occupied territory using powers and authority usually vested in the sovereign within the limits prescribed by the principles of trusteeship, temporariness, and conservation which guide the laws of occupation. The assumption of legislative powers by the occupying power's parliament is an act that essentially constitutes new sovereignty and, therefore, a feature of annexation. International law forbids the unilateral annexation of occupied territory and the transfer of sovereignty to the occupying power.

R.3.1.2 Confiscation of Protected Persons' Private Property

The Regularization Law is a frontal assault on the property rights of thousands, most likely tens of thousands, of Palestinians living under Israeli control and normatively enjoying the status of "protected persons."[46]

The laws of occupation are characterized by their attempt to strike a balance between safeguarding the rights of protected persons and military exigencies. Thus, while the relevant conventions are replete with prohibitions and limitations on the power of the occupying forces and the occupying power in occupied territory, most of them allow for exceptions to the prohibitions in view of military necessity.[47] In line with this logic, damage to property is prohibited unless required for immediate, imperative security considerations: The Hague Regulation 23 and Article 53 of the GC IV do allow physical damage to property, and even its temporary seizure, but only to the extent that such damage or seizure are "imperatively demanded by the necessities of war."

Damage to property is distinct from confiscation. One of the rare *absolute* prohibitions set forth under international law is the one pertaining to

---

[43] These basic tenets are discussed in the Introduction, Section 2.2.
[44] See entry G: Geneva Law.   [45] See entry T: Temporary/Indefinite.
[46] Article 4 of GC IV.
[47] On the construction of *military necessity* in the context of occupation see e.g., Y. Shany and G. Harpaz, "The Israeli Supreme Court and the Incremental Expansion of the Scope of Discretion Under Belligerent Occupation Law" (2010) 43 *Israel Law Review* 514; Y. Dinstein, *The International Law of Belligerent Occupation* (Cambridge: Cambridge University Press, 2009), pp. 89–94.

confiscation of property belonging to protected persons. Article 46 of the GC IV stipulates in no uncertain terms that "Private property cannot be confiscated." This prohibition enjoys an illustrious pedigree: It can be found in the 1863 Lieber Code,[48] the 1874 Brussels Declaration,[49] and the 1880 Oxford Manual on the laws of war on land.[50] In the early twentieth century, the prohibition on confiscating the property of protected persons was entrenched, as noted, in the Hague Regulations and is now considered a customary principle of international law.[51]

R.3.1.3 Discrimination

The Regularization Law is phrased in a manner that guarantees its application only to illegal construction or illegal planting on land owned by Palestinians and only for the benefit of Israeli settlers who illegally built or planted on this land. The law thus lacks general applicability and is blatantly, unabashedly discriminatory on ethnic/national/racial/religious grounds. This discrimination defies the very notion of the rule of law and is specifically prohibited under the laws of belligerent occupation.[52]

The requirement for "state consent" as a condition for "regularizing" illegal construction or planting (Article 3) is what lies at the core of this discriminatory system. It is, as noted earlier, tailor-made for the Israeli settlement "enterprise," which encouraged and incentivized, often in excess of authority, the illegal construction of outposts. The settlements listed by name in the addendum to the law – where, according to Article 11, enforcement measures are suspended – are all Israeli Jewish settlements. The law also instructs that

---

[48] Articles 22, 37–38 of the Instructions for the Government of Armies of The United States in the Field (Prepared by Francis Lieber, promulgated as General Orders No. 100 by president Lincoln, April 24, 1863).

[49] Article 38 of the International Declaration concerning the Laws and Customs of War, Brussels, August 27, 1874.

[50] Articles 54–60 of the The Laws of War in Land, Adopted by the Institute of International Law, Oxford, September 9, 1880 [hereinafter: Oxford Manual], https://ihl-databases.icrc.org/ihl/INTRO/140?OpenDocument.

[51] J.M. Henckaerts and L. Doswald-Beck (eds.), *Customary International Humanitarian Law*, 2 vols. (Cambridge: Cambridge University Press, 2009), vol. I, pp. 179–182 (Rules 51(c)).

[52] Articles 3, 27 of GC IV. It is also prohibited under IHRL, see Article 26 of the International Convent on Civil and Political Rights, opened for signature December 19, 1966, 999 UNTS 171 (entered into force March 23, 1976) prohibits discrimination on grounds of nationality; The International Convention for the Suppression of all forms of Racial Discrimination, opened for signature December 21, 1965, 660 UNTS 195 (entered into force January 4, 1969) (CERD) includes national affiliation in the definition of racial discrimination (Article 1); and prohibits it (Articles 3, 5).

the retroactive allocation and approval of illegal construction or planting be conducted through a "settling body."[53] All of the institutions recognized as settling bodies are Zionist institutions, which, throughout the years, have only built Jewish communities in Israel and in the OPT.

Finally, the law's objective, explicitly stated in Article 1, its legislative history, the explanatory remarks annexed to the proposed bill before it became a law, and the political background for its enactment all indicate it was meant to serve only the settlers' constituency. This service is undertaken at the expense of the Palestinians and in a manner that breaches their rights and their rights only.

R.3.2 *War Crimes*

The Regularization Law is designed to facilitate the transfer of the population of the occupying power to the occupied territory. Such transfer is prohibited under Article 49 paragraph 6 of the GC IV, and is defined as a *grave breach* thereof in Article 85(4)(a) of AP I,[54] and constitutes a war crime under Article 8(2)(b)(viii) of the ICCSt.[55] Adding insult to injury, this law stipulates, in effect, that this facilitation entails – indeed, necessitates and justifies – the commission of three additional crimes, detailed below.

R.3.2.1 Extensive Appropriation of Property not Justified by Military Necessity[56]

Extensive appropriation of property unjustified by military necessity is one of the grave breaches of the Geneva Convention as defined in Article 147 of the GC IV and thus listed as a war crime under Article 8(2)(a) of the Rome Statute.[57]

---

[53] Article 5 of the Regularization Law.
[54] Protocol Additional to the Geneva Conventions of 12 August 1949, and relating to the Protection of Victims of International Armed Conflicts (Additional Protocol I), Geneva, June 8, 1977, 1125 UNTS 3 [hereinafter: *AP I*].
[55] This prohibition is discussed in entry J: Jewish Settlements and entry N: Nomos, Section N.3.
[56] Article 8(2)(a)(iv) of the Rome Statute of the International Criminal Court, UN General Assembly, July 17, 1998, ISBN No 92–9227-227–6 [hereinafter: ICCSt].
[57] It is also listed as a crime under the Article 2(d) of the Statute of the International Criminal Tribunal for the Former Yugoslavia, UN Security Council, May 25, 1993. Nazis were put on criminal trial for this crime already in the postwar trials. See The Krupp Trial, US Military Tribunal Nuremberg, in *Law Reports of Trials of War Criminals* (London, 1949), vol. X, pp. 69, 132; The IG Farben Trial, US Military Tribunal Nuremberg, *ibid.*, pp. 1, 42–51, www.loc .gov/rr/frd/Military_Law/pdf/Law-Reports_Vol-10.pdf.

The word "appropriation" covers the various ways in which property may be taken coercively – temporary seizure, theft, looting (and pillaging), and confiscation.[58] The types of property protected obviously include private property in an occupied territory. As noted earlier, the military necessity exception, which allows temporary appropriation of property, is not relevant to confiscation given that the prohibition on confiscation is absolute and knows no exceptions.[59]

R.3.2.2 Destroying or Seizing the Enemy's Property Unless Such Destruction or Seizure be Imperatively Demanded by the Necessities of War[60]

This war crime, which is complementary to the crime of extensive appropriation of property, derives from the manner with which the prohibition on the destruction or seizure of property is defined in the Hague Regulation 23. The main difference between this crime and the "extensive appropriation" crime is the absence of the element of "extensiveness" (of the seizure or appropriation of property). In other words, the war crime of seizure of enemy property may be committed even when there is no extensive appropriation or harm to protected persons' property and even when there is but one property that has been seized or destroyed without imperative military necessity.

R.3.2.3 Declaring Abolished, Suspended, or Inadmissible in a Court of Law the Rights and Actions of the Nationals of the Hostile Party[61]

The roots of this crime date back to the Hague Regulation 23(h), which forbids to "declare abolished, suspended, or inadmissible in a court of law the rights and actions of the nationals of the hostile party."

This war crime is designed to impose liability on policymakers and criminalize those empowered to abolish the rights of enemy nationals, including protected persons. Indeed, the generic explanation of this crime in literature states that "the *actus reus* may cover both national legislation in a country which would prevent enemy foreigners from taking legal action and administrative acts taken by the Occupying Power in occupied territory."[62]

---

[58] K. Dörmann, *Elements of War Crimes Under the Rome Statute of the International Criminal Court* (Cambridge: Cambridge University Press and the International Committee of the Red Cross, 2003), pp. 89–95.

[59] *Ibid.*, p. 81.   [60] Article 8(2)(b)(xiii) of the ICCSt.   [61] Article 8(2)(b)(xiv) of the ICCSt.

[62] Dörmann, *Elements of War Crimes*, p. 263.

R.4 CONCLUSION: REGULARIZING THE ALREADY REGULAR

Since 1967, Israel has opted for a determined policy of normative indeterminacy for sustaining and entrenching its control over the OPT. This policy, not dissimilar to its policy of ambiguity with respect to its nuclear arsenal,[63] has served its interests well: It has allowed Israel to pursue its objectives ostensibly intra-legem, not extra-legem. In this manner, it engaged in the international legal discourse and was able to use its vocabulary and grammar, benefiting from international law's emphasis on state declarations (or lack of), as well as on its inherent indeterminacies, to argue its positions.

The main normative indeterminacies have related to the legal status of the territories conquered in 1967 and to the applicable normative framework governing the power Israel exercises therein. Thus, the prevalent view of the international community is that the OPT is occupied within the meaning of the term under the law of belligerent occupation. Israel has denied that this is its status, has referred to the West Bank as "administered territories," but has nevertheless refrained from annexing it de jure (with the exception of East Jerusalem). It has thus maintained that it has a claim to sovereignty over the territories, conceding that sovereignty is a matter of dispute to be settled through negotiations.[64] In this manner, while denying that the territories are occupied, Israel has arguably accepted the fundamental tenet of the law: that occupation does not confer title, and that the use of force and conquest are not an accepted way to acquire sovereignty.[65]

Pending the settlement of the dispute over the status of the territory, and in the process generating the temporary/indefinite indeterminacy,[66] the issue of

---

[63] Israel's policy of refraining from revealing its nuclear program's level of development and capabilities has allowed it to evade pressure, mostly from the US, to join the Treaty on the Non-Proliferation of Nuclear Weapons. Treaty on the Non-proliferation of Nuclear Weapons, 729 UNTS 161; 7 ILM 8809 (1968); 21 UST 483. See, "Israel's 'Nuclear Ambiguity' Policy" *Reut Institute* (June 17, 2009), www.reut-institute.org/en/Publication.aspx?PublicationId=3655; "Israel's Atomic Angst: A textile factory with a difference," *The Economist* (May 21, 2016), www.economist.com/news/middle-east-and-africa/21699046-one-worlds-oldest-nuclear-plant s-helped-build-jewish-states-secret; D. Birch and A.J. Smith, "Israel's Worst-Kept Secret," *The Atlantic* (September 16, 2014), www.theatlantic.com/international/archive/2014/09/israel-nuc lear-weapons-secret-united-states/380237/.

[64] See entry G: Geneva Convention; for a thorough analysis of Israel's normative approach to the OPT, see entry N: Nomos.

[65] See Introduction, Section 2.2; Article 47 of GC IV; Pictet, Commentary on GC IV, pp. 275–276; E. Benvenisti, *The International Law of Occupation* (Princeton: Princeton University Press, 1993), p. 5.

[66] See entry T: Temporary/Indefinite.

the applicable normative framework has generated a similar ambiguity: Israel rejected the international legal consensus regarding the applicability of the GC IV and at the same time stated its voluntary undertaking to apply and uphold its humanitarian provisions.[67]

Coupling these indeterminacies regarding the basic normative principles of the regime of belligerent occupation with their application discloses yet additional obfuscations between norm and fact, word and deed: Israel's actual exercise of control over the OPT has mocked both its normative commitment to administer the territory until the dispute is settled in a manner respecting the principle that unilateral use of force is not to produce facts on the grounds and its normative undertaking to apply the "humanitarian" provisions of the GC IV.

Insofar as nonannexation is concerned, over the years Israel has consistently deepened its hold over the OPT, effectively implementing a policy of crawling annexation:[68] It wove the infrastructure of the OPT – the electrical grid, water and sewage networks, roads and communications systems – into its own. It initially opened the borders for the free movement of people and goods (and eventually replaced this policy with the physical and legal barriers designed to halt the movement of Palestinians in order to advance, not halt, its control over the territory)[69] and created a single customs zone.[70] It exploited the OPT's natural resources[71] and suppressed the development of any local leadership that sought to end Israel's control.[72] Above all else, it allowed, encouraged, and incentivized the settlement of its Jewish citizens in the West Bank, in effect transforming the occupation into a regime of settler-colonialism.[73] Complementing these processes, the military commander imported Israeli

---

[67] See entry G: Geneva Law. On Israel's "voluntary" commitment to uphold the humanitarian provisions of the GC IV, see M. Shamgar, "The Observance of International Law in the Administered Territories" (1971) 1 *Israel Yearbook of Human Rights* 117, 266.

[68] See Ben-Naftali, Gross, and Michaeli, "Illegal Occupation," p. 601.

[69] The General Exit Permit (No. 5) Judea and Samaria, 1972 and General Exit Permit (No. 2) The Gaza Strip 5732–1972 collectively permitted Palestinians to exit the West Bank and the Gaza Strip and enter Israel from 5:00 AM to 1:00 AM. The general permit was revoked by the Order regarding Suspension of the General Exit Permit (No. 5) (Temporary) Judea and Samaria, 1991, and "closures" which temporarily denied Palestinian entry to Israel and were first introduced in the 1990s developed into a permanent individual permit system. On the permit regime, see entries B: Border/Barrier and Z: Zone.

[70] HCJ 69/81 *Abu-Itta* v. *The Military Commander of the Judea and Samaria* (1983) PD 37(2) 197.

[71] See entry U: Usufruct; HCJ 2164/09 *Yesh Din – Volunteers for Human Rights* v. *Commander of IDF Forces in the West Bank* (December 26, 2011).

[72] Between October 1979 and July 2012, the military commander made 87 declarations designating hundreds of Palestinian associations as unlawful. The list is available on the Israeli JAG site: www.law.idf.il/163–5149-he/Patzar.aspx.

[73] See entry J: Jewish Settlements.

legislation to the OPT, applying it to Israeli settlers on a personal and personal/
territorial basis, thereby creating two different legal systems in the same
geopolitical area.[74] The lawfulness of these actions was upheld, at times with
minor modifications, by the HCJ. Throughout these processes, Israel's official
position remained that these were "disputed" territories, the future of which
would be determined through negotiations.[75] It is little wonder that the
Palestinians concluded that this conduct is akin to someone eating the cake
while negotiating others' share in it.[76]

Israel's commitment to applying the "humanitarian provisions" of the
GC IV merits a similar assessment. It is difficult to think of a single right
conferred upon *protected persons* by the convention that Israel has not
breached. An incomplete but representative inventory includes the prohibition on destruction of private or public property "not rendered absolutely
necessary by military operations";[77] the prohibition on collective punishment;[78] the prohibition on deportation;[79] the prohibition on transfer of its
own civilian population to the occupied territory;[80] the prohibition on
administrative detention other than as an exception;[81] and the prohibition
on targeting civilians.[82] Most of these common practices qualify as war
crimes.

All these practices were carried out while still maintaining Israel's commitment to abide by the humanitarian provisions of the GC IV and, indeed, were
justified in reference to them. This version of legal *newspeak* was made
possible by the manipulability of the international legal language and the
possibilities thereby presented for the development of a local dialect to this

---

[74]   ACRI, *One Rule, Two Legal Systems.*
[75]   "In legal terms, the West Bank is best regarded as territory over which there are competing
       claims which should be resolved in peace process negotiations," Israeli Settlements and
       International Law, Israeli ministry of foreign affairs website, www.mfa.gov.il/mfa/foreignpo
       licy/peace/guide/pages/israeli%20settlements%20and%20international%20law.aspx.
[76]   "You should tell him you're not going to have the cake and eat it too," transcripts leaked by
       WikiLeaks of a meeting held on October 21, 2009, between the Palestinian negotiator Saeb
       Erekat and the American special enjoy to the peace negotiations, G. Mitchell, "Meeting
       minutes: Saeb Erekat and George Mitchell," *Al Jazeera* (October 21, 2009), http://transpar
       ency.aljazeera.net/en/projects/thepalestinepapers/20121821112587573.html.
[77]   See entries P: Proportionality; J: Jewish Settlements; U: Usufruct.
[78]   See entry H: House Demolitions.   [79]   See entry D: Deportations.
[80]   See entry J: Jewish Settlements.
[81]   Article 78 of GC IV, the ICRC Commentary on internment measures prescribes that "their
       exceptional character must be preserved," Pictet, Commentary on GC IV, p. 368; see entry A:
       Assigned Residence.
[82]   On Israel's engagement in an openly declared policy of targeted killings see entry C:
       Combatants.

language.[83] Litigation and judicial techniques varied. It is sufficient for the purposes of this succinct overview to mention a few of the most commonly used.

Thus, one such technique was to posit that a certain practice – say, deportation – was not a violation of a prohibition because the latter was applicable only to mass deportations but not to individual deportations of Palestinians.[84] A similar reasoning characterized the interpretation given to the prohibition on the transfer of the population of the occupying power to the occupied territory, limiting its application only to forced transfers.[85] Another interpretive technique consisted of jumbling the various documents comprising the Geneva Law, to produce results unintended by any of them, the notable example being the alleged permissibility of targeting civilians denying (properly) the existence of the status of "unlawful combatants" only to recreate it in the form of the "civilians who take direct part in hostilities."[86] By far the most common technique, however, was to posit that a certain practice was indeed prohibited, but that the prohibition was subject to an exception and that the State's action qualifies as such an exception to the prohibition. Thus, for instance, the exception of "imperative military needs" was advanced to support the lawfulness of the otherwise prohibited action of house demolition,[87] and exceptional security reasons justified the routine administrative detention of tens of thousands of Palestinians. This technique has to be appreciated against the observation that the very normative framework of occupation is grounded in the presumption that the situation of occupation itself presents the challenge of the exception to the regular basic norm of sovereign equality between states each exercising effective control over its territory and population.[88] Once thus understood, one could narrate the sorry

---

[83] See O. Ben-Naftali, "The Epistemology of the International Law Closet and the Spirit of Law," in N. Ziv and D. Hecker (eds.), *Does Law Matter?* (Tel Aviv: Tel Aviv University Law Faculty, Ramot Publication, 2011), p. 527 [Hebrew].

[84] HCJ 785/87 *Al-Affu* v. *Commander of the IDF forces in the West Bank* (1988) 42(2) PD 4 [Hebrew; English translation available at (1990) 29 ILM 139].

[85] *Ibid.* See also the Levy Committee Report, ¶ 6. For a discussion see entry N; Nomos, Section N.3.

[86] Article 51(3) *AP I*, HCJ 769/02 *Public Committee against Torture* v. *Government of Israel* (2006) 62(1) PD 507, http://elyon1.court.gov.il/Files_ENG/02/690/007/a34/02007690.a34.pdf.

[87] "Unless such destruction or seizure be imperatively demanded by the necessities of war" (Regulation 23(g) of *HC IV*); "except where such destruction is rendered absolutely necessary by military operations" (Article 53 of *GC IV*).

[88] Article 2(4) of the Charter of the United Nations, United Nations, October 24, 1945, 1 UNTS XVI. On the normative regime of occupation as an exception to the norm, see Introduction, Section 2.2.

story of the Israeli control over the OPT as the story of exceptions trumping norms.

From a perspective internal to international law, there are two major and related reasons that enable, indeed facilitate, sustaining this ostensible reversal of the relations between the norm and the exception and between word and deed: the first is the presumption of the centrality of the principle of sovereign equality to the international legal order. The second is the presumption, underlying the identification of customary international law, that *opinion juris* not merely complements *general practice* but participates in shaping it,[89] and is thus, at least in respect of IHL and IHRL, more important than practice. All evidence to the contrary notwithstanding, the coupling of these normative considerations with political considerations has made it possible for the international community, so long as official Israel has insisted that it does accept the fundamental principles of the law, to exempt itself from treating it as a rogue country. Thus, the charade was sustained both normatively and politically: For more than a quarter of a century, since the Madrid Conference of 1991,[90] the international community has invested itself in a peace process that is meant to implement Israel's declarations about settling the conflict through agreement. The fact that since the 1993 Oslo Accords Israel's long-term hold over the occupied territories has become more deeply entrenched and that the number of Israeli settlers has tripled has failed to produce a qualitative change in this position.[91] The legal discourse of the exceptions – despite the regularization of the latter in practice – was thus preserved at both the domestic and the international levels.

Until and unless one begins from the assumption that law is indistinguishable from violence,[92] there is a distinction to be maintained between arguments made intra-legem and positions taken extra-legem; debating the parameters of a certain exception is substantively different from arguing over the very existence of the rule: the former is an internal argument within the confines of a single discourse shared by the disputants, the latter a repudiation

---

[89] See, e.g., The International Law Commission, Second Report on the Identification of Customary International Law, May 22, 2012, A/CN/4/672.

[90] Madrid Peace Conference on October 30, 1991. See Letter of Invitation to the Madrid Peace Conference issued jointly by the US and the Soviet Union on Israel's MFA site: www.mfa.gov.il/MFA/ForeignPolicy/Peace/Guide/Pages/Madrid%20Letter%20of%20Invitation.aspx.

[91] A good example is the July 2016 Report of the Middle East Quartet which primarily dealt with the apparent Israeli settlement expansion policy, but highlighted Israel's and Prime Minster Netanyahu's "Support for the two-states solution" and the parties' "commitments under existing agreements," www.un.org/News/dh/infocus/middle_east/Report-of-the-Middle-East-Quartet.pdf.

[92] See entry V: Violence.

of the basis for the discourse. This is the reason both Israel and the international community continued to sustain the discourse. On February 6, 2017, Israel's Regularization Law obviated that reason. If upheld, this law should put an end to its participation in that discourse.

The drafters of the Regularization Law could not have chosen a better title to represent its impact on the words/deeds and rule/exception indeterminacies that have hitherto characterized Israeli control over the OPT. The term "regularization" represents the legalization process the law is set to effect on unauthorized Israeli construction in the OPT: from privately initiated trespass to permissible (indeed, a product of allocation, planning, and permit-granting), authorized, and state-sponsored enterprise.

But, aside from legalization, *regularization* further suggests a process of making the *irregular* regular, of normalizing the exception. Consequently, the regularization process works on both facets of the exceptionality of the irregular: its alleged rarity and its being unregulated. Regularization is thus a promise of both regularity and regulation, of high frequency and of administrative propriety.

Finally, regularizing the exception means that henceforth it is the rule. The enactment of this law directly and formally contradicts Israel's express position regarding the status of the territory and its undertaking to uphold the humanitarian provisions of the *GC IV*. The Israeli legislature declared, in effect, that it is the sovereign empowered to determine the law in the OPT and ordered the military authorities to confiscate lands belonging to Palestinians who under the hitherto applicable international legal framework are *protected persons*. In so doing, it crumbled an expertly designed legal edifice that has kept Israel within the bounds of the international legal discourse. It is no wonder then that the entire legal establishment of Israel's executive branch opposed its enactment: the legal advisor to the security establishment, the Knesset's legal advisor, the military advocate general, and the attorney general all objected, and the latter announced that he would not defend the law should a petition for annulling it be filed.[93] Such petitions have been filed.[94]

---

[93] "Position of the Attorney General – Regularization Bill (3433/20)," submitted to the Knesset Joint Committee of the Constitution Law and Justice Committee and the Foreign Affairs and Defense Committee; Opinion of Legal Counsel to the Joint Committee, November 27, 2016; Position of Legal Counsel to the Security Establishment, Ahaz Ben Ari, Transcript of the Joint Committee session dated December 12, 2016 (Transcript No. 5), starting at p. 15.

[94] Two petitions were filed to have the Regularization Law overturned: HCJ 1308/17 *Mayor of Silwad v. Knesset*; HCJ 2055/17 *Head of Ein Yabrud Council v. Knesset*. At the time of publication, they are still pending. The author of this entry represents the petitioners in the second petition. Note that an expert opinion positing that the law is unconstitutional, contravenes IHL and IHRL, and authorizes actions that amount to war crimes was signed by 28

This is how the Regularization Law reforms Israel's OPT words/deeds indeterminacy. The pretense of accepting the principle that the OPT's final status will be determined only through negotiations and consent is reduced to words that ridicule more than affirm it. No more formal commitment to the humanitarian principles of the laws of occupation. No more engaging in the rule/exception charade.

The practices that were presented as exceptions, though for decades over-riding the rules, are now officially, well, *regularized*. The nomos of the regime is out of the closet.

public and international law professors from virtually all law faculties in Israel and submitted as a amicus curia petition accompanying the first petition. For the opinion, see http://media .wix.com/ugd/40845d_3581ccf731794e878bfec9855717f768.pdf [Hebrew].

S

Security Prisoners

Hedi Viterbo

S.1 INTRODUCTION: TERMINOLOGY, FIGURES, AND CONTEXT

Since assuming control of the West Bank and Gaza Strip in 1967, Israel is estimated to have taken between 700,000 and 800,000 Palestinians into custody[1] – the equivalent of about a fifth of the Palestinians currently living in these territories.[2] This mass incarceration mirrors the transformation of the West Bank and Gaza Strip, in general, into a colossal prison of sorts (or rather, a disjointed network of prisons),[3] owing to Israel's severe restriction of Palestinian movement within, between, from, and into these territories.[4]

Israeli law distinguishes "security" from "criminal" prisoners – a distinction that carries manifold implications. "Security prisoners" are held separately and denied many of the rights granted to other inmates in matters including

---

[1] See, respectively, UN Human Rights Council, "Human Rights Situation in Palestine and Other Occupied Arab Territories: Report of the Special Rapporteur on the Situation of Human Rights in the Palestinian Territories Occupied Since 1967, John Dugard" (January 21, 2008) A/ HRC/7/17, www.refworld.org/docid/47baaa262.html; J. Rudoren and K. Abu Aker, "Palestinians Dispute Israel's Findings on a Prisoner's Death," *New York Times* (February 24, 2013), www.nytimes.com/2013/02/25/world/middleeast/palestinians-demand-inquiry-into-detai nees-death-in-israel.html.

[2] United Nations Relief and Work Agency for Palestine Refugees in the Near East (UNRWA), "West Bank & Gaza Strip: Population Census of 2007" (January 2010), www.unrwa.org/user files/2010012035949.pdf.

[3] A. Korn, "The Ghettoization of the Palestinians," in R. Lentin (ed.), *Thinking Palestine* (London and New York: Zed Books, 2008), pp. 116–130; A. Bornstein, "Military Occupation as Carceral Society: Prisons, Checkpoints, and Walls in the Israeli-Palestinian Struggle," in A. Waterston (ed.), *An Anthropology of War: Views from the Frontline* (New York: Berghahn Books, 2008), pp. 106–130 [hereinafter: "Military Occupation as Carceral Society"].

[4] On this restriction of Palestinian movement, see entries B: Barrier/Border, Q: Quality of Life, V: Violence, and Z: Zone.

welfare, education, and family visits.[5] In its regulations, Israel's prison authority, the Israel Prison Service (IPS), generally defines a security offense as an
offense that is either specifically listed in the regulations or is "by its nature or
circumstances a security offense."[6] Each prisoner's classification, as either a
security or a criminal prisoner, is left to the discretion of the IPS, and is often
based on secret information withheld from the prisoner and the defense
attorneys.[7]

This legal category – "security prisoner" – is not only unbounded and
vaguely defined, it also covers physically nonviolent acts, such as membership
of any of the countless organizations proscribed by the military.[8] Further,
unauthorized forms of peaceful political activity – waving or displaying "political flags or symbols," publications "containing material of a political nature,"
and gatherings and processions of ten people or more – have also been
criminalized, and are all punishable by up to ten years in prison, under the
military law Israel applies to Palestinians in the West Bank.[9]

The "security prisoner" category operates primarily along national and
ethnic lines. According to IPS figures, the vast majority of Israel's so-called
security prisoners – 96 percent in April 2013 – are Palestinians (overwhelmingly men)[10] and a meager 0.2 percent are Jews (the rest are foreign Arab
nationals). Of the Palestinians labeled as security prisoners, 85 percent are

---

[5] Articles 1b, 4a of the Israel Prison Service (IPS) Commission Ordinance 03.02.00: Guidelines
     Regarding Security Prisoners, March 15, 2002, www.gov.il/BlobFolder/policy/030200/he/03.0
     2.00%20-%20ביטחוניים%20לאסירים%20הוראת%20ביחס%20כללים.pdf.

[6] Articles 3–4, Appendices A-B of the IPS Commission Ordinance 04.05.00: The Definition of
     Security Prisoner, May 1, 2001. On the Israeli security discourse in general see, e.g., B.
     Kimmerling, "The Code of Security: The Israeli Military-Cultural Complex," in *The
     Invention and Decline of Israeliness: State, Society, and the Military* (Berkeley and Los
     Angeles: University of California Press, 2001), p. 208; J. Ochs, *Security and Suspicion: An
     Ethnography of Everyday Life in Israel* (Philadelphia: University of Pennsylvania Press, 2010).

[7] Y. Berda, "The Security Risk as a Security Risk: Notes on the Classification Practices of the
     Israeli Security Services," in A. Baker and A. Matar (eds.), *Threat: Palestinian Political
     Prisoners in Israel* (London: Pluto Press, 2011), pp. 44, 46.

[8] Article 101(e) of the Counter-Terrorism Law, 2016 (defining membership of a proscribed
     organization as a serious terrorist offense). Until recently, such acts were criminalized and
     classified as "security offenses," respectively, in: Articles 84–85 of Defense (Emergency)
     Regulations, 1945; 1st Annex of Order No. 1651 Concerning Security Provisions (Integrated
     Version) (Judea and Samaria), 2009, www.law.idf.il/Templates/GetFile/GetFile.aspx?FileN
     ame=XGF5b3NoLWRvY3NcdGFmcmloX2hha2lrYVvxiaXRhaG9uXyZfcGxpbGlcb2dkYW5f
     aGFraWthLnBkZg==&InfoCenterItem=true.

[9] Articles 1, 3, 5–6, 10 of Order No. 101 Concerning Prohibition of Incitement and Hostile
     Propaganda, 1967. On Israeli officials' anxieties over physically nonviolent Palestinian protest,
     see entry V: Violence.

[10] On Palestinian women prisoners, see N. Abdo, "Palestinian Women Political Prisoners and
     the Israeli State," in *Threat: Palestinian Political Prisoners in Israel*, p. 57; Addameer, *Occupied*

from the West Bank (excluding East Jerusalem), convicted by the Israeli military court system;[11] around 7 percent are from the Gaza Strip, including prisoners captured during Israel's incursions since its unilateral pullout from this territory in 2005; nearly 4 percent are noncitizen residents from East Jerusalem, which Israel controversially claims to have annexed; and nearly 4 percent are Palestinian citizens of Israel.[12]

Additional figures published by the IPS shed further light on the realities of Palestinians in Israeli custody. Among other things, the proportion of "security offenders" among Israel's prison population has ranged roughly from half to a quarter.[13] Of Palestinians classified as security offenders, two-thirds are prisoners (about a sixth of whom are serving life sentences), a quarter are detainees awaiting trial or on trial, and the rest – around 3 percent, adding up to thousands over the years – are "administrative detainees."[14] The latter are detained without charge or trial, on the basis of secret evidence undisclosed to them or their attorneys. Pursuant to Israeli law, extension of administrative detention is subject to judicial review every six months, with no set limit. This review, unbound by the regular rules of evidence, is based on secret evidence and is held behind closed doors.[15] All of this prevents those placed in so-called administrative detention not only from challenging the suspicions or alleged evidence against them, but also from even knowing how long they are expected to remain behind bars.[16] Even some convicted Palestinian "security prisoners," serving a sentence of a seemingly definite number of years, are not

Lives: Imprisonment of Palestinian Women and Girls (March 2016), www.addameer.org/sites/default/files/publications/international_womens_day_factsheet_o.pdf.

[11] See entry M: Military Courts.

[12] Adalah, *Statistics on Detainees and Prisoners in Israeli Prisons* (April 2013), www.adalah.org/Public/files/English/Newsletter/103-April2013/PalestinianPoliticalPrisoners-Statistics-April-2013.pdf.

[13] IPS, *Statistical Figures – Prisoners* (2015) [Hebrew]. www.ips.gov.il/Web/He/Research/Statistics/Prisoners/Default.aspx (last accessed on September 10, 2016; no longer available online).

[14] Adalah, *Statistics on Detainees and Prisoners in Israeli Prisons.*

[15] Articles 290–291 of Order 1651.

[16] See also Addameer, *Induced Desperation: The Psychological Torture of Administrative Detention* (June 2016), www.addameer.org/sites/default/files/publications/the_psychological_torture_of_administrative_detention.pdf; B'Tselem and Hamoked, *Without Trial: Administrative Detention of Palestinians by Israel and the Internment of Unlawful Combatants Law* (October 2009), www.btselem.org/download/200910_without_trial_eng.pdf; T. Pelleg-Sryck, "The Mysteries of Administrative Detention," in *Threat: Palestinian Political Prisoners in Israel*, pp. 123, 125–126; R. Smith, "'A Danger to the Region': Subaltern Geopolitics of Palestinians Detained in Israeli Prisons" (2013) 16 *Arab World Geographer* 75, 92 [hereinafter: "A Danger to the Region"]. For an ethnographic study showing how soon-to-be-released prisoners in the United States use future-oriented perceptions and practices to realize some degree of selfhood, see J. Seim, "Short-Timing: The Carceral Experience of Soon-to-be-Released Prisoners" (2016) 18 *Punishment & Society* 442.

immune to such uncertainty: immediately or shortly after their scheduled release from prison, some are placed in "administrative detention."[17] Those who are released as planned, now being former prisoners, are subject to continued restrictions by the Israeli authorities which limit their daily movement and freedoms and thus extend their sense of incarceration beyond prison.[18]

Contrary to the language used by the Israeli legal system, many Palestinian inmates self-identify as "political" rather than "security" prisoners. This resistant terminology is meant to underscore the political context of their incarceration – Israel's belligerent regime and the deprivation, domination, and discrimination it engenders – as well as the ideological cause they see themselves as serving. At the same time, when classifying Palestinians as security prisoners, the IPS reportedly considers not only the prisoner's motivation but also the perceived potential harm of the offenses to national security,[19] the result being that not all those who are thus classified actually acted out of ideological opposition to Israel. The distinction between political and criminal prisoners is of some value, as further illustrated in Section S.2.2, but it is not free from pitfalls. Among other things, it might be interpreted as portraying the actions or incarceration of "regular" prisoners as in some sense apolitical, thereby unwittingly masking the inherently political nature of criminal law and criminal justice.[20]

---

[17]   A. al-Bazz (Activestills.org), "Palestinian Prisoner Held in Admin. Detention – After Serving 15 Years," +972 *Magazine* (June 14, 2016), http://972mag.com/palestinian-prisoner-placed-in-admin-detention-after-serving-15-years/120041/; Y. Marom, "An Employee of a Prisoner Rights Organization in Administrative Detention Due to … Connection to Prisoners," *Sicha Mekomit* (June 16, 2016) [Hebrew], http://mekomit.co.il/%D7%A2%D7%99%D7%AA%D7%95%D7%A0%D7%90%D7%99-%D7%A9%D7%A2%D7%95%D7%91%D7%93-%D7%91%D7%90%D7%A8%D7%92%D7%95%D7%9F-%D7%96%D7%9B%D7%95%D7%99%D7%95%D7%AA-%D7%90%D7%A1%D7%99%D7%A8%D7%99%D7%9D-%D7%91%D7%9E./; N. Rotem, "A Person Imprisoned, a Month After His Release Date," *Sicha Mekomit* (April 13, 2016) [Hebrew], http://mekomit.co.il/%D7%91%D7%99%D7%9C%D7%90%D7%9C-%D7%A7%D7%90%D7%99%D7%93-%D7%91%D7%99%D7%93%D7%95%D7%93/. For a more in-depth discussion of the uncertainty inherent to Israel's control over Palestinian lives, see entry M: Military Courts.

[18]   Smith, "A Danger to the Region."

[19]   A. Baker, "Palestinian Prisoners between the Collective and the Individual – A Look from the Inside" 8 *Maasei Mishpat [Law & Social Change]* (forthcoming in 2017) [hereinafter: "Palestinian Prisoners between the Collective and the Individual"].

[20]   For some introductory writing on the latter subject, see, e.g., R. Kennedy, *Race, Crime, and the Law* (New York: Vintage Books 1998); A. Norrie, *Crime, Reason, and History: A Critical Introduction to Criminal Law* (3rd edn., Cambridge: Cambridge University Press, 2014); C. Wells and O. Quick, *Lacey, Wells and Quick – Reconstructing Criminal Law: Text and Materials* (4th edn., Cambridge: Cambridge University Press, 2010); B. Western, *Punishment and Inequality in America* (New York: Russell Saga Foundation, 2006).

Since the early 2000s, Palestinian "security prisoners" have mostly been held in facilities operated by the IPS, though they are also occasionally detained in military custody.[21] However, the formal distinction between these two state organs – the military on the one hand and the supposedly nonmilitary IPS on the other – can be somewhat misleading. This is because, among other reasons, a large portion of IPS staff dealing with Palestinian inmates are soldiers on active duty serving in the IPS. Soldiers make up 51 percent of Ofer Prison staff, for example, as well as 40 percent of Nafha Prison staff.[22] In addition, since combat military service or training is a prerequisite for employment in the IPS, many other IPS staff members are former combat soldiers.[23]

When public attention is paid to the Palestinian inmates in question, it tends to center on relatively isolated cases that are seen as extreme, such as deaths in custody,[24] or hunger strikes, or – at the intersection of these two issues – force-feeding. Hunger strikes – collective and, in recent years, also individual – have taken place every few years since 1968. In the 1970s and 1980s, deaths of Palestinian hunger strikers following force-feeding attempts by the Israeli prison authorities resulted in a supreme court order to cease this practice.[25] Yet, in 2015,

---

[21]   HCJ 2690/09 *Yesh Din v. IDF Commander in the West Bank* (March 28, 2010) [Hebrew], http://elyon1.court.gov.il/files/09/900/026/n05/09026900.n05.htm (an unofficial English translation is available at www.hamoked.org/files/2010/111511_eng.pdf); IPS, *Security Prisoners Incarcerated in the Israel Prison Service* (2007) [Hebrew], http://ips.gov.il/Items/o 5637/bitchonim_heb_2007.pdf.

[22]   See, respectively, N. Telem, "Ofer's Open Eye" (2012) 32 *Seeing Shabas – Journal of the IPS* 12 [Hebrew]; IPS, "Nafha Prison – The Vault" (January 20, 2013) [Hebrew], http://ips.gov.il/Web/ He/News/Articles2/2857.aspx (last accessed on September 10, 2016; no longer available online). Ofer Prison is located in the West Bank, near the Palestinian city of Ramallah; Nafha prison is located in the Naqab/Negev, to the north of Mitzpe Ramon.

[23]   IPS, *A Recruit's Guide* (2012) [Hebrew]. http://ips.gov.il/Items/04381/%D7%9E%D7%AA%D 7%92%D7%99%D7%99%D7%A1.pdf.

[24]   On deaths of Palestinians in Israeli custody, see, e.g., P. Greenwood, "Prisoner Was Tortured Before Dying in Israeli Jail, Says Palestinian Authority," *The Guardian* (February 24, 2013), www.theguardian.com/world/2013/feb/24/violence-west-bank-custody-death; J. R. Hilterman, "Deaths in Israeli Prisons" (1990) 19 *Journal of Palestine Studies* 101; A. Imseis, "Moderate Torture on Trial: Critical Reflections on the Israeli Supreme Court Judgment concerning the Legality of General Security Service Interrogation Methods" (2001) 19 *Berkeley Journal of International Law* 328, 329, 337–338, 344.

[25]   Addameer, *Factsheet: Force-feeding under International Law and Medical Standards* (November 2015), www.addameer.org/publications/factsheet-force-feeding-under-interna tional-law-and-medical-standards; P. Bailey, "Hunger Strike: Still an Effective Mode of Resistance for Palestinian Prisoners?" (May 2014) *Washington Report on Middle East Affairs* 21, www.wrmea.org/2014-may/hunger-strike-still-an-effective-mode-of-resistance-for-palesti nian-prisoners.html; Baker, "Palestinian Prisoners between the Collective and the Individual."

a year after a mass hunger strike by administrative detainees, the Israeli legislature passed a statute permitting force-feeding, which the supreme court later ruled constitutional, thus reintroducing the practice – this time with explicit statutory and judicial authorization.[26]

This entry, however, endeavors to shine a spotlight on seemingly less dramatic, but more routine policies and practices that indiscriminately and directly affect all Palestinians labeled as security offenders. Two specific themes are at the heart of the analysis that follows. The first, discussed in Section S.2, is sociopolitical fragmentation: Israel's isolation of those it deems "security offenders" while splintering them into smaller and uncoordinated groups in prison. The second, examined in Section S.2, concerns rehabilitation, or the lack thereof, and the ways in which it informs, and is informed by, Israel's harshness toward these Palestinian inmates. The Conclusion links these two themes together, demonstrating how incarceration hinders not only Palestinian movement in the physical sense, but also the movement of political thought across time and space.

S.2 SOCIOPOLITICAL FRAGMENTATION

Throughout the years, and with growing force since the 1990s, Israel has deployed an array of practices and policies operating to fragment Palestinians spatially, politically, and socially. It is within this wider context – discussed in depth throughout this book[27] and also touched upon in Section S.2.2 – that Israeli authorities subject Palestinian "security prisoners" in particular to various forms of removal, distancing, and isolation from their society, as well as separation from one another, as discussed throughout this section.

S.2.1 Removal, Distancing, and Isolation

Incarceration, by definition, serves to remove transgressors from the general populace. Yet, in Israeli hands, prisoners removed from Palestinian society are often political activists,[28] including physically nonviolent ones.[29] Thus, unlike

---

[26] HCJ 5304/15 *Israel Medical Association v. Israeli Knesset* (September 11, 2016), http://elyon1 .court.gov.il/files/15/040/053/t11/15053040.t11.pdf.

[27] See entries B: Border/Barrier, F: Future-Oriented Measures (Section F.2), Q: Quality of Life, V: Violence, and Z: Zone.

[28] R. James, "Savage Restraint: Israel, Palestine and the Dialectics of Legal Repression" (2001) 47(4) *Social Problems* 445; E. Nashif, *Palestinian Political Prisoners: Identity and Community* (London: Routledge, 2008).

[29] J. Peteet, "Cosmopolitanism and the Subversive Space of Protests" (2009) 37 *Jerusalem Quarterly* 86; R. Jaraisy and T. Feldman, "Protesting for Human Rights in the Occupied

many criminal justice contexts (though not without analogues elsewhere), Israel's incarceration of those labeled as security offenders is not usually done in the name of protecting the interests or safety of the local (Palestinian) population. Instead, invoking "public order" and (Israel's) "national security," its main aim is to suppress Palestinian resistance.

Even more unique to the Israeli–Palestinian context is that most Palestinian inmates are held in facilities inside Israel "proper" – a practice exemplifying a broader legal–political porosity, as discussed elsewhere in this book.[30] This, combined with restricted access for so-called security reasons as well as the complexity and length of obtaining visit permits, results in the systematic denial of family visits.[31] This practice, petitions to the supreme court have argued, violates *GC IV*, specifically Article 76 ("Protected persons accused of offences shall be detained in the occupied country, and if convicted they shall serve their sentences therein"); Article 49 (prohibiting "forcible transfers, as well as deportations of protected persons from occupied territory to the territory of the Occupying Power"); and Article 80 (ensuring that "[i]nternees shall retain their full civil capacity and shall exercise such attendant rights"). In 1988 and again in 2010, the court rejected these petitions, holding that the legal basis for this practice is Israel's emergency legislation, which according to the court prevails over international law. The court added that rather than "blindly" applying *GC IV*, Israel should adapt it to the local circumstances, which it described as "unanticipated by the Convention's drafters."[32]

Further, some Israeli courts, dealing with remands of noncitizen Palestinians interrogated by the Israeli general security service, are located "inside" Israel (i.e., outside the West Bank). This obstacle to the presence of Palestinian families and attorneys during hearings hinders family contact and

---

Palestinian Territory: Assessing the Challenges and Revisiting the Human Rights Defender Framework" (2013) 5(3) *Journal of Human Rights Practice* 421.

[30] On this porosity, see entry O: Outside/Inside, Section O.3 ("Israeli Law Does Not Stop at the Border").

[31] See Addameer, *Fact Sheet: Families and Family Visits* (October 2014), www.addameer.org/sites/default/files/publications/families-family-visits-october-2014_0.pdf; S. Ben-Ari and A. Barsella, "Family Visits to Palestinian Prisoners Held Inside Israel," in *Threat: Palestinian Political Prisoners in Israel*, p. 201.

[32] HCJ 253/88 *Sajdiyeh v. Minister of Defense* (November 8, 1988) [Hebrew], www.hamoked.org.il/items/4060.pdf; HCJ 2690/09. At the time of the latter judgment, more than 90 percent of noncitizen Palestinian inmates were held inside Israel. *Ibid.*, ¶ 2. For further analysis, see M. Sfard, "Devil's Island: The Transfer of Palestinian Detainees into Prisons within Israel," in *Threat: Palestinian Political Prisoners in Israel*, p. 188.

effective legal representation in this context as well.[33] This practice, like the incarceration of noncitizen Palestinians outside the West Bank and Gaza Strip, has received the supreme court's blessing. In line with its contentious stance on *GC IV*,[34] the court dismissed petitioners' reference, in this context, to Article 66 of the Convention (according to which "the Occupying Power may hand over ... accused [persons resident in the occupied territory] to its properly constituted, non-political military courts, on condition that the said courts sit in the occupied country").[35]

In addition to removing and distancing Palestinian political activists, Israeli authorities also cut them off from outside information and contact accessible to other inmates. The IPS regulations have increasingly restricted Palestinian prisoners' access to media sources, books, and members of Knesset.[36] Those the Israeli authorities regard as especially troublesome, such as hunger strikers, are even more radically isolated from their fellow inmates and the outside world.[37]

S.2.2 *Division*

Israel not only removes, distances, and isolates those it labels as security offenders from the general Palestinian society. It has also been increasingly

---

[33] Yesh Din, *Backyard Proceedings: The Implementation of Due Process Rights in the Military Courts in the Occupied Territories* (2007), pp. 40–41, https://s3-eu-west-1.amazonaws.com/files .yesh-din.org/%D7%9E%D7%A9%D7%98%D7%99%D7%9D+%D7%91%D7%97 %D7%A6%D7%A8+%D7%94%D7%90%D7%95%D7%A8%D7%99%D7%AA/Bac kyardProceedingsfullreportEng+full+report.pdf; Petition HCJ 1958/10 *Palestinian Prisoners Office* v. *Israeli Defense Forces Commander in the Region* (2010) [Hebrew], www.humanrights .org.il/articles/בתי%20משפט%20צבאיים.doc.

[34] See entry G: Geneva Law.

[35] HCJ 6504/95 *Wajiyeh* v. *State of Israel* (1995) [Hebrew], www.hamoked.org.il/files/2011/2350 .pdf; HCJ 2690/09, ¶ 10.

[36] Articles 21a, 21c, 21e of IPS Commission Ordinance 03.02.00 (for the December 26, 2011 version, see www.hamoked.org.il/files/2012/114391.pdf); Temporary IPS Order – Acquisition of Newspapers and Magazines for Criminal/Security Prisoners, December 31, 2013, www.ips.gov .il/Uploads/Commands/PDF/367.pdf; H. Matar, "Israel Bans Palestinian Prisoners from Bringing in Books," +972 *Magazine* (January 27, 2016), http://972mag.com/israel-bans-palesti nian-prisoners-from-bringing-in-books/116350/; J. Khoury, "Prison Service Limiting MP Visits to Security Prisoners," *Haaretz* (August 4, 2016) [Hebrew], www.haaretz.co.il/.premium- 1.3028664.

[37] Article 6a and Appendix A of IPS Commission Ordinance 04.16.00: Prisoners' Hunger Strike, May 1, 2001, www.gov.il/BlobFolder/policy/041600/he/041600.pdf. On the actual use of solitary confinement, see Addameer and Physicians for Human Rights – Israel, *The Sounds of Silence: Isolation and Solitary Confinement of Palestinians in Israeli Detention* (July 2008), www.addameer.org/files/Reports/isolation-eng.pdf; S. Francis and K. Gibson, "Isolation and Solitary Confinement of Palestinian Prisoners and Detainees in Israeli Facilities," in *Threat: Palestinian Political Prisoners in Israel*, p. 212.

separating them from one another while in custody. Time and again, Israeli authorities have cautioned against collective unity among these inmates. As early as 1980, supreme court justice Yehuda Cohen held that "security prisoners are an organized body acting as a uniform ideological body . . . The unique organizational nature of security prisoners justifies [imposing on them] . . . harsher security measures . . . than those applied to criminal prisoners."[38] More recently, in 2007, the IPS likewise described "security prisoners" as endeavoring to "turn prison into a place of training, instruction, [and] forming an ideology," as well as "ensure . . . internal discipline and prevent prisoners from collaborating with the prison management intelligence. In addition, the prisoners try to operate various committees for organizing [education and] . . . instructing prisoners."[39]

In their battle to stymie these collective endeavors, Israeli authorities have deployed an ever-growing array of measures aimed at dividing Palestinian inmates into smaller, uncoordinated groups. This has included barring Palestinian prisoners from electing central prisoner representatives.[40] Article 102 of GC IV gives internees the right to "freely elect . . . members of a Committee empowered to represent them before the Detaining and the Protecting Powers," while Article 79 of GC III entitles war prisoners to "freely elect . . . prisoners' representatives entrusted with representing them before the military authorities [and] . . . the Protecting Powers."[41] Until the 2000s, Palestinian prisoners indeed elected a so-called "dialogue commission" comprising elected prisoner representatives, which was later replaced by individual elected representatives, including ward representatives and central prison representatives. While the IPS regulations used to allow central representatives access to all relevant wards, now the election of such representatives is banned altogether.[42] Similarly divisive, reportedly, has been the collective punishment of Palestinian "security" prisoners for individual violations.[43]

---

[38] HCJ 221/80 *Darwish v. Israel Prison Service* (November 25, 1980), ¶ 5 of justice Yehuda Cohen's opinion [Hebrew], www.hamoked.org.il/items/4640.pdf.

[39] IPS, *Security Prisoners Incarcerated in the Israel Prison Service* (2007), pp. 8, 10 [Hebrew], http://ips.gov.il/Items/05637/bitchonim_heb_2007.pdf.

[40] Articles 6a, 6g of the IPS Commission Ordinance 03.02.00 – 2011 and 2014 versions.

[41] On whether Palestinian prisoners should be considered "war prisoners," see S. Ben-Natan, "Are There Prisoners in This War?," in *Threat: Palestinian Political Prisoners in Israel*, p. 149.

[42] See also M. Rosenfeld, *Confronting the Occupation: Work, Education, and Political Activism of Palestinian Families in a Refugee Camp* (Redwood City: Stanford University Press, 2004) [hereinafter: *Confronting the Occupation*]; Baker, "Palestinian Prisoners between the Collective and the Individual"; W. Daka, "Consciousness Molded or the Re-identification of Torture," in *Threat: Palestinian Political Prisoners in Israel*, p. 234 [hereinafter: "Consciousness Molded"].

[43] *Ibid.*

The IPS has also clamped down on informal study groups run by Palestinian prisoners. These study groups, which many former prisoners have described as a source of empowering political consciousness, have engaged with subjects ranging from Palestinian and Zionist histories, Palestinian culture, and Islam, through Arabic literacy and Hebrew or English as a second language, to security outside prison.[44] This pedagogic-political enterprise did not escape the IPS, which has described prison, in its journal, as "the national Palestinian academy," adding: "For [these] prisoners . . . [Israeli] prison is a stage in . . . national development, personally and collectively. . . . [They] have delved into Israeli issues, mainly by reading books, . . . [and] have had ideological debates on . . . the future character of the Palestinian state."[45] As part of its recent clampdown on Palestinian prisoners' collective activities, the IPS has targeted these study groups as well, placing them under heavy regulation. This has included amending its regulations, in 2011, to prohibit inmates in one cell from attending study groups in other cells.[46] The same amendment also revoked a provision that had allowed "security prisoners" to teach fellow inmates in their ward.[47] As a result of these and other measures, these study groups, though still in operation,[48] have been on the wane.[49]

Attempts at sowing fragmentation have also taken place on a spatial basis, including dividing inmates into different cells, wards, and facilities on the basis of their regions of residence.[50] This geographically based separation resonates with what Israeli officials have publicly called Israel's "separation policy" regarding the West Bank and Gaza Strip.[51] As discussed throughout

---

[44] Rosenfeld, *Confronting the Occupation*; J. Collins, *Occupied by Memory: The Intifada Generation and the Palestinian State of Emergency* (New York: New York University Press, 2004) [hereinafter: *Occupied by Memory*].

[45] R. Shaked, "Security Prisoners in Israeli Prisons" (2008) 23 *Seeing Shabas – Journal of the IPS* 26, 27 [Hebrew], http://ips.gov.il/Items/04423/23.pdf.

[46] Article 21a(1) of the IPS Commission Ordinance 03.02.00, December 26, 2011 version.

[47] Article 21b, *ibid.*

[48] "Interview with Ahmad Saadat: Leading from Prison, Ending Negotiations, and Rebuilding the Resistance" (2014) 43(4) *Journal of Palestine Studies* 49; "Interview with Marwan Barghouti: Life and Politics in Prison, National Unity, and the Resistance" (2014) 43(4) *Journal of Palestine Studies* 57.

[49] Daka, "Consciousness Molded"; Rosenfeld, *Confronting the Occupation*. M. Rosenfed, "The Movement of Palestinian Political Prisoners and the Struggle Against the Israeli Occupation: A Historical Perspective" (Paper presented at the Middle East Studies Association Annual Meeting, Washington DC, November 25, 2014) (in author's possession).

[50] Addameer, *Violations Against Palestinian Prisoners and Detainees in Israeli Prisons and Detention Centers – Annual Report 2010* (2011), www.addameer.org/files/Reports/EN%20Ad dameer%202010%20Violations%20Report.pdf; Daka, "Consciousness Molded."

[51] Gisha, *The Separation Policy: List of References Prepared by Gisha* (2014), http://gisha.org/Us erFiles/File/publications/separation_policy_2014.pdf.

this book,[52] Israel has cut off the Gaza Strip and the West Bank from one another, placing the former under constant (albeit changeable) closure, while enclosing the latter by means of the Separation Wall, subjecting it to restrictions of Palestinian movement, and splintering it into enclaves that each experience Israel's control differently.[53]

The growing spatial separation has also operated along generational lines – separating Palestinian adults and children in Israeli custody. In the past, Israel held all Palestinian child prisoners, as well as detainees older than 15, with Palestinian adults. Inadvertently, this enabled the prisoners to transfer from one generation to another what they regarded as valuable knowledge – including through the study activities now banned by the Israeli authorities – leading many in Palestinian society to view Israeli prison as an "academy of political activism" for young inmates.[54] The Israeli judiciary, however, warned that joint incarceration would expose Palestinian children "to . . . [older] prisoners' ideologies,"[55] and therefore espoused separation as a means for the prison authorities to exert counterinfluences on these children.[56] This idea became a reality over the last 15 years, as a series of amendments and reforms have nearly eliminated joint incarceration.

The detrimental implications of this seemingly benevolent development, however, are alarming. The usual justification for separating children from adult criminals in prison does not seem to apply to the adults in question, who, as explained earlier, are neither criminals in the common sense of the word nor held with those classified as "criminal prisoners." In fact, various sources, including testimonies of Palestinian child ex-detainees, suggest that, prior to this separation, Palestinian adult inmates

---

[52] See entries B: Border/Barrier, Q: Quality of Life, V: Violence, and Z: Zone.

[53] A. Handel, "Where, Where to, and When in the Occupied Territories: An Introduction to Geography of Disaster," in A. Ophir, M. Givoni, and S. Hanafi (eds.), *The Power of Inclusive Exclusion: Anatomy of Israeli Rule in the Occupied Palestinian Territories* (New York: Zone Books, 2009), pp. 179–222.; Bornstein, "Military Occupation as Carceral Society"; Korn, "The Ghettoization of the Palestinians"; Gisha, *A Costly Divide: Economic Repercussions of Separating Gaza and the West Bank* (2015), http://gisha.org/UserFiles/File/publications/a_costly_divide/a_costly_divide_en-web.pdf.

[54] Rosenfeld, *Confronting the Occupation*, pp. 238–265; Collins, *Occupied by Memory*, pp. 125–130; L. Taraki, "The Development of Political Consciousness Among Palestinians in the Occupied Territories, 1967-1987," in J. R. Nassar and R. Heacock (eds.), *Intifada: Palestine at the Crossroads* (New York: Praeger, 1990), pp. 53, 68. See also, on the Palestinian image of imprisonment as a rite of maturation, entry Y: Youth.

[55] MilA 358/03 *E-Nasirat v. Military Prosecutor* (December 18, 2003).

[56] See, e.g., justice Rubinstein's opinion in CrimA 7515/08 *State of Israel v. Gurin* (January 5, 2009) ("Should prison be . . . an academy for terrorism [for Palestinian minors and very young adults], in the absence of any counter-barrier of education and treatment?").

provided their juniors with crucial support, in addition to representing their concerns to the prison authorities. One child who had been detained with adults, for instance, reported to Israeli NGO B'Tselem in 2008: "The [adult] detainees treated us [children] well. ... I felt comfortable. ... At first, I was afraid and cried sometimes, because my family was far away. ... The adult detainees took care of me."[57] Considering that Palestinian children in Israeli custody are often denied contact with their parents, adult Palestinian inmates might have been the closest substitute for parental care, as this child's account indeed suggests. Moreover, separation from these adult inmates has left Palestinian children less protected against abuse and violence – by the Israeli authorities as well as by other children (whose violent disputes adult inmates used to peacefully mediate). Further, most Palestinian child inmates come from poor families, where children and adults sleep in the same room, and might therefore experience such separation as extra punishment.[58]

S.3 (NON-)REHABILITATION

Unlike other prisoners,[59] those classified as security prisoners are not normally referred to Israeli rehabilitation services.[60] The Israeli authorities rarely consider Palestinian rehabilitation facilities a viable

---

[57] "Testimony: 12-Year-Old Beaten and Imprisoned with Adults, Sept. '08," B'Tselem (September 11, 2008), www.btselem.org/testimonies/20080911_muhammad_khawajah_age_12_detained_by_idf.

[58] For further details and critical analysis of this generational segregation of Palestinian inmates, see H. Viterbo, "Rights as a Divide-and-Rule Mechanism: Lessons from the Case of Palestinians in Israeli Custody" Law & Society Inquiry (forthcoming) [hereinafter: "Rights as a Divide-and-Rule Mechanism"]. See also P. Veerman and A. Waldman, "When Can Children and Adolescents Be Detained Separately from Adults?: The Case of Palestinian Children Deprived of Their Liberty in Israeli Military Jails and Prisons" (1996) 4 International Journal of Children's Rights 147. On two of the issues mentioned above – the denial of parental contact and the abuse of Palestinian children in Israeli custody – see entry Y: Youth. In addition to separate detention and separate imprisonment, the Israeli military has also, since 2009, been hearing court cases involving Palestinian child defendants separately from cases of adult defendants. See entry Y: Youth.

[59] Articles 11c–11d of the Prisons Directive [New Version], 1972, www.nevo.co.il/law_html/La wo1/056_002.htm.

[60] Article 1b of the IPS Commission Ordinance 04.54.02: Rehabilitation Frameworks for Prisoners, October 24, 2004, www.ips.gov.il/Uploads/Commands/PDF/161.pdf; Article 4b of the IPS Commission Ordinance 03.02.00; AppR 4612/16 John Doe v. Parole Board (July 26, 2016), ¶ 3, 5, www.hamoked.org.il/files/2016/1160950.pdf; E. Ashkenazi, "Israel Prison Service Begins Rehabilitating Security Prisoners, But Only Jews," Haaretz (February 11, 2013), www .haaretz.com/israel-news/israel-prison-service-begins-rehabilitating-security-prisoners-but-onl y-jews-1.502829.

alternative.[61] For the so-called Palestinian "security prisoners," the ramifications are complex.

On the one hand, they, and Palestinian society generally, do not regard violating Israeli military law – obstructing a soldier, for example, or attending a proscribed demonstration – as criminal behavior requiring rehabilitation. The IPS, when defending its policy on the matter before the supreme court, has cited the prisoners' opposition to rehabilitation, arguing that they "consider themselves neither offenders nor in need of social treatment. [They] ... are generally not interested in any contact with [Israeli] social workers, whom they consider part of the Israeli establishment."[62] Further, even if circumstances exist where rehabilitation may be considered necessary or beneficial, Israeli authorities – whose commitment to Palestinian interests is doubtable – are far from ideal candidates for conducting it.[63]

On the other hand, to be considered for early release, Palestinian prisoners must convince the Israeli parole board that they have undergone ideological transformation, and stand no chance of doing so without participating in the prison's rehabilitation programs.[64] For this reason, some Palestinian prisoners recently petitioned the supreme court against IPS decisions to exclude them, as it usually does, from its rehabilitation programs, but the supreme court has rejected these petitions.[65] In another decision, the court added that "security prisoners" who have not undergone rehabilitation should not be paroled (on the assumption that they remain dangerous), even if it is the prison authorities who decided not to refer them to rehabilitation.[66]

Absent access to the prison's rehabilitation programs, Palestinians classified as security prisoners turned at one point to private mental health professionals to prepare rehabilitation plans for the parole board and also, when applying for temporary home leave, to provide assessments of the prisoners' so-called

---

[61] B'Tselem, *No Minor Matter: Violation of the Rights of Palestinian Minors Arrested by Israel on Suspicion of Stone-Throwing* (2011) [hereinafter: *No Minor Matter*], www.btselem.org/download/201107_no_minor_matter_eng.pdf; MilA 358/03; MilC (Judea) 1261/09 *Military Advocate General* v. *El-Farukh* (February 23, 2009).

[62] Quoted in CrimA 1456/07 *John Doe* v. *State of Israel* (July 10, 2007), ¶ b(3) of justice Rubinstein's opinion.

[63] B'Tselem, *No Minor Matter*. None of this, however, is meant to portray rehabilitation in other circumstances or contexts as necessarily benign or benevolent. For relevant critical literature, see, e.g., M. Foucault, *The Birth of the Clinic: An Archaeology of Medical Perception* (London: Routledge, 1989); M. Foucault, *Discipline and Punish: The Birth of the Prison* (New York: Vintage Books, 1995); N. Rose, *Governing the Soul: The Shaping of the Private Self* (2nd edn, London: Free Association Books, 2007).

[64] Baker, "Palestinian Prisoners between the Collective and the Individual." On the tendency of the IPS to oppose early release of Palestinian "security prisoners," see AppR 4612/16, ¶ 3.

[65] See, e.g., AppR 3770/14 *Kharuve* v. *Prison Service* (December 31, 2014).   [66] AppR 4612/16.

"dangerousness." The IPS, in response, banned contact with private mental health professionals as well, and the Israeli courts, including the supreme court, have denied or rejected Palestinian prisoners' petitions on the matter[67] or, at best, have allowed such contact only on restrictive terms.[68] Though the supreme court recently lifted a blanket ban on access to rehabilitation, it authorized the IPS to continue denying access on a case-by-case basis, and emphasized that "the IPS policy – which the present case does not challenge – is to exclude security prisoners from rehabilitative programs."[69]

S.4 CONCLUSION: INCARCERATING THE MIND

Mass incarceration has long been a keystone of Israel's control over the Palestinian territories. It has rested on the "security prisoner" category, and it has been informed and justified by the legal narratives and mechanisms surrounding this category.[70] As shown in this entry, Israeli authorities have deployed this legal category as grounds to isolate and separate those subject to it from their society and from each other, and also as grounds to deny them the prospect, enjoyed by other inmates, of early release from prison. Both fragmentation and (non-)rehabilitation thus serve, in mutually complementary ways, to sever social and political Palestinian ties as effectively and for as long as possible.

The discourses and practices of fragmentation and (non-)rehabilitation not only complement but also overlap and inform one another. Thus, the growing separation of Palestinian children and adults in Israeli custody[71] has given rise to, or made possible, generationally based distinctions and practices concerning (non-)rehabilitation. On the one hand, the supreme court, while generally authorizing the nonreferral of most "security prisoners" to rehabilitation,[72] has repeatedly called for the now-separated Palestinian child prisoners,[73] "whose

---

[67] See, respectively, CivC (Beer-Sheva Dist. Ct.) 27403–03-14 *Abu Shamma* v. *Prison Service* (April 28, 2014), www.nevo.co.il/psika_html/mechozi/ME-14-03-27403-482.htm; AppR 9109/15 *Awad* v. *Prison Service* (August 1, 2016).

[68] CivC (Nazareth Admin. Ct.) 6244–04-14 *Dweik* v. *Israel Police* (April 4, 2014).

[69] AppR 4644/15 *Ra'ee* v. *Prison Service*, ¶¶ 10, 32 of justice Vogelman's opinion (June 15, 2016). For the blanket ban on access to private mental health professionals, see Prisoner Wing – Reform Division, Temporary Order – Entry of Private Experts to Prison, July 23, 2015.

[70] On the legalistic nature of the Israeli regime more generally, see entries L: Lawfare and V: Violence.

[71] See text accompanying notes 54–58.   [72] See text accompanying notes 59–69.

[73] CrimA 10118/06 *John Doe* v. *State of Israel* (May 2, 2007); Case 1456/07; CrimA 4102/08 *Dirbas* v. *State of Israel* (December 1, 2008); CrimA 7515/08; CrimA 2337/13 *Kawasme* v. *State of Israel* (September 16, 2013); CrimA 8639/13 *Taritari* v. *State of Israel* (March 17, 2014); CrimA 3528/14 *Bakhirat* v. *State of Israel* (September 22, 2014); CrimA 3702/14 *John Doe* v. *State of Israel* (September 28, 2014).

rehabilitation chances are better" (purportedly) than those of their adult counterparts,[74] to be "rehabilitated" in prison. This, the court has suggested, would bring Palestinian children "to function in accordance with norms and productively."[75] The court's calls on the matter have so far remained unheeded by the IPS; but, should they be implemented, they would suffer from the same perils discussed earlier[76] without actually substituting incarceration, since this so-called rehabilitation would operate in prison, not instead of imprisonment. Indeed, supreme court judgments advocating such "rehabilitation" have neither avoided nor reduced, and sometimes have actually increased, the sentences imposed on the Palestinian child appellants concerned.[77] The suggested "rehabilitation" of Palestinian child prisoners therefore represents an attempt at refining, rather than deviating from, the court's general harshness toward Palestinians classified as security prisoners.

At the same time, those at the other side of the generational separation – Palestinian adult prisoners – have had their few rights and entitlements narrowed down and revoked. Among other things, the primary IPS regulations concerning "security prisoners," which hitherto made no reference to either adult or precharge detainees, were recently amended to deny visits to precharge adult detainees suspected of "security offenses."[78] The presumed incorrigibility of Palestinian adults (as opposed to the plasticity of their juniors) has furnished justification for retracting some of their benefits in prison. Thus, in 2011, the Israeli government banned their enrollment in courses provided by the Israeli Open University, which had been highly popular among Palestinian prisoners. In their petition to overturn this decision,[79] prisoners portrayed these studies as facilitating their rehabilitation, an argument reiterated by Open University lecturers who joined the case as amicus curiae.[80] However, the IPS maintained that such prisoners could not be meaningfully rehabilitated, and the supreme court – while pushing for reforming the children among these prisoners – denied the petitions.[81]

---

[74] CrimA 7515/08.   [75] CrimA 10118/06.   [76] See text accompanying notes 62–63.

[77] Viterbo, "Rights as a Divide-and-Rule Mechanism."

[78] IPS Commission Ordinance 03.02.00 – 2011 version; Article 17b of the IPS Commission Ordinance 03.02.00 – 2014 version; see also Article 24 of the IPS Commission Ordinance 04.08.00 Concerning the Detention/Imprisonment of Minors, (December 27, 2009).

[79] Petition (Naz) 16209–09-11 *Sultany v. Prison Service* (September 8, 2011), http://adalah.org/Up/Main/File/Rawi%20sultani%20-%20Academic_Education_Petition_-_Final_7.9.11.pdf.

[80] HCJ 204/13 *Sallah v. Prison Service* (April 14, 2015), http://elyon1.court.gov.il/files/13/040/002/c25/13002040.c25.pdf.

[81] AdminApp 2459/12 *Sallah v. Prison Service* (December 24, 2012), http://elyon1.court.gov.il/files/12/590/024/s07/12024590.s07.htm; HCJ 204/13.

These banned academic studies, as well as the prisoners' study groups that Israel has increasingly restricted,[82] offered platforms for defying dominant Israeli narratives and for transcending the prison walls, ideationally if not physically.[83] Thus, the most popular Open University course among the prisoners characterized Israel's treatment of Palestinians as colonial,[84] and encouraged students to critically draw lessons from the history of Indigenous people in "settler state[s]."[85] Similarly, the prisoners' study groups reportedly placed emphasis on studying the political experience of liberation movements elsewhere, as well as on examining various colonial and military regimes.[86] By clamping down on these studies, Israeli authorities hinder Palestinian prisoners' ability to ideationally traverse the prison's confines, thus imposing a sort of mental incarceration that operates as extra punishment (even if not formally presented as such). Serving a similar function, the increased separation of Palestinian children in Israeli custody minimizes, and aims to undo, their exposure to political knowledge passed on by their elders, thus impeding the movement and continuity of thought from one generation of Palestinian inmates to another.[87]

As this entry has sought to demonstrate, the combination of "security" and incarceration serves to hinder physical movement – the movement of Palestinians from one place to another – as well as the movement of political ideas and communication across time and space. It erects barriers not only between and within territories, but also between those who produce and potentially consume resistant knowledge, as well as between various ideational subjects and sites. At both the individual and collective levels, then, the actual Israeli prison – and to some extent the broader prison that is the West Bank and Gaza Strip – thus operate (albeit never fully coherently, wittingly, or successfully) to incarcerate the Palestinian minds as well as Palestinian bodies.

---

[82] See text accompanying notes 44–49.

[83] On Palestinian prisoners' writing and reading as an attempt to ideationally traverse the prison walls, see Nashif, *Palestinian Political Prisoners*.

[84] A. Jamal, "Racialized Time and the Foundations of Colonial Rule in the Israeli-Palestinian Context," in Y. Auron and I. Lubelsky (eds.), *Genocide: Between Racism and Genocide in the Modern Era* (Raanana: Open University of Israel Press, 2011), p. 185 [Hebrew], http://olvrea der.sefereshet.org.il/Olive/OTB/OpenU/?href=OU03/2008/01/11&usticket=Z3Vlc3 Q&ticket=.

[85] A. Gutfeld, *Genocide in the "Land of the Free": The Indians of North America 1776–1890* (Raanana: Open University of Israel Press 2006), pp. 8–9, 18–24 [Hebrew], http://olvreader .sefereshet.org.il/Olive/OTB/OpenU/?href=OU03/2008/01/02&usticket=Z3Vlc3Q&ticket.

[86] Rosenfeld, *Confronting the Occupation*; see also Collins, *Occupied by Memory*.

[87] For further analysis, see H. Viterbo, "Ties of Separation: Generational Segregation and Analogy in North America, Australia, and Israel/Palestine" (2017) 42 *Brooklyn Journal of International Law*, 686, 691–697.

T

Temporary/Indefinite

Orna Ben-Naftali

T.1 THE CHRONOTOPE OF OCCUPATION

Time and space are categories through which we perceive, make sense of, and structure the world surrounding us. "Chronotope" is a term denoting the varied ways in which these two indicators may interconnect.[1] Such interconnectedness also characterizes the normative framework governing the regime of belligerent occupation.

The normative framework limits the occupant's powers in terms of both material scope and time, forbidding it to act in a manner intended to generate permanent results. Such limitation is evident in the three basic tenets comprising this framework: that occupation does not confer title to the territory; that it is to be managed as a trust; and that it is temporary.[2] It is also evident in the interconnectedness of these tenets: the inalienability of sovereignty is designed to ensure that the effective control the occupying power exercises over a territory is not to be confused with sovereignty. Sovereignty is vested in the population under occupation. The obligation to manage the occupation as a form of trust, the beneficiaries of which are the people under occupation, imposes both the duty to protect the inhabitants' well-being and the duty to abide by the "conservation principle" – that is, to respect the existing laws and legal, economic, and sociopolitical institutions in the territory.[3] This prohibition on the introduction of major systemic changes further underscores the distinction between temporary occupation and sovereignty. The third tenet, decreeing that an occupation is a temporary form of

---

[1]   M. M. Bakhtin, "Forms of Time and of the Chronotope in the Novel: Notes toward a Historical Poetics," in M. M. Bakhtin, *The Dialogic Imagination: Four Essays*, M. Holquist (ed.), C. Emerson and M. Holquist (trans.) (Austin: University of Texas Press, 1981), p. 84. See also M. Valverde, *Chronotopes of Law: Jurisdiction, Scale and Governance* (New York: Routledge, 2015).

[2]   See Introduction text and notes 40–59 for the three basic tenets comprising the normative framework of belligerent occupation.

[3]   Note that the "conservation principle" is jeopardized not only by prolonged occupations but also and even more so by "transformative occupations." On the latter, see N. Bhuta, "The Antinomies of Transformative Occupation" (2005) 16(4) *European Journal of International Law* 721.

control, is implicit in both the principle that occupation does not confer title and in the conservation principle. Indeed, if an occupation could continue indefinitely, the interests the legal regime is to protect would all come to naught. These interests are: first, the inhabitants' interest in regaining control over their life and exercise their right to self-determination; second, the interest of the international system in resuming the normal order of sovereign equality between states; and third, the normative interest of the international rule of law in maintaining the distinction between and the norm (the principle of sovereign equality) and the exception (occupation).

The temporary duration of an occupation is thus normatively written into the DNA of the regime as its working assumption. "The modern law of occupation," writes Graber, "is anchored in the concept that occupation differs in its nature and legal consequences from conquest,"[4] and;

> It is therefore not surprising that the early definitions of the modern concept of occupation are chiefly concerned with the main aspects of this difference, namely the *temporary nature* of belligerent occupation as contrasted with the permanency of conquest, and *the limited, rather than the full powers* which belligerent occupation entails for the occupant.[5]

At the same time, while there is a host of provisions in the various documents comprising the law of occupation which attest to the temporary nature of the regime,[6] the law specifies no limits on its

---

[4] D. A. Graber, *The Development of the Law of Belligerent Occupation 1863–1914 – A Historical Survey* (New York: Columbia University Press, 1949), p. 37.

[5] *Ibid.* (emphasis added).

[6] The Hague Convention (IV) Respecting the Laws and Customs of War on Land and its annex: Regulations concerning the Laws and Customs of War on Land, The Hague, October 18, 1907, 205 CTS 277; 36 Stat 2277, Articles 43 (imposing a duty on the occupant to respect, unless "absolutely prevented," the laws in force in the country) and Article 55 (stating that the occupant is merely to administer and safeguard public buildings, real estate, and the agriculture estates belonging to the state); Geneva Convention Relative to the Protection of Civilian Persons in the Time of War, Geneva, August 12, 1949, 75 UNTS 287 [hereinafter: GC IV], Article 47 (stipulating the rule of nonannexation), Article 54 (stipulating that the status of judges and public officials in the territory shall not be altered, thus reaffirming the maintenance of the territory's judicial and administrative structure administrative structure), and Article 64 (contains a similar provision with respect to the laws in place and "expresses, in a more precise and detailed form, the terms of Article 43 of the Hague Regulations, which lays down that the Occupying Power is to respect the laws in force in the country 'unless absolutely prevented'"); See J. S. Pictet (ed.), *The Geneva Conventions of 12 August 1949, Commentary – IV Geneva Convention Relative to the Protection of Civilian Persons in Time of War* (Geneva: International Committee of the Red Cross, 1958), p. 335. Article 6 of the GC IV and Article 3(b) of the Protocol Additional to the Geneva Conventions of August 12, 1949, and relating to the Protection of Victims of International Armed Conflicts (Additional Protocol I), Geneva, June 8, 1977, 1125 UNTS 3, directly relate to the notion of time and are discussed in Section T.2.

duration:[7] it assumes that an occupation will be of a relatively short duration, but in refraining from regulating the possibility that an occupation will
fail to end and will continue indefinitely, it undercuts its own assumption,
frustrates its own ends, and jumbles the chronotope of occupation: the
coupling of the indeterminacy of the "temporary" with the truism that no
social or political human phenomenon is ever "permanent" obfuscates the
other distinctions upon which the law of belligerent occupation ostensibly
rests, primarily the distinctions between self-determination and foreign control and between the rule and the exception. Such obfuscation, in turn, may
well suggest that the law itself invites the transformation of its preference for
the temporary over the permanent, self-determination over foreign control,
and the rule over the exception, into a dialectical discourse between equally
persuasive positions.

This proposition is substantiated by an analysis of the manner with which
international courts related to the temporal limitations of the regime undertaken in Section T.2 and by a subsequent reading, in Section T.3, of the
manner with which the Israeli judiciary has construed the chronotope of the
OPT. Section T.4 concludes.

T.2 LOST IN THE MISTS OF TIME: INTERNATIONAL JURISPRUDENCE

Given the chronotope of occupation, it is not surprising that courts, faced with
claims concerning the material (physical) effects of prolonged occupations,
had to determine the legal implications of the passage of time. Indeed, both
the Turkish occupation of Northern Cyprus and the Israeli occupation of the
Palestinian Territory have necessitated such a determination. In both, the
judicial engagement failed to cohere between the material and temporal
constraints on the occupant's authority.

In the *Construction of the Wall* Advisory Opinion, the ICJ was quite clear in
finding that "notwithstanding the formal characterization of the Wall by
Israel" as "temporary," "the construction of the Wall and its associated regime
create a 'fait accompli' on the ground that could well become permanent, in
which case ... it would be tantamount to *de facto* annexation."[8] While
properly applying the distinction between the temporary and the permanent

---

[7] See Legal Consequences of the Construction of a Wall in the Occupied Palestinian Territory,
     Advisory Opinion, 2004 ICJ 136, Separate Opinion of Judge Elaraby, ¶ 3.1; Separate Opinion of
     Judge Koroma, ¶ 2.
[8] Construction of a Wall, *ibid.*, ¶ 121.

to the material element of occupation, the court ironically failed to apply it to its temporal element. At issue is the court's reading of Article 6 of the GC IV, the only provision in the Convention that relates most directly to the temporal limits of occupation. It provides in paragraph 3:

> In the case of occupied territory, the application of the present Convention
>   shall cease one year after the general close of military operations; however,
> the Occupying Power shall be bound, for the duration of the occupation, to
> the extent that such Power exercises the functions of government in such
> territory, by the provisions of the following Articles 1 to 12, 27, 29 to 34, 47, 49,
> 51, 52, 53, 59, 61 to 77, 143 . . .

The ICJ read this provision as follows:

> A distinction is also made in the Fourth Geneva Convention between provi-
> sions applying during military operations leading to the occupation and those
> that remain applicable throughout the entire period of occupation . . . Since
> the military operations leading to the occupation of the West Bank in 1967
> ended a long time ago, only those Articles of the Fourth Geneva Convention
> referred to in Article 6, paragraph 3, remain applicable in that occupied
> territory.[9]

This ostensibly textual interpretation generates the conclusion that long-term occupations reduce the responsibilities of occupying powers vis-à-vis the occupied civilian population. It is submitted that this is an absurd reading, unwarranted by the text, incongruent with the nature and purpose of the normative regime of occupation, and one which confuses a problem with a solution.[10]

Textually, Article 6 refers to a "general close of military operations." It does not refer to military operations "leading to the occupation."[11] The latter is

---

[9]   *Ibid.* ¶ 125. In ¶ 126 the court proceeded to identify Articles 47, 49, 52, 53, and 59 of the GC IV
      as relevant to the question at hand. For a similar interpretation, see Y. Dinstein,
      "The International Legal Status of the West Bank and the Gaza Strip – 1998" (1998) 28
      Israel Yearbook on Human Rights 37, 42–44.
[10] The critical review of this aspect of the Advisory Opinion, which the text between notes 12 and
      23 and between notes 30 and 56 reproduces, with the necessary changes, the following
      publications: O. Ben-Naftali, "'A La Recherche Du Temps Perdu': Rethinking Article 6 of
      the Fourth Geneva Convention in the Light of the Legal Consequences of the Construction of
      a Wall in the Occupied Palestinian Territory Advisory Opinion" (2005) 38 *Israel Law Review*
      211; O. Ben-Naftali, A.M. Gross, and K. Michaeli, "Illegal Occupation: Framing the Occupied
      Palestinian Territory" (2005) 23 *Berkeley Journal of International Law*, 551, 592–605.
[11] Construction of a Wall, ¶ 125. Note that in ¶ 135, in the context of addressing the term "military
      operations" in Article 53 in order to determine the existence of military exigencies, the court
      said that such exigencies "may be invoked in occupied territories even after the general close of
      military operations that *led to their occupation*" (emphasis added).

a judicial insertion. The realities of the occupation in general, and the circumstances surrounding the construction of the Wall (itself a military operation) in particular, attest to the fact of ongoing military operations. Thus, even a literal reading of Article 6 should have revealed its inapplicability on its own terms. Indeed, Article 6 lends itself to an entirely different reading.

According to the language of Article 6, in an occupation that lasts longer than one year after the close of military operations, only 23 of the 32 Articles comprising section III of the GC IV, which deals with occupied territories, would continue to apply.[12] The 9 Articles that would cease to apply include, for instance, the occupant's obligation to "facilitate the proper working of all institutions devoted to the care and education of children"[13] and "the duty of ensuring the food and medical supplies."[14] It is unreasonable to assume that the drafters of the convention intended for children to be deprived of proper schooling or for the population to be deprived of medical supplies and food in long-term occupations, as such an intention would defy the convention's main objective. The only reasonable conclusion, therefore, is that the working assumption behind Article 6 was that the situation of an occupation is bound to be relatively short and that responsibilities of this kind would be transferred to local authorities in a process leading to the end of the exceptional situation of occupation.[15] The *travaux préparatoires* and the Commentary confirm this conclusion.[16]

Subsequent legal developments support this proposed reading of the provision: once it became clear that reality defies the drafters' assumption regarding the short duration of occupations, and that this provision may be construed by occupying powers as limiting their responsibilities precisely in situations where they should be expanded, the provision was abrogated: Article 3(b) of AP I provides for the application of the Protocol's provisions until the termination of the occupation.[17]

---

[12] While 43 of the 159 Articles of the GC IV continue to apply, the emphasis is on Articles 47–78 comprising the relevant section III.
[13] GC IV, Article 50. [14] *Ibid.*, Article 55.
[15] The "pick and choose" option introduced in Article 6(3) reflects a potential for a division of responsibilities between the occupying power and the local government during transition periods, and may serve as a basis for a functional approach to occupation. See T. Ferraro (ed.) *Expert Meeting: Occupation and other forms of administration of foreign territory*, report (Geneva: ICRC, 2012), p. 31.
[16] See *Final Record of the Diplomatic Conference of Geneva of 1949*, Volume II, section A, www .loc.gov/rr/frd/Military_Law/pdf/Dipl-Conf-1949-Final_Vol-2-A.pdf, pp. 623–625; Pictet, *The Geneva Convention*, p. 63; A. Roberts, "Prolonged Military Occupations: The Israeli-Occupied Territories since 1967" (1990) 84 *American Journal of International Law* 44, 52–56. Roberts advances four arguments for the inapplicability of Article 6.
[17] Y. Sandoz, C. Swinarski, and B. Zimmermann (eds), *Commentary on the Additional Protocols* (The Hague: Martinus Nijhoff, 1987), p. 66; Roberts, "Prolonged Military Occupation," p. 56.

The argument that Article 6 of the *GC IV* limits the convention's scope of applicability was never raised before Israeli courts, and indeed the Israeli HCJ had applied provisions that would have otherwise become inapplicable in light of the language of Article 6.[18] This practice characterizes other prolonged occupations,[19] thereby lending support to the proposition that Article 3(b) of *AP I* enjoys customary status.

The court's determination regarding the limited scope of applicability of the *GC IV* further contradicts its position regarding the coapplication of various human rights instruments together with humanitarian law in occupied territories, ostensibly to offer greater protection to the civilian population.[20] This contradiction explains the odd conclusion of the court that Israel had violated some of its human rights obligations but not the very same obligations – only far clearer and specifically designed for the situation of occupation – as they appear in the *lex specialis*, the *GC IV*.[21]

It follows that a proper reading of Article 6 should have generated the conclusion that this provision has, as Roberts suggested, "correctly identified a problem" – the problem of a prolonged occupation – but not a solution.[22] It is regrettable that the court confused the solution with the problem. Had it engaged in a discussion of the temporal assumption informing the *GC IV*, it could have produced not merely a better reading of Article 6, but further shed light on the temporal limitations of an occupation. Had it further considered

---

Admittedly, the language of Article 3(b) is unclear, and could be construed as suggesting that it applies the *GC IV* subject to its own terms. For this construction, see Dinstein, "The International Legal Status of the West Bank," pp. 37, 43. Such reading, however, defies both the drafters' intention and a teleological reading of international humanitarian law.

[18] E.g., Article 78 of *GC IV* was applied by the HCJ in HCJ 7015/02 *Ajuri v. IDF Commander in Judea and Samaria* (2002) 56(6) PD 352 [Hebrew]. For an analysis of the case, see entry A: Assigned Residence.

[19] Roberts, "Prolonged Military Occupation," p. 55.

[20] See, e.g., Legality of the Threat or Use of Nuclear Weapons, Advisory Opinion, 1996 ICJ 226, ¶ 25; Construction of a Wall, ¶ 106; Armed Activities on the Territory of the Congo (*Democratic Republic of the Congo v. Uganda*), Judgment, 2005 ICJ Rep 168, ¶¶ 216–217.

[21] See, e.g., Article 50. Protecting children's right to education does not apply, but this very same right as it appears in Article 28 of the Convention on the Rights of the Child, 20 November 1989, 1577 UNTS 3 [hereinafter: *CRC*] and Articles 10, 13, and 14 of the International Convention on Economic Social and Cultural Rights, December 16, 1966, 993 UNTS 3 [hereinafter: *ICESCR*], does apply. Similarly, Articles 55 and 56, which stipulate the duty of the occupant to ensure the population's health through provision of food and medical supplies and the maintenance of medical and hospital establishments, has no applicability while similar duties, far less specific, clear and legally binding, enshrined in Articles 11 and 12 of the *ICESCR* (the right to adequate standard of living and the right to health respectively) and Articles 24 and 27 of the *CRC* (the rights to health and adequate standard of living and development respectively), apply.

[22] Roberts, "Prolonged Military Occupation," p. 57.

the interconnectedness between the material dimension (in this case, the construction of the Wall and the settlements, which it properly assessed as permanent) and the time dimension of this occupation (which it erroneously regarded as temporary),[23] it would have reached the conclusion that Israel has violated not only the trust principle, but also the temporariness principle, and that indeed Israel's control over the OPT reflects the ideology of sovereignty,[24] thus defying the above-described three foundational tenets of the normative regime of occupation.

If one takes the law seriously, the engagement of the European Court of Human Rights with the temporariness of occupations is even more puzzling as it seems to have vitiated this principle altogether. In *Demopoulos v. Turkey*[25] the applicants, Greek-Cypriot refugees since 1974, claimed that the Turkish military deprived them of enjoying their possessions in Northern Cyprus, contrary to Article 1 of the First Protocol to the European Convention of Human Rights as well as the right to return home, protected under Article 8 of the Convention. The court dismissed the claim as inadmissible on procedural grounds of nonexhaustion of local remedies, but grounded its reasoning also in the passage of time:

> In the present case, some thirty-five years have elapsed since the applicants lost possession of their property in Northern Cyprus in 1974. Generations have passed. The local population has not remained static ... Turkish-Cypriot refugees have settled in the north; Turkish settlers from Turkey have arrived in large numbers and established their homes. Much Greek-Cypriot property has changed hands at least once, whether by sale, donation or inheritance.[26]

The court concluded that "with the passage of time the holding of a title may be emptied of any practical consequences" and therefore rejected the remedy of restitution *ad integrum*. This reasoning prefers the principle of *ex factis ius oritur* (the law arises from the facts) over the principle of *ex injuria jus non oritur* (violating the law cannot have legal effects).[27] The court thus seems

---

23   This judicial construction of the "temporary" and the "permanent" does not relate to the relativity of both terms, but rather to the purpose behind the physical construction of the Wall.

24   Y. Blank, "Legalizing the Barrier: the Legality and Materiality of the Israel/Palestine Separation Barrier" (2011) 46 *Texas International Law Journal* 309.

25   *Demopoulos v. Turkey*, Eur Ct HR, App No 46113/99 (March, 1 2010).

26   *Demopoulos*, ¶ 84.

27   The balancing of the principle *ex injuria ius non oritur* against its rival *ex facis ius oritur* is governed by the regime of State Responsibility Rules, which set forth the obligation of restitution and its exceptions. Article 35 provides for restitution subject to two exceptions: restitution is not required if it is "materially impossible," or if it involves "a burden out of all

to have not merely dismissed without much ado the whole rationale of the law of belligerent occupation, but to have further embraced the notion that customary international law changes by means of the violation of its norms.[28] The implications of this judicial reasoning on the ostensible distinction between the norm and the exception, and indeed between the rule of law and violence, upset the very distinction.[29] They may indeed suggest that the court itself, unwittingly no doubt, is "playing against the law."[30]

T.3 THE ALCHEMY OF TIME: THE ISRAELI SUBSTITUTION OF THE INDEFINITE FOR THE TEMPORARY

The chronotope of occupation has found expression in numerous appeals against the construction of settlements and of the separation barrier (Wall), calling on the Israeli HCJ to question "how can a permanent settlement be

proportion to the benefit deriving from restitution instead of compensation." The court seemed to think that the passage of time has rendered restitution materially impossible and that therefore the violation has become irreversible. See Draft Articles on Responsibility of States for Internationally Wrongful Acts, with Commentaries (UN International Law Commission, 2001) http://legal.un.org/ilc/texts/instruments/english/commentaries/9_6_2001 .pdf.

[28] On the nexus between customary international law and violations of the law, see T. L. Stein, "The Approach of the Different Drummer: The Principle of the Persistent Objector in International Law" (1985) 26 *Harvard International Law Journal* 457; R. E. Goodin, "Toward an International Rule of Law: Distinguishing International Law Breakers from Would-Be Law-Makers" (2004) 9 *Journal of Ethics* 225; C. A. Bradley (ed.) *Custom's Future: International Law in a Changing World* (Cambridge: Cambridge University Press, forthcoming 2017).

[29] For support of this reasoning, see A. Zemach, "Frog in the Milk Vat: International Law and the Future of Israeli Settlements in the Occupied Palestinian Territories" (2015) 30 *American University International Law Review* 53 (supports the reasoning of the court and applies it to the Israeli settlements). For a critical review of this reasoning, see L. G. Loucaides, "Is the European Court of Human Rights Still a Principled Court of Human Rights after the Demopoulos Case?" (2011) 24 *Leiden Journal of International Law* 435. A similar critic of the idea that the time factor weighs against claimants in similar situations was made with respect to Palestinians, by K. Lawland, "The Right To Return of Palestinians in International Law" (1996) 8 *International Journal of Refugee Law* 532; and with respect to South Africa by W. Veraart, "Redressing the Past with an Eye to the Future: The Impact of the Passage of Time on Property Rights Restitution in Post South Africa" (2009) 27 *Netherlands Quarterly of Human Rights* 45. See also entry V: Violence.

[30] P. Ewick and S. S. Silbey, "The Social Construction of Legality," in *The Common Place of Law: Stories from Everyday Life* (Chicago: University of Chicago Press, 1998), pp. 48–49. For a discussion of subsequent cases brought before the European Court of Human Rights, dealing with the question of Northern Cyprus, see E. K. Proukaki, "The Right of Displaced Persons to Property and to Return Home after Demopoulos" (2014) 14 *Human Rights Law Review* 701.

construed as a temporary seizure of land?"[31] Unlike the distinction the ICJ made between the permanent nature of the Wall and the settlements, and the temporary nature of occupation, the HCJ repeatedly found both to be temporary, emphasizing the relativity of both the temporary and the permanent.[32]

The coupling of the relativity of time and space with the absence of exact time limits on the duration of occupation has been explained, indeed explained away, by justice Meir Shamgar as being reflective of "a factual situation," generating the conclusion that "pending an alternative political or military solution this system of government could, from a legal point of view, continue indefinitely."[33]

A legal point of view may well wish to turn a blind eye to the political context, but it does not merely reflect a factual situation; it also governs it. The substitution of the "indefinite" for the "temporary" obfuscates the distinct meaning of each adjective: a temporary situation definitely has an end. An indefinite situation may, or may not, have an end. This obfuscation is designed to construct a legal justification for an occupation that has, in fact, ceased to be temporary.

Law, far from constructing time as a natural indefinite, allocates, distributes, and mediates time as a "commodity, the supply of which is not inexhaustible."[34] Indeed, law's capacity to institute, even colonize time, most evidently in its determination of lawful killing, is an aspect of modern sovereignty:[35] law shapes our perceptions of the realities of time as an historical, social, cultural, and political construct:[36] it defines the supposedly natural time of birth and of death; of childhood and of

---

[31] See HCJ 610/78 *Ayyub* v. *The Minister of Defense* (1979) 33(2) PD 113 [Hebrew].

[32] See, e.g., *ibid.* (Opinion of justice Ben-Porat); HCJ 351/80 *Israel Electric Corporation* v. *The Minister of Energy* (1981) 35(2) PD 673 [Hebrew]; HCJ 1361/08 *Filadendrum 12* v. *The IDF Commander in Judea and Samaria* (December 10, 2008) [Hebrew].

[33] M. Shamgar, "Legal Concepts and Problems of the Israeli Military Government – The Initial Stage," in M. Shamgar (ed.), *Military Government in the Territories Administrated by Israel 1967–1980* (Jerusalem: Hemed Press, 1982) p. 43.

[34] W. H. Renquist, "Successful Lawyers Pay the Price" (1996) 82 *American Bar Association Journal* 100.

[35] M. Foucault, *The History of Sexuality Vol. 1: Introduction* (New York: Vintage Books, 1990), pp. 133–160; M. Foucault, *Society Must Be Defended: Lectures at the Collège de France, 1975–76*, M. Bertani and A. Fontana (eds.), D. Macey (trans.) (London: Penguin Books, 2004). See also, L. Barshack, "Time and the Constitution" (2009) 7 *International Journal of Constitutional Law* 533; F. Debrix, "Katechontic Sovereignty: Security Politics and the Overcoming of Time" (2015) 9 *International Political Sociology* 143.

[36] On the ways time is conceived by law, see generally C. J. Greenhouse, "Just in Time: Temporality and the Cultural Legitimation of Law" (1989) 98 *The Yale Law Journal* 1631; R. R. French, "Time in the Law" (2001), 72 *University of Colorado Law Review* 663; T. Rakoff, *A Time for Every Purpose: Law and the Balance of Life* (Cambridge, MA: Harvard University

adulthood;[37] it incorporates certain assumptions about individual and collective time to delineate rights and duties;[38] it shapes our collective memories[39] and engages in the reconstruction of the past from the perspective of the future to govern the present.[40] Indeed, the very principle of legality, as well as foundational legal presumptions, signify embedded conceptions of demarcated time without which they, and law itself, would be meaningless.[41]

Law, then, is preoccupied with time. Given that the distribution of limited resources is a major legal function, the construction of time as a limited resource implies that law is interested in the distribution of time. Time, however, unlike other natural commodities, is *construed* as limited. As such, it cannot be distributed *in abstracto*, but only in relation to a concrete action. It is the very conception of time as a limited resource that endows concrete actions with meaning and requires time allocation relative to competing interests.

It is for this reason that it is unreasonable to place the concrete situation of occupation within an indefinite time frame. If occupation "could, from a legal point of view, continue indefinitely," the interests it is designed to protect – the interest of the occupied people in reaching the point in time where they regain control over their life and exercise their right to self-determination, and the interest of the international system in resuming its ostensibly normal order of sovereign equality between states – would be rendered meaningless. This, indeed, is the rationale behind the temporary – as distinct from the indefinite – nature of occupation.[42]

Press, 2002); J. Rubenfeld, *Freedom and Time: A Theory of Constitutional Self-Government* (New Haven: Yale University Press, 2001).

[37] On law's construction of time relative to childhood see entry Y: Youth. On aspects of law's construction of lawful killing (which may be effected by various means ranging from sending troops to battle to the death penalty and "targeted killings"), see entry C: Combatants.

[38] E.g., statutes of limitations; jurisdictional time limits; civil and criminal procedure laws; the laws of evidence, intellectual property protections; the rule against perpetuities and sentencing are examples that immediately come to mind, and that all embody legal assumptions about human interaction with time.

[39] Most notably in "historical trials," where judges are entrusted with the reductive production of authorized memory. See, e.g., H. Arendt, *Eichmann in Jerusalem: A Report on the Banality of Evil* (New York: Penguin Books, 2006).

[40] C. Douzinas, "Theses on Law, History and Time" (2006) 7 *Melbourne Journal of International Law* 13, 22.

[41] E.g., the principle *nullum crimen sine lege* – that is, of nonretroactivity, is meaningful only due to the centrality of the concept of time. Similarly, any legal presumption would have been rendered meaningless were it not for the temporal dimension which allows for its refutation.

[42] Applying this rationale to the analogous, for the purpose of this discussion, situation of a mandate, a situation where no time limits have been explicitly set, judge Ammoun

The notion of "reasonable time" thus underlies any concrete limits set by law on the duration of an action. The very same rationale holds for setting limits on the duration of actions which are not defined in concrete temporal terms. The conclusion that actions not defined in concrete temporal terms somehow transform the temporary into the indefinite is unreasonable. Indeed, in such situations, the concrete time limit is determined by the legal construct of "reasonable time,"[43] and depends on the nature, purpose, and circumstances of the action.[44]

Given the basic tenets of occupation discussed above, it is clear that the purpose of the regime of occupation is to manage the situation in a manner designed to bring about political change and to generate a resumption of the normal order of the international society. Relevant international norms further decree that this change should come about by peaceful means[45] and realize the principle of self-determination. The standing taken by the ICJ, the General Assembly, and the Security Council with respect to the illegality of South Africa's postmandate presence in Namibia, all serve to emphasize the point. This purpose would be frustrated if the normative regime governance would be construed as indefinite in duration. Such construction may well generate political stagnation rather than the desired change. Such an

concluded that: "Mandates must have an end or are revocable." See Continued Presence of South Africa in Namibia (South West Africa) Notwithstanding Security Council Resolution, 276 (1970), Advisory Opinion, 1971 ICJ 16, Separate Opinion of Vice-President Ammoun, pp. 72–73.

[43] The notion derives from the legal principle of "reasonableness," a general principle of international law. Its application has generated the conclusion that a right cannot be exercised in a wholly unreasonable manner causing harm disproportionate to the right's holder interests. See B. Cheng, *General Principles of Law: As Applied by International Courts and Tribunals* (Cambridge: Grotius Publications, 1987), pp. 121–123; See also, World Trade Organization Appellate Body Report, United States – Standards for Reformulated and Conventional Gasoline, WT/DS2/AB/R (April 29, 1996), reprinted in (1996) 35 *International Legal Materials* 603, 626.

[44] E.g., The Uniform Negotiable Instruments Law sets standards for the measurement of "reasonable time," see R. Speidel and S. H. Nicks, *Negotiable Instruments and Check Collections (The New Law) in a Nutshell*, 4th edn (St. Paul, Minnesota: West Publishing, 1993), pp. 60–61, 148–149, 152; Similarly, "reasonable time" for taking an action is contemplated in the Uniform Commercial Code (Colorado) as depending "on the nature, purpose and circumstances of such action"; see www.law.du.edu/russell/contracts/ucc/4-1-204.htm. It is interesting to note that the Israeli supreme court has itself resorted to the principle of reasonable time in order to determine the time limits of a judicial institutionalization order, see CrimA 3854/02 *Anonymous v. the District Adult Psychiatric Committee* (2003) 57(1) PD 900 [Hebrew]. This determination relied on a similar decision by the US supreme court, *Jackson v. Indiana* 406 US 715, 738 (1972).

[45] Article 2(3) of the UN Charter.

interpretation, then, is unreasonable. Israel's indefinite occupation frustrates the purpose of this regime.

It is not only the purpose of the regime of occupation, but also its essential nature that may well be defied if it is allowed to continue indefinitely: the occupied population under foreign control does not enjoy the full range of human rights, if only because it is deprived of citizenship and the rights attached to that status. The prolongation of such a situation may well be in the interests of an occupying power who may rely on the provisions of the law relative to the maintenance of the status quo, or, conversely, on a need to introduce major changes, and invoke its security concerns, to the detriment of the population. Given that the occupant is likely to treat its own citizens in a manner vastly different from the manner with which it treats the occupied population, the result may well be the de facto institutionalization of apartheid of some sort.[46] Such a scenario, while ostensibly legal in terms of a "rule-book" conception of law, is manifestly illegal in terms of a substantive conception of the rule of law.[47] Indeed, it makes the very rule of law a casualty of an indefinite occupation.[48]

The achievement of the purpose of a peaceful political change is a major policy issue. Matters of policy necessitate planning designed to achieve the desired result. Such planning, especially in respect of complicated and bitterly contested political issues that are not within the absolute control of one party, as is the Israeli–Palestinian conflict, is neither a trivial nor an immediate matter: it is a long-term process; it may be incremental; it may, indeed, fail. It is possible, however, to evaluate whether such a policy was in the making ex ante. This evaluation requires the examination of the circumstances of the specific occupation.

[46] Roberts, "Prolonged Military Occupation," p. 52. See also *Occupation, Colonialism, Apartheid: A re-assessment of Israel's practices in the Occupied Palestinian Territories under International Law* (Cape Town: The Human Sciences Research Council 2009); J. Dugard and J. Reynolds, "Apartheid, International Law, and the Occupied Palestinian Territory" (2013) 24 *European Journal of International Law* 867. See entry G: Geneva Law.

[47] To use Dworkin's reference to a formal and a substantive conception of the rule of law: the former is interested in the enforceability of law regardless of its content, that is, in order; the latter is interested in the substance, nature, and justification of the order, determined by the balance thereby achieved between the individual and society, between liberty and security. See generally, R. Dworkin, *A Matter of Principle* (New York: Oxford University Press, 1985), p. 11.

[48] "[T]he rule of law is one casualty of the conflict in the occupied Palestinian Territory, but the main casualties are the people of Palestine and of Israel." See *Question of the Violation of Human Rights in the Occupied Arab Territories, Including Palestine*, Report of the Special Rapporteur of the Commission on Human Rights, John Dugard, on the Situation of Human Rights in the Palestinian Territories Occupied By Israel Since 1967, UN A/57/366 (August 29, 2002), § 31.

The most relevant circumstances to be examined in this respect are whether the occupying power has annexed the occupied territory or has otherwise indicated an intention to retain its presence there indefinitely. The examination of Israel's annexation of East Jerusalem and its expropriation of vast portions of Palestinian land to establish settlements in the OPT, to construct the bypass roads, and to erect the Wall all suggest such an intention.[49] On the basis of this evidence the ICJ concluded that the "route of the Wall will prejudge the future frontier between Israel and Palestine," and generates "the fear that Israel may integrate the settlements and their means of access" in a manner "tantamount to de facto annexation."[50] Had it entertained the notion that the space between the "temporary" and the "permanent" is inhabited by the "indefinite," its conclusion would have been that this evidence does not indicate a de facto annexation that may happen in the (permanent) future, but rather an annexation that has been effected in the (indefinite) present. When the above-described actions are coupled with the huge investments entailed in the "settlement enterprise," inclusive of the Wall as well as with the observation that such actions realize expansionist ideas within Israel,[51] the only reasonable conclusion is that Israel, far from treating the OPT as a negotiation card to be returned in exchange for peace, has intended to – and de facto did – annex[52] a substantial part thereof; that in fact it does regard itself as the sovereign of these territories, thus frustrating the desired political change.[53]

---

[49] The Special Rapporteur of the UN Commission on Human Rights concluded that "the construction of the Barrier within the West Bank, and the continued expansion of settlements, which, on the face of it have more to do with territorial expansion, de facto annexation or conquest, raise serious doubts about the good faith of Israel's justifications in the name of security," See *Question of the Violation of Human Rights in the Occupied Arab Territories, Including Palestine*, Report of the Special Rapporteur of the Commission on Human Rights, John Dugard, on the Situation of Human Rights in the Palestinian Territories Occupied By Israel Since 1967, UN E/CN.4/2004/6 (September 8, 2003), pp. 7, 15.

[50] Construction of a Wall, ¶ 121.   [51] On these ideas see entry N: Nomos.

[52] Unlike the de jure annexation of East Jerusalem, the actions described in the text lack the official act of annexation, but nevertheless amount to a de facto annexation. As noted by the Special Rapporteur of the UN Commission on Human Rights, John Dugard, "language is a powerful instrument. This explains why words that accurately describe a particular situation are often avoided." Focusing merely on the barrier, the Special Rapporteur observed that "the Wall that Israel is presently constructing within the territory of the West Bank . . . goes by the name of 'Seam Zone', 'Security Fence' or 'Separation Wall'. The word 'annexation' is avoided as it is too accurate a description and too concerned about the need to obfuscates the truth . . . the fact must be faced that what we are presently witnessing in the West Bank is a visible and clear act of territorial annexation under the guise of security . . . Annexation of this kind goes by another name in international law – conquest." See the 2003 Report of the special rapporteur, pp. 6, 8. See entry Z: Zone.

[53] The Judea and Samaria Settlement Regulation Law 2017 underscores this proposition: the Israeli parliament, not the military commander, enacted a law that applies directly to the

The question remains whether Israel's security concerns justify the settlements and the chain of actions generated by their establishment. Up to the first
decade of the twentieth century, Israel has claimed that its actions were
antiterrorist temporary measures justified by legitimate security concerns,
and evidenced no intention to alter political boundaries.[54] This argument,
however, is untenable on the basis of both substantive law and evidence: as
a matter of substantive law, while the law of occupation recognizes the
legitimate security concerns of the occupying power, such recognition does
not extend to all means and methods used to arguably further this security.
Most importantly, it does not extend to settlements: Paragraph 6 of Article 49
of the *GC IV* contains no exception to its prohibition of settlements on the
grounds of such security considerations, and the latter, therefore, do not
render the settlements a valid security measure.[55] Even if, for the sake of
argument, one dissociates the construction of the Wall from the settlements,
and examines the legality of this one measure in isolation, it would be hard to
legally sustain the security claim in view of various factors, the most pertinent
being that the Wall does not only separate Palestinians from Israelis; it also
separates Palestinians from other Palestinians. Given that the Wall, much like
the bypass roads and indeed the settlements themselves, are as inseparable in
reality as they are in applicable law, the legal grounds for the Israeli position
are unconvincing at best.[56]

It follows that an occupation regime that substitutes the "indefinite" for the
"temporary" has ceased to be temporary. Such an occupation, as the discussion pertaining to its purpose, nature, and circumstances demonstrates, has
exceeded its reasonable duration and has violated the basic principle of
temporariness underlying the normative regime of occupation.

The above does not suggest that the occupation is permanent. Walls may,
and do, crumble for various reasons and a political decision, such as the
"disengagement" from the Gaza Strip, can generate the dismantling of
settlements.[57] Political will may lead to the end of occupation.[58] It is instructive to note in this context that, following the political decision to withdraw

---

territory and to its Palestinian inhabitants and enables the confiscation of the latter's private
lands. This is a paradigmatic sovereign act. The law is discussed in entry R: Regularization.

[54]   Construction of a Wall, ¶ 116.   [55]   *Ibid.*, ¶ 135.   [56]   See entry J: Jewish Settlements.
[57]   See Israel's Disengagement Plan: Renewing the Peace Process, Israel Ministry of Foreign
       Affairs (April 20, 2005), http://mfa.gov.il/MFA/ForeignPolicy/Peace/Guide/Pages/Israels%20
       Disengagement%20Plan-%20Renewing%20the%20Peace%20Process%20Apr%202005.aspx.
[58]   Nonetheless, such a decision, when exercised unilaterally and in a diplomatic vacuum, may
       bring about another, equally problematic, time loop: one of recurring surges of violence, to
       which there in no end in sight. For such a discussion, see N. Sultani, "Repetition," in
       H. Tawil-Souri and D. Matar (eds.) *Gaza as Metaphor* (London: Hurst, 2016).

military forces from, and dismantle the settlements in the Gaza Strip, the HCJ emphasized the temporary – as distinct from the indefinite – nature of occupation in order to deny the settlers' claim to remain in the settlements: faced with 12 appeals against the legality of the evacuation of the settlements made by various settlers' groups describing them as "uprooting," "deportation," and "ethnic cleansing," as well as a gross violation of their human rights to dignity, liberty, and property, the court rejected the petitioners' argument that the area was not under temporary belligerent occupation and determined that "The very nature of the area means that the presence of Israelis there is temporary and subject to a peace agreement or a unilateral decision by Israel to withdraw."[59]

The fact that this sound normative decision was never made in order to question the legality of the settlements enterprise in the preceding decades or in later years, demonstrates that the temporary/indefinite indeterminacy is being used to legitimize power, not to contain it: the temporary nature of occupation was resurrected to replace the "indefinite" construction only when a political will to pull out was expressed.

T.4 CONCLUSION: IT'S ABOUT TIME

Prolonged belligerent occupations often require the mitigation of the conservation principle because the duration of military government affects the needs of the occupied people and ergo the scope of the occupant's obligations toward them.[60] Indefinite occupations mock the conservation principle: they generate major systemic changes that effectively erase the limitations on the legislative and administrative authority of the occupying power[61] and, as the discussion above demonstrates, efface the basic principles of the normative regime of belligerent occupation. The chronotope of occupation signifies that the very same actions which indicate that the occupation can no longer be regarded as temporary, also disclose the vitiation of the substantive constraints imposed by the law of occupation on the discretion the occupying power exercises in managing the territory. In the context of the OPT, it engendered

---

[59] HCJ 1661/05 *Gaza Coast Regional Council v. The Israeli Knesset* (2005) 59(2) PD 481 [Hebrew], ¶ 115.

[60] On the need to align the prohibition on changing the existing legal system with the obligations toward the civilian population, see, e.g., HCJ 393/82 *Ascan v. IDF Commander in Judea and Samaria* (1983) 37(4) PD 785 [Hebrew]; HCJ 9717/03 *Na'ale v. The Supreme Planning Committee in Judea and Samaria* (June 14, 2004) [Hebrew]; HCJ 69/81 *Abu Aita v. IDF Commander in Judea and Samaria* (1983) 37(2) PD 197 [Hebrew].

[61] Departing from the ruling of the Nuremberg Tribunal, see *In re Krauch and others (IG Farben trial)* US Military Tribunal at Nuremberg, July 29, 1948, 15 ILR 668, 677.

the de facto annexation of large portions of the occupied territory and defied both the principle of the inalienability of sovereignty and the principle of trust.

The indeterminacy of the "temporary" duration of an occupation created a space between the temporary and the indefinite. That space has not remained empty. It has been filled with judicial narratives further jumbling the chronotope of occupation. Such narratives appear in fragmentary forms in a multitude of administrative actions, such as temporary "requisition for military needs" orders, that seize Palestinian lands which are never returned and on which civilian Jewish settlements are built. They also generate farcical legal assertions, such as the following:[62]

> The State is not prevented from seizing land by means of temporary seizure orders even for the purpose of erecting structures that are not necessarily temporary in nature. By way of illustration: in Judea and Samaria, temporary seizure orders have been used to erect permanent structures of many kinds, such as bypass roads and Israeli communities.

This legal patchwork reflects, as it perpetuates the blurring of boundaries between cause and effects, the temporary and the indefinite, annexation and nonannexation, and between the rule and the exception. Fragmentation and obfuscation have thus operated to don a mantle of legitimacy on the dispossession of the Palestinians while advancing the political agenda of Israel's expansionism. There is an almost invisible – but all the more effective for that – Ariadne's thread that legal *dentelliers* have carefully sewed to hold the mantle together as it hides a naked body, the body politic of the grand narrative of Israel's sovereignty over the territory.

At times, that grand narrative is plainly exposed: the minority position of justice Edmond Levy, the only judge in a panel of 11 judges who accepted the petition submitted by the Gaza Coast Regional Planning against the government's decision to disengage from the Gaza Strip and evacuate the settlers provides a good, albeit thus far rare example:

> Prior to the entry of the State of Israel, there was no sovereign in the area of Judea, Samaria and the Gaza Strip recognized in accordance with international law. Conversely, the State of Israel, which now holds these territories, does so not by virtue of being an "occupying power," but by virtue of the fact that on the one hand it replaced the Mandate government, and on the other hand, it is the representative of the Jewish people. As such it enjoys not only

---

[62] This paragraph is translated from the state attorney's response to the court of first instance in the context of an appeal against the construction of the wall; see *Behind the Barrier: Human Rights Violations as a Result of Israel's Separation Barrier*, Position Paper (Jerusalem: B'Tselem, 2003) (emphasis added).

the historical right to hold and settle in these areas, about which it is not necessary to speak at length but simply to study the Bible, but also a right enshrined in international law.[63]

A similar narrative was articulated in the report of the *Committee to Examine the Status of Building in Judea and Samaria*, established by prime minister Netanyahu and then minister of justice Ne'eman in 2012, in response to public pressure to establish a legal foundation for existing and planned settlements.[64] The report concluded that the West Bank does not qualify as a territory under belligerent occupation. That proposition rested on two legs: the first leg related to time: the report posited that there is no occupation since the law of belligerent occupation is premised on a relatively short duration, whereas Israel's presence and hold over the area has been lasting for decades and "no one can predict its ending, if at all."[65] The second leg on which this proposition rested was that the law applies to territories taken from a sovereign state, whereas there was no sovereign in the area prior to Israel's regaining its historical sovereignty over it.[66]

As the preceding discussion discloses, to the extent that the law of belligerent occupation is taken seriously, neither doctrine nor principle support this line of reasoning: it is true that the normative regime is premised on a relatively short duration. It is equally true that the indefinite duration of the Israeli control over the territory defies that premise. Indefinite belligerent occupations are an anomaly which attests to the failure of political processes. In attempting to transform a political anomaly into a legal justification, the report posits that a wrong can, and does, make a right.[67] It further responds in the positive to the otherwise incredulous biblical question: *"Hast thou killed, and also taken possession?"*.[68]

The report's revisionary reading of international law is grounded in an explicitly stated historical narrative: the grand narrative of the exclusive right of the Jewish people to sovereignty over the land of Mandatory Palestine.[69]

---

[63]   Gaza Coast Regional Council, ¶ 14 of the dissenting judgment.

[64]   *Report on the Legal Status of Building in Judea and Samaria* (June 21, 2012), www.pmo.gov.il /Documents/doch090712.pdf [Hebrew; an English translation of the conclusions and recommendations of the report is available at http://unispal.un.org/UNISPAL.NSF/0/D9D07DC F58E781C585257A3A005956A6]. The Committee was chaired by justice Levy. The report is presented and critiqued in entry N: Nomos.

[65]   *Ibid.*, ¶ 5.   [66]   *Ibid.* This argument is presented and critiqued in entry G: Geneva Law.

[67]   Cf. *Demopoulos v. Turkey.*   [68]   1 Kings 21:19.

[69]   Report on Judea and Samaria, ¶¶ 7–8. For a critical analysis of the report see *Unprecedented: A Legal Analysis of the Report of the Committee to Examine the Status of Building in Judea and Samaria [the West Bank] ("The Levy Committee") – International and Administrative Aspects* (Tel Aviv: Yesh Din – Volunteers for Human Rights and The Emile Zola Chair for Human

This narrative does not justify the legal analysis but it does expose the logic behind the indefinite duration of the occupation, a logic which legal crafts-manship substituting the indefinite for the temporary has advanced as it concealed; a logic that defies both the end of occupation and the ends of its normative regime.[70]

It is also true, however, that the space between the temporary and the indefinite was created by the law itself. In this manner, it frustrated its own objectives and allowed for the transformation of its preference for the temporary over the permanent, for self-determination over foreign control, and for the rule over the exception, into dialectical discourse between positions that are arguably equally persuasive. In this sense, the law incorporates its own revision. In the light of this analysis, it is little wonder that the law of belligerent occupation has offered no solution to the problem. It is part of the problem.[71]

Rights, 2014); O. Ben-Naftali and R. Reznik, "The Astro-Nomos: On International Legal Paradigms and the Legal Status of the West Bank" (2015) 14 *Washington University Global Studies Law Review* 399.

[70] The Levy Committee Report is discussed and critiqued in entry N: Nomos.

[71] For an institutional proposal designed to rectify this problematic lacuna see O. Ben-Naftali, "Belligerent Occupation: A Plea for the Establishment of an International Supervisory Mechanism," in A. Cassese (ed.), *Realizing Utopia: The Future of International Law* (Oxford: Oxford University Press, 2012).

U

Usufruct

Michael Sfard

U.1 GENERAL: TRUST MATTERS

U.1.1 Inspired by Trust: The Rules of Usufruct

The underlying principles of the law of belligerent occupation – that is, that an occupation does not transfer sovereignty, that it is a temporary form of control, and that the administration of the control is a form of trust the beneficiaries of which are the occupied population – limit the managerial powers of an occupant.[1] These principles are detailed in the various provisions of the law of belligerent occupation. The treatment of public immovable property, the rule under review in this entry, specified in the Hague Regulation 55 exemplifies this rationale:[2]

> The occupying State shall be regarded only as administrator and usufructuary of public buildings, real estate, forests, and agricultural estates belonging to the hostile State, and situated in the occupied country. It must safeguard the capital of these properties, and administer them in accordance with the rules of usufruct.

Regulation 55 thus clarifies that the occupant is "only" an administrator (rather than an owner/sovereign), and that the administration of the public immovable property of the occupied territory must "safeguard its capital," thus adhering to the principle of conservation that is derived from the underlying idea that the occupation is a form of trust and of limited duration. Lastly, it determines that the administration of public immovable property should

---

[1] For a discussion of these principles see the Introduction at Section 2.2; see also entry T: Temporary/Indefinite, Section T.1.

[2] The Hague Convention (IV) Respecting the Laws and Customs of War on Land and its annex: Regulations concerning the Laws and Customs of War on Land, The Hague, October 18, 1907, 205 CTS 277; 36 Stat 2277 [hereinafter: *HC IV*].

follow the *rules of usufruct*: the occupying power is only the usufructuary of the property.

Usufruct tolerates only ordinary wear and tear of the capital: It signifies a "right to use another's property for a time without damaging or diminishing it, although the property might naturally deteriorate over time."[3]

This provision is as old as IHL itself. The Lieber Code,[4] the Brussels Declaration,[5] and the Oxford Manual,[6] using identical or very similar language,[7] all present the same idea: The occupying power may only use the proceeds derived from immovable public property, but is prohibited from diminishing its capital. It is a trustee administering the territory for the benefit of its local inhabitants, as distinct from a colonizing power who exploits local resources for its own benefit.

Rules of usufruct thus limit the *type* of use of the subject of their application, but arguably their formal definition does not limit the *purpose* of permissible use. A question, therefore, may arise as to whether proceeds and revenues earned from the use of immovable public property, in accordance with the rules of usufruct (while safeguarding its capital), may be directed for any purpose, including for the benefit of the occupying army, and indeed for the benefit of the economy of the occupying power itself. The rules of interpretation of the Vienna Convention on the Laws of Treaties mandate a negative answer:[8] Regulation 55 must be interpreted in the context and in the light of the fundamental principle of trust underlying the law of belligerent occupation, a trust the beneficiaries of which are the "protected persons."[9]

This conclusion receives additional support when read in the light of the law regulating movable public property: The law allows the use of movable public property for military operations. To that end, "cash, funds, and

3   B. A. Garner and H. C. Black, *Black's Law Dictionary* (7th edn, St. Paul: West Group, 1999), p. 1542.
4   Article 31 of Instructions for the Government of armies of the United States in the Field (Prepared by Francis Lieber and promulgated as General Order No.100 by president Lincoln, April 24, 1863) [hereinafter: The Lieber Code].
5   Article 52 of Project of an International Declaration concerning the Laws and Customs of War, Brussels, August 27, 1874.
6   Article 52 of The Laws of War on Land, Oxford, September 9, 1880 [hereinafter: The Oxford Manual].
7   The Oxford Manual, for example, defines the occupant as a "provisional administrator." The Lieber Code maintains that the victorious army may "sequester the revenues" of immovable property.
8   See Articles 31(1) and 31(2) of the Vienna Convention on the Law of Treaties, May 23, 1969, 1155 UNTS 331.
9   Article 4 of Geneva Convention IV Relative to Protection of civilian Persons in Times of War (1949) [hereinafter: GC IV].

realizable securities, depots of arms, means of transport, stores and supplies"[10] and other public movables may even be confiscated.[11] But it does not allow use of movable public property for any purpose other than "military operations." In fact, the principle which allows for the use of movable public property for military operations is an exception to the prohibition on pillage of property and on plundering the resources of the occupied country.[12] Hence, the administration of public property, movable as well as immovable, which is not needed for military operations, is governed by the principle of trust. The trusteeship model dictates that public property may only be used to further the interests of its beneficiaries. The occupying power's authority is thus restricted on two cumulative levels: The *type* of use may only be one that meets the rules of usufruct, and the *purpose* of use must remain within the confines of a trust unless it serves a military necessity. Use of public property for any other purpose, especially for the economic benefit of the occupying power, is therefore considered looting, a practice which was customary in ancient times, but which the modern laws of war set to eradicate.

U.1.2 *A Trust Betrayed: Exploitation of Palestinian Soil and People*

In a laudable passage in a landmark case of the Israeli HCJ, the court reiterates the principle of trust:[13]

---

[10] Regulation 53 of the *HC IV*.

[11] Regulation 53 and 23(g) of the *HC IV*; Article 53 of the *GC IV*; see J.M. Henckaerts and L. Doswald-Beck, *Customary International Humanitarian Law*, 2 vols. (Cambridge: Cambridge University Press, 2009), vol. I: Rules, pp. 178–179 (Rule no. 51(a)).

[12] The International Military Tribunal in Nuremberg ruled that "under the rules of war, the economy of an occupied country can only be required to bear the expense of the occupation": International Military Tribunal, *Trial of the Major War Criminals before the International Military Tribunal, Nuremberg, 14 November 1945 – 1 October 1946* (Nuremberg: 1947), vol. I, pp. 239, In the *Krupp case*, one of the subsequent Nuremberg trials held by the American Military Courts in the occupied zone of Germany, the court ruled that use of resources of occupied territory beyond the military needs constitute the crime of plunder: "having exploited, as principals or as accessories, in consequence of a deliberate design and policy, territories occupied by German armed forces in a ruthless way, *far beyond the needs of the army of occupation and in disregard of the needs of the local economy*" (emphasis added), Krupp Trial, "US Military Tribunal Nuremberg (31.7.1948)," in *Trials of War Criminals Before the Nuremberg Military Tribunals Under Control Council No. 10, Nuremberg, October 1946 – April 1949* (Washington, DC: US Government Printing Office, 1949), vol. IX, p. 1337; See also: M. A. Lundberg, "The Plunder of Natural Resources During War: a War Crime?" (2008) 39 *Georgetown Journal of International Law* 513–514.

[13] HCJ 393/82 *Jam'iyyat Iskan v. IDF Commander in Judea and Samaria* (1982) 37(4) PD 785, 794–795.

The military commander may not weigh the national, economic and social interests of his own country, insofar as they do not affect his security interest in the Area or the interest of the local population. Military necessities are his military needs and not the needs of national security in the broader sense. A territory held under belligerent occupation is not an open field for economic or other exploitation.

In this particular judgment, the court, having offered properly a narrow construction of the scope of military necessity and a broad construction of the principle of trust and the limits it imposes on the managerial powers of the occupant, authorized the confiscation of Palestinian land for the building of a road that was ostensibly to benefit the Palestinian inhabitants. That road, as discussed in entry G: Geneva Law, eventually became forbidden for Palestinian traffic.[14]

In reality, Israeli policies have exploited almost every facet of the OPT's economy: Jewish settlements used, among many other resources, land and water;[15] Israeli employers utilized cheap Palestinian labor;[16] the Israeli arms industry turned the OPT into its testing grounds;[17] and Israeli retailers and service providers profited from the Palestinian captive market. The occupation has been transformed into colonization, that is a province for economic exploitation, "undermining the original sources of all wealth: the soil and the workers."[18]

The distance between judicial rhetorical adherence to the principle of trust and a reality which consistently and persistently defies that very principle was challenged in a petition to the HCJ concerning the operation of Israeli quarries in the OPT.[19] The petitioner, the Israeli Human Rights NGO Yesh Din, demanded a complete shut-down of all quarries run by Israeli companies in the territories, arguing that the mining violates both the trusteeship principle and the rules of usufruct. The judgment rejected the petition and approved the continuous exploitation of Palestinian resources by the occupying power and by its private business sector for the benefit of the Israeli economy. It subverted altogether the three basic tenets of the law of belligerent

---

[14] See G: Geneva Law, Section G.3.   [15] See entry J: Jewish Settlements.

[16] *The Situation of Workers of the Occupied Arab Territories: Report of the Director General* (Geneva: International Labor Office, 2015), p. 25.

[17] See entry X: X-ray.

[18] K. Marx, *Capital: A Critique of Political Economy* (London: Penguin Classics, 1990), vol. I, p. 638.

[19] HCJ 2164/09 *Yesh Din – Volunteers for Human Rights v. Commander of IDF Forces in the West Bank* (December 26, 2011) [hereinafter: HCJ 2164/09]. The petitioner was represented by the author of this entry, Michael Sfard.

occupation, while speaking the language of trust. This reading of the law is a form of judicial newspeak:[20] It transforms limitations on the powers of the occupant to exploit the natural resources of an occupied territory into an authorization to advance the very colonial enterprise they were set to eliminate.

This judgment is the focus of the present entry. In order to substantiate the argument Section U.2 describes Israeli mining practices in the OPT; Section U.3 details the petition, the response and the judgment and proceeds to offer a critique of the latter. Section U.4 concludes.

U.2 ISRAEL'S WEST BANK QUARRY INDUSTRY

The hills that make up the West Bank mountain ridge are rich in aggregate stone deposits. Before the occupation of the West Bank by Israel, quarrying of these substances existed on a small scale and supplied only local building materials. In 1967, the military commander of the West Bank signed an order authorizing the custodian of government property, an official in the civil administration of the OPT, to take possession of government property.[21] In keeping with the principles underlying the laws of belligerent occupation, the order did not grant the custodian ownership of the property, but limited him to possession and management. Pursuant to this order, since the early 1970s, the civil administration has granted Israeli corporations mining concessions in the West Bank. As of 2009, ten Israeli companies had mining licenses in the area.

All quarrying sites run by these companies are new and operate on a commercial scale. The main types of materials mined in these quarries are stone, gravel (aggregates), and gypsum. In addition to these quarries, nine Palestinian-owned quarries operated in Area C of the West Bank, as of 2009.[22] According to figures the state provided to the HCJ, Israeli quarries export 94 percent of their products to Israel, supplying 20–30 percent of the country's demand for mined materials.[23] Mining companies are required to pay yearly royalties as part of their concession agreements. As the petition was litigated, it came to light that many royalty payments were never collected, and those collected since the Oslo Accord have been transferred to the State of Israel, rather than to the civil administration.[24] Use of materials quarried in the West

---

[20] G. Orwell, *1984* (London: Secker & Warburg, 1949).
[21] Order Regarding Government Property (Judea and Samaria) (No. 59), 1967.
[22] HCJ 2164/09, Response on behalf of the Respondents, pp. 3–4. [23] *Ibid.*, p. 5.
[24] The state comptroller has found that the custodian of government and abandoned property has failed entirely to collect due royalties (State Comptroller, *Annual Report A56* (2005), pp. 218). In addition, and more grievously, the state's response in the *Yesh Din* petition revealed

Bank has been integrated into Israel's economy to such an extent that an economic policy paper produced in the ministry of the interior on the planning of future construction in Israel includes deposit materials in the West Bank in its calculations as providing a major part of Israeli consumption over the next 30 years.[25]

U.3 QUERYING THE QUARRY CASE

U.3.1 The Legal Challenge to Quarry Licensing

The petition for the cessation of all Israeli quarrying in the West Bank[26] was based, first and foremost, on the argument that this activity was a violation of Regulation 55: Quarrying fails to comply with the demand for conservation of capital as required under the rules of usufruct; and further, since this activity benefits the occupying power's economy rather than advances the well-being of the occupied population, it is a violation of the trust principle.

Quarrying natural resources is a way of using of public immovable property. Since ground deposits are, by definition, a nonrenewable resource, quarrying diminishes capital, and therefore, appears to be a breach of the prohibition stated in Regulation 55. At the same time, the economy of an occupied territory often relies on coal, oil, minerals, and other natural resources produced by mines and wells located there, and thus, restoring public life may entail using them. This gives rise to the question of whether Regulation 55 requires a complete shut-down of these industries for the duration of the occupation. Positions on this issue range from complete denial of the legality of operating quarries and wells[27] to a more nuanced approach, which is based on the tension between Regulation 55 and Regulation 43,[28] and allows for

that the royalties that have been collected have been transferred to the Israel land administration, an agency that operates in Israel. The response stated that a reform has been introduced which would see the royalties paid to the civil administration. However, no assurances were given that the money would be used solely for the benefit of the protected persons, and therefore it is clearly being used as part of the general expenses in the West Bank, including ones related to the Israeli settlements.

25 Ministry of Interior, Planning Department, *Masterplan 14b – National Masterplan for Quarrying and Mining Sites for the Construction Sector* (2010) (assessment of existing potential of raw materials). The document was prepared by Lerman Architects and Urban Planners Ltd. and Aviv Engineering and Information System Management Ltd.

26 HCJ 2164/09.

27 For a discussion of that stand see J. Stone, *Legal Controls of International Conflict* (Sydney: Maitland Press, 1954), p. 714.

28 Regulation 43 of the *HC IV*: "The authority of the legitimate power having in fact passed into the hands of the occupant, the latter shall take all the measures in his power to restore, and

limited operations. The second approach centers on the principle of continuity, which mainly concerns the continuation of policies and practices that predate the occupation.[29] It follows that although the principle of continuity does allow the occupying power to operate quarries in the occupied territory, such use is limited to the policy and the de facto rate of exploitation of natural resources in the occupied territory that prevailed prior to the occupation, with an attendant prohibition on expanding quarrying operations, opening new quarries, or developing plans for exploitation of natural resources that were not in place prior to the occupant's entry into the territory.[30]

The petition further posited that the use made of quarrying materials by the occupant's companies, which generates profit for the economy of the occupant, was also illegal: Under the above-noted principle of continuity, any production of natural resources must be carried out in a manner that ensures that the returns serve the occupied people exclusively. It is indeed for this very reason that the letter sent by the occupying powers in Iraq, headed by the USA, to the UN Security Council stated that all proceeds from the sale of Iraqi petroleum would benefit the Iraqi people and would be kept in a fund only a recognized representative of the Iraqi people could use.[31] The petition substantiated this argument by reference to a scholarly consensus on the issue: There is wide agreement that the exploitation of public property for the benefit of the occupant's economy is a violation of the

---

ensure, as far as possible, public order and safety, while respecting, unless absolutely prevented, the laws in force in the country."

[29] R. Dufresne, "Reflections and Extrapolations on the ICJ's Approach to Illegal Resource Exploitation in the Armed Activities Case" (2008) 40 *New York University Journal of International Law and Politics* 200; E. R. Cummings, "Oil Resources in Occupied Arab Territories under the Law of Belligerent Occupation" (1974) 9 *Journal of International Law and Economics* 533–593; A. Crivellaro, "Oil Operations by a Belligerent Occupant: The Israel-Egypt Dispute" (1977) 3 *The Italian Yearbook of International Law* 171–187; United States Department of the Army, *Field Manual 27–10, The Law of Land Warfare* (Washington, 1976), ¶ 402.

[30] Dufresne, "Reflections and Extrapolations," p. 200.

[31] "All export sales of petroleum, petroleum products, and natural gas from Iraq following the date of the adoption of this resolution shall be made consistent with prevailing international market best practices, to be audited by independent public accountants reporting to the International Advisory and Monitoring Board ... in order to ensure transparency, [and that] *all proceeds from such sales shall be deposited into the Development Fund for Iraq* until such time as an internationally recognized, representative government of Iraq is properly constituted" (emphasis added), quoted in E. Benvenisti, "Water Conflicts During the Occupation of Iraq," in: "Agora (Continued): Future implication of the Iraq Conflict" (2003) 97 *American Journal of International Law* 864.

international laws of occupation. Many also believe that under certain conditions, such exploitation constitutes the war crime of looting.[32]

U.3.2 *The Position of the Respondents*

The respondents (the military commander of the West Bank and the head of the civil administration[33]) denied both the interpretation of Regulation 55 as preventing any quarrying operations and the principle of continuity. The Israeli government's position was that the laws of occupation do allow for quarrying if it exploits the natural resources of the occupied territory in a "reasonable" manner and does not cause "significant" harm to the capital.[34] In fact, the respondents argued, the occupier has a *right* to use natural resources in a reasonable manner.[35] In their reading, thus, only "exhaustive," "negligent," or "wasteful" use is prohibited.[36] They further posited that the occupier's duties under Regulation 43 in fact oblige it to make sure the economy of the occupied territory does not stagnate, and in prolonged occupation this means more flexibility in interpreting the restrictions Regulation 55 imposes on the occupying power. The juxtaposition of these arguments with the figures the state provided – according to which, West Bank quarries transfer about seven million tons of material to Israel each year, while the quarrying potential is in the billions of tons – compels the conclusion that the use is reasonable. The state also announced that, in keeping with policy amendments following submission of the petition, quarrying royalties would be used henceforth by the treasury of the civil administration, and "as a rule" (i.e., barring exceptions), no new quarries the main purpose of which is to market to Israel will be opened.

---

[32] A resolution of the London International Law Conference of 1943, quoted in full in G. von Glahn, *The Occupation of Enemy Territory* (Minneapolis: The University of Minnesota Press, 1957), pp. 194–195; International Military Tribunal, Trial of the Major War Criminals, vol. 1, pp. 238–239; 6 F. R. D. 69, 120; H. Lauterpacht, *Annual Digest and Reports of Public International Law Cases* (Cambridge: Cambridge University Press, 1946), vol. 13, pp. 203, 214–215; E. Benvenisti, "Water Conflicts During the Occupation of Iraq" (2003) 97 *American Journal of International Law* 860, 864; J. J. Paust, "The US as an Occupying Power Over Portion of Iraq and Special Responsibilities Under the Law of War" (2003) 27 *Suffolk Transnational Law Review* 12, 12–13; Armed Activities on the Territory of the Congo (*Democratic Republic of the Congo* v. *Uganda*), Judgment (2005) ICJ 168.

[33] The ten concessions holding quarrying companies were also respondents in this petition, but the response of the government is the one relevant for our purposes.

[34] HCJ 2164/09, Response on behalf of the Respondents, ¶ 38.   [35] *Ibid.*, 41.   [36] *Ibid.*, 43.

U.3.3 *The Judgment and Its Critique*

The HCJ dismissed the petition for several threshold reasons:[37] It ruled that the Interim Agreement between Israel and the PLO provided for the operation of Israeli quarries during the interim period and that therefore any intervention in this matter would be predominantly political by nature.[38] Another reason for dismissal was laches, given that the quarries had been operating since the 1970s.[39] It also found the petition to be overly general since it included allegations regarding ten different quarries in one petition.[40] Yet despite the dismissal on threshold arguments, the court did devote the second part of its judgment to a discussion – and dismissal – of the substantive legal arguments made in the petition. It appears that the court believed such a fundamental issue could not be ruled on threshold arguments alone, and, in contrast to the ruling on settlements, which avoided a decision precisely because of what the court found to be issues that are predominantly political,[41] here it chose to opine on the legal questions, making extensive use of its power to use obiter dicta.

Substantively, the court adopted an exceedingly narrow interpretation of the restrictions imposed by Regulation 55 on the use of public immovable property:

> According to its language, this Article contains limited license which allows a state that holds another territory under belligerent occupation, to act as the administrator and usufructuary of public buildings, real estate, forests, and agricultural land belonging to the hostile state, and situated in that territory, while refraining from damaging the capital of these assets. Hence, a state holding such territories may administer the property of the hostile state situated in the occupied territory and *enjoy its fruits.*[42]

---

[37] HCJ 2164/09. The panel presiding included then chief justice Dorit Beinisch, justice Miriam Naor, and justice Esther Hayut.

[38] This position is based on Article XXXI of The Israeli-Palestinian Interim Agreement on the West Bank and the Gaza Strip Oslo II (September 28, 1995), 36 ILM 551, which transferred powers regarding quarries in Areas A and B to the Palestinian Authority and left the transfer of powers and responsibility over quarries in Area C to the interim process (which never materialized). The agreements left all core issues in the conflict to the final agreement. This interpretation lends itself to the argument that the Palestinians agreed to the settlements as well, which is clearly not the case. In addition, at the time the judgment was given, 16 years had gone by since the interim agreement was signed – the deadline for the interim period had long since passed, the al-Aqsa Intifada had broken out, and the peace process, for all intents and purposes, collapsed.

[39] HCJ 2164/09, ¶ 6.   [40] *Ibid.*   [41] See Entry J: Jewish Settlements.

[42] HCJ 2164/09, ¶ 7 (emphasis added).

This interpretation removes the phrase "rules of usufruct" from its normative context. It effectively allows using quarrying products for the benefit of the occupying power, thus disregarding the principle of trusteeship.

Proceeding to determine how much quarrying is permitted, the court accepted the state's position that the principle of continuity must be rejected as it is ill-suited for prolonged occupation and that a more flexible standard for permitted use of public property must be adopted. The court adopted the stance that subjecting usufruct to the principle of continuity constitutes a narrow interpretation of Regulation 55, "which is not only unnecessary, but may lead to economic stagnation and harm the interests of the Area."[43] It ruled that traditional laws of occupation must be adapted "to the prolonged duration of the occupation, to the continuity of normal life in the Area and to the sustainability of economic relations between the two authorities – the occupier and the occupied."[44] The court makes a distinction between the occupier's obligation to restore life under Regulation 43 in a situation of short-term occupation, when it must preserve the status quo, and its obligations under prolonged occupation, lasting five decades, in which the occupier must adjust civil life to the changing world, and hence, develop the economy and infrastructure of the occupied territory. The court, in fact, uses the rhetoric of the interests of the occupied to justify the mining concessions:[45]

> There is concern that adopting the Petitioner's strict view might result in the military commander's failure to perform his duties pursuant to international law. For instance, adopting the stance that under the current circumstances the military commander must cease quarrying operations might impair existing infrastructure and result in a shut-down of the industry, which may consequently harm, of all things, the interests of the local population.

The judgment does not specify which interests of the local population are served by the quarrying industry and vaguely refers to the economy of the area. It does, however, refer to the state's position, which, in turn, relied on a previous HCJ's judgment rendered in a petition filed by residents of the settlement of Naale, who sought to prevent the operations of a quarry in their area, cynically invoking Regulation 55 and the prohibition on exploiting

---

43 *Ibid.,* ¶ 8.
44 *Ibid.,* ¶10. In the Hebrew original the terms used for the two authorities mentioned (the occupier and the occupied) are "holding" and "held."
45 *Ibid.,* ¶13.

natural resources in occupied land.[46] In that case, the court ruled, in reference to its previous judgments,[47] that the "local population" whose interests the quarry must serve includes Israeli settlers in the West Bank. The citation of these judgments implies an approach whereby the requirement that use of public resources in occupied territory must benefit the local population is fulfilled if such use serves Israeli settlers, as they are part of the local population. This approach would seem to embrace the notion that *ex injuria jus oritur* (a legal norm produces a legal right). In the *Yesh Din* case, the court stopped short of explicitly saying as much, but the reference to the Naale judgment as part of the discussion on the need to adapt the laws of occupation to prolonged occupation does imply it.

There is, however, one specific benefit to the Palestinian population mentioned by the court: Relying on data provided by the state and by some of the Israeli quarrying companies, according to which several hundred Palestinians are employed in the quarries and make a living from them, the court concluded that the Israeli development of the quarrying industry in the West Bank advances the interests of the local population, thus meeting the duty imposed on the occupier in Regulation 43.[48] This, in combination with the finding that the exploitation of natural resources in the West Bank had a minor effect on the reservoir of quarrying materials in the West Bank and the policy change that new quarries serving the Israeli market will be opened in exceptional cases only, generated the judicial conclusion that the quarrying industry is lawful under the laws of belligerent occupation.[49]

The rules of usufruct are meant to draw the boundaries of permitted exploitation of the public immoveable property of the occupied land, and place the line squarely between exploitation of the capital and enjoyment of the fruits. They thus signify that in the context of an occupation, the extraction of wealth entails the burying of trusteeship. In the quarry case, however,

---

[46] HCJ 9717/03 *Naale – Association for Samaria Settlement of Israel Aerospace Industries* v. *Judea and Samaria Area Supreme Planning Council – Subcommittee for Quarrying and Mining* (2004) 58(6) PD 97.

[47] HCJ 256/72 *Jerusalem District Electric Co. Ltd.* v. *Minister of Defense* (1972) 27(1) PD 124.

[48] The court also notes the argument made by the companies that their operations contribute to the "economic development and modernization of the Area in many ways, such as training of employees, payment of royalties and supplying quarrying products necessary for construction purposes," HCJ 2164/09, ¶13.

[49] A motion for a further hearing by an extended panel was filed with respect to this judgment. Deputy supreme court president Eliezer Rivlin rejected the motion on the basis that the court's comments on the legality of the quarries were obiter dictum, and therefore do not constitute new law that can be the subject of further hearing. HCJFH 316/12 *Yesh Din – Volunteers for Human Rights* v. *Commander of IDF Forces in the West Bank* (July 25, 2012).

the judgment manages to achieve the authorization of the former while positing that it is nothing short of advancing the responsibilities attached to trusteeship.

Furthermore, on the whole, Regulation 55 must be read in the context of the legal order of which it is part. The immediate context is the constitutional order of the regime of occupation. The latter is grounded in the two pillars of military necessity on the one hand, and of trusteeship on the other hand. Such reading clarifies the restrictions on the exploitation of the fruits of immovable public property: They may only be exploited for either the interests of the occupied people as the beneficiaries of the trust or for military purposes. The wider significant context is the nexus between the jus in bello (of which the law of belligerent occupation is a part) and the objectives of the jus ad bellum: The latter, concerned with the raison d'être of the very use of force to self-defense, limits it essentially to individual or collective self-defense.[50] The outlawing of the plundering of an occupied country's resources in the jus in bello, serves this objective as it is designed to eradicate the economic incentive for the occupation of foreign lands.

The HCJ neither denied the applicability of the Hague Regulation 55, nor challenged its meaning. It simply carved a formidable exception into its very heart. For the exception to yield the required fruit for the occupying power, yet not be seen as a decree of divorce from the international laws of belligerent occupation, it had to be wide enough to allow the extensive mining practice, but still rhetorically loyal to the foundational principles of IHL. The latter is required in order to ensure that the court is not seen as stepping outside the common legal discourse, but merely as opting for a certain interpretation within it. This is necessary always and a fortiori in cases such as this, where a certain understanding of a rule enjoys wide consensus. In this manner, the judicial discourse is framed as an *internal* disagreement between "schools" of interpretation within IHL. The art of carving out an exception that frustrates the major value underscoring the rule without suffering a serious blow to legitimacy is the art of turning those very values against themselves; it is a judicial engagement in the art of make-believe.

In the quarries case, such an exception was molded by resorting to the obligation toward the occupied people in the Hague Regulation 43 and reading it in the light of the long, indeed indefinite duration of the occupation.

---

[50] The UN Charter matrix prohibits, in Article 2(4), the use of force in international relations subject to two exceptions: the use of force in individual or collective self-defense under Article 51 and the use of force upon the decision on the Security Council under Chapter VII, United Nations, Charter of the United Nations, October 24, 1945, 1 UNTS XVI.

This duration led to the seemingly logical conclusion that it has a significant effect on the scope of the occupier's obligations and hence on its powers. The court's analysis was predicated on the reality of a decades-long occupation with no end in sight, which it treated as a given. According to the court's reasoning, the changing economic needs of any society over decades, including a society under occupation, indeed justify injecting new meaning into the obligation to restore and ensure civil life. The reasons the occupation lasts decades, including the exploitation of the land's resources and Israel's various policies aimed at deepening its military and civilian presence in the territory and colonizing it, are all left outside the legal analysis, discarded as irrelevant to the discussion on the nature of Regulation 43 obligations.

In this manner, the court's power to choose a frame for its legal analysis and determine the legal narrative allows it to base one breach of the founding principles of the regime of occupation on the outcomes of another. Since the new breach is articulated as an exception, and is alleged to be grounded in the desire to fulfill obligations intrinsic to the legal field, it can be and is presented as complying with the normative framework rather than being a deviation from it. One wrong produces another, and two wrongs produce a positive answer to the biblical question *"hast thou killed, and also taken possession?"*[51]

This methodology sustains the façade of remaining within the realm of IHL while subverting its rules, objectives, and underlying principles. Worse still, in positing that the "long term" warrants an exception to the rule it actually stretches the temporal application of the exception indefinitely. That, by definition, makes the exception a rule.[52]

U.4 CONCLUSION: THE COLONIALIST STATE OF MIND

This HCJ's reading of the Hague Regulations 55 and 43 defies the basic tenets of the law of belligerent occupation which these provisions seek to specify. Indeed, given that outlawing the plunder of an occupied country's resources was designed not only to limit the occupying power's authority and shoulder it with the responsibility to advance the well-being of the occupied population, but also to reduce the economic incentive for the occupation of foreign lands, such a reading seems to have frustrated the objective of both the rules governing the very use of force (jus ad bellum) and humanitarian rules (jus in bello).

---

[51] 1 Kings 21:19. [52] See entry T: Temporary/Indefinite.

The rules of usufruct were put in place to protect the rights of the occupied population to the wealth of their land. They thus set limits on the authority of an occupying power which is designed to distinguish between belligerent occupation and colonization. In the quarries judgment, they were extracted out of this normative context and stripped of their normative content: The judgment regrouped them under the obligation to restore civil life in "long-term," indeed indefinite occupation, thereby, in effect, making the latter quite indistinguishable from colonization: this new reading of the rules of usufruct under the laws of occupation allows the exploitation of natural resources in the occupied land to furnish the economy of the settlements. It also allows for the economic exploitation of the occupied territory as a whole by the occupying power and its private business sector.

The most striking move made by the court is its use of Regulation 43 obligations to legitimize the policy. The plunder is passed off as benefiting the occupied. It drives their economy. It provides them with employment opportunities. It modernizes their land. This is the ultimate colonialist argument and state of mind: the subjugation and exploitation of the occupied to the occupier is rationalized by the court in the best tradition of colonial apology for conquest and the superiority of the conqueror: the colonized are actually far better off than they were before they were colonized; their life conditions improve;[53] and the rules of usufruct indeed serve their interests not by restricting the occupiers' exploitation of the land and resources, but by the opposite – that is, by incentivizing them to get involved in its economy. This judicial knowledge of the native population whose inferiority is demonstrated by their material conditions[54] is not merely used instrumentally in service of power. It is itself a form of power.[55]

---

[53] One of the respondent companies indeed brought evidence in its brief to prove that the Palestinian workers of the quarry now have cars and credit cards, which they did not have before. Unpublished, copy at author's archive.

[54] A. Memmi, *The Colonizer and the Colonized* (Boston: Beacon Press, 1967), pp. 70–71, 74.

[55] E.W. Said, *Orientalism* (New York: Pantheon Books, 1978).

V

Violence

Hedi Viterbo

V.1 TERMINOLOGY

Violence is a key concern of the international law of armed conflict. The Geneva Conventions all prohibit *"violence to life and person"* toward "[p]ersons taking no active part in the hostilities," listing "in particular murder of all kinds, mutilation, cruel treatment and torture."[1] *GC III* also awards "prisoners of war" the right to protection from *"acts of violence or intimidation,"*[2] and *GC IV* provides similar protection to "protected persons."[3] *GC I* and *II* further stipulate: "Any attempts upon their lives, or *violence to their persons*, shall be strictly prohibited; in particular, they shall not be murdered or exterminated, subjected to torture or to biological experiments; they shall not wilfully be left without medical assistance and care, nor shall conditions exposing them to contagion or infection be created."[4] In addition, *GC I* requires the "civilian population" of an occupying force to "abstain from offering them *violence*."[5] At one point, *GC III* also makes reference to *"violence against life or limb"* committed by prisoners of war, "such as offences against public property, theft," or fraud.[6]

Despite its invocations of the term, the international law of armed conflict offers no definition of violence. The language in use, however, betrays two

---

[1] Common Article 3 of the Geneva Conventions, Geneva Convention for the Amelioration of the Condition of the Wounded and Sick in Armed Forces in the Field, Geneva, August 12, 1949, 75 UNTS 31 [hereinafter: *GC I*]; Geneva Convention for the Amelioration of the Condition of Wounded, Sick and Shipwrecked Members of Armed Forces at Sea, Geneva, August 12, 1949, 75 UNTS 85 [hereinafter: *GC II*]; Geneva Convention Relative to the Treatment of Prisoners of War, Geneva, August 12, 1949, 75 UNTS [hereinafter: *GC III*]; Geneva Convention Relative to the Protection of Civilian Persons in the Time of War, Geneva, August 12, 1949, 75 UNTS 287 [hereinafter: *GC IV*] (emphasis added).
[2] Article 3 of *GC III* (emphasis added).   [3] Article 27 of *GC IV*.
[4] Common Article 12 of *GC I* and *GC II* (emphasis added).
[5] Article 18 of *GC I* (emphasis added).   [6] Article 93 of *GC III* (emphasis added).

assumptions. The first, a normative assumption: that illegal violence is undesirable and reprehensible, and should therefore be banned. This represents a broader social denouncement of unauthorized or illegal violence, a sentiment prevalent primarily in democracies in the Global North. Murder or theft, for instance, are regarded as acts of violence deserving of punishment, whereas the death penalty or taxation are carried out under legal auspices and therefore perceived as nonviolent and legitimate.[7]

Accordingly, this view proscribes the use by the politically disempowered and subjugated of so-called physically "violent" resistance, which is regarded as transgressing the law. This has been a key factor in Israel's opposition to the First Additional Protocol to the Geneva Conventions (API), which extends the rules of armed conflict to "conflicts in which peoples are fighting against colonial domination and alien occupation and against racist regimes in the exercise of their right of self-determination."[8] By refusing to sign and ratify the API, Israel has held to its characterization of Palestinian resistance as illegal and hence illegitimate. The battle over the legitimacy (and meaning) of violence, then, largely revolves around the bounds of law, in line with what Walter Benjamin described as "law-preserving violence" – "the subordination ... to laws" in order to sustain the desired political order.[9]

In principle, according to Israel's approach, physically "nonviolent" Palestinian protest remains potentially legitimate. In reality, however, Israeli officials have expressed concern over precisely the global legitimacy of Palestinian "non-violence."[10] Illustrating this is Israel's response to two expressions of Palestinian resistance that are generally regarded as "nonviolent":

---

[7]   The critique of this assumption in this entry draws, in part, on R. P. Wolff, "On Violence" (1969) 66:19 *Journal of Philosophy* 601; W. de Haan, "Violence as an Essentially Contested Concept," in S. Body-Gendrot and P. Spierenburg (eds.), *Violence in Europe: Historical and Contemporary Perspectives* (New York: Springer, 2008), pp. 27–40. See also F. Fanon, "Concerning Violence," in *The Wretched of the Earth* (New York: Grove Press, 2001), pp. 27–84. A specific illustration of this approach is Israel's use of the category "unlawful combatants" to deny Palestinians in Israeli custody prisoner-of-war status. See entry E: Export of Knowledge.

[8]   Article 1(4) of the Protocol Additional to the Geneva Conventions of August 12, 1949, and relating to the Protection of Victims of International Armed Conflicts (Additional Protocol I), Geneva, June 8, 1977, 1125 UNTS 3 [hereinafter: *AP I*]. On Israel's opposition to Article 1(4), see R. Lapidot, Y. Shany, and I. Rosenzweig, *Israel and the Two Protocols Additional to the Geneva Conventions* 25–26 (Jerusalem: Israel Democracy Institute Policy Paper 92, 2011) [Hebrew], www.idi.org.il/m edia/5085/pp_92.pdf. For further discussion of *AP I*, see entry C: Combatants.

[9]   W. Benjamin, "Critique of Violence," in P. Demetz (ed.), *Reflections: Essays, Aphorisms and Autobiographical Writings* (Berlin: Schoken, 1986), pp. 227, 284.

[10] See, e.g., A. Pfeffer, "Security Officials: We Would Struggle to Handle Non-Violent Demonstrations," *Haaretz* (September 5, 2011) [Hebrew], www.haaretz.co.il/news/politics/1 .1447782 (quoting classified documents published by Wikileaks, which record concerns Israeli security officials voiced on the matter in 2010).

prisoner hunger strikes and appeals to international legal and political forums. As described elsewhere in this book, these Palestinian actions have been met with harsh Israeli reactions, including the enactment of legislation authorizing force-feeding of hunger strikers.[11]

A second assumption evident in the language of the international law of armed conflict concerns the nature of violence – an ontological assumption. Violence is understood, first, as a primarily physical and psychological phenomenon, and second, as consisting of discrete, easily identifiable events or outcomes.[12] Indeed, the above quotes from the Geneva Conventions focus on violence to life and person, such as murder and torture, and generally equate violence with acts involving individual perpetrators and individual victims.

Much of the violence experienced by Palestinians – such as deadly attacks by Israeli forces, or abuse and torture in Israeli custody – seems to meet this definition. According to the UN Office for the Coordination of Humanitarian Affairs, for example, 2015 saw the highest number of Palestinian casualties in the West Bank in the last decade, and 2014 the highest number ever in the West Bank and Gaza Strip.[13] Of more than 100 Palestinians who were recently detained by Israel, the vast majority reported experiencing physical violence prior to their interrogation, and an eighth reported being subjected to physical violence during interrogation.[14] More than 800 complaints of torture or abuse during interrogation were also submitted to the Israeli authorities between 2001 and 2014.[15] Yet, as illustrated in this entry, the Geneva Conventions' conceptualization of violence, while covering such phenomena, excludes

---

[11] On prisoner hunger strikes and Palestinians' resort to international forums, see, respectively, entries S: Security Prisoners and L: Lawfare.

[12] For scholarship espousing this narrow conception of violence see, e.g., C. A. J. Coady, "The Idea of Violence" (1986) 3 *Journal of Applied Philosophy* 3; R. Williams, "Violence," in *Keywords: A Vocabulary of Culture and Society* (2nd edn., New York: Oxford University Press, 1983), pp. 329, 331.

[13] United Nations Office for the Coordination of Humanitarian Affairs (UNOCHA), Fragmented Lives: Humanitarian Overview 2015 (June 2016), www.ochaopt.org/sites/default/files/annual-humanitarian-overview_10_06_2016_english.pdf.

[14] B'Tselem and Hamoked, *Backed by the System: Abuse and Torture at the Shikma Interrogation Facility* (December 2015), www.btselem.org/sites/default/files2/201512_backed_by_the_syste m_eng.pdf.

[15] Public Committee Against Torture in Israel, *Prosecutorial Indifference: Systematic Failures in the Investigation of Soldier Violence against Detainees in the Occupied Palestinian Territories* (June 2014), p. 5, http://stoptorture.org.il/wp-content/uploads/2015/10/%D7%91%D7%9E%D 7%A6%D7%97-%D7%9C%D7%90-%D7%A0%D7%97%D7%95%D7%A9%D7%94-%D7%9 2%D7%A8%D7%A1%D7%94-%D7%91%D7%90%D7%A0%D7%92%D7%9C%D7%99%D7 %AAProsecutorial-Indifference.pdf. However, none of these complaints resulted in a criminal investigation. See also entries L: Lawfare and I: Investigations.

other important forms of violence, which are perhaps sometimes less immediately observable yet no less potent.

The dominant conception of violence, then, acknowledges certain manifestations while overlooking others; it delegitimizes certain expressions of
protest while justifying purportedly "counter-violent" responses to them.
Both this conceptual exclusion and legitimation are themselves violent, inas-
much as they mask and thus facilitate violence. Those who espouse this
socially and legally dominant conception by appealing to "ordinary language"
or to "common sense" do little more than potentially obfuscate the inherent
violence of this conception,[16] and of language itself.[17]

Alternative definitions, such as the widely cited one advanced by
Norwegian sociologist Johan Galtung,[18] may help lay bare some of the
excluded, legitimized, or depoliticized violence. According to Galtung, "violence is present when human beings are being influenced so that their actual
somatic and mental realizations are below their potential realizations. . . .
Violence is here defined as the cause of the difference . . . between what
could have been and what is." In contrast to acts of interpersonal physical or
psychological violence, then, there is also "structural or indirect" violence
"built into the [social] structure," which "shows up as unequal power and
consequently as unequal life chances."[19] This structural violence interrelates
with "cultural violence": "those aspects of culture, the symbolic sphere of our
existence – exemplified by religion and ideology, language and art, . . .
science" – and, one could add, law – "that can be used to justify or legitimize
direct or structural violence."[20] In similarly broad terms, the French theorist
Michel Foucault described a "relationship of violence" as one that "acts upon

[16] For a similar criticism, see Y. Winter, "Violence and Visibility" (2012) 34 *New Political
Science* 195.

[17] On the violence of language, see, e.g., J. Derrida, *Of Grammatology*, G. Spivak (trans.)
(Baltimore: Johns Hopkins University Press, 1976), p. 112; J. Derrida, "Force of Law:
The 'Mystical Foundation of Authority'" (1990) 11 *Cardozo Law Review* 921, 995; J. Galtung,
"Cultural Violence" (1990) 27:3 *Journal of Peace Research* 291, 299–300; T. de Lauretis,
"The Violence of Rhetoric: Considerations on Representation and Gender," in
N. Armstrong and L. Tennenhouse (eds.), *The Violence of Representation: Literature and
the History of Violence* (New York: Routledge, 1989), pp. 239, 240; S. Žižek, *Violence: Six
Sideways Reflections* (New York: Picador, 2008), pp. 58–72.

[18] See V. Bufacchi, "Two Concepts of Violence" (2005) 3 *Political Studies Review* 193 (describing
Galtung as "perhaps the best known advocate" of a broad understanding of "violence as
violation," and also analyzing the competing, minimalist conception of "violence as force").

[19] J. Galtung, "Violence, Peace, and Peace Research" (1969) 6:3 *Journal of Peace Research* 167.

[20] Galtung, "Cultural Violence." For similar conceptualizations, see, e.g., R. Nixon, *Slow
Violence and the Environmentalism of the Poor* (Cambridge, MA: Harvard University Press,
2011), p. 2 (using the term "slow violence" to denote "the violence that occurs gradually and out
of sight, a violence of delayed destruction that is dispersed across time and space, an attritional

a body or upon things; it forces, it bends, it breaks on the wheel, it destroys, or it closes the door on all possibilities. . . . [I]f it comes up against any resistance, it has no other option but to try to minimize it."[21]

Through such conceptualizations, violence can be delineated beyond law's restrictive perimeters – beyond the equation of violence with illegality (assumption 1, as discussed above) and also beyond its equation with discrete incidents of physical or psychological harm (assumption 2). Contrary to the view represented by the Geneva Conventions, violence can be understood as often operating indirectly; nonpersonally; in ways irreducible to, though still potentially eventuating in, physical harm; and not in disregard of the law but in close relation to it.

Treading along this alternative conceptual line, this entry examines two aspects of Israel's violence toward the Palestinians under its control: legality and invisibility. Section V.2 deals with the former: law's centrality in shaping and legitimizing Israel's violence, an issue explored from different angles in some of this book's other entries.[22] Section V.3 turns to the latter theme – invisibility – in two senses of the word: a visual (or literal) sense, concerning Israel's attempts to hide its violence from the public, and a figurative sense, concerning Israel's slow, remote, structural – and therefore, perhaps, less easily detectible – violence. Finally, the concluding section highlights connections between these two dimensions – legality and invisibility – with a focus on law's contribution to rendering the violence of Israeli authorities publicly invisible. By shedding light on these issues, this entry seeks to provide a richer and more critical account of Israel's rule over the West Bank and Gaza Strip than would be possible within the legally and socially dominant understanding of violence.

---

violence that is typically not viewed as violence at all . . . a violence that is neither spectacular nor instantaneous, but rather incremental and accretive, its calamitous repercussions playing out across a range of temporal scales"); B. E. Hernández-Truyol, "Sex, Culture, and Rights: A Re/Conceptualization of Violence for the Twenty-First Century" (1997) 60 *Albany Law Review* 607 (developing a gender-sensitive reconceptualization of violence as including male dominance and the subordination, marginalization, and subjugation of women).

[21] M. Foucault, "The Subject and Power" (1982) 8:4 *Critical Inquiry* 777. Also noteworthy is Pierre Bourdieu's writing on "symbolic violence" within the realm of law: P. Bourdieu, "The Force of Law: Toward a Sociology of the Juridical Field" (1987) 38 *Hastings Law Journal* 805. As the translator of this piece usefully clarifies, Bourdieu understood "symbolic violence" as "the imposition of . . . symbolic representations (languages, conceptualizations, portrayals), on recipients who have little choice about whether to accept or reject them"; according to Bourdieu, such violence involves the use of "symbolic capital," consisting of "[a]uthority, knowledge, prestige, reputation, academic degrees" and so forth. R. Terdiman, "Translator's Introduction to Pierre Bourdieu's The Force of Law: Toward a Sociology of the Juridical Field" (1987) 38 *Hastings Law Journal* 805, 805–813.

[22] See in particular entries L: Lawfare and M: Military Courts, as well as G: Geneva Law and S: Security Prisoners.

Violence

V.2 LAW'S VIOLENCE

Violence is often regarded, rightly, as integral to the foundation of a new legal order, or even to the transformation of an existing order. Yet, it is equally part and parcel of the routine operation of the law,[23] of every legal decision and interpretation.[24] Law realizes itself through violence, occasions violence, justifies violence, and fundamentally depends on violence.[25] This violence is sometimes less direct, immediate, or visible than the sort of acts law itself selectively defines or perceives as violence. And this invisibility of law's violence, in turn, is by no means coincidental; in fact, part of law's function is to deny its own violence.[26] More than simply a field of violence, then, law is itself a mode of violence endowed with elevated social legitimacy, a violence that simultaneously denies and affirms physical and symbolic violence.

As this book demonstrates, Israel has developed and legitimized its policies and actions concerning the West Bank and Gaza Strip through legal mechanisms and legal professionals. As one of Israel's incumbent supreme court justices, Uri Shoham, claimed when he was still the military advocate general: "all Israeli governments ... have laid down a strict requirement that all activities of the Israeli military in the control of the Territories must adhere to the principle of 'the rule of law'."[27] In fact, several years before Israel actually assumed control over the West Bank and Gaza Strip, another key figure in the country's legal history[28] – Meir Shamgar, who also served as the military advocate general before eventually becoming chief justice[29] – had

---

[23] Benjamin, "Critique of Violence," pp. 277, 284.
[24] R. M. Cover, "Violence and the Word" (1986) 95 *Yale Law Journal* 1601.
[25] Benjamin, "Critique of Violence"; Cover, "Violence and the Word." For further discussion, see, e.g., A. Sarat (ed.), *Law, Violence and the Possibility of Justice* (Princeton: Princeton University Press, 2001); A. Sarat and T. R. Kearns (eds.), *Law's Violence* (Ann Arbor: University of Michigan Press, 1993).
[26] Cf. E. Grosz, "The Time of Violence: Deconstruction and Value" (1998) 2 *Cultural Values* 190, 193–194 (following Jacques Derrida, characterizing what "we sometimes name the law, right, or reason" as "a kind of counter-violence whose violence consists in the denial of violence. ... This is a violence that describes and ... structures itself as lawful, and thus beyond or above violence, that which judges violence").
[27] U. Shoham, "The Principle of Legality and the Israeli Military Government in the Territories" (1996) 153 *Military Law Review* 245, 246.
[28] Decades later, supreme court chief justice Aharon Barak would praise Shamgar's historical importance in this regard: "President Shamgar was unique. As Military Advocate General he determined the pattern for this role. At the center of his work – the preparation of the infrastructure for the domination by the state and the army of the territories that came into our control after the Six Day War." Quoted in I. Zertal and A. Eldar, *Lords of the Land*, V. Eden (trans.) (New York: Nation Books, 2007), p. 343.
[29] For discussion of this professional trajectory of some prominent Israeli state lawyers, see, e.g., Zertal and Eldar, *ibid.*, pp. 341, 343–344, 361–371; H. Viterbo, "Rights as a Divide-and-Rule

already devised with other state lawyers the necessary legal infrastructure for governing occupied territories and had started inculcating it among military officers.[30] Over time, lawyers from the military advocate general corps, currently numbering around a thousand (300 of whom are on active duty),[31] have also played a growing role in planning, advising on, and executing the Israeli military's operations.[32]

Repeatedly citing international law (as they interpret it), Israeli authorities have enacted thousands of laws, regulations, and military orders affecting virtually every aspect of Palestinians' lives. The military court system, whose operation Israel has justified on the basis of GC IV, convicts thousands of noncitizen Palestinians every year for violating these laws.[33] The Israeli prison system has harnessed legal rhetoric, including international legal norms, in the service of the fragmentation of Palestinian society.[34] Laws have also been utilized, among other things, to detain thousands of Palestinians without charge or trial, and the HCJ has been reluctant to interfere in military court reviews of such detentions.[35]

The HCJ's stance on the latter issue symptomizes its broader record regarding the West Bank and Gaza Strip. Palestinian petitioners are rarely successful, and the court has shown consistent deference to Israeli security forces. Israeli authorities widely publicize those exceptional decisions in favor of Palestinian petitioners, yet these rulings have generally had little to no long-term impact, aside from making Israel come up with new laws or legal interpretations on which to base its contentious practices.[36] And even rulings that have been heralded as victories for human rights often contain loopholes[37] that leave the door open for continued violations: an example is a 1999 supreme court

Mechanism: Lessons from the Case of Palestinians in Israeli Custody" (forthcoming) *Law & Social Inquiry*.
[30] See entry O: Outside/Inside, Section O.2 ("Before 1967").
[31] M. N. Schmitt and J. J. Merriam, "The Tyranny of Context: Israeli Targeting Practices in Legal Perspective" (2015) 37 *University of Pennsylvania Journal of International Law* 53, 82.
[32] See entry L: Lawfare.   [33] See entry M: Military Courts.
[34] See entry S: Security Prisoners.
[35] See entries M: Military Courts and S: Security Prisoners.
[36] R. Shamir, "'Landmark Cases' and the Reproduction of Legitimacy: The Case of Israel's High Court of Justice" (1990) 24 *Law & Society Review* 781; Y. Dotan, "Judicial Rhetoric, Government Lawyers, and Human Rights The Case of the Israeli High Court of Justice during the Intifada" (1999) 33 *Law & Society Review* 319; D. Kretzmer, *The Occupation of Justice: The Supreme Court of Israel and the Occupied Territories* (Albany: State University of New York, 2002); G. Harpaz and Y. Shany, "The Israeli Supreme Court and the Incremental Expansion of the Scope of Discretion under Belligerent Occupation Law" (2010) 43 *Israel Law Review* 514; D. Kretzmer, "The Law of Belligerent Occupation in the Supreme Court of Israel" (2012) 94 *International Review of the Red Cross* 207. Many of the present book's entries expand on current manifestations of this trend in specific legal–political contexts.
[37] On the role of loopholes and exemptions in Israeli law, see entry Y: Youth.

judgment, which prohibited "physical pressure" in interrogations but granted impunity to interrogators who employ it in so-called "exceptional circumstances" under the "necessity defense."[38]

Rather than ignoring international law, then, Israel has engaged with it, going to remarkable lengths to design and justify its conduct through legal arguments and mechanisms.[39] In the words of the former chief justice Dorit Beinisch, "the international community does not agree with the [HCJ's] interpretation ... of some of the [Geneva] Convention's articles. ... Yet, [this is] ... *a creative and original interpretation of international law.*"[40] The complicity not only of the Israeli legal system but of international law in state violence is neither unique to Israel[41] nor extraordinary. Concepts such as "proportionality," "necessity," "humanitarianism," "combatants," "torture," "wartime," "custom," or, indeed, "legality," are inevitably fluid,[42] allowing international law sufficient malleability in the service of state violence.[43] As Eyal Weizman, drawing on David Kennedy's writing on the subject,[44] has remarked, international treaty law "is fundamentally *indeterminate* and subject to constant struggles over interpretation," while customary international law "means that military practice can continue to shape the law." Hence, "[r]ather than being simply positioned as a restraint to violence," the

---

38 HCJ 5100/94 *Public Committee Against Torture in Israel* v. *Israeli Government* (1999) 53(4) PD 817, http://elyon1.court.gov.il/files_eng/94/000/051/a09/94051000.a09.pdf. For critical analysis, see B. Cohen, "Democracy and the Mis-Rule of Law: The Israeli Legal System's Failure to Prevent Torture in the Occupied Territories" (2001) 12 *Indiana International & Comparative Law Review* 75, 82–84; C. M. Grosso, "International Law in the Domestic Arena: The Case of Torture in Israel" (2000) 86 *Iowa Law Review* 305, 327; A. Imseis, "'Moderate' Torture on Trial: Critical Reflections on the Israeli Supreme Court Judgment Concerning the Legality of the General Security Service Interrogation Methods" (2001) 5 *International Journal of Human Rights* 71, 80. Hundreds of sworn affidavits collected from Palestinian detainees since this ruling indicate the persistence of interrogational torture and abuse. B. Shoughry-Badarne, "A Decade After the High Court of Justice 'Torture' Ruling, What's Changed?," in A. Baker and A. Matar (eds.), *Threat: Palestinian Political Prisoners in Israel* (London: Pluto Press, 2011), pp. 114, 116.

39 See also E. Playfair, "Playing on Principle? Israel's Justification for its Administrative Acts in the Occupied West Bank," in E. Playfair (ed.), *International Law and the Administration of Occupied Territories* (Oxford: Clarendon Press Oxford, 1992), p. 205.

40 D. Beinisch, "The Rule of Law in Times of War" (2004) 17 *Mishpat ve-Tsava* 19, 24–25 [Hebrew], www.law.idf.il/SIP_STORAGE/files/9/309.pdf (emphasis added).

41 See also entry E: Export of Knowledge.

42 D. Kennedy, "Lawfare and Warfare," in J. Crawford and M. Koskenniemi (eds.), *The Cambridge Companion to International Law* (Cambridge: Cambridge University Press, 2012), pp. 158, 162–172.

43 C. Jochnick and R. Normand, "The Legitimation of Violence: A Critical History of the Laws of War" (1994) 35 *Harvard International Law Journal* 49.

44 D. Kennedy, *Of War and Law* (Princeton: Princeton University Press, 2006).

international law of armed conflict "is developed and reshaped through innovation in the field of military violence."[45]

That the Israeli military is well aware of this is evidenced, for example, by a statement one of its top lawyers made in 2009:

> If you do something for long enough, the world will accept it. The whole of international law is now based on the notion that an act that is forbidden today becomes permissible if executed by enough countries. . . . International law progresses through violations. We invented the targeted assassination thesis and we had to push it. At first there were protrusions that made it hard to insert easily into the legal moulds. Eight years later it is in the center of the bounds of legitimacy.[46]

Even Israeli policies and practices that seem to unashamedly fly in the face of legal norms are linked to, if not dependent upon, these norms. A case in point is the so-called "Dahiya doctrine," which advocates using disproportionate force in order to turn the enemy's civilians against their governments. First developed and used by the Israeli military in Lebanon, this doctrine was subsequently deployed in Israel's assaults on the Gaza Strip,[47] and continues to receive endorsement from high-ranking security officials.[48] This policy is not altogether indifferent to the international legal principle of proportionality, which it presents itself as negating. Rather, its threat of "disproportionate force" derives its communicative impact from the legal principle of proportionality, and particularly from the understanding that this principle is otherwise upheld.[49]

---

[45] E. Weizman, "Legislative Attack" (2010) 27 *Theory, Culture & Society* 11, 19 (emphasis in the original).

[46] Y. Feldman and U. Blau, "Consent and Advise," *Haaretz* (January 29, 2009), www.haaretz .com/consent-and-advise-1.269127.

[47] For further discussion, see H. Marouf, *Israel's Military Operations in Gaza: Telegenic Lawfare and Warfare* (New York: Routledge, 2016), pp. 42–61; A. Craig, *International Legitimacy and the Politics of Security: The Strategic Deployment of Lawyers in the Israeli Military* (Lanham: Lexington Books, 2013), pp. 161, 174–176.

[48] See, e.g., D. Liel, "Eizenkot: 'IDF Using Disproportionate Force in Gaza to Prevent Firing'," *Channel 2 News* (March 22, 2017) [Hebrew], www.mako.co.il/news-military/secur ity-q1_2017/Article-7c77ef89bf4fa51004.htm (quoting Israel's chief of the general staff as reporting to the Knesset that "the IDF has been using disproportionate force in Gaza to prevent firing").

[49] Weizman, "Legislative Attack," p. 19. As noted earlier, Weizman's analysis draws on the work of David Kennedy, who argued, on this particular point, that "legal categorization . . . is a communication tool," and that "defining the battlefield is . . . also a rhetorical and legal claim." Kennedy, *Of War and Law*, p. 122; Kennedy, "Lawfare and Warfare," pp. 158, 166.

V.3 INVISIBLE VIOLENCE

The violence of Israel's rule over the West Bank and Gaza Strip owes much of its impact to its invisibility. This is invisibility in the literal (or visual) sense, created by a state apparatus that keeps Israel's violence toward Palestinians out of public sight and knowledge. It is also invisibility in the figurative sense, relating to phenomena or forces that are not easily identified as violence. As touched upon in Section V.1, invisibility in this latter sense characterizes structural or slow violence (as opposed to direct, interpersonal incidents), and it also characterizes violence that occurs under the auspices of the formal law (in contrast to soldiers' failure to follow orders, for example).

The former – visual – aspect of this invisibility concerns the concealment of potentially incriminating sights or information from Palestinian individuals, the general public, or both. Israel's violence comprises not only Palestinians' corporeal encounter with Israeli security forces, but also the web of forces and factors that determines, among other things, by whom and to what extent this encounter can be seen and known. Included here are practices such as the widespread blindfolding and hooding of Palestinians in Israeli custody;[50] the use of torture methods that leave no lasting visible physical marks;[51] or Israel's obstruction of media coverage of its actions in the West Bank and Gaza Strip.[52]

Moreover, in comparison with the events that are traditionally equated with violence, Israel's violence toward Palestinians is also invisible in a less literal

---

[50] See, e.g., B'Tselem and Hamoked, *Kept in the Dark: Treatment of Palestinian Detainees in the Petah Tikva Interrogation Facility of the Israeli Security Agency* (October 2010), pp. 14–16, 41, 49–51, 59, www.btselem.org/download/201010_kept_in_the_dark_eng.pdf.

[51] J. Ron, "Varying Methods of State Violence" (1997) 51 *International Organization* 275, 276, 285–86. See also G. E. Bisharat, "Courting Justice? Legitimation in Lawyering under Israeli Occupation" (1995) 20 *Law & Society Inquiry* 349, 379–380.

[52] See, e.g., P. Beaumont, "Israeli Soldiers Attack Journalists on West Bank," *The Guardian* (September 25, 2015), www.theguardian.com/world/2015/sep/25/israeli-soldiers-attack-agence-france-presse-journalists-west-bank; Committee to Protect Journalists, "Journalists under fire in Israel and the Occupied Palestinian Territory" (March 24, 2014), https://cpj.org/2014/03/jo urnalists-under-fire-in-israel-and-the-occupied.php; Committee to Protect Journalists, "Palestinian Photojournalist Held Without Charge by Israel" (May 19, 2016), https://cpj.org /2016/05/palestinian-photojournalist-held-without-charge-by.php; L. Goldman, "WATCH: Israeli Border Police Assault, Pepper Spray Palestinian Journalists," +972 *Magazine* (October 30, 2015), http://972mag.com/photos-israeli-border-police-assault-pepper-spray-palestinian-journalists/113402/; G. Izikovich and AP, "Foreign Journalists Speak Out Against Ban on Entry to Gaza," *Haaretz* (November 28, 2011), www.haaretz.com/foreign-journalists-speak-out-against-ban-on-entry-to-gaza-1.258420; Reporters Without Borders, "Israeli Troops Take Aim at Photojournalists Covering Protest in West Bank" (February 14, 2012), https://rsf .org/en/news/israeli-troops-take-aim-photojournalists-covering-protests-west-bank.

sense: it occurs indirectly, slowly, or routinely. A case in point is the violence to which Israel has subjected Gazans since unilaterally withdrawing from the Gaza Strip in 2005, and with increased intensity since pronouncing it an "enemy entity" in 2007. On the one hand, Israel's periodic military offensives have been manifestly violent, directly causing thousands of Palestinian casualties and severe damage to property and infrastructure. On the other hand, the constant (albeit changeable) closure of the Gaza Strip has not usually been classified as "violence" per se, despite violently restricting the movement of people and goods.

Embodying what Galtung, Foucault, and others portray as violence, the closure normally prevents medical teams and technical experts from traveling between the Gaza Strip and the West Bank. It bars students from studying outside the Gaza Strip, even in Palestinian universities in the West Bank. It rarely permits family reunions, for which only first-degree relatives are eligible in the first place.[53] According to the Israeli branch of Physicians for Human Rights, about a fifth of the applications for a medical exit permit are rejected. Moreover, as a prerequisite for having their application for a permit considered, the Israeli Security Agency requires Palestinian patients to attend security interrogations, during which they are requested to become informants or at least provide some information on other Palestinians.[54] Israeli authorities also place obstacles in the way of exports, and limit fishing – the largest local industry – to only three miles from the shore. Building a seaport is forbidden, as is the rebuilding of Gaza's airport. The entry of fuel, building materials, communications equipment, and medical equipment is also heavily restricted.[55]

Not only does the closure limit Palestinians' life chances and inflict mass suffering, it also leads to harm to property and actual loss of lives. By virtue of its relatively slow or mediate nature, however, it does so in a seemingly

---

[53] On other Israeli practices that fragment Palestinian society, see also entry S: Security Prisoners.

[54] Physicians for Human Rights – Israel, *#Denied: Harassment of Palestinian Patients Applying for Exit Permits* (June 2015), pp. 19–21. http://cdn3.phr.org.il/wp-content/uploads/2015/06/Denied.pdf.

[55] On related issues concerning the Gaza Strip, see also entries Q: Quality of Life and Z: Zone. For further details, see, e.g., Gisha, *Scale of Control: Israel's Continued Responsibility in the Gaza Strip* (November 2011), http://gisha.org/UserFiles/File/scaleofcontrol/scaleofcontrol_en.pdf; Gisha, *Gaza Up Close*, http://features.gisha.org/gaza-up-close/; S. Bashi, "Controlling Perimeters, Controlling Lives: Israel and Gaza" (2013) 7:2 *Law & Ethics of Human Rights* 243; A. Gross and T. Feldman, "'We Didn't Want to Hear the Word "Calories"': Rethinking Food Security, Food Power, and Food Sovereignty – Lessons from the Gaza Closure" (2015) 33 *Berkeley Journal of International Law* 379.

invisible manner. In an attempt to connect these unseen dots, Israeli NGO Gisha opened one of its reports with a description of an illustrative incident, from May 2016, concerning a deadly fire that burned to the ground a home in a-Shati Refugee Camp and killed three of the family's children. The fire reportedly broke out due to candles that had been burning in the children's room, a fact the Gisha report contextualizes in relation to Israel's actions:

> Candles are often used for lighting in Gaza due to an ever-present and severe electricity shortage. . . . [This] family's tragedy was a sad statistical addition to a slew of deaths that have taken place in Gaza under similar circumstances over the past several years. Even where the electricity shortage does not end in injuries or fatalities, it wreaks havoc . . . on the lives of all of Gaza's . . . residents. . . . [From 1967 to 2005, throughout Israel's] direct control over the Gaza Strip, . . . it refrained from investing the resources required for developing independent civilian infrastructure.[56] . . . [Since the 2005 pullout] . . . Israel's severe restrictions on the entry of construction materials, spare parts, fuel, travel for experts and technicians to and from the Strip . . . [have] hampered the ability of local authorities in Gaza to develop infrastructure that can meet the needs of the population. . . . Electricity blackouts in Gaza last between 8–12 hours each day, and have sometimes even reached 20 hours straight. . . . Without a consistent supply of electricity, it is impossible to provide sufficient health, education and welfare services. . . . This acute shortage in energy is not predestined, nor is it a result of a natural disaster. It is the product of neglect and destruction, economic hardship, political strife and severe restrictions on the entry of equipment and technicians into the Gaza Strip.[57]

At one point, the report mentions the death of 29 Gazans between 2010 and mid-2016 in accidents described as resulting from the electricity shortage.[58] Considering the above, however, Israel's policy could also be linked, more

---

[56]   The political economist Sara Roy has described Israel's policy during this period as the "de-development" of the Gaza Strip, a term denoting "a process which undermines or weakens the ability of an economy to grow and expand by preventing it from accessing and utilizing critical inputs needed to promote internal growth beyond a specific structural level." See S. Roy, "The Gaza Strip: A Case of Economic De-Development" (1987) 17 *Journal of Palestine Studies* 56, 56. Minutes of a 1968 parliamentary meeting were recently declassified, in which the Israeli commander of the Gaza Strip argued that Gaza unemployment serves Israeli interests as long as its gravity is short of encouraging dissent. Foreign Affairs and Security Committee – 6th Knesset, Meeting Minutes No. 102 (January 19, 1968), p. 8 [Hebrew], http://akevot.org.il /wp-content/uploads/2017/02/FDC102.pdf.

[57]   Gisha, *Hand on the Switch: Who's Responsible for Gaza's Infrastructure Crisis?* (January 2017), pp. 1, 3–4, http://gisha.org/UserFiles/File/publications/infrastructure/Hand_on_the_Switch-EN.pdf.

[58]   *Ibid.*, p. 3.

extensively, to numerous other deaths, such as those caused by hospital equipment malfunctions due to unstable electrical currents. In addition, the difficulties in keeping medicine chilled given the electricity shortages, as well as the lack of adequate water and sanitation infrastructure, gravely impact public health and can be life threatening.[59]

Thus, though the escalated violence of Israel's military assaults tends to be viewed distinctly from the closure's everyday violence,[60] the two are, in fact, interconnected. The closure not only shuts the door on the realization of Palestinians' interests, wishes, and potential (to rephrase Galtung and Foucault);[61] despite not usually being labeled as "violence" per se, it also wreaks even the sort of "violence to life and person" that the Geneva Conventions narrowly associate with violence.[62]

Further, these seemingly disparate forms of violence reinforce one another in two additional ways. First, the concentrated damage brought about by Israel's military offensives aggravates the harm already caused to the local economy and infrastructure, incrementally, by Israel's closure and de-development policies. And second, the routine violence of the closure has helped keep the immediate or direct violence of Israel's military offensives out of public sight: by signaling a shift from boots on the ground to remote military violence,[63] it has distanced the violence in the Gaza Strip from the Israeli public's experience and discourse.[64] In addition, as part of the closure, Israel has placed restrictions on the entry of journalists[65] and human rights organizations[66] to the Gaza Strip, thus further limiting the sights of violence available to the public.

---

[59] For further details, see *ibid.*, pp. 3, 10–16.

[60] L. Allen, "The Scales of Occupation: 'Operation Cast Lead' and the Targeting of the Gaza Strip" (2012) 32 *Critique of Anthropology* 261, 262 [hereinafter: The Scales of Occupation] ("the violence ... unleashed on Gaza-as-target made the attacks there seem ... somehow unique and distinct from the rest of the occupation. The everyday violence of occupation was left ... diminished in significance and generally prompting less outrage").

[61] See text accompanying notes 18–21.   [62] See text accompanying notes 1–6, 12–17.

[63] See, e.g., E. Weizman, *Hollow Land: Israel's Architecture of Occupation* (London and New York: Verso, 2007), pp. 237–240.

[64] See also Allen, "The Scales of Occupation," p. 262 ("the perceived physical distance between the Gaza Strip and the rest of Palestine/Israel has allowed Gaza and its inhabitants to come to be seen as uniquely other, and thereby especially targetable").

[65] On this and other restrictions Israeli authorities have placed on the media, see note 52 and its accompanying text. On how protesters and journalists, within and outside the Gaza Strip, acted to challenge dominant media representations of the Israeli bombing in 2014, see A. Ramamurthy, "Contesting the Visualization of Gaza" (2016) 9 *Photographies* 31.

[66] See, e.g., "Human Rights Watch, Unwilling or Unable: Israeli Restrictions on Access to and from Gaza for Human Rights Workers" (April 2017), www.hrw.org/report/2017/04/03/unwilling-or-unable/israeli-restrictions-access-and-gaza-human-rights-workers.

At the same time, states often complement their invisible violence with hypervisible violence, provided they still get to choose the audiences that will witness their violence. Thus, in the West Bank, hypervisible military brutality is meant to "display presence" and "sow fear" among Palestinians.[67] In the Gaza Strip, the hypervisibility of the abovementioned "Dahiya doctrine"[68] aims to "sear the Palestinian consciousness,"[69] while reportedly providing some Israelis with a spectacle to watch from nearby hilltops.[70] In cases where state agents deem the visibility of their violence self-jeopardizing, however, invisibility is likely to prevail: in 2002, for instance, four Israeli Border Police soldiers videotaped their killing of a Palestinian in the West Bank, but destroyed the video once they realized its incriminatory nature.[71]

V.4 CONCLUSION

Israel's violence in the West Bank and Gaza Strip functions, is made possible, and is experienced in ways that exceed the legally and socially prevalent conception of violence. Two of its key dimensions, in particular, tend to remain out of sight and mind: legal violence, a phrase used here to denote the complicity of legal rhetoric, legal institutions, and legal professionals in bringing about and legitimating violence toward Palestinians; and invisible

---

[67] M. Zagor, "'I Am the Law!' – Perspectives of Legality and Illegality in the Israeli Army" (2010) 43 *Israel Law Review* 551, 573.

[68] See text accompanying notes 47–49.

[69] A. Shavit, "Has the Disengagement Been Successful?," *Haaretz* (July 5, 2006), www.haaretz .co.il/misc/1.1118413 (English translation available at www.imra.org.il/story.php3?id=29953 and http://israelvisit.co.il/BehindTheNews/Archives/Jul-07-06.htm#perspective) (quoting Israel's minister of justice at the time, Moshe Ya'alon, as saying: "When the present confrontation [concerning the Gaza Strip] began, in 2000, . . . I said we had to sear the Palestinian consciousness. . . . The fact that we did not stick to our promise that if Qassam rockets were fired after the disengagement we would react with all our force, eroded our deterrence").

[70] R. Mackey, "Israelis Watch Bombs Drop on Gaza From Front-Row Seats," *New York Times* (July 14, 2014), www.nytimes.com/2014/07/15/world/middleeast/israelis-watch-bombs-drop-on-gaza-from-front-row-seats.html?_r=0; H. Sherwood, "Israelis Gather on Hillsides to Watch and Cheer as Military Drops Bombs on Gaza," *The Guardian* (July 20, 2017), www .theguardian.com/world/2014/jul/20/israelis-cheer-gaza-bombing. On violence as a spectacle, see also A. L. Wood, *Lynching and Spectacle: Witnessing Racial Violence in America, 1890–1940* (Chapel Hill: The University of North Carolina, 2009).

[71] The soldiers also disposed of other incriminating evidence, coordinated their stories to avoid suspicion, denied all accusations during the police investigation, and threatened a colleague who testified against them in court. CrimC (Jer) 907/05 *State of Israel v. Bassem* (September 22, 2005), www.nevo.co.il/psika_html/mechozi/m05000907.htm; CrimC (Jer) 157/03 *State of Israel v. Butvika* (September 9, 2008), www.nevo.co.il/psika_html/m 03000157-324.htm; CrimC (Jer) 3172/07 *State of Israel v. Lalza* (April 28, 2008), www.nevo.co.il /psika_html/mechozi/m07003172-297.htm.

violence, referring to the operation of violence out of public sight, or slowly, or through structural processes rather than discrete personal acts.

These legal and invisible dimensions of Israel's violence are tightly intertwined and mutually dependent.[72] All too often, Israeli authorities design, justify, or conceal their violence in the West Bank and Gaza Strip by actively relying on law, or at least by benefiting from law's indifference. In large measure, the invisibilities of violence, such as those examined in this entry, are thus imputable to law.

Israel's so-called "targeted killings," examined in other entries in this book,[73] illustrate this interplay of legality and invisibility. In 2008, former soldier Anat Kamm leaked to an Israeli journalist classified military documents, which suggested the military had violated a supreme court ruling by assassinating Palestinians who could have been arrested.[74] While the attorney general refused to investigate the reportedly unlawful "targeted killing,"[75] the Israeli legal system prosecuted and convicted those who exposed this information. The leaker, Kamm, was initially sentenced to four and a half years in prison, and later had her penalty reduced to three and a half years;[76] the journalist, Uri Blau, was sentenced to four months' community service.[77] In a rhetorical twist, the judgments on their matter portrayed their unauthorized possession of this information as a "ticking bomb"[78] – an image usually invoked to justify state violence.[79]

---

[72] For further analysis of the relationship between legality and visibility in state violence, see also H. Viterbo, "Seeing Torture Anew: A Transnational Reconceptualization of State Torture and Visual Evidence" (2014) 50:2 *Stanford Journal of International Law* 281.

[73] For in-depth discussion of Israeli "targeted killings" and their legal context, see entries C: Combatants and F: Future-Oriented Measures.

[74] U. Blau, "License to Kill," *Haaretz* (November 27, 2008), www.haaretz.com/license-to-kill-1.258378.

[75] D. Izenberg, "Stamp of Approval from Attorney-General," *Jerusalem Post* (April 13, 2010), www.jpost.com/Israel/Stamp-of-approval-from-attorney-general.

[76] CrimC 17959–01-10 (Tel Aviv Dist. Ct.) *State of Israel v. Kam* (October 30, 2011), www.psakdin.co.il/kAnnex/nws_nkqa_1.pdf; CrimA 8445/11 *Kam v. State of Israel* (December 31, 2012), http://elyon1.court.gov.il/files/11/450/084/o9b/11084450.o9b.pdf.

[77] CrimC (Tel Aviv Meg. Ct.) 10677–07-12 *State of Israel v. Blau* (September 3, 2012), www.nevo.co.il/psika_html/shalom/SH-12-07-10677-22.pdf.

[78] CrimC 10677–07-12, pp. 4, 11; CrimA 8445/11, ¶ 5.

[79] In the "ticking bomb" scenario, state torture is presented as justified because the captive knows of the whereabouts of a bomb that is about to explode, or knows how to defuse it. On the factual and ethical flaws of this scenario, see, e.g., Y. Ginbar, *Why Not Torture Terrorists?: Moral, Practical, and Legal Aspects of the "Ticking Bomb" Justification for Torture* (Oxford and New York: Oxford University Press, 2008). For a critical analysis of Israel's use of this scenario, see Public Committee Against Torture in Israel, *"Ticking Bombs": Testimonies of Torture Victims in Israel* (May 2007), http://stoptorture.org.il/wp-content/uploads/2015/10/ticking-bombs-2009.pdf.

Another area where law shrouds Israel's violence, by commission or omission,[80] is detention and incarceration. In contrast to the domestic law applicable to Israeli suspects, which generally mandates videotaping police interrogations,[81] the military law that Israel applies to Palestinians in the West Bank includes no such provision to minimize interrogational abuse.[82] In 2013, the HCJ rejected a petition requiring the General Security Service to video-tape interrogations of suspected "security offenders,"[83] the overwhelming majority of whom are Palestinians.[84] Further, as shown in another entry, judicial reviews of so-called "administrative detention" – incarceration with-out charge or trial for indeterminate periods of time – also produce invisibility: they are held behind closed doors and are based on secret evidence not disclosed to the defense.[85] The Israeli military law also authorizes keeping Palestinians' arrest secret for up to 12 days.[86]

Lady Justice, the allegorical personification of law,[87] is often portrayed as holding a sword – an emblem of law's violence. Yet, in view of the above, it is the blindfold she is commonly depicted as wearing that may embody law's violence no less than her sword. Though this visual element has come to symbolize the impartiality of the law, in the past it critically represented law's inability to deliver justice.[88] Revisiting this disused yet relevant image, Lady Justice's blindfold brings to mind a bidirectional flow of invisibility and concealment: on the one hand, the blindfold keeps those who are subjected

---

[80] On omissions as acts of violence, see J. Harris, "Violence and Responsibility" (1980) 56 *Philosophy* 273.

[81] Articles 4, 17 of the Criminal Procedure Law (Interrogation of Suspects), 2002, www.nevo.co.il /law_html/law01/999_542.htm.

[82] On the abuse and torture of Palestinians in Israeli custody, see, e.g., B'Tselem and Hamoked, *Absolute Prohibition: The Torture and Ill-treatment of Palestinian Detainees* (2007), www .btselem.org/download/200705_utterly_forbidden_eng.pdf; Public Committee Against Torture in Israel, Prosecutorial Indifference.

[83] HCJ 9416/10 *Adalah* v. *Ministry of Public Security* (February 6, 2013), http://elyon1.court.gov.il /files/10/160/094/s07/10094160.s07.pdf.

[84] See entry S: Security Prisoners.   [85] See entry S: Security Prisoners.

[86] Article 55 of Order No. 1651 Concerning Security Provisions (Integrated Version) (Judea and Samaria), 2009.

[87] For relevant discussions of visual representations of Lady Justice, see J. Resnik and D. Curtis, *Representing Justice: Invention, Controversy and Rights in City-States and Democratic Courtrooms* (New Haven: Yale University Press, 2011), pp. 62–105; L. Mulcahy, "Imagining Alternative Visions of Justice: An Exploration of the Controversy Surrounding Stirling Lee's Depictions of Justitia in Nineteenth-Century Liverpool" (2013) 9 *Law Culture & Humanities* 311.

[88] E. Panofsky, *Studies in Iconology: Humanistic Themes in the Art of the Renaissance* (New York: Harper & Row, 1972), pp. 109–10; M. Jay, "Must Justice Be Blind?: The Challenge of Images to the Law," in C. Douzinas and L. Nead (eds.), *Law and the Image: The Authority of Art and the Aesthetics of Law* (London and Chicago: The University of Chicago Press, 1999), pp. 19, 19–21 [hereinafter: *Law and the Image*].

to law's violence out of its sight or interest, while on the other hand preventing these targets of violence from knowing the direction of law's gaze.

This inability to see the law is experienced not only by those Palestinians who, as previously mentioned, are actually blindfolded in Israeli custody;[89] it also has to do, in part, with the difficulty of tracing the origin and location of many of the decisions taken by Israeli authorities with regard to Palestinians.[90] Furthermore, there is a more fundamental connection between law, invisibility, and violence at work, which is by no means unique to Israel/Palestine. Just as in Kafka's parable "Before the Law" – as jurist Costas Douzinas points out – the law is, to some degree, "always somewhere else, in the next room, deferred and unseen, ... a sign of the transcendent apprehended in its absence."[91] Law, then, not only enables but also always operates through invisibility, a dynamic particularly central to Israel's violence in the West Bank and Gaza Strip. To tackle this dynamic, one must first envisage violence beyond its dominant conception, as embodied in the international law of armed conflict.

---

[89] See text accompanying note 50.

[90] In the context of Israel's permit regime in the West Bank, sociologist Yael Berda has called this dynamic "phantom sovereignty." Y. Berda, *The Bureaucracy of the Occupation: The Permit Regime in the West Bank* (Jerusalem: Van Leer Institute and Hakibbutz Hameuhad, 2012) [Hebrew].

[91] C. Douzinas, "Prosopon and Antiprosopon: Prolegomena for a Legal Iconology," in *Law and the Image*, pp. 36, 58. See also P. Goodrich, "The Iconography of Nothing: Blank Spaces and the Representation of Law in Edward VI and the Pope," in *Law and the Image*, pp. 89, 94, 100 (discussing the facelessness and unrepresentability of the source and power of law).

W

War Crimes

Orna Ben-Naftali

W.1 GENERAL: INTERNATIONAL CRIMES AND PUNISHMENT

W.1.1 *War Crimes: Substance and Jurisdiction*

International criminal law (ICL) is concerned with the substantive determination of international crimes and with enforcement mechanisms designed to ensure that perpetrators of such crimes would not enjoy impunity. In essence, it is designed to provide a judicial response to the commission of international crimes by holding individuals responsible for having abused human rights and humanitarian norms, believing that they do so with impunity.

War crimes are one category of international crimes.[1] It comprises serious violations of international humanitarian law (IHL). Such violations, thus, are occasioned in the context of an armed conflict, whether international or noninternational.[2] They may be committed by military personnel as well as by civilians whose conduct is linked to the armed conflict[3] against enemy combatants or civilians.[4] Serious violations are grave deviations from a rule

---

[1] Other categories are Crimes against Humanity, Genocide, Aggression, Torture, Terrorism, and Piracy.

[2] The rationale for expanding the applicability of war crimes to noninternational armed conflicts is articulated in the Tadić case, Tadić, Appeal Chamber Opinion and Judgment, ICTY-94-1-A (July 15, 1999), ¶ 95.

[3] On the link with an armed conflict see, e.g., Kunarac, Kovac, and Vuković, Appeal Chamber Judgment, ICTY-96-23 & 96-23/1-A (June 12, 2002), ¶¶ 57–59.

[4] *The Government Commissioner of the General Tribunal of the Military Government for the French Zone of Occupation in Germany* v. *Röchling*, Judgment of the General Tribunal of the Military Government of the French Zone of Occupation in Germany (January 25, 1949), Volume XIV, TWC, Appendix B, 1061. The Kapo trials conducted in Israel also charged civilians who themselves were persecuted people with war crimes. On the Kapo Trials, see O. Ben-Naftali and Y. Tuval, "Punishing International Crimes Committed by the Persecuted: The Kapo Trials in Israel (1950s–1960s)" (2006) 4 *Journal of International Criminal Justice* 128;

which protects normatively important values, and entail severe consequences for the victim. The normative sources of these rules are treaty law, primarily the Geneva Law,[5] and customary law. Indeed, most conventional rules have currently attained the status of custom and are therefore applicable regardless of ratification by any individual state. The most recent codification of war crimes, comprising 50 such crimes, exists in Article 8 of the Statute of the International Criminal Court (ICCSt).[6]

The applicable jurisdictional regime provides a globalized criminal jurisdictional network comprising traditional state-centered jurisdiction, centralized international jurisdiction, and decentralized universal jurisdiction. Given that these obligations are not merely technical, but "are fundamental to the respect of the human person,"[7] they too are considered part of customary international law.[8]

The combination of substantive law and a global jurisdictional network for its enforcement was ostensibly designed to replace a "culture of impunity" with a "culture of accountability."[9]

W.1.2 *A Culture of Impunity*

The term "culture of impunity" became common currency in the early 1990s.[10] It signifies that a distinct group of perpetrators of international crimes are systematically exempt from accountability. The rationale for this

---

O. Ben-Naftali, "10 entries on Holocaust Trials in Israel," in A. Cassese (ed.), *The Oxford Companion to International Criminal Justice* (Oxford: Oxford University Press, 2009).

[5] See entry G: Geneva Law.

[6] Article 8 of the Rome Statute of the International Criminal Court, UN General Assembly, July 17, 1998, ISBN No 92–9227-227–6 [hereinafter: ICCSt]. The long, though nonexhaustive list of 50 such crimes comprises four categories: (a) grave breaches of the 1949 Geneva Conventions; (b) other serious violations of the law and customs of war applicable to international armed conflicts; (c) serious violations of Common Article 3 of the 1949 Geneva Conventions applicable to noninternational armed conflicts; and (d) other serious violations of the laws and customs applicable to noninternational armed conflicts. While it is commonly accepted that the crimes listed in the ICCSt codify existing rules, it has been argued that some of them, such as the launching of an attack knowing that it will cause significant damage to the environment (Article 8(2)(b)(4)) or the insertion of the word "indirectly" to the prohibition on the transfer of the population of the occupying power to occupied territories (Article 8(2)(b)(8)), have not reflected custom prior to their inclusion in the Statute.

[7] Legality of the Threat or Use of Nuclear Weapons, Advisory Opinion, 1996 ICJ 226, ¶ 79.

[8] See J.M. Henckaerts, "The Grave Breaches Regime as Customary International Law" (2009) 7 *Journal of International Criminal Justice* 683, 693–700.

[9] ICCSt Preamble, ¶ 5.

[10] In a manner that parallels the reference to "international criminal court," see J. B. Michel, Y. K. Shen, A. Presser Aiden, A. Veres, and M. K. Gray, "Quantitative Analysis of Culture Using Millions of Digitized Books" (2011) 331 *Science* 176, 176–182, cited in K. Engle,

development, as articulated by Amnesty International in 1991, does not see impunity merely as a postfactum failure to remedy violations through the decision not to prosecute perpetrators, but as the cause of the violations.[11]

The campaign against the "culture of impunity" generated the inclusion of an accountability mandate in numerous inquiry and fact-finding UN missions;[12] a surge in attempts to bring perpetrators to justice through the exercise of universal jurisdiction;[13] and the establishment of the ICC and extensive jurisprudence holding states accountable for the criminal investigation, prosecution, and punishment of human rights violations, including invalidating amnesty laws.[14]

This focus on criminal processes as the master paradigm to counter a culture of impunity, through punishment, deterrence, and the exposure of truth,[15] also generated a critique.

The starting point of the critique is that the very reference to "culture" indicates that international crimes do not occur as a result of sporadic or arbitrary individual decisions, but in a sociopolitical, ideologically driven, and institutionally sanctioned context. It is this context, or *nomos*,[16] that explains not only the systematic nature of both the crimes and the impunity, but also why the criminal process which focuses on individuals is ill-suited to achieve its stated objectives: focusing on individual accountability de-contextualizes

---

"Anti-Impunity and the Turn to Criminal Law in Human Rights" (2015) 100 *Cornell Law Review* 1069, 1078.

[11] Amnesty International Policy Statement on Impunity, in N. J. Kritz (ed.), *Transitional Justice: How Emergency Democracies Reckon with Former Regimes* (Washington DC: United States Institute of Peace, 1995), vol. I, p. 219.

[12] L. van den Herik, "An Inquiry into the Role of Commissions of Inquiry in International Law: Navigating the Tension between Fact-Finding and Application of International Law" (2014) 13 *Chinese Journal of International Law* 507.

[13] See, e.g., *R. v. Bow Street Stipendiary Magistrate and others, ex parte Pinochet Ugarte (Amnesty International and others intervening) (No. 3)* in [1999] *All E.R.* 97; M. Langer, "Universal Jurisdiction is not Disappearing" (2015) 13 *Journal of International Criminal Justice* 245.

[14] The trend began in the Inter-American Commission on Human Rights in *Velásquez-Rodriguez* v. *Honduras*, Inter-Am Ct HR (ser. C) No 4 (July 29, 1988), ¶¶ 172–174, determining that state accountability requires due diligence to prevent the violation or respond to it. See also *Marguš* v. *Croatia*, Eur Ct HR (Grand Chamber), App No 4455/10 (May 27, 2014), ¶¶ 124–128.

[15] On the emergence of the "right to truth" in this context, see e.g., *Barrios Altos* v. *Peru*, Inter-Am Ct HR (ser. C) No. 83 (March 14, 2001), ¶ 48; *Almoacid-Arellano* v. *Chile*, Inter-Am Ct HR (ser. C) No 154 (September 26, 2006), ¶ 148; *Gomes Lund* v. *Brazil*, Inter-Am Ct HR (ser. C.) No 219 (November 24, 2010), ¶ 151. See also, L. Bilsky, "Transitional Justice as a Modern Oedipus: The Emergence of a Right to Truth" (2015) 2 *Critical Analysis of Law* 446.

[16] R. Cover, "The Supreme Court, 1982 Term – Foreword: Nomos and Narrative" (1983–1984) 97 *Harvard Law Review* 4. Cover uses the term "nomos" to signify a normative universe, comprising both rules and the narratives that give them meaning.

our understanding of the nature of such crimes, belies deterrence, distorts the very search for truth, and contaminates the judicial process.

The challenges presented to the criminal system by focusing on the individual who acted in the context of criminal normality, relate to both the accused and to the court: the accused, as Arendt observed,[17] genuinely believes that his deeds were both lawful and moral, and thus lacks *mens rea*. Institutionally, the engagement of a judicial text which focuses on the individual in an often bitterly disputed political context situates the court, as Koskenniemi wrote, between the "Scylla of impunity" and the "Charybdis of show trials."[18] If the court exercising jurisdiction is foreign or international, it will invariably be charged with having taken a political side that has contaminated the process, producing neither justice nor peace.[19] If the court is domestic, and the trial does not take place in postconflict circumstances which invite critical self-reflection, it is often part of the culture on the culpability of which it is to adjudicate. Under such conditions, the most that could be expected of it is to relate to the perpetrator as an exception, a bad apple in an otherwise well-cultivated orchard.[20] In so doing, it will invariably extract the crime from its context, thus reinforcing the perpetuation of criminal normality, reproducing neither truth nor deterrence, but rather the conditions of possibility for the thriving of false collective consciousness of moral blamelessness, and ergo for the crimes carried out in its name. The judicial process is thus likely to be co-opted into what Arendt had aptly termed "the banality of evil."[21] The result would be the fertilization of a culture of impunity in which the domestic justice system is implicated, not its replacement by a culture of accountability. This entry substantiates this general critique in respect of the Israeli justice system: while allegations of war crimes committed in the context of maintaining Israel's control over the OPT have been made against both parties,[22] the

---

[17]   H. Arendt, *Eichmann in Jerusalem: A Report on the Banality of Evil* (New York: Penguin Books, 2006), pp. 289–290. Arendt nevertheless thought that the greatness of the judicial system lies in providing a forum which focuses on individual responsibility, as the individual was not to be exempt from responsibility for having forfeited his ability to think critically about what he was doing. K. Sikkink, *The Justice Cascade: How Human Rights Prosecutions Are Changing World Politics* (New York: W. W. Norton & Company, 2011).

[18]   M. Koskenniemi, "Between Impunity and Show Trials" (2002) 6 *Max Planck Yearbook of United Nations Law* 1, 19.

[19]   The position taken by Milošević vis-à-vis the ICTY is a case at point, see, e.g., S. Swimelar, "Guilty Without a Verdict: Bosniaks" Perception of the Milošević Trial," in T. W. Waters (ed.), *The Milošević Trial: An Autopsy* (Oxford: Oxford University Press, 2013), p. 189.

[20]   Engle, "Anti-Impunity," p. 1120.   [21]   Arendt, *Eichmann in Jerusalem*.

[22]   See e.g., UN Human Rights Council [hereinafter: UNHRC], Report of the United Nations Fact-Finding Mission on the Gaza Conflict, "Human Rights in Palestine and other Arab

focus of this entry is on the implication of the Israeli justice system in cases that involve such allegations against Israelis.

W.1.3 *Israel and the "Justice Cascade"*[23]

The "justice cascade," equated with the view that criminal prosecutions of individuals for severe human rights violations are legally required to combat a culture of impunity, has met with Israeli resistance. Israel has stood in less than splendid (near) isolation in its suspicion toward the globalization of ICL[24] and is not a party to the ICCSt.[25] This position is directly related to Israel's control over the OPT: the prolonged occupation has increasingly generated charges, that sustaining it entails the commission of war crimes.[26] These charges, in turn, led to attempts by other states to exercise universal jurisdiction over Israeli political and military leaders;[27] to the inclusion, in the ICCSt of Article 8(2)(b)(viii), which defines the direct or indirect transfer by the occupying power of its

---

Occupied Territories" (September 25, 2009) A/HRC/12/48, §§ xx–xxv [hereinafter: The Goldstone Report], www.refworld.org/docid/4ac1dd252.html.

[23] Sikkink, *The Justice Cascade*.

[24] The USA is the other Western democracy that refrained from ratifying the ICCSt. On its position, see e.g., D. J. Scheffer, "The United States and the International Criminal Court" (1999) 93 *American Journal of International Law* 12. For the common position of states comprising the EU, see European Council Common Position of 11 June 2011 on the International Criminal Court, 2001/443/CFSP, http://eur-lex.europa.eu/legal-content/EN/T XT/PDF/?uri=CELEX:32001E0443&from=EN.

[25] Israel signed the ICCSt on December 31, 2000, adding a political declaration which clarified that the signature is to be understood as a moral identification with the objectives of the court, but conveys no intention of becoming a party to its statute. See Statement of 3 January 2001, by Alan Baker, the Israeli Foreign Ministry Legal Advisor, http://mfa.gov.il /MFA/MFA-Archive/2001/Pages/International%20Criminal%20Court%20-%20Press%20Bri efing%20by%20I.aspx.

[26] See, e.g., M. Lanz E. Max, and O. Hoehne, "The Conference of High Contracting Parties to the Fourth Geneva Convention of 17 December 2014 and the Duty to Ensure Respect for International Humanitarian Law" (2014) 96 *International Review of the Red Cross* 1115; The Goldstone Report; UNHRC, Report of the Independent Commission of Inquiry Established Pursuant to Human Rights Council Resolution S-21/1, UN Doc A/HRC/29/52 (June 25, 2015), ¶ 74; UNHRC, Report of the Independent International Fact-Finding Mission to Investigate the Implications of the Israeli Settlements on the Civil, Political, Economic, Social and Cultural Rights of the Palestinian People throughout the Occupied Palestinian Territory, including East Jerusalem, UN Doc A/HRC/22/63 (February 7, 2013), ¶ 104.

[27] See, e.g., UN General Assembly Meeting Coverage, Experts Suggest Invoking Universal Jurisdiction among Legal Options to Address Israeli Settlements, as International Meeting on Palestine Question Continues, GA/PAL/1346 (September 8, 2015); B. Quinn, "Former Israeli Minister Tzipi Livni to Visit UK after Change in Arrest Law," *The Guardian* (October 4, .2011), www.theguardian.com/world/2011/oct/04/tzipi-livni-arrest-warrant.

civilian population to an occupied territory as a war crime; and to the specter of the ICC assuming jurisdiction over Israeli citizens.[28]

A culture of impunity/accountability has a public and a legal dimension. The latter is expressed in the quality of the four main components of the criminal process: criminal legislation that defines certain acts as war crimes; investigations geared toward the exposure of the relevant facts; diligent prosecution of suspects; and an independent judicial system that renders a reasoned judgment and determines the appropriate punishment.

Israeli legislation refrains from classifying war crimes as a criminal offense. The notable exception is contained in the Nazis and Nazi Collaborators (Punishment) Law,[29] an enactment that is chronologically and geographically

---

[28] On January 2, 2015, Palestine deposited its instrument of accession to the ICCSt, along with a declaration giving the ICC jurisdiction over crimes committed in the OPT from June 13, 2014, See "The State of Palestine Accedes to the Rome Statute," *ICC Press Release* (January 7, 2015), www.icc-cpi.int//Pages/item.aspx?name=pr1082_2; State of Palestine, Declaration Accepting the Jurisdiction of the International Criminal Court (December 31, 2014), https://unispal.un.org/D PA/DPR/unispal.nsf/0/93EEF1935D2E78E285257DC4006B7C2F, a time frame indicating Palestine's wish that the ICC investigates crimes committed during the 2014 Operation "Protective Edge" in Gaza. On April 1, 2015, Palestine became the 123rd state party to the Statute: see, "ICC Welcomes Palestine as a new State Party," *ICC Press Release* (April 1, 2015), www.icc-cpi.int/Pages/item.aspx?name=pr1103. On January 16, 2015, the ICC Prosecutor opened a preliminary examination into the situation in Palestine: see, "The Prosecutor of the International Criminal Court, Fatou Bensouda, Opens a Preliminary Examination of the Situation in Palestine", *ICC Press Release* (January 16, 2015), www.icc-cpi.int/Pages/item.aspx? name=pr1083. Presently, the ICC Prosecutor is conducting a preliminary investigation into both alleged crimes committed during the 2014 operation "Protective Edge," and other alleged crimes, primarily the settlements. The preliminary examination is designed, as per Article 15 of the ICCSt to "assess whether a situation warrants investigation." Should the Prosecutor decide to open an investigation *proprio motu*, then under Article 15(3) of the ICCSt, the issue of jurisdiction will be determined by a pretrial chamber. Under Article 17 of the Statute, the issue of admissibility is determined by two criteria: gravity and complementarity. In view of the conclusion of the commission appointed by the Human Rights Council to investigate the 2014 operation "Protective Edge" in Gaza that serious violations of IHL that may amount to war crimes have been committed by both Israelis and Palestinians, the gravity criterion is likely to be met. See UNHRC, Report of the Independent Commission of Inquiry (June 25, 2015), ¶ 74. It is equally likely that Israel would raise the issue of complementarity, arguing that it has already investigated the matter and concluded that no war crimes were committed. On the Israeli investigation, see The Public Commission to Examine the Maritime Incident of 31 May 2010, Second Report: Israel's Mechanisms for Examining and Investigating Complaints and Claims of Violations of the Laws of Armed Conflict According to International Law (February 2013), www.turkel-committee .gov.il/files/newDoc3/The%20Turkel%20Report%20for%20website.pdf; L. Yavne, *Alleged Investigation: The Failure of Investigations into Offenses Committed by IDF Soldiers against Palestinians* (Tel Aviv: Yesh Din, 2011), goo.gl/kq0PF2. The Prosecutor, however, stated she would also focus on other alleged crimes, primarily the settlements, an issue over which there is already an international determination that they appear to breach Article 8 of the ICCSt.

[29] The Nazis and Nazi Collaborators (Punishment) Law, 1950. Israel also enacted the Crime of Genocide (Prevention and Punishment) Law, incorporating the Convention on the

delimited to the period of the Nazi regime.[30] Subject to this exception, some of the crimes classified under the ICCSt as "war crimes" are thus indistinguishable from other crimes in the Israeli penal legislation. This omission and its impact on investigations and prosecutions are discussed in entry I: Investigations. Insofar as the courts are concerned, this legal silence and its bearing on investigations and prosecutions, results in very few cases in which courts exercise judgment over conduct that may otherwise qualify as a war crime. On such occasions, the judicial discourse, discussed in Section W.2, frames the conduct as an exception to the normal military ethos and praxis or otherwise extracts it from the context in which it has taken place. The political/public discourse, however, often does not regard such conduct as exceptional, but rather as reflecting normal routine. This discourse is the focus of Section W.3. Section W.4 concludes with a reflection on the nature of the dynamics between the judicial and the political discourses in the making of a culture of impunity.

W.2 THE JUDICIAL DISCOURSE: THE EXCEPTION AND ITS DISCONTENT

Both courts-martial and the HCJ can be engaged in judging conduct that may amount to war crimes: the former, in direct adjudication; the latter, in

---

Prevention and Punishment of the Crime of Genocide. In 1966, the Annulment of Statutory Limitations on Crimes against Humanity Law was enacted, establishing that there would be no statute of limitations on crimes under this law and under the Nazis and Nazi Collaborators (Punishment) Law.

[30] Section 16(a) of the Israeli Penal Code, 1977, provides that "Israel's penal laws will apply to foreign offenses, which Israel has, under multilateral conventions that are open to accession, committed itself to punish, even if they are perpetrated by a person who is neither a citizen nor a resident of Israel, and irrespective of the place in which the offense was committed." This section thus provides the source of universal jurisdiction in Israeli law, but does not establish offenses additional to those listed in the Israeli Penal Code for Israeli citizens. The Penal Code, however, does not list war crimes as offenses nor is there any legislation that incorporates war crimes into Israeli criminal law through reference to relevant provisions of international law. Legislation by reference to international law may follow the static referral, or "cut and paste" approach (a model followed by the UK) or the dynamic approach, which refers generally to the laws of war or to customary international law (a model followed by the USA) or by a mixed approach employing both models model (e.g., Finland). See generally, K. Dormann and R. Geiss, "The Implementation of Grave Breaches into Domestic Legal Order" (2009) 7 *Journal of International Criminal Justice* 703; S. J. Hankins, "Overview of Ways to Import Core International Crimes into National Criminal Law," in M. Bergsmo, M. Harlem, and N. Hayashi (eds.), *Importing Core International Crimes into National Law* 7 (Oslo: FICHL, 2010); L. Yavne, *Lacuna: War Crimes in Israeli Law and Court Martial Rulings* (Tel Aviv: Yesh Din, 2013), pp. 18–22, http://files.yesh-din.org/userfiles/file/Reports-English/Y esh%20Din%20-%20Lacuna%20Web%20-%20English.pdf.

exercising its oversight authority over the military enforcement system. Section W.2.1 offers a brief review of relevant courts-martial jurisprudence. Section W.2.2 focuses on a test case where the HCJ exercised its oversight function.

W.2.1 Courts-Martial

The vast majority of indictments of soldiers accused of offenses against Palestinians and of judgments rendered by courts-martial refers neither to protected persons nor indeed to the Geneva Conventions or to other normative international sources, that may be relevant and that emphasize the special responsibility owed to protected persons in an occupied territory. Instead, soldiers are charged with ordinary criminal offenses, and commonly with offenses such as "conduct unbecoming" (improper behavior) which do not reflect the gravity of the offense and carry no criminal record.[31] In most cases, a plea bargain is concluded and adopted by the courts and punishment, referring to the past record of the soldier, tends to be lenient in relation to the conduct.[32]

The exceptions to this assessment are few and far between. The most notable such judgment predates the 1967 occupation: in 1956, in what would become known of the "Kafr Qasim massacre," an IDF border police battalion killed, upon order, 48 Arab civilian men, women, and children who, unaware that a curfew had been imposed, were returning from work. Many more were injured and left unattended. Following an inquiry commission's recommendation, 11 soldiers and commanders were charged with murder. The defense rested on the duty to obey orders. On October 16, 1958, 8 of them were found guilty and sentenced to prison terms. The judgment is known for having articulated the test for the duty not to obey a manifestly illegal order, as follows:[33]

---

[31] E.g., the indictment for using Palestinians as "human shields," a practice which the HCJ classified in reference to the Geneva Law, as impermissible, "cruel[,] and barbarian" (see, HCJ 3799/02 *Adalah* v. *GOC Central Command*, IDF (2005) 60(3) PD 67, ¶ 21) [Hebrew; English translation available at http://elyon1.court.gov.il/Files_ENG/02/990/037/A32/02037990.a32.pdf]. The indictment charged the offenders with at most "exceeding authority to the extent of risking life or health" which carries a maximum penalty of three years in prison, and even that charge was reduced as part of the plea bargain. For a survey of relevant cases see Yavne, *Lacuna*, pp. 37–41.

[32] For a review of sample cases substantiating this assessment see Yavne, *Lacuna*, pp. 43–49.

[33] MilC Center 3/57 *Military Prosecutor* v. *Melinki*, ¶ 90 [Hebrew]. The test was upheld by the military appeals court, Mil. Appeal 279–283/58 *Ofer* v. *Chief Military Prosecutor* [Hebrew].

The hallmark of manifest illegality is that it must wave like a black flag over the given order, a warning that says: "forbidden!" Not formal illegality, obscure or partially obscure, not illegality that can be discerned only by legal scholars, is important here, but rather, the clear and obvious violation of law ... Illegality that pierces the eye and revolts the heart, if the eye is not blind and the heart is not impenetrable or corrupt – this is the measure of manifest illegality needed to override the soldier's duty to obey and to impose on him criminal liability for his action.

The attempt to balance discipline and the rule of law by introducing an equation between morality and legality is problematic: it substitutes the meta-legal rationale underlying accountability for the normative content of a crime. It further fails to provide a "clear and obvious" guidance, especially in situations where it is precisely the obviousness of the moral outrage that is lacking in the context within which the crime is committed. Yet, these ethically evocative but legally hollow words remain, to date, the only test by which the issue is determined.[34] No substantive reference to international law was made then or since.[35] By November 1959, and following various pardoning procedures, all those convicted were out of prison.[36]

The exceptionality of an indictment for murder is underscored not merely by the fact that this trial took place some six decades ago, but also by later data: between September 2000 and October 2016, the IDF killed some 9,200 Palestinians. Investigations were opened in only 203 instances; of these, only 6 soldiers were prosecuted for manslaughter, not for murder. Of these, 3 were convicted of minor offenses carrying no prison sentence,[37] the trial of 1 is still underway, and 2 soldiers were convicted of this offense: a Bedouin who killed a British citizen in Gaza,[38] and a soldier who executed a wounded Palestinian

---

[34] Other judgments that applied this test include MilC South 24/88 (Giv'ati A) [Hebrew]; MilC North 556/88 (Golani) [Hebrew].

[35] A survey conducted by the NGO Yesh Din found that references to international and foreign legal sources exist under the heading "universal values and morality in combat" in a judgment of the Appeal Court Martial on looting, an offense that is included in the Military Justice Act, and that a reference to the Rome Statute as an interpretative source was made by a court martial acquitting an accused of killing a Palestinian girl, Iman al-Hams. A poor harvest indeed. See Mil. Appeal 62/03 *Chief Military Prosecutor v. Sergeant A.A.* (May 27, 2003) [Hebrew]; MilC South 400/04 *Military Prosecutor v. Captain R.* (November 15, 2005) [Hebrew], p. 72, respectively. See Yavne, *Lacuna*, pp. 48–50.

[36] For a review of the impact of the judgment, see L. Bilsky, *Transformative Justice: Israeli Identity On Trial* (Ann Arbor: University of Michigan, 2004), pp. 166–197.

[37] G. Cohen, "IDF Soldiers Have Been Tried for Manslaughter – but Most Were Not Convicted," *Haaretz* (August 28, 2016), www.haaretz.com/israel-news/.premium-1.739021.

[38] A. Feldman, "'Neutralize' a Terrorist? Just Say a Bullet to the Head," *Haaretz* (August 30, 2016), www.haaretz.com/opinion/.premium-1.739272.

in Hebron.[39] The latter is the focus of Section W.3. The "black flag" is yet to be waved.

W.2.2 *The HCJ – The Ashraf* Abu Rahme *Case*[40]

The *Abu Rahme* case merits attention for two main reasons: first, the judgment, in which the HCJ concluded that the decision of the military advocate general (MAG) to charge two soldiers who cruelly abused a Palestinian merely with "conduct unbecoming" was exceedingly unreasonable, presents the HCJ taking the most active stand it has taken before or since to ostensibly promote a culture of accountability. Second, the relevant facts, which, as shall be posited, present a textbook case of a war crime, do not emanate from a large-scale military operation of the kind that spawns allegations that war crimes have been committed.[41] Rather, they disclose the routine interaction between the occupied people and the occupying army. This routine is often overlooked; knowledge and public discourse about the nature of the actions necessary to carry it out are suppressed;[42] and law is kept at bay. An incident that becomes visible and consequently triggers both public reaction and law enforcement, thus offers a unique opportunity to appreciate the legal framing of this routine and its construction of the relationship between the norm and the exception. The *Abu Rahme* case is such an incident.

---

[39] MilC (Center) 182/16 *Military Prosecutor* v. *Azaria* (January 4, 2017) [Hebrew]. This case is discussed in Section W.3.

[40] HCJ 7195/08 *Abu Rahme* v. *the MAG* (2009) 63(2) PD 325 [Hebrew; English translation available at http://elyon1.court.gov.il/files_eng/08/950/071/r09/08071950.r09.pdf]. The discussion below reproduces, mutatis mutandis, the analysis in O. Ben-Naftali and N. Zamir, "Whose 'Conduct Unbecoming'? The Shooting of a Handcuffed, Blindfolded Palestinian Demonstrator" (2009) 7 *Journal of International Criminal Justice* 155.

[41] Large-scale operations such as those undertaken periodically in Gaza attract international attention, allegations of war crimes, the establishment of international commissions of inquiry, and reports that conclude that such crimes have been committed. See, e.g., The Goldstone Report.

[42] The legislative and discursive attempts to suppress Israeli NGOs working to expose the legal violations that sustaining the occupation entails is a case at point. See e.g., Draft Bill Amending the National Education Law (Preventing Activities of Organizations Subverting the Objectives of Education and the IDF), 2017, HH p/20/3643 [Hebrew]. Breaking the Silence, an NGO which collects testimonies of soldiers who have served in the OPT, especially in Hebron, "to force Israeli society to address the reality that it created" has been the target of most of the wrath of those who insist on the IDF being "the most moral army in the world." On Breaking the Silence see the NGO's website: www.shovrimshtika.org/about_ e.asp. On the alleged superior morality of the IDF, see, e.g., Chief of Staff Lt. Gen. Gabi Ashkenazi quoted in Yaakov Lappin, "Ashkenazi: IDF Most Moral Army in World," *Jerusalem Post* (March 23, 2009), www.jpost.com/Israel/Ashkenazi-IDF-most-moral-army-in-world.

W.2.2.1 The Factual Framework

The incident took place during a period of routine demonstrations by Palestinians, some Israelis, and international supporters against the construction of the Separation Wall on Palestinian lands.[43] On July 7, 2008, during one such usual demonstration in Ni'lin, a village in the West Bank,[44] Israeli border policemen stopped, handcuffed, and blindfolded a 27-year-old Palestinian demonstrator, Ashraf Abu Rahme. He was taken to an army jeep, beaten, and driven to the village's entrance, where he was left for some two hours.[45] Thereafter, still handcuffed and blindfolded, an IDF Lt. Col. led him by the arm to stand next to a jeep and asked him, in Hebrew: "well, will you now stop participating in demonstrations against the IDF forces?" The detainee responded in Arabic in a manner that made it clear that he does not understand Hebrew. The officer then asked a soldier, who stood some two meters away: "What do you say, shall we take him aside and 'shoot rubber' at him"? The soldier responded, also in Hebrew: "I have no problem shooting him." The officer then instructed the soldier to load the bullet and the soldier responded that he had already done so. The soldier aimed his weapon at Abu Rahme's legs and fired a rubber-coated steel bullet at him, hitting a toe on his left foot.[46]

---

[43]   See entry B: Border/Barrier.

[44]   Ni'lin is a Palestinian village located 17 km west of Ramallah in the central West Bank. In May 2008, work began on the construction of the Separation Wall in the village's land. The route of the Wall – designed to secure the neighboring settlements – requires confiscation and destruction of agricultural lands, including the olive groves which are the main source of the villager's livelihood. Organized demonstrations against the construction of the Wall take place on a regular basis, involving the Palestinian villagers, Israelis, and internationals (mainly from the International Solidarity Movement). See, e.g., Reuters, "Israel Extends Curfew in Palestinian Town," *ynet* (July 7, 2008), www .ynetnews.com/articles/0,7340,L-3564808,00.html. Note that the judgment describes the demonstration as "violent," *Abu Rahme*, ¶ 3.

[45]   The petition disclosed that Abu Rahme was beaten; in the judgment, the court notes that he was detained in view of his active engagement in disrupting orders and is silent on the alleged beating; *Abu Rahme*, ¶ 3.

[46]   The so-called "rubber bullets" are steel bullets, coated with thin rubber. They are used to disperse demonstrations based on the belief that such bullets are less lethal than live ammunition and that they are therefore appropriate for use in situations that pose no threat to the IDF soldiers' lives. Yet they can be lethal, a fact acknowledged by the drafters of the Open-Fire Regulations, which stipulates, inter-alia, a minimum range for firing them of 40 m. In fact, "rubber bullets" have caused the deaths of dozens of Palestinians, and it is probable that the fact that they are perceived as "less lethal" generates a light trigger-finger. See generally, B'Tselem, *Crowd Control: Israel's Use of Crowd Control Weapons in the West Bank* (2013), www.btselem.org/download/201212_crowd_control_eng .pdf, p. 21.

The incident was videoed by Salaam Amira, a 15-year-old girl from Ni'lin, from her home.[47] On July 20 B'Tselem received the video clip she shot and distributed it on national and international media, demanding that a military police investigation be opened and that the soldier – Staff Sergeant L. – and the officer – who turned out to be the battalion commander, Lt. Col. Omri Borberg – be brought to justice. It was only then, some two weeks after the shooting, that the MAG ordered an investigation.

Following the investigation, the MAG decided to prosecute both the soldier and the commander for "conduct unbecoming."[48] According to the indictment, the commander intended merely to frighten the detainee (a justification hard to reconcile with the fact that he knew that the blindfolded detainee does not speak Hebrew), whereas the soldier understood that he had been ordered to shoot.[49] Ample evidence indicates various other questionable incidents under the command of Lt. Col. Borberg, which included shootings at Palestinian civilians with both rubber bullets and live ammunition, denying injured Palestinians access to medical care, and detainees' beatings.[50]

Evidence further suggests that this incident reflects common and systematic military practices in response to Palestinian demonstrations against the continuous occupation in general and the construction of the Wall in particular. As stated in the 2008 report of the Special Rapporteur on the Situation of Human Rights in the Occupied Palestinian Territories, Israeli security forces use both rubber-coated steel bullets and live ammunition as a means to disperse demonstrations in the OPT.[51] In its 2007 annual report, B'Tselem stated that more than 1,000 civilians protesting against the Wall have required medical attention since 2004 due to injuries from "rubber" bullets, beatings, and tear gas inhalation, and that 320 of them were injured during 2007 alone, the year the *Abu Rahme* incident took place.[52] According to testimonies, most

---

[47]   The day following the release of the video, Salaam's father, Jamal, was detained by the IDF for 26 days, probably as a vengeful measure for the release of the video clip, a connection acknowledged even by the military court which, having found no evidence to justify his continued detention, ordered his release. See G. Levy, "Twilight Zone Caught on Camera," *Haaretz* (August 28, 2008), www.haaretz.com/twilight-zone-caught-on-camera-1.252782.

[48]   Criminal Register and Rehabilitation Law, 1981 (Regulations 1984) [Hebrew]. Conviction in this offense may lead to a maximum of one year in prison and carries no criminal record.

[49]   Cited in the petition, ¶ 17, www.acri.org.il/pdf/petitions/hit7195.pdf [Hebrew]; *Abu Rahme*, ¶ 3.

[50]   *Abu Rahme* Petition, ¶ 20.

[51]   UN General Assembly, Situation of Human Rights in the Palestinian Territories Occupied since 1967: note by the Secretary-General, A/63/326 (September 25, 2008), https://unispal.un.org/DPA/DPR/unispal.nsf/0/061F1F4FBDECFFE5852574D60065B4BA, ¶ 26.

[52]   See B'Tselem, *Human Rights in the Occupied Territories: Annual Report 2007* (2008), www.btselem.org/download/200712_annual_report_eng.pdf, p. 27.

of the incidents involved no threat to the lives of the soldiers or policemen.[53] In a letter dated August 31, 2008, B'Tselem requested the Israeli attorney general to review the escalating occurrence of ostensibly illegal shootings with rubber-coated steel bullets by the security forces. The letter draws attention to the fact that fired from a short range, rubber-coated steel bullets are lethal and in violation of the army's rules of engagement. The latter are quite permissive when it comes to Palestinians, and the problem is exacerbated by the fact that the rules that do exist are consistently violated.[54] The finger on the trigger has become unbearably light. Against this background, the fact that the MAG only ordered a criminal investigation of the incident some two weeks after it had taken place, and only in response to pressure generated by the distribution of the video clip, lends support to the assessment that instilling a culture of accountability is not a priority of the military justice system.

On August 19, Ashraf Abu Rahme and a coalition of human rights organizations filed an urgent petition to the HCJ against the MAG's decision, demanding that the indictment be altered to reflect the gravity of the offense.[55] The HCJ issued an interim injunction requiring the MAG to justify his decision. On September 28, the HCJ held a hearing on the petition and ordered the MAG to reconsider the indictment and to inform the court of its decision within 40 days.[56] On November 4, following extensive consultations with the top echelons of the military and the government legal advisors, including the state attorney general, the MAG decided to retain the original indictment.[57] On July 1, 2009, the court rendered its judgment in the case. Having concluded that "phenomena characterized by exceeding gravity in that they offend the public's accepted moral norms must be matched by an appropriate punitive norm that is as

---

[53] For example, Amnesty International reports that soldiers standing on rooftops of Palestinian houses shoot at Palestinian children throwing stones. See Amnesty International, "Bullets Greet Anti-Wall Protesters," in *Enduring Occupation: Palestinians under Siege in the West Bank* (2007), www.amnesty.org/download/Documents/MDE1440932016ENGLISH.PDF.

[54] The rules of engagement themselves, distinguishing between demonstrations that involve Israelis and those that do not, were also subject to criticism from human rights organizations. The letter was written following incidents involving injury to Jewish–Israeli protesters. See e.g., www.btselem.org/press_releases/20080901; R. Sharon, "Rules of Engagement for Arabs Only," NRG (June 4, 2007), www.nrg.co.il/online/1/ART1/590/452.html [Hebrew].

[55] *Abu Rahme* Petition. The petitioning NGOs were B'Tselem; The Association for Civil Rights in Israel (ACRI); The Public Committee Against Torture in Israel (PCATI) and Yesh Din.

[56] See HCJ decision of 28.9.2008, http://elyon1.court.gov.il/files/08/950/071/r04/08071950.r04 .pdf [Hebrew].

[57] See B'Tselem, "Judge Advocate General Informs the High Court that he will not Amend the Indictment in the Shooting of a Bound Palestinian in Ni'lin" (November 4, 2008), www .btselem.org/firearms/20081104_nilin_state_response.

grave as the action,"[58] it determined that the MAG's decision was "extremely unreasonable" and ordered him to change the indictments to reflect the nature of the facts and the actions committed.[59] This decision is meritorious. Other than characterizing the facts of harming a helpless detainee as a "severe and cruel" conduct,[60] however, the court was not required to, and indeed refrained from, setting out the relevant normative framework within which the conduct is to be analyzed. This framework is the focus of the following subsection.

W.2.2.2 The Normative Framework: An Analysis in the Light of IHL and ICL

International humanitarian law provides the primary normative framework applicable to this case. The treatment of Mr. Abu Rahme, a "protected person,"[61] violates Articles 27 and 32 of the GC IV.[62] Article 27 is considered the "basis of the Convention, stipulating the principles upon which the whole of the 'Geneva Law' is founded," primarily "the principle of respect for the human person and the inviolable character of the basic rights of individual men and women."[63]

---

[58] *Abu Rahme*, ¶ 37.

[59] *Ibid.*, ¶ 92. The court further decided to revoke the order concealing the name of Sergeant L. (Koroa Leonardo).

[60] *Ibid.*, ¶ 41.

[61] According to Article 4 of the Geneva Convention Relative to the Protection of Civilian Persons in the Time of War, Geneva, August 12, 1949, 75 UNTS 287 [hereinafter: GC IV], Mr. Abu Rahme qualifies as a "protected person" since he is in the hands of the occupying power of which he is not national.

[62] "Protected persons are entitled, in all circumstances, to respect for their persons, their honour ... They shall at all times be humanely treated, and shall be protected especially against all acts of violence or threats thereof." Article 32 of GC IV specifies the principle stated in Article 27, by clarifying that the prohibition on taking measures "of such a character as to cause physical suffering" extends to "any ... measures of brutality." Note the similarity between this provision and the prohibition set forth in Article 27 of GC IV on "acts of violence." Note further that the drafters substituted a causal criterion ("of such a character as to cause") for a criterion of intention ("likely to cause," which appeared in the original draft), thereby expanding the scope of the prohibition. See J. S. Pictet (ed.), *The Geneva Conventions of 12 August 1949, Commentary – IV Geneva Convention Relative to the Protection of Civilian Persons in Time of War* (Geneva: International Committee of the Red Cross, 1958), p. 222. In the context of a noninternational armed conflict (NIAC), Common Article 3 of the Geneva Conventions, a "Convention in miniature," Pictet, *ibid.*, p. 34, reiterates the principle according to which "persons not taking active part in the hostilities shall in all circumstances be treated humanely" and acts consisting inter-alia, of cruel treatment and "outrages upon personal dignity, in particular humiliating and degrading treatment," are prohibited.

[63] Pictet, *ibid.*, p. 200.

The obligation to treat protected persons humanely, writes Pictet, is "in truth, the 'leitmotiv' of the four Geneva Conventions"; it is to be construed broadly "as applying to all aspects of man's life"; it is absolute in character, valid in all circumstances and at all times, and "remains fully valid in relation to persons in prison or interned . . . It is in such situations, where human values appear to be in greatest danger, that the provision assumes its full significance."[64]

The conduct of the IDF personnel toward Abu Rahme violated his human-ity, dignity, and person. Under customary international law, such conduct breaches the basic IHL principles described earlier and, qualifying as inhu-mane and degrading treatment, constitutes a war crime.

It is instructive to note in this context that the HCJ itself characterized the conduct as "cruel," and that ICL does not distinguish between "inhuman" and "cruel" treatment as the degree of physical or mental suffering required to prove either one of those offenses is the same.[65] "Inhumane treatment," which according to Article 147 of the GC IV is a grave breach of the convention,[66] is (a) an intentional act or omission, that is an act which, judged objectively, is deliberate and not accidental; (b) causes serious mental harm or physical suffering or injury or constitutes a serious attack on human dignity; and (c) is committed against a protected person.[67] The elements of crimes for Article 8(2)(a)(ii) (infliction of *inhuman* treatment in an international context), and Article 8(2)(c)(i) (violence to life and person, in particular *cruel* treatment in a noninternational context) are identical,[68] requiring that the "perpetrator inflicted severe physical or mental pain or suffering upon one or more persons."[69]

---

[64] *Ibid.*, p. 205.
[65] Naletilić and Martinović, Trial Chamber Judgment, ICTY-98–34-T (March 31, 2003), ¶¶ 245–246.
[66] Pictet, *Geneva Conventions*, p. 596; See also Delalić, Trial Chamber Judgment, ICTY-96–21-T (November 16, 1998), ¶¶ 516–534.
[67] Blaškić, Appeals Chamber Judgment, ICTY-95–14-A (July 29, 2004), ¶ 665. Cruel treatment under Common Article 3 of the Geneva Conventions applicable to noninternational armed conflicts is similarly defined. See Blaškić, *ibid.*, ¶ 595; Limaj, Bala, and Musliu, Trial Chamber Judgment, ICTY-03–66-T (November 30, 2005), ¶ 231; Strugar, Trial Chamber Judgment, ICTY-01–42-T (January 31, 2005), ¶ 261.
[68] A. Zimmermann, "Article 8 – War Crimes, para 2(c)-(f)," in O. Triffterer (ed.), *Commentary on the Rome Statute of the International Criminal Court – Observers' Notes, Article by Article* (2nd edn, Oxford: Hart Publishing, 2008), p. 490.
[69] Assembly of States Parties to the International Criminal Court, *First Session, New York, 3–10 September 2002: Official Records* (New York: United Nations, 2002), ICC ASP/1/3, https://documents-dds-ny.un.org/doc/UNDOC/GEN/N02/603/35/PDF/N0260 335.pdf?OpenElement.

It is further significant to note that the state response to the petition in the *Abu Rahme* case, including the argument that since the physical effect of the shooting was merely an injury to a toe, the conduct fails to meet the standard of severe pain accompanying serious physical injury, is not supported by relevant jurisprudence.[70] The appeals chamber of the ICTY in the *Braanin* case rejected a similar argument, holding that "acts inflicting physical pain amount to torture even when they do not cause pain of the type accompanying serious injury."[71] This is a fortiori the case when the conduct considered falls short of torture.[72] When coupled with the severe mental effect, being detained for hours while blindfolded and then shot at from short range is bound to have an effect akin to that of a mock execution – which has been considered torture[73] – hence, the appropriate classification of the conduct is not merely "unbecoming"; it constitutes a war crime.[74]

The petition to the HCJ included extensive references to war crimes.[75] The judgment's brief summary of the petitioners' arguments merely states that "international law regards inhuman and degrading behavior as grave breaches obliging the state to prosecute and to punish the perpetrators."[76] No reference to war crimes is made, and the Geneva Law is mentioned in the independent

[70] The state's response to the *Abu Rahme* petition, p. 27.
[71] Brdanin, Trial Chamber Judgment, ICTY-99-36-T (November 28, 2003), ¶ 521.
[72] For further discussion on the differences between "torture" and "inhuman treatment" see C. M. De Vos, "Mind the Gap: Purpose, Pain, and the Difference between Torture and Inhuman Treatment" (2007) 14 *Human Rights Brief* 4.
[73] See Commission on Human Rights, Torture and Other Cruel, Inhuman or Degrading Treatment or Punishment: Report of the Social Rapporteur, UN ESCOR, E/CN.4/1986/15 (February 19, 1986), ¶ 119.
[74] At a minimum, it constitutes "other acts contravening the fundamental principle of humane treatment, in particular those which constitute an attack on human dignity." While an attack on human dignity is an element of the crime of inhumane/cruel treatment under customary law, under the normative framework of the ICCSt it is not. Rather, a conduct amounting to an attack on human dignity falls under the crime of "committing outrages upon personal dignity, in particular humiliating and degrading treatment" laid out in Article 8(2)(c)(ii) of the ICCSt with respect to international armed conflicts and in Article 8(2)(b)(xxi) with respect to NIAC. Like the crime of "inhumane and cruel treatment," these provisions, as well as their respective elements of crimes, are identical. The elements required are that "the perpetrator humiliated, degraded or otherwise violated the dignity of one or more persons" and that "the severity of the humiliation, degradation or other violation was of such degree as to be generally recognized as an outrage upon personal dignity."
[75] The petition referred extensively to international law, and the judgment acknowledges that the petitioners argued that "international law regards inhuman and degrading behavior as grave breaches obliging the state to prosecute and to punish the perpetrators," but otherwise refrains from basing its decision on international law.
[76] *Abu Rahme*, ¶ 7.

opinion of justice Rubinstein only to signal its inadequacy, and indeed irrelevance:[77]

> [T]he 1949 Geneva Conventions and the 1907 Hague Regulations before them, were designed and signed in a period different from ours. The terror which the States of the world have to face, and Israel is surely not different, presents them with difficult challenges since terrorist bodies do not abide by this or that Convention.

Given that terrorism was not at issue in the context of the appeal but that the occupation was, this skewed reading of the Geneva Law intimates that even when ostensibly exercising oversight function over military law enforcement, the court is engaged in "state lawfare."[78]

The judgment does regard the conduct as "severe and cruel",[79] but refrains from framing it within IHL and ICL. Instead, the normative sources within which it is framed include the fundamental principles of Israeli administrative,[80] criminal,[81] and constitutional law,[82] and Israel's "Jewish and democratic values."[83] The individual opinions of justices Rubinstein and Melcer refer to the ethical code of the IDF[84] as well as to Jewish law,[85] the writings of Israel's first prime minister, David Ben-Gurion, and to Israeli poetry[86] as additional sources of both normative and eth(n)ical behavior. Comparative law and European human rights jurisprudence is also mentioned in the individual opinion of justice Melcer, with a view to positing Israel's good standing among nations.[87]

That the absence of an analysis of the issue in the light of international law from the judgment was not an oversight, but a conscious decision, becomes evident in the individual opinion of justice Melcer:[88]

[77] *Ibid.*, justice Rubinstein, ¶ 1.   [78] See entries G: Geneva Law; L: Lawfare.
[79] *Abu Rahme*, ¶ 42.   [80] *Ibid.*, ¶¶ 66–84.   [81] See, for example, *ibid.*, ¶¶ 35–38, 43.
[82] See, for example, *ibid.*, ¶ 40.   [83] *Ibid.*, ¶ 90.   [84] *Ibid.*, justice Rubinstein, ¶ 11.
[85] *Ibid.*, ¶¶ 14–18. Rubinstein further indicates that the conduct at issue amounts to "*Hillul Hashem*," or defamation of God. This is noteworthy as it reflects his understanding of the "imagined community" to whom the judgment is addressed, as indeed otherwise there seems to be little reason to engage God in the matter.
[86] Both Rubinstein and Melcer refer to, and the latter quotes from the poetry of, Nathan Alterman, the late distinguished Israeli poet and publicist, who, horrified by abuses of military power that occurred in 1948, wrote condemning and widely publicized poems heralding the value of "purity of arms" and behavior restrained by law. See e.g., *Abu Rahme*, justice Melcer, ¶¶ 11, 14.
[87] *Ibid.*, ¶¶ 8–10. The comparison proposes that Israel fares better than other states insofar as the functioning of its military prosecution works and that according to the standard established by *Öcalan* v. *Turkey*, Eur Ct HR, App. No. 46221/99 (2003) 37 EHRR 10, detaining civilians, blindfolding them etc., does not amount to inhumane behavior.
[88] *Abu Rahme*, justice Melcer, ¶ 7.

This is the place to emphasize that even from the perspective of the respondents ... indicting them for ... improper behavior ... would prove to be counter-productive in the final analysis. The reason for that is that it is possible, once the court martial renders its final judgment, for someone to argue that given the nature of the indictment, they would not be able to avail themselves of the "double jeopardy" defense under international criminal law, and I shall not expand on this point, though it brings us to a brief discussion of comparative law.

This reference to ICL does not convey the deontological value of a culture of accountability. Alluding to the principle of complementarity, it advances a utilitarian rationale for the decision, explaining to the perpetrators (as well as to the military justice personnel and to the public at large) that given the specter of the exercise of international or universal jurisdiction, they stand to gain from a more severe domestic prosecution.[89]

W.2.2.3 Exceptionalizing the Norm

To the extent that the treatment of Mr. Abu Rahme, far from being an isolated and an exceptional incident, actually conforms to a pattern of similar incidents, the effort of the HCJ's judgment to frame both the conduct of the soldiers and the MAG's failure to exercise properly his authority over the administration of justice as exceptional, merits a closer look.

In the court's view the "severity of the event from a normative and an ethical perspective is great and exceptional."[90] This alleged exceptionality, in turn, justifies the truly exceptional decision to overturn the MAG's decision, as the court finds it necessary "to eradicate phenomena of exceptional conduct amongst IDF soldiers and commanders vis-à-vis local inhabitants."[91]

In reality, the only exceptionality of the event is that it was videoed and widely publicized. The possibility that the conduct to be eradicated is quite

---

[89] The ICCst provides in Article 10 of the Preamble and in Article 1 that the court established under the statute "shall be complementary to national criminal jurisdictions." See also Articles 15, 17, 18, and 19 of the ICCst. See generally, E. C. Rojo, "The Role of Fair Trial Considerations in the Complementarity Regime of the International Criminal Court: From 'No Peace without Justice' to 'No Peace with Victor's Justice'?" (2005) 18 *Leiden Journal of International Law* 829; The Goldstone Report, ¶¶ 1804–1835.

[90] *Abu Rahme*, ¶ 73. It should be noted that the petitioning human rights organizations equally referred to the event as exceptional. This is noteworthy since much of the data suggesting that the incident is far from exceptional is painstakingly gathered by them. The explanation for this apparent discrepancy is as clear as it is indicative of the paradox inherent to their activities: the price of defending the interests of a particular client is collaboration with the system they otherwise oppose.

[91] *Abu Rahme*, ¶ 88. For a similar framing of the event as exceptional see justice Melcer, ¶ 11.

common is nowhere contemplated in the text. The routine presence and activities of the IDF in the territories are never placed within the context of the occupation, but within the context of "the fight against terror" and the "inherent tension between human rights and security."[92] This is problematic not only because neither terror nor security were at issue, but primarily because in this manner the judgment contributes to the normalization of the occupation and legitimizes the violence required to sustain it. The question of why was Abu Rahme detained at all given that nowhere is it mentioned that he acted violently, and indeed the very legality of suppressing demonstrations against the construction of the Wall so long as they are nonviolent, are not raised.[93] Having their eyes wide shut to this reality allows the justices to sweeten the bitter pill they have otherwise ordered the MAG to swallow, by engaging in extensive praise for the adherence of the IDF to the values of human dignity and purity of arms as the source of its "qualitative, moral and intellectual superiority."[94] In this narrative, the offensiveness of the perpetrators' conduct seems to reside less in the harm to the victim or in grave breaches of the GV IV but in the blemish thereby caused to an otherwise untainted moral army. Indeed, even the perpetrators are not treated as war criminals: rather, they are men without whom "we would not have been able to sit here," and their significant contribution to the fight against Palestinian terror is not to be forgotten just because of a single moment, an exceptional moment, of "mischievous folly."[95]

Given that the reality is very different, the judicial text does not merely ignore it, but produces a narrative that replicates, and ipso facto augments, the problem. Indeed, the judgment fuses law and morality to conceal the ever-greater divide between the normative (detailed in the numerous and diversified sources on which the judgment relies to assert the ethical underpinnings of the IDF and of Israel) and the descriptive (evidence pertaining to widespread violations, coupled with a systematic lack of law enforcement). This normative/descriptive obfuscation fits neatly within the matrix of the occupation regime, and further contributes to the reversal of the relationship between the rule and the exception. The impact of such reversal on the very conditions of possibility for the rule of law, becomes evident once the legal discourse

[92] *Ibid.*, justice Rubinstein, ¶ 64.
[93] On the status of the right to demonstrate in the OPT, see Association for Civil Rights in Israel, *The Status of the Right to Demonstrate in the Occupied Territories* (2014), www.acri.org.il/en/wp-content/uploads/2014/12/Right-to-Demonstrate-in-the-OPT-FINAL.pdf.
[94] E.g., *Abu Rahme*, ¶¶ 72–73; justice Melcer, ¶¶ 11–12.
[95] *Ibid.*, justice Rubinstein, ¶¶ 1, 23 respectively.

meets the political/public discourse. This junction is the focus of the following section.

W.3 THE POLITICAL DISCOURSE: "THE CENTER CANNOT HOLD"[96]

On March 24, 2016, two Palestinians stabbed an IDF soldier and moderately wounded him in the Tel-Rumeida neighborhood in old Hebron.[97] Both were shot by IDF soldiers, resulting in the immediate death of one of them. The other, Abed al Fatah al-Sharif, was lying severely wounded and incapacitated on the road, yet still moving his head. Soldiers around him, including medics, refrained from offering him any medical treatment, and indeed ignored him altogether. Eleven minutes later, a soldier approached him and fired at his head from about three meters. None of the bystanders (IDF soldiers, medics, and settlers[98]) seems to have been perturbed by the execution.

The execution was videoed by a Palestinian, Imad Abushamsiya, and the video, distributed by B'Tselem, went viral on social media.[99] Subsequently, both a judicial process and a public controversy began: this ostensibly clear-cut war crime led to the prosecution of the soldier, Sergeant Elor Azaria, an IDF medic, before a court martial. In the light of the previous discussion, it is not surprising that he was not charged with a war crime, and not even with murder, but rather with manslaughter under the criminal code and with "conduct unbecoming a non-commissioned officer" under the Military Justice Act. The trial opened on May 9, 2016 and a judgment, rendered on January 4, 2017, convicted him of both offenses.[100] Azaria's lawyers announced they would appeal. Even before the judgment was rendered, the current minister of defense (Avigdor Lieberman) and minister of education (Naftali Bennet) alluded to a presidential pardon.[101] This allusion is part of the

---

[96] W.B. Yeats, "The Second Coming," in *The Collected Poems of W.B. Yeats* (London: Wordsworth Poetry Library, 2008), p. 158.

[97] On the situation in Hebron, see entry Z: Zone, Section Z.2.2.2.1.

[98] On the interaction between settlers and soldiers and its impact on the latter, see a report by Breaking the Silence, *The High Command: Settler Influence on IDF Conduct in the West Bank* (January 2017), www.breakingthesilence.org.il/inside/wp-content/uploads/2017/01/The-High-Command-Shovrim-Shtika-Report-January-2017.pdf.

[99] B'Tselem, Video: Soldier executes Palestinian lying injured on ground after the latter stabbed a soldier in Hebron (March 24, 2016), www.btselem.org/video/20160324_soldier_executes_palestinian_attacker_in_hebron.

[100] *Military Prosecutor v. Azaria.*

[101] A. Ben Zikri, "Lieberman Slams Israeli Media: A Soldier Can't Fulfill His Mission with a Lawyer beside Him," *Haaretz* (August 29, 2016), www.haaretz.com/israel-news/1.739222;

public controversy that has transformed the judicial process into a show trial even before it began, with the incident becoming "the Azaria Affair." This controversy is the focus of the present section.

The public discourse consists of three narratives: one narrative, advanced by the top echelons of the military, maintains that Azaria is an exception, a rotten apple: the shooting is a moral failure that, in the words of the chief of staff, "represents neither the IDF's nor Jewish values."[102] In this narrative, the IDF is under an obligation to take a moral stand even when that stand meets public outrage, and the soldier, who was motivated by a "twisted ideology,"[103] has to be held accountable.[104]

Tellingly, this "twisted ideology" appears to enjoy not only wide public support but also the approval of some of the major political players: thus, for instance, the minister of defense at the time of the incident, Yaalon, was fired by prime minister Netanyahu, pursuant to taking a position that supported the chief of staff's standing on the matter.[105] He was replaced by Lieberman, who publicly expressed support for Azaria, stating that it is unreasonable to expect IDF soldiers to go into battle with a lawyer and that resources should be devoted to fighting the enemy rather than to deterring Israeli soldiers from doing their job.[106] Prime minister Benjamin Netanyahu holds the rope at both ends: on the one hand, he stated that the incident deviates from the IDF's esprit de corps and that the open-fire instructions should be obeyed;[107] on the other hand, he telephoned Azaria's father to support him in his hour of need, replaced the minister of defense ostensibly for his standing on the matter, and called for the conduct of a "balanced" trial.[108] This position is silent on the interests that are to be balanced, but the silence echoes as it orchestrates the

---

H. Keinon, "Bennett Affirms: Azaria should be Pardoned," *Jerusalem Post* (October 10, 2016), www.jpost.com/Breaking-News/Bennett-affirms-Azaria-should-be-pardoned-469807.

[102] I. Sharon, "Netanyahu, Ya'alon Slam Hebron Shooting as IDF Vows Probe," *Times of Israel* (March 24, 2016), www.timesofisrael.com/idf-vows-probe-into-hebron-shooting-these-arent-jewish-values.

[103] B. Bryant, "Exclusive: Leaked IDF Report States Soldier Who Shot Palestinian Attacker Driven by 'Twisted Ideology'," *Vice News* (April 28, 2016), https://news.vice.com/article/exclusive-leaked-idf-report-states-soldier-who-shot-palestinian-attacker-driven-by-twisted-ideology-1.

[104] Sharon, "Netanyahu, Ya'alon Slam Hebron Shooting."

[105] Y. Karni, M. Azoulay, Y. Ziton, and K. Nachshony, "Ya'alon Leaves Defense Ministry: Netanyahu Abandoned Me," *ynet* (May 22, 2016), www.ynetnews.com/articles/0,7340,L-4806114,00.html.

[106] Ben Zikri, "Lieberman Slams Israeli Media."

[107] Sharon, "Netanyahu, Ya'alon Slam Hebron Shooting."

[108] T. Pileggi, "Netanyahu Urges 'Balance' in Trial for Hebron Shooter," *Times of Israel* (April 19, 2016), www.timesofisrael.com/netanyahu-urges-leniency-for-in-trial-for-hebron-shooter.

vocal public support for Azaria. The implicit directive to the judicial system undermines its credibility and independence.

Indeed, the Azaria Affair indicates that the very distinction between the center and the margins insofar as the occupation is concerned has become obscure if not altogether obsolete: it is the narrative of the IDF's leadership, the very body responsible for sustaining the occupation, which has become the gatekeeper of morality, the rule of law, and accountability, and attempts to represent the center, but the "center cannot hold":[109] the narrative presenting the execution as an exception to, rather than a reflection of the system and a realization of its values, is rejected as hypocritical by both the two other narratives.

The narrative of the "Azarian Camp," which a poll found comprises the majority of the Israeli public,[110] holds that not only had he done nothing wrong, but that he is indeed a role model, realizing the values of both Zionism and the IDF and heroically defending them against enemies within and without and against the culture of political correctness.[111] These values decree that a wounded soldier is not to be left behind in the battlefield; his comrades take care of him. The battlefield has simply been moved from the OPT to the judicial arena. In this narrative, bringing him to justice is a show trial against Zionism. Armed with this narrative, a former MP initiated a head-start project to finance Azaria's legal defense, raising within hours a very substantial amount.[112] Rallies attracting thousands of supporters identify with this narrative.[113] On September 30, 2016, the eve of the Jewish new-year, Azaria was selected by a major newspaper as "Man of the Year."[114] In this narrative, the killer is the victim.

From a normative perspective, in addition to attempts to exculpate Azaria, a young frightened soldier who acted in the heat of the moment in a complex situation, the main line of defense was "*tu quoquo*," that is, the defense attempted to discredit the validity of the prosecutor's – and the military

---

[109] Yeats, "The Second Coming."

[110] P. Beaumont, "Most Israelis Support Soldier Accused of Shooting Palestinian, Says Poll," *The Guardian* (March 29, 2016), www.theguardian.com/world/2016/mar/29/most-israelis-support-soldier-accused-of-shooting-palestinian.

[111] M. Lipman, "Elor Azaria: First Show Trial in Israel Against Zionism," *News1* (September 6, 2016), www.news1.co.il/Archive/003-D-114297-00.html [Hebrew].

[112] See www.headstart.co.il/project.aspx?id=19464.

[113] R. Mackey, "Thousands of Israelis rally in support of soldier who executed wounded Palestinian," *The Intercept* (April 20, 2016), https://theintercept.com/2016/04/19/thousands-israelis-rally-support-soldier-executed-wounded-palestinian.

[114] Y. Hollander, "People of the Year: Elor Azaria," *Makor Rishon* (September 28, 2016), www.makorrishon.co.il/?p=3998.

leadership's – narrative, by asserting the system's failure to act consistently with its alleged position in other cases.[115] Thus, the defense brought as witnesses a long line of retired generals who testified, both in court and publicly, that in similar cases of killing Palestinians, including cases where the victims did not assault Israeli soldiers and presented no danger whatsoever, no one was prosecuted.[116] The testimony of Gen. (retired) Uzi Dayan reflects succinctly the message the system has been consistently sending to the soldiers in this respect: "every terrorist has a death sentence over his head, regardless of whether or not they [*sic*] pose a risk at the moment ... I ordered to kill terrorists simply because they were terrorists, regardless of whether they endangered or didn't endanger."[117] Past generals testifying for the defense further expressed concern that the very prosecution of Azaria may cause other soldiers to refrain from shooting altogether as they would henceforth fear prosecution.[118]

The intimation is that the unwritten contract between the IDF and its soldiers is that Israel's security rests on the soldiers' knowledge that they are immune from prosecution.[119] A culture of impunity is thus the cornerstone of the occupation regime and is required for the proper functioning of the army sustaining it. Azaria is not an exception to this culture; he exemplifies its normative order. Data on the working of law enforcement in the OPT corroborate this narrative.[120]

The third narrative is identical to that of Azaria's defense from a descriptive perspective, but reflects its mirror image from a normative perspective: in this narrative, Azaria's conduct is indeed no exception; it merely exposes the routine criminality that sustaining the occupation entails. Azaria has committed a war crime, and should be held accountable, but the accountability is not his alone to shoulder: it resides also, and indeed primarily, with those

---

[115]   Interestingly, this was the line of defense chosen by Klaus Barbie's lawyer, Jacques Vergès, to critique the hypocrisy of the French State in accusing Barbie of racist acts that had been routine parts of its own colonial warfare, particularly in Algiers. See Koskenniemi, "Between Impunity and Show Trials," pp. 29–31.

[116]   "No MAG, No Military Police and Nobody Else," *Arutz* 7 (July 27, 2016), www.inn.co.il/Ne ws/News.aspx/327040.

[117]   JNi.Media, "Former Deputy Chief of Staff: Every Day Sgt. Azaria is On Trial Damages the IDF," *The Jewish Press* (September 19, 2016), www.jewishpress.com/news/breaking-news/for mer-deputy-chief-of-staff-every-day-sgt-azaria-is-on-trial-damages-the-idf/2016/09/19.

[118]   S. Pulwer, "Officer in Hebron Shooter's Company Says Other Soldiers Now Gun-Shy," *Haaretz* (September 2, 2016), www.haaretz.com/israel-news/.premium-1.739870.

[119]   D. Zonsheine, "The Israeli Military's Unspoken Contract with its Soldiers," *Haaretz* (September 12, 2016), www.haaretz.com/opinion/.premium-1.741101.

[120]   See above text and notes 36–37. For comprehensive analysis of the law-enforcement system, see entry I: Investigations.

responsible for normalizing the occupation,[121] including the military and political leadership whose narrative, as discussed earlier, attempts to designate Azaria's conduct as the exception rather than as a normal, and indeed inevitable consequence of the occupation.[122]

Both this narrative and the narrative of Azaria's supporters thus agree that Azaria is a scapegoat and that his prosecution is a clear case of selective enforcement. Where they differ is in the direction of the punch to the soft belly of the culture of impunity the Azaria Affair is dealing in: the camp which unfolds the third narrative wishes to expose it; Azaria's supporters wish to seal it. This difference becomes palpable in the reaction of each camp to disclosure of evidence that Azaria's conduct is anything but exceptional: members of the "Azaria camp" threatened the life of the Palestinian photographer who videoed the execution of al-Sharif,[123] and, more broadly, they and their representatives in government and in parliament are designating Israeli soldiers who attest to the routine violations of the Geneva Law as traitors.[124]

The predicament of the legal system is clear: it cannot, by definition, endorse a culture of impunity, and must therefore frame the Azaria case as an exception and extract the incident from the context of the occupation. At the same time, this very framing not only augments the culture of impunity which it denies, but also fails to convince, let alone affect, public consciousness across the political spectrum. It is little wonder that, under these circumstances, the judgment did not bring the issue to a close.

The judgment, consisting of 309 paragraphs, is solidly based on evidence and applicable law. The court martial acknowledges at the very beginning that "the affair has generated wide public interest and extensive public debate," and proceeds to state that this debate is irrelevant to its determination, which is based solely on the legal and factual arguments and evidence submitted to it.[125] For the purposes of the present discussion, it is sufficient to highlight

---

[121] H. El-Ad, "A Once-in-a-Decade Show Trial," +972 (September 7, 2016), http://972mag.com /a-once-in-a-decade-show-trial/121768.

[122] Feldman, "'Neutralize' a Terrorist?" See also, J. Cook, "Execution of Palestinian exposes Israel's military culture," *Common Dreams* (April 3, 2016), http://commons.commondreams .org/t/execution-of-palestinian-exposes-israel-s-military-culture/20627.

[123] J. Brown, "Threats to Life of Photographer Who Documented the Shooting of Azaria in Hebron," *Local Conversation* (September 2, 2016), goo.gl/ohHQVF [Hebrew].

[124] The public reaction to "Breaking the Silence," an Israeli NGO that collects and publicizes testimonies from ex IDF soldiers relative to the nature of the actions they routinely perform in the OPT, is a case at point. See, e.g., A. Pfeffer, "Why Breaking the Silence became the Most Hated Group in Israel," *Haaretz* (December 17, 2015), www.haaretz.com/israel-news/ .premium-1.692373.

[125] *Military Prosecutor v. Azaria,* ¶ 4.

briefly some narrative and normative aspects of the judgment that together suggest the nomos of the court.

From a narrative perspective, two points are noteworthy. First, the court refers consistently and amply (312 times) to the victim as "the terrorist." Inversely, there is not one reference to the occupation. Given that the victim, Abed al Fatah al-Sharif, attacked an armed soldier, not a civilian, he does not qualify as a terrorist. The implication, well attuned with both public perception and other judicial narratives, is that a Palestinian is indistinguishable from a terrorist. Second, given further that al-Sharif, a civilian presumably engaged in this attack as an act of resistance to the soldiers' role in sustaining the occupation, the omission of any judicial reference to the occupation extracts the events from their context.

Two points merit attention from a normative perspective. First, the judgment, having rejected all Azaria's defenses and justifications, concluded that Azaria shot "the terrorist" in the head with the intention to kill him, or, in his own words, because "he deserved to die," and convicted him of manslaughter.[126] The judgment refers neither to international law nor to war crimes. Indeed, given that the elements of the crime as determined by the court suggest murder, rather than manslaughter, the judgment refrains from referring to that possibility as well. Second, the rejection by the court of the "selective enforcement" defense is the weakest normative link in an otherwise solid judgment: the defense relied on two cases to establish this argument: the relevance of the first was dismissed by the court martial because the HCJ determined that the soldier honestly believed that the Palestinian presented a threat to life. The second case related to a 2015 shooting in the head of a 17-year-old Palestinian, Muhamad el-Kasbah, by Col. Israel Shumar. Pursuant to the MAG's decision, neither a disciplinary nor a criminal process was pursued in this case. In the Azaria judgment, the court determined that, despite the fact that parts of the MAG's opinion were transmitted to the defense, the latter failed to use it to support its argument.[127] This judicial position is unconvincing: given that the MAG decided to close the case, it is obvious that his opinion was of no use to the defense. The court concludes this part of the judgment by stating, correctly, that in order to establish "selective enforcement" it is not enough to point to one case, and that the accused has to show that "over time and systematically (or close to that) the decisions of the administrative authorities in similar cases were different than those made in the case at hand."[128] It is true that the defense failed to do that. It does not follow, as was discussed earlier, that the reason it has thus failed is lack of

---

[126]   *Ibid.*, ¶¶ 298–299.   [127]   *Ibid.*, ¶¶ 236–242.   [128]   *Ibid.*, ¶ 243.

evidence of systematic failure over time of law enforcement over Israelis in the OPT.

The last substantive paragraphs of the judgment determine that Azaria is guilty of "conduct unbecoming" as well. In this context, the court cites at length and reiterates excerpts from the above-discussed *Abu Rahme* judgment relative to the importance of "upholding the rule of law and recognizing human rights which characterize the concept of democracy at the core of the Israeli system of government" and to the observation that "the spirit of moral character of the IDF depends, *inter alia*, on safeguarding purity of arms and respect for the individual whoever he is."[129] The discussion thus far suggests an inverse relation between the exceptional rites of judicial purification and the routine staining of the "purity of arms" ethos. In this sense, the Azaria judgment is a show trial. Azaria is a cog in the machine, not its engineer. It is thus little wonder that the judgment did not generate any change in the above-discussed narratives. Worse still, the court martial seems to have been attentive to the popular narrative far more than the other way around: having convicted Azaria on January 4, 2017, of manslaughter, an offense which carries a maximum penalty of twenty-years' imprisonment, it sentenced him, on February 21, 2017, to 18 months in prison.[130] The culture of impunity inhabits the gap between the possible and the actual sentence.

The historical judgment on the functioning of the legal and judicial processes, even when they reach a well-grounded legal conclusion, is likely to pronounce them guilty of having failed to deliver either truth or justice.

W.4 CONCLUSION: THE NORM AND ITS DISCONTENT

A culture of impunity may, but does not necessarily, signify disregard for law: it may well be that its progenitors are a regime characterized by the reversal of the relationship between the rule and the exception, and a particular nomos, a political space comprising both rules and the narrative which gives them meaning. Once the exceptional regime and the nomos are joined, a space is created where the exception and the rule, the fact and the norm, are indistinguishable.[131] The culture of impunity generated by this union does not signify disregard for law, but rather that law itself has become

---

[129] *Ibid.*, ¶¶ 303–308 (citing *Abu Rahme*, ¶¶ 89–90).
[130] MilC Center 182/16 *Military Prosecutor v. Azaria* (February 21, 2017). The sentence also included a suspended one-year sentence and demotion from the rank of sergeant to the rank of private.
[131] Cover, "Nomos and Narrative."

interchangeable with a certain political morality and is at once all pervasive and meaningless.

In the context of the Israeli control over the OPT, law is all pervasive in the sense that both the military and the public discourses justify military actions in reference to legal terms such as proportionality, deterrence, necessity, obeying orders, and self-defense. Law, at least in the conventional understanding of the rule of law, is meaningless insofar as these references are made to circumvent legal constraints, not to constrain military conduct.

IDF soldiers have been told by the highest court in the country that each of them "carries in his backpack the norms of customary public international law which deal with the laws of war as well as the basic norms of the Israeli administrative law";[132] they have been told by former and current chiefs of staff that the IDF is "the most moral army in the world"; and they have been interacting closely with settlers and told by some of their rabbis that Jewish law decrees the permissibility of committing crimes against Palestinians with impunity.[133] Equipped with these discursive messages, they also engage in practical operations the legality of which, they are aware, while dubious at best, will invariably be rationalized in legal terms and entail no accountability.[134] This legal consciousness is a product of, and reproduces a culture of impunity.[135]

Having endowed the practice of rule breaking with an aura of rule keeping, Israeli law enforcement mechanisms have been complicit in the construction of this culture.[136] Once thus implicated, their fidelity to a conventional understanding of the rule of law which would compel them to designate perpetrators of grave breaches as exceptions, would clash with the unconventional understanding of the rule of law they have otherwise endorsed. The net result would be both an engagement in a show trial and the perpetuation of criminal normality.

---

[132] See, e.g., HCJ 393/82 *Almalmon v. the Commander* of the IDF, 37(4) PD 785, 810 [Hebrew].

[133] See Institute for Middle East Understanding, *A Culture of Impunity: Violence against Non-Jews in Israel & the Occupied Territories* (2012), http://imeu.org/article/a-culture-of-impunity-violence-against-non-jews-in-israel-the-occupied-terr, listing 11 cases of Incitement by Jewish Religious Leaders, only in 2010–2012.

[134] For an illuminating analysis of the various constructions of legal consciousness of IDF soldiers based on testimonies of ex-soldiers by Breaking the Silence, see M. Zagor, "'I am the Law!' – Perspectives of Legality and Illegality in the Israeli Army" (2010) 43 *Israel Law Review* 551.

[135] On the production of legal consciousness see P. Ewick and S.S. Silbey, "The Social Construction of Legality" in *The Common Place of Law: Stories from Everyday Life* (Chicago: University of Chicago Press, 1998), p. 43; see also Introduction, Section 2.4.

[136] On this "organizational decoupling" of rules and practices, see J. Ron, "Savage Restraint: Israel, Palestine and the Dialectics of Legal Repression" (2000) 47 *Social Problems* 445, 452–453.

X

X Rays

Orna Ben-Naftali

X.1 GENERAL: THE GAZE

X rays are a form of electromagnetic radiation. Discovered in 1895, they have since been put to numerous beneficial medical and scientific uses, covering the gamut from diagnostics to dental care, cancer treatment to cosmic explorations.[1] They also present health hazards and have been classified as a carcinogen. While the long-term health risks of low-level radiation remain to be determined, research concluded that the more radiation a person gets, even if in small dozes at a time, the greater the increase in her/his cumulative risk of dying of cancer, and that the risk of radiation is greater to fetuses.[2]

Due to their ability to penetrate and offer a visualization of certain otherwise concealed materials, they are commonly used for medical imaging, for various evaluation and testing applications, for military purposes, and for transportation security inspections of cargo, luggage, and passengers. This ability, well captured in the metaphor of having "X-ray vision," connotes a power to "see though" objects and people, to reveal their secrets and expose their true nature. The various ways in which Israel exercises this power over the Palestinians are explored in this entry.

The power of an omniscient gaze, hitherto assigned to divine providence (or to magic), currently serves another theology, the security theology.[3] The latter is a conceptual paradigm that sees the world as divided between those who

---

[1] See, e.g., British Medical Association, A-Z *Family Medical Encyclopedia* (London: DK, 2014), p. 811.

[2] Committee on Airport Passenger Screening: Backscatter X-Ray Machines, *Airport Passenger Screening Using Backscatter X-Ray Machines: Compliance with Standards* (Washington, DC: National Academies Press, 2015).

[3] On the term "security theology," see Y. Berda, "The Security Risk as a Security Risk: Notes on the Classification and Practices of the Israeli Security Services," in A. Baker and A. Matar (eds.), *Threat: Palestinian Political Prisoners in Israel* (London: Pluto Press, 2011), pp. 44–55;

present a security risk and those who do not. Such schematic friend/foe division is characteristic of fundamentalist theologies and while originally conceived as closely affiliated with nondemocratic politics, it is increasingly penetrating democracies as well.[4] Its primary edict is to eliminate the risk. Obeying it requires the power, the authorization and the means to classify individuals, groups, and populations accordingly. Such classification, involving technologies of identification, surveillance, and profiling, is currently known as "risk management,"[5] a title suggesting that the management of a risk is preferred to, or at least more achievable than, the resolution of the conflict from which the risk emanates. The construction of the category of "objective enemies" is coherent with this preference.[6] This entry focuses on Israel's practices of risk management in relation to its conflict with the Palestinians.

Israel is not the only state to be concerned with risk management: perceived threats from refugees, immigrants, and terrorists have been interwoven into a suspect class of fearsome people, generating a global security obsession and a sense of insecurity that feeds a booming security industry.[7] Israel is a key player in this security market and has positioned itself as a successful model of a security state that is also democratic: with a population of only eight million, it ranks among the five largest weapons and surveillance technologies global exporters.[8] This success is due to various factors, including its close alliance with the United States, which has opened up markets for its products, and the

N. Shalhoub-Kevorkian, *Security Theology, Surveillance and the Politics of Fear* (Cambridge: Cambridge University Press, 2015), pp. 16–20.

[4] C. Schmitt, *The Concept of the Political*, Expanded Edition, G. Schwab (trans.) (Chicago: University of Chicago Press, 2007), pp. 26–57. The global reach of the security theology and the related of practice of risk management by democratic states is discussed in Section X.3.

[5] See entry F: Future-Oriented Measures.

[6] On the notion of "objective enemies" who, due to who they are in terms of their group affiliation, rather than to what each of them does, are perceived as tending to present a danger to the security of the state, and on the role of the secret service in their identification, indeed production, see H. Arendt, *The Origins of Totalitarianism* (Cleveland: Meridian Books, 1958), pp. 423–430.

[7] On the weaving together of crime, immigration, and terror into a paradigm of suspicion, see R. Shamir, "Without Borders? Notes on Globalization as a Mobility Regime" (2015) 23 *Sociological Theory* 197.

[8] See N. Gordon, "Working Paper III: The Political Economy of Israel's Homeland Security/ Surveillance Industry," *The New Transparency* (April 28, 2009), www.sscqueens.org/sites/defa ult/files/The%20Political%20Economy%20of%20Israel%E2%80%99s%20Homeland%20Secu rity.pdf; The Israel Export & International Cooperation Institute, *Israel Homeland Security Industry* (2012), www.export.gov.il/uploadfiles/11_2012/cyber%20security_pages.pdf; G. Cohen, "Israel is World's Largest Exporter of Drones, Study Finds," *Haaretz* (May 19, 2013), www .haaretz.com/israel-news/israel-is-world-s-largest-exporter-of-drones-study-finds.premium-1.524 771. Israel's export of weapons and surveillance systems extends also to governments engaged in

intimate collaboration characterizing the relationship between its military and industrial sectors.[9] But mainly, it is due to its experience and expertise in the production, deployment, and use of both weapons and surveillance-related technologies in the laboratory known as the OPT.[10]

Profiling, inscribing on the human body a designated category of collective suspicion – usually assigned to minorities within a given society – stands at the apex of present-day surveillance technology. Israel has been using it in relation to its Arab/Palestinian citizens from the early days of the state, extended it to the permit regime governing Palestinian movement between the OPT and Israel and within the OPT, perfected it in its airports, and exported it globally as a successful risk management tool. Thus, a practice originally justified on the basis of the military regime which was imposed on Arab citizens of Israel between 1948 and 1966,[11] has since 1967 been extended to all areas under Israeli control and exported globally.[12]

Indeed, the logic underlying the use of surveillance technologies employed by Israel to control the Palestinians, is the same logic of exclusion driving the global risk-management society and its mobility regime: just as the mobility regime is in effect an immobility regime,[13] the surveillance technologies, which make the Palestinians utterly visible, are used in order to ensure their invisibility. This type of exclusionary gaze, the colonial legacy of which is palpable[14] even

---

grave violations of human rights and crimes against humanity, such as South Sudan. See, e.g., *Final Report of the Panel of Experts on South Sudan Established Pursuant to Security Council resolution 2206 (2015)* (January 22, 2016), www.un.org/ga/search/view_doc.asp?symbol=S/2016/70. A petition made by MP Tamar Sandberg against the Israeli Defense Minister, requesting the HCJ to cancel or at least suspend the license to export surveillance systems to South Sudan, has been rejected (HCJ 3893/16; judgment was not published due to a gag order).

9 See N. Gordon, "Israel's Emergence as a Homeland Security Capital," in E. Zureik, D. Lyon, and Y. Abu-Laban (eds.), *Surveillance and Control in Israel/Palestine: Population, Territory and Power* (Oxford: Routledge, 2011), p. 153 [hereinafter: *Surveillance and Control*].

10 See entry E: Export of Knowledge.

11 See, e.g., I. S. Lustick, *Arabs in the Jewish State: Israel's Control of a National Minority* (Austin: University of Texas Press, 1980); A. Korn, "Crime and Legal Control: The Israeli Arab Population during the Military Government Period (1948–66)" (2000) 40 *British Journal of Criminology* 574.

12 See entry O: Outside/Inside.   13 See entry Z: Zone, Section Z.2.3.2.

14 Surveillance literature notes three (and somewhat overlapping) types of surveillance: (a) "colonial surveillance," referring to the then new administrative means and methods and the use of statistics to discipline population considered antagonistic to the ruler, see M. Foucault, *Security, Territory, Population*, M Senellart (ed.), G. Burchell (trans.) (New York: Palgrave Macmillan, 2007), p. 35. On the colonial gaze which "corresponds to the grand-autre [the process of Othering, whereby the colonizer's self-affirmation and identity construction is configured on the basis of stigmatizing and denigrating the identity of the Other, the colonized]," see B. Ashcroft, G. Griffiths, and H. Tiffin, *Post-Colonial Studies: The Key Concepts* (Oxford: Routledge, 1998), p. 226; (b) "inclusive surveillance," indicating

when camouflaged in a sophisticated actuarial jargon,[15] is a far cry from the use of inclusive surveillance technologies by modern democratic states, technologies the stated purposes of which are to embrace, protect, and enable the free movement of citizens under normal circumstances. The globalization of exclusionary surveillance attests to both the obfuscation of the alleged distinction between emergency situations and normal times, and to the risk a risk-management society presents to democratic values.[16]

Within democratic regimes, the tension between security and human rights wrought by surveillance technologies is usually framed in terms of the right to privacy. Given that the concept underlying privacy, be it the right to be left alone or the right to have control over one's life,[17] is individually based, the right to privacy provides a fairly inadequate basis for countering group surveillance – that is, profiling. This is a fortiori the case when surveillance is undertaken in the context of a belligerent occupation, where it is embedded in a comprehensive control system exercised by a state which even within its own internationally recognized borders, maintains a permanent emergency situation since its inception. Israel is such a state, and it is thus not surprising that its political and legal culture has internalized the security discourse in a manner that far too often trumps human rights.[18]

In order to substantiate these propositions, Section X.2 offers a brief survey of some of the main surveillance technologies employed by Israel and their modus operandi in the OPT. Section X.3 focuses on profiling the Palestinian population and the role law has played in this respect. Section X.4 concludes with a reflection on the genealogy of the biopolitical "objective enemy" in risk-

---

a shift from disciplinary societies to control societies where gathering of information through, for instance, passports and identity cards is used to benefit the population; and (c) "exclusionary surveillance," whose objective is to identify specific groups in order to exclude them from the rest, the primary example being the Apartheid regime. See A. Handel, "Exclusionary Surveillance and Spatial Uncertainty in the Occupied Palestinian Territories," in *Surveillance and Control*, p. 259.

[15] On profiling as a technology which fuses the insurance-oriented risk-management techniques and sentencing paradigms used by the criminal justice system, see Shamir, *Without Borders*, pp. 210–211.

[16] For the judicial discourse in the US on the dilemmas wrought by the globalization of the policy and practice of racial/religious profiling, see, e.g., Center for Constitutional Rights, Supreme Court to review case against Ashcroft and other Bush officials for post 9–11 racial and religious profiling (October 11, 2016), https://ccrjustice.org/home/press-center/press-releases/s upreme-court-review-case-against-ashcroft-and-other-bush-officials.

[17] See *Olmstead v. United States*, 277 US 438 (1928); A. F. Westin, *Privacy and Freedom* (London: The Bodley Head, 1970).

[18] Israel has been in a declared state of emergency since its establishment. A petition to the HCJ requesting it to terminate the prolonged state of emergency was rejected in 2012, HCJ 3091/99 *The Association for Civil Rights in Israel v. The Knesset* (May 8, 2012) [Hebrew].

management societies; the means, including the legal mechanisms that facilitate its construction in Israel, and the relationship between the profile of the enemy thus generated and the democratic profile of the society.

X.2 ISRAEL'S SURVEILLANCE TECHNOLOGIES: DETECTING THE RISK VIRUS

X.2.1 *General*

The Palestinians inhabit a surveilled nomos[19] wherein Israel's power is ever-present in time, space, and perception: they are surveilled by state agencies, by private individuals, and by machines; by nontechnical means as well as by low-tech and hi-tech means; their experience and consciousness, body and mind, are subject not only to the direct gaze of the panopticon designed to ensure that each individual assumes that s/he is being constantly surveilled, thus internalizing the disciplinary gaze,[20] but also to the indirect, postpanopticon gaze[21] that subjects them to statistical analysis and restructures their identity as carriers of the risk virus. The Ariande's thread weaving through these various practices reflects the logic and the objectives of the material occupation of the land: to fragment the land (West Bank) or disengage from it while practically sealing it from the world (Gaza Strip),[22] to exclude and dehumanize the people and to debilitate their capacity to create and sustain a political community, let alone exercise anything other than simulated sovereignty. The various means and methods of surveillance discussed below do not exhaust the arsenal but are nevertheless sufficient to substantiate this assessment.

X.2.2 *Direct Surveillance: People Watching People*

People watching people is the most traditional system of surveillance. Israel has created spy networks and embedded them within its local Arab

---

[19]   See R. Cover, "The Supreme Court, 1982 Term – Foreword: Nomos and Narrative" (1983–1984) 97 *Harvard Law Review* 4, 24–25 (Defining "Nomos" as the normative universe which we inhabit, a universe comprised of law and narrative and held by interpretive commitments regarding what the law means). See entry N: Nomos.

[20]   M. Foucault, *Discipline and Punish: The Birth of the Prison*, A. Sheridan (trans.) (New York: Vintage Books, 1995), pp. 195–230.

[21]   A. Martziano, "A Critical Reflection on the Israeli Biometric Project" (2016) 46 *Theory and Criticism* 41, 44 [Hebrew].

[22]   See entry Z: Zone, section Z.2.2.1–2. Note that the impact of the Oslo Accords on the fragmentation of the OPT, discussed in entry Z: Zone, spreads to other means of control, including surveillance technologies, as is substantiated in the following discussion.

communities since 1948. Comprising Arab collaborators seduced or coerced to cooperate due to economic and personal reasons, they have been gathering information about opposition groups; Palestinians refugees from 1948 and 1967 who attempted to come back; the presumed loyalty of Arab teachers, etc. An added value of this system was the sowing of suspicion within the communities – that is, the advantage inherent in the tried and true "'divide-and-rule" method.[23] Since 1967, a similar surveillance system has been operating in the OPT, where information about available Palestinian land has been added to the list of necessary knowledge, and where, since the institution of the permit regime, there are ever-greater opportunities to coerce Palestinians into collaboration.[24] At times, special undercover units comprising IDF soldiers dressed in civilian clothes and pretending to be Arabs, have been used in Palestinian villages in Israel and in the OPT for both the gathering of information and for combat action. The Israeli supreme court had related occasionally to the consequences of such operations in the OPT, but did not discuss issues relative to the very legality of operations that clearly defy the principle of distinction and may well amount to forbidden perfidity.[25]

X.2.3 Technological Surveillance 1.0: Identity Documents

Face-to-face surveillance is complemented with technical surveillance systems. Identity documents (IDs) exemplify an initially low-tech, though increasingly digitized and biometricized, such system. These documents are instruments of bureaucratic control used by modern states to render their

---

[23] See E. Zureik, "Colonialism, Surveillance and Population Control: Israel/Palestine" in *Surveillance and Control*, pp. 18–21.

[24] See entry Z: Zone, section Z.2.3.2; Y. Berda, *The Bureaucracy of the Occupation: The Permit Regime in the West Bank* (Tel Aviv: Van Leer Institute, 2012) [Hebrew], pp. 137–141.

[25] Such undercover military unites are known as "Mista'arvim." In *Ex Parter Quirin*, 317 US 1 (1942) the US supreme court designated such soldiers as "unlawful combatants." For a critique of that notion, see entry C: Combatants. Soldiers who are captured while undercover lose their combatants' privileges. Perfidity is prohibited under Article 23 of The Hague Convention (IV) Respecting the Laws and Customs of War on Land and its annex: Regulations concerning the Laws and Customs of War on Land, The Hague, October 18, 1907, 205 CTS 277; 36 Stat 2277, and Article 37 of the Protocol Additional to the Geneva Conventions of August 12, 1949, and relating to the Protection of Victims of International Armed Conflicts (Additional Protocol I), Geneva, June 8, 1977, 1125 UNTS 3 [hereinafter: *AP I*]. For Israeli judgments that dealt with the consequences of such operations in the OPT see e.g., CA 3569/03 *Savaana* v. *Military Commander in the West Bank* (November 4, 2010) [Hebrew]; CA 3866/07 *State of Israel* v. *Almakusi* (March 21, 2012) [Hebrew]; HCJ 474/02 *Thabet* v. *Attorney General* of Israel (January 30, 2011) [Hebrew].

population legible: to supervise growth, social composition, spatial distributions, and the granting or withholding of rights and entitlements, covering the
whole gamut from suffrage through welfare, health, and education to family
rights.[26] In the OPT, they regulate mobility and residency far more than they
bestow rights.

Israel introduced mandatory IDs upon its establishment in 1948. Those IDs
detailed the ethnic/national identity of the holder. That designation was
removed in 2002, only to be replaced by differentiating numerical codes
conveying the same information. Upon establishing its control over the OPT
in 1967, Israel introduced IDs for Palestinians in the West Bank and Gaza,
which differ in both color and numerical codes from those issued to its own
citizens as well as from those issued to Palestinian residents of East Jerusalem.
In 1989, the IDF required workers from Gaza to carry a magnetic card as
a precondition to enter Israel or the settlements. As of 1991, all Palestinians
residing in the OPT must have an individual permit to enter Israel, including
East Jerusalem. Since then, magnetic cards are required for all OPT residents
above the age of 16.[27] Up to 2007, the magnetic card indicated that its holder
was not designated by either the police or the General Security Services (GSS)
as a security threat. Thereafter, it was given to all Palestinians, including those
who have been classified as a security threat. The reason is twofold: first, since
2005, the magnetic card has been biometricized and includes fingerprints and
a photo, information that Israel wants; second, the magnetic card – much like
the ID, and indeed even a work permit – provides no guarantee of entry; it is
merely a prerequisite for such entry. These regulations – as the different color
coding evidences – signify a policy of controlling through fragmentation of
territory and people and controlling different populations unevenly in terms of
rights allocation. This reflects the logic of the regime, a logic that the Oslo
process did not challenge. Quite tellingly, in 1994, and pursuant to the Oslo
Accords, the PA began issuing IDs and travel documents. The numbers it uses,
however, are allocated by Israel. This simulated Palestinian sovereignty thus
both conceals and attests to the real, ever-present locus of power.

It is impossible to meet any of the necessities of daily existence, from
registering birth and death to applying for a job, without an ID. Coupled
with the permit regime, the ID is also an internal travel document, determining eligibility for mobility within various parts of the OPT, to East Jerusalem
and to Israel. The ID thus effectively controls both how and where

---

[26] H. Tawil-Souri, "Colored Identity: The Politics and Materiality of ID Cards in Palestine/
      Israel" (2011) 29 *Social Text* 67, 73.
[27] On the link between IDs and the mobility regime, see entry Z: Zone, Section Z.2.2.3.1.

a Palestinian can go about the business of making a life and making a living. In that sense it defines, confines, and borders identity.[28] IDs must be carried at all times. The penalty for having been unable to present it upon the request of every soldier and other authorized personnel is up to one year imprisonment, and they are authorized to confiscate it. Given that it is impossible to function without it, the power to confiscate does not even have to be exercised; the mere threat is sufficient to guarantee obedience.[29] This power further signifies that the ID is not necessarily proof of the legal identity of its Palestinian holder, but rather a text open to interpretation and ergo producing uncertainty and angst.[30]

The site where the controlling, excluding, and immobilizing nature of this tactile technology is most obvious is the physical barrier. "[T]he Palestinian experience," as Rashid Khalidi observed some three decades ago, "takes place at a border, an airport, a checkpoint: in short, at any of those modern barriers where identities are checked and verified."[31] This experience as it takes place at the modern, technologically enhanced checkpoints known as "terminals" is the focus of the next section.

X.2.4 Technological Surveillance 2.0: The Terminal

The terminals are a relatively new form of modernized checkpoint. Situated along the separation barrier, they echo its logic in two significant ways: first, in securing the border without securing an agreement on Israel's borderline, in effect simulating a border on Palestinian Territory;[32] second, in availing Israel of the power to remote-control the Palestinians through surveillance technologies.

Israel, as noted by Eyal Weizman, "sees through" the Wall: in the areas where the barrier consists of fences, it is located on a higher terrain which allows for spatial and population control through visual domination; in areas where it is made of concrete, the walls are equipped with a variety of vision and radar sensors directed at Palestinians on the other side.[33] The terminals,

---

[28] Tawil-Souri, "Colored Identity," pp. 77, 89–90.
[29] N. Abu Zhara, "Identity Cards and Coercion in Palestine," in R. Pain and S. Smith (eds.), *Fear: Critical Geopolitics in Everyday Life* (Farnham: Ashgate, 2008), pp. 175, 177–180, 189.
[30] Zureik, "Colonialism, Surveillance and Population Control," p. 30. On un/certainty governance, see entry M: Military Courts.
[31] R. Khalidi, *Palestinian Identity: The Construction of Modern National Consciousness* (New York: Columbia University Press, 1997), p. 1.
[32] Tawil-Souri, "Colored Identity," p. 70.
[33] E. Weizman, "Seeing through Walls: The Split Sovereign and the One Way Mirror" (2006) 24 *Grey Room* 89, 96.

constructed since 2005, rely heavily on technology and are equipped with a myriad of technological devices, including security cameras, electric turnstiles made of iron, x-ray machines, and biometric identification devices. Communication with the soldiers and, more recently, with the private security guards who replaced them, is conducted via an intercom, allowing the security personnel to remain invisible. These devices are ostensibly designed to minimize friction and appear to offer more humane conditions than those that exist in the traditional checkpoints.[34]

Appearances, however, are notoriously deceiving.[35] This particular charade begins upon arrival: on first sight the terminal resembles any international terminal, complete with digital "welcome" signs and covered with peace slogans. It takes some mental effort to recall that they are located within the OPT rather than on an internationally recognized border; that they extend welcome greetings not to international visitors but to local Palestinians attempting to go about their daily business, a business which the terminal disrupts; and that the peace slogans do not reflect reality, but rather camouflage the face of the occupation as they sustain its violence.

The Palestinian who has turned a blind eye, so to speak, to this dissonance, as she invariably does, enters through barricaded walkways, passes through the electronic turnstiles, scans her magnetic card, submits her paperwork, and passes through detection – both x-ray and biometric machines. Each of these sign-spots is prone to functioning in a somewhat skewed manner. First, unless she is classified as a VIP and is directed to a special lane, she has to follow a lane which corresponds to her place of residence, as there are separate and differently colored lanes which replicate the differently colored IDs that, in turn, reflect as they reinforce the Oslo zoning of the OPT. If she is lucky, all lanes would be open; otherwise, a lane may be shut down while people are waiting, invariably causing the very havoc the orderly structure of the terminal was intended to prevent.[36]

Second, once she passes through the electronic turnstiles, if she happens to be with a child, has to use a walking aid, or simply carries a bag, she is likely to get stuck. This is so because the turnstiles are tighter than the acceptable standard and there is little room between their metal arms. Consequently, the

[34] H. Kotef and M. Amir, "Between Imaginary Lines: Violence and Its Justifications at the Military Checkpoints in Occupied Palestine" (2011) 28 *Theory, Culture and Society* 55, 70.

[35] See judge Krylov in his dissenting opinion in Conditions of Admission of a State to Membership in The United Nations, Advisory Opinion, 1948 ICJ 57, 107.

[36] Zureik, "Colonialism, Surveillance and Population Control," pp. 31–32.

seemingly orderly arrangement habitually collapses into chaos as inevitably people get trapped and bags burst open.[37]

Third, it is not uncommon for the magnetic card to fail to display the coded information due to technical problems related to the wear of the magnetic stripe.[38] Technical problems may also beset the detection machines to which she has to submit her body along the terminal's via dolorosa: the biometric checks of fingerprints and palm-prints, ensuring that the Israeli databases would be more complete than the Palestinian's,[39] all too often do not recognize the person, especially if the person happens to make a living through manual labor, which tends to render the fingerprints and palm-prints less legible.[40] Many of the Palestinians passing through the terminal are thus engaged.

X-ray machines, a technology designed to undress us while we are dressed, also tend toward dysfunction, especially when a person sweats, a fairly common reaction to the environmental and presumably also the psychological conditions on site.[41] On such occasions, the person is requested to pass through the machine several times and ultimately to undergo a physical search and undress down to her underwear. The process is both humiliating and time consuming, and may well result in a loss of the transport to work that awaits on the other side of the promised land, and thus in the waste of a day's work.[42]

The need to submit to this technology has also generated health concerns. These range from requests for a medical certificate that the machines do not present a health hazard made by Palestinians who attribute their failing health to frequent radiation as they are exposed to it regularly and, at times, more than once a day,[43] to complaints that even pregnant women and people, including children, who have medical certificates stating that health reasons

---

[37] E. Weizman, *Hollow Land: Israel's Architecture of Occupation* (London: Verso, 2007), pp. 150–151; Kotef and Amir, "Between Imaginary Lines," pp. 71–73.

[38] See, e.g., Check Point Watch Organization (CPWO) Report, Tarqumia Checkpoint, June 9, 2013, https://machsomwatch.org/he/node/21692 [Hebrew].

[39] Weizman, "Seeing through Walls," 96.

[40] CPWO Report, Etzion Checkpoint, July 11, 2013, https://machsomwatch.org/he/reports/check points/11072016/morning/53461 [Hebrew]; Azun Atma Checkpoint, May 20, 2013, https://ma chsomwatch.org/he/node/21517 [Hebrew].

[41] CPWO Report, Tarqumia checkpoint, June 10, 2013, https://machsomwatch.org/he/node/216 15 [Hebrew].

[42] CPWO Report, Etzion checkpoint, July 11, 2013; Tarqumia checkpoint June 9, 2013; Barta'a checkpoint, January 11, 2011, https://machsomwatch.org/he/node/16357 [Hebrew].

[43] CPWO Report, Hashmona'yim checkpoint, February 18, 2014, https://machsomwatch.org/he/ node/23288 [Hebrew]; Artach Checkpoint, February 9, 2011, https://machsomwatch.org/he/n ode/16583 [Hebrew].

exempt them from undergoing the radiation are forced to pass through such machines.[44] These requests and complaints remain unheeded, and no legal process has been initiated in their respect. Interestingly, concerns over loss of privacy associated with a technology that strips people and deprives them of their control over their own bodies – concerns that were translated into judicial proceedings in Western countries, and surely an issue of particular sensitivity in traditional communities – have not been recorded, and no legal proceedings have been initiated in Israel. This may not be altogether surprising given that courts faced with such claims tend to give preference to national security over the right to privacy.[45]

Passage through some of the terminals turns into a truly uncanny experience when the person submits her papers for inspection to a Palestinian official. The reason is that both know that the Palestinian officer transfers the documents through a tinted glassed one-way mirror to an Israeli official. The latter is invisible but his gaze is all the more penetrating for that.[46] This arrangement, detailed in the Oslo Accords,[47] signifies the macabre – albeit grounded in a much praised international agreement – dissonance between fabricated Palestinian sovereignty and the occupying power's actual control.

The concealed, absent/present violence of the terminal extends beyond the Palestinian person to Palestinian time: its working assumption is the dangerousness of the person and the insignificance of her time.[48] The disruption of life such an assumption generates potentially presents opportunities to counter it through the use of digital and cellular technologies. Such use, for instance, may inform people of delays; suggest alternative routes of passage, etc.

---

[44] CPWO Hebron checkoint, April 4, 2012, https://machsomwatch.org/he/node/19355 [Hebrew]; Qalandia checkpoint, November 24, 2013, https://machsomwatch.org/he/node/22645 [Hebrew].

[45] See *Sima Prod. Corp.* v. *McLucas*, 612 F 2d 309 (7th Cir. 1980) (concerned with violation of privacy by x-raying baggage); *Gilmore* v. *Gonzales*, 435 F 3rd 1125 at 1137–39 (9th Cir. 2006) (concerned with violation of privacy by identification requirements); *United States* v. *Aukai*, 497 F 3d 955 (9th Cir. 2007) (concerned with violation of privacy by magnometers); *Elec. Privacy Info. Ctr.* v. *United States Department of Homeland Security*, 653 F 3d 1 at 6 (D.C.Cir. 2011) (concerned with violation of privacy by body scanners). For a comprehensive analysis of the right to privacy in the context of the use of body scanners by American airport securities, see Y. Tirosh and M. Birnhack, "Naked in Front of the Machine: Does Airport Scanning Violate Provacy" (2013) 74 *Ohio State Law Journal* 1263.

[46] Weizman, "Seeing through Walls," pp. 89–90; E. Zureik, "Constructing Palestine through Surveillance Practices" (2001) 28 *British Journal of Middle Eastern Studies* 205.

[47] Article X of Annex I to the Agreement on the Gaza Strip and the Jericho Area (May 4, 1994), 33 ILM 622.

[48] A. Jamal, "On the Troubles of Racialized Time," in Y. Shenhav and Y. Yona (eds.), *Racism in Israel* (Jerusalem: Van Leer Institute, 2008), p. 376 [Hebrew].

The Israeli control over the digital landscape, discussed in the following section, all too often hampers this potential benefit for Palestinians while advancing Israeli business interests.

X.2.5 *Surveillance Technologies 3.0: "Smart" Techno-occupation*

Digital technology facilitates Palestinian communication with other Palestinians and with the world beyond their surrounding walls, and contributes to economic development. Given, however, that the technology is premised on the continuous importance of space rather than on its disappearance, it is not surprising that the technology allows for ever more penetrating surveillance, reflects Israeli control of the Palestinian space, and augments economic exploitation.[49]

Putting technology at the service of gathering personal, indeed intimate information about Palestinians is the expertise of "Israel's Cyber Spy Agency":[50] an elite IDF intelligence unit known as "8200," uses state-of-the-art signal wiretapping technologies in an enterprise of "sucking in and analyzing vast amounts of electronic data, from wiretapped phone calls and emails to microwave and satellite broadcasts."[51] A glimpse into the objectives of this enterprise was offered in an open letter to the Israeli prime minister,[52] sent in September 2014, by 43 of the unit's reservists.[53] The letter, declaring the signatories' decision to refuse "to take part in actions against Palestinians," indicated that the information collected by the unit "is used for political persecution and to create divisions within Palestinian society by recruiting collaborators and driving parts of Palestinian society against itself." More so, the letter describes the work of the unit as a "thorough and intrusive supervision and invasion of most areas of life." Some details of the

---

[49] H. Tawil-Souri, "Between Digital Flows and Territorial Borders: ICTs in the Palestine-Israel-EU Matrix," in R.A. Del Sarto (ed.), *Fragmented Borders, Interdependence and External Relations: The Israel-Palestine-European Union Triangle* (Basingstoke: Palgrave Macmillan, 2015), pp. 107–110.

[50] J. Reed, "Unit 8200: Israel's Cyber Spy Agency," *Financial Times* (July 10, 2015), www.ft.com/content/69f150da-25b8-11e5-bd83-71cb60e8f08c.

[51] M. Kalman, "Israeli Military Intelligence Unit Drives Country's Hi-Tech Boom," *The Guardian* (August 12, 2013), www.theguardian.com/world/2013/aug/12/israel-military-intelligence-unit-tech-boom.

[52] The full text can be found at *The Guardian*, "Israeli Intelligence Veterans' Letter to Netanyahu and Military Chiefs – in full" (September 12, 2014), www.theguardian.com/world/2014/sep/12/israeli-intelligence-veterans-letter-netanyahu-military-chiefs.

[53] G. Cohen, "Reservists from Elite IDF Intel Unit Refuse to Serve over Palestinian 'Persecution'," *Haaretz* (September 12, 2014), www.haaretz.com/israel-news/1.615498.

type of information gathered – which include sexual, health, and financial information – were given in interviews with the reservists.[54]

Control over the digital space facilitates the achievement of additional objectives. It mirrors the control over the material space, and in this context, too, the Oslo Accords determined the distribution of power between Israel and the PA: the latter was authorized to build its own telecommunication network, but Israel retained the ultimate control to determine the infrastructure.[55] Its control extends to the location of infrastructure, its maintenance and accessibility, the kind of equipment that could be purchased, the allocation of spectrum bandwidth, access speed, and area codes, etc.[56] This distribution of power, grounded in Israeli security concerns, accounts not merely for the fact that there is no access to Google maps and GPS unless one subscribes to Israeli providers,[57] and that Israel can and does disrupt reception of Palestinian networks and surveys cell phone users for intelligence purposes, but also for the political and economic face of a digitized occupation: thus, for instance, Israel has used its control over the bandwidth as a negotiating card in attempts to halt Palestinian moves relative to the International Criminal Court,[58] and its own cellular companies, unhampered by bandwidth constraints, profit handsomely from Palestinian dependence on their services.[59]

The story of the illegal outpost[60] known as Migron and the cellular antennas provides a microcosmic illustration of the interfacing of material and digital occupation and the role law has played in this respect. In 2000, shortly after the

---

[54] E. Levi, "We Were There, We Did it, and We Are Not Able to Keep Doing it: The 8200 Refuseniks Speak Out," *ynet* (September 12, 2014), www.ynet.co.il/articles/0,7340,L-4570055,00.html [Hebrew].

[55] Article II of Annex II to the Agreement on the Gaza Strip and the Jericho Area.

[56] H. Tawil-Souri, "Occupation Apps" (2015) *Jacobin* 17, www.jacobinmag.com/2015/03/occupation-apps-souri-palestine.

[57] This restriction generated the development of various Palestinian applications designed to report of traffic jams, possibilities of sharing a taxi, and provide information on conditions at various checkpoints. For a comprehensive and critical survey, see Tawil-Souri, "Occupation Apps."

[58] See Tawil-Souri, "Occupation Apps"; A. Shatz, "The Mobile Phone War," *London Review of Books* (October 30, 2009), www.lrb.co.uk/blog/2009/10/30/adam-shatz/the-mobile-phone-war.

[59] In settlements, outposts, bypass roads, buffer zones, and other locations all along the Wall, Israeli cellular towers beam strong signals. This is so because Israeli cellular companies enjoy two thousand times more spectrum allocation than the combined allocation of their Palestinian counterparts. The Palestinians are a no-cost captive market for their services (purchasing cellular phones or paying roaming charges) both because no additional investment in infrastructure is required and because of Israel's control over additional aspects of the technology discussed in the text above. See Tawil-Souri, "Occupation Apps."

[60] "Outposts" is a term denoting unauthorized settlements, i.e., settlements established without official government approval. See entries Z: Zone, Section Z.2.1, note 19; O: Outside/Inside; R: Regularization.

outbreak of the second Palestinian uprising (Intifada),[61] settlers requested that
the IDF improve cellular connectivity in certain parts of Area C, not far from
Ramallah, ostensibly for security purposes. In order to accommodate this
request, a private cellular communications company erected a broadcasting
tower and a cellular antenna on a hill some 6 km east of Ramallah. Once the
tower was erected, the Israeli electric company engaged in infrastructure work
in the area, and once electricity was available a group of settlers established the
outpost. Within a year, pursuant to a governmental decision, an access road to
the outpost was paved; light poles were installed; and IDF soldiers, an electric
fence, security cameras, and dogs appeared to provide additional security.
As the years went by, the outpost flourished, with some 50 Jewish families and
3 additional broadcasting towers of other companies providing cellular reception to the settlers and to the drivers on route 60, Area C's main Palestinian-
free road.[62] Given that outposts were, at the time, illegal even under Israeli
law,[63] in 2012, pursuant to an HCJ decision,[64] Migron was evacuated and the
land returned to its lawful owners. The dismantling of the settlement did not
include the broadcasting towers, even though demolition orders against three
of them were pending. In 2015, the HCJ accepted a petition from the four
cellular communication companies and determined that the order to evacuate Migron does not apply to them.[65] The decision – reached even though the
companies had never received authorization to place the antennas there and
even though demolition orders were pending against three of them[66] –
was based on both procedural grounds and on the security communication
needs in the nearby area, which were deemed to be independent of the
existence of the outpost.[67] Given that the Migron settlers were relocated to

---

[61]   On the second Intifada, see O. Ben-Naftali and A. Gross, "The Second Intifada" in
      A. Dworkin, R. Gutman, D. Reiff, and S. A. Mendez (eds.), *Crimes of War (0.2): What the
      Public Should Know* (New York: W. W. Norton & Company, 2007).

[62]   See entry Z: Zone, Section Z.2.2.4.

[63]   Note that in response to settlers' pressure, the Netanyahu government established an expert
      committee of jurists and entrusted them with the task of finding ways to legalize the outposts.
      The Report of the committee accommodated the political will and even exceeded it in
      determining that settlements too are legal under international law. For the report and its
      critique, see entry N: Nomos. This report eventually paved the way for the enactment of a law
      that purports to regularize the outposts. See The Judea and Samaria Settlement Regulation
      Law, 2017. The law is discussed in entry R: Regularization.

[64]   HCJ 8887/06 *El Nabuth* v. *Minister of Defense* (August 2, 2011) [Hebrew].

[65]   HCJ 3905/14 *Pelephone Communication Ltd* v. *Minister of Defense* (July 22, 2015) [Hebrew].

[66]   The court noted that its judgment does not preclude the State from implementing the
      demolition orders issued previously against the construction and that given that they were
      construed on private Palestinian land it should indeed do so. *Ibid.,* ¶ 27.

[67]   *Ibid.,* ¶ 21. The procedural grounds revolved around the fact that the companies were not
      a party to the judicial process that determined the dismantling of the outpost.

a nearby hill,[68] and that the whole area is dotted with settlements and outposts, it is reasonable to conclude that the court had their security interests in mind. Indeed, they too contribute to the official effort to place Palestinians under intimidating surveillance, availing themselves of the technology – and the dogs – at hand.[69] There are hundreds of Israeli antennas and broadcasting towers throughout Area C generally and along route 60 specifically, facilitating not merely communication between, but the very construction, of settlements in the area.[70] The story of Migron is the story of a combined political, commercial, and legal cooperation to enhance material and digital control over Palestinian space and people. It is the story of a "smart" techno-occupation designed to extend Israel's sovereignty over land.[71]

It is, however, in the allegedly unoccupied Gaza Strip from which Israel ostensibly disengaged[72] that the X factor for Israel's phenomenal success in the global security market is located. The following section focuses on Gaza as the showcase of Israeli weapon and surveillance technology.

X.2.6 *Gaza.com*

Gaza is surrounded by a "smart" security fence: the material construction has integrated video cameras, ground sensors, motion detectors, and satellite monitoring. The Israeli company which had built it and assisted in constructing barriers along the Egyptian and Jordanian borders, and which had signed a draft agreement with an Israeli town on the southern edges of Tel Aviv to turn it into a "smart city" by lining its street with hundreds of cameras linked to alarm systems, intercoms, and emergency buttons in public spaces, is hoping that US president Trump's plan to build a barrier along the 2,000 mile-long border between the US and Mexico to stop illegal immigration will be realized.[73] It is

---

[68] Migron's relocation was to a land privately owned by Palestinians, and the court ordered dismantling of the outpost. See El Nabuth, decision of August 29, 2012 [Hebrew].

[69] For a description of surveillance, intimidation, and violence toward Palestinians by settlers organized within the "Tag Mehir's" [Hebrew for "Price Tag"], see Shalhoub-Kevorkian, *Security Theology*, pp. 38–40 (focusing on testimonies from East Jerusalem). On Tag Mehir see N. Shalhoub-Kevorkian and Y. David, "Is the Violence of Tag Mehir a State Crime?," *British Journal of Criminology* (October 27, 2015), http://bjc.oxfordjournals.org/content/early/2015/10/27/bjc.azv101.

[70] N. Alexander, "The Israeli Control over the Digital and Cellular Space in the Territories" (an interview with Helga Tawil-Souri), *Haaretz* (March 31, 16), www.haaretz.co.il/magazine/.premium-1.2899665 [Hebrew].

[71] See entry Z: Zone, Sections Z.1, Z.3.   [72] See entry Z: Zone, Section Z.2.2.1.

[73] See, J. Ferziger, "The Israeli Company that Fenced Gaza Eyes Trump's Mexico Wall," *Bloomberg* (August 2, 2016), www.slidedoc.us/bloomberg-businessweek-middle-east-august-16-2016-pdf.

presently competing for a contract to build the planned 425-mile fence between Kenya and Somalia. Its CEO considers that it is better placed than competing companies to win the bid not only because it had already built and operates the perimeter security system in Nairobi's airport, but also because "anyone can give you a very nice Powerpoint, but few can show you such a complex project as Gaza that is constantly battle tested."[74] Immigrants, refugees, people under occupation, and others who belong to the "wretched of the earth"[75] are good for the security business. Gaza is a laboratory[76] that contributes to Israel's economy. Indeed, "smart fences" are not the only export. Thus, for instance, remote-controlled urban and aerial warfare, perfected in the recurrent military operations in Gaza, has been emulated in the drone wars over Afghanistan, Pakistan, Yemen, and in urban warfare waged in Iraq and in Syria.[77]

The 2005 "disengagement" from Gaza is echoed in the material/digital interplay. The physical dismantling of the settlements and ground withdrawal did not mean the end of control, but the development of hi-tech forms of remote control where the geographic distance loses its relevance. It also meant that Israeli providers do not service the people in Gaza anymore, but given that the infrastructure remained exclusively in Israeli hands, Israel has complete control over communications to and from Gaza.[78] This allows the IDF, for instance, to halt internet access, pinpoint the location of signals and interrupt them, and call both cellular and landline phones to "warn" civilians in Gaza that their house is about to be bombed. Such advance warnings, first used in the 2008–2009 Gaza operation, and then used by the USA when it bombed ISIS targets in Iraq,[79] expose the nature of the interaction of technology with politics and law.

Warning before bombing in Gaza consisted of two steps: first, a general warning directed at all Gazans and communicated by breaking into

---

[74] *Ibid.* The CAO, together with other businessmen, was part of a delegation headed by prime minister Netanyahu to Africa in July 2016.

[75] F. Fanon, *The Wretched of the Earth*, C. Farrington (trans.) (London: Penguin Classics, 2001).

[76] See the Documentary film "The Lab," Y. Feldman (dir.) (Gum Films, 2013), which investigates how Israeli companies develop and test the vessels of future warfare, which are then sold worldwide by private Israeli agents.

[77] S. Dawes, "The Digital Occupation of Gaza: An Interview with Helga Tawil-Souri" (2015) 8 *Networking Knowledge*, http://ojs.meccsa.org.uk/index.php/netknow/article/view/374/204. See also entry E: Export of Knowledge.

[78] H. Tawil-Souri, "The Technological End between the 'Inside' of Gaza and 'Outside' of Gaza," *7iber* (September 29, 2014), http://7iber.com/2014/09/the-technological-end-between-the-inside-of-gaza-and-the-outside-of-gaza/#.V_IJRvB97IU.

[79] See B. Starr, "Pentagon adopts Israeli tactic in bombing ISIS," *CNN* (April 27, 2016), http://edition.cnn.com/2016/04/26/politics/u-s-uses-israeli-tactic-isis-bombing.

Palestinian TV or radio broadcasts, leaflets dropped from the air, and text messages sent to all cellular phone subscribers; and second, a specific warning directed at people whose houses were targeted. The specific message included two steps: a "knock on the door" and a "knock on the roof." The former comprised a phone call informing the inhabitants that their home will be destroyed within a few minutes, and the latter consisted of either warning shots or a rocket to scare the inhabitants into escaping. Warnings may indeed save lives – at least for those who are able to flee. Yet, the devastation to life and limb in Gaza was augmented rather than decreased, suggesting that there may be other purposes, both political and legal, behind the practice.

Politically, it indicates to the civilian population that things could get worse; that they could be bombed out of existence without warning. When people are suspended between life and death and threatened with escalation, they have a good incentive to pressure their government into acquiescence.[80] From a legal perspective, the warning technology appears at first sight to comply with the requirement for "effective advance warning" stipulated in Article 57 of the *AP I*. This provision proceeds, however, to state that the advanced warning may not be construed as "authorizing any attacks against the civilian population, civilians and civilian objects."[81] The legal logic driving the Israeli warnings was to counter that caveat, by positing that persons who received a warning and chose to ignore it (notwithstanding their ability to do so in terms of time allowed, physical condition, and the availability of nearby shelters) have forfeited their civilian status and have henceforth become human shields and thus a legitimate target, and one affecting the proportionality embedded in risk management.[82] Indeed, the logic of risk management is one and the same whether it is used in combat or in regular situations that are considered to be security-related.

This interpretative logic indicates more than law's elasticity; it signifies that Gaza is not just a military, but also a legal laboratory experimenting with a mutation of lawfare that takes law into consideration in a manner that renders it indistinguishable from violence.[83]

---

[80]   E. Weizman, "Legislative Attack" (2010) 27 *Theory, Culture & Society* 11, 21–22.

[81]   Article 57 of *AP I*. On the legal debate whether Israel's warning policy complied with Article 57 or violated it see e.g., J. Dill, "Israel's Use of Law and Warnings in Gaza," *Opinio Juris* (July 30, 2014), http://opiniojuris.org/2014/07/30/guest-post-israels-use-law-warnings-gaza.

[82]   See entry P: Proportionality.

[83]   Weizman, "Legislative Attack," p. 24. See also entries L: Lawfare; V: Violence.

X.3 THE PALESTINIAN PROFILE: WRITTEN
ON THE BODY (POLITIC)

X.3.1 Inherent Enmity

Risk management has become a global security enterprise with legal dimensions. Its legal consciousness is framed within the matrix of exceptional times, an emergency wrought by the confluence of terrorists, refugees, immigrants, and criminals, which requires and indeed legitimates special security measures.[84] The security measures require surveillance technologies to identify the risk and generate a variety of preemptive procedures designed to contain if not altogether eliminate it.[85] Profiling – that is, the classification of population into those who are risk carriers and those who are not according to race, ethnicity, class, religion, or national origin – has emerged as the governing procedure in this respect. The human body thus becomes the site of risk management by the body politic. The biopolitical state takes upon itself to single out "the biological threats posed by the other, the sub-race, the counter-race that we are, despite ourselves, bringing into existence."[86] The enemy may well be within and enmity resides in his being, not in his action.[87] These threats thus do not abide by the peace/war dichotomy any more than they abide by an external/internal dichotomy. From the perspective of the legal order, they blur the norm/exception relations and generate a permanent state of emergency.[88]

As noted, in Israel, a state of emergency has been the defining matrix of the normative order since its establishment. The threat within was perceived to emanate mainly from the Arab/Palestinian minority in Israel, conceived of as potential enemies. It was then expanded to Palestinians classified as de facto enemies – that is, those who attempted to return to Israel from neighboring countries pursuant to the 1949 Armistice agreements,[89] and eventually to the Palestinian residents of the OPT

---

[84] Shamir, *Without Borders*, p. 200.   [85] See entry F: Future-Oriented Measures.

[86] M. Foucault, *Society Must Be Defended: Lectures at the Collège de France, 1975–76*, M. Bertani and A. Fontana (eds.), D. Macey (trans.) (London: Penguin Books, 2004), pp. 256, 261–262.

[87] H. Arendt, *On Revolution* (Harmondsworth: Penguin, 1965), p. 100. Note that while Foucault does not refer to Arendt, his biopolitical reading of enmity is clearly influenced by her notion of the "objective enemy."

[88] G. Agamben, *State of Exception*, K. Attell (trans.) (Chicago: University of Chicago Press, 2005).

[89] Hashemite Jordan Kingdom – Israel: General Armistice Agreement, UN Doc S/1302/Rev1 (April 3, 1949), adopted by the Security Council in SC Res 72, UN Doc S/RES/72 (August 11, 1949).

including East Jerusalem.[90] This section complements the previous discussion by focusing on profiling in the context of Israeli airports. Airport security is not, alas, the only site where ethnic profiling is practiced and receives judicial approval as a legitimate tool of risk management. The Palestinian family is another such site. An amendment Israel introduced to its Citizenship and Entry into Israel Law, bars Palestinian spouses of Israeli citizens from entering Israel on the grounds of the security risk they inherently present.[91] This profiling of the Palestinian family is discussed in entry K: Kinship.

X.3.2 *Profiling the Palestinian Passenger in Israeli Airports and El-Al Flights*

Israel began to engage in airport security and in related profiling in 1968, in response to a hijacking of an El-Al air plane en route from Rome to Tel Aviv by the Popular Front for the Liberation of Palestine and its forced landing in Algiers. Its General Security Services (GSS) are responsible for determining the criteria comprising the profile and for training the airport security personnel. The criteria remain secret. An appeal by the Freedom of Information Movement to disclose whether the criteria differentiate between passengers on the basis of religious, national, or ethnic origin was dismissed: the court determined that according to the GSS Law, this information is privileged and its disclosure is a criminal offense. The court further commented that in Israel, terrorist attacks are not exceptional but "a way of life," intimating that even if the criteria are discriminatory, the Israeli public has no interest in disclosing information which may "expose its personal security to constant danger."[92] That the "constant danger" emanates from Arab/Palestinian identity is, however, commonly known, and has been acknowledged openly by both the GSS and the HCJ. The latter is yet to determine that a practice which differentiates between Israeli citizens on the basis of their ethnicity/religion undermines the basic tenets of liberal democracy.

---

[90]   See Section X.2.3; see also entry Z: Zone, Section Z.2.2.3.1.

[91]   The Citizenship and Entry into Israel Law (temporary provision), 2003. The Amendment was introduced in 2003 and has been annually renewed since. See also entry O: Outside/Inside.

[92]   Administrative Petition (Tel Aviv) 1555/06 *The Freedom of Information Movement v. the Airports Authority* (November 12, 2006) [Hebrew]. That comment was made in response to a comparison the petitioner presented with changes made to discriminatory profiling procedures in the USA.

This profiling was challenged in a petition submitted by the Association for Civil Rights in Israel (ACRI) to the HCJ in 2007.[93] The petition details the following factual background: the GSS has determined profiling criteria focusing on those who are considered "potential suspects." Its acknowledged justification for this profiling is utilitarian, that is, its assessment that the time it would take to subject all passengers to an intensive search would be too long, and that consequently the harm done to Arab passengers is both necessary and proportionate. Passengers belonging to the Arab minority are ipso facto "potential suspects" and are subjected to a more thorough check than the one which Jewish passengers undergo. The use of an Arab ethnicity as an indicator for suspicion makes traveling a humiliating experience. This humiliation is public: thus, for instance, when the scanning machines malfunction, Arab passengers – and only Arab passengers – have to undergo a security check in plain view, and at times the Arab passenger is accompanied to the flight by a security guard.[94] Occasionally, the nature and duration of the security check cause Arab passengers such distress that they are either forced to, or chose to, give up the flight altogether.[95]

Referring to the negative impact generated by racial profiling of minority groups – a practice which exacerbates prejudices, racism, discrimination, and hostility – on both members of that group and on the members of the majority,[96]

---

[93] HCJ 4797/07 *Association for Civil Rights in Israel* v. *the Airport Authority* (March 10, 2015) [Hebrew].

[94] E.g., Small Claims 48058-07-15 *Shdud* v. *El-Al Israeli Airlines* (May 16, 2016) [Hebrew] (the court rejecting a claim for compensation in view of a security check on the body of the passenger who, upon refusing to take off her bra, was told that she would not be allowed to board the aircraft. The court determined that she did not prove that the security check was related to her Arab origin and that the fact that she was the only passenger to undergo such a search does not prove that she was discriminated against due to her origin).

[95] The petition in HCJ 4797/07, www.acri.org.il/pdf/petitions/hit4797.pdf [Hebrew], ¶¶ 6, 8. See, e.g., Civil Claim 6783-11-09 *Kevorkian* v. *the Airport Authority* (February 15, 2015) [Hebrew] (Prof. Kevorkian was scheduled to participate in a conference in Tunis. Pursuant to an extensive security check at Tel Aviv airport she was notified that she would not be allowed to board the plane with her laptop. She decided not to board the plane and gave up participating in the conference. She claimed 75,000 NIS as compensation for humiliating treatment and injury to her dignity, freedom, privacy, and equality. The court, rejecting her argument that the checkup reflected any national hostility rather than regrettable lack of professional behavior on the part of the security personnel, awarded her 7,500 NIS).

[96] HCJ 4797/07 petition, ¶¶ 25–28. The "expressive harm" hypothesis, according to which profiling minorities may result in significant equity costs because it echoes the discrimination they suffer in other spheres of life, has been supported by numerous empirical studies interested in an economic analysis of profiling. See, e.g., D. Barak-Erez, "Terrorism and Profiling: Shifting the Focus from Criteria to Effects" (2007) 29 *Cardozo Law Review* 1; B. Hasisi, Y. Margalit, and L. Orgad, "Ethnic Profiling in Airport Screening: Lessons from Israel, 1968-2010" (2012) 14 *American Law and Economics Review* 517.

the petition proceeded to present its legal grounds: racial profiling, it argued, violates a myriad of constitutional and international human rights, including human dignity, in that it relates to a person as a means to others' ends, the right to equality, various antidiscrimination laws, the prohibition on racial and ethnic discrimination, and the right to privacy. Such profiling does not meet any of the constitutional conditions that may render it legally valid: the GSS is authorized to employ measures designed to prevent illegal acts against the security of the state, but it is not authorized to engage in discriminatory practices, and this is a fortiori the case when the security reasoning camouflages as it enhances a reality of racism, exclusion, and suppression. Ethnic profiling is thus a disproportionate means in the service of a discriminatory end.[97]

The HCJ delivered its judgment in 2014. It concluded that the introduction of HBS (Hold Baggage Screening) technology that allows for the screening of baggage without the presence of the passenger and of advanced body screening gates has reduced, if not altogether eliminated, the discomfort of Arab passengers.[98] The coupling of these technological innovations with secret information pertaining to the procedures of the security checks, and with the observation that the level of the risk is not determined exclusively on the basis of one criterion, generated the conclusion that the petition has exhausted itself at this point.[99] The court invited ACRI to submit another petition in the future, should it find that the changes are insufficient and that "the distinction, especially the overt distinction" between Israeli citizens, persists.[100]

The HCJ thus dismissed the petition without determining any of the principled issues relative to the harm caused by ethnic profiling to human dignity, equality, freedom of movement, and privacy on either the deontological or the utilitarian levels.[101] Technology and procedural justice may indeed alleviate the public humiliation suffered as a result of discriminatory processes, but they do not erase the consciousness of members of the minority that their state of citizenship holds them suspect because of their being, not action. The court in effect accepted that security considerations justify the harm caused by discrimination, a harm that cannot be legally justified in democratic regimes on the basis of utilitarian considerations.

---

[97] HCJ 4797/07 petition, ¶¶ 41–108.   [98] HCJ 4797/07 judgment, ¶¶ 3–10.
[99] *Ibid.*, ¶¶ 11–12.   [100] *Ibid.*, ¶ 13.
[101] The HCJ acknowledged that it makes no determination on these issues. *Ibid.*

X.4 CONCLUSION

All theologies are devoted to the rational study of their subject of worship. The security theology is no exception. Its devotion to the study of security entails the study of the nature of the enemy. The nature relevant scholarship ascribes to the enemy has changed over time. The gradual fading of the interstate war era has blurred the profile of the equal enemy, the combatant imagined by the laws of war. Wars in the open seas, belonging to no state, have seen the emergence of the *hostis humanis generis*, the "enemy of humanity"; a global criminal to be squashed by states fighting not to advance their own interests, but to protect an imagined community: humanity. The profile evolved with the changing face of war: the "real enemy," the partisan or freedom fighter, who is neither a criminal nor an equal combatant, appeared and was soon followed by its radical version, the "absolute enemy," a world aggressor requiring absolute destruction and rendering all distinctions other than the distinction between friend and foe meaningless.[102] The emergence of the "objective enemy,'" a mirror image of the "real enemy," whose status, and guilt, are (pre) determined by his mere being, not by his action, further collapsed the distinctions between politics and culture, the individual and the collectivity, the citizen and the Other.[103] The transformation of the concept of war from an outward activity limited in space and time to a constant activity flowing across and within borders, has generated the invisible enemy, a hidden carrier of risk, a contaminating virus lurking within the population. His profile is determined by biopolitics.[104] Given his invisibility, identifying him requires both devotion and expertise. The clergy entrusted with this task are the security services. Risk management is their proper rite. The fundamental edict of risk management is the axiomatic existence of an enemy who presents a risk and that the risk can and must be managed, not questioned.

A wealth of means is needed to perform the rite. These include surveillance technologies required for identification; interdisciplinary knowledge and analytical tools employed in, and borrowed from, benevolent industries

---

[102]   C. Schmitt, *Theory of the Partisan: Intermediate Commentary on the Concept of the Political*, G. L. Ulmen (trans.) (New York: Telos Press Publishing, 2007). For a brief review of the intellectual genealogy of the "enemy," see M. Thorup, *Total Enemies: Understanding "The Total Enemy" through Schmitt, Arendt, Foucault and Agamben* (January 1, 2014), www .libraryofsocialscience.com/essays/thorup-total-enemies/.

[103]   Arendt, *On Revolution.*   [104]   Foucault, *Society Must Be Defended.*

such as health, insurance, and law enforcement, for constructing the enemy profile; the development of preventive procedures designed to eliminate the risk;[105] and authorization to operate all these. Given the indeterminate and chaotic yet omnipresent nature of a risk that obeys neither borders nor other boundaries, its expert management further requires a permanent sense of urgency and emergency as well as cooperation with like-minded clergies worldwide. It also requires that devout followers willingly accepting the cost in terms of human rights that successful management necessitates. Fear has proven to be an excellent antidote to critical sensibilities and is instilled to mobilize support for the risk that risk management presents to democratic sensibilities. In the security theology, self-preservation both precedes and is independent of the self.

In the globalized risk-management league, Israel is in a class of its own. As discussed in the present entry, it owes its pivotal position to both consciousness and experience with the enemy thus construed within and across its (indeterminate) borders, and to hands-on expertise with technologies of population management in Israel and the OPT. The effort to maintain its cutting-edge position is ceaseless, as evidenced by the initiative, hitherto absent in democratic regimes, to create a comprehensive biometric database for governmental use, especially for its various security authorities.[106] Linking its actuarial collection of demographic, ethnic, and socioeconomic data used for profiling with biometric technologies designed to measure and analyze biological and behavioral characteristics of a person for identification and control, such a database will augment the aggregate power of the state vis-à-vis the human subject.[107] The latter, speaking through her body, is otherwise silenced and objectified.[108] A petition challenging the legality of this initiative on the basis of the harm thereby entailed to privacy, human dignity, liberty, and indeed democracy was dismissed by the HCJ as premature.[109] Both the initiative and the judicial

---

[105] See entry F: Future-Oriented Measures.
[106] Comprehensive biometric data bases exist in nondemocratic states such as Pakistan and Indonesia. In democracies, the technology is used for issuing of IDs and travel documents not linked to biometric databases and for specific databases relative to convicted criminals, refugees, and people on welfare and accessible only to the corresponding governmental entities. See Martziano, "A Critical Reflection on the Israeli Biometric Project," pp. 52–53.
[107] See entry O: Outside/Inside.
[108] *Ibid.*, pp. 44–45; I. van der Ploeg, "Biometrics and the Body as Information: Normative Issues of the Socio-technical Coding of the Body," in D. Lyon (ed.) *Surveillance as Social Sorting: Privacy, Risk and Digital Discrimination* (Oxford: Routledge, 2003), p. 57.
[109] HCJ 1516/12 *Nahon v. the Knesset* (July 23, 2012) [Hebrew].

dismissal of the petition are coherent with the political culture in Israel. They also underscore the devotion of its legal institutions, both legislative and judicial, to the security theology.[110]

---

[110] Legislation that authorizes surveillance practices includes, for instance, the Law for fighting Terrorism, 2016; the Law for the Prevention of Infiltration (Offences and Jurisdiction), 1954; the Law of The General Security Service, 2002. The rejection by the HCJ of a petition to cancel the state of emergency in HCJ 3091/99 Association for Civil Rights, equally attests to its contribution to the normalization of exceptional measures and the consequential "security as trump" jurisprudence.

Y

Youth

Hedi Viterbo

Y.1 INTRODUCTION

As part of modernity's obsession with age-related norms and distinctions,[1] young people are commonly conceptualized through various terms – "youth," "children," "adolescents," and so forth. These age categories reinforce presumptions about young people's supposedly unique traits and needs. The UN Secretariat, UNICEF, UNESCO, the UN Population Fund, the World Health Organization, and the International Labor Organization all define "youth" as "persons between the ages of 15 and 24," while other international legal texts, as well as some UN documents, define this term differently.[2] Some of the above UN bodies also speak of "children" (in relation to individuals under 15) and "adolescents" (for those aged 10–19 years).[3] In comparison, the UN Convention on the Rights of the Child – the world's most

---

[1] See, e.g., H. P. Chudacoff, *How Old Are You: Age Consciousness in American Culture* (Princeton and Oxford: Princeton University Press, 1989); N. Lesko, *Act Your Age!: A Cultural Construction of Adolescence* (New York and London: Routledge, 2001).

[2] See, e.g., Security Council Resolution 2250 (2015), www.un.org/press/en/2015/sc12149.doc.htm (defining "youth" as "persons of the age of 18–29 years old"); UN Habitat, "Urban Youth Fund," http://unhabitat.org/urban-initiatives/initiatives-programmes/urban-youth-fund/ (demarcating youth as "people aged 15–32 years"); definitions section of African Union, African Youth Charter, July 2, 2006, www.refworld.org/docid/493fe0b72.html (defining "youth" as "every person between the ages of 15 and 35 years").

[3] For a useful overview, see UN Department of Economic and Social Affairs, "Definition of Youth," www.un.org/esa/socdev/documents/youth/fact-sheets/youth-definition.pdf. See also, e.g., Secretary-General's Report to the General Assembly, December 17, 1981, A/36/215; Secretary-General's Report to the General Assembly, December 18, 1985, A/40/256; United Nations Secretariat – Division for Palestinian Rights, Palestinian Children in the Occupied Palestinian Territory, March 31, 1990, https://unispal.un.org/DPA/DPR/unispal.nsf/0/46762C CC39F84A4385256II20067C84F ("For the purpose of this study, Palestinians under 15 years of age are considered as children"); UNESCO, "What Do We Mean by 'Youth'?," www.unesco .org/new/en/social-and-human-sciences/themes/youth/youth-definition/.

widely ratified treaty[4] – generally classifies anyone under the age of 18 as a "child,"[5] and so do other international legal documents,[6] while Israeli law labels them "minors."[7] In addition to categories such as these, international law and Israeli law alike apply a range of age thresholds.[8] Such overlapping, complementary, and competing age demarcations, and the norms and expectations potently enforced on their basis, are among the means through which childhood, as some suggest, has become "the most intensively governed sector of personal existence."[9]

Like their elders, young Palestinians are affected by Israel's rule in virtually every area of their lives. Yet, more than in any other legal field, it is in criminal law – whether under Israel's military legal system or its domestic system – that a separate set of laws for noncitizen Palestinian children has been developed.[10] And, partly for this reason, it is on this particular legal context that this entry focuses. Following law's broader preoccupation with age divisions, Israel's military criminal law, to which most noncitizen Palestinians in the West Bank

---

[4]   The only country not to have ratified it is the United States.
[5]   Article 1 of the Convention on the Rights of the Child, November 20, 1989, 1577 UNTS 3.
[6]   Article 2 of the African Charter on the Rights and Welfare of the Child, July 11, 1990, CAB/ LEG/24.9/49.
[7]   In the past, the age of criminal majority for Palestinians under Israeli military was 16 years – see discussion in Section Y.4 and in the entry M: Military Courts. For the current law concerning noncitizen Palestinians in the West Bank, see Article 136 of Order No. 1651 Concerning Security Provisions (Integrated Version) (Judea and Samaria), 2009 [hereinafter: Order 1651] (amended in 2011 by Article 3 of Order No. 1676 Concerning Security Provisions (Judea and Samaria) (Amendment No. 10), 2011 [hereinafter: Order 1676]). Regarding Israelis and others, see Article 1 of Youth Law (Adjudication, Punishment, and Modes of Treatment), 1971 [hereinafter: Youth Law]. Beyond the criminal law context, see, e.g., Article 3 of Law of Legal Competence and Guardianship, 1962.
[8]   Examples of thresholds, set at the ages of 15 or 18 years, are: Article 6 of International Convent on Civil and Political Rights, opened for signature December 19, 1966, 999 UNTS 171 (entered into force March 23, 1976); Preamble and Articles 1–4 of Optional Protocol to the Convention on the Rights of the Child on the Involvement of Children in Armed Conflict, May 25, 2000, 2173 UNTS 222; Article 77 of the Protocol Additional to the Geneva Conventions of August 12, 1949, and relating to the Protection of Victims of International Armed Conflicts (Additional Protocol I), Geneva, June 8, 1977, 1125 UNTS 3; Articles 4, 6 of the Protocol Additional to the Geneva Conventions of August 12, 1949, and relating to the Protection of Victims of Non-International Armed Conflicts (Additional Protocol II), Geneva, June 8, 1977, 1125 UNTS 609.
[9]   N. Rose, *Governing the Soul: The Shaping of the Private Self* (2nd edn., London and New York: Free Association Books, 1999), p. 121. See also A. McGillivray (ed.), *Governing Childhood* (Aldershot: Dartmouth, 1997); K. Heltqvist and G. Dahlberg (eds.), *Governing the Child in the New Millennium* (New York and London: Routledge Falmer, 2001).
[10] Family law proceedings are normally dealt with by Palestinian courts, as are most intra-Palestinian cases. See, regarding the Palestinian Authority's courts in the West Bank, entry M: Military Courts. Regarding Palestinian courts in the Gaza Strip, see Human Rights Watch, *Abusive System: Failures of Criminal Justice in Gaza* (2012), pp. 8–23, www.hrw.org/sites/def ault/files/reports/iopt1012ForUpload_0.pdf.

are subject, further divides Palestinian suspects under the age of 16 into three subgroups, differing in their legal status and entitlements: "children" (defined as those under the age of 12), "youth" (aged 12–13), and "tender adults" (aged 14–15).[11] Relatedly, the UN Rules for the Protection of Juveniles Deprived of Their Liberty, also known as the "Havana Rules," refer to those under 18 as "juveniles."[12]

An essentialist[13] preoccupation with age is, on the one hand, problematic and simplistic, for reasons largely exceeding this entry. Among other things, it effaces the culturally and historically contingent nature of the constructs "childhood" and "adulthood," the infinite disparities among "children," their weighty commonalities with "adults," and the social forces invested in reproducing seemingly natural age-based differences.[14]

On the other hand, an age prism also foregrounds important aspects of life under Israeli rule in the West Bank and Gaza Strip. It highlights the relatively young composition of the local population – almost every other person is under the age of eighteen[15] – as well as the key role of youth in the political

---

[11] Article 1 of Order 1651. On the legal consequences of these age categories, see H. Viterbo, "The Age of Conflict: Rethinking Childhood, Law, and Age through the Israeli-Palestinian Case," in M. Freeman (ed.), *Law and Childhood Studies – Current Legal Issues* (Oxford: Oxford University Press, 2012), vol. XIV, pp. 133, 137–138 [hereinafter: "The Age of Conflict"]. On the adoption of these subcategories and other child-related measures from the British mandate law, see H. Viterbo, "Ties of Separation: Analogy and Generational Segregation in North America, Australia, and Israel/Palestine" (2017) 42 *Brooklyn Journal of International Law*, 686, 730.

[12] Article 11(a) of Annex to the UN Rules for the Protection of Juveniles Deprived of their Liberty, General Assembly, April 2, 1991, A/RES/45/113, p. 205.

[13] Crudely defined, essentialism is the belief that a type of person or thing (in this case, a person belonging to a certain age group) has a true, intrinsic, constitutive and invariant nature. D. Fuss, *Essentially Speaking: Feminism, Nature and Difference* (New York and London: Routledge, 1989), p. 2.

[14] For critical discussion, see, e.g., M. J. Kehily (ed.), *An Introduction to Childhood Studies* (3rd edn., Berkshire: Open University Press, 2015); E. Burman, *Deconstructing Developmental Psychology* (Hove and New York: Routledge, 2007); A. James, C. Jenks, and A. Prout, *Theorizing Childhood* (Cambridge: Polity Press, 1998); C. Jenks, *Childhood* (2nd edn., New York and London: Routledge, 2005); D. Kennedy, *The Well of Being: Childhood, Subjectivity, and Education* (Albany: State University of New York Press, 2006); H. Montgomery, *An Introduction to Childhood: Anthropological Perspectives on Children's Lives* (Chichester: Wiley-Blackwell, 2009); J. Ainsworth, "Youth Justice in a Unified Court: Response to Critics of Juvenile Court Abolition" (1995) 36 *Boston College Law Review* 927; D. M. Rosen, "Child Soldiers, International Humanitarian Law, and the Globalization of Childhood" (2007) 109 *American Anthropologist* 296; P. Kelly, "The Brain in the Jar: A Critique of Discourses of Adolescent Brain Development" (2012) 15 *Journal Youth Studies* 944.

[15] Regarding the Palestinian population, see UNWRA, *West Bank & Gaza Strip Population Census of 2007* (2010), p. 21, www.unrwa.org/userfiles/2010012035949.pdf (reporting that 57.52 percent of Palestinians in the West Bank and Gaza Strip are under 19, according to

history of Israel/Palestine.[16] In the criminal law context, specifically, Palestinians in Israeli custody are generally over the age of 12 – the age of criminal responsibility under Israeli law[17] – and the great majority of child inmates are aged 16 or older.[18] At the same time, on numerous occasions, Israeli authorities have arrested Palestinians aged as young as 5,[19] and entire families have also been detained overnight with toddlers as young as 2.[20]

No clear aggregate figures are available about noncitizen Palestinian under-18s in Israeli custody. Absent such clear information, estimates range between 8,500 and 12,000 since the year 2000,[21] not including East Jerusalem, where nearly 800 Palestinians in this age group have been detained in a single year alone.[22] These relatively high numbers, coupled with the political conscious-ness young Palestinians have reported acquiring in Israeli prisons, may explain

information provided by the Palestinian Central Bureau of Statistics). Regarding Israeli settlers, see Central Bureau of Statistics, *Selected Data for International Child Day* (2008), p. 2 [Hebrew], www.cbs.gov.il/reader/newhodaot/hodaa_template.html?hodaa=200811235 (reporting that 46 percent of Israeli settlers are under 18).

[16]   See, e.g., J. Collins, *Occupied by Memory: The Intifada Generation and the Palestinian State of Emergency* (New York: New York University Press, 2004), pp. 2, 11–14, 17–20, 35–74; D. Rosen, *Armies of the Young: Child Soldiers in War and Terrorism* (New Brunswick and London: Rutgers University Press, 2005), pp. 91–131.

[17]   Article 191 of Order 1651.

[18]   B'Tselem, "Statistics on Palestinian Minors in the Custody of the Israeli Security Forces" (January 6, 2017) [hereinafter: "Statistics on Palestinian Minors"], www.btselem.org/statistics/ minors_in_custody.

[19]   See, e.g., Association for Civil Rights in Israel, *Arrests, Interrogations and Indictments of Palestinian Minors in the Occupied Territories: Facts and Figures for 2014* (February 2016), pp. 4–5, www.acri.org.il/en/wp-content/uploads/2016/02/arrests-minors-OPT2014-ENG.pdf; B'Tselem, "Video Footage: Soldiers Detain Palestinian Five-year-old in Hebron" (July 11, 2013), www.btselem.org/press_releases/20130711_soldiers_detain_5_year_old_in_hebron; N. Hasson, "Israel Police Arrest 6-year-old East Jerusalem Boy Suspected of Stoning Bus," *Haaretz* (April 30, 2015), www.haaretz.com/news/diplomacy-defense/1.654234; Ma'an, "Israeli Forces 'Detain-6-year-old' in Jerusalem," *Ma'an News Agency* (January 4, 2011), www.maannews.net/eng/ViewDetails.aspx?ID=449915; CC (Jerusalem Magistrate Ct.) 11330/08 *Matir* v. *State of Israel* (October 28, 2008).

[20]   See, e.g., N. Hasson, "Palestinian Family Taken into Custody, Two-year-old Toddler Spends Four Hours in Jail," *Haaretz* (March 1, 2016), www.haaretz.com/israel-news/.premium-1.706354.

[21]   See, respectively, Defence for Children International – Palestine, Madaa Silwan Creative Center, YMCA East Jerusalem, and War Child Holland, *Israel's Compliance with the International Covenant on Civil and Political Rights – Shadow Report to the Fourth Periodic Report of Israel*, 112th Session of the Human Rights Committee (October 2014), http://tbinternet .ohchr.org/Treaties/CCPR/Shared%20Documents/ISR/INT_CCPR_CSS_ISR_18219_E.doc x; Addameer, "Imprisonment of Children" (February 2016), www.addameer.org/the_prison ers/children. For monthly figures obtained from the Israeli authorities, see B'Tselem, "Statistics on Palestinian Minors."

[22]   Addameer, "Joint Report Estimates that 6440 Palestinians Arrested in 2016" (January 2, 2017), www.addameer.org/news/joint-report-estimates-6440-palestinians-arrested-2016 (estimating

the image, in Palestinian discourses, of incarceration as a rite of passage from childhood to adulthood.[23] To this one may add that many child detainees are denied contact with their parents,[24] usually either on "security" grounds or due to their transfer to facilities inside Israel "proper," out of their families' reach.[25]

This entry examines the treatment of young Palestinians suspected of violating Israeli law – be they classified as "youth," "minors," "children," or otherwise – with a focus on the relationship, in this context, between the rule and the exception. While many of this book's entries tackle this subject in terms of the distinction between what is commonly considered the rule and exception of the international law of belligerent occupation, this entry primarily engages with another important yet under-examined aspect: the design and application of statutory rules and exceptions within Israel's own law.

As Section Y.2 demonstrates in depth, the Israeli military has, since its early years in the West Bank and Gaza Strip, undermined its professed rules and/or rendered them the de facto exception. Several manifestations of this "rule of exception" are analyzed in what follows. Section Y.3 turns to comparable phenomena in two Israeli legal contexts outside the military law: first, Israeli authorities' handling of Palestinian children in East Jerusalem, under the domestic law; and second, Israeli authorities' approach to international children's rights law. Section Y.4 explains that due, among other legal issues, to the reversal of the formal rule and exception, Israel's recent reforms concerning

---

that Israeli authorities arrested some 1,332 children from the West Bank in the year 2016, 757 of whom were from East Jerusalem); Association for Civil Rights in Israel, *Arrested Childhood: The Ramifications of Israel's New Strict Policy toward Minors Suspected of Involvement in Stone Throwing, Security Offenses, and Disturbances* (February 2016), p. 9 [hereinafter: *Arrested Childhood*], www.acri.org.il/en/wp-content/uploads/2016/02/Arrested-Childhood0216-en.pdf ("According to police figures, 792 Palestinian minors were arrested in East Jerusalem in 2014"). On Israeli authorities' treatment of noncitizen Palestinian in East Jerusalem, specifically, see below notes 48–54 and their accompanying text.

[23] J. Peteet, "Male Gender and Rituals of Resistance in the Palestinian Intifada – A Cultural Politics of Violence," in M. Ghoussoub and E. Sinclair-Webb (eds.), *Imagined Masculinities: Male Identity and Culture in the Middle East* (London: Saqi Books, 2000), pp. 103–126; E. Nashif, *Palestinian Political Prisoners: Identity and Community* (London: Routledge Studies in the Arad-Israeli Conflict, 2008); S. Quota, R.L. Punamäki, and E. El Sarraj, "Prison Experience and Coping Styles Among Palestinian Men" (1997) 3(1) *Peace and Conflict: Journal of Peace Psychology* 19.

[24] See, e.g., B'Tselem, *No Minor Matter: Violation of the Rights of Palestinian Minors Arrested by Israel on Suspicion of Stone-Throwing* (2011) [hereinafter: *No Minor Matter*], www.btselem.org/download/201107_no_minor_matter_eng.pdf; Defence for Children International – Palestine, *No Way to Treat a Child: Palestinian Children in the Israeli Military Detention System* (2016) [hereinafter: *No Way to Treat a Child*], https://d3n8a8pro7vhmx.cloudfront.net/dcipalestine/pages/1527/attachments/original/1460665378/DCIP_NWTTAC_Report_Final_April_2016.pdf.

[25] For further discussion of the latter issues, see entry S: Security Prisoners.

Palestinian children lack any meaningful impact. The concluding section provides an overview of the entry's main themes and findings.

In tackling these issues, it is crucial to remain critical and skeptical toward legal "rules" and "exceptions." As explained elsewhere in this book,[26] these terms, and the distinctions between them, are conceptually, normatively, and historically questionable. Further, rather than being necessarily antithetical to violence, so-called legal rules or norms may well be violent. For these and other reasons, the reversal of the rule and exception is not, in and of itself, necessarily deplorable. What do warrant criticism, as shown below, are the concrete consequences of this reversal in the specific context under examination: Israel authorities' pursuit of public legitimacy by claiming to enforce and comply with what they present as statutory rules, while at the same time turning these purported rules into exceptions and thus denying Palestinian children the protections they appear to offer.

Y.2 THE RULE OF EXCEPTION IN ISRAELI MILITARY LAW

Rules, exceptions, and distinctions are all products of the social imaginary,[27] and as such are produced and molded in discourse and social actions, including legal texts. Indeed, Israel's military orders, like statutes elsewhere, brim with provisions, guarantees, or safeguards – presented as the rules – as well as their imagined exceptions: exemption or qualification clauses. Upon careful inspection of Israeli military law, however, particularly as regards Palestinian youth, the formal or seeming statutory exception is often found to be the de facto rule.

This phenomenon can be traced back to at least the early days of Israel's rule in the West Bank and Gaza Strip. In 1967, shortly after it assumed control over these territories, the Israeli military enacted Order Number 132 Concerning the Adjudication of Young Offenders. Among other things, the order limited to a year the maximum prison sentence for Palestinian defendants aged 14 and 15 at the time of their sentencing. Initially, the order excluded from this limitation a handful of offenses related to political expression, such as flying political flags or symbols, disseminating political documents, and taking part in unlicensed marches or gatherings.[28] Less than three years later, the order

---

[26] See Introduction, Section 2.3 ("Critiquing Against/With the Law"), as well as entry V: Violence.

[27] This in no way makes them any less "real," as Benedict Anderson explained regarding another product of the social imaginary: nationality. See B. Anderson, *Imagined Communities: Reflections on the Origin and Spread of Nationalism* (London and New York: Verso, 1983).

[28] Article 5 of Order No. 132 Concerning the Adjudication of Young Offenders, 1967.

was amended to exclude from the maximum sentence limitation all offenses that otherwise carry a maximum penalty of five years.[29] This was a considerable expansion of the exception clause, because all common charges against Palestinian children are punishable by more than five years, and hence the amended exception clause almost always applies. As a case in point, the most common charge – stone-throwing – carries a maximum prison sentence of 10 years, or even 20 years if perpetrated against a moving vehicle.[30] The all-embracing exception thus swallowed the maximum sentence rule, effectively rendering it void.

In more recent years, Israel has made a series of statutory reforms concerning noncitizen Palestinians under the age of 18, which likewise contain broad exception clauses. Among the reforms are two amendments to the military law from 2011: a requirement to inform parents or adult relatives of Palestinian children's arrest, and a reduction of the statute of limitations for children from two years to one. Shortly after enacting them, the Israeli military issued public statements in both Hebrew and English, describing these and other amendments as "yet another significant step in strengthening the protection of the rights of [Palestinian] minors in Judea and Samaria [i.e., the West Bank]."[31] Yet, in reality, these have been token reforms, largely due to their all-encompassing exception clauses.

Specifically, one type of exception clause, common to both amendments, precludes them from applying to suspected "security offenders."[32] The statutory term "security offenses" is broad and vague,[33] encompassing almost all of the common charges against Palestinian minors, such as stone-throwing, membership of associations proscribed by the Israeli military, and obstructing

---

[29]   Order No. 132 (Amendment No. 3), 1970.   [30]   Article 212 of Order 1651.

[31]   Defense Forces Spokesperson's Office, "Amendment to the Military Law: The Age of Minority in Judea and Samaria Raised from 16 to 18," *IDF* (October 10, 2011) [hereinafter: "Amendment to the Military Law"] [Hebrew], www.idf.il/1133–13409-he/Dover.aspx; MAG Corps, "Security Legislation Amended to Define 'Minors' under 18" (October 6, 2011); Office of the Legal Advisor to the IDF in the West Bank, "Statutory Amendment: The Age of Minority in the Judea and Samaria Region Raised to 18," *IDF MAG Corps* (October 5, 2011) [hereinafter: "Statutory Amendment"] [Hebrew], www.mag.idf.il/163 4736-cn/patzar.aspx.

[32]   Articles 4, 5, and 7 of Order 1676. Palestinian minors suspected of "security offenses" are subject to a longer (two-year) statute of limitations. See also Article 54(a) of Order 1651 (authorizing the military and the police not to inform of arrests of those suspected of a charge for which the sentence exceeds three years, subject to approval by a military court judge). In recent years, "security offenders" have constituted between half to a third of Israel's total child inmate population. See Knesset Research and Information Center, *Children in Israel: Select Issues Concerning Rights, Needs, and Services* (2015), http://main.knesset.gov.il/Activity/Info/MMMSummaries19/Children.pdf.

[33]   For further information on the scope and application of this and related terms, see entry S: Security Prisoners.

a soldier.[34] As a result, the formal exception to these amendments is applied as a matter of norm, thus operating as the actual rule. Alongside these blanket "security offenses" clauses, two other exceptions operate to preserve the latitude and ad hoc discretion of Israeli authorities. One such clause exempts Israeli authorities from informing parents or relatives of children's arrest, in the name of safeguarding "national security," "the success of the interrogation," or "the child's wellbeing"[35] – open-ended terms allowing for virtually unrestricted discretion. Another exception clause likewise authorizes the military, at its discretion, to prosecute Palestinian children even after the one-year statute of limitation expires.[36]

As these examples illustrate, the Israeli military has designed and enforced statutory exceptions, time and again, as the de facto rules. This, however, has not been the military's only way of reversing the formal rule and exception. Some provisions in military orders are effectively the exceptions not due to some exemption or qualifications clauses, but because, contrary to public Israeli statements, they only apply to very rare circumstances. In 2009, for instance, two amendments were made to the military law, concerning witness examination: the first, requiring military judges to assist unrepresented Palestinian children in examining witnesses; and the second, entitling parents to examine witnesses. In a public statement, the military's legal advisor in the West Bank extolled these and other amendments as being "practical and important provisions" that take "into account the principle of the best interests of the minor."[37] The reality, however, is quite different: these publicly lauded new rules are likely to have little if any impact in the Israeli court system, where witness examination is a rare exception. Full evidentiary trials, in which witnesses give testimony, are a rarity – reportedly constituting less than one percent of military court trials in 2010.[38] Moreover, even on the rare occasions that Palestinian parents could potentially examine witnesses, military judges have been reported to often not inform them of this right,[39] and the military court of appeals has also ruled that they can be denied access to some of their

---

[34] H. Viterbo, "Rights as a Divide-and-Rule Mechanism: Lessons from the Case of Palestinians in Israeli Custody" (forthcoming) *Law & Social Inquiry* [hereinafter: "Rights as a Divide-and-Rule Mechanism"].

[35] Article 4 of Order 1676 (amending Article 136b of Order 1651).

[36] Article 144 of Order 1651.

[37] Legal Advisor to the IDF, "The Establishment of a Military Juvenile Court in Judea and Samaria," *IDF MAG Corps* (August 26, 2009) [Hebrew], www.law.idf.il/163–3161-he/patzar .aspx.

[38] See entry M: Military Courts.

[39] No Legal Frontiers, *All Guilty! Observations in the Military Juvenile Court* (2011), p. 34 [hereinafter: *All Guilty!*], http://nolegalfrontiers.org/images/stories/report_2011/report_en.pdf.

child's hearings on "security grounds."[40] Like other recent amendments discussed earlier, then, these are also token reforms – an issue this entry shall revisit later.

In addition to making formal rules the actual exception, the military legal system has also, by applying some child-related statutory rules incoherently, undermined their professed status as rules. Thus, like many other jurisdictions, Israel has in its law – including the military orders applied to Palestinians – a requirement for the courts to consider children's age when determining their sentence.[41] Yet, the military courts have been inconsistent in applying this statutory requirement. Some military judgments have followed the socially dominant view that youth is a potentially mitigating consideration,[42] whereas others disregarded this consideration in their judgments,[43] and some even treated it as an aggravating factor, for the purpose of deterrence.[44] Further, while the statutory military law mentions only chronological age, some military judgments show consideration of the appearance of Palestinian children's physical age, meaning that defendants may be treated differently because they look younger or older than their peers.[45] Moreover, for several years, in spite of the unequivocal definition of "minor" in the relevant military order, military judges applied competing definitions, and sometimes did so in explicit defiance of this statutory definition.[46]

Y.3 THE RULE OF EXCEPTION BEYOND ISRAELI MILITARY LAW

Far from being unique to the military law, the rule of exception extends to Israel's domestic law, as well as to Israeli authorities' approach to international

---

[40] MilC (Mil. Ct. App.) 1236/15 *Military Prosecution v. John Doe* (April 1, 2015), www.nevo.co.il/psika_word/army/ARMY-15-1236-33.doc.

[41] See, in the military and domestic law respectively, Article 168(a) of Order 1651; Article 25(c) of Youth Law.

[42] See, e.g., MilC (Ramalah Mil. Ct.) 2167/82 *Military Advocate General v. Ta'amra* (July 7, 1983), in General Military Corps, *Selected Rulings of the Military Court of Appeals in the Administered Territories* (General Staff – General Corps, 1987), vol. IV(II), pp. 368, 387; MilC (Mil. Ct. App.) 58/00 *Hatib v. Military Advocate General* (May 30, 2000); MilC (Mil. Ct. App.) 63/02 *Military Advocate General v. Hanawi* (February 9, 2003).

[43] Yesh Din, *Backyard Proceedings: The Implementation of Due Process Rights in the Military Courts in the Occupied Territories* (2007), p. 160 [hereinafter: *Backyard Proceedings*], https://s3-eu-west-1.amazonaws.com/files.yesh-din.org/%D7%9E%D7%A9%D7%A4%D7%98%D7%99%D7%9D+%D7%91%D7%97%D7%A6%D7%A8+%D7%94%D7%90%D7%97%D7%95%D7%A8%D7%99%D7%AA/BackyardProceedingsfullreportEng+full+report.pdf.

[44] Viterbo, "The Age of Conflict," pp. 142–144.   [45] *Ibid.*, pp. 144–147.

[46] For further discussion of this latter issue, see entry M: Military Courts.

legal norms. Regarding the former, given the unique status of Palestinian residents of East Jerusalem, one might expect their situation to be rather different to that described above. As part of its controversial annexation of East Jerusalem,[47] Israel tries these Palestinians under its domestic law (in civil courts), thereby formally expanding their legal rights far beyond those of Palestinians in other parts of the West Bank.[48] The context of custodial sentences provides some illustrative differences between the domestic law (applied, among other things, in East Jerusalem), which is generally considered to conform to international legal norms,[49] and the military law (applied to Palestinians in the rest of the West Bank). The domestic law sets the minimum age for imposing a custodial sentence at 14 years,[50] for example, as compared with only 12 years under the military law.[51] And while Israel's domestic legal system imposes custodial sentences on 6.5 to 20.6 percent of child defendants, the military courts, with barely any acquittals, sentence the vast majority of Palestinian child defendants (93.55 percent) to prison, usually in addition to fines (96.77 percent) and probationary sentences (98.71 percent).[52]

Yet, despite this legal and political disparity, reports suggest that Israeli authorities heavily rely on statutory exceptions when handling Palestinian children in East Jerusalem as well.[53] Exemplifying this are two statutory provisions concerning interrogations. The first entitles children to have a

47   On the status of East Jerusalem under Israeli law, see entries B: Border/Barrier, J: Jewish Settlements, M: Military Courts, and Z: Zone.

48   See also entries Z: Zone and M: Military Courts, as well as P. Veerman and B. Gross, "Implementation of the United Nations Convention on the Rights of the Child in Israel, the West Bank and Gaza" (1995) 3 *International Journal of Children's Rights* 296, 322–327; Viterbo, "The Age of Conflict," pp. 136–138.

49   See, e.g., T. Morag, "The Case Law Following the Ratification of the UN Convention on the Rights of the Child – A New Era?" (2006) 22 *Ha-Mishpat* [The Law] 22 [Hebrew]; T. Morag, "The Effect of the Commission for Examination of the Basic Principles Concerning the Child and the Law on the Israeli Case Law's Underlying Conceptions" (2010) 3 *Mishpaha Ba-Mishpat* [Family in Law] 67, 68–70 [Hebrew].

50   Article 25(b) of Youth Law.

51   Israeli military law includes no restriction on the minimum age for custodial sentences. Such sentences can therefore be imposed on all Palestinians aged 12 years (the age of criminal responsibility) or older.

52   Viterbo, "Rights as a Divide-and-Rule Mechanism."

53   Association for Civil Rights in Israel, *Violations of the "Youth Law (Adjudication, Punishment and Methods of Treatment) – 1971" by the Israeli Police in East Jerusalem* (2011), pp. 9–14, http://reliefweb.int/sites/reliefweb.int/files/resources/Full_Report_1007.pdf; Association for Civil Rights in Israel, Arrested Childhood, p. 9; B'Tselem, *Caution: Children Ahead – The Illegal Behavior of the Police toward Minors in Silwan Suspected of Stone Throwing* (2010), pp. 18–19, www.btselem.org/download/201012_caution_children_ahead_eng.pdf; Defence for Children International – Palestine, *Voices from East Jerusalem: The Situation Facing Palestinian*

parent or relative present at their interrogation, and also to consult with them, preferably prior to the interrogation. The second is a general requirement to avoid interrogating children "at night" (defined as 20:00–7:00 for those under 14 and 22:00–7:00 for older children). The latter provision is unequivocally framed in rule/exception terms in the police regulations: "As a rule, a minor shall be interrogated at daytime." Both provisions, however, contain expansive and widely used exemption clauses. The domestic law thus exempts the police – and this exemption is used in three out of four cases according to one report – from providing family presence and contact during or before interrogation, on grounds such as preventing harm to the interrogation or to national security. Invoking a similar exception clause, the Jerusalem police have also been reported to detain many Palestinian children at night. By normalizing such statutory exceptions and undermining the professed rules, Israeli authorities thus deny Palestinian children in East Jerusalem their formal protections.[54]

The rule of exception across both sides of the pre-1967 border resonates with two wider issues discussed elsewhere in this book. First, it exemplifies the legal continuities and parallels between what many Israelis imagine as the normal space of Israel "proper" and the supposedly exceptional space of the West Bank and Gaza Strip. And second, it resonates with the normalization of supposedly exceptional legal measures across the world for at least a century now.[55]

Moreover, Israel's reversal of the formal rule and exception within its laws also shares some parallels with its position regarding the applicability of international law.[56] Israeli governments have considered the West Bank and Gaza Strip as spaces of exception. In line with their general stance on the applicability of international law, and not unlike the rule of exception in Israel's own law, they have placed these territories outside the international norms of children's rights to which Israel has otherwise pledged allegiance. In statements widely rejected internationally – including by the UN Committee on the Rights of the Child, among many others[57] – Israeli governments have

---

children (2011), pp. 42–44, https://d3n8a8pro7vhmx.cloudfront.net/dcipalestine/pages/1297/att achments/original/1433986700/DCIP_east_jerusalem_final.pdf?1433986700.

[54] The above provisions and exceptions appear in Article 9h of Youth Law; Article 3(c)(2)(a) of Police Ordinance No. 14.01.05 Concerning the Police Handling of Minors, 2004.

[55] See, respectively, entries O: Outside/Inside, Sections O.3 ("Israeli Law Does Not Stop at the Border") and O.4 ("Conclusion"); Introduction, Section 2.3 ("Critiquing Against/With the Law").

[56] On this position, see entry G: Geneva Law.

[57] See, e.g., UN Committee on the Rights of the Child, Consideration of Reports Submitted by States Parties under Article 8 of the Optional Protocol to the Convention on the Rights of the

posited that the UN Convention on the Rights of the Child, to which Israel is a signatory,[58] do not bind Israeli authorities in the Palestinian Territory. Similarly nonbinding, the claim goes, are international treaties with child-related provisions, including GC IV, the Covenant on Civil and Political Rights, and the Convention against Torture.[59] The military court system has generally treaded a similar line. In cases involving noncitizen Palestinian children, Israeli military judges have only rarely and sporadically made reference to international legal norms: the prohibition, in the UN Convention on the Rights of the Child, on sentencing children to life;[60] the weight accorded by the Convention to child offenders' age;[61] the Convention's influence on Israeli domestic law;[62] and various child-related international humanitarian law provisions.[63] This body of international law, the military courts nonetheless made sure to consistently emphasize, is nonbinding to noncitizen Palestinians under Israeli rule. Somewhat similarly to Israeli authorities' selective invocation of Israel's own statutory norms, then, the military courts have invoked these international legal rules while undoing their power as rules.

Y.4 TOKEN REFORMS BEYOND THE RULE OF EXCEPTION

Israel's use of legal exceptions also opens a broader window into its recent reforms concerning Palestinian children in Israeli custody. Some of these

Child on the Involvement of Children in Armed Conflict – Concluding Observations: Israel, January 29, 2010, CRC/C/OPAC/ISR/CO/1, ¶ 4, www2.ohchr.org/english/bodies/crc/docs/C RC-C-OPAC-ISR-CO-1.pdf. See also, e.g., Legal Consequence of the Construction of a Wall in the Occupied Palestinian Territory, Advisory Opinion, 2004 ICJ 136, ¶¶ 102–113, www.icj-cij.org/files/case-related/131/131-20040709-ADV-01-00-EN.pdf; UN Committee Against Torture, Consideration of Report Submitted by States Parties under Article 19 of the Convention – Israel: Concluding Observations, May 14, 2009, CAT/C/ISR/CO/4, ¶ 11, www2.ohchr.org/english/bodies/cat/docs/cobs/CAT.C.ISR.CO.4.pdf.

[58] Israel, however, is not party to the two 1977 additional protocols of GC IV concerning victims of armed conflicts, including children.

[59] For discussion of this position, see, e.g., O. Ben-Naftali and Y. Shany, "Living in Denial: The Application of Human Rights in the Occupied Territories" (2003) 37 *Israel Law Review* 17, 18–28. On the supreme court's somewhat more nuanced approach, see, e.g., *ibid.*, p. 24.

[60] MilC (Mil. Ct. App.) 128/02 *Kudsi* v. *Military Advocate General* (December 23, 2002); MilC (Mil. Ct. App.) 346/03 *Military Advocate General* v. *Jawadra* (July 1, 2004).

[61] MilC (Judea Mil. Ct.) 4941/08 *Military Advocate General* v. *K.D.* (August 6, 2009).

[62] MilC (Mil. Ct. App.) 2912/09 *Military Prosecution* v. *Abu Rahma* (August 31, 2009).

[63] MilC (Judea Mil. Ct.) (unnumbered) *Military Advocate General* v. *Salem* (2003); MilC (Beit El Mil. Ct.) 41867/01 *Military Advocate General* v. *Abu Ish-Shabab* (April 7, 2003); MilC (Mil. Ct. App.) 1/07 *Meshbaum* v. *Military Advocate General* (January 29, 2007); MilC (Mil. Ct. App.) 3335/07 *Dar-Halil* v. *Military Prosecution* (May 29, 2008).

reforms, as shown, have been either devoured by exception clauses or designed to only apply in exceptional circumstances, and have consequently been deprived of most of their potential impact. These, however, are only part of an array of token reforms Israeli authorities have introduced and hailed in recent years.

This systematic use of token reforms is clearly evidenced in the three most high-profile reforms to date. The first is Israel's establishment, in 2009, of the world's first and only[64] "military youth court." For the first time, this first-instance court was legally required to hold proceedings of Palestinian children separately, "as much as possible," from those of their adult counterparts.[65] But contrary to self-congratulatory statements by the Israeli military legal system,[66] military youth court hearings are not actually significantly different from the previous system. And though military youth court judges are required by law to undergo "appropriate training," the exact nature of this training is not publicly known.[67]

A second high-profile reform, taking place in 2011, was the military's raising of the statutory age of criminal majority from 16 to 18 years,[68] which brought 16- and 17-year-old Palestinian defendants within the definition of "minors." The military, in special Hebrew and English statements, lauded this amendment as having "great significance" and "substantial implications."[69] In reality, however, this terminological change had no discernible impact on the adjudication, sentencing, or incarceration[70] of those newly classified as "minors." The sentences imposed on this age group have reportedly remained

---

[64] United Nations Children's Fund (UNICEF), *Children in Israeli Military Detention: Observations and Recommendations* (February 2013), www.unicef.org/oPt/UNICEF_oPt_C hildren_in_Israeli_Military_Detention_Observations_and_Recommendations_-_6_Marc h_2013.pdf.

[65] Article 1 of Order 1644 Concerning Security Provisions (Temporary Order) (Amendment No. 109), 2009 (amending Articles 136–143 of Order 1651).

[66] Legal Advisor to the IDF, *The Establishment of a Military Juvenile Court in Judea and Samaria*; T. Yaniv and D. Yom-Tov, "A Military Youth Court Established," *IDF Spokesperson* (November 2, 2009) [Hebrew], www.idf.il/1133–8498-hc/Dover.aspx.

[67] Defence for Children International – Palestine, "Israeli Juvenile Military Court – Four Months On" (February 16, 2010), http://right2edu.birzeit.edu/israeli-juvenile-military-court-f our-months/.

[68] Article 3 of Order 1676 (amending Article 139 of Order 1651).

[69] Defense Forces Spokesperson's Office, "Amendment to the Military Law"; MAG Corps, "Security Legislation Amended to Define 'Minors' under 18" (October 6, 2011), www.mag.id f.il/163–4736-en/patzar.aspx; Office of the Legal Advisor to the IDF in the West Bank, "Statutory Amendment".

[70] On the pitfalls of Israel's shift toward separating Palestinian children and adults, see entry S: Security Prisoners.

unchanged,[71] and the sentencing guidelines relating to them are still no different from those applied to adults.

The third of these high-profile reforms was described, in Israeli authorities' responses to petitions on the matter,[72] as "shortening, very substantially, the [maximum] detention periods for [Palestinian] minors in Judea and Samaria [i.e., the West Bank]."[73] Consisting of a series of amendments, which the military made in 2012 and 2013 following these petitions, this reform has in fact not necessarily reduced the time Palestinian children can be detained. Instead, it merely modified the procedures for extending their detention. For instance, in their responses to the petitions, Israeli authorities described one of the amendments as reducing the maximum detention period prior to first judicial review from eight days to shorter periods depending on the child's age and offenses.[74] Later, Israeli authorities added that the military court, which had previously been authorized by law to extend a child's detention at this stage for up to 90 days, could now – following the reform – only do so for 40 days.[75] Despite these changes, however, the amendments kept detention potentially unlimited, by explicitly preserving the military court of appeals' authority to continue extending it for additional periods of 90 days each, with no aggregate maximum.[76] The Israeli authorities have similarly boasted of having "significantly shortened" the maximum detention period at a later stage of the legal process – remand until the end of proceedings – from 18 months to a year.[77] Yet, at this stage, too, detention can be extended every 3 months, with no set limit.[78]

---

[71] B'Tselem, *No Minor Matter*.

[72] Petition in HCJ 4057/10 *Association for Civil Rights in Israel and others* v. *IDF Commander in the Judea and Samaria Region* (May 25, 2010), www.acri.org.il/pdf/petitions/hit4057.pdf; Petition in HCJ 3368/10 *Palestinian Ministry of Prisoners' Affairs and others* v. *Minister of Defense* (May 3, 2010) (on file with the author). Due to their overlap, the supreme court decided to consider these two petitions together.

[73] Update statement by the State in HCJ 3368/10 and 4057/10 (December 16, 2016) [hereinafter: Update statement December 16, 2016], www.acri.org.il/he/wp-content/uploads/2012/12/hi t4057idkun1212.pdf.

[74] These shorter maximum periods, according to the state's response to the petitions, are: a day (24 hours) for under-14-year-olds; 2 days for those aged 14–15; and, for 16–17-year-olds, 4 or 2 days, depending on whether or not they are suspected of "security offenses." *ibid.*

[75] Further update statement by the State in HCJ 3368/10 and 4057/10 (October 29, 2013), www .acri.org.il/he/wp-content/uploads/2014/04/hit4057meshivim1013.pdf.

[76] Article 38 of Order 1651 (amended by Articles 5–6 of Order 1685 Concerning Security Provisions (Amendment No. 16) (Judea and Samaria), 2012; and Articles 1–2 of Order 1726 Concerning Security Provisions (Amendment No. 34) (Judea and Samaria), 2013).

[77] Update statement December 16, 2016.

[78] Article 2 of Order 1711 Concerning Security Provisions (Judea and Samaria) (Amendment No. 25), 2012 (amending Article 44 of Order 1651).

Rather than reducing the maximum duration of detention, then, this reform has merely modified the points in time at which each Israeli legal authority extends the detention. This procedural change is unlikely to have much of an effect on the actual length of detention, given the military courts' deference to, and preference for, the wishes and interests of Israeli agencies over those of Palestinian detainees. Among other things, the military court of appeals is twice more likely to accept appeals by the military prosecution against the leniency of first-instance court decisions than appeals by Palestinian defendants. Further, confessions extracted during the interrogation – the main and sometimes only evidence against Palestinian child defendants – are seldom later excluded by the military court. In fact, military judges have openly admitted their tendency to take Israeli interrogators' word over that of Palestinian detainees.[79] This is despite repeated reports of Israeli interrogators coercing Palestinian children into potentially false confessions through physical violence, threats, and protracted handcuffing or binding in stress positions.[80] Reports also abound of Israeli authorities' attempts to recruit Palestinian children as informants, through threats and inducements during and in between interrogations.[81]

Against this backdrop, Israeli military judges seem likely to usually extend detention at the interrogators' request. Indeed, in recent years, the military courts have been found to remand the vast majority (81.7 percent) of Palestinian child defendants until the end of proceedings, and only 14.5

[79] See entry M: Military Courts; L. Hajjar, *Courting Conflict: The Israeli Military Court System in the West Bank and Gaza* (London: University of California Press, 2005), p. 109. See also the 2011 documentary film *The Law in These Parts* (2013; Dir.: Ra'anan Alexandrowicz; American Documentary/POV), specifically the interviews with former military judges Oded Pessenson ("as a rule, I didn't doubt what they [the Security Service interrogators] said. ... When a detainee tells me what they did to him, I'm pretty suspicious. Because he has his interests") and Jonathan Livny ("As a military judge you don't just represent justice. ... As a military judge you represent the authorities of the occupation. ... You're conducting a trial against your enemy").

[80] See, e.g., United Nations Children's Fund (UNICEF), *Children in Israeli Military Detention: Observations and Recommendations – Bulletin No. 2* (February 2015), www.unicef.org/oPt/C hildren_in_Israeli_Military_Detention_-_Observations_and_Recommendations_-_Bulleti n_No._2_-_February_2015.pdf; B'Tselem, *No Minor Matter*; Defence for Child. Int'l – Palestine, No Way to Treat a Child; No Legal Frontiers, *All Guilty!*; Madaa Creative Center, *The Impact of Child Arrest and Detention* (2012), https://resourcecentre.savethechil dren.net/sites/default/files/documents/2012-madaa-report-on-child-arrest-and-detention-in-sil wan.pdf.

[81] Addameer, Imprisonment of Children; Defence for Children International – Palestine, *Recruitment and Use of Palestinian Children in Armed Conflict* (2012), http://arabic.dci-pales tine.org/sites/default/files/recruitment_report_-_final.pdf; Madaa Creative Center, *The Impact of Child Arrest and Detention*.

percent were released on bail.[82] In contrast to Israel's domestic law, which stipulates that detention should be a last resort,[83] no equivalent provision exists in the military law. The question also arises of how seriously military judges consider remand given the relative hastiness of military court proceedings:[84] in some observations, detention hearings involving under-18s were found to last no longer than 3 minutes and 20 seconds on average.[85] Moreover, even if the above procedural reform would somehow actually shorten detention, it has no direct effect on the period of time to which most complaints of ill-treatment relate: the first 24 hours following Palestinian children's arrest.[86]

To a large extent, then, what the recent amendments provide is not a meaningful change to the treatment of Palestinian children. Rather, while preserving the powers and latitude of Israeli authorities, they provide a legal veneer to potentially legitimize Israel's continued rule in the Palestinian territories.

Y.5 CONCLUSION: THE RULE OF EXCEPTION

This entry has sought to highlight and explore the key role of so-designated "rules" and "exceptions" in Israel's dealing with young Palestinians. Beginning at least in the early days of Israel's rule over the West Bank and Gaza Strip, and continuing vigorously to the present day, Israeli authorities have pursued a two-pronged legal endeavor. On the one hand, they have continuously enacted new provisions, guarantees, and safeguards, often publicly praising them as introducing new statutory rules beneficial to Palestinian children. On the other hand, on both sides of the pre-1967 border – through the military law applied to most Palestinians in the West Bank as well as the domestic law applied to other noncitizen Palestinians – Israeli authorities have rendered these formal rules the de facto exception.

This has been achieved in two central ways: first, designing broad exemption or qualification clauses, and heavily invoking such clauses, so that the statutory exception swallows the formal rule; and second, introducing statutory provisions that only affect very rare circumstances, contrary to self-

---

[82]   Viterbo, "Rights as a Divide-and-Rule Mechanism."   [83]   Article 10a of Youth Law.
[84]   See entry M: Military Courts.   [85]   Yesh Din, *Backyard Proceedings*, p. 160.
[86]   Military Court Watch, *Children in Military Custody: Progress Report – 2 Years on* (September 2014), pp. 14, 17, www.militarycourtwatch.org/files/server/CHILDREN%20IN%20MILITARY% 20CUSTODY%20-%202%20YEARS%20ON%20(1).pdf; G. Horton, "Assessing Developments in Israel's Juvenile Military Courts," +972 *Magazine* (December 7, 2013), http://972mag.com/ assessing-developments-in-israels-juvenile-military-courts/83196/. Interestingly, these reports did not notice that the amendments in question merely modified the remand procedures rather than actually reducing the maximum detention periods.

congratulatory Israeli statements. In addition, the Israeli legal system has also undermined the professed status of some statutory rules as rules, by either applying them inconsistently or even breaching them outright. Somewhat comparably, while occasionally invoking international children's rights norms, Israeli authorities have relegated noncitizen Palestinians to a space of exception, supposedly outside the binding power of these legal norms.

Due to this rule of exception, as well as other factors identified above, Israel's recent amendments concerning Palestinians under the age of 18 are not much more than mere token reforms. These amendments preserve the latitude and ad hoc discretion of Israeli authorities, without substantially changing the actual treatment of young Palestinians. Israel thus seems resolute in shaping and potentially legitimizing its often-violent practices through legal means – statutes, amendments, judgments, and law enforcement – illustrating law's violence, an issue examined further elsewhere in this book.[87]

In principle, rules and norms can be no less violent than their supposed exceptions. Moreover, the very distinction between rule and exception is conceptually, normatively, and historically questionable.[88] Therefore, the reversal of the rule and exception is not innately deplorable. As this entry has shown, what warrants criticism in the present context is Israel's use of seeming rules and exceptions: its self-legitimizing claim to enforce and comply with what it presents as statutory rules, while turning these ostensible rules into exceptions and thus denying Palestinian children their purported protections.

---

[87] See entries V: Violence and L: Lawfare, as well as Introduction, Section 2.3 ("Critiquing Against/With the Law").

[88] See Introduction, Section 2.3 ("Critiquing Against/With the Law") and entry V: Violence.

Z

Zone

Orna Ben-Naftali

Z.1 GENERAL: ON THE LEGAL CONSTRUCTION OF OCCUPIED TERRITORY

Z.1.1 *The Discomfort Zone*

The term "zone" commonly denotes a material area or a stretch of land that is subject to particular legal restrictions related to its assigned purpose or use. IHL generally, and the law of belligerent occupation specifically, regulate certain areas designated as "danger zones," "safety zones," and "neutralized zones" to advance humanitarian purposes, but do not otherwise specify spatial regulation.[1] From the perspective of the law of belligerent occupation, an occupied territory in its entirety is one zone, a delimited and exceptional space, subject to its regulation. The exceptionality of the space derives from the severance of the normal link between sovereignty and effective control exercised over it. The law of belligerent occupation regulates this exceptionality in two primary ways: first, it prohibits the occupying power from annexing the territory and from otherwise introducing therein major systemic changes, including the transfer of its own population to the

---

[1] The terms "safety zones" and "neutralized zones" are referred to in Articles 14–15 and in Annex I of the Geneva Convention Relative to the Protection of Civilian Persons in the Time of War, Geneva, August 12, 1949, 75 UNTS 287 [hereinafter: GC IV]. The term "danger zones" is referred to in Article 28 of the GC IV, and the term "demilitarized zones" in Article 60 of the Protocol Additional to the Geneva Conventions of August 12, 1949, and relating to the Protection of Victims of International Armed Conflicts (Additional Protocol I), Geneva, June 8, 1977, 1125 UNTS 3 [hereinafter: AP I]. The Hague Convention (IV) Respecting the Laws and Customs of War on Land and its annex: Regulations concerning the Laws and Customs of War on Land, The Hague, October 18, 1907, 205 CTS 277; 36 Stat 2277 [hereinafter: the Hague Regulations], contains the term "zone" only once in the context of the definition of spies, Article 29, and otherwise refers only to the term "territory," mainly in the context of occupied territory, Articles 42–56.

occupied territory;[2] second, it entrusts the occupant with the management of the territory in a manner designed to protect the well-being of the occupied population, designated as "protected persons."[3]

This legal perspective thus conceives of an occupied territory as "the fixed" and "the undialectical"[4] upon which legal norms are applied. This perspective ignores the legal production of space: space itself is a sociopolitical configuration. The spatial and the sociopolitical are dialectically related, each affecting the other,[5] thus signifying the way power is written on the ground.[6] Law, far from providing a neutral framework, is one mechanism that produces material, social and mental spaces.[7] The legal production of the occupied Palestinian space is the focus of this entry.

Z.1.2 *The OPT as a No-place*

The Israeli–Palestinian conflict has been about territory since its very beginning. A cursory glance at maps, from the United Nations partition plan to date,[8] tells the story of the expansion of Israeli space at the expense of Palestinian space.[9] This story, however, is but the tip of the iceberg in a hot

---

[2] Article 49(6) of the GC IV. For a discussion of this prohibition, see entry J: Jewish Settlements.

[3] On the basic purposes and related principles of the law of belligerent occupation see the Introduction, Section 2.2; G: Geneva Law, Section G.1.1; T: Temporary/Indefinite, Section T.2. On the status of "protected persons" see article 4 of the GC IV.

[4] M. Foucault, *Questions on Geography* in *Power/Knowledge: Selected Interviews and Other Writings 1972–1977*, C. Gordon (ed.) (New York: Pantheon Books, 1980), p. 70, cited in Y. Blank and I. Rosen-Zvi, "The Spatial Turn in Legal Theory" (2010) 10 *Hagar: Studies in Culture, Polity and Identities* 39.

[5] E. Soja, "The Socio-Spatial Dialectic" (1980) 70 *Annals of the Association of American Geography* 207, 225, cited in T. Mahmud "Geography and International Law: Towards a Postcolonial Mapping" (2007) 5 *Santa Clara Journal of International Law* 525.

[6] M. Foucault, *Dits et Ecrits*, Volume III (Paris: Gallimard, 1994), pp. 28–40 [French].

[7] H. Lefebvre, *The Production of Space*, D. Nicholson-Smith (trans.) (Oxford: Blackwell Publishers, 1991) introduced the material, social (where people interact), and mental-subjective (the way space is experienced by people) aspects of space. Blank and Rosen-Zvi, "The Spatial Turn," provide an illuminating exposé of the various ways law influences and is influenced by these spaces.

[8] The Partition Plan, GA Res 181 (II), UN Doc A/RES/181(II) (November 29, 1947).

[9] For the notion that the maps are misleading first because they assume that both Israelis and Palestinians share the same space whereas the spatial control exercised by Israel creates a division, and second, because they create a false picture of symmetry in the sense that every piece of land taken from one party is added to the other, thereby obfuscating the asymmetry in the actual possibility of using the land, see A. Handel, "Where, Where to, and When in the Occupied Territories: An Introduction to Geography of Disaster," in A. Ofir, M. Givoni, and S. Hanafi (eds.), *The Power of Inclusive Exclusion: Anatomy of Israeli Rule in the Occupied Palestinian Territories* (Cambridge, Ma: MIT Press, 2009), pp. 179–180.

land. The story that the maps fail to tell is that, to the extent a place is the meeting point of space with people, the OPT has become a no-place for Palestinians. It is a territorial project undertaken by Israel, a de-bordered State which exercises intense border policing throughout the land.[10] It is a project the underlying logic of which relates to the territory as *terra nullius*,[11] an empty space, "a land without people" to be restored "to a people without a land."[12] In this land there are no Palestinians endowed with a right to self-determination. The land is impregnated with Jewish sovereignty. The project is designed to deliver that sovereignty.

In this project, the Palestinians have no place:[13] they inhabit an extreme form of heterotopia, where they are separated from their land, from other Palestinians and from Israelis, yet closely controlled by the latter;[14] a land where it has become impossible for them to lead a normal life, a life the sine qua non condition for which is the ability to use space in a predictable manner that allows one to engage in the routine activities comprising it.

---

[10] Israel is a de-bordered State in two senses: first, while 20 percent of Israelis are non-Jews, it is defined as a Jewish State and as the nation for the world's Jewry not only for Israelis; see Law of Return, 1950. Second, it is yet to define its borders with Syria, Lebanon, and Palestine/ Palestinian Authority (PA). On the gap between Israel's lack of defined borders and zeal for border control, see, H. Tawil-Souri, "Uneven Borders, Coloured (Im)mobilities: ID Cards in Palestine/Israel" (2012) 17 *Geopolitics* 153, 154–155.

[11] See Western Sahara, Advisory Opinion, 1975 ICJ 12, ¶¶ 79–80 ("[T]he State practice of the relevant period indicates that territories inhabited by tribes or peoples having a social and political organization were not regarded as *terrae nullius* . . . the acquisition of sovereignty was not generally considered as effected unilaterally through 'occupation' of *terra nullius* by original title but through agreements concluded with local rulers").

[12] This phrase, attributed to British writer Israel Zangwill, was first used in the writings of nineteenth-century Evangelical writers. On its genesis, see D. Muir, "A Land without People for a People without a Land" (2008) XV *Middle East Quarterly* 55. This view explains, inter alia, Israel's refusal to admit the de jure applicability of the GC IV to the OPT, see entry G: Geneva Law. For a discussion of the role this view plays in the current politics of Israel, see entry N: Nomos.

[13] "No-Place" should be distinguished from "Non-Place": The latter, first introduced by Augé, is used to oppose the concept of a sociological "place": If a place can be defined as relational, historical, and concerned with identity, then it is a "place"; the rest would be "non-places," such as, for example, highways, airports, and supermarkets. See M. Augé, *Non-places: Introduction to Anthropology of Supermodernity*, J. Howe (trans.) (London: Verso, 1995).

[14] M. Foucault, *Discipline and Punish: The Birth of the Prison*, A. Sheridan (trans.) (New York: Vintage Books, 1995), p. 198. The OPT is an extreme form of heterotopias because, as Ronen Shamir observed "Foucault's evocative image of the lepers – those who gave rise to rituals of exclusion; transferred, deported, locked away, rendered invisible – and the plague – inviting the careful partitioning of space and surveillance – rendering them hypervisible – collapses here: the occupation relies on both modalities of power," R. Shamir, "Occupation as Disorientation: The Impossibility of Borders" in A. Ofir, M. Givoni, and S. Hanafi, *The Power of Inclusive Exclusion*, pp. 587, 591. See also entry X: X Rays.

This space which is no-place and is inhabited by bare life is nevertheless not lawless.[15] Indeed, it overflows with laws and regulations that have played a major role in its production. This role is detailed in Section Z.2, focusing on two enabling legal technologies: the division of the territory (Z.2.2) and the major control mechanisms employed by Israel over both mobile subjects and immobile objects within it (Z.2.3). The story which unfolds is the story of the legal shaping of facts on the grounds in a manner that exposes the infrastructure of the A to Z of the Israeli control over the OPT. Section Z.2 concludes with a focus on law's role and modus operandi in the landscaping the Palestinian space to advance the Israeli territorial project.

Z.2 THE LEGAL REGULATION OF THE PALESTINIAN SPACE

Z.2.1 *Of Land and People*

Like many unhappy marriages, Israel entered its relationship with the occupied Palestinians in 1967, coveting "the dowry but not the bride,"[16] and turning a blind eye to the fact that she was "married to another man."[17] Its interest in the dowry, the territory of the West Bank, remains the driving logic of the occupation: Jerusalem was annexed and the first Jewish settlement in the West Bank was built in 1967.[18] Presently, approximately 50 percent of the land of the West Bank has been expropriated;[19] 125 settlements, home to close to 370,000 Jewish–Israeli settlers, and some 100 "outposts" where additional 10,000

---

[15] On "bare life," see G. Agamben, *Homo Sacer: Sovereign Power and Bare Life*, D. Heller-Roazen (trans.) (Stanford: Stanford University Press, 1988), pp. 50–55; see also the Introduction, Section 2.2.

[16] In 1967, in a Labor Party meeting, then MP Eshkol said to then general secretary of the party, MP Meir: "you covet the dowry, not the bride": See S. Gazit, *The Carrot and the Stick – Israel's Policy in Judea and Samaria 1967–1968* (Washington, DC: B'nai B'rith, 1995), p. 135.

[17] See G. Karmi, *Married to Another Man: Israel's Dilemma in Palestine* (London: Pluto Press 2007).

[18] Basic Law: Jerusalem Capital of Israel, Article 5; the first settlement was Kfar Etzion. The territory on which the settlement had been established was officially seized by the military commander for military purposes, following a governmental decision to resettle the Hebron area, see Civil Case (District Court, Jerusalem) 2581/00 *G.A.L Ltd* v. *State of Israel* (October 30, 2007) [Hebrew]. The settlements project is discussed in entry J: Jewish Settlements.

[19] N. Shalev, *Under the Guise of Legality: Israel's Declaration of State Land in the West Bank* (Jerusalem: B'Tselem, 2012), pp. 47–55; Y. Lein, *Land Grab: Israel's Settlement Policy in the West Bank* (Jerusalem: B'Tselem, 2002), p. 47. See also, Y. Holzman-Gazit, *Land Expropriation in Israel: Law, Culture and Society* (Hampshire: Ashgate, 2007).

settlers live, were built.[20] Approximately 211,000 Jewish Israelis reside in East Jerusalem.[21] The Gaza Strip, "the forgotten corner of Palestine,"[22] has been separated from the West Bank and essentially sealed off from the rest of the world. What has changed over time is the attitude toward the bride, the Palestinians: whereas between 1967 and the beginning of the Oslo process in the early 1990s, Israel shouldered the responsibility for the management of Palestinian civil society institutions, it has since outsourced them to the Palestinian Authority (PA): The eight Oslo agreements[23] disclose that responsibilities related to the management of the population were transferred to the PA but that spatial control was retained by Israel. In that sense, the Oslo process has not been about Israel's withdrawal from the West Bank, much less about the dismantlement of settlements; it has been about the fragmentation of the OPT and the reorganization of Israeli

[20]   "Outposts" is a term denoting unauthorized settlements, i.e., settlements established without government approval. These are communities that formally do not comply with one or more of the following conditions: (1) governmental authorization to build the settlement; (2) the land is state land or owned by Jews; (3) the settlement is built according to a master plan, pursuant to which building permits may be issued; (4) the community's jurisdiction is determined by order of the commander of the area. See T. Sasson, *Interim Report on the Subject of Unauthorized Outposts* (Jerusalem: 2005) [Hebrew; an English summary of the report is available at www.mfa .gov.il/mfa/aboutisrael/state/law/pages/summary%20of%20opinion%20concerning%20unau thorized%20outposts%20-%20talya%20sason%20adv.aspx], pp. 20–21. The report was presented to late prime minister Sharon in February 2005. Government Resolution No 3376, www.pmo .gov.il/Secretary/GovDecisions/2005/Pages/des3376.aspx [Hebrew] endorsed the report's findings and recommendations on March 13, 2005. The term "unauthorized outposts" is designed to differentiate them from the settlements. Note that from an international legal perspective there is no difference between an "unauthorized outpost" and a settlement: both are equally unauthorized as they violate Article 49(6) of the GC IV. Currently, the Israeli government is devising legal ways and means to retroactively authorize such outposts; see Z. Stahl, *From Occupation to Annexation: the Silent Adoption of the Levy Report on Retroactive Authorization of Illegal Construction in the West Bank* (Tel Aviv: Yesh Din, 2016). See entry R: Regularization.

[21]   Central Intelligence Agency (CIA), *The World Factbook – Middle East: The West Bank*, https://www.cia.gov/library/publications/the-world-factbook/geos/we.html. On Jerusalem, see Section Z.2.2.3.

[22]   A. M. Lesch, "Gaza: Forgotten Corner of Palestine" (1985) 15 *Palestinian Studies* 43. See Section Z.2.1. Other than in the context of periodic eruptions of violence, Gaza and its inhabitants still remain the "forgotten corner of Palestine."

[23]   The agreements comprise of the following: Declaration of Principles on Interim Self-Government Arrangements (September 13, 1993), 32 ILM 1525; The Paris Protocol on Economic Relations (April 29, 1994); Agreement on the Gaza Strip and the Jericho Area (May 4, 1994), 33 ILM 622; Agreement on Preparatory Transfer of Powers and Responsibilities Between Israel and the PLO (August 29, 1994), 34 ILM 455; The Israeli-Palestinian Interim Agreement on the West Bank and the Gaza Strip Oslo II (September 28, 1995), 36 ILM 551 [hereinafter: Oslo II]; Protocol Concerning the Redeployment in Hebron (January 17, 1997), 36 ILM 653 [hereinafter: the Hebron Protocol]; The Wye River Memorandum (October 23, 1998), 37 ILM 1251; The Sharam el-Sheikh Memorandum (September 4, 1999), 38 ILM 1465.

power:[24] henceforth, Palestinians would cease to be of interest to Israel, other than for the purpose of their exclusion.

The separation thus affected, is not about separating the state of Israel from a nascent Palestinian state. It is about separating Palestinians from their land, from other Palestinians and from Israelis. It is not about borders between states; it is about bordering the Palestinians in order to realize Israel's sovereignty throughout much of their land. The production of this relationship between place and people in a manner that affects peoples' sense of belonging and shapes the economic, social and political course of their life and identity, has been affected by law and legal practices. Section Z.2.2 outlines the fragmentation of the OPT and discusses the material and legal means used to affect this separation and produce this relationship between place and people.

Z.2.2 Territorial Fragmentation: Too Many Zones, No Place

The OPT is dissected into the following main zones:

Z.2.2.1 The Sui Generis Status of the Gaza Strip

The Gaza Strip is located on the eastern coast of the Mediterranean Sea, bordering Egypt on the southwest and Israel on the east and north. With a population of some 1.85 million people, and comprising 365 square kilometers, some of which are depopulated buffer zones on both the Egyptian and the Israeli sides, it is one of the most densely populated areas in the world. The territory was captured from Egypt in 1967 and remained under Israeli military administration until 1994. Pursuant to the Oslo Accords, the PA assumed the management of civilian life in Gaza and Israel retained control of airspace, territorial waters, and borders crossings, with the exception of the border with Egypt.[25] In 2005, the Israeli parliament approved a unilateral disengagement plan, evicted some 9,000 settlers from the territory and declared an end to the military occupation of the area.[26] Since 2007 – and following the 2006 election of Hamas as the government of Gaza – the territory has been subject to a blockade maintained by both

---

[24] N. Gordon, "From Colonization to Separation: Exploring the Structure of Israel's Occupation" (2008) 29 *Third World Quarterly* 25, 34–35.

[25] Oslo II. Egypt controls its border with Gaza.

[26] Disengagement Plan Implementation Law, 2005, http://fs.knesset.gov.il//16/law/16_ls r_299869.pdf [Hebrew]. See also HCJ 1661/05 *Gaza Coast Regional Council v. The Israeli Knesset* (2005) 59(2) PD 481 [Hebrew].

Egypt and Israel.[27] Periodic eruptions of lethal violence between Israel and Hamas have further devastated the area.[28]

The status of Gaza received international legal attention revolving around the question of whether, following its disengagement, Israel still exercises sufficient effective control over the Gaza Strip to qualify as its occupying power. In a nutshell, Israel's position is that since it no longer continuously maintains forces on the ground, it no longer has effective control over the territory and cannot, therefore, shoulder the responsibilities imposed by the law of belligerent occupation on an occupying power. From Israel's perspective, allowing the passage of basic provisions and unspecified humanitarian assistance to Gaza exhaust its obligations.[29] This position, based on a narrow interpretation of "effective control," has been embraced by the HCJ in numerous decisions.[30] It is also supported by some leading international jurists.[31] An opposite perspective, interpreting the notion of "effective control" broadly and deriving from a teleological reading of IHL and from the large degree of control Israel still exercises over Gaza, also enjoys strong institutional and scholarly support.[32] In between these polar positions is the functional approach to the law of belligerent occupation, positing that the

[27]   See Y. Shany, "Binary Law Meets Complex Reality: The Occupation of Gaza Debate" (2008) 41 *Israel Law Review* 68 (2008); S. Solomon, "Occupied or Not: The Question of Gaza's Legal Status after the Israeli Disengagement" (2011) 19 *Cardozo Journal of International and Comparative Law* 59.

[28]   Including operation "Autumn Clouds" in 2006, which cost the lives of 82 Palestinians and 1 Israeli; operation "Cast Lead" in 2008–2009, in which the Palestinian death toll stood at 1,417, and the Israeli at 13; operation "Pillar of Defense" in 2012, causing approximately 150 deaths on the Palestinian side, and 6 on the Israeli one; and operation "Protective Edge" in 2014, taking approximately 2,200 Palestinian lives and 72 Israeli ones. See www.btselem.org/statistics.

[29]   *The 2014 Gaza Conflict: Factual and Legal Aspects* (The State of Israel, 2015), ¶¶ 45, 374, http://mfa.gov.il/ProtectiveEdge/Documents/2014GazaConflictFullReport.pdf.

[30]   The leading precedent is HCJ 9132/07 *Elbassiuni v. The Prime Minister of Israel* (January 30, 2008) [Hebrew].

[31]   E.g., E. Benvenisti, *The International Law of Occupation*, 2nd edn (Princeton: Princeton University Press, 2004), pp. 211–212; A. Roberts, "The Termination of Military Occupations." In *Occupation and Other Forms of Administration of Foreign Territory: Expert Meeting* (Geneva: ICRC, 2012), www.icrc.org/eng/assets/files/publications/icrc-002-4094.pdf, p. 41; Y. Shany, "Binary Law Meets Complex Reality." The notion that "boots on the ground" is a sine qua non condition for "effective control" has found judicial support in Armed Activities on the Territory of the Congo (*Democratic Republic of the Congo v. Uganda*), Judgment, 2005 ICJ Rep 168, ¶ 173; *Banković v. Belgium*, Eur Ct HR, App no 52207/99; *Chiragov v. Armenia*, Eur Ct HR, App No 13216/05; *Sargsyan v. Azerbaijan*, Eur Ct HR, App No 40167/06.

[32]   E.g., UN Security Council Resolution 1860, UN Doc S/RES/1860 (January 8, 2009); UN General Assembly Resolution 63/96, UN Doc A/RES/63/96 (December 18, 2008); UN General Assembly Resolution 64/92, UN Doc A/Res/64/92 (December 10, 2009); UN Human Rights Council, Report of the United Nations Fact-Finding Mission on the Gaza Conflict, UN Doc A/HRC/12/48 (September 25, 2009), §§ 276–280; Report of the International

level of responsibility to be shouldered has to relate to the actual power exercised.[33] The debate attests to the malleability of the law of belligerent occupation. It is thus not entirely surprising that it provides fertile grounds for the position that Gaza is actually a sui generis case which fits no recognized international definition, framework, or norm.[34] It is equally not surprising that the people of Gaza found themselves in the same normative vacuum.

The status of Gaza's inhabitants received much less attention than the status of the territory. Few Israeli laws and numerous other enactments regulate their access to and from the West Bank and elsewhere via Israel. They do so in a manner that obfuscates their status and invites arbitrary decisions.[35] Thus, they are often regarded as alien residents of Gaza, as tourists, who have no right of access into Israel. This means that their right of movement is not a matter of law but a matter of discretion and

Fact-Finding Mission to Investigate Violations of International Law, Including International Humanitarian and Human Rights Law, Resulting from the Israeli Attacks on the Flotilla of Ships Carrying Humanitarian Assistance, UN Doc A/HRC/15/21 (September 27, 2010), §§ 63–64; Report of the Detailed Findings of the Independent Commission of Inquiry Established Pursuant to Human Rights Council Resolution S-21/1, UN Doc A/HRC/29/ CPR.4 (June 24, 2015), §§ 26–30; T. Ferraro, "Determining the Beginning and End of an Occupation Under International Humanitarian Law" (2012) 94 *International Review of the Red Cross* 133; P. Maurer, "Challenges to International Humanitarian Law: Israel's Occupation Policy" (2012) 94 *International Review of the Red Cross* 1508; Y. Dinstein, *The International Law of Belligerent Occupation* (Cambridge: Cambridge University Press, 2009), pp. 277–280; I. Scobbie, "An Intimate Disengagement: Israel's Withdrawal from Gaza, the Law of Occupation and of Self-Determination" (2006) 11 *Yearbook of Islamic and Middle Eastern Law* 3; N. Stephanopoulos, "Israel's Legal Obligations to Gaza After the Pullout" (2006) 31 *Yale Journal of International Law* 524; S. Darcy and J. Reynolds, "An Enduring Occupation: the Status of the Gaza Strip from the Perspective of International Humanitarian Law" (2010) 15 *Journal of Conflict and Security Law* 215, 235. This position too finds support in determination of various international tribunals, e.g., *Nuremberg Tribunal, US v. List* (1949) VIII *Law Reports of Trials of War Criminals* 38, 55–56; ICTY, *Prosecutor v. Naletilic and Martinovic*, IT-98-34-T (March 31, 2003) §§ 214–217.

33   E.g., A. Gross, "The Binary Approach to Occupation: A Double Bind?" *Opinion Juris* (April 26, 2012), http://opiniojuris.org/2012/04/26/the-binary-approach-to-occupation-a-double-bind/; A. Gross, *The Writing on the Wall: Rethinking the International Law of Occupation*, (Cambridge: Cambridge University Press, 2017), pp. 52–135.

34   Israel refers to Gaza by a variety of names, such as "a hostile territory," "an enemy entity," "a danger zone," and "an area controlled by a terrorist organization," the common denominator of which is that they are devoid of internationally recognized legal meaning. See e.g., Darcy and Reynolds, "An Enduring Occupation," pp. 240–241; C. James, "Mere Words: The Enemy Entity Designation of the Gaza Strip" (2009) 32 *Hastings International And Comparative Law Review* 643, 653–655.

35   For an excellent study of the legal status of Gaza's residents see M. Luft, *The Legal Status of the Residents of Gaza and Israel's Attitude Towards Them* (an LL.M research seminar paper on file with author) [Hebrew].

humanitarian grace.[36] At other times, however, when Israel had an interest in detaining them within its territory, it argued that they are not to be regarded as foreigners or tourists but rather as "special" cases whose foreign status is unique. The HCJ embraced this inconsistency.[37] They are not accorded the status of "protected persons" although Israel retains and routinely exercises effective control over a wide array of matters relative to their daily life, including access of foreign visitors and goods to Gaza, Gaza's population registry, family unification with Palestinians from the West Bank, transfer of money, and the supply of water, electricity, and other essential materials.[38] Given further Israel's negation of the extraterritorial application of IHRL, power is exercised in a normative vacuum. The suspension of the law by an entity which exercises this kind of power renders life a "bare life."[39]

A few other issues – primarily, the legality of the blockade and the devastation wrought by the periodic eruptions of armed violence – were also subject to international legal concern.[40] Otherwise, Gaza remains a sui generis black box, an out of zone ghetto in both the material and the legal sense.

Gaza is also sui generis in that Israel lacks an interest not only in its inhabitants but also in the territory. When former prime minister Rabin said during a 1988 election campaign that he "would like to see Gaza drown in the sea,"[41] he succinctly expressed the sentiment of most of the Israeli constituency. This lack of concern stands in sharp contrast to Israel's territorial interest in the West Bank.

Z.2.2.2 The Land-locked "Islands" of the West Bank

The West Bank is a land-locked territory. It borders (as demarcated by the 1949 Jordanian–Israeli armistice line, known as the "Green Line") to the west, north, and south with Israel, and to the east, across the Jordan River, with Jordan. Its land area comprises some 5,600 square kilometers (excluding East

[36] See, e.g., HCJ 9657/07 *Garbua* v. *IDF Commander in the West Bank* (July 24, 2008) [Hebrew]; HCJ 1912/08 Physicians for Human Rights v. *IDF Commander in Gaza* (April 16, 2008) [Hebrew].
[37] HCJ 9329/10 *Anonymous* v. *Minister of Defense* (March 8, 2011) [Hebrew], ¶ 20.
[38] This control is discussed in entry Q: Quality of Life.
[39] Agamben, *Homo Sacer*, pp. 50–55.
[40] UN Human Rights Council, Fact-Finding Mission on the Gaza Conflict; International Fact-Finding Mission to Investigate Israeli Attacks on the Flotilla of Ships Carrying Humanitarian Assistance; UN Human Rights Council, Independent Commission of Inquiry Established Pursuant to Human Rights Council Resolution S-21/1.
[41] United Nations Department of Public Information, *Promoting a Culture for Peace in the Middle East: an Israeli-Palestinian Dialogue* (1994), p. 139.

Jerusalem), and its water area of 220 square kilometers consists of the northwest quarter of the Dead Sea. Close to 2.8 million Palestinians and approximately 375,000 Jewish–Israeli settlers inhabit the land.[42] Since it was captured from Jordan in June 1967, Israel has exercised the power of a belligerent occupant over the territory and the population until the Oslo Accords introduced a distribution of powers between Israel and the PA, as detailed throughout the remainder of this chapter.

Z.2.2.2.1 THE PARTITION OF THE WEST BANK INTO AREAS A, B, AND C The Interim Agreement on the West Bank and the Gaza Strip (Oslo II),[43] designed to implement the Oslo Agreement[44] divided the West Bank into three areas.[45] Area A, where 26 percent of the Palestinian population resides in the major cities, consisted in 1995 of 3 percent of the West Bank. Due to later arrangements, it presently comprises 18 percent of the land,[46] and is divided into 11 clusters. Area B, where 70 percent of the population resides, currently amounts to 22 percent of the land, and is divided into 120 clusters. Four percent of the Palestinian population lives in villages in Area C. It comprises the rest of the West Bank, primarily covering the Jordan Valley and areas where most of the Jewish settlements are located. Area C disrupts the territorial continuity of the West Bank. These internal boundaries, each with its own laws and regulations, signify the Oslo-generated new distribution of power between Israel and the PA: In all three areas the PA assumed full responsibility over civil institutions; in Area A, it was given full responsibility for law and public order;[47] in Area B, the PA shoulders responsibility for public order, and Israel maintains overriding responsibility for security. In both Areas A and B, the PA was given "civil powers and responsibilities, including planning and zoning."[48] In Area C, Israel retains full responsibility for security and public order as well as for civil issues related to territory, including zoning and planning. In this manner, Israel was relieved of Palestinian pressure relative to building permits in Areas A and B, yet retained control over planning and building permits in Area

---

[42] CIA, *The World Factbook.* [43] Oslo II.

[44] Declaration of Principles on Interim Self-Government Arrangements between Israel and the PLO (The Oslo Accords).

[45] Oslo II, Annex 1, Article V(2)-(3). It also divided the city of Hebron, discussed in Section Z.2.2.3 and Gaza, a division that eventually lost its meaning as discussed in Section Z.2.2.1.

[46] The Wye River Memorandum; The Sharam el-Sheikh Memorandum.

[47] This formal provision does not exist in reality, as Israeli military law retains jurisdiction over Area A. See entry M: Military Courts.

[48] Oslo II, Article XI(2)(c).

C – that is, over expansion of settlements.[49] Indeed, over the years, the Palestinian space was further curtailed by both the expansion of settlements and various control of movement and construction control apparatuses, discussed in Section Z.2.3.

The net result of this division was to separate Palestinians from other Palestinians as well as from Israelis and to leave Israel, to enjoy much of the dowry without the burden of caring for the bride.[50]

Z.2.2.2.2 THE PARTITION OF HEBRON INTO ZONES H-1 AND H-2 Hebron was the last of the major cities of the West Bank which was subject to a redeployment agreement,[51] dividing it internally into two zones: H-1 and H-2, the Palestinian- and the Israeli-controlled sectors, respectively.[52] The redline map attached to the Hebron Protocol further provides for a buffer zone and numerous checkpoints, police stations, and other security arrangements. Over H-1, comprising 80 percent of Hebron, and home to some 140,000 Palestinians, the PA has powers similar to those it has over Area A. The rest is H-2, comprising the entire old city, including the Cave of the Patriarchs, the al-Ibrahimi Mosque, and five settlements, where Israel retains all powers and responsibilities for

---

[49] N. Shalev and A. Cohen-Lifshitz, *The Prohibited Zone: Israeli Planning Policy in the Palestinian Villages in Area C*, S. Vardi (trans.) (Jerusalem: BIMKOM, Planners for Planning Rights, 2008), p. 7.

[50] Oslo II envisioned a phased redeployment of the Israeli military from the three areas, with complete redeployment within 18 months of the inauguration of the Palestinian government (Article X(2)). In Area C, Israel would remain in control of both police and security but would turn them over the PA by the end of the 18 months period (Article XIII). Between 1995 and 1996, the initial deployment of areas A and B occurred mostly on schedule. With Rabin's murder and the election of Netanyahu, the third deployment still awaits implementation: Israel maintains full control over Area C where the Palestinians are subject to its planning and security policy. *Ibid.* See also, Gordon, "From Colonization to Separation," pp. 35–37.

[51] This was due to the explosive religious sensitivity of Hebron: Hebron is where the Jews established their oldest legal deed, with Abraham buying a burial place, known today as the Cave of the Patriarchs from the Hittite for 400 pieces of silver (see Genesis 23:8–16), and where, it is believed that Abraham, Isaac, Jacob, and some of their wives are buried. It is one of Judaism four holy cities. Following a 1929 massacre resulting in the murder of 69 Jews, the remaining community of 400 people fled the town. On the significance of the 1929 events for the formation of national consciousness, see H. Cohen, *Year Zero of the Arab-Israeli Conflict: 1929*, H. Weitzman (trans.) (Lebanon: Brandeis, 2015). Settlers returned to the heart of Hebron in 1968. Muslims, who also venerate Abraham, father of Ishmael, have lived continuously in Hebron for more than 1,300 years. In the thirteenth century, they converted the tomb of the Patriarchs and the surrounding compound into the al-Ibrahimi mosque. In 1995 Baruch Goldstein, a settler, murdered 29 Muslim worshippers there. See text between notes 55–56. See J. R. Weiner, "The Hebron Protocol: The End of the Beginning or the Beginning of the End of the Israeli-Palestinian Peace Process" (1997) 15 *Boston University International Law Journal* 373, 375.

[52] The Hebron Protocol.

internal security and public order.[53] Some 800 Jewish settlers live in H-2 and some 7,000 more live in the adjacent settlement of Kiryat Arba. The number of Palestinians who live in H-2 is consistently declining, and currently comprises some 30,000 people.[54] This decline signifies population transfer even if, much like that famous rose, it goes "by any other name" and smells less sweet.[55]

In many ways, Hebron is a microcosm of the control Israel exercises over the West Bank.[56] This control guarantees that the interests of the settlers, often themselves armed, and protected by the presence of some 2,000 IDF soldiers, prevail consistently over those of the Palestinian population. Thus, for instance, pursuant to the 1995 al-Ibrahimi Mosque massacre by Dr. Baruch Goldstein, a Jewish settler who went on a shooting spree and murdered 29 Muslim worshippers, Israel placed Palestinians under a strict curfew and closed off al-Shuhada Street, once the thriving market-place of old Hebron, to all Palestinians. The street remains closed to Palestinians to date. Settlers and other Israelis enjoy free access. Consequently, Palestinian economic life in the area collapsed and most Palestinian families who lived there were effectively displaced.[57]

Businesses were closed down by direct military orders. Various measures restricting Palestinian freedom of movement further contributed to what is in effect a population transfer. These range from the blocking of the main north–south traffic artery of the city, along with the movement of Palestinian vehicles – and in some sections the movement of Palestinian pedestrians – is forbidden (with the exception of the street's few remaining residents who hold a special permit); to the designation of certain areas inhabited by Palestinians as "closed military zones";[58] to curfews, closures, and the installation of permanent and flying checkpoints connecting Hebron to

---

53 When the protocol was signed, there were four settlements in the heart of old Hebron. In 2014, a fifth one was established.

54 See P. Beaumont, "Inside Hebron's Pressure Cooker: the West Bank's most Troubled City," *The Guardian* (November 14, 2015), www.theguardian.com/world/2015/nov/14/hebron-west-bank-troubled-city-palestine-israel; AL-HAQ, *Special Focus on Hebron: A Microcosm of the Israeli Occupation* (2015), www.alhaq.org/images/stories/PDF/2012/Special.Focus.on.Hebron .Nov.2015.pdf; O. Foyerstein, *Ghost Town: Israel's Separation Policy and Forced Eviction of Palestinians from the Center of Hebron* (Jerusalem: B'Tselem and the Association for Civil Rights in Israel, 2007); Peace Now, *Hebron: Settlements in Focus* (2005), https://peacenow.org /entry.php?id=10149#.WjFoiothBE4; Temporary International Presence in Hebron, *Hebron*, http://www.tiph.org/hebron/.

55 W. Shakespeare, *Romeo and Juliet*, Act II, Scene II: "What's in a name? that which we call as rose by any other name would still smell as sweet."

56 AL-HAQ, Special Focus on Hebron. 　 57 Foyerstein, *Ghost Town*.

58 On "closed military zones" see Section Z.2.2.5.1.

other Palestinian towns and villages.[59] The increased presence of soldiers and police, and their close contact with the settlers, further generate daily harassment, including arbitrary house searches, seizure of houses, and detention of passersby.[60]

The right of worship in the al-Ibrahimi Mosque has also been periodically restricted: Palestinians were prohibited from entering it for a period following the massacre; thereafter, it was divided so that a synagogue was also established on the premises. Throughout the years, Israel has repeatedly closed the mosque off to Muslim worshippers in order to accommodate Jewish worship. During these closures, the mosque is also prohibited from making the call to prayer. Further, the common reaction to escalation of violence in the area, occasioned by both Palestinians and Jews, is to close the road leading to the mosque, thus barring Palestinians from reaching it.[61]

These measures are coupled with routine settler violence against Palestinians in H-2.[62] Whenever the situation escalates and Palestinians use violent means of resistance, they are met with what appears to be excessive and lethal force by the IDF.[63]

In light of the above, it is little wonder that Palestinians find life in old Hebron unsustainable and that many have left. The HCJ engagement in this process merits attention.

In a series of cases, the court repeatedly found that the settlers' security and human rights override Palestinian rights.[64] The succinct – yet all the more

[59] Foyerstein, *Ghost Town*, pp. 17–40.
[60] AL-HAQ, Special Focus on Hebron; Foyerstein, *Ghost Town*. See entry W: War Crimes, Section W.3.
[61] Foyerstein, *Ghost Town*, p. 20.
[62] Beaumont, "Inside Hebron's Pressure Cooker"; AL-HAQ, *Special Focus on Hebron*; Foyerstein, *Ghost Town*.
[63] In 2015 alone, Palestinians reported over 200 violent attacks by settlers, Albawaba News, *West Bank: Israeli Settlers Attack Palestinian Mother and Child in Hebron* (May 14, 2016), www.albawaba.com/news/west-bank-israeli-settlers-attack-palestinian-mother-and-child-hebron-840152; see also, www.btselem.org/ota?tid=155; entry W: War Crimes.
[64] E.g., HCJ 72/86 *Zalum v. Military Commander for Judea and Samaria* (1987) 41(1) PD 528 [Hebrew] (settlers' security justifies preventing Palestinian access to their stores; and indeed their shutting down); HCJ 7007/03 *Kawasme v. IDF Commander for Judea and Samaria* (April 19, 2005) [Hebrew] (settlers' security justifies the shutting down of Palestinian stores, i.e., the elimination of their livelihood); HCJ 3435/05 *Elnatsha, Director of the Wakf in Hebron v. IDF Commander for Judea and Samaria* (September 12, 2005) [Hebrew] (seizure of Palestinian land within H-2 to build an "emergency road" safeguarding settlers' security is justified); HCJ 4661/06 *The Committee for the Development of Hebron v. The State of Israel* (June 27, 2006) [Hebrew] (security concerns override Palestinian freedom of religion); HCJ 10356/02 *Hass v. Commander of the IDF forces in the West Bank* (2004) 58(3) PD 443 [Hebrew; English translation available at http://elyon1.court.gov.il/files_eng/02/970/104/r15/02104970

telling for that – judgment in the *Chalbi* case provides a good illustration:[65] The petitioner is a Palestinian woman who had left her home pursuant to settlers' harassment. When she wanted to return, a barbed wire fence prevented her access. Thereafter, a gate was installed and she was given a key, only to find that the IDF changed the lock and refused to give her the new key. Faced with her petition, the IDF proposed an arrangement requiring her to call its local station to coordinate each entry, whereupon a soldier would be sent with a key. The obvious concerns of the petitioner regarding the reasonableness of an arrangement forcing her to coordinate every entry to and exit from her home with the occupying authorities were dismissed by the court. Extracting the petition from the context of the occupation, and from the illegality of the presence of settlers in the occupied zone, it determined that the settlers' right to security, which the military is to protect, overrides her right to freely access her home. In this and other cases, human rights law, specifically the human rights of settlers, has been used not to complement the *lex specialis*, IHL, but to undermine it, effectively eradicating the guarantees of the "protected persons" status.[66]

The combination of severe restrictions on Palestinian movement, daily harassment, and a systematic failure – indeed, unwillingness – to enforce law and order on the settlers reflects a policy of separation which generated a virtually Palestinian-free zone. The HCJ has never sanctioned this policy explicitly, but its judgments did contribute to its realization.

Z.2.2.3 The Liminal Zone of Jerusalem

Jerusalem is yet another sui generis zone: whereas much of Area C of the West Bank land is being annexed de facto,[67] East Jerusalem and 28 neighboring villages were annexed de jure two weeks after the 1967 war ended. This clear contravention of international law was rejected by the international

---

.115.pdf] (Palestinian land seizure and buildings' demolition is justified to secure the settlers' access to the Cave of the Patriarchs). For a critical analysis of this judgment see A. Gross, "Human Proportions: Are Human Rights the Emperor's New Clothes of the International Law of Occupation?" (2007) 18 *European Journal of International Law* 1.

[65] HCJ 4547/03 *Chalbi v. The Prime Minister* (May 30, 2005) [Hebrew].

[66] In Gross, "On Human Proportions," the author offers an insightful critique of the HCJ's resort to human rights in a manner that undermines the principles and specific provisions of the law of belligerent occupation. See also Gross, *The Writing on the Wall*, pp. 338–396.

[67] Stahl, *From Occupation to Annexation*. In February 2016, The Minister of Justice, Ms. Ayelet Shaked, said she intend to promote a law that would apply Israeli law to Jewish settlers in the West Bank. See T. Tsimuki, "Shaked Seeks to Apply Israeli Law on West Bank Jewish Settlers," *ynet* (February 5, 2016), www.ynetnews.com/articles/0,7340,L-4798296,00.html.

community which regards the area as occupied territory.[68] Yet, while Israel declared sovereignty over the entire city, incessantly refers to a "unified Jerusalem," and has moved some of its governmental offices to the east side, notably the ministry of justice, it also acts in a manner that defies these very claims: the route of the separation barrier does not merely separate Jerusalem from the rest of the West Bank, it also, as it partly follows the 1949 Green Line and partly cuts through the city, effectively undoes any unity. Some of its neighborhoods have thus been rendered a no man's land where virtually no sovereign responsibilities are exercised.[69]

There are some 300,000 Palestinians living in Jerusalem, comprising 37 percent of its population. More than 25 percent of them reside in neighborhoods that the barrier has disconnected from the rest of the city.[70] The status of the inhabitants differs, and they are subject not only to starkly different treatment but also to different legal systems. Jerusalem is a liminal zone[71] wrought by the logic informing Israel's control: coveting Palestinian land and forsaking Palestinians. The brief discussion which follows, focusing on the legal status of the Palestinian inhabitants of Jerusalem, various mechanisms that affect Palestinian housing, and the effects of the separation barrier on municipal services, substantiates this proposition.

---

[68] Israel imposed its law and administration on East Jerusalem on June 28, 1967. It initially objected to the use of the term "annexation" to describe this move, claiming it was done for purely municipal and administrative reasons. The Basic Law: Jerusalem, The Capital of Israel, put this objection to rest. From an international legal perspective the annexation of East Jerusalem (expanding gradually its boundaries from 6.5 to 71 square kilometers) is illegal. This illegality was affirmed by both the Security Council and the General Assembly and the ICJ. See SC Res 478, UN Doc S/RES/478 (August 20, 1980); GA Res 35/169E, UN Doc A/RES/35/169E (December 15, 1980); SC Res 673, UN Doc S/INF/46 (October 24, 1990); Consequences of the Construction of a Wall in the Occupied Palestinian Territory, Advisory Opinion, 2004 ICJ 136, ¶ 74–75, 120–122. It should be noted that on December 6, 2017, President Trump announced his decision to recognize Jerusalem as the capital of Israel. See Statement by President Trump on Jerusalem, December 6, 2017, www.whitehouse.gov /the-press-office/2017/12/06/statement-president-trump-jerusalem. The rest of the international community rejected this decision, stating it is in violation of both UN resolutions and international law. See United Nations, Meetings Coverage, *United Nations Position on Jerusalem Unchanged, Special Coordinator Stresses, as Security Council Debates United States Recognition of City.* SC/13111, December 8, 2017, www.un.org/press/en/2017/sc13111 .doc.htm.

[69] These neighborhoods are Kafr 'Aqab and Semiramis, Ras Khamis, Ras Shehada, Dahiyat al-Salam, and the Shuafat Refugee Camp.

[70] Association for Civil Rights in Israel (ACRI), *East Jerusalem 2015: Facts and Figures*, www.acri .org.il/en/wp-content/uploads/2015/05/EJ-Facts-and-Figures-2015.pdf, p. 1.

[71] M. Klein, "Old and New Walls in Jerusalem" (2005) 24 *Political Geography* 53.

Z.2.2.3.1 PALESTINIAN LEGAL STATUS Following the annexation of East Jerusalem, its inhabitants were not automatically granted Israeli citizenship. In 1967, a census was conducted. At the time, 66,000 Palestinians resided there, but only those physically present received residency status. Of these, those who could demonstrate allegiance to Israel, Hebrew proficiency, and the relinquishing of other citizenships – all conditions not required of Jews who wish to become Israeli citizens – were eligible to apply for Israeli identity cards (IDs). Few availed themselves of this option. Given that the PA has not been authorized to grant them Palestinian citizenship, most are thus bereft of any citizenship.[72] Instead, they are permanent residents of Israel. This status does not grant them the right to vote or seek election to the Israeli parliament, but it entitles them to all other rights and social services provided to Israeli citizens and to vote to or seek office in the Jerusalem municipality. Since voting may be construed as legitimizing the annexation, they generally do not participate in it. The net result is that they have not been engaged in policy decisions at the national and the municipal levels that shape their lives.[73]

Permanent residents have blue IDs, externally identical to those of Israeli citizens, though distinct by various internal indicators. In this manner, they are differentiated from Israeli citizens, including Palestinian citizens of Israel;[74] from Palestinian residents of the West Bank, who hold green IDs; and from Palestinians with previous arrest records, who hold orange IDs. This color-coded bureaucratic mechanism signifies both the fragmentation of the Palestinian society and uneven mobilities based on ethno-national and spatial distinctions.[75]

Palestinian residents of the OPT who are married to Palestinian permanent residents of East Jerusalem, as well as children with one parent who is a resident of the territories, also live in Jerusalem. Their status is unregulated due to amendments introduced since 2003 to the Law of Citizenship and Entry into Israel[76] in order to freeze family unification processes in Israel and prevent residents of the OPT from obtaining residency.[77] From the

---

[72] Tawil-Souri, "Uneven Borders, Coloured (Im)mobilities," pp. 157–160.

[73] ACRI, East Jerusalem 2015, p. 3.

[74] In 1952 Israel granted its citizenship to Palestinians who could prove continuous residence in Israel between 1948 and 1952. See Nationality Law, 1952. Some 160,000 Palestinians thus became citizens and they and their off springs have blue IDs. Palestinians who fled or were expelled during the 1948 war, and thereafter designated as "absentees," were not eligible; unlike Jews worldwide, they do not enjoy a right of return.

[75] Tawil-Souri, "Uneven Borders, Coloured (Im)mobilities," p. 155. This point is amplified in Section Z.2.3.2.

[76] The Citizenship and Entry into Israel Law (temporary provision), 2003.

[77] See entry K: Kinship.

perspective of international law, all Palestinian noncitizens of Israel residing in Jerusalem are "protected persons" under the law of belligerent occupation; for those who are not permanent residents, this status remains, at least in theory, their only legal umbrella. From the Palestinian domestic perspective, the fragmentation of the Palestinian family and the insecurities wrought by these amendments are further exacerbated by internal tensions generated in situations where some family members have blue IDs which allow them both more mobility and accessibility to work and other social services, while others do not.[78]

Finally, the status of permanent residency is conditional. Palestinians have been required to prove time and again to the bureaucracy of the Israeli ministry of the interior that they did not leave Jerusalem for an extended period of time and that it remains the center of their lives. If they fail to do that, their status may be revoked and they would be barred from returning to live in their place of birth. In this manner, between 1967 and 2015, the permanent residency status of 14,416 Palestinian residents of Jerusalem has been revoked.[79] Only in March 2017 was this practice put to rest by the supreme court.[80]

z.2.2.3.2 PALESTINIAN HOUSING Another means to control the number of Palestinian residents in East Jerusalem is to minimize their living space. Three main mechanisms are employed for this purpose:

Judaization Activities   Direct Judaization activities have two main forms. The first is expropriation: since 1967 Israel has expropriated approximately 26,300 dunams (the equivalent of 26,300,000 square meters) in East Jerusalem for the purpose of building Jewish neighborhoods and government offices. The result is a significant reduction in land reserves that would have enabled the natural growth of Palestinian neighborhoods.[81] The second form consists of establishing settlements mainly amidst Palestinian neighborhoods in properties that were owned by Jews before 1948 and where Palestinians have resided since. The result is both the eviction of Palestinians from homes

---

[78]   N. Shalhoub-Kevorkian, "Counter-Spaces as Resistance in Conflict Zones: Palestinian Women Recreating a Home," in P. Lyness (ed.), *The Politics of the Personal in Feminist Family Therapy* (New York: Routledge, 2005), pp. 109, 127.

[79]   ACRI, *East Jerusalem 2015*, p. 3. See also, HCJ 7603/96 *Wafa* v. *Director of Civil Registry, Ministry of Interior* (2005) 59(4) PD 337 [Hebrew]; HCJ 282/88 *Awad* v. *The Prime Minister and Minister of Interior* (1988) 42(2) PD 242 [Hebrew].

[80]   In AA 3268/14 *Al Huq* v. *Ministry of the Interior* (March 14, 2017) [Hebrew].

[81]   ACRI, *East Jerusalem 2015*, pp. 7–10.

they have occupied for decades, and the destruction of the fabric of life in the neighborhoods. The Israeli legal system and the courts enable this process for Jews but not for Palestinians who owned property prior to 1948 in the Western part of the city or elsewhere in Israel.[82]

A unique zone which demands a closer look in this context is E-1, an area located east of the Jerusalem municipal boundary, between Jerusalem and the settlement town of Ma'aleh Adummim. It covers some 12,000 dunams (the equivalent of 12,000,000 square meters) and functions as the main artery between the northern and southern West Bank which runs through it. Israel began construction in the area in 2004. In 2005, the municipality of the settlement approved two detailed urban plans for the development of the area, one for approximately 3,500 housing units, a commercial center, etc.,[83] and the second for police headquarters. Neither of the plans refer to the local 15,000 Palestinians who reside there. Pursuant to strong pressure from the US government and the European Union, the execution of the first plan was frozen; however, drawing an analogy between such construction and the establishment of military bases, building of the police headquarters continued. In 2012, ostensibly in response to the Palestinian statehood bid at the UN, the Israeli government announced that it will promote a zoning plan for E-1 which will allow the construction of 3,000 housing units for Jews.[84] Once fully executed, the Palestinian neighborhoods of East Jerusalem will be cut off from the West Bank, effectively preventing the emergence of a contiguous Palestinian state. Demolition of Palestinian houses in the area has already begun.

Urban Planning Failure   The Jerusalem municipality has failed to shoulder its responsibility to plan adequately in East Jerusalem. The result is housing shortage, inadequate urban development and an appalling lack of infrastructure and public structures including schools, roads, transportation, water and sewage networks, parks, and playgrounds.[85]

---

[82] See, e.g., CA 4126/05 *Hajazi v. Sephardic Community Committee* (June 20, 2006) [Hebrew]; HCJ 6358/08 *Alkord v. Land Registration and Settlement of Rights* Department (November 11, 2008) [Hebrew].

[83] Ir Amim, *E-1 Settlement is not Ma'aleh Adummim*, Position Paper (December 2012), http:// www.ir-amim.org.il/sites/default/files/%D7%93%D7%95%D7%97%20%D7%90%D7%99%2 0%D7%93%D7%A6%D7%9E%D7%91%D7%A8%202012.pdf [Hebrew].

[84] JStreet, *E1 Development Would Be "The Death Knell for the Two-State Solution,"* http://jstreet .org/press-releases/e1-development-would-be-the-death-knell-for-the-twostate-solution/# .WjFswUthBE4.

[85] ACRI, *East Jerusalem 2015*, p. 7. This reality places the concern expressed by the HCJ when it authorized the canceling of a rare building permit that had been granted to build housing for Palestinian teachers and the ensuing confiscation of their land in its proper context. See HCJ

In areas for which outline plans exist for Palestinian neighborhoods, they do not conform to the planning level that is considered acceptable elsewhere in Israel. Further, in these plans, the area designated for construction is limited since most of the land is reserved as an open landscape.[86] Some 55 percent of the requests for building permits in these areas are approved, compared to approval rate of some 85 percent in West Jerusalem.[87] In areas for which there are no outline plans, applying for a building permit is both useless and costly.

The net result is that Palestinian residents are forced by law to violate the law. Some 40 percent of Palestinian structures – amounting to some 20,000 buildings – have been built without a permit. Their owners are thereby exposed to demolition orders, legal proceedings, fines, and loss of their home.[88] A loss of a home shatters a person's sense of belonging and of safety. For Palestinians, this experience of uprooting often resurrects past traumas.[89]

Welfare and Municipal Services Not all discriminatory practices are created equal. Lack of governmental allocation of resources to East Jerusalem in general, and especially when compared to West Jerusalem, attests to governance failure. Lack of any resources or services provided to the Palestinian neighborhoods which found themselves on the "other side" of the separation barrier sheds a dim light on the nature of Israel's self-proclaimed sovereignty over the territory.

This assessment rests on clear indicators. A few examples suffice: 75 percent of Palestinians and close to 84 percent of Palestinian children in East Jerusalem live below the poverty line. This staggering rate is mainly due to

---

145/80 *Jamayit Iskan* v. *Minister of Defense* (1980) 35(2) PD 285 [Hebrew]. For a discussion of this case, see entry G: Geneva Law, Section G.3.2.

[86] It should be noted that in 2014–2015 a plan for Arab a-Sawahra, a neighborhood in the southeastern part of the city, was approved. It covers an area of 1,500 dunams and includes an option for building 2,200 housing units. The approval is a first step in a process that may take years to materialize. ACRI, *East Jerusalem 2015*, p. 8.

[87] BIMKOM, Planners for Planning Rights, *Survey of Palestinian Neighborhoods in East Jerusalem: Planning Problems and Opportunities* (2013), http://bimkom.org/eng/wp-content/uploads/survey-of-the-Palestinian-neighborhoods-of-East-Jerusalem.pdf.

[88] Residents who receive demolition orders often prefer to demolish their houses themselves in view of the costs imposed on them when the demolition is executed by the authorities. See ACRI, *East Jerusalem 2015*, p. 9. See also N. Shalhoub-Kevorkian, *Security Theology, Surveillance and the Politics of Fear* (Cambridge: Cambridge University Press, 2015), pp. 73–115.

[89] Building without a permit is but one venue to lose a home. Demolishing or sealing family houses of Palestinians who were engaged in terrorist activities is another venue. See entry H: House Demolitions.

the impact of the separation barrier: severing Jerusalem from the West Bank, disconnecting Palestinian neighborhoods from each other and cutting off some of them from other parts of the city altogether, it also halts economic, commercial, and tourist activities and reduces the accessibility of social services. This explains, at least partly, why only 11.3 percent of the residents of East Jerusalem are treated by the welfare services. The same percentages of Jewish residents are thus treated, though the poverty rate in the Jewish population is much lower. Of the 48 postal offices in Jerusalem, only 8 service Palestinian neighborhoods. Basic infrastructure is in a dismal state, with only 64 percent of Palestinian households connected officially to the city's water network and a shortage of some 30 kilometers of sewage pipes.[90] But the situation could get worse, and for tens of thousands of Palestinian residents of the five neighborhoods that have been completely isolated by the separation barrier, it did.

In those areas, the water and sewage systems have collapsed; garbage collection, road repair, street lightening, and other basic services are not provided; there are neither hospitals nor emergency and rescue services. Law and order forces, enter those areas to quash demonstrations against Israel, but not otherwise. In order to access the rest of the city, residents, including workers and school children,[91] spend hours queuing at checkpoints. The HCJ rejected petitions against the construction of the separation barrier in these areas.[92] Its determination that the harm to the residents' rights is reasonable and proportionate in relation to Jewish security thereby achieved, rested, inter alia, on governmental and municipal commitments to set up arrangements and provide the services that would enable the conduct of what is seen as normal life.[93] A decade later, these commitments are yet to be honored. The space bordered by a barrier which does not signify a boundary is populated by bare lives.[94] It is a forsaken no man's land which Israel insists is part of "unified Jerusalem" subject to its sovereignty.

---

[90] ACRI, East Jerusalem 2015, p. 2.

[91] There are only four public schools in these neighborhoods, and none of them are for girls.

[92] HCJ 5488/04 *Alram Local Council* v. *Government of Israel* (December 13, 2006) [Hebrew]; HCJ 4289/05 *Bir Nabala Local Council* v. *Government of Israel* (November 26, 2006) [Hebrew]; HCJ 940/04 *Abu Tir* v. *Military Commander for Judea and Samaria* (November 24, 2004) [Hebrew].

[93] Government Decision no 3783 (July 10, 2005), www.pmo.gov.il/Secretary/GovDecisions/200 5/Pages/des3873.aspx [Hebrew], obliged various government ministries and the Jerusalem Municipality, to develop and supply services, including health, education, welfare, employment, and postal services, to these neighborhoods.

[94] Agamben, *Homo Sacer*, pp. 50–55.

Neglect, isolation, extreme poverty, discriminatory practices, and the elimination of the conditions of possibility to engage in what is seen as the normal
course of productive life are forcing Palestinian relocation.

Z.2.2.4 The Enclaves: Palestinian Islands in an Israeli-controlled Sea[95]

"Our very presence or mobility makes contiguous Arab control more
difficult . . . Jewish presence in the settlements, and the connections between
them, will in effect confine the area of influence of the Arab block," wrote
one of the leaders of the settlement community in the West Bank. He
proceeded to suggest that in addition to the settlements and other measures
designed to ensure their interconnectedness, another technology is required
to achieve the objective of exclusive Israeli sovereignty over the area:
"The block, if only for the sake of future generations, must be cut into
slices."[96] This vision materialized. Palestinians land and communities
have indeed been cut into slices.

This feat was achieved not merely by the above-described fragmentation of
the OPT, but also through the construction of material and legal barriers
within these fragments. Material barriers include the separation barrier,[97]
other forms of physical blockades, and a web of highways and roads connecting the settlements between themselves and to Israel proper while separating
them from Palestinian areas and from the "fabric of life" roads designed for
Palestinian movement.[98] Legal barriers are attached to the material ones and
equally create boundaries comprising additional land-control and population-
control mechanisms.[99] Some 200 Palestinian "enclaves" have been generated
by the juxtaposition of the material and legal aspects of the barriers. They
inscribe on both land and life the logic of Israel's expansion, Palestinian
constriction, separation, and exclusion.[100]

---

95 The metaphor was used in Weiner, "The Hebron Protocol," p. 394.
96 P. Wallerstein, "That's how we will Prevent the Establishment of a Palestinian State" (1994)
    182 *Nekudah* 28–29, cited in A. Handel, "Gated/Gating Community: the Settlement
    Complex in the West Bank" (2013) 39 *Transactions* 504, 510.
97 See entry B: Border/Barrier.
98 On the roads, see N. Gordon, *Israel's Occupation* (Oakland: University of California Press,
    2006); E. Weizman, *Hollow Land: Israel's Architecture of Occupation* (London: Verso, 2007);
    Construction of a Wall.
99 Land-control and population-control mechanisms are discussed in Sections X.2.3.1 and
    X.2.3.2, respectively.
100 On the hybrid nature of the separation barrier see, Y. Blank, "Legalizing the Barrier: the
    Legality and Materiality of the Israel/Palestine Separation Barrier" (2010–2011) 46 *Texas
    International Law Journal* 309.

The enclaves are areas throughout the West Bank, where some 300,000 Palestinians live, cut off from other areas as well as from their agricultural land in a manner that adversely affects all aspects of their lives. There are two types of enclaves: "seam enclaves" and "internal enclaves."[101]

"Seam enclaves" epitomize Palestinian exclusion. They are home to Palestinian communities trapped between the separation barrier and the Green Line. Their residents' entry to other areas of the West Bank is restricted by the barrier; their entry to Israel is restricted by checkpoints and not by the barrier, thus exposing the falsity of Israel's argument that the separation barrier is designed to prevent entry into Israel.[102] The military order which designated the seam zone as a "closed military zone," states in its first provision that no one may enter it and that anyone in it must leave immediately. Its second provision allows all kinds of people, with the exception of its Palestinians inhabitants, to enter it.[103] The trapped Palestinians must have a "permanent resident permit," which has to be renewed every three months, in order to continue living in their homes. Noninhabitants, classified into various categories, must enter the bureaucratic maze of requesting a special permit, normally given only for a day at a specifically named entrance gate.

"Internal enclaves" have been generated by the road of the barrier and its encounter with other physical barriers such as roads prohibited for Palestinians, fences, and checkpoints, preventing access to the rest of the West Bank; agricultural lands; the settlements; and Israel. The reference to the roads requires a pause: the roads stretch over hundreds of kilometers, bypassing Palestinian villages and cities and connecting the settlements to each other and to Israel west of the Green Line. These roads, thus, are an integral part of the "settlement enterprise," as it is known in Israel: strengthening and connecting the settlements, they pull apart and weaken the Palestinian communities,[104] generating a sense of displacement and insecurity[105] and the destruction of the Palestinian fabric of life. This destruction, which the HCJ authorized so long as it is "reasonable" and

---

[101]   BIMKOM, Planners for Planning Rights, *Between Fences: The Enclaves Created by the Separation Barrier* (2006), http://bimkom.org/eng/wp-content/uploads/Between-Fences.pdf.

[102]   See, e.g., HCJ 2056/04 *Beit Sourik Village Council v. Government of Israel* (2004) 58(5) PD 807, 816 [Hebrew; English translation available at http://elyon1.court.gov.il/Files_ENG/04/560/020/A28/04020560.A28.pdf].

[103]   Order Regarding Defense Regulations (Judea and Samaria) (No 378) 1970, Declaration Regarding Closure of Area No s/2/03 (Seam Area).

[104]   The legal aspect of the roads is discussed in entry G: Geneva Law, Section G.3.2.

[105]   T. Kelly, "Returning Home? Law, Violence and displacement Among West Bank Palestinians" (2004) 27 *PoLAR* 95, 96.

"proportionate,"[106] has been further affected by a few additional zoning designations discussed in Section Z.2.2.5.

Z.2.2.5 Additional Zoning Designations

A multiplicity of zoning designations has devastated the Palestinian space. These cover the whole gamut from the classification of vast areas as "state land," as distinct from privately owned land, on which the HCJ authorized the construction of settlements,[107] to various zoning decisions made by both the military and the civil administration in the OPT.

z.2.2.5.1 MILITARY ZONING A military commander of a certain area, both in Israel proper and in the OPT, is legally authorized to designate the area or parts of it as a "closed military zone."[108] He may do so at his full discretion in terms of reason and duration. Pursuant to such designation, entry into, and exit from the zone requires a special permit.

In the West Bank, some areas have been designated as a "closed military zone" or as a "special security zone." The latter designation refers to areas outside of Jewish settlements, where there is no separation barrier. Indeed, the construction of separation barriers is neither necessarily nor exclusively a material matter.[109] It may be generated by nothing more than a legal order. The effect of this designation, the exact location and scope of which is not marked, has been twofold: first, to expand the de facto territory of Jewish settlements without legally expropriating Palestinian land;[110]

---

[106] In various appeals against the route of the separation barrier, the HCJ followed the logic of its first decision on the matter in the *Beit Sourik* case. Thus, for instance, in HCJ 7957/04 *Mar'abe v. Prime Minister of Israel* (2005) 60 PD 477 [Hebrew], it determined that the route of the barrier failed to meet the "least injurious means" test and ordered the army to devise new plans. By the same logic, in other decisions, it was determined that the injury to Palestinian rights was proportionate. See e.g., HCJ 426/05 *Bido Village Council v. The Government of Israel* (September 10, 2006) [Hebrew]. A critical discussion of the separation barrier jurisprudence is offered in entry B: Border/Barrier.

[107] This designation is discussed in entry J: Jewish Settlements.

[108] Regulation 125 of the Defense (Emergency) Regulations, 1945. About 25 percent of the territory within Israel proper is thus designated, see HCJ 2281/06 *Even Zohar v. the State of Israel* (April 28, 2010), justice Procaccia's opinion, ¶ 9. This authority with respect to the West Bank is stipulated in Article 318 of Order Concerning Security Provisions (Judea and Samaria) (no 1651), 2009.

[109] Blank, "Legalizing the Barrier," p. 322.

[110] *Access Denied: Israeli Measures to Deny Palestinians Access to Land around Settlements* (Jerusalem: B'Tselem, 2008), www.btselem.org/download/200809_access_denied_eng .pdf.

and second, to further restrict Palestinian movement by means of uncertainty.[111]

Approximately 18 percent of the West Bank, a space larger than Area A, has been designated as a "firing zone," a special category of a "closed military zone" for training. This category turns the inhabitants into illegal residents, unless they can prove permanent residency.[112] The exact boundaries of the firing zones, which are not clearly marked on the ground, have remained unchanged since they were thus designated in the 1970s and 1980s, and despite clear evidence that virtually no military training has taken place in many of them. Located mostly in the Jordan Valley, the Dead Sea area, or the South Hebron hills, they are home to particularly vulnerable Bedouin and herding communities comprising some 5,000 people. They also include a few Jewish settlers' outposts. The humanitarian impact of the longstanding designation of the areas as "firing zones" has been catastrophic, covering the whole gamut from no infrastructure and no access to services, to reduced access to grazing areas which are the main source of livelihood, confiscation of property, subjection to settlers' harassment, and demolition of structures and deportations.[113] The purpose and combined effect of these actions is to generate a Palestinian-free area. Such actions constitute grave breaches of the GC IV, which recognizes no distinction between permanent and other residents who are "protected persons."[114]

A legal battle which began in 1999 with two petitions following the forced transfer of 700 residents of an area designated as "Firing Zone 918" has thus far generated interim orders to halt the process, and two failed mediation processes, but still awaits judicial determination.[115] It is instructive to note that this

[111] A. Handel, "Controlling Space through the Space: Uncertainty as a Control Technology" (2007) 31 *Theory and Criticism* 101, 110 [Hebrew].

[112] See the state's response to one of petitions regarding "Firing Zone 918" (HCJ 413/13), discussed below in text and notes 115–117, available at www.acri.org.il/he/wp-content/uploads/2013/07/hit413tguva.pdf (July 29, 2013) [Hebrew].

[113] UN Office for the Coordination of Humanitarian Affairs, Occupied Palestinian Territory, *The Humanitarian Impact of Israeli-Declared "Firing Zones" in the West Bank* (2012).

[114] An expert opinion written by international law scholars in support of local residents who petitioned against their planned eviction from the firing zone (HCJ 413/13, currently pending) further stresses that international customary law forbids unconditionally both deportation of protected persons to places outside of the occupied area, and transferring them to a different place within it. Evacuation is permitted only temporarily and under certain conditions, which do not apply in the area, such as an urgent military operation or the conditions relative to assigned residence under Article 78 of the GC IV (discusses in entry A: Assigned Residence). For the expert opinion, see. www.acri.org.il/he/wp-content/uploads/2013/01/hit413expert1.pdf.

[115] For a detailed account of the proceedings, see Association for Civil Rights in Israel, *Info-sheet: The 12 Villages of Firing Zone 918 in the South Hebron Hills* (February 21, 2016), www.acri.org.il/en/2016/02/21/firing-zone-918-infosheet.

specific zone, located in South Hebron Mountain, covering approximately 30,000 dunams (equivalent to 30,000,000 square meters), 12 tiny villages, and some 1,200 residents, was originally incorporated into the "Israeli" side of the separation barrier. This inclusion was overruled by the HCJ in the *Beit Sourik* case.[116] Coupling this fact with strong evidence – though disputed by the military – that virtually no military training has taken place in the area throughout most of these years,[117] it is plausible to conclude that the designation of the area as a firing zone is but a different means to achieve the same result the original route of the separation barrier was designed to achieve: the de facto annexation of the land without its Palestinian inhabitants.

z.2.2.5.2 CIVILIAN ZONING The civil administration of the military commander has designated certain zones in a manner designed to restrict Palestinian construction, even in those lands not allocated for settlements in Area C. Thus, for instance, the 1991 plan for roads in the West Bank, in addition to connecting the main roads to Israel to maximize their use value for Jewish settlers, further imposed excessive right of way and building lines, as compared to those applicable in Israel, where construction is prohibited.[118] Areas designated as "natural reserves," a worthy cause no doubt, and on which construction is forbidden, have limited Palestinian development only to be amended periodically to allow the construction of Jewish settlements on those very lands.[119] A similar cynicism characterizes the designation of national parks.[120] Finally, due to different types of planning for the settlements and for the Palestinian communities, areas designated as "archeological sites" generate sweeping prohibitions on Palestinian construction, whereas in the settlements they do not.[121]

Use of zoning laws and regulations to separate, discriminate, dispossess, and force the transfer of Palestinians has been complemented by bureaucratic

---

[116]   *Beit Sourik*. For an analysis of this judgment see entry B: Border/Barrier.
[117]   See the petition in HCJ 413/13, available at www.acri.org.il/he/wp-content/uploads/2013/01/h it413.pdf [Hebrew]; and the state's response, www.acri.org.il/he/wp-content/uploads/2013/07/ hit413tguva.pdf.
[118]   Norwegian Refugee Council, *A Guide to Housing, Land and Property Law in Area C of the West Bank* (2012), p. 68.
[119]   *Ibid.*, pp. 69–70, details the example of the designation, in 1985, of 350 dunams of the land of the Palestinian village of Bil'in, as a nature reserve due to old oaks planted in 35 dunams of the land. In 1993 an amendment reduced the natural reserve to 35 dunams; in 1999 it was reduced to 30 dunams and in 2007 to 25.5 dunams. In all these cases the land was used for settlement construction.
[120]   *Ibid.*, p. 70. This is by a military order.   [121]   *Ibid.*

apparatuses exercising control through permit regimes. These regimes are discussed in Sections Z.2.3.1 and Z.2.3.2 respectively.

Z.2.3 *Prohibitive Permit Regimes*

Z.2.3.1 Control Over Planning and Building

The main feature of the planning process in Area C is that it is controlled exclusively by Israel; Palestinians are prevented from participating in the shaping of their space. The planning regime consists of planning laws, planning authorities, outline plans, and decisions relative to building permits, as briefly detailed below.

In 1966, a year before Israel took control of the OPT, Jordan enacted a planning law providing for a planning regime that recognized local interests and left details of planning to local and district authorities. In 1967 Israel kept the Jordanian law, ostensibly to comply with the conservation principle,[122] only to modify it significantly in 1971, in military order no. 418.[123] The order abolished the local committees that existed under the Jordanian law, transferring their power to a Supreme Planning Committee (SPC), comprising Israeli military and civilians but no Palestinians. It then authorized the military commander to set up a Special Local Planning Committee in any area that does not include a city or a village council – that is, in Jewish settlements. Thus, a separate and discriminatory planning system was set up for settlements, where local committees comprising settlers approve plans, submit plans to the SPC, and issue building permits. Palestinian villages depend on the civil administration for these functions.[124]

There are currently two types of outline plans for Area C: regional outline plans prepared during the British Mandate, and a special outline plan made by the civil administration. All but ten Palestinian villages are still subject to the mandatory plan under which most of the area was classified as an agricultural zone where, subject to certain specified exceptions, no construction is allowed. It may be recalled in this context that, in addition, much of the

---

[122] The principle forbids an occupying power from changing the laws and legal institutions in place in an occupied territory. See Article 43 of the Hague Regulations; Article 64 of GC IV. See entry T: Temporary/Indefinite.

[123] Order Concerning Towns, Villages and Buildings Planning Law (Judea and Samaria) (No 418), 1971. It has been amended numerous times since.

[124] Shalev and Cohen-Lifshitz, *The Prohibited Zone*, pp. 55–58; See also the background review provided in S. Leighton, "Al-'Aqaba: What One Village Can Teach us About the Law of Occupation" (2014) 45 *Georgetown Journal of International Law* 524, 535.

area has also been designated as a "closed military zone" where construction is prohibited. It is thus perfectly legal to reject Palestinian requests for building permits, and to classify villages that were not named in this plan as "unrecognized." Lack of updated plans further prevents many villages from building crucial infrastructure, including roads and structures for water and electricity. The plans issued by the civil administration, in effect restrict Palestinian construction to existing built-up areas, thus arresting their development.[125]

A building permit is required in order to add a new building or construct to an existing one. This normal process is, however, fraught with difficulties and very costly: the petition must include registration certificates, which most owners do not have for a variety of reasons, proof of ownership, a land survey, constructions plans, etc.[126] Landowners whose petition was denied by a local committee may appeal to a subcommittee of the SPC and thereafter to the HCJ. Less than 6 percent of petitions for building permits are approved.[127]

It is thus not surprising that many buildings are constructed without a permit. Illegal construction generates demolition orders. Thousands have been executed; thousands more are pending.[128] Palestinian petitions challenging the composition of the SPC, the process of issuing building permits, and demolition orders were rejected by the HCJ.[129]

The net result is that the permit regime governing construction in Area C is for all practical purposes a *non*permit regime. The occupied Palestinian space provides ever diminishing space for Palestinian habitats.

---

[125] Shalev and Cohen-Lifshitz, *The Prohibited Zone*, pp. 60–72.
[126] Israel Military Order No 291 Concerning the Settlement of Disputes over Titles in Land and the Regulation of Water, 1968, froze the land registration process that began during the mandate in 1928, leaving 66 percent of the West Bank and 69 percent of Area C unregistered. Even when registration was allowed, many Palestinians avoided registration for a combination of tax reasons and a traditional system of communal ownership. They also fear that if registration is denied, the land will be confiscated.
[127] Shalev and Cohen-Lifshitz, *The Prohibited Zone*, pp. 73–84.
[128] United Nations Office for the Coordination of Humanitarian Affairs, *Under Threat: Demolition Orders in Area C of the West Bank* (September 2015), www.ochaopt.org/sites/def ault/files/demolition_orders_in_area_c_of_the_west_bank_en.pdf.
[129] HCJ 11/5667 *Dirat-Al Rfai'ya Village Council v. Minister of Defense* (June 9, 2015) [Hebrew]. (Following the establishment of a new procedure in September 2014, for planning in Area C – according to which the civil administration will conduct consultations with the local population regarding plans which impact civil life, prior to the discussion in the planning committees thus providing a chance for Palestinians to voice reservations, if not fully participate in the decision-making process – the court concluded that the balance between security considerations and the interests of the local population is reasonable. It was also decided that after three years of operating this procedure, the issue will be re-examined by the minister of defense and the attorney general.)

Z.2.3.2 Control Over Movement

The logic which has been driving the spatial violation of the OPT through zoning also dictated the development of movement control technologies.[130] Ranging from low-tech (e.g., a flying blockade) to high-tech (e.g., "terminals"), such technologies too need the appearances of law.[131] The bureaucratic apparatus known as "the permit regime" supplies them with this appearance.

The "permit regime" is a regulatory system administered by several district liaison and coordination offices (DCLs), established pursuant to the Oslo Accords.[132] It requires every Palestinian who wishes to travel between the West Bank and Israel (including East Jerusalem), Gaza, as well as within some parts of the West Bank,[133] to obtain a special permit. Given that every human interaction that necessitates traveling between zones – be it for accessing medical and educational services, work, engaging in commercial transactions, or visiting relatives – requires a permit, the meaning of the regime far exceeds restrictions on freedom of movement: it impacts accessibility to most rights and the ability to realize them, thus shaping both private and community life. Indeed, the very condition of possibility to lead a normal life depends on one's ability to navigate in the bureaucratic maze comprising the regime.[134]

This navigation requires, first, knowledge of the criteria for submitting requests and of the criteria according to which they may be accepted or rejected. Such knowledge, alas, has hardly been made publicly available, let alone accessible to the relevant Palestinian public: only in the mid-2000s, and

---

[130] In 1972, an "open borders" policy was declared between Gaza, the West Bank, and Israel. The genesis of the permit regime began in 1989, when the IDF demanded that workers from Gaza carry a magnetic card as a prerequisite for obtaining permission to enter Israel. In 1991, during the first Gulf War, the general permit of entry was canceled and a new military decree required Palestinians to obtain individual permits for entry into Israel at the full discretion of the military commander distribution. During the 1990s closure became institutionalized as the rule and the exit permit became the exception. The fragmentation of the OPT and the reorganization of power bureaucratized the permit process.

[131] These technologies are discussed in entry X: X Rays.

[132] For the DCLs, see Oslo II, second Annex. The structural coordination relative to the permit regime between Israel and the PA ended with Palestinian suicide bombing in the late 1990s and the second Intifada is its graveyard. It has since been operated under the full discretion of the civil administration of the military commander.

[133] Especially in the seam zone, see Section Z.2.4. On the operation of the permit regime in the seam zone, see A. Cahana and Y. Kanonich, *The Permit Regime: Human Rights Violations in the West Bank Areas Known as the "Seam Zone"* (Jerusalem: Hamoked – Center for the Defense of the Individual, 2013).

[134] For a most comprehensive and insightful analysis of the structural underpinnings of the permit regime, see Y. Berda, *The Bureaucracy of the Occupation: the Permit Regime in the West Bank* (Tel Aviv: Van Leer Institute, 2012) [Hebrew].

only in response to petitions made pursuant to the 1998 Freedom of Information Law,[135] was information gradually released. In March 2016, a document comprising a comprehensive list of permit categories was finally published, albeit only in Hebrew, not in Arabic.[136]

Some features of this document merit attention: first, its general part, having grounded the rationale for the permit regime in security, proceeds to "recall," in paragraph 6, that "a Palestinian resident has no vested right to enter into Israel and an Israeli has no vested right to exit to the Gaza Strip." The permit regime is thus a by-product of both the separation and the discrimination principles and practices that drive Israel's policy and are given the force of law and regulations. Indeed, the notion that there is no right of entry to a sovereign state borrows from the language of relations between sovereign states, thus obfuscating the entirely different context in which the regime operates. Second, an internal discrimination between Palestinians from Gaza and Palestinians from the West Bank operates. The document makes clear that while as a rule both do not enjoy a right to freedom of movement, there are nevertheless important distinctions between them: 8 broad categories and 48 subcategories of permits are listed for Palestinians from the West Bank, as compared with 3 categories and 11 subcategories for Gazans. Third, while documents that should accompany each request are listed, forms that may be required are absent. The inaccessibility of such forms, in both material and language terms, exacerbates an already arduous process.

Finally, in most categories the classification of an applicant as "denied entry for reasons of security," or the requirement that s/he be subject to such a classification process, suspends the permit process. Hundreds of thousands of Palestinians are thus classified. The criteria for this classification are not published since the information itself has been construed as a security threat. One may be thus classified by either the police[137] or the General Security Service (GSS). The information on whether one is denied entry for having been thus classified, though not its reasons, may be obtained only through the database of the civil administration; in the computer system of the ministries

---

[135]   Administrative Petition (Tel Aviv) 27605-01-11 *Gisha v. Civil administration in the West Bank* (May 19, 2013) [Hebrew].

[136]   Coordinator of Government Activities in the Territories, *Unclassified status of permits for the entry of Palestinians into Israel, their crossing between the zone of Judea and Samaria and the Gaza Strip and for their exit abroad* (updated May 10, 2016), www.gisha.org/UserFiles/File/LegalDocuments/procedures/general/50.pdf [Hebrew].

[137]   This classification includes people who have pending cases in criminal or civil courts, cases open by the police though never investigated, people who served a jail sentence for any charge and are denied entry after release, and people who have not paid their traffic tickets. Berda, *The Bureaucracy of the Occupation*, pp. 111–132.

of the interior and of the economy, all are classified as denied entry for security reasons without further specification.[138] There are a few venues to challenge this classification, but they too withhold this information from the person concerned or his/her lawyer, on the basis of secret evidence. Experience seems to suggest that an acceptance of an offer to collaborate with the GSS is the surest way to change the classification.[139]

Knowledge of the applicable rules is a necessary but not a sufficient condition to receive a permit. The process engages a wide array of administrative bodies and departments headed by the civil administration of the military and realized by liaison officers, representatives of the GSS and the Israeli police, investigation units of the border police, the ministry of the interior, the ministry of the economy, the office for foreign workers, the command of the coordinator of government action in the territories, and military courts. The practices of these bodies may conflict, and an applicant is often sent from one office to another in the quest for a permit, only to find out that the working hours of or indeed access routes to the offices have changed, as they regularly do.[140] This bureaucracy may appear inefficient insofar as its working is evaluated in the light of its stated objective: regulating movement. But insofar as it is evaluated in the light of its otherwise hidden objective, the prevention of Palestinians from using the space, and the production of constant uncertainty, it is quite effective.[141] Indeed, even if a Palestinian successfully navigates through this exhausting, humiliating, often costly and ultimately uncertain process – a navigation s/he is to repeat in view of the

---

[138] On the combined basis of experience in representing hundreds of Palestinians requesting permits and research, Berda suggests that the reasons for this classification, which are otherwise unknown, include the following: if a family member of the applicant was killed or injured by the IDF, all family members, including women and the elderly, would be thus classified; as a general rule, subject to unspecified exception, if a family member is serving sentence in Israel for a security offense or is in administrative detention, the applicant would be thus classified; if the GSS has received information about the political or military activities of the applicant, information the source of which may be a family or neighborly or labor dispute; if the applicant resides in a village that has been declared a security threat then the whole community would be thus classified; if the applicant has refused a proposition by the GSS to work as an informer. This practice, completely prohibited under Article 31 of the GCIV, further generates suspicions within the community and the family. Berda, *The Bureaucracy of the Occupation*, pp. 137–141.

[139] *Ibid.*, pp. 138, 149–152.

[140] A. Handel, "Exclusionary Surveillance and Spatial Uncertainty in the Occupied Palestinian Territories," in E. Zureik, D. Lyon, and Y. Abu-Laban (eds.), *Surveillance and Control in Israel/Palestine: Population, Territory and Power* (Oxford: Routledge, 2011), pp. 259, 268–270.

[141] The process has been aptly characterized by Berda as one of "effective ineffectiveness." Berda, *The Bureaucracy of the Occupation*, pp. 88–110. On governance through (un)certainty see entries M: Military Courts and K: Kinship.

time limits attached to permits – s/he may find out that a permit is of little value in the face of a closed checkpoint or an unaccommodating soldier.

This routine production of Palestinian "procedural bare life"[142] by the permit regime stems from the spatial reorganization of the OPT. It does not regulate movement in and between the OPT and Israel; it minimizes Palestinian – and only Palestinian – movement. It disrupts Palestinians' ability to use their land in a predictable manner that allows them to engage in the routine activities comprising life. The HCJ, acknowledging that the permit regime "does lead to a severe infringement on the right of the Palestinian residents," nevertheless determined the infringement to be proportionate and dismissed a petition against it.[143]

Z.3 CONCLUSION

The Israeli-controlled legal production of the occupied Palestinian space has generated a Palestinian no-place: the combined effect of its material regulations (such as those designed to encourage the thriving of Jewish settlements) and material deregulation (such as its lack of planning and building permits) with the dissection of the land, various barrier artifacts, and their attendant permit regime, has created a socially and mentally distorted Palestinian space.[144] It is socially distorted because it prevents Palestinians from engaging in routine socioeconomic, personal, and political activities that comprise life. It is mentally distorted because of the sense of disorientation, displacement, anxiety, and uncertainty experienced by the Palestinians caught in its violent orbit.[145] This "spacio-cide"[146] or "geography of continuous disaster,"[147] wherein one finds oneself homeless in her own home, is a site of constant, and indeed recurrent, loss.[148]

---

[142]   *Ibid.*, pp. 133–161. The study posits that, structurally, the permit regime is a combination of a colonial bureaucracy (inherited from the British Mandate and initially applied by Israel within Israel to the Arab minority during 1948–1966, the years of the military government) and a Schmittian "security theology," which sees every Palestinian as a foe, a security threat.

[143]   HCJ 9961/03 Hamoked – *Center for the Defense of the Individual* v. *Government of Israel* (April 5, 2011) [Hebrew]. The court did find that the military commander must relax the rules applicable to Palestinians in living in the "seam zone" and instructed the respondent to establish a clear and efficient timetable for processing applications. In this manner, it rejected the petition in principle but opened the door for specific petitions. For a discussion of "proportionality" see entry P: Proportionality.

[144]   Blank and Rosen-Zvi, "The Spatial Turn."   [145]   Kelly, "Returning Home?," pp. 96–97.

[146]   S. Hanafi, "Explaining Spacio-cide in the Palestinian Territory: Colonization, separation, and state of exception" (2013) 61 *Current Sociology* 90.

[147]   Handel, "Where, Where to, and When in the Occupied Territories," pp. 216–217.

[148]   Shalhoub-Kevorkian, "Counter-Spaces as Resistance in Conflict Zones," pp. 118–119.

What the discussion above further discloses is that the territory/population tension has been replicated in the modus operandi of the various legal technologies employed to control the Palestinian space. This modus consists of a series of indeterminacies which include, but are not limited to, the borders/boundaries, occupation/annexation, de jure annexation/de facto annexation, and exclusion/inclusion regulatory mechanisms.[149]

These indeterminacies characterized the legalization of the settlement enterprise from its very beginning.[150] It reached its logical conclusion with the HCJ's later determinations that the route of the separation barrier was occasioned by security consideration rather than by the politics of expansionism.[151] These decisions provided the legal grounds for further indeterminacies.[152] These legal obfuscations do more than reflect the legal nature of the control Israel exercises over the OPT. They also donned a legal mantle on the making of a Jewish utopia and the related transformation of the Palestinian space into a heterotopia, a space containing the undesirable bodies, Palestinian bare life, that make the utopian space possible.[153]

---

[149] See note 14.

[150] HCJ 390/79 *Dweikat* v. *Government of Israel* (1979) 34(1) PD 1 [Hebrew]; D. Kretzmer, *The Occupation of Justice* (Albany: SUNY Press, 2002), p. 7. See generally, I. Zertal and A. Eldar, *Lords of the Land*, V. Eden (trans.) (New York: Nation Books, 2007); entry J: Jewish Settlements.

[151] *Beit Sourik*. This position was reiterated in HCJ 7957/04 *Mara'abe* v. *Prime Minister of Israel* (2005) 60(2) PD 477 [Hebrew], a judgment rendered after the ICJ advisory opinion, *Consequences of the Construction of a Wall*. See entry B: Border/Barrier.

[152] Blank, "Legalizing the Barrier'; M. Koskenniemi, "Occupied Zone – 'A Zone of Reasonableness'?" (2008) 41 *Israel Law Review* 13.

[153] Foucault, *Discipline and Punish*.

Index

Abayat, Hussein, 64–66
"absolute enemy" principle, surveillance
    technology and, 496–498
Abu Hilo v. Government of Israel (1973), 27(2)
    PD 169, 205–211
Abu-Rahme, Ashraf, 196–199, 460–461
Abu-Rahme, Bassem, 196–199
Abu Rahme v the MAG (2009) 63(2) PD 325,
    457–467
Abu Ramah, Jawaher, 196–199
Abu Safiyeh v Minister of Defense (2009) 63(3)
    PD 331, 149–152, 155–161
Abushamsiya, Imad, 467–473
accountability. *See* impunity, culture of
actus reus
    inadmissibility in court of law, 375
    military/domestic law overlap in definitions
        of, 315–319
Additional Protocol I (1977), 11–12
    Article 3(b), 404–405
    Article 51(3), 68–70
    Article 51(5)(b), 327–331
    Article 54, 351–355
    Article 57, 489–491
    Article 85(4)(a), 289–291
    belligerent occupation and, 141–144
    collective punishment prohibition in,
        167–170
    distinction principle in, 68–70
    inter-state context of armed conflict in,
        71–74
    Israel's rejection of, 431–435
    Jewish settlements as violation of, 289–291
    proportionality principle in, 327–331
    status of combatants and, 60–64
    Targeted Killing case and, 71–74

violence terminology in, 431–435
Additional Protocol II (1977), collective
    punishment prohibition in, 167–170
administrative detentions
    of African asylum seekers, 322–323
    HCJ authorization of, 109
    Israeli supreme court review of, 273–274
    military courts' review of, 271
    Palestinian prisoners and, 385–386
    pre-1967 use of, 306–312
    as preventive strategy, 130–133
    as state violence, 446
African asylum seekers, Israeli law and, 319–324
against the law approach
    law-rule-exception relationship and, 7–8
    overview of, 17–21
    Regularization Law and, 362–364
Agamben, Giorgio, 6–7, 325–326
    on law-preserving violence, 20–21
    on state of exception, 18–19
    on suspension of rule of law, 9–10
age of criminal majority, 268–270, 499–504,
    511–512
Aharonovitch, Yitzhak, 321–322
airport security, Palestinian profiling and,
    492–495
Ajuri, Ahmed Ali, 29, 34–35, 38–39
Ajuri, Amtassar, 29, 34–35
Ajuri, Kipah, 29, 34–35
*Ajuri v Commander of the IDF in Judea and
    Samaria* (2002) 56(6) PD 352, 28, 30–35
    applicability of facts in, 38–39
    applicability of law in, 34–35
    critical analysis of judgment in, 35–39
    dynamic and teleological interpretation of,
        35–38

law *vs.* fiction in, 39–42
narrative framework of, 30–32
normative framework for, 32–33
Al-Affo v Commander of the IDF in the West Bank (1988) 42(2) PD 4, 85
Al-Bassiouni Petition, 351–357
Al-Fasfous, Mahmoud, case of, 162–164, 179–181
Alfe Menashe Case. *See Mara'abe v Prime Minister of Israel* (2005) 60(2) IsrSC 477
al-Hadi Muhsin al-Fasfous v Minister of Defense (1989) 43(3) PD 576., 162–164
Al Huq v Minsitry of the Interior (14.3.2017), 226n.39
al-Ibrahimi Mosque, 524–529
al-Sharif, Abed al Fatah, 467–473
Alterman, Nathan, 464n.86
Amira, Salaam, 459–460
Amit, Yitzhak (Justice), 302–303, 322
Amnesty International, 449–452
Amoore, Louise, 139–140
annexation
chronotope of occupation and, 401–406
crawling annexation in OPT, 377–378
in East Jerusalem, 529–536
indefinite status of, 411
Regularization Law and, 371–372
separation fence project and, 54–56
Apartheid in South Africa, seam zone permit regime case compared with, 335–337
applicability of law
assigned residence and, 34–35
HCJ belligerent occupation jurisprudence and, 149–152
appropriation of property, in Regularization law, 374–375
Arab Revolt of 1937, 167n.18
Arendt, Hannah, 9n.34, 451–452
armed conflict, law of
identity of parties in, 71–74
Israeli investigation mechanisms for claims involving, 187n.21
normative framework for targeted killing policy based on, 67–68
proportionality principle and, 329n.7
Red Lines policy in framework of, 351–355
violence terminology in, 431–435
war crimes and, 448–449
"warning" procedures as preemptive defense and, 126–129

Armistice line of 1949, 294, 304, 312, 325–326, 331–333. *See also* Green Line
zone divisions in West Bank and, 524–529
Armistice Line of 1949, 47–48, 295–297
separation fence project and, 51–52, 58–59, 331–333
zone divisions in West Bank and, 524–529
Asida, Aber, 29, 34–35
assigned residence
analysis of Fourth Geneva Convention Article 78 and, 33–34
applicability of facts in, 38–39
applicability of law and, 34–35
in context of Ajuri case, 28–32
law *vs.* fiction in policies of, 39–42
narrative framework for, 30–32
normative framework of, 26–28
Association for Civil Rights in Israel (ACRI), 85, 93–94, 493–495
Attorney General, oversight mechanisms of, 193–196
Ayub v Minister of Defense (1979) 33(2) PD 113 (Beit El case), 206–211
Azaria, Elor, 467–473
Azoulay, Ariella, 303–304

Bach, Gavriel (Justice), 85, 90
Baker, Alan, 282
Balfour Declaration of 1917, 282, 291–294
Barak, Aharon (Justice), 30–35, 56–58
Beit Surik case, 333–335
on Citizenship and Entry Law, 232–233
deportations halted by, 93–94
on "focused preemption" policy, 124–125
house demolitions and, 164–165n.11
teleological interpretations by, 87n.41, 90–94
"bare life" paradigm, 9n.34
barriers
legal definition of, 44–46
natural barriers, 45n.11
physical implications of, 48–50
seam zone in, 49–50
Basic Law: Human Dignity and Liberty, 48–50, 232–233
"Before the Law" (Kafka), 447
before the law approach
law-rule-exception relationship and, 7
Regularization Law as expression of, 362–364
Begin, Menachem, 210–211
Beinisch, Dorit (Chief Justice), 124–125, 156n.78, 159–161, 335–337, 438–439

Beit El case. *See Ayub v Minister of Defense*
    (1979) 33(2) PD 113
Beit Surik case, 333–335, 339–340,
    538n.106, 540
belligerent occupation, law of, 9n.32
    annexation prohibitions and, 54–56
    applicability of law and, 149–152
    assigned residences justification and, 32–33
    chronotope ideology and, 399–401
    deportations and, 80
    "effective control" concept and, 355–357
    emergency regulations of British Mandate
        and, 167–172
    exploitation of natural resources in, 422–424
    Gaza Strip management and, 521–524
    Geneva Convention Article 2 and, 146
    historical evolution of, 141–144
    international law and, 11–12, 176–178
    investigations and, 182–183
    Israeli interpretation of, 144–149
    Israel to Greater Israel framework for,
        152–159
    Jewish settlements in OPT, HCJ
        jurisprudence based on, 206–211
    Levy Committee disregard of, 278–280,
        291–294
    nomos of Israeli law concerning, 281–284
    normative framework for, 159–161
    origin of concept, 4–6
    prohibition of settlements and, 200–202
    prolonged occupations, legal issues
        surrounding, 284–285
    proportionality and, 337–340
    quality of life and, 345–347
    Regularization Law violations of, 370–375
    temporary/indefinite control in, 406–416
    trust principles in, 419–421
    usufruct principles and, 417–419
Ben-Gurion, David, 306–312, 463
Benjamin, Walter, 6–7, 18–19
    on law-preserving violence, 20–21, 432
Bennet, Naftali, 467–473
Berda, Yael, 447n.90, 475n.3, 543n.134,
    545n.138, 545n.141
Berlin Wall, 45n.10
Beth El case. *See Ayub v Minister of Defense*
    (1979) 33(2) PD 113
big data, growth of administrative detentions
    and use of, 132
biometric surveillance tools, 484, 496–498
    inherent enmity ideology and, 492–493

biopolitics, inherent enmity ideology and,
    492–493
Blau, Uri, 69n.53, 347–350, 445
Blum, Yehuda, 146
Borberg, Omri (Lt. Col.), 459
border/barrier distinction
    multiple facets of walls and, 43–47
    separation fence project and, 51–54
borders
    legal definition of, 43–44
    legal and political porosity of, 117, 302, 304,
        312–324
Branin, Trial Chamber Judgment, ICTY-99-
    36-T, 463
Breaking the Silence NGO, 457n.42
Brillat-Savarin, A., 360–361
British Mandate for Palestine (1922–1947), 165,
    246–250
    draconian powers of, 167–172
    emergency regulations of, 167–172, 305–306
    influence on Israeli military law, 311–315
    justification of settlements based on, 282
    Levy Committee's interpretation of, 291–294
    regional outline plans under, 541–542
Brussels Declaration, 246–247, 345n.9,
    372–373, 417–419
    law of belligerent occupation and, 9n.32
B'Tselem (Israeli Information Center for
    Human Rights in the Occupied
    Territories), 114–115, 189–192, 194–199,
    251–256
    Abu Rahme case and, 459–460
    child prisoners and, 390–394
    war crimes investigations and, 467–473
building permits
    house demolitions and, 162–164
    housing shortages in East Jerusalem and,
        533–534
    as invisible violence, 441–443
    Israeli control in OPT over, 118–119, 152–154
    planning and building control and, 541–542
Bureau of Alcohol, Tobacco, Firearms and
    Explosives (U.S.), Israeli training
    programs for, 100–101

catastrophization, politics of, 360n.78
cellular communications technology, Israeli
    control of, 486–489
Center for Constitutional Rights, 253–254
"center of life" standard, family unification and
    separation and, 237–241

Central Intelligence Agency (CIA), enhanced
    interrogations by, 106–107
Chalbi v The Prime Minister (30.5.2005),
    528–529
Cheshin, Mishael, 56–58, 232–233
Chief Military Prosecutor's Directives, 185–186
children. *See* youth justice
chronotope of occupation
    definition and terminology, 399–401
    indefinite occupation and, 413–416
    international jurisprudence and, 401–406
    Israeli substition of indefinite for temporary,
        406–413
Churchill, Winston, 292–293
Ciechanover Commission, 187–188, 194–196
Citizenship and Entry into Israel Law
    (Temporary Order), 48–50, 223–225,
    226n.39, 492–493
    amendment of 2003 to, 229–230
    categories of people in, 228n.52
    citizenship status of Palestinians and,
        531–532
    international law and, 232–233
    kinship ties and impact of, 241–242
    profiling of Palestinians as enemy and, 234,
        237n.97
    restrictions on foreigners critical of
        settlements in, 234n.79
    suspension of families as result of, 237–241
citizenship status
    familes, unification and separation and,
        225–228
    military prosecution of Israeli citizens,
        312–315
    for Palestinians, 531–532
Civil Administration of the OPT
    civilian zoning and, 540–541
    regional outline plans under, 541–542
    West Bank quarry industry and, 421–422, 424
civilians
    in AP I Article 51(3), 68–70
    IDF investigations in death of, 191–192n.38
    law enforcement and, 182–183
    principle of distinction and, 68–70, 111–112,
        128–129
    Targeted Killings judgment and legal status
        of, 71–74
coercion of evidence
    administrative detentions and, 130–133
    direct surveillance and, 479–480
    military court proceedings and, 273–274

Cohen, Haim (Justice), 84
Cohen, Yehuda, 391
collaborators. *See* informants
collateral damage, proportionality principle
    and, 329n.7
collective punishment, prohibition of
    house demolitions jurisprudence and,
        172–179
    Israeli methods in violation of, 179n.79
    Palestinian prisoners, treatment as violation
        of, 390–394
    Regulation 119 as violation of, 167–170
collective suspicion, surveillance technology
    and principle of, 477–478
colonialism
    house demolitions under, 165
    Israeli settler-colonial project, 202–204
    Jewish settlements jurisprudence and,
        216–217
    in Levy Committee report, 280, 291–294
    sovereignty as distinct from occupation and,
        13–14
    surveillance and, 477–478n.14
    usufruct principles and, 429–430
Comaroff, Jean, 243–246
Comaroff, John, 243–246
combatant status
    AP I Article 51(3) and, 68–70
    fluidity of, 438–439
    HCJ judgment concerning, 66–70
    legal principles concerning, 60–64
    principle of distinction and, 68–70, 111–112,
        128–129
    privileges and rights under, 68n.47
    targeted killing policy and, 64–66
Comey, Michael, 146
command responsibility principle, military law
    and, 186–189
*Commission on the Responsibility of the
    Authors of the War and on Enforcement
    of Penalties*, 169–170
*Committee to Examine the Status of Building
    in Judea and Samaria*, 415
common law rule, HCJ deportation rulings
    and, 83–84
complementarity, principle of, 351n.37
confessions, coercion of, 130–133, 273–274
confiscation of property
    Israel to Greater Israel framework for,
        152–159
    in OPT, 360–361

confiscation of property (cont.)
  Regularization Law and, 368–370, 372–373
conquest, sovereignty and, 13–14
conservation principle
  house demolitions and, 172–176
  indefinite occupation and, 413–416
  respect for domestic law and, 176–178
  sovereignty vs. temporary occupation, 15–16
"constant danger" principle, airport
      surveillance and, 493–495
constants, proportionality principle and
      abandonment of, 337–340
construction and planning
  illegal construction and, 541–542
  Regularization Law and, 362–364, 370
Construction of the Wall advisory opinion,
      chronotope of occupation and, 401–406
continuity, principle of, legal challenge to
      quarry licensing and, 422–429
contra-legem principle, Israeli settler-colonial
      project, 202–204
control
  occupation as temporary control, 16–17,
      141–144
  over interned persons, 26–28
counterterrorism
  cross/self-referential loop in transfer of
      knowledge about, 104–112
  Israeli training programs in, 99–104
courts martial
  military law and, 186–189
  war crimes and, 455–457
Cover, Robert, 277–278
criminal law
  future-oriented elements of, 129–130
  Israeli war crimes law and, 183–185
  military/domestic law overlap in, 315–319
  Palestinian prisoners and, 383–384
  youth justice and, 499–504
critiquing against the law
  law-rule-exception relationship and, 7–8
  overview of, 17–21
critiquing before the law
  basic principles of, 8–17
  law-rule-exception relationship and, 7–8
  occupation as form of trust and, 14–16
  occupation as temporary control and, 16–17
  sovereignty as distinct from occupation,
      13–14
cross/self-referential loop, in Israeli-U.S.
      transfer of knowledge, 104–112, 115–117

custodial sentencing, youth justice in domestic
      law and, 507–510
customary international law
  belligerent occupation and, 141–144
  Jewish settlements in OPT, HCJ
      jurisprudence based on, 206–211
  property destruction prohibition and,
      170–172
  status of combatants and, 60–64
  war crimes and, 448–449

Dahiya doctrine, 439, 444
Danon, Danny, 321–322
Danun, 'Aziz Muhammad, 64–66
Dayan, Moshe, 103–104, 205n.19, 308–309,
      310n.60
Dayan, Uzi (Gen.), 469–470
de facto occupying power
  chronotope of occupation and, 401–406
  indefinite occupation and, 411n.52, 413–416
  Israeli occupation of OPT and, 146–149
  sovereignty and, 143n.12
  youth justice and, 505–507
Defense Regulations, emergency regulation
      112, deportations under, 225–228
Defense (Emergency) Regulations,
      deportation of Palestinian militants and
      political leaders out of, 81–82
de jure occupation
  Israeli occupation of OPT framed as,
      146–149
  Regularization Law and, 371–372
demographic anxiety about Jewish majority
  Citizenship and Entry into Israel Law
      amendments and, 229–230
  citizenship status and, 225–228
  HCJ judgments, critique of, 230–237
  human rights law on, 220–223
  international humanitarian law and, 219–225
  Israeli freeze on Palestinian unification in
      2002, 228–229
  kinship and, 218–219
  as preemptive/preventive strategy, 118–119
  profiling of Palestinians as enemy and,
      234–237
  reunification laws and, 223–225
Demopoulos v Turkey, Eur Ct HR, App No
      46113/ 99, 405–406
Dempsey, Martin, 102–103
deportations
  forcible transfers and, 200–202

GC IV prohibition on, HCJ disregard of,
  78–81, 86–90
HCJ rulings on, 83–90
Israeli practices of, 81–83
military commanders' authority concerning,
  32–33
normative framework for law on,
  78–83
Palestinian court petitions involving, 85
teleological interpretation of, 91–94
Deri, Aryeh, 211–212n.39
Derrida, Jacques
  on justice, 20–21
  on meaning and différance, 23
detention periods, youth justice in Israel and,
  510–514
deterrence
  collective punishment and, 167–170
  in criminal law, 129–130
  as future-oriented strategy, 118–122
  house demolitions as tool for, 166, 172–176,
    178–179
Dichter, Avraham, 253–254
"direct participation" in hostilities
  in AP I Article 51(3), 68–70
  ICRC study of, 71–74
direct surveillance, 479–480
distinction, principle of
  combatant status and, 60–64, 111–112,
    128–129
  lesser evils perspective in, 327–331
  targeted killing policy and, 68–70
District Liaison and Coordination Offices
  (DCLs), 543–546
division
  direct surveillance and, 479–480
  of Palestinian prisoners, 390–394
domestic law
  belligerent occupation law and, 172–176
  family rights in, 220–223
  international law and, 176–178
  Israeli duality in, 301–305
  Jewish settlements and, 368–370
  jurisdiction beyond borders of, 312–315
  military law overlap with, 315–319
  suppression of criticism using, 260
  temporal and spatial aspects of, 312–324
  war crimes in Israeli domestic legislation,
    187–188
  youth justice and rule of exception in,
    507–510

drone strikes
  targeted killings and, 65, 65n.27–66n.27
  U.S. authorization of, 106–107
Dugard, John, 54–55, 411n.52
Dunlap, Charles, 113–115, 243–246
Dweikat v Government of Israel (1979) 34(1) PD
  1, 149–152
Dworkin, Ronald, 341–342

East Jerusalem
  Jewish settlements in, 202–204, 520–521
  judaization activities in, 532–533
  legal commonality with rest of West Bank,
    315–319, 507–510
  liminal zone of, 529–536
  Palestinian citizenship status in, 226n.39,
    531–532
  urban planning failure in, 533–534
  welfare and municipal services in, 534–536
economic development, West Bank quarry
    industry jurisprudence and invocation
    of, 425–429
effective control
  Gaza Strip and, 521–524
  law of belligerent occupation and, 355–357
  Red Lines policy and concept of, 351–355
El-Al high-jacking, 493–495
Elon Moreh case, 209–211, 213–214, 285–289.
  See Dweikat v Government of Israel
  (1979) 34(1) PD 1
emergency regulations
  under British Mandate, 167–172, 305–306
  framing of Palestinians and, 234–237
  global increase in scope of, 18–19
  inherent enmity ideology and, 492–493
  jurisdiction beyond borders of, 312–315
"enclave law"
  separation fence project and, 51–52
  sociopolitical fragmentation and, 536–538
enemy aliens, profiling of Palestinians as,
    233–237
erga omnes rights, of Palestinians, 295–297
European Convention on Human Rights,
    221–222n.16
European Court of Human Rights
  concept of family in, 219–220
  temporariness of occupations in cases
    before, 405–406
European Directive on the Right to Family
    Reunification, 223–225
Ewick, Patricia, 7, 21–22

exception, rule of. *See also* law-rule-exception
    relationship
  absence of, in Jewish settlements case,
    215–216
  Agamben's discussion of, 9–10
  civilian direct participation in hostilities
    and, 75–77
  critiquing against the law and, 18–19
  deportations and, 78–80
  in domestic law, 507–510
  expansion of, after *Targeted Killings* case,
    75–77
  future issues with, 514–515
  Jewish settlements in OPT and, 212–216
  justifications for, 20–21
  law of belligerent occupation and, 11–12
  in military law, 504–507
  military necessity defense and forcing of,
    213–214
  Regularization law and, 379–380
  war crimes and, 454–467
excessive harm hypothesis
  airport security profiling and, 494n.96
  proportionality principle and,
    329–331
exclusionary surveillance, 477–478n.14
Executive Order 13769 (U.S.), 234–237
Executive Order 13780 (U.S.), 234–237
ex factis ius oritur (the law arises from the facts),
    chronotope of occupation and,
    405–406
ex injuria jus non oritur (violating the law
    cannot have legal effects)
  chronotope of occupation and, 405–406
  West Bank quarry industry jurisprudence
    and, 425–429
exploitation, sovereignty as distinct from
    occupation and, 13–14
export of security knowledge
  common terminology used in, 113–115
  cross/self-referential loop in, 104–112
  international legal discourse on, 105–111
  interrelations and convergence of U.S.-
    Israeli discourse and practices, 115–117
  by Israel, overview of, 95–99
  security knowledge, U.S-Israeli transfer of,
    99–104
ex post facto laws, military/domestic law
  overlap in definitions of, 315–319
extra-judicial/extra-legal killings
  human rights references to, 66n.30

  as preemptive strategy, 124–126
extraterritorial application of law
  Regularization Law and, 362–364
  separation fence project and, 52–53

"fabric of life" crossings, barrier entry gates
    and, 48n.25
fact-driven norms, proportionality and, 329
families, unification and separation of
  Citizenship and Entry into Israel Law
    amendments and, 229–230
  citizenship status and, 225–228
  HCJ judgments, critique of, 230–237
  human rights law on, 220–223
  international humanitarian law and, 219–225
  Israeli freeze on Palestinian unification in
    2002, 228–229
  kinship and, 218–219
  profiling of Palestinian familiy and, 234–237
  profiling of Palestinians as enemy and,
    233–234
  reunification laws and, 223–225
  surveillance technology and, 492–493
  suspended families and, 237–241
  unification restrictions and, 109–110, 118–119
  youth justice and, 504–507
family, legal concept of, 219–220
family resemblance theory, 23
Fatah, Palestinian Hamas reconciliation with,
    122–123
Federal Bureau of Investigation (FBI), Israeli
    training programs for, 100–101
Feldman, Avigdor, 85–86, 209–211
Feldman, Tamar, 353–355
Feldman, Yotam, 347–350
"financial guarantees," military law imposition
    of, 318
firing zones, creation of, 538–540
First Geneva Convention for the Amelioration
    of the Condition of the Wounded and
    Sick in Armed Forces in the Field,
    431–435. *See also* Geneva Conventions,
    Common Article 3
Five Broken Cameras (documentary), 198n.73
"focused preemption" policy, 124–125
"Food Consumption in the Gaza Strip – Red
    Lines" (Feldman & Blau), 347–350
food security
  Gaza Flotilla incident and, 353–355
  international human rights law and,
    357–359

forced transfer
  deportation *vs.*, 79n.4
  Jewish settlements in context of, 211–212
  Regularization law and, 379–380
force-feeding of Palestinian prisoners, 105,
    387–388
  HCJ authorization of, 109, 388
forcible transfers, deportation and, 200–202
'for such time' principle, in AP I Article 51(3),
    68–70
Foucault, Michel, 24, 140
  biopower concept of, 77n.88
  on violence, 434–435, 440–444
Fourth Geneva Convention Relative to the
    Protection of Civilian Persons in Times
    of War, 11–12. *See also* Geneva
    Conventions, Common Article 3
  Ajuri case and, 28–32, 35–38
  annexation prohibitions and, 54–55
  Article 6, 17n.70, 401–406
  Article 23, 351–355
  Article 27, 220–223, 431–435, 461–465
  Article 28, 78–81
  Article 32, 461–465
  Article 46, 372–373
  Article 49, 78–81, 83–90, 91–94, 364–368,
    388–390
  Article 53, 170–172, 372–373
  Article 55, 355–357
  Article 59, 355–357
  Article 64, 178
  Article 66, 388–390
  Article 76, 388–390
  Article 78, 26–28, 32–33, 35–38
  Article 80, 388–390
  Article 102, 390–394
  Article 146, 183–185
  Article 147, 374–375
  assigned residence concept in, 26–28
  belligerent occupation law and, 141–144,
    149–152
  collective punishment prohibition, 167–170
  concept of family in, 219–220
  de jure non-applicability, Israeli position on,
    72n.67
  HCJ interpretations of, 83–90, 205–211
  inhabitants' rights in, 14–16
  Israeli control of OPT as violation of, 144–146
  Israeli disregard of, 268–270, 281–284
  Jewish settlements as breach of, 278–280,
    289–291

legal construction of combatants/civilians
    in, 72–73
  Levy Committee interpretation of, 285–289
  military courts use of, 268–270
  Palestinian prisoners and, 388–390
  prohibition of settlements in, 200–202
  property destruction prohibition in, 170–172
  war crimes and, 461–465
  youth justice and, 509–510
Freedom of Information Movement, 493–495
freedom of movement. *See also* HaMoked:
    Center for the Defense of the
    Individual
  control of occupying power over, 26–28
  identity documents as control over, 480–482
  permit regime and control of, 543–546
future-oriented strategies
  Massumi's perspective on, 120–121
  penalty of potential threats and, 129–137
  preemptive military attacks, 122–129
  results and consequences of, 137–140

Galtung, Johan, 434–435, 440–444
Gaza Coast Regional Planning Council
  Levy Committee and, 284–285
  petition by, 279n.11, 414–415
Gaza Flotilla incident, 256–262, 348–349,
    352–353
  alternative normative frameworks for,
    355–359
  laws of armed conflict and, 351–355
Gaza Strip
  as Administered Territory, 305–306
  assigned residence in, 33–34
  blockade and closure of, 187n.21, 440–444
  deportation of of Palestinian militants and
    political leaders out of, 81–82
  "disengagement" judgment regarding,
    26–27n.4, 489–491
  family separation and unification in, 237–241
  "Hunger Games" of 2007-2010 in, 350–359
  Israeli control over, 37–38, 120, 264–267,
    301–305, 440–444
  Israel's occpation in 1950s of, 308–309
  open borders policy in, 543n.130
  Palestinian prisoners in, 383–388
  preemptive strikes in, 122–123
  Red Lines policy in, 347–350
  rhetoric justifying occupation of, 261–262
  security training programs in, 101–104
  separation from West Bank, 442n.56

Gaza Strip (cont.)
  sui generis status of, 521–524
  surveillance technology in, 489–491
  temporal and spatial aspects of Israeli law in, 312–324
  "warning" procedures in, 126–129
  youth justice in, 499–504
GC I. *See* First Geneva Convention for the Amelioration of the Condition of the Wounded and Sick in Armed Forces in the Field
GC II. *See* Second Geneva Convention for the Amelioration of the Condition of the Wounded, Sick and Shipwrecked Members of Armed Forces at Sea
GC III. *See* Third Geneva Convention Relative to the Treatment of Prisoners of War
GC IV. *See* Fourth Geneva Convention Relative to the Protection of Civilian Persons in Times of War
General Security Service (GSS), 310–311, 312–315
  airport surveillance and, 493–495
  interrogations by, 388–390, 446
General Staff Order 33.0133, 186
Geneva Conventions. *See also* Fourth Geneva Convention Relative to the Protection of Civilian Persons in Times of War
  Article 2, 146–149, 285–289
  collective punishment prohibition in, 167–170
  Common Article 3, 431, 449, 461–462
  HCJ jurisprudence and, 149–159
  laws of war and, 246–247
  legal and judicial legacy of, 159–161
  Levy Committee interpretations of, 285–289
  normative framework of belligerent occupation in, 141–146
  principle of distinction and, 68–70
  property destruction prohibition in, 170–172
  protected persons status in, 461–465
  Regularization Law violations of, 371–372
  Targeted Killing case and, 71–74
  violence terminology in, 431–435
  war crimes and, 448–449
geopolitics
  borders *vs.* barriers and, 43–44
  of West Bank, 1n.1
Gisha – the Center for Freedom of Movement, 347–350, 441–443

Goldstein, Baruch, 193–194, 527–528
Goldstone Report, 9–10
Gorenberg, Gershom, 205n.19
governance, quality of life and, 343–345
government legal system, rule over Occupied Palestinian Territory and, 2–3
"Greater Israel" vision, Regularization Law and, 364–368
Green line. *See* Armistice Line of 1949
Gross, Aeyal, 233–234, 353–355
Guantánamo, US detention facility
  Israeli references to, 104–105, 109, 114–115
  legal scholarship on, 18–21, 264–267, 326

Hague Regulations Respecting the Laws and Customs of War on Land (1907), 11–12
  Article 23, 372–373, 375
  Article 23(g), 205–211, 213–214
  Article 43, 14–16, 143n.15, 154–159, 178, 345–347, 422–429
  Article 46, 220–223
  Article 55, 417–419, 422–429
  assigned residences and, 32–33
  belligerent occupation and, 141–144
  collective punishment prohibition in, 167–170
  laws of war and, 246–247
  principle of distinction and, 68–70
  property destruction prohibition in, 170–172
  quality of life under occupation and, 345–347
  respect for domestic law in, 176–178
  systemic change, occupation as form of trust precluding, 143n.15
Hamas
  economic warfare on, 348–349
  Israeli civil litigation against, 256–262
HaMoked: Center for the Defense of the Individual, 93–94
  house demolitions report, 166n.15
  seam zone permit regime case, 335–337, 543–546
Havana Rules. *See* UN Rules for the Protection of Juveniles Deprived of Their Liberty
Hayut, Esther (Justice), 175
Head of Ein Yabrud Council v Knesset, 381–382n.94
health concerns
  barriers to medical care for Palestinians and, 441–443
  in surveillance technologies, 484–485

Hebron, partition of, 526–529
Hebron Massacre, 193–194, 526n.51
Hebron Protocol, 526–529
heterotopia, OPT as no-place and, 517–519
Hezbollah, Israeli war against, 126–129
High Court of Justice (HCJ)
  Abu Rahme case and, 457–467
  Ajuri case judgment by, 28–32
  analysis of Fourth Geneva Convention
    Article 78 and, 33–34
  Beit Surik case, 333–335
  belligerent occupation jurisprudence of,
    149–159
  data on judgments by, 4n.16
  deportation rulings by, 83–94
  dynamic and teleological interpretations by,
    35–38, 73–74
  exceptions in Jewish settlement
    jurisprudence, 214–215
  family reunification petitions and, 228–237
  Geneva Convention Article 2 interpretation
    by, 146
  Hold Baggage Screening (HBS) technology
    and, 495
  indefinite occupation in settlement
    jurisprudence, 406–413
  institutional non-justiciability in Jewish
    settlements jurisprudence, 211–212
  Israel to Greater Israel framework and,
    152–154
  Jewish settlements in OPT, jurisprudence
    on, 205–212, 282, 285–289
  judicial inertia regarding house demolitions
    in, 172–176
  Military Advocate General investigations
    and, 196–199
  narrative framework of Ajuri judgment by,
    30–32
  national constituency for rulings by, 5n.18
  normative framework in *Targeted Killings*
    case, 67–68
  oversight mechanisms of, 193–196
  partition of Hebron and, 528–529
  pitfalls and advantages of litigation in,
    251–252
  principle of distinction in *Targeted Killings*
    case, 68–70
  proportionality principle and jurisprudence
    of, 155–159, 329–331
  quality of life under occupation and
    jurisprudence of, 346–347

  references to U.S. law by, 107–108
  Regularization Law and, 364–368
  rule over Occupied Palestinian Territory
    and, 1–4
  selective and dynamic interpretation of
    targeted killing policy by, 75–77
  separation fences and walls project case,
    56–58, 331–333
  support of "focused preemption" policy in,
    125–126
  Targeted Killings case jurisprudence and,
    64–70, 71–74
  trust principle invoked by, 419–421
  violence and rule of law and, 437–438
  war crimes case law of, 457–467
  West Bank quarry case and, 422–429
Hold Baggage Screening (HBS)
  technology, 495
home, personhood and, 26–28
hostile party rights and action, inadmissibility
  in court of law, 375
hostilities, in AP I Article 51(3), 68–70
hostis humanis generis (enemy of humanity),
  surveillance technology and, 496–498
house demolitions
  case law involving, 162–164
  as catalyst for violence, 179–181
  critique of jurisprudence involving, 176–179
  impact of, 162–164
  judicial inertia concerning, 172–176
  lack of permit as basis for, 533–534
  planning and building control using,
    541–542
  as punitive action, 164–166
  Regularization Law and, 364–368
  Regulation 119 case law, 167–176
  surveillance technology and, 489–491
housing policies, minimization of Palestinian
  living space, 532–536
humanitarian issues
  Israeli Red Lines policy, 347–350
  occupant's obligation concerning, 14–16
  Regularization law and, 378–379
human rights
  citizenship rights and, 9–10
  criticism of administrative detentions as
    violation of, 133
  quality of life and, 343–345
  "transformative" occupations and, 16n.68
"human shields" defense
  war crimes and, 455n.31

"human shields" defense (cont.)
  "warning" procedures and, 126–129
"Hunger Games" of 2007-2010, 350–359
hunger strikes. *See* force-feeding of Palestinian
  prisoners

identity documents
  citizenship status of Palestinians and,
    531–532
  permit regime and, 543n.130
  as surveillance, 480–482
"The IDF Spirit,"186
imperial nomos, 277n.3
impunity, culture of, 196–199
  Israeli military law and, 196–199
  "justice cascade" and, 452–454
  war crimes and, 449–452, 470–474
incarceration
  as legal violence, 446
  mass incarcerations in OPT, 383–388
  removal, distancing and isolation and,
    388–390
  of young offenders, 504–507
inclusive surveillance, 477–478n.14
indefinite occupation. *See* chronotope of
  occupation; temporary duration
  principle
individual responsibility, collective
  punishment prohibition and, 167–170
informants, 118–119, 131, 273, 306–307, 309, 311,
  441, 513
  children recruited as, 513
  before 1967, 305–312
  asylum seekers recruited as, 319–324
  closeted homosexuals recruited as, 308–309
  as evidence source for administrative
    detentions, 131n.68,69,69
  paid informants, administrative detentions
    and, 130–133
inherent enmity ideology, 492–493
inhumane and cruel treatment principle, war
  crimes jurisprudence and, 463n.74
institutional non-justiciability, Jewish
  settlements cases and, 211–212
Interim Agreement on the West Bank and
  Gaza Strip (Oslo II), 524–529
International Committee of the Red Cross
  (ICRC)
  collective punishment study by, 167–170
  commentary on GC IV prohibition on
    deportation of protected persons, 78–81

commentary on Jewish settlements, 200–202,
  289–291
'direct participation in hostilities' reviewed
  by, 71–74
property destruction prohibition and,
  170–172
International Convention on the Condition
  and Protection of Civilians of Enemy
  Nationality Who Are on Territory
  Belonging to or Occupied by a
  Belligerent, Tokyo draft, deportations
  and, 80
International Court of Justice (ICJ)
  Beit Surik case and, 333–335
  Construction of the Wall advisory opinion,
    401–406, 411
  international *vs.* domestic norms and,
    176–178
  Israeli criticism of, 256–262
  lawfare and, 254–256, 262–263
  on Israeli-Palestinian Conflict, 295–297
  Israeli separation fence and, 54–56
International Covenant on Civil and Political
  Rights
  Israel's rejection of Article 9 in, 18–19n.75
  youth justice and, 509–510
International Criminal Court (ICC), 35n.37
  collective punishment prohibition and,
    167–170
  deportation of protected persons in, 200–202
  lawfare and, 254–256, 262–263
  Jewish settlements and Statute of,
    289–291Statute of (*See* Rome Statute)
international criminal law (ICL)
  Ajuri judgment and, 35n.37
  culture of impunity and, 449–452
  Israeli isolation from, 452–454
  war crimes and, 448–449, 461–465
International Criminal Tribunal for Rwanda
  (ICTR), 169–170
International Criminal Tribunal for the former
  Yugoslavia (ICTY), 36–37
  deportation interpretations by, 88
  status of combatants and, 63–64
  war crimes jurisprudence and, 463
international humanitarian law (IHL)
  Ajuri case based on, 35–38
  approaches to forced transfer in, 78–79n.3
  belligerent occupation under, 11–12, 141–144
  chronotope of occupation and, 401–406
  defined, 3n.12

domestic law *vs.*, 176–178
family life and unity in, 219–225
family separation and reunification and, 232–233
food security and, 357–359
house demolitions as violation of, 172–176
inherent violence in, 19–20
Jewish historical narrative *vs.*, 415–416
lesser evils perspective in, 327–331
Levy Committee report and, 278–280
Levy Committee's interpretation of, 291–294
nomos/nomoi of, 284–298
norm *vs.* principle of sovereign equality and, 16n.68
occupied territories and application of, 14–16
precedence over domestic law, 178
principle of distinction and, 68–70
quality of life under occupation and, 345–347
Red Lines policy and, 351–355
Regularization Law and, 364–368
usufruct principles and, 417–419
violence in Israeli law and, 438–439
war crimes and, 448–449, 461–465
youth justice in domestic law and, 509–510
international human rights law (IHRL)
belligerent occupation and, 141–144
chronotope of occupation and, 404–405
defined, 3n.12
family life in, 220–223
food security and, 357–359
occupied territories and application of, 14–16
International Law Commission (ILC), 289–291
International Law Department (MAG), 246–250. *See also* Military Advocate General (MAG) Corps
deployment of law against criticism by, 256–263
international legal community, nomos of, 284–298
International Military Tribunal in Nuremberg, 419n.12
international tribunals, Israeli lawfare and, 254–256
interrogation methods
commonly U.S.-Israeli terminology in discourse on, 113–115
necessity defense invoked for, 105–111
youth justice in domestic law and, 507–510
Intifada uprisings
Abu Safiyeh case and, 155–159

barrier system in wake of, 47–48
family unification freeze following, 228–229
house demolitions and, 164–166
Israeli reoccupation of West Bank following, 28–32, 64n.22
"targeted killing policy" in wake of, 64–66
transfer of security knowledge and, 99–104
intra-legem principle, Israeli settler-colonial project, 202–204
investigations
oversight mechanisms, 193–196
in practice, 189–192
rule of law and, 182–183
invisible violence, Israeli practices of, 440–444
Iraq
influence of Israeli security tactics, 101–104
Israeli references to, 102–103, 114–115
occupation of, 4–6, 13–14
sanctions against, following first Gulf War, 349n.26
U.S. expropriation of petroleum in, 423–424
Iskan cases, 155–159
Islamic State, U.S.-Israeli military collaborations and, 102–103
Israel
birthrate in, 221–222n.16
control regime of, 22–25, 301–305
deportation of Palestinian militants and political leaders by, 81–83, 93–94
divergence from law of belligerent occupation, 144–146
export of security knowledge by, 95–99
Geneva Convention Article 2 interpretation and, 146
law-rule-exception relationship and control regime of, 21–22
Palestine-Eretz Israel partitioning and, 47–48
pre-1967 military regime of, 306–312
rule over Occupied Palestinian Territory, 1–4
separation fence project in, 46–47
state lawfare in, 246–250
state of exception in, 18–19
"targeted killing policy" of, 64–66
transfer of security knowledge with U.S., 99–104
Israeli Basic Law: Human Dignity and Liberty, 230–237
Israeli Defense Forces (IDF)
Abu Rahme case involving, 457–467

Israeli Defense Forces (IDF) (cont.)
   law enforcement in West Bank by, 189–192
   military law and, 185–189
   targeted killing policy and, 64–70
   unit '8200,' 486–489
   war crimes committed by, 456–457, 467–473
Israeli law
   jurisdiction beyond borders of, 312–315
   rule over Occupied Palestinian Territory
      and, 2–3
   temporal and spatial aspects of, 312–324
Israeli Open University, 396–398
Israeli-Palestinian Interim Agreement on the
      West Bank and the Gaza Strip, 33–34,
      65n.23, 425–429
Israeli Penal Code, 183–185
   military law and, 185–189
   war crimes and, 452–454
Israeli settler-colonial project, Jewish
      settlements in OPT as expansion of,
      202–204
Israeli Supreme Court, rule over Occupied
      Palestinian Territory and, 2–3, 314
Israel Prison Service (IPS)
   division of Palestinian prisoners by, 390–394
   restrictions on Palestinian prisoners of,
      388–390
   security offenses defined by, 383–384
"Israel proper" framework, 304–305
   jurisdiction across borders and, 312–315
   outside/inside duality and, 325–326
   Palestinian incarceration in, 388–390

Jamayit Iskan v Minister of Defense (1980) 35(2)
      PD 285, 154–159
Jewish Agency, 369
Jewish settlements in OPT, 1–4
   exceptions and, 212–216
   as expansion of settler-colonialism, 202–204
   Gaza Strip "disengagement" judgment and,
      26–27n.4
   HCJ jurisprudence on, 205–212, 216–217
   Israeli administrative and constitutional law
      and, 3n.13
   jurisdiction over, 264–267, 312–315
   legal regulation of Palestinian space and,
      519–546
   Levy Committee report on, 278–280
   military purposes of, 205–211
   outposts as distinct from, 203n.13
   population transfers prohibition and, 211–212

   pre-1967 settlements, 308–309
   as private property issue, 205–211
   Regularization Law and, 364–368
   as violation of Geneva Conventions,
      285–289
Jewish settlements OPT, legal prohibition of,
      200–202
judaization activities
   before 1967, 305–306
   land expropriation and, 532–533
Judea and Samaria Settlement Regulation Law
      2017, 286n.50, 362–364, 411–412n.53
judicial review
   of administrative detentions, 130–133
   exemption of extrajudicial assassinations
      from, 125–126
   war crimes and, 454–467
jus ad bellum
   assigned residence decisions and,
      39–42
   proportionality and, 328
jus in bello
   assigned residence decisions and, 39–42
   proportionality and, 328
justiciability, principle of, targeted killing
      policy and, 70

Kafka, Franz, 447
'Kafr Qasim massacre,' 455–456
Kamm, Anat, 69n.53, 445
Kaplinsky, Moshe (Maj. Gen.), 56–58
Karp, Yehudit, 193–194
Karp Report of 1982, 193–194
Kasher, Asa, 102–103
Kemp, Adriana, 303
Kennedy, David, 438–439
Khalidi, Rashid, 482
Khoury, Elias, 209–211
King's Order in Council, deportation of of
      Palestinian militants and political
      leaders out of, 82–83
kinship
   Citizenship and Entry into Israel Law
      (Temporary Order) and, 241–242
   Palestinians and disintegration of,
      218–219
Koskenniemi, Martti, 451–452
Kretzmer, David, 85–86, 205n.19

laches principle, West Bank quarry industry
      jurisprudence and, 425–429

Lambermont, Auguste, 345n.9
Landau, Uzi, 101, 205–211
land expropriation
    direct surveillance as tool for, 479–480
    as indefinite occupation, 411
    Israel to Greater Israel framework for,
        152–159
    judaization activities and, 532–533
    legal regulation of Palestinian space and,
        519–546
    in OPT, 360–361
    Regularization Law and, 368–370, 372–373
    usufruct principles and, 419–421
    West Bank quarry industry jurisprudence
        and, 425–429
language
    common language used in Israeli-U.S.
        security knowledge transfers, 113–117
    in future-oriented strategies, 137–140
    growth of administrative detentions and role
        of, 132
    law and, 22–25
law enforcement
    investigations and, 182–183
    oversight of, 193–196
    prosecution and investigation in practice
        and, 189–192
    substantive legislation on, 183–189
lawfare
    evolution of, 243–246
    expansion of, 262–263
    Israeli deployment of law against, 256–262
    Israeli's critics and, 251–256
    of Israeli State, 246–250
    legal challenges and, 113–115
Law for the Internment of Unlawful
        Combatants (Israel), 74n.71
The Law in These Parts (documentary),
        182–183, 267n.21
Law of Return (Israel)
    barrier entries and, 49–50
    separation fences and walls project and,
        331–333
Law of the Regularization of Settlement in
        Judea and Samaria 2017. *See*
        Regularization Law
Law of War Manual (U.S. Dept. of Defense),
        107, 110–112
law-rule-exception relationship
    convergence and divergence of critiques on,
        21–22

critiquing against the law and, 17–21
critiquing before the law approach and,
    8–17
Israeli war crimes jurisprudence and, 465–467
in military law, 504–507
outside/inside duality and, 325–326
overview, 6–8
Regularization law and, 380–382
youth justice and, 499–504, 514–515
laws of war, lawfare and, 243–246
Lebanon, Israeli war against Hezbollah in,
    126–129
legal normalcy, law-rule-exception
    relationship and, 7
lesser evil concept, proportionality principle
    and, 327–331, 337–340
Levy, Edmond E. (Justice), 26–27n.4, 156n.78,
    414–415
Levy Committee
    establishment of, 277n.3
    international legal discourse and work of,
        278–280, 284–298
    nomos in findings of, 281–284
    Regularization Law and, 367–368
    sovereignty perspectives on, 298–300
    understanding of international law by,
        283–284
lex generalis, 157–159
lexicon format, overview of, 22–25
lex specialis
    belligerent occupation and, 141–144
    Gaza Flotilla incident and, 352–353
    HCJ interpretations of, 157–159
    law of belligerent occupation and, 11–12
    normative framework for targeted killing
        policy based on, 67–68
Lieber Code (1863), 60–61
    deportations and, 80
    family life in, 220–221n.11
    laws of war and, 246–247
    property rights in, 372–373
    usufruct principles and, 417–419
Lieberman, Avigdor, 308, 467–473
limited duration, occupation as temporary
    control and, 16–17, 141–144
limited scope of powers, law of belligerent
    occupation and, 11–12
livelihood, protection of, occupant's obligation
    concerning, 14–16
Livni, Jonathan, 267n.21
Livni, Tzipi, 256–262

Madrid Conference of 1991, 380–382
Manual for the Military Advocate General in Military Government, 310–311
"mappings," 135–137, 517–519
Mara'abe v Prime Minister of Israel (2005) 60(2) IsrSC 477, 56–58
Maritime Incident of 31 May 2010, 187–188
marriage of Palestinians and Israelis. *See also* families, unification and separation of
  Citizenship and Entry into Israel Law amendments and, 229–230
  citizenship status and, 225–228
  HCJ judgments, critique of, 230–237
  human rights law on, 220–223
  international humanitarian law and, 219–225
  Israeli freeze on Palestinian unification in 2002, 228–229
  kinship and, 218–219
  as preemptive/preventive strategy, 118–119
  profiling of Palestinians as enemy and, 233–234
  reunification laws and, 223–225
  surveillance technology and, 492–493
  suspended families and, 237–241
Massumi, Brian, 120–121
Mayor of Silwad v Knesset; HCJ 2055/17, 381–382n.94
Mazuz, Menachem (Justice), 176, 278–279
Mbembe, Achille, 77n.88
medical care, barriers for Palestinians to, 441–443
Meir, Golda, 308–309
Melcer, Hanan (Justice), 109–110, 461–465
Mendelbit, Avichai, 113–115, 243–246, 256–262
mens rea
  culture of impunity and, 451–452
  military/domestic law overlap in definitions of, 315–319
Meron, Theodor, 146, 288–289
Migron outpost case, 487–489
Military Advocate General (MAC) Corps, 194. *See also* International Law Commission (ILC); military law
  Abu Rahme case and, 457–467
  B'Tselem investigation of, 196–199
  deployment of law against critics of, 256–262
  lawfare and, 246–250, 262–263
  legal infrastructure of, 436–437
  Turkel Commissions recommendations concerning, 194–196
  war crimes case law involving, 457–467

military commanders, authority of
  administrative detentions and, 130–133
  analysis of Fourth Geneva Convention Article 78 concerning, 33–34
  applicability of law and, 34–35
  assigned residence and, 30–35
  barrier entries and, 48–50
  belligerent occupation and, 149–152
  criminal liability recommendations, 187–188
  family unification and separation and, 225–228
  Hague Convention Article 43 and, 154–159
  Jewish settlement case law and, 206–211
  Levy Committee interpretations of, 285–289
  "mappings" and, 135–137
  normative framework for, 32–33
  punitive demolitions and, 165
  Regularization Law and, 371–372
  Regulation 119 codification of, 167–176
  West Bank quarrying operations and, 424
military courts
  academic neglect of, 275–276
  characteristics of, 264–267
  control of West Bank and Gaza through rulings of, 275–276
  conviction rate in, 273–274
  jurisdiction beyond borders of, 312–315
  legal discrepancies in, 268–270
  legal rhetoric of, 437–438
  military youth court, 511
  youth courts, establishment of, 315–319
  pitfalls and advantages of litigation in, 251–252
  pre-1967 establishment of, 310–311
  trial and sentencing procedures in, 271–272
  uncertainty in governance of, 270–274
Military Justice Act 1955 (MJA), 185–189
military law. *See also* Order Concerning Security Provisions (1651); Order Concerning the Adjudication of Juvenile Delinquents (No.132)
  African asylum seekers and, 324
  applicataion to Palestinians before 1967, 305–306
  British Mandate law, influence on, 311–315
  exception rule in, 504–507
  Israeli duality in, 301–305
  Israeli system of, 185–189
  jurisdiction beyond borders of, 312–315
  law enforcement practices and, 189–192

as legal violence, 446

military courts' divergence from, 268–270

operational inquiry prior to criminal investigation in, 191–192

overlap with domestic law, 315–319

Palestinian prisoners and violation of, 394–396

rule over Occupied Palestinian Territory and, 2–3

temporal and spatial aspects of, 312–324

military necessity exception

Jewish settlements jurisprudence and, 213–214

property destruction prohibition and, 170–172

military prosecutors, qualifications of, 265n.9

military zoning, 538–540

minors. *See* youth justice

"mista'arvim" ("Arabized" forces), 311–312, 479–480

Montevideo Convention, 43–44

annexation prohibitions and, 54–55

moral judgment

proportionality and, 329

war crimes and, 456–457

municipal services, barriers for Palestinians to, 534–536

Namibia, South African post-mandate occupation of, 409–410

Naor, Miriam (Justice), 176n.70, 176

national courts, criticism of Israeli lawfare in, 253–254

national liberation movements, legal framework for, 142n.9

natural reserves and parks, zoning for, 540–541

Nazi *Judenrein* policies, Levy Committee Report invocation of, 288–289

Nazis and Nazi Collaborators (Punishment) Law, 183–185, 452–454

necessity defense. *See also* military necessity

fluidity of concept, 438–439

torture justification under, 105–111

necropolitics, *Targeted Killings* case and expansion of, 77n.88

Ne'eman, Ya'akov, 415

negligence, military/domestic law overlap in definitions of, 315–319

Netanyahu, Benjamin, 104–105

on African asylum seekers, 319–324

Azaria affair and, 468–469

opposition to Palestinian unity by, 122–123

"roof knocking" tactics defended by, 126–129

settlement policies and, 415

on stone throwing regulations, 318–319

NGO lawfare, 251–256

1967 War (Six-Day War), 1–4, 47–48

as preemptive strike, 122–123

punitive house demolitions following, 164–166

Nomos and Narrative (Cover), 277–278

nomos/nomoi

Cover's concept of, 277–278

culture of impunity and, 449–452

IDF war crimes and, 470–474

of international legal community, 284–298

in Levy Committee findings, 281–284

padeic and imperial versions of, 277n.3

sovereignty of Jewish people and, 298–300

surveillance of Palestinians, 479

noncitizen Palestinians

incarceration of, 388–390

statistics on youth incarceration for, 499–504

nongovernmental organizations (NGOs)

criticism of Israeli lawfare by, 251–256

as Israeli allies, 256–262

Israeli authorities' clampdown on, 260

non-justiciability principle

HCJ minimization of, 214–215

Israeli lawfare and, 253–254

Jewish settlements in OPT and, 211–212

non-state lawfare, 243–246

non-violent protest, violence terminology and, 431–435

"normal" legal order, critiquing against law and, 19–20

normative framework. *See also* nomos/nomoi

assigned residences justification and, 32–33, 35–38

of belligerent occupation law, 149–152, 159–161

chronotope of occupation and, 399–401

civilian/combatant status and, 73–74

for deportations policies, 78–84

family reunification laws and, 223–225

future-oriented strategies in context of, 137–140

Gaza Flotilla incident and, 355–359

house demolitions in context of, 176–178

for IDF war crimes, 470–473

normative framework (cont.)
  indeterminacy in, Regularization Law and,
    376–382
  for Jewish settlements in OPT, 205–211
  proportionality and, 329
  for Red Lines policy, 351–355
  for targeted killing policy, 67–68
  war crimes and exceptionalization of,
    465–467
  war crimes petitions in *Abu Rahme* case,
    461–465
nuclear weapons policies, proportionality and,
  340–341n.44

Obama, Barack, 75, 106–107
obiter dictum
  house demolitions jurisprudence and,
    172–176
  rulings on deportations and, 85
  West Bank quarry industry jurisprudence
    and, 425–429
"objective enemies," surveillance ideology
  and, 475–479
occupation
  as form of trust precluding systemic change,
    14–16
  sovereignty as distinct from, 13–14
  as temporary control, 16–17
Occupied Palestinian Territory (OPT)
  closure of towns and villages in, 179n.79
  deportation of of Palestinian militants and
    political leaders out of, 81–83
  divergence from law of belligerent
    occupation in, 144–146
  family unification and separation in, 225–228
  house demolitions in, 162–164
  inapplicability of Geneva Convention in,
    85–86
  indefinite status of, 117
  Israeli nomos in, 277n.3
  "Israel proper" and, 304 305, 312–315
  Jewish settlements in, 1–4
  law enforcement in, 182–183, 196–199
  legal construction of, 516–519
  legal regulation of Palestinian space in,
    519–546
  mass incarcerations in, 383–388
  as a no-place, 517–519
  normative indeterminacy of Israeli law in,
    376–382
  origin of term for, 1–4

  overview of legal research on, 4–6
  profiling of Palestinian families in, 234–237
  prohibition against Jewish settlements in,
    200–202
  Regularization Law and, 362–364
  Six-Day War and, 1–4
  territorial fragmentation, 521–546
  zones of, 521–546
occupied territories, suspension of law in, 8–9
Olmert, Ehud, 348–349
operational inquiry, precedence over criminal
  investigation, in Israeli military law,
    191–192
"Operation Cast Lead," 249–250
"Operation Patient," 81–82
"Operation Protective Edge," 64–66, 101,
    453n.28
Ophir, Adi, 303–304
opinion juris, Regularization law and,
    380–382
Order Concerning Security Provisions (1651),
    130–133, 268–270, 312–319, 383–384
Order Concerning the Adjudication of
    Juvenile Delinquents (No.132),
    269n.31, 504–507
Orientalist paradigm, in Levy Committee
    report, 280, 291–294
Oslo Accords, 4n.16, 301–305, 380–382
  Gaza Strip in, 521–524
  Palestinian civil society institutions and,
    520–521
  power distribution between Israel and
    Palestinian Authority in, 486–489
  surveillance technology in, 480–482,
    485–486
  zone divisions in West Bank and, 524–529
outposts
  expropriation of Palestinian through,
    364–368
  legal regulation of Palestinian space and,
    519–546
  regularization of status of, 362–364, 368–370
  settlements *vs.*, 203n.13
  surveillance technology and, 487–489
  unauthorized status of, 278–279n.9
outside/inside duality, 301–326
  Israeli duality toward West Bank and Gaza
    Strip, 301–305
  pre-1967 history and, 305–312
  spatial and temporal aspects of Israeli law
    and, 325–326

temporal and spatial aspects of Israeli law, 312–324
oversight mechanisms, investigations and, 193–196

padeic nomos, 277n.3
Palestine
  Israeli duality toward, 301–305
  Palestine-Eretz Israel partitioning and, 47–48
  UN partition of, 282–283
  UN recognition of, 254–256
  Zionism and Jewish home in, 292–293
Palestine Gazette Extraordinary (No. 675), Memorandum on the Palestine (Defense) Order in Council, Supplement No. 2, 167n.18
Palestine Liberation Organization (PLO), Israeli civil litigation against, 256–262
Palestinian Authority
  civil litigation against, 256–262
  inter-Palestinian matters, jurisdiction over, 264–267
  Israeli jurisdiction over, 312–315
  Palestinian civil society institutions and, 520–524
  petitions by, 254–256
  status of combatants and, 60–64
  transfer of authority over Gaza to, 347–350
"Palestinian chair" torture device, 113–115
Palestinian Declaration of Independence (1988), 295–297
Palestinian Hamas, reconciliation with Fatah, 122–123
"Palestinian hanging" technique, 113–115
"Panel of Inquiry on the 31 May 2010 Flotilla Incident" (Palmer Panel)., 352–353
Paris Conference (1919), 169–170
Partition Plan, 47–48
  Levy Committee perspective on, 294
  UN General Assembly Resolution 181 and, 282–283
Peace Now, 211–216, 369
Peres, Shimon, 306–312
Performance Based Roadmap to a Permanent Two-State Solution to the Israeli-Palestinian Conflict (30 April, 2003), 365n.9, 366n.12
performative speech, language of law and, 24n.99
permit regime

before 1967, 305–306
control over movement and, 543–546
direct surveillance as tool for, 479–480
as invisible violence, 441–443
planning and building control with, 541–542
seam zone permit regime case, 335–337
separation fences and walls project and, 331–333
values and proportionality in cases involving, 337–340
personhood, home and, 26–28
Phillips, David, 282
Physicians for Human Rights, 441–443
Pictet, Jean Simon, 461–465
pipelining, separation fence project and, 51–52
police departments in U.S., Israeli training programs for, 100–101
political assassinations
  human rights' organizations' criticism of, 66n.30
  post-September 11 increase in, 75–77
  as preemption, 124–126
political prisoners, "security prisoners" as, 386–387
Political Theology (Schmitt), 9–10
political unity of Palestinians
  division of security prisoners as tool against, 390–394
  Israeli perception of threat of, 122–123
politics
  cross/self-referential loop in knowledge transfer and, 104–112
  Jewish settlements in OPT and, 209–211
  suspension of norms and, 20
  war crimes in context of, 467–473
Politics as Vocation (Weber), 179n.80
Popular Front for the Liberation of Palestine
  El-Al high-jacking by, 493–495
  prisoner of war (POW) status denied for members of, 111–112
potential threats
  administrative detention on basis of, 130–133
  "mappings" and, 135–137
  penalty of, 129–137
  preemptive arrest based on, 133–135
preemption
  extrajudicial assassinations as, 124–126
  as future-oriented strategy, 118–122
  preemptive arrest, 133–135
  preemptive military attacks, 122–129
  preemptive strikes, 122–123

preemption (cont.)
  "warning" procedures as, 126–129
"prevailing view" principle, Levy Committee
      Report and, 285–289
Prevention of Infiltration Law, 319–324
preventive attacks
  as future-oriented strategy, 118–122
  targeted killing policy justification on basis
      of, 66–67
preventive detention. *See* administrative
      detentions
prisoner of war (POW) status, U.S.-Israeli
      reciprocal referencing concerning,
      111–112
prisoners. *See also* hunger strikes
  children as, 505–507
  division of, 390–394
  family visits, restriction of, 383–384,
      388–390, 499–504
  mental incarceration of, 396–398
  non-rehabilitation of, 394–398
  parole of, 394–396
  removal, distancing and isolation and,
      388–390
  separation of child prisoners, 390–394,
      396–398
  sociopolitical fragmentation and, 388–394
  terminology, statistics and context for,
      383–388
prisoner study groups, "security prisoners"
      barred from, 390–394, 396–398
privacy, right to, surveillance technology
      and, 478
private property. *See* property rights
  proportionality in Beit Surik case and,
      333–335
profiling
  inherent enmity ideology and, 492–493
  surveillance and, 477–478, 492–495
prolonged occupation, sovereignty and, 13–14
property rights
  appropriation of property under
      Regularization law, 374–375
  damage *vs.* confiscation, 372–373
  destruction of property, Regularization Law
      violations, 375
  Jewish settlements in OPT and issue of,
      205–211
  occupant's obligation concerning, 14–16
  prohibition on property destruction not
      justified by military necessity, 170–172

Regularization Law as violation of, 362–364,
      372–373
Regulation 119 as violation of, 167–172
West Bank quarry industry jurisprudence
      and, 422–429
proportionality, principle of
  abusive application of, 341–342
  Beit Surik case, 333–335
  boundaries of power and, 340–341
  combatant status and, 69–70
  family separation and reunification law and,
      230–237
  fluidity of, 438–439
  HCJ interpretations of, 155–159, 331–337
  lesser evils perspective and, 327–331
  military authority and, 33–34
  normative framework for targeted killing
      policy and, 67n.36
  nuclear weapons and, 340–341n.44
  seam zone permit regime case, 335–337
  values and, 337–340
prosecution, in practice, 189–192
protected persons
  belligerent occupation and status of,
      159–161
  family unification and separation and,
      225–228
  GC IV prohibition on deportation of,
      78–81
  IHL and ICL framework for war crimes
      against, 461–465
  Israeli enforcement mechanisms and,
      182–183
  Israeli occupation framed as, 146
  occupied territories and concept of,
      14–16
  proportionality and rights of, 337–340
  Regularization Law as violation of rights of,
      372–373
  Regulation 119 as violation of property rights
      of, 167–172
  war crimes courts martial and, 455–457
protest. *See also* separation fences and walls
      project (Israel); stone throwing,
      military and domestic laws concerning
  military courts, enforcement and regulation
      of, 268–270
  non-violent protest, violence terminology
      and, 431–435
protest regulation, military courts'
      enforcement of, 268–270

Public Committee Against Torture v Government of Israel (2006) 62(1) PD 507
  context of judicial text in, 64–66
  critical analysis of judgment in, 71–74
  judgment in, 66–70
public land, Jewish settlements on, 210–211
punitive house demolitions
  deterrence justification for, 178–179
  evolution of, 164–166
"pure combat" circumstances, deaths of civilians and, 191–192n.38

Qasem Qawasmeh v Minister of Defense (1980) 35(3) PD 113, 84
Qawasmeh case. See Qasem Qawasmeh v Minister of Defense (1980) 35(3) PD 113
quality of life
  alternative normative frameworks for, 355–359
  chronotope of occupation and, 404–405
  "Hunger Games" in Gaza and, 350–359
  international human rights law and, 357–359
  Israeli Red Lines policy and, 347–350
  law of belligerent occupation and, 355–357
  under occupation, 345–347, 360–361
  permit regime and, 543–546
  research approaches to, 343–345
quarries in OPT
  colonialism in jurisprudence involving, 429–430
  Israeli operation of, 419–421
  legal challenge to licensing, 422–424
  West Bank quarry industry, 421–429

Rabin, Yitzhak, 146, 211–212n.39
racist regimes, sovereignty as distinct from occupation and, 13–14
Radin, Margaret, 26n.3
Rafah Approach Case, Jewish settlements in, 205n.19, 212–216. *See also Abu Hilo v. Government of Israel* (1973), 27(2) PD 169
rationae temporis, Regularization law and, 370
ratione materiae
  military authority and, 157–159
  Regularization Law and, 369
ratione personae authority
  Regularization Law and, 368–370
  scope of military authority and, 157–159
"real enemy" principle, surveillance technology and, 496–498

reasonable doubt, military/domestic law overlap in definitions of, 315–319
Red Lines policy, 347–350
  alternative normative frameworks for, 355–359
  international human rights law and, 357–359
Regularization Law
  annexation in, 371–372
  discrimination in, 373–374
  intentionally wrongful acts in, 370–375
  motivations for, 364–368
  normative indeterminacy, 376–382
  outposts' status in, 368–370
  rule of law and rule by law and, 362–364
  war crimes and, 374–375
Regulation 119
  case law involving, 167–176
  house demolitions under, 164–166, 176–179
  judicial inertia concerning, 172–176
  legal issues in, 167–172
rehabilitation programs, barriers for "security prisoners" to, 394–396
Reisner, Daniel, 75–77
Report on the Legal Status of Building in Judea and Samaria. See Levy Committee
restitution *ad interegnum*, chronotope of occupation and, 405–406
retroactive liability, military/domestic law overlap in definitions of, 315–319
Rhodes Agreements, 47–48, 295–297
  separation fence project and, 51–52, 58–59
right to life, occupant's obligation concerning, 14–16
risk management
  surveillance ideology and, 475–479
  surveillance technology and, 479–491
Road 443 project, law of belligerent occupation and, 152–159
Roman-Commissarial model, 11–12
Rome Statute
  deportation of protected persons and, 200–202
  Israeli criticism of Palestinian recognition in, 256–262
  Israeli isolation from, 452–454
  Jewish settlements and, 289–291
  Palestinian accession to, 453n.28
  recognition of Palestine and, 254–256
  war crimes and, 448–449

"roof knocking" tactics, 126–129
  Israeli-US military collaborations and,
    102–103
  surveillance technology and, 489–491
Rostow, Eugene, 282
royalties from quarries, Israeli expropriation of,
    421–422n.24
rubber bullets, IDF use of, 458n.46
Rubinstein, Amnon, 303, 463
Rubinstein, Elyakim (Justice), 176n.70,
    461–465
rule of law
  belligerent occupation and, 159–161
  investigations and, 182–183
  law-rule-exception relationship and, 7
  quality of life and, 343–345
  Regularization Law and, 362–364
  state violence and, 179–181
  violence and, 436–439
  war crimes and, 473–474

Sa'ar, Gideon, 322–323
Sabra massacre, 253–254
Said, Edward, 291–294
San Remo Manual on International Law
    Applicable to Armed Conflicts at Sea,
    353–355
San Remo Resolution of 1920, 282, 291–294
Sasson, Talia, 193–194
Sasson Report of 2005, 193–194, 369
Schmitt, Carl, 6–7, 9–10
  on state of exception, 18–19
seam zone
  annexation argument concerning, 54–55
  barriers and, 49–50
  extra-territorial legislation and, 52–53
  Palestinian enclaves and, 536–538
  permit regime case, 335–337
  political results of, 53–54
  separation fences and walls project and,
    51–52, 331–333
Second Geneva Convention for the
    Amelioration of the Condition of the
    Wounded, Sick and Shipwrecked
    Members of Armed Forces at Sea,
    431–435. *See also* Geneva Conventions,
    Article 3
secret evidence, administrative detentions
    based on, 130–133, 446
security blocks
  Palestinian enclaves and, 536–538

separation fence project and, 52–53
security issues
  Beit Surik case, 333–335
  indefinite occupation justification on,
    412–413
  Jewish settlements in OPT, HCJ
    jurisprudence based on, 206–211
  military/domestic law overlap concerning,
    315–319
  permit regime and, 543–546
  surveillance and, 475–479, 496–498
security knowledge
  common terminology used in transfer of,
    113–115
  cross/self-referential loop in transfer of,
    104–112
  Israeli market dominance in, 475–479
  U.S-Israeli transfer of, 99–104, 115–117
"security prisoners." *See* prisoners
"selective enforcement" defense, war crimes
    jurisprudence and, 472–473
self-defense
  justification of torture and interrogation
    using, 105–111
  preemptive strikes justified as, 122–123
self-determination
  annexation prohibitions and, 55n.56
  indefinite occupation and, 409–410
  Israeli denial to Palestinians of, 295–297
  law of belligerent occupation and, 291–294
  occupation as temporary control and, 16–17
  occupied people, sovereignty vested in, 13–14
  sovereignty and, 8–9
self-investigation mechanisms, complaints by
    Palestinians and, 251–256
separation fences and walls project (Israel),
    46–47
  annexation argument concerning, 54–56
  Beit Surik case, 333–335
  border issues and, 51–54
  division of Palestinian prisoners and,
    390–394
  economic impact of, 534–536
  HCJ jurisprudence involving, 56–58,
    331–333
  as indefinite occupation, 412–413
  Palestine-Eretz Israel partitioning and,
    47–48
  Palestinian demonstrations against, 458–461
  smart fence technology and, 489–491
  sovereignty and, 58–59

terminals in, as surveillance tool, 482–486
values and proportionality in cases involving, 337–340
separation of powers, international vs. local law and, 178
September 11, 2001 attacks
expansion of political assassination after, 75–77
export of security knowledge in wake of, 105–111
HCJ rulings and, 109–110
settlements. *See* Jewish settlements in OPT
"settling bodies," private settlement institutions as, 369
Shahin, Rahmeh, 64–66
Shamgar, Meir (Justice), 85, 86–94
Al-Fasfous case and, 162–164
on duration of occupation, 406–413
house demolitions and, 172–176
pre-1967 contingency plans for military occupation, 310–311
reference to U.S. law by, 107–108
on rule of law, 436–437
Shamgar Commission of Inquiry, 193–194
Shani, Ehud, 166
Sharon, Ariel, 253–254, 278–279
Shatilla massacre, 253–254
Shehadeh, Salah, assassination of, 125
Shenhav, Yehuda, 303–304
Shikma interrogation facility, 114–115
Shoham, Uri, 114–115, 302–303, 436–437
Shurat HaDin, 256–262
Silbey, Susan, 7, 21–22
smart fence technology, 489–491
"smart" techno-occupation, 486–489
social media
growth of administrative detentions and use of, 132
preemptive arrest based on posts to, 133–135
sociopolitical fragmentation
direct surveillance and, 479–480
division and, 390–394
family life and strategy of, 219–225
Israeli strategy of, 388–394
mental incarceration and, 396–398
Palestinian enclaves and, 536–538
Palestinian political unity and, 122–123
removal, distancing and isolation, 388–390
zone divisions in West Bank and, 524–529
zones of occupation and, 516–519

South Africa, post-mandate occupation of Namibia by, 409–410
sovereign equality between states, occupation as temporary control and, 16n.68
sovereignty
belligerent occupation and, 141–144
border/barrier distinction and, 43–44
chronotope of occupation and, 399–401
conservation principle and, 15–16
critiquing before the law approach and, 8–9
de facto occupying power and, 143n.12
family reunification laws and, 223–225
of Jewish settlements in West Bank, 281–284
Levy Committee interpretations of, 284–298
occupation as distinct from, 13–14
Regularization Law as expression of, 362–364
Regularization Law violations of, 371–372
separation fence project and, 58–59
spatial regulation
of Palestinian space, 519–546
zones of occupation and, 516–519
Special Rapporteur on the Situation of Human Rights in the Occupied Palestinian Territories, 459–460
state
assassinations, 66n.30
Israeli state lawfare, 246–250
lawfare and, 243–246
law-rule-exception relationship and, 6–7
state agencies in U.S., Israeli training programs for, 100–101
state consent requirement, in Regularization Law, 373–374
state violence
house demolitions as, 179
hypervisible violence, 444
invisible violence, 440–447
Israeli lawfare and, 246–250
legal violence, 436–439, 444–447
outposts as expression of, 364–368
preservation of law and, 20–21
quality of life under, 360–361
Regularization Law as expression of, 362–364, 380–382
of surveillance terminals, 482–486
terminology of, 431–435
Statute of the Special Court of Sierra Leone (SCL), 169–170
Stone, Julius, 282

stone throwing, military and domestic laws
concerning, 318–319, 505–507
St. Petersburg Declaration, 60–61, 246–247
strict liability, military/domestic law overlap in
definitions of, 315–319
Supreme Planning Committee (SPC), 541–542
surveillance
airport profiling and, 493–495
categories of, 477–478n.14
direct, 479–480
in Gaza Strip, 489–491
inherent enmity ideology, 492–493
nomos of Palestinian surveillance, 479
profiling and, 492–495
risk detection and, 479–491
security theology and, 475–479, 496–498
'smart' techno-occupation, 486–489
technological surveillance, 479–491
underlying logic of, 475–479
systemic change, occupation as form of trust
precluding, 14–16, 141–144

Tadić, Appeal Chamber Opinion and
Judgment, ICTY-94-1-A (15.7.1999),
36–37
Taking Rights Seriously (Dworkin),
341–342
targeted killing policy. *See also Public
Committee Against Torture v
Government of Israel* (2006) 62(1)
PD 507
critical analysis of judgment conceing,
71–74
HCJ judgment on, 66–70
Israeli implementation of, 64–66
as lawfare, 253–254
legal principles as basis for, 246–250
as preemptive action, 124–126
selective and dynamic interpretation of,
75–77
as state violence, 444–447
U.S. courts' support for, 111–112
technological surveillance
identity documents, 480–482
'smart' techno-occupation, 486–489
terminals as tool for, 482–486
telecommunications infrastructure, Israeli
control of, 486–489
teleological interpretations of HCJ
Ajuri case, 35–38
deportations cases, 86–94
Targeted Killings case, 73–74
temporary duration principle

family reunification law and, 223–225
indeterminacy of, 413–416
international jurisprudence and,
401–406
Jewish settlements in OPT and, 206–211
law of belligerent occupation and, 11–12
Levy Committee reliance on, 284–285
normative indeterminacy in Regularization
law and, 376–382
Regularization Law, 370
substition of indefinite for temporary in
settlement jurisprudence, 406–413
temporary/indefinite control
chronotope of occupation and, 399–401
international jurisprudence on, 401–406
Israeli substitution of indefinite for
temporary, 406–413
occupation as, 16–17, 141–144
terminals, technological surveillance using,
482–486
terra nullius
OPT as no-place and, 517–519
West Bank as, 295–297
terrorism
exceptionalization of war crimes on grounds
of, 465–467, 472
house demolitions justification on basis of,
172–176
Israeli characterization of lawfare as,
256–262
justification of assigned residence and,
39–42
Third Geneva Convention Relative to the
Treatment of Prisoners of War, 60–64,
431–435. *See also* Geneva Conventions,
Article 3
Article 79, 390–394
time, law's preoccupation with, 406–413
torture. *See also Public Committee Against
Torture v Government of Israel* (2006) 62
(1) PD 507
common U.S.-Israeli terminology in
discourse on, 113–115
Israel's claims about, 261–262
legal prohibition of, 431–435
methods that leave no marks, 440–444
necessity defense for justification of,
105–111
unaccountability for, 433–434
"transformative" occupations
conservation principle and, 16n.67
human rights and, 16n.68
sovereignty and, 13–14

Trump, Donald, 97, 104–105, 234–237
trust
  exploitation of Palestian land and people as
    violation of, 419–421
  occupation as form of, 14–16, 141–144,
    399–401
  "tu quoquo" defense, Azaria affair and, 469–470
Turkel Commissions (Israel), 110–111, 187–188,
    194–196
  Gaza Flotilla incident and, 352–353
  "twisted ideology" principle, war crimes by
    IDF and, 467–473

ultra vires principle
  belligerent occupation and, 149–152
  Road 443 project and, 157–159
"un/certainty governance," of military court
    proceedings, 270–274, 275–276
UN Committee on Economic, Social and
    Cultural Rights, Comment 12, 357–359
UN Convention on the Rights of the Child,
    499–504, 509–510
UN Convention Relating to the Status of
    Refugees, African asylum seekers in
    Israel and, 319–324
undercover soldiers, 118–119, 305–312, 479–480
UN General Assembly Resolution 181,
    282–283, 294
UN Human Rights Committee, family rights
    and, 221–222n.16
United Nations Fact Finding Mission on the
    Gaza Conflict, 189–192
United States. *See also* Guantánamo, US
    detention facility
  expansion of political assassination in, 75–77
  export of security knowledge by, 95–99
  HCJ references to law in, 107–108
  influence on Israeli law and politics of, 98,
    105–111
  Israeli civil litigation in, 256–262
  security knowledge collaboration with
    Israel, 99–104, 475–479
Universal Declaration of Human Rights,
    357–359
  quality of life in, 343–345
universal jurisdiction
  assigned residences and, 35n.37
  Israeli criticism of, 256–262
  lawfare and doctrine of, 253–254
unlawful combatant status
  international law concerning, 72–73

Regularization law and, 379–380
U.S.-Israeli reciprocal referencing
    concerning, 111–112
UN Office for the Coordination of
    Humanitarian Affairs, 433–434
UN Rules for the Protection of Juveniles
    Deprived of Their Liberty, 499–504
UN Security Council
  Resolution 62 (1948), 295–297
  Resolution 2334, 298–300
  resolutions on Palestine in, 95–99
urban planning failure, in East Jerusalem,
    533–534
Urban Warfare Training Center, 100
US Army War College, 100
use of force, gradual international
    renunciation of, 13–14
usufruct, rules of
  colonialism and, 429–430
  exploitation of Palestinian land and people
    and, 419–421
  trust as inspiration for, 417–419
  West Bank quarry industry jurisprudence
    and, 421–429
Uzi, Vogelman (Justice), 156n.78

variables, proportionality principle and
    embrace of, 337–340
Vienna Convention on the Law of Treaties
  Article 27, 84n.31, 144n.20
  international *vs.* domestic norms in, 176–178
  rules of treaty interpretation in, 87–88
Vietnam, U.S. war in, Israeli cooperation on,
    103–104
violence. *See also* state violence
  in Gaza Strip, 521–524
  hypervisible violence, 444
  invisible violence, 440–447
  legal violence, 436–439, 444–447
  terminology of, 431–435

war crimes
  courts martial and, 455–457
  culture of impunity and, 449–452
  exceptionalization of normative framework
    and, 465–467, 473–474
  exception principle and, 454–467
  HCJ case law and, 457–467
  IHL and ICL framework for, 461–465
  international crimes and punishment,
    448–454

war crimes (cont.)
  Israeli "cascade of justice" and, 452–454
  Israeli mlitary law and, 186–189
  Israeli Penal Code, 183–185
  nationals' exemption from prosecution for,
    110–111
  political discourse on, 467–473
  Regularization law and, 374–375
  substance and jurisdiction concerning,
    448–449
"warning" procedures, as preemptive policy,
  126–129
Weber, Max, 179n.80
Weisglass, Dov, 348–349
Weizman, Eyal, 347–350, 438–439, 482–483
welfare services, barriers for Palestinians to,
  534–536
West Bank
  as Administered Territory, 305–306
  geopolitical boundaries of, 1n.1
  IDF law enforcement in, 189–192
  illegal Israeli construction in, 95–99
  Israeli control over planning and building
    permits in, 118–119
  Israeli duality toward, 301–305
  Israeli rhetoric justifying occupation of,
    261–262
  Israeli security training programs in, 101–104
  Jewish settlements in, 202–204
  Jordanian waiver of sovereignty over,
    295–297
  Levy Committee report on settlements in,
    278–280
  military zoning in, 538–540
  non-territorial status claimed for, 415
  open borders policy in, 543n.130
  Palestinian prisoners in, 383–388
  partition of Hebron in, 526–529
  pre-1967 infrastructure in, 305–312
  quarry industry in, 421–422
  regulation of Palestinian space in, 519–546
  seam zone in, 51–52
  security provisions order and, 268–270
  Six-Day War and, 1–4, 47–48
  temporal and spatial aspects of Israeli law in,
    312–324
  youth justice in, 499–504
  zone divisions in, 524–529
Westphalian international order, critiquing
  before the law and, 8–9
White, James Boyd, 271

wiretapping, Israeli surveillance technology
  for, 486–489
Witkon, Alfred (Justice), 205–211
Wittgenstein, Ludwig, 23
women, Israeli family separation and
  unification laws and, 237–241
World Zionist Organization, 369

X-rays
  at separation terminals, 482–486
  surveillance and profiling with, 475–479

Ya'alon, Moshe, 124–125, 166, 468–469
Yesh Din – Volunteers for Human Rights,
  189–192, 271–272, 419–421
Yishai, Eli, 228–229, 319–324
youth justice
  age of criminal majority in Israeli military
    law, 268–270, 511–512
  detention periods in, 511–512
  domestic law and rule of exception for,
    507–510
  exception in military law and, 504–507
  historical evolution of, 499–504
  Israeli token reforms in, 510–514
  mental incarceration and, 396–398
  military/domestic law overlap and, 315–319
  military youth court, 511
  rule of exception and, 514–515
  security offenses clauses, 505–507
  separation of child prisoners and, 390–394

Zichroni, Ammon, 209–211
Ziegler, Jean, 54–55
Zionism, 292–293
  Regularization Law and, 369
  war crimes defenses in context of, 469–470
zones
  before 1967, 305–306
  civilian zoning, 540–541
  control over movement with, 543–546
  in Gaza Strip, 521–524
  in Jerusalem, 529–536
  judaization activities and, 532–533
  military zoning, 538–540
  in Occupied Palestinian Territory, 516–519,
    546–547
  Palestinian enclaves and, 536–538
  permit regimes and, 541–546
  in West Bank, 524–529
Zussman, Yoel (Chief Justice), 89

CPSIA information can be obtained
at www.ICGtesting.com
Printed in the USA
LVHW081829080319
610002LV00018B/358/P